CLASSICAL RHETORIC FOR THE MODERN STUDENT

CLASSICAL RHETORIC
for the Modern Student

THIRD EDITION

EDWARD P. J. CORBETT

NEW YORK OXFORD OXFORD UNIVERSITY PRESS 1990

Oxford University Press

Oxford New York Toronto
Delhi Bombay Calcutta Madras Karachi
Petaling Jaya Singapore Hong Kong Tokyo
Nairobi Dar es Salaam Cape Town
Melbourne Auckland

and associated companies in
Berlin Ibadan

Published by Oxford University Press, Inc.,
200 Madison Avenue, New York, New York 10016

Oxford is a registered trademark of Oxford University Press

Library of Congress Cataloging-in-Publication Data

Corbett, Edward P. J.
Classical rhetoric for the modern student / Edward P. J. Corbett.—3rd ed.
p. cm.
Includes bibliographical references.
ISBN 0-19-506293-0
1. Rhetoric, Ancient. 2. English language—Rhetoric. I. Title.
PN175.C57 1990
808—dc20 89-22981
CIP

9 8 7

Printed in the United States of America
on acid-free paper

This book is gratefully dedicated to my deceased wife and to my children, whose persistent image of me is that of a man hunched over a typewriter

PREFACE

The first edition of *Classical Rhetoric for the Modern Student* had a more favorable reception and a wider classroom use than I had dared to hope for when the book was published in 1965. Part of the success of the book was due undoubtedly to the revival of interest in formal rhetoric at the time. That wave of interest had ebbed somewhat when the second edition appeared in 1971, but rhetorical activity had increased at an astounding rate. The second half of the 1960s was marked by a feverish increase of demonstrations of various kinds, both "verbal rhetoric" and "body rhetoric": marches, boycotts, sit-ins, take-overs, and riots, on college campuses and in large cities all over the country. The nation was in a state of ferment about many social, political, and cultural issues, and many ordinary citizens—especially young people—had assumed the mission of righting the wrongs that they perceived to be rampant in our society and of restoring the rights that they felt many members of our society had been denied. The rhetoric that was exerted in those causes was frequently a much different kind of rhetoric from the one that had come down to us from the Greeks and the Romans. It was often (1) *non-verbal,* more disposed to putting bodies on the line than words; (2) *gregarious,* involving clusters of people rather than the single orator on the podium; (3) *coercive,* making non-negotiable "demands" rather than persuasively formulated "requests"; (4) *non-conciliatory,* more inclined to shock and even alienate an audience than to use ingratiating techniques. That new style of rhetoric—if it really was new—was frequently effective in producing reforms or influencing attitudes. It certainly seemed to fit the mood of the times.

But when the civil-rights movement lost some of its steam and the United

States withdrew its troops from the Vietnam War, the nation as a whole seemed to slip into a conservative mood. The rhetoric exerted by the conservative forces in our society was as different from classical rhetoric as was the "body rhetoric" of the later 1960s. The prime exemplar of this brand of rhetoric was our "great communicator," Ronald Reagan. But about this same time, we were exposed to an even stranger kind of rhetoric, the rhetoric of the Middle Eastern world, exerted by the people of countries such as Iran, Lebanon, and Israel. This was a rhetoric that seemed to play by none of the rules that had come down to us from a tradition of rhetoric that had been practiced by the reigning nations of the Western World for over 2000 years. And then there is the distinctive rhetoric of the Oriental world. . . . But those are rhetorics that we still have to study and analyze and codify.

Meanwhile, there is evidence that some of the principles and practices of classical rhetoric are still operative in our society as we head into the last decade of the twentieth century. Although we are paying increasing attention to those emotional, psycho-physical dynamics that affect people's responses and actions, it does not seem likely that people will entirely abandon the strategy of appealing to the rationality, the reasonableness, the moral consciousness of the human animal. One of the most salutary lessons to come down to us from the Greek rhetoricians and philosophers is that unless we regard human beings as complexes of intellect, will, passions, and physicality, we will not produce well-integrated citizens for any society.

The point of all of the above is that rhetoric, of some sort, is always and still with us. The exercise of rhetoric seems to be as natural and as necessary for human creatures as breathing. The Greeks had that insight when they first formulated an art of rhetoric. Later peoples expanded and refined the art to fit the needs and the temper of their times. Undoubtedly, there will be a "new rhetoric" for the twenty-first century, a rhetoric that will be more comprehensive than any that has been devised so far, an international rhetoric that will be congenial for people of many nations and cultures. But in that new rhetoric there will be noticeable residues of classical rhetoric. So a quarter of a century after the appearance of the first edition, I am not hesitant about issuing yet another edition of *Classical Rhetoric for the Modern Student.*

The basic structure of the book remains the same as it was in the first two editions. The first chapter of the book gives a brief explanation of the kind of rhetorical training that flourished in the schools of the West for over two thousand years. The next three chapters develop the three vital parts of classical rhetoric: Chapter II, Discovery of Arguments; Chapter III, Arrangement of Material; Chapter IV, Style. The Appendix provides a brief history of rhetoric and a bibliography for those who want to pursue their interest in the subject.

The contents of that basic structure remain largely the same as in the previous editions. I was disposed to change more of the contents than I ultimately did, but many teachers and some students pleaded with me not to drop those parts of the book that had become their "favorites." But I did make some changes. The principal changes that I made were to remove where possible the blatantly sexist language that pervaded the book and to give greater representation to women than they had in the two previous editions. The removal of sexist language will be noticeable only to those who were painfully aware of its presence in the first and second editions. But the greater representation of women will be conspicuous to all. Many of the new readings in the book are by women, and some of the rhetorical analyses of the readings are done on the prose pieces authored by women. Whereas only *one* woman was represented in the previous editions among the Specimen Passages for Imitation in the chapter on Style, there are now seventeen. In the Survey of Rhetoric in the final chapter, I have remarked about the conspicuous absence of women in all of the histories of rhetoric and have explained why women were not prominent practitioners or theoreticians of rhetoric in earlier ages. I observed, however, that some scholars now are turning their attention to women in rhetoric. They are finding isolated instances in ancient times of women who could be called rhetoricians, and they will discover many more when they turn their attention to the nineteenth and twentieth centuries.

I have changed other readings in the book too, often substituting shorter, timelier selections for some of the venerable but stodgy pieces I used previously. In the introductory chapter, for instance, I substitute a one-page magazine ad for a fairly lengthy prose selection that was in the second edition, and I do an extensive analysis of the rhetoric of that ad. In the section on External Aids to Invention in Chapter II, I have added a new section on A Search Strategy prepared for this edition by Virginia Tiefel, the Director of Library-User Education at Ohio State University. In the chapter on Style, I have given, in parentheses, phonetic spellings of the names of the tropes and figures, names which were derived, by and large, from Greek and Latin words.

I hope that these changes will make the book more useful and appealing.

As usual, I owe a great debt of gratitude to the many teachers and students who wrote me or buttonholed me at professional meetings to tell me what they liked about the book and what they did not like. I learned a great deal from those unsolicited remarks. I also learned a lot from users of the book who were formally engaged by the publisher to write reviews of the edition that was to be replaced. I cannot adequately acknowledge the debt I owe to my colleagues and to the many graduate students I have had in seminars over the years for their insights and suggestions. I refrain from naming those colleagues and students only because I know that I would omit several people who deserve to be named. And I am profoundly grateful to the editorial staff of the Oxford University Press for their consistently wise counsel and their continuing faith in the book. I alone am responsible for the shortcomings of this third edition.

E.P.J.C.

Columbus, Ohio
January 1990

CONTENTS

CLASSICAL RHETORIC FOR THE MODERN STUDENT

I / INTRODUCTION

Rhetoric is the art or the discipline that deals with the use of discourse, either spoken or written, to inform or persuade or motivate an audience, whether that audience is made up of one person or a group of persons. Broadly defined in that way, rhetoric would seem to comprehend every kind of verbal expression that people engage in. But rhetoricians customarily have excluded from their province such informal modes of speech as "small talk," jokes, greetings ("Good to see you"), exclamations ("What a day!"), gossip, simple explanations ("That miniature calculator operates on dry-cell batteries"), and directions ("Take a left at the next intersection, go about three blocks to the first stoplight, and then . . ."). Although informative, directive, or persuasive objectives can be realized in the stop-and-go, give-and-take form of the dialogue, rhetoric has traditionally been concerned with those instances of formal, premeditated, sustained monologue in which a person seeks to exert an effect on an audience. This notion of "an effect on an audience"—a notion that gets at the very essence of rhetorical discourse—is implicit in such definitions as Marie Hochmuth Nichols's: "a means of so ordering discourse as to produce an effect on the listener or reader"; Kenneth Burke's: "the use of language as a symbolic means of inducing cooperation in beings that by nature respond to symbols"; or Donald Bryant's: "the function of adjusting ideas to people and of people to ideas." The classical rhetoricians seem to have narrowed the particular effect of rhetorical discourse to persuasion. Aristotle, for instance, defined rhetoric as "the faculty of discovering all the available means of persuasion in any given situation." But when one is reminded that the Greek word for *persuasion* derives from the Greek verb "to believe," one sees that Aristotle's definition can be made to comprehend not only those

3

At Smith Corona, simplicity is the mother of invention.

Our engineers racked their brains so you won't have to.

We started out with a very simple idea.

To make electronic typewriters and word processors that have lots of great features but are very simple to use.

We make the simplest typewriters in memory.

So simple you don't have to keep one eye on your typing and one eye on the instruction manual.

So simple you don't need a degree in computer programming to operate them.

So simple they can even make a confirmed non-typist comfortable at the keyboard.

Call it human engineering if you like. Or call it ergonomics. Or call it plain old inspiration.

What we came up with is a line of remarkable typewriters that are sophisticated without being complicated.

In fact, they're unlike any other typewriters you've ever seen before... or used before...or muttered at before.

Take our new Smith Corona XD 5500. (Lots of people are going to.)

We call the XD 5500 the Memory Typewriter. You just may call it the simplest typewriter in memory.

It features a 7,000 character editable memory you can access with the mere flip of a switch.

Combined with the 16 character LCD display, you can proofread, correct and make changes before you ever put anything down on paper.

Of course, should you want to

Give your typing a screen test.

make changes on paper, we've made that simpler than ever too.

On the XD 5500, as well as on every new Smith Corona typewriter, you'll find our new correcting cassette.

It's an easy-to-load, drop-in correction tape you can insert in seconds.

There are no spools to unwind. No complicated threading. No tangles.

So now correcting mistakes is as easy as making them.

We've reformed the correction system.

Add features like a Spell-Right™ 50,000 word electronic dictionary, WordFind® WordEraser® Full Line Correction and much more and you've got a typewriter that's not just incredibly simple to use, but simply impossible to pass up.

Of course, the same goes for every other Smith Corona typewriter and word processor as well.

Which is why we recommend that you hurry to your nearest store and try our machines yourself.

Obviously, they won't come to you. Yet.

SMITH CORONA

TOMORROW'S TECHNOLOGY AT YOUR TOUCH

For more information on this product, write to Smith Corona Corporation, 65 Locust Avenue, New Canaan, CT 06840 or Smith Corona (Canada Ltd.), 440 Tapscott Road, Scarborough, Ontario, Canada M1B 1Y4.

modes of discourse that are "argumentative" but also those "expository" modes of discourse that seek to win acceptance of information or explanation.

But whether we are seeking, as the eighteenth-century Scottish rhetorician George Campbell put it, "to enlighten the understanding, to please the imagination, to move the passions, or to influence the will," we must adopt and adapt those strategies that will best achieve our end. *Strategies* is a good rhetorical word, because it implies the *choice* of available resources to achieve an end. It is no accident that the word *strategy* has military associations, for this word has its roots in the Greek word for *army*. Just as a general will adopt those resources, those tactics, which are most likely to defeat the enemy in a battle, so the marshaller of language will seek out and use the best argument, and the best style to "win" an audience.

Let us look at one of the commonest forms, in our society, of a discourse designed to influence an audience, a magazine advertisement. Following the ad, there will be an analysis of the rhetoric of that piece of discourse.

Analysis of the Smith Corona Ad

Perhaps the most common, most ubiquitous, form of persuasive discourse in our society is advertising. Whether in the visual medium or in the sound medium, advertising is inescapable. Ads appear in newspapers, in magazines, in catalogues, in flyers, on billboards, on the radio, on the television. They are primarily forms of deliberative rhetoric: spoken or graphic discourses (or combinations of spoken and graphic discourses, such as the commercials on TV) that try to get the reader or the listener to buy a product or a service. A huge industry has developed in our society to prepare and disseminate these ads. "Madison Avenue" is the figurative way of referring to this industry. (In the chapter on style, you will find out that the figure of speech represented by the term Madison Avenue is *antonomasia*.) Ad-writers are some of the most skillful rhetoricians in our society. They may never have studied classical rhetoric, but they employ many of the strategies of this ancient art to influence the attitudes and actions of those who are exposed to the ads that they compose. The analysis that follows will point out some of the rhetorical strategies that the ad-writers used in the Smith Corona magazine ad.

The so-called "communication triangle" is frequently used as a graphic representation of the components of the rhetorical act:

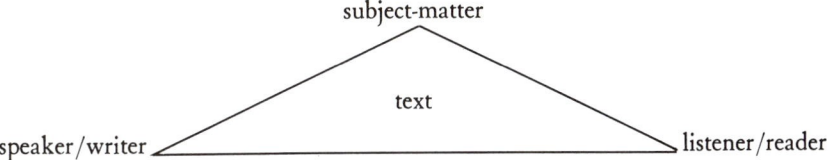

In most ads, as in most forms of technical writing, the least prominent of the components is the speaker/writer. Who is addressing us in the ad? Most ads are composed by the staff of the ad agency that the company or the manufacturer hired. The speaker or writer in an ad—unlike the speaker or writer in a speech or an essay—is not a particular person; it is usually a corporate persona created by the ad agency. The very first word of the sentence under the picture at the top of the page is *our*, and the very first word of the text under that picture is *we*. To whom does that first-person plural pronoun refer? Obviously, the pronoun does not refer to the three engineers in the picture. (The three men who appear in the picture are probably not engineers employed by Smith Corona; they are probably professional actors hired by the ad agency to pose for the picture.) The pronoun *we/our* probably stands for the Smith Corona Corporation, but that corporate persona is a vague, amorphous entity, whose personality it is difficult for us to discern.

But an *ethos* does come through the ad. The smiling, friendly faces of the three men standing behind a Smith Corona typewriter make us readers feel comfortable and confident. The Smith Corona logo at the end of the ad, with its slogan "Tomorrow's Technology at Your Touch," and the Smith Corona seal, with its motto "Commitment to Excellence," is also intended to make us feel comfortable and confident about the *ethos* or the *voice* that comes through to us from the ad. A good deal of the ethical appeal of this ad is exerted by what is said and how it is said—more specifically, by the credibility of the appeals to our reason and by the impressiveness of the style of the ad.

Another component that does not come through clearly is the listener/speaker. Whom is the ad addressing? The most obvious general answer to that question is "It is addressing the reader of the ad," referred to frequently by the second-person pronoun *you/your*. But just who is that *you*? For one thing, is the *you* singular or plural? In other words, does the *you* stand for an individual or for a group of people?

One possible candidate as an antecedent for the pronoun *you* is the administrative office of a company that is responsible for purchasing equipment, such as typewriters and word processors, for the workers. In that case, the *you* stands for a group of people. On the other hand, the *you* may stand for an individual out there who is in the market for a new typewriter. (A college student, for instance, who wants to buy a typewriter for class assignments might be that *you*.) The point is that the audience for most ads is not as easily definable as is the audience, for instance, for a nomination speech at a national political convention. We just sense that there is somebody out there—preferably thousands of people—that the ad-writer wants to persuade to buy something.

The rhetorical components that are most prominent in advertisements are the subject-matter and the text that is talking about that subject-matter. In this case, the subject-matter is the new Smith Corona typewriters and word processors, and the text is the full-page ad printed in the pages of a national magazine that is read each week by thousands of literate people. From here on, this analysis will focus on the rhetoric of the text as it attempts to persuade the readers of the ad that if they are in the market for a new typewriter or word processor, the Smith Corona products are a "good buy."

What first catches our eye in the ad is the headline, printed in big, bold-faced letters: "At Smith Corona, simplicity is the mother of invention." That headline introduces the name of the company; it adumbrates the theme of the ad with the use of the word *simplicity;* and, for many people, the main clause of the headline cleverly echoes a folk expression: "Necessity is the mother of invention." (*Simplicity* here neatly matches the word *necessity* in the number of syllables in it and in the suffix that ends the word, *-ity.*) There are many plays on words in the ad and many echoes of familiar phrases given a new twist. For instance, there are clever twists on phrases in all of the captions under the pictures: (1) "racked their brains"; (2) "in memory"; (3) "a screen test"; (4) "reformed the correction system." For people who recognize and value plays on words, these puns are delightful and help to establish a favorable ethos for the "voice" in this ad.

We have already remarked about the function of the first picture of the ad in creating a favorable image of the "seller," so we will go on to the text of the ad.

The first sentence of the text picks up on the main theme of the ad, simplicity. The next four sentences—actually they are sentence fragments, a very common stylistic feature of printed advertisements—elaborate on the theme. The second "sentence" of the text—"To make electronic typewriters…."—articulates the full theme of the ad: a typewriter with "great features" and "simplicity" of operation. The next three "sentences," all beginning with the same words, "so simple," spell out the sense in which these typewriters can be called simple. (Incidentally, beginning successive sentences with the same words is a figure of speech that the Greek rhetoricians called *anaphora.*) There are at least two more examples of anaphora in the ad: (1) the triple repetition of "call it" in the next paragraph; (2) the triple repetition of the initial word *no* in the next-to-last paragraph of the second column—"no spools," "no complicated threading," "no tangles." In the next-to-last paragraph of the first column, there is an example of just the opposite kind of figure—ending successive clauses or sentences with the same word or words (here, ending the three verb phrases with the word *before*).

Speaking of paragraphs, you may have noted how short the paragraphs are in this ad. In fact, all but four paragraphs in this ad consist of a single sentence. Brevity of sentences and paragraphs is another common stylistic feature of printed advertisements. The average length of the 32 sentences in this ad is 11.61 words, let's say 12 words, per sentence—a short sentence even by modern standards. There are different conventions of sentence length and paragraph length in newspaper copy and advertising copy from those in other kinds of prose in our society.

Note the clever downshifting in the vocabulary in the next paragraph: "Call it human engineering if you like. Or call it ergonomics. Or call it plain old inspiration." The designation of what is responsible for the kind of simplicity mentioned in the previous three paragraphs moves from the buzz phrase *human engineering* to the technical term *ergonomics* to an ordinary word wrapped in colloquial phrasing *plain old inspiration*. Some readers will know what all of these words mean; but all readers will be able to understand the third phrase.

This may be a good place to mention another stylistic feature that subtly influences the reactions of readers to the ad: the colloquial quality of the language. This colloquial quality manifests itself in the use of such phrases as the one we just mentioned, "plain old inspiration," in the frequent use of sentence fragments, and in the use of contractions such as *won't, don't, they're, you've, we've, that's*. The conversational tone created by these devices helps to establish a cozy relationship between the speaker in the ad (whoever that is) and the readers of the ad (whoever they are).

The ad is divided into three main sections:

1. A series of claims about the efficiency and the simplicity of the Smith Corona typewriters and word processors. (paragraph 1–8)
2. A series of substantiations of the claims made in the previous section. (paragraphs 9–18)
3. A final pitch to the readers. (paragraphs 19–22)

The first section sets forth the theme of the ad and makes a number of assertions about the Smith Corona products. Now what is needed to convince the readers of the truth of the assertions is some *proof* of the assertions. So in the second major section, the ad focuses on a specific model of a Smith Corona product, the SD 700, and cites some features of this model that help to confirm the previous claims about the efficiency and simplicity of Smith Corona products. Since the details offered in this section are presumably "facts," the method of proof offered here is what the classical rhetoricians called the "logical appeal" or the "appeal to reason."

The third major section begins with the question-begging phrase "of course." We are told in this 19th paragraph that "of course" everything said in the previous section about the SD 700 model "goes for every other Smith Corona typewriter and word processor as well." Since no proof of this latter claim is offered, we just have to take the word of the corporate persona speaking in the ad. The final pitch is delivered in the next paragraph, where the readers are urged to hurry to the nearest store where Smith Corona products are sold and find out for themselves just how efficient and simple the machines art.

The most brilliant touch in the ad occurs in the final paragraph. Having made the obvious point in the next-to-last paragraph that potential customers should go out to see the efficient, simple machines because the machines cannot go out to see the customers, the ad-writers conclude the pitch with a one-word paragraph—*Yet*. The implication of that one-word paragraph is that Smith Corona has made so many advances in the efficiency and simplicity of its typewriters and word processors that in the very near future these machines may be able to come to the customer instead of the customer having to go to the machines. The ad-writer who thought up that brilliant way of concluding the ad should get some kind award from the advertising profession.

The bottom line about the effectiveness of this magazine ad is whether a significant number of readers of the ad have been persuaded enough by the claims and the proofs of the ad that they are prepared to go out and test the Smith Corona products. We can admire in the abstract the cleverness of this piece of rhetoric, but the ultimate pay-off, as far as the ad agency and the company are concerned, is whether a number of people are moved to buy the product. If you were in the market for an electronic typewriter and could afford to buy one, would you be induced by this ad to go out and buy one of the latest Smith Corona typewriters?

Lest we think, however, that this display of deliberative rhetoric is another of the glorious products of our technological age, let us look at one more example of this kind of persuasive effort. The example is taken from one of the world's great masterpieces, written many centuries before the art of rhetoric was even formulated. It is the famous scene in Book IX of Homer's *Iliad* in which Odysseus, Phoinix, and Ajax come to Achilles' camp and plead with him to return to battle. Achilles has been sulking in his tent ever since Book I, when Agamemnon, the leader of the Greek forces besieging the city of Troy, affronted Achilles by taking the woman named Briseis, one of his prizes of war. After Achilles withdrew his troops from the front lines, the fortunes of war went from bad to worse for the Greeks. Agamemnon's army is now desperate. The envoys must succeed in persuading Achilles to return to battle.

We will look at only the first two speeches in this scene—Odysseus' plea to Achilles and Achilles' reply.

Homer: The Envoys Plead with Achilles

1 "Your health, Achilles! With all these appetizing dishes to dispose of, we cannot complain of our rations, either in my lord Agamemnon's hut or here again in yours. But at the moment the pleasures of the table are far from our thoughts. We are confronted by a disaster, your highness, the magnitude of which appals us. Unless you rouse yourself to fight, we have no more than an even chance of saving our gallant ships or seeing them destroyed. The insolent Trojans and their famous allies are bivouacking close to the ships and wall. Their camp is bright with fires. They are convinced that there is nothing left to stop them now from swooping down on our black ships. Zeus the Son of Cronos has encouraged them, with lightning flashes on the right. Hector has run amuck, triumphant and all-powerful. He trusts in Zeus, and fears neither man nor god in the frenzy that possesses him. His one prayer is for the early coming of the gracious Dawn, for he is itching to hack the peaks from the sterns of our ships, to send up the ships themselves in flames, to smoke us out and to slaughter us by the hulls. And indeed I am terribly afraid that the gods may let him carry out his threats—that it may be our fate to perish here, far from Argos where the horses graze. Up with you then, if even at this late hour you want to rescue the exhausted troops from the Trojans' fury. If you refuse, you yourself will regret it later, for when the damage has been done there will be no mending it. Bestir yourself, before that stage is reached, to save the Danaans from catastrophe.

2 "My good friend, when your father Peleus sent you from Phthia to join Agamemnon, did he not admonish you in these words: 'My son, Athene and Here, if they wish you well, are going to make you strong. What *you* must do is to keep a check on that proud spirit of yours; for a kind heart is a better thing than pride. Quarrels are deadly. Be reconciled at once; and all the Argives young and old will look up to you the more"? Those were the old man's precepts—which you have forgotten. Yet even so, it is not too late for you to yield. Give up this bitter animosity. Agamemnon is ready to make you ample compensation the moment you relent. If you will listen, I will enumerate the gifts he destined for you in his hut. Seven tripods, untarnished by the flames; ten talents of gold; twenty cauldrons of gleaming copper; and twelve powerful, prize-winning race-horses. He said that with nothing more than the prizes they had won for him, a man would not be

From Homer, *The Iliad*, trans. E. V. Rieu (Penguin Classics, 1950). Copyright © the Estate of E. V. Rieu, pp. 167–72.

badly off or short of precious gold. In addition, he will give you seven women, skilled in the fine crafts, Lesbians whom he chose for their exceptional beauty as his part of the spoils when you yourself captured the city of Lesbos. These you shall have from him, and with them the woman he took from you, the daughter of Briseus. Moreover, he will give you his solemn oath that he has never been in her bed and slept with her, as a man does, your highness, with a woman. All these gifts shall be put in your hands at once. Later, if the gods permit us to sack the great city of Priam, you must come in with us when we are sharing out the spoils, load your ship with gold and bronze to your heart's content, and pick out twenty Trojan women for yourself, the loveliest you can find after Argive Helen. And if in due course we get back to Achaean Argos, the richest of all lands, you can become his son-in-law, and he will treat you as he does Orestes, his own beloved son, who is being brought up there in the lap of luxury. He has three daughters in his palace, Chrysothemis, Laodice and Iphianassa. Of these you shall choose for your own whichever you like best and take her to Peleus' house without making the usual gifts. In fact, he will pay *you* a dowry, a generous one, bigger than anybody has ever given with his daughter. Not only that, but he will give you seven fine towns, Cardamyle, Enope and grassy Hire; holy Pherae and Antheia with its deep meadows; beautiful Aepeia, and Pedasus rich in vines. They are all near the sea, in the farthest part of sandy Pylos. Their citizens are rich in flocks and cattle. They would do homage and pay tribute to you as though you were a god, acknowledging your sceptre and prospering under your paternal sway. All this he will do for you, if you relent. But if your hatred of Atreides, gifts and all, outweighs every other consideration, do have some pity on the rest of the united Achaeans, lying dead-beat in their camp. They will honour you like a god. Indeed, you could cover yourself with glory in their eyes, for now is the time when you could get Hector himself. He fancies that he has no match among all the Danaans whom the ships brought here, and he may even venture near you, in his insensate fury.'

3   "Royal son of Laertes, Odysseus of the nimble wits," replied Achilles the great runner; "to save you from sitting there and taking it in turns to coax me, I had better tell you point-blank how I feel and what I am going to do. I loathe like Hell's Gates the man who thinks one thing and says another; so here I give you my decision. You can take it that neither my lord Agamemnon nor the rest of the Danaans are going to win me over, since it appears that a man gets no thanks for struggling with the enemy day in, day out. His share is the same, whether he sits at home or fights his best. Cowards and brave men are equally respected; and death comes alike to one who has done nothing and one who has toiled hard. All I have suffered by constantly risking my life in battle has left me no better off than the rest. I have been like

a bird that brings every morsel she picks up to her unfledged chicks, however hard it goes with *her*. I have spent many a sleepless night and fought through many a bloody day—against men who, like us, are fighting for their womenfolk. I have captured twelve towns from the sea, besides eleven that I took by land in the deep-soiled realm of Troy. From each I got a splendid haul of loot, the whole of which I brought back every time and gave to my lord Agamemnon son of Atreus, who had stayed behind by the ships, and who, when I handed it over, gave a little of it out, in bits, but kept the lion's share. What he did give to the princes and kings in recognition of their rank is safe in their possession; and I am the only one he has robbed. It is not as though he had no wife. He *has* one, of his own choice. Let him sleep with her and be content.

4 "For that matter, what drove the Argives to make war on Troy? What did Atreides raise an army for and bring it here, if not for Helen of the lovely hair? And are the Atreidae the only men on earth who love their wives? Does not every decent and right-minded man love and cherish his own woman, as I loved that girl, with all my heart, though she was a captive of my spear? But now that he has snatched her from my arms and swindled me, don't let him try his tricks on me again. I know him too well. He will not succeed.

5 "No, Odysseus, he must look to you and the other kings if he wants to save the ships from going up in flames. He has already done marvels without me. He has built a wall, I see, and dug a trench along it, a fine broad trench, complete with palisade. But even so he cannot keep the murderous Hector out! Why, in the days when I took the field with the Achaeans, nothing would have induced Hector to throw his men into battle at any distance from the city walls. He came no farther than the Scaean Gate and the oak-tree, where he took me on alone one day, and was lucky to get home alive. But things have changed, and now I do not choose to fight with my lord Hector. So to-morrow I am going to sacrifice to Zeus and all the other gods, then lade and launch my ships. The very first thing in the morning, if you have the curiosity to look, you will see them breasting the Hellespont where the fishes play, and my men inside them straining at the oar. And in three days, given a good crossing by the great Sea-god, I should set foot on the deep soil of Phthia. I left a rich home there when I had the misfortune to come here; and now I shall enrich it further by what I bring back, the gold, the red copper, the girdled women, and the grey iron that fell to me by lot—everything, in fact, but the prize of honour that was given me and insultingly withdrawn by one and the same man, his majesty King Agamemnon son of Atreus.

6 "Tell him all I say, and tell him in public, so that the rest may frown on any further efforts he may make to overreach a Danaan prince, unconscionable schemer that he always is. And yet he would not dare to look me in

the eye, for all his impudence. No; I will help him neither by my advice nor in the field. He has broken faith with me and played me false: never again shall I be taken in by what he says. So much for him. Let him go quietly to perdition. Zeus in his wisdom has already addled his brains.

7 "As for his gifts, I like them just as little as I like the man himself. Not if he offered me ten times or twenty times as much as he possesses or could raise elsewhere, all the revenues of Orchomenus or of Thebes, Egyptian Thebes, where the houses are stuffed with treasure, and through every one of a hundred gates two hundred warriors sally out with their chariots and horses; not if his gifts were as many as the grains of sand or particles of dust, would Agamemnon win me over. First he must pay me in kind for the bitter humiliation I endured.

8 "Again, I will not have any daughter of Agamemnon son of Atreus for my wife. She could be lovely as golden Aphrodite and skilful as Athene of the Flashing Eyes, and yet I would not marry her. He can choose some other Achaean, someone more royal than me and on a level with himself. If the gods allow me to get safely home, Peleus will need no help in finding me a wife. Up and down Hellas and Phthia there are plenty of Achaean girls, daughters of the noblemen in command of the forts. I have only to choose one and make her my own. There were often times at home when I had no higher ambition than to marry some suitable girl of my own station and enjoy the fortune that my old father Peleus had made. For life, as I see it, is not to be set off, either against the fabled wealth of splendid Ilium in the peaceful days before the Achaeans came, or against all the treasure that is piled up in Rocky Pytho behind the Marble Threshold of the Archer-King Apollo. Cattle and sturdy sheep can be had for the taking; and tripods and chestnut horses can be bought. But you cannot steal or buy back a man's life, when once the breath has left his lips. My divine Mother, Thetis of the Silver Feet, says that Destiny has left two courses open to me on my journey to the grave. If I stay here and play my part in the siege of Troy, there is no home-coming for me, though I shall win undying fame. But if I go home to my own country, my good name will be lost, though I shall have long life, and shall be spared an early death.

9 "One more point. I recommend all the rest of you to sail home too, for you will never reach your goal in the steep streets of Ilium. All-seeing Zeus has stretched out a loving hand above that city, and its people have taken heart. So leave me now and report to the Achaean lords in open council, as you seniors have the right to do—they must think out some better way of saving the ships and all the troops beside them, now that these overtures to me have met with blank refusal. But Phoenix can stay here and spend the night with us. Then he could embark for home with me in the morning— that is to say, if he wants to. There will be no compulsion."

Analysis of "The Envoys Plead with Achilles"

The situation dramatized in this scene from the *Iliad* is one that we see enacted frequently today, possibly in our own lives, certainly in public life: one person or a group of persons trying to persuade someone to do something or to assent to something. Today it may be a young man pleading with his father to let him use the family car for a Saturday night date, or it may be a delegation of party bosses trying to induce a reluctant candidate to run for a high political office. This rather common situation calls for uncommon rhetorical powers.

Viewed from the standpoint of narrative, this is an intensely dramatic scene that Homer has posed in the ninth book of his epic; viewed from the standpoint of rhetoric, this is a situation that will call upon all the resources of the men sent on this crucial mission. Agamemnon chose his ambassadors shrewdly: Odysseus, "the man who was never at a loss"; Ajax, reputed to be the mightiest Greek warrior after Achilles; Phoinix, Achilles' beloved old tutor. Each of them will work on the aggrieved and disgruntled Achilles in his own way.

The Homeric heroes took as much pride in their skill with words as in their skill with arms. When Phoinix rose to plead with Achilles, he reminded his former pupil of how he had schooled him to be "both a speaker of words and a doer of deeds." And throughout the *Iliad,* Achilles boasts of, and his companions acknowledge, his skill in oratory. Odysseus knows that he is not as great a warrior as Achilles, but he is conscious that he is superior to Achilles in rhetorical prowess. In Book III of the *Iliad,* Antenor described Odysseus when he came to the Trojan court to negotiate for the return of Helen: "But when he uttered his great voice from his chest, and words like unto snowflakes of winter, then could no mortal man contend with Odysseus." And it was Odysseus, remember, who in Book II restrained the Greeks, by the power of his rhetoric, from rushing off to their ships and sailing home. Phoinix too is on his mettle in this scene. As Quintilian said, "The teacher should therefore be as distinguished for his eloquence as for his good character, and like Phoinix in the *Iliad* be able to teach his pupil both how to behave and how to speak" (*Institutio Oratoria,* II, iii, 12).

It is no wonder that rhetoricians found Homer a rich mine for quotations and illustrations, for the *Iliad* and the *Odyssey* are filled with models of almost every kind of eloquence. Quintilian remarked that the magnificent speeches in the first, second, and ninth books "display all the rules of art to be followed in forensic or deliberative oratory" (*Institutio Oratoria,* X, i, 47). Today we find it almost laughable to read about warriors pausing in the heat of battle, as they do in some of the scenes of the *Iliad,* to hurl long speeches at one another. But the tradition of oratory was already well established—if not yet well formulated—in Homer's time, and this tradition persisted and grew stronger throughout the Golden Age of Athens. So we must take the oratory displayed in this scene as seriously as the participants took it, and we must savor the relish with which they indulged in this battle of words.

The participants in this battle of words are clearly engaged in what the classical rhetoricians called *deliberative* discourse. In classifying the three kinds of oratory, Aristotle pointed out that deliberative oratory is concerned with *future* time; that the means used in this kind of oratory are *exhortation* and *dissuasion;* and that the special topics that figure most prominently in this kind of discourse are the *worthy* and the *worthless,* or the *advantageous* and the *injurious.* In other words, when we are trying to persuade a person to do something, we try to show that the recommended course of action is either a good in itself (and therefore worthy of pursuit for its own sake) or something that will benefit the person. The envoys are trying to exhort Achilles to undertake an action in the future (on the morrow, if he will) that will be advantageous both to himself and to the Greeks. Achilles is engaged in refuting the exhortations.

Our selection from this scene reproduces only Odysseus' plea to Achilles and Achilles' reply to Odysseus. Let us look at the strategies of argument in these two speeches.

We have already remarked that Odysseus was reputed to be the most accomplished speaker among the Greeks. And indeed his speech here is a model, in miniature, of the well-organized oration. It has an exordium, a narration, a proof, and a peroration. None of these parts is developed to the extent that it would be in a full-fledged deliberative oration, but the speech does conform to the standard *dispositio* or arrangement laid down by the teachers of rhetoric.

Odysseus begins his speech by offering a toast to Achilles. Here he is doing what is often done in the exordium or introduction to a discourse: attempting to ingratiate himself with his audience, to conciliate his audience that is indifferent or reluctant or hostile (whichever term best describes Achilles' mood at the moment). All the rhetoricians emphasize the importance of putting the audience in a receptive frame of mind, especially if the audience is suspicious or hostile. The need to dispose an audience favorably explains why so many speakers begin their talk with a joke or a humorous anecdote.

Odysseus then proceeds to the *narratio,* or the exposition of the state of affairs at the moment (paragraphs 2 and 3). He describes for Achilles the desperate straits in which the Greeks now find themselves. In doing this, he employs the device of *enargeia,* which, as Quintilian puts it, "makes us seem not so much to narrate as to exhibit the actual scene, while our emotions will be no less actively stirred than if we were present at the actual occurrence" (*Institutio Oratoria,* VI, ii, 32). Thus Odysseus pictures for Achilles the countless watch-fires burning in the Trojan bivouac outside the line of the Greek ships; the favorable omen given by Zeus's lightning; and the "devouring flame" that threatens to engulf the ships. All these fire images are subtly calculated to arouse Achilles' anger, since to the Greek mind fire was intimately associated with the emotion of anger. By picturing Hector in his frenzied, arrogant, triumphant assault on the ships, Odysseus seeks to touch Achilles' pride and envy. He is needling Achilles. Are you going to let Hector make good his boast that he will chop down our ensigns and smother our ships with fire and smoke? If an appeal like this does not touch Achilles' pride, perhaps it will touch his sense of loyalty and patriotism.

Odysseus then launches into that part of his speech that the Latin rhetoricians called the *confirmatio*—the proof of one's case. In this section the speaker brings to bear "all the available means of persuasion" to support the cause he is espousing.

Odysseus first tries to influence Achilles by reminding him of his father Peleus' warning that he should restrain his proud temper and avoid quarrels. Not only is restraint of temper a good in itself, but it disposes a man to fight more effectively, and it disposes the gods, in whose hands our fortunes rest, to look with favor on our cause. Odysseus is here appealing to filial piety. Achilles is not as distinguished for *pietas* as was that later epic hero Aeneas, but in a strongly patriarchal society such as existed in ancient Greece, a son would not be entirely impervious to the advice of his father. If this reminder of a forgotten warning does not prevail with Achilles, it is only because Achilles feels that there is an over-riding justification for his anger.

After this, Odysseus catalogues for Achilles all the gifts that Agamemnon is prepared to give him if he will return to battle. Aristotle pointed out in his *Rhetoric* that *exhortation* and *dissuasion* turn ultimately on considerations of happiness or, more generally, the Good. Whenever we try to persuade someone to do something, we try to show the benefits that will result from action. Some of the goods that most people agree upon as contributing to happiness are such external goods as a respected family, loyal friends, wealth, fame, honor, and such personal excellences as health, beauty, strength. Of all these goods, Odysseus comes down heaviest on wealth. He entices Achilles with the list of all the gold, the horses, the servant women, and the property that Agamemnon will bestow on him. Not only will he get back the girl Briseis, the object of the quarrel with Agamemnon in the first place, but he will be honored with one of Agamemnon's daughters as a bride.

Odysseus is plainly appealing to Achilles' self-interest here. Achilles could not help being tempted by the king's generous offerings, for in this aristocratic society one of the marks of honor for a hero was abundant possessions. And, besides, these generous offerings would be a manifestation of Agamemnon's humiliating capitulation to Achilles. We shall see, when we consider Achilles' rebuttal, why it is that he was able to resist the tempting offer of these goods.

Odysseus did not, of course, have to *invent* these appeals. He is merely repeating, verbatim, the offer that Agamemnon had made, at the beginning of Book IX, before the council that immediately preceded this embassy. Odysseus was using the available means of persuasion, but he didn't have to discover these means.

One point needs to be made, however, about this verbatim retailing of Agamemnon's offer. The shrewd Odysseus did leave out one part of Agamemnon's council speech. At the very end, Agamemnon had said: "All this will I accomplish so he but cease from wrath. Let him yield; Hades I ween is not to be softened neither overcome, and therefore is he hatefullest of all gods to mortals. Yea, let him be ruled by me, inasmuch as I am more royal and avow me to be the elder in years." Odysseus knew that if he were to repeat these words, he would only increase Achilles' anger. For these words reveal that Agamemnon's capitulation is grudging and half-hearted. And certainly the king's insistence that he is still the superior man would have antagonized rather than conciliated Achilles.

Odysseus concludes his appeal by playing a slightly different note. If Achilles cannot rise above his hatred of Agamemnon, let him consider the honor he can win for himself by destroying Hector and rescuing the Greeks. This is another appeal to self-interest, but it is self-interest on a higher plane than the previous reminder of material rewards. For the Homeric hero, personal glory was the highest good. Odysseus has reserved the strongest appeal for the climax of his argument.

Achilles' reply is immediate and impulsive. There is no reflective pause to weigh the arguments. One gets the impression that Achilles had given only half an ear to Odysseus' plea and that he has been waiting impatiently for Odysseus to stop speaking so that he can have his say. One is not surprised then to find Achilles' speech emotionally charged—and, as a consequence, disorganized.

Achilles seems not so much to answer Odysseus as to express, vigorously and repeatedly, his scorn of Agamemnon's offer and to declare his determination not to fight. At first he talks as though he had not listened to Odysseus at all. He says he won't fight any more because he gets no thanks or reward for risking his life. But Odysseus has just told him of the thanks and reward he will get if he returns to battle. He will get not only what he had before the quarrel but additional rewards in superabundance.

As Achilles' torrent of speech tumbles on, however, it is clear that he *has* heard Odysseus. Achilles shows himself to be aware of all the details of Agamemnon's offer. But he spurns the offer. He is not just holding out for a higher price. No, he would reject the offer even if it were infinitely greater than it is. Some other considerations are now influencing Achilles.

Something has happened to Achilles while he has been brooding in his tent. He has been evaluating the rationale of war in general and this war in particular. Why have they been fighting here for ten years? To rescue Helen? But that is an inane cause to fight and die for. Why should hundreds of wives be widowed so that the king's brother can recover his wife? The sheer stupidity of the war and the egregious arrogance of Agamemnon in marshalling so many noble warriors to fight such a war magnifies the insult that Achilles has sustained. Does Agamemnon really think that he can compensate for all this with his paltry gifts?

Nor has Achilles been deaf to Odysseus' plea on the grounds of personal honor. As we have pointed out, the prospect of winning personal glory exercised a strong attraction for the Greek heroes. But having seen this war in proper perspective, Achilles no longer finds the attraction of personal honor as potent as it once was for him. There is something more dear to him now than honor and wealth—life. Achilles says, "For life, as I see it, is not to be set off, either against the fabled wealth of splendid Ilium in the peaceful days before the Achaeans came, or against all the treasure that is piled up in Rocky Pytho behind the Marble Threshold of the Archer-King Apollo." And a little later on he says, "But if I go home to my own country, my good name will be lost, though I shall have long life, and shall be spared an early death." Achilles has decided at this point that life is a higher good than fame or wealth.

In making this decision, Achilles has employed one of Aristotle's common topics—the topic of degree. When people deliberate about a course of action, the choice is not always between a good and an evil; sometimes the choice is between two or more goods. In making a choice from among several goods, people decide on the basis of degree: which of these goods is the greater good or the greatest good? And that is the topic that Achilles resorts to here. As readers of the *Iliad* know, Achilles later changes his mind and elects honor over life. But at the moment and in answer to Odysseus' persuasive appeals, he declares his preference for life over wealth and honor.

This is all the argument that one can make out of Achilles' rebuttal. Most of his speech is taken up with impassioned but eloquent ranting. One thing is clear, though, at the end of his speech: he will not fight. And it appears that Odysseus, the renowned orator, the man who was never at a loss, has utterly failed to move Achilles. It is now Phoinix's turn to appeal to him, and then Ajax's. But we have not reproduced these two speeches in our selection.

.   .   .

What lessons about rhetoric can we learn from a study of this episode, which constitutes a dramatic scene in a narrative poem but which is presented in the form of an oratorical debate? We learn, for one thing, that despite the hundreds of years that separate our society from Homer's, people acted and responded then in much the same way that they do today. People still sulk because of a real or supposed affront to their pride or dignity; other people try to salve the wounds of the insult. The dominant values of a society may change with the passage of time—today, for instance, we put more of a premium on actions that contribute to the common welfare than on actions that contribute only to a person's honor—but the basic human passions and motivations are the same today as they were in Homer's day.

In this episode, we see men arguing in much the same way as we argue today. What do we do when we want to change someone's attitude or get someone to do something? Like Odysseus, Phoinix, and Ajax, we resort to a variety of appeals, hoping that one or other of the appeals or the combination of them will persuade the person to change his or her mind or to act in a certain way. We may try to show the person that a proposed course of action is a good in itself or that it will result in substantial personal benefits. The material rewards we suggest may not be fancy tripods and swift race horses, but they will be similar lures—money or expensive automobiles or fur coats. Or we may try to show the person how much honor or power or fame he or she will reap. Or we may try to show how foolish or how dangerous the failure to act will be.

If these appeals to personal interest fail to move the person, we may resort to other approaches. We may try to induce such emotions as anger, fear, pity, shame, envy, contempt. Since the will controls whether a person will act or not and since an appeal to emotions is one of the most potent means of moving the will, we may find that in some circumstances, an emotional appeal is the most effective tactic. We would rely too on ethical appeal to influence the reluctant person. If someone perceives from our persausive efforts that we are men and women of intelligence, good character, and good will, that person will be disposed to listen and respond to our logical and emotional appeals.

In short, what we learn from the display of rhetoric in this episode from the *Iliad* is that in similar circumstances, we employ the same strategies of appeal that the envoys did. We make use of "all the available means of persuasion in any given case." We may use more or different arguments, we may arrange them in a different way, we may use a more temperate or a more florid style in which to convey our arguments; but fundamentally our strategies will be the same as those used by the envoys.

This text will be concerned with the strategies of discourse directed to a specific audience for a specific purpose.

A Brief Explanation of Classical Rhetoric

We have just seen two examples of persuasive discourse. The analyses of these two pieces introduced some terminology that may be unfamiliar. The terminology is strange because it belongs to an art that was formulated many centuries ago and that ceased to be a vital discipline in our schools sometime in the nineteenth century. Although modern students may often have heard the term *rhetoric* used, they probably do not have a clear idea of what it means. Their uncertainty is understandable, because the word has acquired many meanings. Rhetoric may be associated in their minds with the writing of compositions and themes or with style—figures of speech, flowery diction, variety of sentence patterns and rhythms—or with the notion of empty, bombastic language, as implied in the familiar phrase "mere rhetoric." Maybe tucked away somewhere in their consciousness is the notion of rhetoric as the use of language for persuasive purposes.

What all these notions have in common is that rhetoric implies the use or manipulation of words. And, indeed, a look at the etymology of the word *rhetoric* shows that the term is solidly rooted in the notion of "words" or "speech." The Greek words *rhēma* ("a word") and *rhētor* ("a teacher of oratory"), which are akin, stem ultimately from the Greek verb *eirō* ("I say"). Our English noun *rhetoric* derives from the Greek feminine adjective *rhetorikē,* which is elliptical for *rhetorikē technē* ("the art of the rhetor or orator"). English got its word immediately from the French *rhétorique.*

This investigation of the etymology of the term brings us somewhat closer to the original meaning of rhetoric: something connected with speaking, orating. From its origin in fifth-century Greece through its flourishing period in Rome and its reign in the medieval *trivium,* rhetoric was associated primarily with the art of oratory. During the Middle Ages, the precepts of classical rhetoric began to be applied to letter-writing, but it was not until the Renaissance, after the invention of printing in the fifteenth century, that the precepts governing the spoken art began to be applied, on any large scale, to written discourse.

Classical rhetoric was associated primarily with persuasive discourse. Its end was to convince or persuade an audience to think in a certain way or to act in a certain way. Later, the principles of rhetoric were extended to apply to informative or expository modes of discourse, but in the beginning, they were applied almost exclusively to the persausive modes of discourse.

Rhetoric as persuasive discourse is still very much exercised among us, but modern students are not likely to have received much formal training in the art of persuasion. Frequently, the only remnant of this training in the schools is the attention paid to argumentation in a study of the four forms of discourse: Argumentation, Exposition, Description, and Narration. But this study of argumentation usually turns out to be an accelerated course in logic. For the classical rhetorician, logic was an ancillary but distinct discipline. Aristotle, for instance, spoke of rhetoric as being "an offshoot" or "a counterpart" of logic or, as he called it, dialectics. The speaker might employ logic to persuade the audience, but logic was only one among many "available means of persuasion." So those who study argumentation in classrooms today are not really exposed to the rich, highly systematized discipline that earlier students submitted to when they were learning the persuasive art.

Although classical rhetoric has largely disappeared from our schools, there was a time when it was very much alive. For extended periods during its two-thousand-year history, the study of rhetoric was the central discipline in the curriculum. Rhetoric enjoyed this eminence because, during those periods, skill in oratory or in written discourse was the key to preferment in the courts, the forum, and the church. One of the reasons why the study—if not the practice—of rhetoric has declined in our own times is that in an industrial, technological society like our own, there are avenues to success other than communication skills. Part of the folklore of America is that in the years from about 1870 to 1910, some barely literate men became millionaires—some of whom, ironically, later founded libraries and endowed universities.

One fact that emerges from a study of the history of rhetoric is that there is usually a resurgence of rhetoric during periods of social and political upheaval. Whenever the old order is passing away and the new order is marching—or stumbling—in, a loud, clear call goes up for the services of the person skilled in the use of spoken or written words. One needs only to hearken back to such historical events as the Renaissance in Italy, the Reformation in England, and the Revolution in America to find evidence of this desperate reliance, in times of change or crisis, on the talents of those skilled in the persuasive arts. As Jacob Burckhardt has pointed out in *The Civilization of the Renaissance in Italy,* the orator and the teacher of rhetoric played a prominent role in the fifteenth-century humanistic movement that was casting off the yoke of the medieval church. After Henry VIII broke with Rome, the Tudor courts of England resounded with the arguments of hundreds of lawyers engaged to fight litigations over confiscated monastic properties. Students of the American Revolution need recall only Tom Paine's incendiary pamphlets, Patrick Henry's rousing speeches, Thomas Jefferson's daring Declaration of Independence, and Hamilton's and Madison's efforts to sell constitutional democracy in the *Federalist Papers* to be convinced that in time of change or upheaval, we rely heavily on the services of those equipped with persuasively eloquent tongues or pens. Something of the same kind of rhetorical activity is raging today among the nationalists fighting for independence in African and Asian countries. More recently in our own country, we witnessed the furious rhetorical activity, expressed in both words and physical demonstrations, in the civil-rights movement of the 1960s.

Those who want to learn something about the long history of rhetoric can read the Survey of Rhetoric in the Appendix of this book and can pursue their interest by reading some of the primary and secondary texts on rhetoric listed in the Bibliography. Before getting into the study of rhetoric in the next chapter, however, students may want to gain some general knowledge of the classical system of rhetoric and its terminology. By the time Cicero came to write his treatises on rhetoric, the study of rhetoric was divided, mainly for pedagogical convenience, into five parts: *inventio, dispositio, elocutio, memoria,* and *pronuntiatio.* Since this text professes to be an adaptation of classical rhetoric, students may appreciate an explanation of these and other key terms so that they might better understand the kind of rhetoric presented in the next three chapters.

The Five Canons of Rhetoric

Inventio is the Latin term (*heuresis* was the equivalent Greek term) for "invention" or "discovery." Theoretically, an orator could talk on any subject, because rhetoric, as such, had no proper subject matter. In practice, however, each speech that the orator undertook presented a unique challenge. He had to find arguments that would support whatever case or point of view he was espousing. According to Cicero, the speaker relied on native genius, on method or art, or on diligence to help find appropriate arguments. Obviously, that individual was at a great advantage who had a native, intuitive sense for proper arguments. But lacking such an endowment, a person could have recourse either to dogged industry or to some system for finding arguments. *Inventio* was concerned with a system or method for finding arguments.

Aristotle pointed out that there were two kinds of arguments or means of persuasion available to the speaker. First of all, there were the non-artistic or non-technical means of persuasion (the Greek term was *atechnoi pisteis*). These modes of persuasion were really not part of the art of rhetoric; they came from outside the art. The orator did not have to *invent* these; he had merely to use them. Aristotle named five kinds of non-artistic proofs: laws, witnesses, contracts, tortures, oaths. Apparently, the lawyer pleading a case in court made most use of this kind of proof, but the politician or the panegyrist could use them too. The representatives today, for instance, who are trying to persuade the citizens to adopt a sales tax quote statistics, legal contracts, existing laws, historical documents, and the testimony of experts to bolster their case. They do not have to invent these supporting arguments; they already exist. True, there is a sense in which they have to find such supporting arguments. They have to be aware that they exist, and they have to know what departments or records to go in order to discover them. (One of the sections in the next chapter will provide expositions of some of the standard reference books that can supply the facts, figures, testimonies to support arguments.) But the representatives do not have to imagine these arguments, to think them up—to invent them, in the classical sense of that term.

The second general mode of persuasion that Aristotle spoke of included artistic proof—"artistic" in the sense that they fell within the province of the art of rhetoric: *rational* appeal (*logos*), *emotional* appeal (*pathos*), and *ethical* appeal (*ēthos*). In exercising the rational appeal, the speaker was appealing to the audience's reason or understanding. The speaker is "arguing," in other words. When we argue, we reason either *deductively* or *inductively*—that is, we either draw conclusions from affirmative or negative statements (e.g., No man can attain perfect happiness in this life; John is a man; therefore John cannot attain perfect happiness in this life) or make generalizations after observing a number of analogous facts (e.g., Every green apple that I bit into had a sour taste. All green apples must be sour.) In logic, the deductive mode of arguing is commonly referred to by the term that Aristotle used, the *syllogism*. In rhetoric, the equivalent of the syllogism was the *enthymeme*. The rhetorical equivalent of *full induction* in logic is the *example*. Since the next chapter will provide an elaborate explanation of syllogism, enthymeme, induction, and example, we will not dwell on them here.

A second mode of persuasion is the emotional appeal. Since people are by nature rational animals, they should be able to make decisions about their private and public lives solely by the light of reason. But they are also endowed with the faculty of free will, and often enough their will is swayed more by their passions or emotions than by their reason. Aristotle expressed the wish that rhetoric could deal exclusively with rational appeals, but he was enough of a realistic to recognize that a person is often prompted to do something or accept something by his or her emotions. And if rhetoric was, as he defined it, the art of discovering "all the available means of persuasion," then he would have to give a place in his *Rhetoric* to an investigation of the means of touching the emotions. Accordingly, he devoted the major portion of Book II of his *Rhetoric* to an analysis of the more common human emotions. This was the beginning of the science of human psychology. If the orator was to play upon people's emotions, he must know what those emotions were and how they could be triggered off or subdued.

A third mode of persuasion was the ethical appeal. This appeal stemmed from the character of the speaker, especially as that character was evinced in the speech itself. A person ingratiated himself or herself with an audience—and thereby gained their trust and admiration—if he or she managed to create the impression that he or she was a person of intelligence, benevolence, and probity. Aristotle recognized that the ethical appeal could be the most potent of the three modes of persuasion. All of an orator's skill in convincing the intellect and moving the will of an audience could prove futile if the audience did not esteem, could not trust, the speaker. For this reason politicians seeking election to public office take such great care to create the proper image of themselves in the eyes of the voters. It was for this reason also that Cicero and Quintilian stressed the need for high moral character in the speaker. Quintilian defined the ideal orator as "a good man skilled in speaking." In his *Nicomachean Ethics,* Aristotle explored the *ēthos* proper for the individual; in his *Politics,* the *ēthos* proper for individuals living together in a society.

The method that the classical rhetoricians devised to aid the speaker in discovering matter for the three modes of appeal was the *topics. Topics* is the English translation of the Greek word *topoi* and the Latin word *loci.* Literally, *topos* or *locus* meant "place" or "region" (note our words *topography* and *locale*). In rhetoric, a topic was a place or store or thesaurus to which one resorted to find something to say on a given subject. More specifically, a topic was a general head or line of argument which suggested material from which proofs could be made. To put it another way, the topics constituted a method of probing one's subject to discover possible ways of developing that subject. Aristotle distinguished two kinds of topics: (1) the special topics (he called them *idioi topoi* or *eidē*); (2) the common topics (*koinoi topoi*). The special topics were those classes of argument appropriate to particular kinds of discourse. In other words, there were some kinds of arguments that were used exclusively in the law courts; some that were confined to the public forum; others that appeared only in ceremonial addresses. The common topics, on the other hand, were a fairly limited stock of arguments that could be used for any occasion or type of speech. Aristotle named four common topics: (1) more and less (the topic of degree); (2) the possible and the impossible (3) past fact and future fact; (4) greatness and smallness (the topic of size as distinguished from the topic of degree). In the text itself we will see how the topics are put to work.

All of the considerations reviewed in the last two or three pages fell within the province of *inventio.* Chapter II, entitled "Discovery of Arguments," will be concerned with this aspect of rhetoric—how to "discover" something to say on some given subject, which is the crucial problem for most writers. The chief reason for writers' inarticulateness on certain subjects is the lack of experience or reading background that can stock their reservoir of ideas. At other times, their inarticulateness stems from their inability to look into a subject to discover what they already know about the subject. Since *inventio* is a systematized way of turning up or generating ideas on some subject, writers may find this rhetorical approach helpful.

The second part of rhetoric was *dispositio* (Greek, *taxis*), which may be translated as "disposition," "arrangement," "organization." This was the division of rhetoric concerned with the effective and orderly arrangement of the parts of a written or spoken discourse. Once the ideas or arguments are discovered there remains the problem of selecting, marshalling, and organizing them with a view to effecting the end of the discourse.

In the simplest terms, one might say that any discourse needs a beginning, a middle, and an end; but this division is self-evident and not much help. Rhetoricians spelled out the division of a discourse more specifically and functionally. Aristotle held that there were really only two essential parts of a speech: the statement of the case and the proof; but he was ready to concede that in practice orators added two more parts: an introduction and a conclusion. Latin rhetoricians, like the author of the *Ad Herennium,* further refined these divisions, recognizing six parts: (1) the introduction (*exordium*); (2) the statement or exposition of the case under discussion (*narratio*); (3) the outline of the points or steps in the argument (*divisio*); (4) the proof of the case (*confirmatio*); (5) the refutation of the opposing arguments (*confutatio*); (6) the conclusion (*peroratio*).

Such a division may strike writers as being arbitrary, mechanical, and rigid. Two things may be said in defense of this conventional pattern. It did set forth clear principles of organization, and inexperienced writers need nothing so much as simple, definite principles to guide them in arrangement of material. Then too the rhetoricians allowed for some adjustments in this scheme. Accepting the Aristotelian notion of the "available means of persuasion," they acknowledge that on some occasions it was expedient to omit certain parts altogether (for instance, if one found it difficult to break down the opposing arguments, it might be advisable to omit the stage of *confutatio*) or to re-arrange some of the parts (for instance, it might be more effective to refute the opposing arguments *before* advancing one's own arguments).

Unquestionably, there is a close interrelation between *inventio* and *dispositio,* and in many rhetoric books these two divisions were treated under one head. Disposition was looked upon as just another aspect of invention; *inventio* was the originative aspect, and *dispositio* was the organizing aspect. As one may learn from the history of rhetoric in the Appendix, Peter Ramus and his followers, like Francis Bacon, wanted to relegate invention and disposition to the province of logic and to limit rhetoric to considerations of style, memory, and delivery. Chapter III of this text, entitled "Arrangement," will deal with this aspect of rhetoric.

.   .   .

The third part of rhetoric was *elocutio* (Greek, *lexis* or *hermēneia* or *phrasis*).
The word *elocution* means something quite different to us from what it
meant to the classical rhetorician. We associate the word with the act of
speaking (hence, the elocution contest). This notion of speaking is, of course,
implicit in the Latin verb from which this word stems, *loqui,* "to speak" (cf.
Greek, *legein,* "to speak"). We have a number of English words based on
this Latin verb: *loquacious, colloquial, eloquence, interlocutor.* It was after
the revival of interest in delivery in the second half of the eighteenth century
that the word *elocution* began to take on its present meaning. But for the
classical rhetorician, *elocutio* meant "style."

Style is a difficult concept to define, although most of us feel we know what
it is. Famous definitions of style, like Buffon's "style is the man," Swift's
"proper words in proper places," Newman's "style is a thinking out into
language," and Blair's "the peculiar manner in which a man expresses his
conceptions," are apt, but they are just vague enough to tease us out of
thought and just general enough to give us a sense for style without giving
us a clear definition of it. None of the major rhetoricians attempted to give
a definition of style, but most of them had a great deal to say about it; in
fact, some of the Renaissance rhetorics were devoted exclusively to a consideration of style.

One of the points that elicited a great deal of discussion was the classification of styles. Various terms were used to name the kinds of style, but
there was fundamental agreement about three levels of style. There was the
low or *plain* style (*attenuata, subtile*); the *middle* or *forcible* style (*medi-
ocris, robusta*); and the *high* or *florid* style (*gravis, florida*). Quintilian proposed that each of these styles was suited to one of the three functions that
he assigned to rhetoric. The plain style was most appropriate for instructing
(*docendi*); the middle for *moving* (*movendi*); and the high for *charming*
(*delectandi*).

All rhetorical considerations of style involved some discussion of *choice of
words,* usually under such heads as correctness, purity (for instance, the
choice of native words rather than foreign words), simplicity, clearness, appropriateness, ornateness.

Another subject of consideration was the *composition or arrangement of
words* in phrases or clauses (or, to use the rhetorical term, *periods*). Involved
here were discussions of correct syntax or collocation of words; patterns of
sentences (e.g. parallelism, antithesis); proper use of conjunctions and other
correlating devices both within the sentence and between sentences; the
euphony of sentences secured through the artful juxtaposition of pleasing
vowel and consonant combinations and through the use of appropriate rhythmical patterns.

A great deal of attention was paid, of course, to *tropes* and *figures* (Greek, *schēmata,* hence the English term *schemes,* which was often used in place of *figures*). Since the concept of tropes and schemes is very complex, it is better that we defer any definition and illustration of these terms to the appropriate section of the text.

Also involved in considerations of style were arguments about (1) the functional vs. the embellishing character of style; (2) Asianism vs. Atticism; (3) the written style vs. the spoken style; (4) economy of words vs. copia of words. These points of discussion are rather peripheral matters, but it is remarkable how much time and energy the rhetoricians devoted to such controversies. The final chapter of this book will be devoted to consideration of style.

The fourth part of rhetoric was *memoria* (Greek, *mnēmē*), concerned with memorizing speeches. Of all the five parts of rhetoric, *memoria* was the one that received the least attention in the rhetoric books. The reason for the neglect of this aspect of rhetoric is probably that not much can be said, in a theoretical way, about the process of memorizing; and after rhetoric came to be concerned mainly with written discourse, there was no further need to deal with memorizing. This process did receive, however, some attention in the schools of rhetoric set up by the sophists. The orator's memory was trained largely through constant practice (just as professional actors today acquire an amazing facility in memorizing a script), but the rhetors did suggest various mnemonic devices that facilitated the memorizing of speeches. The courses that one sometimes sees advertised in newspapers or magazines—"I Can Give You a Retentive Memory in Thirty Days"—are modern manifestations of this division of rhetoric. There will be no consideration in this book of this aspect of rhetoric.

The fifth division of rhetoric was *pronuntiatio* (Greek, *hypokrisis*) or delivery. As in the case of *memoria,* the theory of delivery was conspicuously neglected in the rhetoric texts until the elocutionary movement began about the middle of the eighteenth century. But most rhetoricians would acknowledge the importance of effective delivery in the persuasive process. When Demosthenes, the greatest of the Greek orators, was asked what he considered to be the most important part of rhetoric, he replied, "Delivery, delivery, delivery." Despite the neglect of delivery in the rhetoric books, a great deal of attention was devoted to this aspect in the Greek and Roman schools of rhetoric. Skill in delivery can best be acquired, of course, not by listening to theoretical discussions of this art but by actual practice and by analyzing the delivery of others. Understandably enough, discussions of delivery, as well as of memory, tended to be even more neglected in rhetoric texts after the invention of printing, when most rhetorical training was directed primarily to written discourse.

Involved in the treatment of delivery was concern for the management of the voice and for gestures (*actio*). Precepts were laid down about the modulation of the voice for the proper pitch, volume, and emphasis and about pausing and phrasing. In regard to action, orators were trained in gesturing, in the proper stance and posture of the body, and in the management of the eyes and of facial expressions. What this all amounted to really was training in the art of acting, and it is significant that all the great orators in history have been great "hams."

There is no denying the importance of delivery in effecting the end that one sets for oneself. Many speeches and sermons, however well prepared and elegantly written, have fallen on deaf ears because of inept delivery. Writers lack the advantage a speaker enjoys because of their face-to-face contact with an audience and because of their vocal delivery; the only way in which writers can make up for this disadvantage is by the brilliance of their style.

The Three Kinds of Persuasive Discourse

All rhetoricians distinguished three kinds of orations, and this tripartite classification is well-nigh exhaustive. First, there was *deliberative* oratory, also known as *political, hortative,* and *advisory,* in which one deliberated about public affairs, about anything that had to do with politics, in the Greek sense of that term—whether to go to war, whether to levy a tax, whether to enter into an alliance with a foreign power, whether to build a bridge or a reservoir or a temple. More generally, however, deliberative discourse is that in which we seek to persuade someone to do something or to accept our point of view, as in the two pieces we considered at the beginning of this chapter. According to Aristotle, political oratory was always concerned about the *future* (the point at issue is something that we will or will not do); its special topics were the *expedient* and the *inexpedient;* and its means were *exhortation* and *dehortation.*

Second, there was *forensic* oratory, sometimes referred to as *legal* or *judicial* oratory. This was the oratory of lawyers in the courtroom, but it can be extended to cover any kind of discourse in which a person seeks to defend or condemn someone's actions. (Richard Nixon's famous "Checkers" speech before a nationwide television audience can be considered as an example of forensic rhetoric; and Newman's *Apologia Pro Vita Sua* is another example of forensic discourse.) Forensic oratory, according to Aristotle, was concerned with *past* time (court trials are always concerned with actions or crimes that took place in the past); its special topics were *justice* and *injustice;* and its means were *accusation* and *defense.*

Third, there was *epideictic* oratory. This species has had a variety of other titles: *demonstrative, declamatory, panegyrical, ceremonial.* It is the oratory of display, the kind of oratory exemplified in the *Gettysburg Address* and in the old-fashioned Fourth of July speeches. In this kind of discourse, one is not so much concerned with persuading an audience as with pleasing it or inspiring it. *Ceremonial* discourse—the term we use in this text—is the most "literary" and usually the most ornate of the three kinds of discourse. Aristotle had to strain to fit a proper time-province to this form of oratory, but in the interests of neatness he laid it down that ceremonial oratory was concerned primarily with the *present.* Its special topics were *honor* and *dishonor,* and its means were *praise* and *blame.* The ancients made no provision in their rhetorics for sermons or homiletics. But later, when rhetoric was studied in a Christian culture, the art of preaching was usually considered under the head of epideictic oratory—even though preachers are also concerned with people's past and future actions.

The Relevance and Importance of Rhetoric for Our Times

The kind of complicated, formalized system of rhetoric described in the previous sections may seem to be remote from the concerns and needs of contemporary society. Indeed, some exercises that students in Greek and Roman schools were subjected to are totally dispensable. Practices and principles should not be retained simply because they are venerable with age. They should be retained only if they prove relevant and useful.

Let it be said, first of all, that rhetoric is an inescapable activity in our lives. Every day, we either use rhetoric or are exposed to it. Everyone living in community with other people is inevitably a rhetorician. A parent constantly uses rhetoric on a child; a teacher, on his or her students; a salesperson, on customers; a supervisor, on workers. During every half hour that we spend in front of a television set, we are subjected three or four times to somebody's efforts to get us to buy something. During election time, we are bombarded by candidates' appeals for our vote. Even when we are driving on the streets and highways, our eyes are constantly assaulted by sales pitches on huge billboards.

Advertising may be the most ubiquitous example of an activity that practices what Aristotle preached. But many other fields of endeavor in modern life rely on rhetoric too. The diplomat is a traveling rhetorician with portfolio. The public-relations agent is a practitioner of ceremonial rhetoric, that variety of rhetoric that seeks to reflect credit on a person or an institution. Law is such a many-faceted profession today that many lawyers never get a chance to practice the forensic brand of rhetoric in the courtroom; but even those lawyers whose principal function is to prepare briefs for the Clarence Darrows of the courtroom can be said to be engaged in the *inventio* and *dispositio* aspects of rhetoric. Insurance agents and sales personnel of various kinds practice deliberative rhetoric, often very effectively, every day. Preachers, press-agents, senators and representatives, counsellors, union leaders, business executives, lobbyists are as actively exercising their rhetorical skills today as they ever were.

There are some forms of rhetoric practiced today that we regard with suspicion, even disdain. One of these is propaganda. The term *propaganda* was once a neutral word, signifying the dissemination of truth. But because some people have used propaganda for unscrupulous purposes, *propaganda* has taken on decidedly unfavorable connotations. Closely allied to this disreputable form of rhetoric is demagoguery. The names of the most successful of the twentieth-century demagogues are etched so deeply into our memories that they need not be specified here. These were the exploiters of specious arguments, half-truths, and rank emotional appeals to gain personal advantage rather than to promote the public welfare. Another variety of dangerous rhetoric is brainwashing. A definitive analysis of this diabolical technique has yet to be written, but a beginning has been made in the terrifying final chapters of George Orwell's novel *1984.* Another term has been taken from Orwell's novel to designate another dangerous form of rhetoric, *doublespeak*—a deliberate attempt to use language in such a way as to deceive or confuse listeners or readers. A good argument for an intensive study of rhetoric is that citizens might thereby be put on their guard against the onslaughts of these vicious forms of persuasion.

If "rhetoric" is such a pervasive activity in contemporary society, it behooves us to be aware of the basic strategies and principles of this ancient art. If nothing else, a knowledge of this art will equip us to respond critically to the rhetorical efforts of others in both the oral and written forms. As originally conceived, rhetoric was primarily a synthetic art—an art for "building up," for "composing," something. But rhetoric can also be used as an analytical art—an art for "breaking down" what has been composed. As such, it can make us better readers. As Malcolm Cowley once pointed out, the New Criticism of writers like Cleanth Brooks and Robert Penn Warren represented an application of rhetorical principles to the close reading of poetic texts. Mortimer Adler's *How to Read a Book* presented a rhetorical technique for the reading of expository and argumentative prose. Wayne C. Booth, in his book *The Rhetoric of Fiction,* has shown us the subtle operations of rhetoric in such narrative forms as the short story and the novel. And a knowledge of rhetoric can help us to respond critically and appreciatively to advertisements, commercials, political messages, satires, irony, and doublespeak of all varieties.

Rhetoric can also assist us in becoming more effective writers. One of the chief values of rhetoric, conceived of as a system for gathering, selecting, arranging, and expressing our material, is that it represents a *positive* approach to the problems of writing. Students have too often been inhibited in their writing by the negative approach to composition—don't do this, beware of that. Classical rhetoric too had its negative prescriptions, but, in the main, it offered positive advice to help writers in the composition of a specific kind of discourse directed to a definite audience for a particular purpose. Rhetoric cannot, of course, tell us what we must do in any and every situation. No art can provide that kind of advice. But rhetoric can lay down the general principles that writers can adapt to fit a particular situation. At least, it can provide writers with a set of procedures and criteria that can guide them in making strategic decisions in the composition process.

Students may fear that an elaborately systematized approach to composition will inhibit rather than facilitate writing. There is no denying that formula can retard and has retarded inventiveness and creativity. But to admit that formula *can* inhibit writers is not to admit that it invariably does. Almost every one of the major English writers, from the Renaissance through at least the eighteenth century—Chaucer, Jonson, Shakespeare, Milton Dryden, Pope, Swift, Burke—had been subjected to an intensive rhetoric course in their grammar school or university. If one cannot claim that the study of rhetoric made them great writers, one might yet venture to say that the study of rhetoric did not prevent them from becoming great writers and might even have made them better writers than they would have been on genius alone.

Lest any false hopes be raised, however, let it be affirmed that this adaptation of classical rhetoric offers no magic formula for success in writing. Students will have to work hard to profit from the instruction offered in this book, for it is not all easy to understand, and what is learned must be applied.

The road to eloquence is a hard road and a lonely road, and the journey is not for the faint-hearted. But if, as we are told, the ability to use words to communicate thoughts and feelings is our most distinctively human accomplishment, there can be few satisfactions in life that can match the pride a person feels when he or she has attained mastery over words. As Quintilian said, "Therefore let us seek wholeheartedly that true majesty of expression, the fairest gift of God to man, without which all things are struck dumb and robbed both of present glory and the immortal acclaim of posterity; and let us press on to whatever is best, because, if we do this, we shall either reach the summit or at least see many others far beneath us."

Formulating a Thesis

The beginning of all discourse is a topic, a question, a problem, an issue. This topic or question or problem or issue can be said to be the *subject* of the discourse. Subject is the *res* of the *res-verba* combination that the Latin rhetoricians talked about. The discovery of the *res* (*what* is said) became the province of that part of rhetoric that dealt with "invention." *Verba* (*how* it is said) was the concern of two other parts of rhetoric, "style" and "delivery." Obviously, we cannot make any sensible decisions about the expression part of our discourse until we have clearly and firmly defined the subject-matter.

Frequently, our subject-matter is assigned to us. Our teacher announces in class, "For next Friday I want you to write a 500-word letter to the editor of the school newspaper, giving your views on the proposed increase in tuition." Or the editor of a magazine writes to us and asks us to do a 3000-word piece on the demonstrations against the building of a nuclear powerplant in our community. Or the president of the company for which we work asks us to prepare a report for the next business meeting on the success of the latest advertising campaign. Occasionally, we choose our own subject, but more frequently when we are engaged in major writing project, we are dealing with a subject that has been assigned to us.

But the choice or designation of a subject is only a beginning; in fact, it can be a dead-end if something further is not done to define the subject. It is not enough for us to decide that we are going to write on "democracy." Before "democracy" can become a real subject for a discourse, something must be *predicated* of it. The subject must be converted into a thesis; it must, to use a term from logic, be stated in the form of a *proposition,* a complete sentence that asserts or denies something about the subject. So our vague subject "democracy" must be turned into a sentence like "Democracy is the form of government that best allows its citizens to realize their potentialities as human beings" or "A democracy cannot function effectively if its citizens are illiterate." Now we have a theme or a thesis to write about—a precise notion of what we are going to say about the subject of "democracy."

John Henry Newman, in a section called "Elementary Studies" in his *Idea of a University*, points out the importance of stating a subject in the form of a proposition. His fictitious Mr. Black is commenting on a composition written by a boy named Robert:

> "Now look here," Mr. Black says, "the subject is *'Fortes fortuna adjuvat'* [Fortune favors the brave]; now this is a *proposition;* it states a certain general principle, and this is just what an ordinary boy would be sure to miss, and Robert does miss it. He goes off at once on the word *'fortuna.'* *'Fortuna'* was not his subject; the thesis was intended to *guide* him, for his own good; he refuses to be put into leading strings; he breaks loose, and runs off in his own fashion on the broad field and in wild chase of 'fortune,' instead of closing with a subject, which, as being definite, would have supported him.
>
> "It would have been very cruel to have told a boy to write on 'fortune'; it would have been like asking him his opinion 'of things in general.' Fortune is 'good,' 'bad,' 'capricious,' 'unexpected,' ten thousand things all at once (you see them all in the Gradus), and one of them as much as the other. Ten thousand things may be said of it: give me *one* of them, and I will write upon it; I cannot write on more than one; Robert prefers to write upon all."

Hundreds of Roberts and Robertas are defeated every year in their composition classes because they will not or cannot define their subject. The Latin rhetoricians used a formula, referred to as *status* or *stasis,* for determining the point at issue in a court trial, a formula that might help students decide on a thesis. The formula consisted of three questions that were asked about the subject of dispute or discussion:

> *An sit* (whether a thing is)—a question of fact
> *Quid sit* (what is it?)—a question of definition
> *Quale sit* (what kind is it?)—a question of quality

In a murder trial, for instance, the case for the prosecution and the defense could turn on one of three issues:

1. Did Brutus, as has been alleged, kill Caesar? (whether a thing is)
2. If it is granted that Brutus *did* kill Caesar, was the act murder or self-defense? (what is it?)
3. If it was in fact murder, was Brutus justified in murdering Caesar? (what kind is it?)

The application of this formula settles the issue in a trial and in turn suggests the topics that lawyers resort to in arguing their case.

The use of this formula will not establish the thesis of a discourse, but it can help students determine what aspect of the subject they are going to treat, and then they are in a position to formulate a thesis. Let us suppose that the teacher has asked her students to write a letter to the editor about the increase in tuition. First of all, they must determine what aspect of the subject they are going to talk about. Is there actually going to be an increase in tuition next term, or has the increase only been proposed or rumored? Some of the students may know that the Board of Trustees has been considering an increase in tuition but has not yet formally voted on the proposal. If so, the burden of the letter they would write would be something like the following: "The students of this university have been in an uproar about something that is not yet a fact. If they had taken the trouble to determine the facts, they would know that they do not yet have any just cause for complaint."

Suppose, however, that the report about the increase in tuition charges per credit-hour has been confirmed. What aspect is there left to discuss? Well, the students could direct their attention to the question of definition. Is the change from $48 to $52 per credit-hour really an *increase* in tuition costs? Not if one considers that the Board of Trustees has also voted to reduce the number of credit-hours that students will be allowed to take in any one semester. So although the cost per credit-hour will go up, the total cost of tuition per semester will remain the same. It is apparent that in this instance, a discussion of the definition of *increase* could turn into a mere quibble about words, but with other subjects, like "democracy" or "socialized medicine," there would be more of an opportunity to deal, in a substantive way, with the definition of key terms.

But suppose that a change in tuition has been approved and that this change does constitute a substantial increase in the cost of tuition. Now the third question (*quale sit*) can disclose the real focus of the discussion. Was the increase necessary? Can it be justified? In comparison with the general rise in the cost of living, does the increase in tuition turn out to be minimal? Will the increase in tuition ensure the continuance of, or even an improvement in, the quality of the education the students receive? Or will the increase prevent many students from continuing their education? The application of the third question turns up a number of significant areas of discussion.

The subject-matter considered in relation to the current situation or occasion and to the audience often dictates which of the three questions is most applicable. In any case, however, the application of the pertinent question of *status* does help to define the aspect of the subject that is to be discussed. Once that aspect has been determined, the students should be prepared to formulate a thesis sentence. Once the subject has been narrowed down, what do individual students want to say about that subject?

The cardinal principle is to *state the thesis in a single declarative sentence.*

It is important that the thesis be formulated in a single sentence. Making use of a second sentence to state the thesis is likely to introduce foreign or subsidiary matter and thereby to violate the unity of the thesis. It is equally important to formulate the thesis in a *declarative* sentence. Hortatory sentences like "Let us fight to preserve the integrity of our democracy" and interrogatory sentences like "Is democracy a feasible form of government?" leave the subject fuzzy; both kinds of sentence have a tentative or uncertain air about them. The thesis will be clearly and firmly stated if the predicate *asserts* or *denies* something about the subject: "The integrity of our democracy can be preserved only if we fight to maintain it"; "Democracy is (is not) a feasible form of government."

The thesis sentence is a good starting-point in the composition process because it forces the writer to determine at the outset just what it is that he or she wants to say about the chosen or the designated subject. Moreover, it lays the foundation for a unified, coherent discourse. Then, too, it often suggests some of the *topics* that can be used to develop the subject.

Say, for instance, that for a paper you were going to write for a political science course, you settled on the thesis "Democracy is a feasible form of government for the newly emergent countries of South Africa." That statement precisely defines the proposition that you want to argue for in your paper: a democratic form of government will work in South Africa. If you keep that objective in mind, it is likely that your paper will achieve a tight unity. But the mere verbalization of the thesis also suggests some lines of development. Will you not, for instance, have to define at the beginning of your essay at least two of the key terms in your thesis sentence—*democracy* and *feasible?* Will it not also be advisable for you to specify which countries of South Africa you have in mind? Is there a possibility that you could strengthen your argument about the feasibility of a democratic government in certain countries of South Africa by comparing the situation in these countries with the situation in other countries where democracy has proven successful? As you can see, the statement of your thesis has already suggested the topics of *definition* and *comparison* as possible lines of development and has also suggested a possible organization of your essay that will be conducive to coherence.

Defining the thesis in a single declarative sentence will also help you determine whether you can adequately handle the given or chosen subject within the word limit set for you. The subject "democracy" is so broad that you could not forecast how much development would be necessary to adequately treat that subject. A proposition like "Democracy is the best form of government" is still somewhat broad and vague, but at least it fixes some limits to the subject. You perhaps could not do justice to such a thesis in 500 words, but you might be able to treat it satisfactorily in 1500–2000 words. On the other hand, a proposition like "Representative democracy allows each citizen to exercise some voice in the conduct of the government" might very well be adequately treated in 500 words.

Simple as the principle is, some writers have difficulty in framing their thesis in a single declarative sentence. Part of their difficulty stems from the fact that they do not have a firm grasp on their ideas before they sit down to compose a thesis sentence. Thought and language interact with each other. Hugh Blair, the eighteenth-century Scottish rhetorician, once said, "For we may rest assured that whenever we express ourselves ill, there is, besides the mismanagement of language, for the most part, some mistake in our manner of conceiving the subject. Embarrassed, obscure, and feeble sentences are generally, if not always, the result of embarrassed, obscure, and feeble thought."

It often takes considerable practice before students acquire the ability to define a thesis sharply. They can foster the development of this ability if they will make a habit of formulating a thesis sentence for any formal prose they read. Sometimes the author of the prose they are reading will help them by actually stating the thesis somewhere in the essay, and in that case, their job is to locate that thematic sentence. In some cases, however, the central idea of an essay is nowhere explicitly stated, and the readers must be able to abstract the central idea from the whole essay. The ability to generalize in this way is often the last ability we acquire in learning how to read. If we cannot abstract a thesis from what we read, it is not likely that we will have much success in formulating our own thesis sentences.

We must acquire this ability if we hope to be able to communicate clearly and coherently with others through the medium of written prose. Failure to sharply define one's subject is the chief cause of fuzzy, disunified discourse. Vague beginnings invite chaotic endings. The audience for a discourse, whether written or spoken, can achieve no firmer grasp of the thesis than the writer or the speaker has. As a matter of fact, if we make allowance for what is inevitably lost in the process of transmission, the audience's grasp will always be *less* than the writer's or the speaker's.

So we round back to what was said earlier in this chapter: the beginning of coherent, unified writing is a sharply defined thesis. But as soon as that general principle is enunciated, it invites some qualification. Someone once said, "I don't really know what I want to say until I have said it." And indeed there may be times when it may be advantageous for us to start writing *before* we have a firm, clear idea of what our thesis is. In such cases, the act of writing out our yet unfocused thoughts could become part of the invention process, could lead to the discovery of what we finally want to say about the subject we had chosen, or been delegated, to write on. The articulation of our thesis would not come until *after* we had written our rough draft. We could still say, however, that even in those cases, the articulation of the thesis would be the starting-point, the catalyst, the focusing device for the writing of the final product.

The Three Modes of Persuasion

The thesis we formulate serves as an objective for the discourse we intend to compose. It specifies the idea that we would like to "put across" to others. In argumentative discourse, the thesis indicates the truth or proposal that we want our audience to accept or act upon. But how do we get others to accept our point of view? How do we get others, in Kenneth Burke's terms, "to identify" with us?

Aristotle said that we persuade others by three means: (1) by the appeal to their reason (*logos*); (2) by the appeal to their emotions (*pathos*); (3) by the appeal of our personality or character (*ēthos*). We may use one of these means exclusively or predominantly, or we may use all three. Which of these means we use will be partly determined by the nature of the thesis we are arguing, partly by current circumstances, partly (perhaps mainly) by the kind of audience we are addressing. Everyone develops some instincts for adapting means to fit the subject, occasion, and audience, but by experience and education some people so refine these instincts that their success in dealing with others can be attributed to an art rather than to a mere knack. And when persuasive activities approach the condition of art they can be said to fall within the province of rhetoric.

Before we discuss the *topics*, the system that the classical rhetoricians devised to help one find something to say on any given subject, we will consider the strategies of these three modes of appeal.

The Appeal to Reason

Rationality is humanity's essential characteristic. It is what makes people human and differentiates them from other animals. Ideally, reason should dominate all of people's thinking and actions, but actually, they are often influenced by passions and prejudices and customs. To say that people often respond to irrational motives is not to say that they never listen to the voice of reason. We must have faith not only that people are capable of ordering their lives by the dictates of reason but that most of the time they are disposed to do so. Because the rhetoricians had that faith in people, they thought of rhetoric as an offshoot of logic, the science of human reasoning. "Rhetoric is the counterpart of dialectics," Aristotle said in the first sentence of his *Rhetoric*. Aristotle had dealt with strict logic in the six treatises that collectively have been called the *Organon,* and in two of these treatises, the *Prior Analytics* and the *Posterior Analytics,* he had dealt primarily with deductive and inductive reasoning. Dialectics was the popular form of "analytics" or logic, in the same way that rhetoric was the popular form of the strict demonstration that took place in the sciences. Plato's *Dialogues,* with their give-and-take of question and answer, are good examples of the informal way in which people argue logically with one another. Similarly, rhetoric is the practical art by which we learn how to manipulate all the available means of persuading a large, heterogeneous, perhaps uneducated audience. The appeals to reason that an orator might use do not violate the principles of strict logic; they are merely adaptations of logic. So, whereas the syllogism and induction are the forms that reasoning takes in logic, the enthymeme and the example are the forms that reasoning takes in rhetoric.

Whenever formal deductive or inductive logic is "an available means of persuasion," we should, of course, make use of it. In literary and scientific journals, we often find the authors of articles presenting masses of evidence or employing full-fledged deductive reasoning to convince their professional colleagues of the soundness of their experiments or theses. Even in popularized articles on abstruse subjects, where we do not expect to get the full panoply of logical demonstrations, those authors who are jealous of their professional reputations will take care not to violate the principles of logical reasoning.

As a foundation for the discussion of the rhetorical appeals to reason, we will review some of the principles of logic. First, let us consider the matter of definition.

Principles of Definition

Exposition and argumentation often turn on definition. Exposition, in fact, is a form of definition. In order to *explain* something, we have to tell what a thing is or describe it or enumerate its parts or demonstrate its operation. A dictionary is an expository work—a work that defines, not things, but words that stand for things. All "how to" books are primarily expository, because, by showing how something works or operates, these books are in a sense explaining or defining that thing. Discourses that analyze or classify things are also instances of expository definition.

In the *Topica,* one of his treatises on logic, Aristotle lays down the principles governing what is commonly referred to as an "essential definition." An essential definition is one that designates that which makes a thing what it is and distinguishes that thing from all other things; in other words, it is one that spells out a thing's fundamental nature. For instance, the widely accepted essential definition of *man* is as follows: "A man is a rational animal." The predicate term "rational animal" designates a man's essence and cannot be used of any other creature.

One of the tests by which we can determine whether we have arrived at an essential definition is to see whether we can *convert* the proposition—that is, interchange the subject and predicate terms without destroying the truth of the proposition. The proposition "A man is a rational animal" can be converted to "A rational animal is a man." The proposition is as true in its second form as it is in its first. Let us apply the test to another definition of man, "Man is a biped animal." When we convert the proposition to "A biped animal is a man," we can readily see that the "truth" has been upset, because while it is true that every man is a biped animal, it is not true that every biped animal is a man. "Two-footedness" is a characteristic of man, but it does not designate the essence of man. "Rationality" does designate man's essence, not only because it is characteristic of man, but because it "belongs" exclusively to man.

In an essential definition, the subject and predicate are equivalent terms. In a loose sense, an essential definition sets up an equation: *man* equals *rational animal; rational animal* equals *man.* To use another analogy, the subject term in an essential definition must "weigh" as much as the predicate term. We must be able to interchange the weights on the scale and still keep the scale in balance. That's the trouble with the terms *man* and *biped animal*—they do not "weigh" the same.

It was Aristotle, with his biologist's passion for classification, who showed us how to formulate an essential definition. We put the "thing to be defined" (the *definiendum*) into a *genus* or general class and then give the *differentiae* or the specific differences that distinguish this thing from every other thing comprehended in the same general class. In the essential definition that we used, "animal" is the *genus,* and "rational" is the *differentia* that distinguishes man from every other creature that can be classified as an animal.

The student must not get the idea that the *differentia* will always be given in a single word, as in our definition of man. Sometimes we have to designate several differences to distinguish the thing from other things in the same class. Consider this definition for instance: "An automobile is a vehicle that runs on four wheels." We have the *genus* (vehicle) and a *differentia* (runs on four wheels), but obviously this *differentia* is not sufficient to distinguish an automobile from other vehicles that run on four wheels. The etymology of the word suggests another *differentia* that would help to distinguish an automobile—*auto,* "self-," and *mobilis,* "movable." So we would add that this four-wheeled vehicle is propelled by an internal engine. If this were not sufficient to distinguish an automobile we could add *differentiae* which specify the kind of engine that propelled it, the material the vehicle is made of, its shape, and what it is used for.

The *differentiae* in a definition often specify one or more of the four causes of a thing: the *material,* the *formal,* the *efficient,* and the *final.* For instance, if one were explaining a table, one might say that a table is a piece of furniture (the *genus*) made by a carpenter (efficient cause) from wood (material cause) with a broad, flat top resting horizontally on four legs (formal cause) on which one puts things, often dishes for a meal (final cause, the end or purpose of the thing). It goes without saying that the *differentiae* will change as we attempt to define various kinds of tables. Some tables are made of metal or stone by metalworkers or stonemasons; some tables rest on three legs, others on six; people use tables for a variety of purposes, e.g. to sit or stand at while they are writing or drawing or cutting cloth.

Students will find it instructive to open their dictionaries at random and look at the definitions of nouns on the page they opened. They will find that most definitions of nouns follow the Aristotelian pattern; the substantive is assigned to a general class and then differentiated in one or more ways. They will also find that a dictionary does not often attain or even strive for an essential definition. For practical purposes, we do not often need the precision or exclusiveness of an essential definition. And besides, it is extremely difficult to arrive at, or to know when we have arrived at, an essential definition. Most of us would find it frustrating to specify the essence of a typewriter (even though we would be able to pick out a typewriter from a group of other artifacts), and unless we have desperate need of an essential definition, we do not take the trouble to seek one. We will settle for a serviceable definition of a typewriter. On the other hand, philosophers have sought an essential definition of *man* because it has seemed important to determine just what man's essence is.

Definitions of anything will vary, of course, according to the definer's point of view and one's particular basis of classification. In fact, one of the ways to distinguish the various branches of knowledge is to note the methods and bases of definition used by each science. A biologist, for instance, might define a man as "an erect, bipedal, giant mammal relatively unspecialized in body form." Or if attempting an operative definition, the biologist might define man as "the only creature capable of modifying his evolutionary future." A behavioral scientist might define man as a "social animal" or a "tool-making creature" or "a creature that prepares its food with fire." A theologian might define man as "an adopted son of God." Each of these definitions is true in its own way, and each tells us something useful to know about man. For some purposes, we will find the biologist's definition of man more useful than the logician's definition. (In Vercors's fascinating novel *You Shall Know Them,* a murder trial turns on whether the strange creatures that a scientist has discovered in the jungle and brought back to civilization can be classified as human. In our space age, we may be faced with a similar problem if we find some form of primate life on other planets.) A rhetorician is especially interested in the fact that words admit of a variety of valid definitions.

Other Methods of Definition

Synonyms

There are other ways to define words besides the Aristotelian method of giving the genus and the specific differences. One of the common ways is to cite synonyms. We often resort to this method in the case of adjectives, nouns, and verbs. So if we want to convey the meaning of *inflexible,* we might cite such synonyms as *adamant, implacable, obdurate, stiff, unbending;* to clarify the meaning of *infer* we might offer such synonyms as *deduce, conclude, judge, gather.* Aristotle questioned this method of definition; he maintained that a real definition could be rendered only in a phrase. And he was probably right, for although a synonym can illuminate the meaning of a strange word, it does not really inform us about the mode of being of that word. Still and all, synonyms do play a useful part in clarifying the words used to convey ideas or feelings.

Etymology

Closely allied to definition by synonyms is definition by reference to etymology. One might explain the meaning of *inflexible* by pointing out that the word derives from the Latin prefix *in-,* meaning in this case "not," the Latin verb *flectere,* meaning "to bend," and the suffix *-ible,* meaning "able to be"—hence "not able to be bent." A study of etymology can throw light on the meaning of words, can suggest subtle shades of meaning, and can serve as a mnemonic device—especially for those who have some knowledge of the parent languages. But there is one caution about relying on etymology for the meaning of words: the meanings frequently drift far from the etymological roots. The English word *police,* to take only one example, has strayed considerably from its root in the Greek word *polites,* meaning "citizen." Citing the etymology of *democracy* might stir up more arguments than it would settle.

Description

Another method of definition, frequently used to convey a notion of a complex organization or mechanism, is the extended description. These descriptions often mention the *genus* and several of the *properties* and *accidents* of the thing to be defined, but the definition is presented in discursive prose rather than in the tight, unitary phrases that a dictionary uses. Comparisons, analogies, metaphors, and similes are frequently employed to facilitate definitions by description.

Example

A method especially useful in defining abstractions is giving an example. The dubious syntax, "Honesty is when..." is usually a signal that we are about to get a definition by this method. A definition by example might run something like this:

> You ask me what *honesty* is. Well, I'll tell you. One night about 10:30 while a rather elderly man was walking to the subway after work, he spied a black purse lying in the gutter. Some woman must have dropped it as she was getting into a cab. He looked about him. There was no one else on the street at the moment. He picked up the purse and opened it. Inside the purse was a bundle of ten-dollar bills bound with a rubberband. Riffling through the bills, he estimated that there was 150 to 200 dollars in the bundle. The only identification in the purse was an envelope bearing the name and address of a lawyer. What should he do? Nobody had seen him pick up the purse. The woman who had dropped the purse obviously didn't need the money as desperately as he did. The money could solve a lot of his financial problems at home. He was tempted. But he knew he wouldn't sleep at night if he took the purse home. He snapped the purse shut and walked two blocks out of his way to turn the purse in at the police station. You ask me what honesty is. *That* is honesty.

Defining by example has long been a favorite device of preachers, orators, and teachers. The *exemplum,* an anecdote or short tale with a moral, once played a prominent part in literature. Aesop's *Fables* and Chaucer's *Pardoner's Tale* are just two instances of this genre.

In conclusion, here are three rules that should govern our attempts to define terms:

> 1. The defining terms should be clearer and more familiar than the term to be defined.

This principle is so self-evident that it hardly needs to be enunciated, yet it does need some qualification. Dr. Johnson's notorious definition of a *network* as a "reticulated fabric, decussated at regular intervals, with interstices at the intersections" is not very enlightening to someone who has no notion of a network—although this much-ridiculed definition is remarkably accurate and precise. By using more familiar words, modern dictionaries succeed in conveying a clearer notion of a network. The real difficulty in observing the first rule presents itself when one has to define a relatively simple, everyday object. How does one define an *egg?* Will not the defining terms necessarily be "harder" words than the term to be defined?

> 2. The definition should not repeat the term to be defined or use synonymous or derivative terms.

As we said above, synonyms do not really define; they are merely similar, perhaps more familiar words, which may illuminate the meaning of an unknown word. Nor can the repetition of the same word or of an inflectionally derivative word do much to clarify the meaning of the *definiendum.* So we should avoid definitions like these: "Justice is a virtue which prompts a man to deal justly with another man"; "Man is a creature possessing a human nature"; or definitions like Bardolph's in *King Henry IV,* Part Two, Act III, scene ii: "Accommodated: that is, when a man is, as they say, accommodated; or when a man is, being, whereby 'a may be thought to be accommodated—which is an excellent thing."

> 3. The definition, wherever possible, should be stated positively, not negatively.

The phrase "wherever possible" has to be inserted here because sometimes a concept is so obscure or ambiguous that it is difficult to define it positively; in such cases we realize some gain if we are told at least what the concept is *not.* Of course, concepts that are themselves negative in meaning can hardly be defined positively. So a concept like *darkness* has to be defined negatively as "the absence of light." There can be a rhetorical advantage also in the use of negative definitions—for instance, a series of statements telling what a thing is *not* before one comes forth with the statement of what a thing is. The kind of definition that the third rule cautions against is one like this: "Democracy is that form of government which does not deprive its citizens of their civil liberties." If this is the *only* definition of democracy offered, no one is going to have much of an idea about what democracy *is.*

The Syllogism

The syllogism was a schematic device that Aristotle invented to analyze and test deductive reasoning. People in real life rarely argue in a strict syllogistic form, but the syllogism is a useful device for analyzing the method or form that people observe when they reason deductively. We cannot give a full course in logic here, but we can set down some of the basic principles governing this form of deductive reasoning.

The syllogism reasons from statements or propositions. These propositions are called *premises*. The reasoning follows this course: if *a* is true, and *b* is true, then *c* must be true. Before we consider the syllogism itself, we should say something about the kinds of propositions that appear in categorical syllogisms. Let us start out with the *square of opposition,* a device that logicians invented mainly for mnemonic purposes (see figure below).

The square of opposition presents schematically the four kinds of *categorical propositions*—that is, propositions that either assert or deny something, without conditions or alternatives proposed.

> The A-proposition (All men are mortal beings) is a *universal affirmative.*
>
> The E-proposition (No men are mortal beings) is a *universal negative.*
>
> The I-proposition (Some men are mortal beings) is a *particular affirmative.*
>
> The O-proposition (Some men are not mortal beings) is a *particular negative.*

The letters attached to these propositions happen to be the first four vowels in the English alphabet, but these letters were chosen to label the propositions because they are the first two vowels in two pertinent Latin verbs:

> *AFFIRMO* (I affirm)—so the A and I are attached to the affirmative propositions.
>
> *NEGO* (I deny)—so the E and O are attached to the negative propositions.

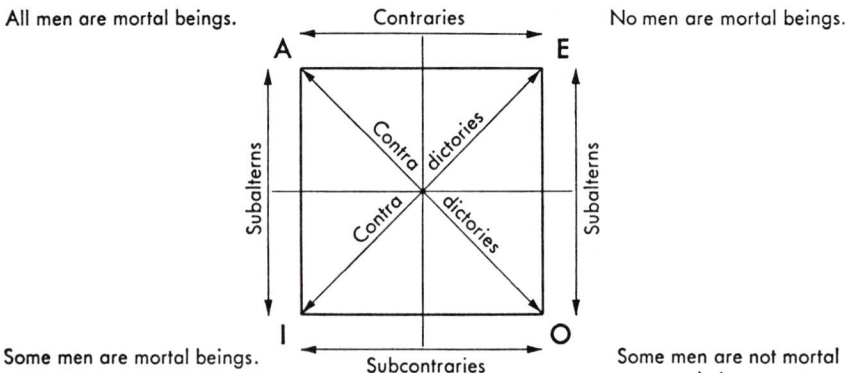

In argument, it is frequently necessary that one be able to classify propositions as to their *quantity* and *quality*. When we ask about the quantity of a proposition, we are seeking to determine whether the proposition is *universal* or *particular*—that is, whether a statement is being made about a whole class or about only part of a class. When we ask about the quality of a proposition, we are seeking to determine whether the proposition is *affirmative* or *negative*—that is, whether the predicate asserts something about the subject or denies something about the subject. Notice that the two propositions above the horizontal line drawn through the square of opposition are *universal* propositions; the two below the line are *particular* propositions. The two propositions to the left of the vertical line are *affirmative* propositions; the two propositions to the right of the vertical line are *negative* propositions.

Each language has its own lexical and grammatical devices for indicating the quantity and quality of propositions. In English, universal propositions are signalled by such words as *every, all, no* before the subject term of the propositions. Particular propositions are signalled by such words as *some, most, many, a few, the majority of.* The presence of the adverb *not* in the predicate indicates that a proposition is negative. But propositions can also be rendered negative in English by the presence of *no, none, none of the, not all, not any of the* in the subject.

In classifying propositions, one never has any difficulty determining whether a proposition is affirmative or negative. One does have difficulty at times, however, determining the quantity of a proposition. What is the quantity, for instance, of a proposition with a proper name as the subject, e.g., "John Smith is mortal"? It seems that since we are asserting something about a particular person, the proposition must be particular. Most logicians, however, would classify this as a universal affirmative, because mortality is being predicated of the entire subject in the same way as in the proposition, "All men are mortal," mortality is being predicated of the whole class of men. By the same reasoning, "John Smith is not mortal" would be classified as a universal negative.

How do we classify the quantity of a proposition like "Men are more stable emotionally than women"? If we are arguing face to face with someone, we can stop our opponent and ask him to clarify the quantity of his statements:

> "Look, you just said that men are more stable emotionally than women. Do you mean *all* men or just *some* men?"
>
> "I mean *some* men ... no, I'll go so far as to say the *majority* of men."
>
> "All right, go on—but remember now what limits you have placed on the extension of your term."

Whenever we are engaged in discussions or arguments with someone present before us, we frequently stop him to ask for clarifications of statements. But when we see a categorical statement in print we cannot call upon the author for clarification. The common practice in such circumstances is to assume, especially if the assertion has the air of a general statement—e.g., "Quakers are zealous, sincere pacifists" or "Birds are feathered creatures"— that the author meant the statement to be taken as a universal. In reconstructing the argument for the purpose of analysis, we would put an "all" in front of the subject term.

How do we classify a proposition like "All men are not mortal"? It is clearly a negative proposition, but despite the "All" in front of the subject term, this proposition does not have the same meaning as the E-proposition, "No men are mortal." "All men are not mortal" is the contradictory form of "All men are mortal." In the square of opposition, contradictory propositions are opposed diagonally. So "All men are not mortal" is really an O-proposition, equivalent in meaning to "Some men are not mortal." The same would be true if the statement took the form of "Not all men are mortal." The final test must always be the *meaning*, not the *form*, of the statement.

It is customary and useful to put categorical statements in the following form:

(Quantity word)   (substantive)   (copulative verb)   (substantive)
Example: All   men   are   mortal beings

Oftentimes, statements put in this form will be awkward and unidiomatic. "All men are mortal" is certainly more idiomatic than "All men are mortal beings." Frequently, too, assertions are made with transitive or intransitive verbs—e.g., "Men run faster than women" and "Most men can hit a golf ball farther than most women can." Putting such categorical statements into the prescribed form frequently results in some very awkward locutions:

> "Men run faster than women." > "All men are faster runners than women." "Most men can hit a golf ball farther than most women can." > "Some men are athletes capable of hitting a golf ball farther than most women can."

The reason for putting statements into the prescribed form is that when these statements occur in syllogisms it is easier for the beginner to pick out terms. As we will see, some of the rules for a valid syllogism involve the distribution of terms. So it is important that we be able to ascertain the terms. Substantives with their cluster of modifiers are easier to pick out than terms hidden in predicate adjectives or action verbs. After students have had practice analyzing arguments, they can dispense with this conversion process and deal with statements in their natural form.

We can learn a great deal about the process of deductive reasoning from studying the relationships of propositions in the square of opposition. Here are the valid deductions we can make from the various propositions:

1. If the A-proposition is true, the I-proposition must be true; like-wise, if the E-proposition is true, the O-proposition must be true.

   If it is true that *all* men are mortal, it logically follows that *some* men are mortal. And if it is true that *no* men are mortal, it is equally true that *some* men are not mortal.

2. If the I-proposition is true, no deduction can be made about the A-proposition; likewise, if the O-proposition is true, no deduc-tion can be made about the E-proposition.

   If we determine that *some* men are mortal, we cannot infer from that fact that *all* men are mortal. In other words, we cannot *infer* the truth of the universal proposition from the particular proposition; we have to *prove* the truth of the universal.

3. If the A-proposition is true, the E-proposition is false; likewise, if the E-proposition is true, the A-proposition is false.

   We know *a priori* that if one of a pair of *contrary* propositions is true, the other is necessarily false. Common sense tells us that if *all* men are mortal, the contrary proposition "No men are mor-tal" must be false.

4. If the A-proposition is false, no deduction can be made about the E-proposition; likewise, if the E-proposition is false, no deduction can be made about the A-proposition.

   Although, as we saw in (3), contrary propositions cannot both be true, they both may be false. So if the proposition "No men are mortal" is false, we may not conclude that all men are mortal. That proposition may also be false.

5. In the case of contradictory propositions (A and O; E and I), one of them must be true and the other false. Accordingly, these are the valid deductions we may make about the propositions opposed diagonally in the square of opposition:

    a. If A is true, O must be false.
    b. If A is false, O must be true.
    c. If O is true, A must be false.
    d. If O is false, A must be true.
    e. If E is true, I must be false.
    f. If E is false, I must be true.
    g. If I is true, E must be false.
    h. If I is false, E must be true.

The law of contradiction is based on the principle that a thing cannot at the same time be and not be. This law plays an important part as one of the means of logical proof in persuasive discourse.

6. If the I-proposition is true, no deduction can be made about the O-proposition; likewise, if the O-proposition is true, no deduction can be made about the I-proposition.

If the I-proposition is false, the O-proposition is true; likewise, if the O-proposition is false, the I-proposition is true.

In the case of subcontraries (the propositions opposed horizontally at the bottom of the square of opposition), both of them can be true, but both of them cannot be false (compare this with the relationship between contrary propositions). It is easier to see that both the subcontraries could be true if we take the propositions "Some men are Republicans" and "Some men are not Republicans." But we cannot deduce the truth of one from the truth of the other. We can, however, infer the truth of one from the falsity of the other.

We are now ready to look at a syllogism. The following syllogism has become Exhibit A in almost every elementary book of logic:

All men are mortal beings.
Socrates is a man.
Therefore, Socrates is a mortal being.

This syllogism sets forth the full chain of reasoning that is implicit in a statement like this: "Socrates is bound to die too, because he is, like the rest of us, a human being." The syllogism is made up of three categorical propositions, the first two of them being called *premises,* the last one being the *conclusion* drawn from these premises. The categorical syllogism is built on three terms: a major term, a minor term, and a middle term. Here are the simple criteria for picking out these terms:

The *major term* is the predicate term of the conclusion ("mortal beings").

The *minor term* is the subject term of the conclusion ("Socrates").
The *middle term* is the term that appears in both of the premises
but does not appear in the conclusion ("men" and its singular
form "man").

The syllogism is made up of three propositions: a major premise, a minor
premise, and a conclusion. The major premise is the proposition that contains the major term ("All men are mortal beings"). The minor premise is
the proposition that contains the minor term ("Socrates is a man"). In con-
structing a syllogism, we usually put the major premise first—although it
should be understood that in actual deductive reasoning the major premise
could occur in any order and, in fact, need not be expressed at all (see the
later discussion of the enthymeme).

It is not so easy to define the conclusion. We could say that the conclusion
is the proposition deduced from the two premises or that the conclusion is
the proposition that contains both the major term and the minor term but
not the middle term. But such definitions involve us in a circular argument.
We cannot determine the major and minor premises unless we know the
major term and the minor term, and we cannot determine the major and
minor terms unless we know which proposition is the conclusion. If we were
to remove the word *Therefore* from the third proposition in our model syllogism and if we were then to scramble the order of the propositions, it
would be impossible to tell which of the propositions was the conclusion.
Any one of the propositions could serve as the conclusion, although only
one combination—the combination in our model—would produce a valid
syllogism.

The main point of this is that we cannot reconstruct a syllogism from
deductive reasoning as we are likely to find it in argumentative discourse
unless we can pick out the conclusion. In the enthymeme, "Socrates is bound
to die too, because he is, like the rest of us, a human being," the first clause
is clearly the conclusion; *because* signals one of the reasons or premises for
the conclusion. In argumentative discourse, conclusions are often signalled
by the use of such function words as *therefore, thus, hence, consequently, so.*
The context of an argument will also serve as a guide to the conclusion.

So much for the form of the syllogism. Before we set down the rules for
a valid syllogism, we need to establish two important points. The first is
the distinction between *truth* and *validity*. Truth has to do with the *matter*
of the syllogism; validity has to do with the *form* of the syllogism. When we
inquire about the truth of a syllogism, we are asking whether a proposition
is true or false. "All men are mortal beings." Is that a true statement? Do
you agree? When we inquire about the validity of a syllogism, we are not
at all concerned about whether the propositions are true; we are concerned
only with whether the inferences are justifiable, whether we can logically

draw this conclusion from those premises. All the rules for the syllogism concern the form, the validity, of the syllogism.

It is extremely important that students keep this distinction in mind. If they withhold their assent to a conclusion, they must know whether they are objecting to the truth of the premise or the validity of the reasoning. If they detect an invalid argument, they can utterly destroy their opponent's argument in a matter of minutes. If they object to the truth of a proposition, they have a harder task on their hands, for it may take a long time to demonstrate that their opponent's statement is false. We must be satisfied about *both* the truth of the premises and the validity of the reasoning before we will give our assent to a conclusion. But the peculiar force of a syllogistic argument resides in this: *if* we assent to the truth of the premises and *if* we agree that the reasoning is valid, we *must* grant the conclusion. Under these conditions, rational people cannot resist the conclusion.

The second point we need to establish is the meaning of the term *distribution*. In logic, distribution signifies the full extension of a term to cover all the objects or individuals in the class denoted. In the phrase "all men," the term *men* is said to be distributed because the *all* designates the total number of individuals in the class of *men*. In the phrase "some men," *men* is undistributed because the *some* designates something less than the total number of individuals in the class. Sometimes we speak of a distributed term as being a *universal term* and of an undistributed term as being a *particular term*.

In the syllogism, we usually have no difficulty determining whether the subject term of propositions is distributed, because the quantity words (*all, every, no, some, most*), if present, will tell us. Since, as we have pointed out, most logicians regard a proposition that has a proper name as the subject as being a universal proposition ("Socrates is a rational animal"), the proper name may be regarded as a distributed term (the predicate applies to the *entire* subject).

It is a little more difficult to determine—or at least to recognize—whether predicate terms are distributed. For beginning students, it is just as well that they use this simple formula:

1. The predicate terms of all *affirmative* propositions (all A- or I- propositions) are *undistributed*.
2. The predicate terms of all *negative* propositions (all E- or O- propositions) are *distributed*.

Let us see why this is so. When we assert "All men are mortal beings," it is clear that "mortal beings" is predicated of every member of the class of men. At the same time, however, we are not saying, "All men are all the mortal beings that are." Perhaps this can be clarified with a system of circles. Let one circle represent the entire class of men and another circle represent the entire class of mortal beings. Now here is a picture of the proposition "All men are mortal beings":

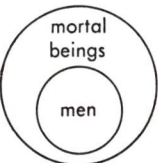

The proposition asserts that the entire class of men is "in" the class of mortal beings, but as the circles make clear, the class of men does not have as wide an extension, does not cover as much area, as the class of mortal beings. There are other mortal beings (birds, animals, fish) that are not men. We have then made an assertion about the entire class of men but not about the entire class of mortal beings. So the term *men* is distributed, but the term *mortal beings* is undistributed.

Now here is a picture of the proposition "No men are mortal beings":

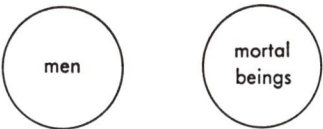

We have asserted that *none* of the class of men is "in" the class of mortal beings: or, to put it another way, the entire class of men is excluded from the entire class of mortal beings. Both terms are being used in the widest possible extension, and therefore both the subject term and the predicate term of an E-proposition are distributed.

The scheme of circles can also illustrate the distribution of the predicate terms in I- and O-propositions:

I-proposition:

Some men are mortal beings.

O-proposition:

Some men are not mortal beings.

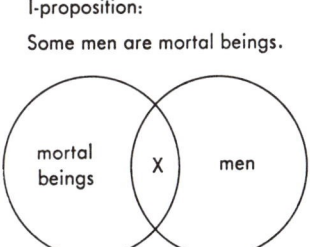

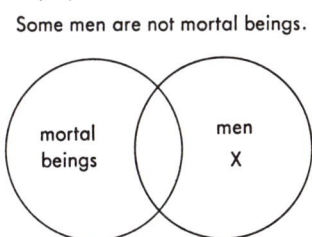

In the I-proposition, part of the *men* circle (the checkmarked area) overlaps part of the *mortal being* circle, and so it is clear that neither the subject term nor the predicate term is distributed—in neither case is the entire class involved. In the O-proposition, part of the *men* circle (the checkmarked area) falls outside the *mortal being* circle; consequently, the subject term *men* is undistributed (a predication is made about something less than the whole class of men), but the predicate term *mortal beings* is distributed (the "some men," represented by the checkmark, is wholly outside the entire class of mortal beings).

The distribution of predicate terms is not an easy concept to grasp. If the circle diagrams have not clarified this concept, it would be well for students to rely, until the light strikes them, on the simple formulas that the *predicate terms of all affirmative propositions are undistributed* and that the *predicate terms of all negative propositions are distributed*. This matter of distribution is important, because two of the rules for a valid syllogism involve distribution of terms and because many of the fallacies in deductive reasoning are the result of an inference being drawn from undistributed terms.

We are ready now to look at the rules for a valid syllogism. Remember that these rules concern the form or the logic of the argument, not the truth of the propositions:

1. There must be three terms and only three terms.
2. The middle term must be distributed at least once.
3. No term may be distributed in the conclusion if it was not distributed in the premise.

Most invalid syllogisms will be detected by the application of these three rules. Occasionally, however, a syllogism will pass the test of these three rules and yet will not be a valid syllogism. So we must add three more rules:

4. No conclusion may be drawn from two *particular* (as opposed to *universal*) premises.
5. No conclusion may be drawn from two negative premises.
6. If one of the premises is negative, the conclusion must be negative.

Let us apply these six rules to our model syllogism and see whether the reasoning is valid. Here is the syllogism again:

All men are mortal beings.
Socrates is a man.
Therefore, Socrates is a mortal being.

The first rule is that there must be *three terms and only three terms*. In the elementary stages of testing syllogisms, students must actually count the terms.

Once they have counted three terms, they may not stop there; they must go on to make sure that there are *only* three terms. In the first proposition, there are two terms, *men* and *mortal beings*. In the next proposition, there are two terms, *Socrates* and *man*. Since *Socrates* is a term clearly distinct from the *men* and *mortal beings* of the first proposition, we have now determined that there are three terms in this syllogism. But we must now go on to check that the syllogism has no more than three terms. What about *man* in the second proposition? Is it not a fourth term? Is it not different from *men* in the first proposition? *Men* does differ grammatically from *man*, being the plural form of the singular noun, but lexically the two terms do not differ, since they both have the same referent. Terms are the "same"— are *univocal*, to use the logician's term—if the referent of the terms is identical. If, for instance, we substituted *He* for *Socrates* in the conclusion, we would not be introducing a fourth term into the syllogism because the referent or antecedent of *He* is, presumably, *Socrates*. (We would, of course, be introducing another term if the antecedent of the pronoun were not *Socrates*.) Sometimes in arguing with someone we call for a clarification of the ambiguity of pronoun reference. "Who is *they?*" we ask our opponent, just to make sure that he hasn't shifted referents. Likewise we can use synonyms or periphrasis without introducing a new term. If in the conclusion we were to substitute "a man who will die" for *mortal being*, we would not be introducing another term. In such cases, of course, we must be satisfied that the synonym or periphrasis means the same as the term for which it is substituting.

What we must be especially on our guard against is the use of the same term with different meanings. To do this is to be guilty of what the logicians call *equivocation*. Let us look first at an obvious example of equivocation:

> All men have hearts.
> All celery plants have hearts.

No native speaker of English would be deceived by the shift of meaning in the two uses of the word *hearts*. The second *hearts* is clearly a new term. It is subtle shifts of denotation that can trap us. We must be alert enough to catch a subtle shift like this:

> All draftsmen are designing men.
> All politicians are designing men.

The point might be made here that from the logician's point of view shifts in denotation will result in fallacious reasoning, but that from the rhetorician's point of view shifts in denotation can be used for certain stylistic effects, in which case the audience is aware of both meanings. The pun, the figure of speech that rhetoricians called *paronomasia*, is an example of this kind of shift in denotation. One of the famous examples of paronomasia was Christ's promise to the chief of his apostles: "Thou art Peter [Greek, *petra,* rock], and upon this rock I will build my church." Rhetorical effects are also achieved by shifts in the connotation of words. We will discuss this further in the chapter on style.

Let us go back now to counting the terms in our model syllogism. We had gone through the two premises and discovered that we had three distinct terms and decided that *man* in the second premise was not a fourth term. In the conclusion, *Socrates* is a repetition of a term in the minor premise, and *mortal being* is a repetition, in singular form, of a term in the major premise. So our model syllogism passes the first test: it has three terms and only three terms.

Now to test the syllogism by the second rule: *the middle term must be distributed at least once.* The middle term, we said, was the term that occurred in both premises but not in the conclusion. Our middle term here is *men (man).* We must determine whether it is distributed, whether it is used, at least once, to include the whole class. "All men are mortal beings" is our major premise. The middle term *men* is distributed. We can tell that it is distributed by noting the *All.* Is the middle term distributed in the minor premise, "Socrates is a man"? No, it is not; here it is the predicate term of an affirmative proposition, which, as we have said, is never distributed. But since our middle term is distributed *once,* our syllogism passes the test of the second rule. Later on, we shall see examples of the fallacy of the undistributed middle—one of the commonest fallacies in deductive reasoning.

According to the third rule for a valid syllogism, *no term may be distributed in the conclusion if it was not distributed in the premises.* The conclusion of our model syllogism is "Therefore, Socrates is a mortal being." If, as we observed, propositions with a proper noun as subject must be regarded as universal propositions, *Socrates* is a distributed term. So we must check to see whether this term was distributed in the premise. *Socrates,* we find, is the subject term of the same kind of proposition in the minor premise and is therefore a distributed term. *Socrates* is distributed in the conclusion, but *Socrates* is also distributed in the premise; hence our third rule is satisfied. The predicate term *(mortal being)* of the conclusion is undistributed (remember, the predicate term of affirmative propositions is undistributed). If we find any term in the conclusion to be undistributed, we can stop right there; we do not have to check to see whether the term is distributed in the premise.

Our model syllogism has passed the test of the first three rules, and generally this indicates that the reasoning is valid. But, just to be sure, we have to apply the fourth, fifth, and sixth rules. We can do that hurriedly. The fourth rule is that *no conclusion may be drawn from two particular premises.* Both of the premises in our model syllogism are universals. The fifth and sixth rules do not apply at all because neither of the premises is negative.

So the reasoning in our model syllogism is unshakably valid. We are satisfied about the *form* of the argument. Now before we assent to the conclusion, we must be satisfied about the *matter* of the argument—that is, about the truth of the premises. Is it true that all men are mortal, that all men are destined to die? Do we agree that Socrates is a man, that Socrates is a species of the genus *man*? If we answer "yes" to both of those questions, we must grant the conclusion.

If, on the other hand, we deny the truth of either premise, we will have to settle down to demonstrating that the premise is false or to listening to our opponent's arguments that the premise is true. Arguments about the truth of premises can go on for a long time and even then not be settled. Usually, arguments that go on and on are arguments about the truth or falsity of propositions. Even those arguments that are stalemated by the lack of agreement about the definition of terms are arguments about the matter and not about the form of the argument. Whenever it can be shown that the mode of arguing is illogical, the dispute can be settled very quickly. The rules for a valid syllogism were derived inductively from a study of the way in which the human mind reasons, and no one has successfully challenged the validity of these rules. Even one who has no formal training in logic and its technical terminology can be shown very quickly, in layperson's terms, that his or her reasoning is invalid, if it is.

Once students have been instructed about the form, the terminology, and the rules for the syllogism, it is simply a matter of practice with sample syllogisms before they acquire a proficiency in detecting fallacies in deductive reasoning. A number of syllogisms have been provided in the exercises immediately following this section. In the beginning stages, students may have to apply the rules, one by one, in a mechanical fashion. After they have had some practice in dealing with syllogisms, they will be able to tell at a glance whether the syllogism is valid or not. For instance, any time they find a syllogism taking this form, they will detect the Fallacy of the Undistributed Middle:

> All A is B.
> All C is B.
> ∴ All C is A.

Whenever the middle term (B) is the predicate term of two affirmative premises, the middle term will be undistributed, and consequently no conclusion can logically follow from those premises.

Since the arguments based on the topic of antecedent and consequent often take the form of a hypothetical or conditional proposition, we should consider the principles that govern validity of reasoning in the hypothetical syllogism. When we argue in the form of a hypothetical proposition, we are proposing that the truth of the antecedent (the *if* clause) implies the truth of the consequent (the main clause). So we say, "If he has leukemia, he will die." The truth of the consequent, however, does not necessarily imply the truth of the antecedent: "If he dies, he has leukemia" is not necessarily true.

If we construct a deductive argument from the hypothetical proposition, we can detect, from another angle, that the truth of the antecedent does not follow from the truth of the consequent. First, let us look at a valid deductive argument:

> 1. If he has leukemia, he will die.
>   He has leukemia.
>   Therefore, he will die. (VALID)

Here the second premise affirms that the antecedent is true. If it is confirmed that a man has leukemia and if everyone afflicted with leukemia invariably dies, then it logically follows that this man will die.

Now let us see what happens to the validity of the argument when the second premise affirms the consequent:

> 2. If he has leukemia, he will die.
>   He will die.
>   Therefore, he has leukemia. (INVALID)

Confronted with this argument, most of us would be prompted to say, "Somehow I don't feel that the conclusion follows from the premise." Our feeling about the conclusion would be right. A logician labels this form of argument "the fallacy of affirming the consequent." Common sense tells us that from this sequence of propositions one may not validly infer that the man has leukemia from the affirmation that the man is going to die.

If the consequent is *denied,* a valid conclusion may be drawn. We can use the same sort of propositions to illustrate this form of argument:

> 3. If he has leukemia, he will die.
>   He will not die.
>   Therefore, he does not have leukemia. (VALID)

The validity of this conclusion may not be immediately apparent, but if we reflect a moment on what the premises say, we are forced to agree to the conclusion. If a man afflicted with leukemia inevitably dies and if a doctor affirms that this man is not in apparent danger of death, the one thing we can assert definitely is that this man does not now have leukemia.

Let us look at an example of "the fallacy of denying the antecedent":

> 4. If he has leukemia, he will die.

He does not have leukemia.
Therefore, he will not die. (INVALID)

Common sense tells us that even if both premises are true, the conclusion does not follow, because we recognize that a man could die from something other than leukemia.

Here is a simple table of criteria for testing the validity of hypothetical syllogisms:

> If the minor premise (that is, the second premise)
> (1) affirms the antecedent—the conclusion is valid (see syllogism 1 above)
> (2) affirms the consequent—the conclusion is invalid (see syllogism 2)
> (3) denies the consequent—the conclusion is valid (see syllogism 3)
> (4) denies the antecedent—the conclusion is invalid (see syllogism 4)

Since arguments based on the topic of contradiction sometimes take the form of "either/or," or disjunctive, propositions, we might take a look at some of the principles governing this kind of deductive reasoning.

The issue in an argument might take this form: "Either he committed the murder, or he did not commit the murder." We recognize that these are the only two possibilities. Therefore, if one of the possibilities is disproved, the other one must be true. As anyone knows who has witnessed a fictional or real-life courtroom drama, it sometimes takes a protracted trial to prove or disprove one of the alternatives posed in our sample disjunctive proposition. But once we have proved one of the alternatives to be true, we automatically prove the other to be false.

In setting up the disjunctive proposition, however, we must take care to set up *mutually exclusive* alternatives. The proposition "She is either a student or a teacher" has the form of a disjunctive proposition, but the alternatives, the matter of the disjunctive statement, are not mutually exclusive. For she could be a teacher and a student in any one period. However, if we were to say, "Either she is a teacher, or she is not a teacher," we have set up mutually exclusive alternatives, for being a teacher and not being a teacher are the only two possibilities in this instance.

Exercise

Test the following syllogisms for validity. Wherever necessary, convert the propositions into the form of substantive terms on both sides of a copulative verb. Where no quantity word is expressed, presume that *All* precedes the subject term if the proposition is affirmative or that *No* precedes the subject term if the proposition is negative—e.g., *Men are not happy > No men are happy people.* Since we should not be at all concerned with the truth of the propositions when we are testing a syllogism for validity, nonsense words or symbols will occasionally be used for the terms of the propositions.

1.   No out-of-state students are taxpayers.
     Some freshmen are out-of-state students.
     ∴ Some freshmen are taxpayers.

2.   All Catholics are Protestants.
     All Protestants are Baptists.
     ∴ All Catholics are Baptists.

3.   All typhoons are destructive windstorms.
     All cyclones are destructive windstorms.
     ∴ All cyclones are typhoons.

4.   All college graduates are potential wage-earners.
     No high-school graduates are college graduates.
     ∴ No high-school graduates are potential wage-earners.

5.   No Russians are democratic.
     All Americans are democratic.
     ∴ All Americans are Russians.

6.   All those who contribute to the Community Chest are charitable.
     John Smith does not contribute to the Community Chest.
     ∴ John Smith is not charitable.

7.   All horse-race betting is gambling.
     Some gambling is illegal.
     ∴ Some horse-race betting is illegal.

8.   Some Marines have been awarded the Distinguished Service Cross.
     No civilians have been awarded the Distinguished Service Cross.
     ∴ Some civilians are not Marines.

9.   Those who get good grades study diligently.
     All students are anxious to get good grades.
     ∴ All students study diligently.

10. All brilligs are slithy toves.

No slithy toves are borogoves.
∴ No borogoves are brilligs.

11. No planets are suns.
No planets are satellites.
∴ No satellites are suns.

12. All cosmonauts are highly trained men.
Some test pilots are not highly trained men.
∴ Some cosmonauts are not test pilots.

13. All A is B.
Some B is C.
∴ Some C is A.

14. Some A is B.
All B is C.
∴ Some C is A.

15. Anything I possess is mine.
I possess your pen.
∴ Your pen is mine.

16. All contracts are based upon an agreement between two parties.
The United Nations is based upon an agreement among several
countries.
Therefore the United Nations can also be classified as a contract.

17. Because most Americans are industrious and all of them love freedom, most industrious people love freedom.

18. Since robins are two-legged creatures and since all birds are two-
legged creatures, it follows that all robins are birds.

19. Since only radicals want to subvert the duly constituted government
of a country, this man can't be a radical because he wants to preserve
the government of the country.

20. Prabusks are certainly not panbuls. I know that because plocucks
are panbuls and prabusks are plocucks.

The Enthymeme

Our treatment of the categorical, hypothetical, and disjunctive syllogisms
was sketchy, but all the fundamentals were touched on. These fundamental

principles should provide us with sufficient guidance for the construction or analysis of deductive reasoning according to the laws of formal logic. We have by no means exhausted all the facets and complexities of Aristotelian or scholastic logic, nor have we touched on symbolic logic, which has developed from the mathematical studies of men like Gottlob Frege, Alfred North Whitehead, and Bertrand Russell and from studies in semantics by men like C. K. Ogden, I. A. Richards, and Alfred Korzybski. But our primary concern is with rhetoric, and we can linger in the province of logic only long enough to gather some useful basic principles.

We turn now to a consideration of the enthymeme, which is the rhetorical equivalent of the syllogism. In modern times, the enthymeme has come to be regarded as an abbreviated syllogism—that is, an argumentative statement that contains a conclusion and one of the premises, the other premise being implied. A statement like this would be regarded as an enthymeme: "He must be a socialist because he favors a graduated income-tax." Here the conclusion (He is a socialist) has been deduced from an expressed premise (He favors a graduated income-tax) and an implied premise (either [a] Anyone who favors a graduated income-tax is a socialist or [b] A socialist is anyone who favors a graduated income-tax). Incidentally, the student who has developed some skill in analyzing the validity of syllogisms will detect that if the implied premise is [b], the conclusion (He is a socialist) is invalidly drawn because the middle term (anyone who favors a graduated income-tax) is undistributed in both of the premises of the fully reconstructed syllogism.

The modern notion of the enthymeme as a truncated syllogism is probably implicit in Aristotle's statement, "The enthymeme must consist of few propositions, fewer often than those which make up a normal syllogism" (*Rhetoric*, I, 2). But according to what Aristotle said in the *Prior Analytics* (Bk. II, Ch. 27), the essential difference is that the syllogism leads to a necessary conclusion from universally true premises but the enthymeme leads to a tentative conclusion from probable premises. In dealing with contingent human affairs, we cannot always discover or confirm what is the truth. Think of how difficult it often is to prove that the defendant is guilty of the crime with which he or she is charged; how much more difficult it is to prove the wisdom or advantage of a future course of action—for instance, that a proposed tax cut will contribute to the general prosperity of the country. But frequently, in the interests of getting on with the business of life, we have to make decisions on the basis of uncertainties or probabilities. The function of rhetoric is to persuade, where it cannot convince, an audience. And in matters where the truth cannot be readily ascertained, rhetoric can persuade an audience to adopt a point of view or a course of action on the basis of the merely probable—that is, on the basis of what usually happens or what people believe to be capable of happening.

We can illustrate the difference by looking at a syllogism and an enthymeme. Our model syllogism is a good example of the kind of deductive reasoning that can lead to an irresistible conclusion. The major premise of that syllogism—"All men are mortal"—states a universal truth. Both history and the evidence of our own senses tell us that all men must die. The minor premise—"Socrates is a man"—is a truth that can be unmistakably verified. From these two "truths" then we can arrive at the infallible conclusion that Socrates too will die.

But suppose someone argues this way: "John will fail his examination because he hasn't studied." Here we have an enthymeme, both in the sense of a truncated syllogism and in the sense of a deductive argument based on probable premises. The truth of the minor premise here—"John hasn't studied"—could be confirmed. The probable premise resides in the unexpressed proposition—"Anyone who doesn't study will fail his examination." We all know that the latter proposition is not universally true. But we also know that those who do not study usually fail their examinations. It is, in other words, probable that those who do not study will fail. For all practical purposes, that probability is enough to persuade us that next week we will see John's name on the Dean's list of failures.

Aristotle was shrewd enough to see that we base persuasive arguments not only on what usually or generally happens but also on what people believe to be true. For that reason, those who seek to persuade a select audience must apprise themselves of the generally held opinions of that group. If it is known, for instance, that a certain group of people believe that the Fire God causes the rainfall, we could use that received opinion to persuade our audience that it is their failure to propitiate the Fire God that is responsible for the protracted drought. Every civilization has a body of accepted opinions that influence the conduct of its affairs—a body of "truths" that have never really been demonstrated but in which the people have faith, almost to the point of accepting them as self-evident.

The enthymeme then—"a kind of syllogism," as Aristotle puts it—is the instrument of deductive reasoning peculiar to the art of rhetoric. It often suppresses some of the links in the chain of argument because the audience is impatient with, or incapable of attending to, the kind of closely reasoned, full-scale argument associated with formal logic. And the audience can be satisfied with probable conclusions because it recognizes the contingent nature of the things that rhetoric deals with.

Since the enthymeme partakes of the nature of the syllogism, its mode of inference is similar to that of the syllogism. One of the premises may be missing, but the missing premise is as readily supplied as the missing parts of an elliptical grammatical structure. When we are seeking to refute someone else's enthymeme, it may be the missing premise that we should attack, because the implied proposition may be the vulnerable spot in the other person's argument.

For instance, take the enthymeme, "He must be a Communist because he advocates civil rights for minority groups." We cannot really judge the validity of the conclusion ("He must be a Communist") until we look at the implied premise. We might *sense* that the conclusion is unwarranted, but until we exposed the implied proposition, we could not demonstrate that the conclusion was unwarranted. We cannot determine, in other words, whether the conclusion follows logically until we study the conclusion in relation to the expressed premise *and* the implied premise.

What is the implied premise in this instance? In the discussion of the syllogism, we said that if we can determine which proposition in a deductive argument is the conclusion we can reconstruct the full syllogism. The minor term, we learned, is the subject of the conclusion; the major term is the predicate of the conclusion. Since "he" is the subject term of the conclusion, we know that the expressed premise (he advocates civil rights for minority groups) is the minor premise of the full syllogism. We also know that the major premise of the full syllogism will contain the predicate term of the conclusion ("a Communist"). But although we know that the implied premise will contain this term, we do not know for sure whether this major term is the subject term of the major premise or the predicate term of the major premise. The implied premise could take either of these forms:

All Communists are advocates of civil rights for minority groups.
All advocates of civil rights for minority groups are Communists.

It is important that we be able to determine which form the implied premise takes, because until we do so, we cannot determine whether and where the argument is vulnerable. If the person who advanced the enthymeme meant to imply that "all Communists advocate civil rights for minority groups," we would not have to spend our time discussing whether that proposition was true; we could very quickly point out that this argument is invalid because the middle term ("advocates of civil rights"), being the predicate term of two affirmative propositions, is undistributed. If our opponent did not understand what it meant to say that a term was "undistributed," we could point out to him that his argument had not established that only Communists advocate civil rights for minority groups. At bottom, this is the fallacy behind all assertions of guilt by association.

If, on the other hand, the implied premise is "All advocates of civil rights for minority groups are Communists," the reasoning will be valid, because now the middle term is distributed (*"All* advocates"). Hence we can impugn only the truth of the implied proposition. Is it true that anyone who advocates civil rights is a Communist? Whether we judged this proposition from the viewpoint of what is necessarily true (the province of strict logic) or from the viewpoint of what is probably true (the province of rhetoric), we would have to deny that this proposition is true. So although the argument in this case is valid, we would not grant the conclusion because the implied premise is patently false.

Aristotle said that the materials of enthymemes are *probabilities* and *signs.* We have already treated of the probable propositions, which constitute the premises of an enthymeme and which constitute, in Aristotle's eyes, the essential distinction between enthymemes and syllogisms. A sign is an indication or concomitant of something else; it may occur before or simultaneously with or after something else. Smoke, for instance, is a sign of fire; lightning is a sign that thunder is about to rumble; thunder is a sign that lightning has flashed. A sign is not a cause or reason for something else happening; it is merely an indication that something has happened, is happening, or will happen. Signs, like probabilities, can constitute the premises of an enthymeme.

Aristotle distinguished two kinds of signs that figure in an enthymeme— *infallible* and *fallible.* An infallible sign is that which invariably accompanies something else. It is said, for instance, that smoke invariably accompanies fire. Accordingly, whenever we see smoke or smell smoke we conclude that there is a fire someplace. And if it was really smoke we saw or smelled, there will of course *be* a fire someplace. Now, what makes a conclusion drawn from this kind of sign infallible is not only that smoke invariably accompanies fire but that smoke accompanies fire exclusively. If what we commonly know as smoke sometimes accompanied something else besides fire, we could not conclude infallibly that the presence of smoke was a sign of the presence of fire.

If a sign does not invariably and exclusively accompany something else, it is fallible—that is, any conclusion drawn from a sign of this kind will always be open to refutation. For instance, fast breathing is often a sign that a person has a fever. But because fast breathing does not always accompany a fever and because fast breathing sometimes attends other physical conditions, we cannot conclude infallibly that a person has a fever from the fact that the individual breathes rapidly. The condition of fast breathing would justify us in concluding that the person probably has a fever, but no more than that. The probability of that person's having a fever increases, of course, if the fast breathing is accompanied by other signs or symptoms of fever—high temperature, flushed cheeks.

Circumstantial evidence in a court trial is usually based on a series of fallible signs. The prosecuting lawyer reminds the jury of a number of suspicious circumstances: the accused was discovered with blood on his coat; his face was badly scratched; his shirt was torn; there was an ugly purplish bruise on his skin. "Are these not signs," the prosecutor asks the jury, "of a fierce physical struggle?" The prosecutor hopes that the jury mentally answers "yes" to this rhetorical question. Circumstantial evidence can never prove absolutely that a person is guilty, and for this reason many states will not allow the death penalty to be imposed on someone convicted by this evidence alone. But circumstantial evidence, especially when it has acquired cumulative force from the citation of a large number of incriminating particulars, can have great persuasive power with a jury.

So rhetoricians will use infallible signs for their enthymemes whenever such signs are available. But they will also use fallible signs, because they too can have persuasive force. They will remain aware, however, that arguments built upon fallible signs are always open to challenge. Fallible signs are like analogies: they never prove, but they can persuade.

Let us stress again two points about the use of the rhetorical enthymeme: (1) it is important to ascertain the implied premise of an enthymeme, because the implied premise or assumption may be the vulnerable spot in the argument; (2) the probable propositions and the fallible signs used in rhetorical enthymemes do not lead to necessarily and universally true conclusions, but they can be effectively persuasive.

How can students recognize an enthymeme when they meet one in ordinary discourse? Fortunately, enthymemes assume a fairly common syntactic pattern accompanied by a limited number of function words. Enthymemes often take the form of a compound sentence, with the two clauses joined by co-ordinating conjunctions *for* or *so* or linked logically by such conjunctive adverbs as *therefore, hence, consequently;* or they take the form of a complex sentence, with the clauses joined by such subordinating conjunctions as *since* or *because.*

Let us illustrate the syntactic form of the enthymeme by taking two propositions and linking them grammatically in a variety of ways to form an enthymeme. These are the two propositions:

> John Smith would not make a good governor. He has Communist leanings.

These two independent clauses, juxtaposed paratactically, could constitute an enthymeme. The context in which those two sentences occurred might suggest to the hearer or reader a logical relationship between the two statements: the second statement gives the grounds for the first assertion. An alert, sophisticated audience will readily detect the connection between these two statements. Rather than rely on the implied relationship, however, most speakers or writers will tie the two statements together explicitly. Note the various ways in which they could link the clauses:

John Smith would not make a good governor, *for* he has Communist leanings.
          because he has Communist leanings.
          since he has Communist leanings.

John Smith has Communist leanings, *so* he would not make a good governor.

John Smith has Communist leanings; *therefore* he would not make a good governor.
          consequently he would not make a good governor.
          hence he would not make a good governor.

But not every sentence employing linking words like *for, because,* and *therefore* will constitute an enthymeme. Take, for instance, a statement like this: *He didn't go to the lecture last night, because he had a headache.* Here the *because*-clause merely gives a *reason* for his not going to the lecture; it is not a premise from which the conclusion is deduced. If we link the first statement with a different statement, however, we will have an enthymeme: *He didn't go to the lecture last night, so he must differ ideologically with the guest speaker.* Now the first statement becomes the ground or the premise for the inference stated in the second clause.

Sometimes there will be an ambiguity about the relationship of the clauses. Take this statement for instance: *He did not kill his mother because he loved her.* What is the import of this statement? Is this statement merely denying the reason given for the murder? It may mean something like this: he did not kill his mother because he loved her and wanted to relieve her of any further agony from her incurable disease; no, he killed her because he wanted to collect on her insurance. Or it may mean this: he loved his mother; therefore it is ridiculous to suggest that he killed her. If the statement means the latter, we would have a true enthymeme. The import of the statement depends upon whether the *because*-clause is *restrictive* or *nonrestrictive*. If the clause is restrictive, we are denying the reason alleged for the crime. If the clause is nonrestrictive, we are stating a premise upon which we have based our conclusion that he did not murder his mother. If we were speaking this sentence, we would indicate whether the clause was restrictive or nonrestrictive (and therefore the import of the entire statement) by some phonemic device of intonation. If we were writing that sentence, we could clarify the meaning by one of two courses: (1) recasting the sentence to remove the ambiguity; (2) putting a comma before *because* if the clause is nonrestrictive or leaving the comma out if the clause is restrictive. Unless we *wanted* the statement to be ambiguous, it would probably be better to reword the sentence so that our meaning would be clear.

Speakers and writers will sometimes deliberately leave statements of this kind ambiguous. They sometimes seek to discredit someone by innuendo. If they render the relationship between statements vague, they may trap the audience into accepting an implication that is unwarranted by the facts. We must be alert enough to detect such chicanery and scrupulous enough not to employ such devious means ourselves. This is not to deny that ambiguity can be an effective and legitimate literary device, as in a poem, for instance.

Exercise

Expressions of deductive reasoning in practical discourse will most often take the form of the statements in the following Exercise—that is, the form of the enthymeme. In order to test the *truth* and the *validity* of the reasoning, convert these statements into a full syllogism, supplying the missing, implied premise. Sometimes the implied premise may take two forms, and in those cases, you will have to consider both forms of the premise. For instance, in the enthymeme "That must be a sour apple, because it's hard and green," the implied premise may be either (a) All hard and green apples are sour, or (b) All sour apples are hard and green. If the implied premise was (b), you would reject the conclusion because the reasoning is invalid (the middle term "hard and green" is undistributed in both premises). If the implied premise was (a), you might reject the conclusion because you did not agree that all hard, green apples are sour. Sometimes in reconstructing the full syllogism, you may have to rephrase the propositions, but if you do, be sure to preserve the sense of the original statement. For example, the enthymeme "Where would our country be today if it were not for our long tradition of free enterprise?" might be recast in this fashion:

> Anything that promotes prosperity is good.
> The free-enterprise system is something that promotes prosperity.
> Therefore, the free-enterprise system is good.

1. He must be happy, because he's smiling all the time.

2. A nuclear war is inevitable, for our sworn enemy, Communist China, now has the hydrogen bomb.

3. He would not take the crown. Therefore 'tis certain he was not ambitious. —Shakespeare, *Julius Caesar,* III, ii, 118.

4. Because 29.8 percent of Thurber's sentences are simple sentences, we can say that a good part of his essay is easy to understand. —Student theme

5. Since you didn't speak up in my defense at the meeting, you must be as much against me as the rest of them are.

6. John definitely didn't drive the car home last night. He never puts the car in the righthand side of the garage.

7. No, the fuse isn't blown. It's the light bulb that is bad. When you flip the wall-switch, all the other lights in the room go on, don't they?

8. In your statement you assert that our actions, even though peaceful, must be condemned because they precipitate violence. —Martin Luther King, Jr., "Letter from Birmingham Jail"

9. Since the bullet obviously entered through his back, we have to rule out suicide; quite certainly he was murdered.

10. We must conclude that she's not a natural blonde. Otherwise, how do you explain those clearly visible black roots in her hair?

11. Blessed are the poor in spirit, for they shall see God.

12. The most convincing evidence that cigarette-smoking causes lung cancer is that the number of nonsmokers who die from lung cancer is so minimal as to be negligible.

13. The Civilization of the Dialogue is the only civilization worth having and the only civilization in which the whole world can unite. It is, therefore, the only civilization we can hope for, because the world must unite or be blown to bits. —Robert M. Hutchins, "Morals, Religion, and Higher Education"

14. You've come a long way, baby. You can't deny that all those electrical appliances have freed you from slavery to your household.

15. My girl doesn't love me anymore. The last three times I called her for a date, she said she had to stay in and catch up on her schoolwork.

16. It is better to die, for death is gentler than tyranny. —Aeschylus, *Agamemnon,* lines 1450–51.

17. She must have lost her car keys somewhere between the checkout counter and the parking lot, because she remembers taking the keys out of her purse when she was paying her bill and laying them on the counter.

18. You say he's a great hitter. Hogwash! A great hitter doesn't strike out 113 times a season.

19. Since cultivation of mind is surely worth seeking for its own sake, there is a knowledge which is desirable, though nothing come of it. —John Henry Newman, *The Idea of a University*

20. How do I know that the "silent majority" is indeed a majority? Well, they elected a conservative President, didn't they?

The Example

All knowledge is acquired and all proof is achieved through either deduction or induction. The syllogism is the formal device that Aristotle invented to analyze and systematize deductive reasoning. The enthymeme, as we have just seen, is a kind of imperfect syllogism, which produces, not the conclusive demonstration that we get in science and logic, but belief or persuasion.

Just as deductive reasoning has its rhetorical equivalent in the enthymeme, so inductive reasoning has its rhetorical equivalent in the *example*. In induction we proceed from the particular to the general. Hence in a scientific demonstration or in logic, we arrive inductively at a generalization through observation of a series of particulars. The validity and truth of the generalization will be in direct proportion to the *number* of pertinent particulars studied. The generalization, "Women are more careful drivers than men," will be "truer" and will be more validly derived if it was based on a study of the driving habits of a million men and women than if it was based on a study of only 100,000 men and women—presuming, of course, that the same criteria for carefulness were used in both studies.

The reason for the greater reliability of the generalization made from a number of instances is that there is less of an "inductive leap." Both deduction and induction make use of inference. The difference is that deduction makes inferences from *statements,* while induction makes inferences from *verifiable phenomena.* Induction leaps from known, observed facts, over an area of unknown, unobserved instances, to a generalization. The more facts or instances that are observed, the narrower will be the gap of the unknown that has to be leaped and accordingly the more reliable will be the generalization.

Aristotle realized that an orator addressing an audience could not adduce a whole series of particular instances to substantiate a generalization. Scientists of course must offer the supporting evidence of hundreds, even thousands, of experiments if they are to convince their colleagues of the validity of their generalization. But an orator has only a limited amount of time, and a writer has only a limited amount of space, to present their case to an audience, and they cannot risk boring their audience with an exhaustive catalogue of supporting evidence. Normally they will offer only one or two cogent examples to support their generalizations.

Let us illustrate the use of the rhetorical example by imagining the kind of argument that we might employ in trying to persuade our colleagues in the Senate not to declare war against a neighboring country. The point that we want to make, the generalization that we seek to establish, is that waging war against a neighbor will prove disastrous for the country initiating the war. If we had time, we could recite from world history dozens of instances of how wars waged against neighbors proved to be disadvantageous to the country precipitating the conflict. Instead we cite a single example, analogous to the present situation, preferably one from American history and recent enough to be impressive. We might, for instance, cite the example of the Spanish-American War or the Mexican War. We might say something like this:

> Look, it's true that we won this war, but consider the price we paid for waging war on a neighboring country. We disrupted our economy by expending millions of dollars to finance the invasion. We sent ten thousand young men to an early death, at a time when the labor market at home was ominously sparse. Millions of dollars worth of American property was damaged or destroyed. Besides, we alienated the good will of the dominant European powers. And instead of retaining an unaggrieved buffer state on our southern border, we produced at our threshold a hostile, vindictive nation that at the first opportunity would gladly enter into an alliance with any major power that sought to invade us. The price we paid for that war far exceeded the benefits we reaped. Gentlemen, I tell you that a war now against neighboring ——— would have equally disastrous consequences.

One of the strategies open to those senators who advocate going to war against the neighboring country would be to offer examples of other wars waged against neighbors that did *not* prove disastrous for the aggressor. Many considerations would determine which of these conflicting examples would produce more belief in the audience, but one of the considerations certainly would be the degree of similarity in the past and present situations.

An argument by example does not really prove anything, for like the rhetorical enthymeme, the example leads, most of the time, to a mere probability. But because a probability is what usually happens or what is believed to happen, the example has persuasive value. The example, of course, is always exposed to challenge and refutation. The opposition can counter with the reminder that on the grounds of strict logic a single example does not *prove* anything—no more than a single swallow makes a summer. Another way for the opposition to counteract the persuasive force of the example is, as we have pointed out, to cite another similar example where the outcome was just the opposite of the one cited. In such cases, the issue will be decided by a complex of attendant considerations: (1) the relative impressiveness and pertinence of the conflicting examples; (2) the persuasiveness of the other arguments offered in support of the contention; (3) the persuasiveness of the styles of the discourses; (4) the "ethical appeal" of the two people offering examples: (5) the force of the "emotional appeals"; (6) the emotional climate of the times. (See treatment of Example under topic of Testimony, pp. 131–32.)

The Fallacies

Before we end this section on the logical modes of appeal, we should consider, at least briefly, the common fallacies in deductive and inductive reasoning. An awareness of these fallacies can be of help to us when we are seeking to refute arguments that oppose the position we maintain, and it can also prevent us from indulging in specious reasoning in our own discourses.

In common parlance, the word *fallacy* has two meanings: (1) a false, erroneous statement, an untruth; (2) invalid, specious, or deceptive reasoning. The first of these meanings has to do with the *matter* of the argument; the second, with the *form* or *mode* of argument. Formal logic is concerned primarily, although not exclusively, with the form of argument, but since *fallacy* denotes for most people a "false statement," we should say a few words about fallacious matter.

Fallacies of Matter

A false statement can be detected and refuted only if we know what the truth is. The claim that the earth was the center of our solar system was not detected as a falsehood until Copernicus discovered the corrective fact: that the sun was the center of our universe. We may suspect a statement—as Copernicus must have suspected the Ptolemaic view of the universe—but we cannot disprove the statement until we have discovered the facts. One of the cardinal principles of argument is that the burden of proof rests upon the one who challenges the generally accepted view of things. Since most astronomers hold that human life as we know it does not exist on the other planets in our solar system—in other words, since the testimony of experts concurs—the burden of proof that there *is* life on these other planets rests on those who make the counterclaim. Exploration of outer space may turn up the "facts" that will either confirm or correct the generally received view.

Since truth is the only corrective of falsity, it is extremely important that all of us learn, through experience or education, as many facts about our world as are necessary for our effective and purposeful existence, or at least learn how and where to acquire facts. The person of inferior or inadequate knowledge will always be at a disadvantage in dealings with other people. How often all of us have been frustrated in an argument by having to admit, "I can't discredit your assertion because at the moment I don't know the facts." If in the course of an argument about the rate of economic growth someone makes the telling point that at least a third of the families in the country have a total annual income of less than $2000, we cannot discredit that claim by saying simply, "That's not so." We can call for and challenge the source of someone's information, but we will most effectively undermine an assertion by adducing evidence that a claim is false. The next best thing to having the refutative information at our fingertips is to know where we might find the facts that will discredit our opponent's statement.

One point needs to be made very strongly here: mere assertion, on either side of an argument, does not constitute proof. It is amazing how often argument is conducted solely with assertions and counterassertions. Conducting an argument in this fashion is like two young boys standing toe to toe and shouting at one another, "My pa can lick your pa," "No, he can't," "Yes, he can," "Oh, yeah!" An argument like this gets nowhere, but a surprising number of people seem to think that it does. (Just take a look at the letters-to-the-editor column of your local newspaper.)

This is not to say that every time we make a categorical statement we need to substantiate our statement. There are some statements that most people regard as being self-evident—e.g., a whole is equal to the sum of all of its parts. The writers of the Declaration of Independence made some statements in the opening paragraphs of that document that they asserted were self-evident: "that all men are created equal," "that they are endowed by their Creator with certain unalienable rights." A self-evident proposition has been defined as a statement that all or most people would immediately assent to once they understand the terms of the statement. Being self-evident, such statements do not have to be proved.

Another kind of statement that normally does not have to be proved is the statement regarded as "true by definition": "Two plus two equals four"; "Democracy is government of the people, by the people, and for the people"; "A majority is any plurality in excess of 50 percent of the total number." Such statements are "true" in the sense that a consensus has defined them. Sometime in the future, consensus could establish that a majority was a plurality of 60 percent of the total number. Most laws and statutes, for instance, can be regarded as "true by definition."

The third kind of statement that does not demand proof is the statement about matters that even the minimally informed person should know: "There are fifty states in the United States"; "All wage-earning adults in America must file an income-tax report once a year"; "A vast body of water separates North America from Europe." The nature of the subject matter and the composition of the audience will largely determine which statements of this kind need to be substantiated. Many statements about physics that might need to be substantiated for an audience of laypeople would not have to be proved for an audience of physicists.

Nor should we demand more precision and accuracy in statements than the occasion demands. When our opponent claims that "150,000 home owners defaulted on their mortgage payments last year," we make ourselves appear silly by countering, "According to the Government Bureau of Statistics only 146,987 home owners defaulted on their mortgage payments last year." A corrective statement like this is mere punctilio and does nothing to advance our own argument or to weaken our opponent's argument. There are occasions, of course, when strict accuracy should be insisted on. When someone, in order to advance an argument, claims that the successful candidate for the office of the President received a clear majority of the electoral votes, it might be useful for our purposes to point out that the successful candidate had a margin of only 345,330 votes, a bare 0.1 percent of the total popular vote, and that therefore he did not receive an overwhelming mandate from the people.

Beware also of the fallacy of the half-truth, which can be a particularly vicious but surprisingly effective tactic in argument. In the half-truth everything that is said is true, that is, verifiable as a fact; but because not enough is said, the total picture is distorted. Such omission of details conceals or distorts the context of a situation. Imagine someone seeking to impugn the loyalty of a nuclear scientist with a narrative like this: "For years Professor X carried on an active correspondence with top Soviet scientists. He subscribed to at least six Russian scientific journals. In 1956 he was observed having lunch in a New York restaurant with four Soviet scientists. In 1958 he took a trip to Moscow. A strange pattern of affinity with Soviet ideology, is it not?" Professor X did, and would admit that he did, everything ascribed to him here; but he would not admit the implications drawn from these facts. He would not admit the implications because a number of relevant facts that would put his relationship with Soviet scientists in the proper perspective have been omitted. He did correspond with Soviet scientists, but all of these letters were cleared by the State Department. He did subscribe to six Russian journals, but every scholar who wanted to keep up on the developments in science had to read the periodical literature from other countries. He did have lunch with four Russian scientists, but also present at that luncheon were four other American physicists, including Professor Y, whose loyalty no one called into question. The trip he took to Moscow in 1958 was sponsored by the Atomic Energy Commission after he had been cleared by an intensive investigation by the FBI.

This is a bald example of the fallacy of the half-truth, but its very obviousness helps to illustrate how more subtle examples of this fallacy operate. It shows how what is left unsaid can distort the total picture. It is for this reason that witnesses in court are made to swear that they will tell "the *whole* truth and nothing but the truth."

Because every categorical statement is, in a sense, unique, we can hardly do more here than lay down the general cautions and principles in regard to fallacies of matter. Each statement of a purported fact must be examined on its own terms and in its own context. The falsity of a statement—if the statement is false—can be detected and exposed only by one's knowledge of the facts. Mere assertion does not constitute proof, but not every statement needs to be substantiated. Nor should punctilious accuracy be insisted on where such precision is irrelevant or inconsequential. We should, however, bear in mind that by indulging in the half-truth we can, paradoxically, tell lies by speaking "nothing but the truth."

Fallacies of Reasoning

All fallacies of reasoning, whether inductive or deductive, could be classified as *non sequiturs*—that is, as conclusions or generalizations that "do not follow" from the premises. A logical fallacy is, at bottom, an instance of incoherence—the chain of reasoning does not link together.

Since we have dealt at length in previous sections with inductive and deductive *non sequiturs,* we will here merely list the fallacies, with a minimum of comment and with cross references to the sections where these fallacies have been elaborated on.

A. *Fallacies of Reasoning in Deduction*

1. *Equivocation:* This is the fallacy of using the same term with two or more meanings or referents. In syllogistic reasoning, equivocation introduces a fourth term into the process. No conclusion can be validly drawn from premises that have four terms. Equivocation could also invalidate inductive reasoning. If the referent of the term used to specify the particulars keeps shifting, no valid generalization can be made about the series of particulars. (See SYLLOGISM, pp. 52–54.)

2. *Undistributed Middle Term:* This common fallacy results basically from a failure to supply a link in the chain of arguments, a failure to establish that the major term and the minor term coincide. A diagram of one form of this fallacy will point up the missing link.

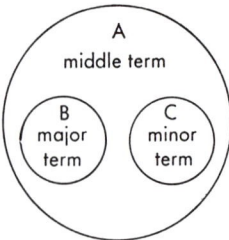

This arrangement of circles could be a schematic representation of an argument like the following:

> All Communists are people.
> All Americans are people.
> Therefore, all Americans are Communists.

The B and C circles are shown to be comprehended within the larger A-circle, but the C-circle does not fall inside the B-circle, nor does it even overlap the B-circle. In other words, the two premises have not established that there is any connection between B and C. That failure to establish a connection is the missing link in this kind of argument, and until the link is supplied, we cannot arrive at any conclusion. (See SYLLOGISM, p. 54.)

3. *Illicit Process:* This is the fallacy in which a term in the conclusion has a wider extension than it has in the premises; or, to put it another way, a term is distributed or universal in the conclusion, but was undistributed or particular in the premise. It stands to reason that we cannot draw any conclusion about *all men* if in the premises we have been talking only about *some men.* Such a conclusion simply "does not follow." (See SYLLOGISM, p. 54.)

4. *Conclusion from Two Negative Premises:* Because two negative premises establish no relationship among all three terms in a syllogistic chain of reasoning, no conclusion, either affirmative or negative, can be drawn. Negative premises exclude relationships. Unless one of the premises is affirmative so that it can include a relationship, we cannot validly arrive at any conclusion. (See SYLLOGISM, p. 52.)

5. *Affirmative Conclusion from a Negative Premise:* Since a negative premise excludes a relationship between two of the terms in a syllogism, the only kind of conclusion that can be arrived at logically is a proposition that excludes any relationship between one of these terms and a third term.

This is a diagrammatic representation of the following two premises, with the × indicating the area specified by the second premise:

> No Russians are free men.
> Some Russians are atheists.

It should be apparent from the diagram that it is logically impossible to get the terms *free men* and *atheists* together in any kind of affirmative predication. There *may be* an affirmative relationship between *free men* and *atheists* (for instance, the area of the *atheist* circle that is outside the *Russian* circle could fall inside the *free men* circle). But that relationship has to be demonstrated; it cannot be inferred from this set of premises. From this set of premises, we can logically deduce only this conclusion: *Some atheists are not free men.* (Since the X-area is inside the *Russian* circle and since no part of the *Russian* circle is in the *free men* circle, it stands to reason that the X-area cannot be in the *free men* circle.) The moral of this explication: do not allow anyone, including yourself, to draw an affirmative conclusion from a negative proposition. (See Syllogism, p. 52.)

6. *"Either/Or" Fallacy:* This is a common fallacy of those who tend to judge life by a two-valued rather than a multi-valued system. Psychologists designate this tendency as the "black-or-white syndrome." There are some either/or situations from which we may draw valid inferences; the condition for valid inference is that the alternatives be exhaustive. If we start from the premise, "Either he voted for the candidate or he didn't vote for him," we can legitimately infer one alternative from the proof or disproof of the other alternative. We can make this inference validly because one or the other of the situations *must* exist. As the premise is phrased, no other situation is possible. But if we start from the premise, "Either he voted for the candidate or he voted for the candidate's opponent," we have not posed alternatives which take all the possible actions in the case into account. Voting for this or that candidate is not the only possibility; the man might not have voted at all or might have voted for a third candidate. So if we prove that he didn't vote for the candidate, we may not infer that he must have voted for the candidate's opponent; we have to go on to prove that he voted for the candidate's opponent. (See Disjunctive Syllogism, p. 57.)

7. *Fallacy of Affirming the Consequent:* This is the fallacy occurring in de-ductive reasoning that starts out with a hypothetical proposition. For ex-ample:

> If he makes concessions to the Russian ambassador, the prestige of the United States will decline.

The consequent is affirmed: "The prestige of the United States has declined." The fallacy now is the conclusion drawn from this affirmation of the conse-quent: "He must have made concessions to the Russian ambassador." That conclusion is clearly a *non sequitur.* (See HYPOTHETICAL SYLLOGISM, pp. 56–57.)

8. *Fallacy of Denying the Antecedent:* This is another fallacy that can occur in reasoning from hypothetical propositions. For example:

> If she captures the undecided votes, she will win the election.

The antecedent is denied: "She did not capture the undecided votes." The fallacy now is the conclusion drawn from this denial: "She did not win the election." This conclusion would follow if it had been established that the *only* way to win the election is to capture the undecided votes. We would have to start out with, and secure agreement on, this premise: "Only if she captures the undecided votes, will she win the election." (See HYPOTHETICAL SYLLOGISM, pp. 56–57.)

B. *Fallacies of Reasoning in Induction*

1. *Faulty Generalization:* We are liable to this fallacy when we "jump to a conclusion" from inadequate evidence. Evidence can be inadequate in a number of ways: (1) the particulars may be irrelevant; (2) the particulars may be unrepresentative; (3) the particulars may not be numerous enough to warrant the conclusion. All of these inadequacies concern evidence gathered by observation or study. Sometimes our generalizations are based on evidence derived from authority. Generalizations based on evidence de-rived from authority can be faulty when the authority quoted is (1) biased or prejudiced, (2) incompetent, (3) outmoded. Even when the authority quoted is objective, competent, and reliable, a generalization from the evi-dence supplied by this authority can be faulty if the authority is (1) inac-curately quoted, (2) misinterpreted, (3) quoted out of context. (See COM-MON TOPICS, p. 124.)

2. *Faulty Casual Generalizations:* These are fallacies to which all cause-and-effect inferences are liable. These fallacies can occur when we argue (1) from an effect to a cause or (2) from a cause to an effect. We offend in the first way (1) when we assign an inadequate cause to an effect; (2) when we

fail to take into account the fact that there could be more than one cause for the same effect. We offend in the second way (1) when we fail to establish that a potential cause of an effect could and did operate in a particular situation; (2) when we fail to take into account that the same cause can produce diverse effects. One of the commonest instances of faulty causal generalization is the fallacy commonly referred to as *post hoc, ergo propter hoc* ("after this, therefore because of this"). This fallacy results from the assumption that because there is a temporal relationship between events (something happened *after* something else) there is also a causal relationship—e.g., "Our sales shot up 25 percent after we started using that musical jingle in our advertising campaign." The use of the musical jingle *may* have been a cause for the increase in sales. But we may not assume that it was a cause; we must prove that it was a cause. (See COMMON TOPICS, pp. 112–13.)

3. *Faulty Analogy:* Argument by analogy is always the most vulnerable of all modes of argument. It is always exposed to the charge, "The analogy does not hold." But some analogies are more vulnerable than others. They are especially vulnerable when they concentrate on irrelevant, inconsequential similarities between two situations and overlook pertinent, significant dissimilarities. The analogical argument, "Where there is smoke, there is fire," commonly used to throw suspicion on someone's character or activity, is frequently open to the objection that the persuasiveness of the similarities is weakened, if not entirely nullified, by the dissimilarities. While it is true that argument by analogy always rests on shaky ground, it is possible for someone to become so niggling in his attitude toward all analogy that he is liable to strain at a gnat and swallow a camel. Perhaps we can avoid this carping habit by remembering that an analogy never proves anything; at best, it persuades someone on the grounds of probability. It is the *degree* of probability that will be susceptible to challenge.

C. Miscellaneous Fallacies

A number of fallacies will be grouped here under the heading "Miscellaneous" because they are not peculiar to either inductive or deductive reasoning and because they are a blend of material fallacies, formal fallacies, and emotional fallacies.

1. *Begging the Question:* This fallacy (labelled *petitio principii* by the scholastic logicians) is found more often in deductive reasoning than in inductive reasoning. Basically, this is the fault of circular reasoning. In syllogistic reasoning, for instance, this fallacy occurs when we assume in the premise the conclusion that we are trying to prove. A lawyer would be guilty of "begging the question" if he or she pleaded before a jury, "My client

would not steal because he is an honest man." We can more readily detect the *petitio principii* if we reconstruct the full chain of reasoning from the lawyer's enthymeme:

> Any man who is honest will not steal.
> My client is honest.
> Therefore, my client would not steal.

The second premise and the conclusion say the same thing in different words, because of the tautological definition set up in the first premise. The argument eddies around in a circle; it doesn't go anywhere. We get this same kind of circular argument in a sequence like this: "God exists." "How do you know that God exists?" "The Bible says so." "Why should I put my credence in what the Bible says?" "Because it's the inspired word of God." God is worthy of a more cogent argument than this.

One of the commonest and subtlest forms of this fallacy is the question-begging epithet: "This *murderer* should be put away for life." "We don't want any *controversial* figures as lecturers in this state." "This *creeping socialism* won't fool the American people." The occurrence of certain formulas should alert us that an instance of question-begging may be lurking in the verbiage. We should be on our guard whenever we meet expressions like "obviously," "of course," "as everyone knows," "really," "unquestionably." (Whenever you see one of these expressions in this textbook, take another look at the sentence in which these expressions occur to see whether what the author has said *is* obvious or unquestionable.)

2. *Argument* Ad Hominem (*"to the man"*): This is a form of emotional argument, the fallacy of switching the argument from a discussion of issues to a discussion of personalities. If we find that we cannot refute someone's argument, we might attack the person's character. "My opponent's arguments are very impressive, but remember, this is the man who deserted his faithful wife and family after he had won his first political victory." Judged by its prevalence throughout history, this tendency to denigrate the character of one who espouses a cause or argument rather than to evaluate the cause or argument on its own merits seems to be natural. We sometimes see this sort of thing in literary criticism. Attention is diverted from the literary work itself to a discussion of the vicious character of the author; the work is assumed to be foul because the author is a notorious rake. As Alexander Pope said,

> Some judge of authors' names, not work, and then
> Nor praise nor blame the writings, but the men.
>
> *An Essay on Criticism*, II, 412-13.

A person's character can have some relevance to an argument—when, for instance, we are attempting to assess the reliability of someone's testimony or the likelihood of someone having done something—but a discussion of a person's character becomes an irrelevancy—and thereby a form of fallacy—when such a discussion is used merely to distract attention from the issue at hand. Beware of the "poisoned spring" tactic.

3. *Argument* Ad Populum *("to the people")*: This is another devious emotional appeal, similar to the argument *ad hominem*. This is the tactic of appealing to irrational fears and prejudices to prevent audiences from squarely facing the issues. Honorific terms—*Americanism, patriotism, motherhood, rugged individualism*—are used to stir up a favorable emotional climate; pejorative terms—*socialism, godlessness, radical, reactionary*—are used to arouse hostile reactions. None of these terms are "good" or "bad" in themselves. They become "weasel words" when they so color the emotional atmosphere of a discussion that people are disposed to accept as proven what has only been asserted. Appeals to emotions are legitimate—in fact, rhetoricians maintained that people often could not be moved to action unless their emotions were touched—but appeals to emotions are reprehensible when they cloud the issue, when they anesthetize people's rational faculties, when they move people to do things or accept things which they would not do or accept if their conscience or reason were allowed to operate.

4. *The "Red Herring"*: This is another diversionary tactic. "Red herring" is a term adopted from hunting and refers to the practice of dragging a herring across the trace in order to lead the hounds astray from their pursuit of the prey. The classical term for this fallacy is *ignoratio elenchi* (literally, "ignorance of the refutation"). This is another device, like the *ad hominem* or *ad populum* arguments, of ignoring or avoiding the issue. Backed into a corner in an argument, all of us are prone to steer the discussion to a side issue. "You accuse me of cheating on my income tax, but doesn't everybody cheat a little bit?" "So what if the general did lose that battle? Think of all his glorious victories in the past." The disputant who allows her opponent to "change the subject," to dodge the main issue, may soon find herself losing the argument because her opponent has shifted his position to safer ground.

5. *The Complex Question*: An oft-quoted example of this is the question, "When did you stop beating your wife?" It is impossible to give a simple answer to such a question without incriminating oneself. What is wrong here is that a question like this has two parts. It combines these questions:

"Do you beat your wife?" and "When did you stop beating her?" It is a form of question-begging. Just as a defending lawyer would jump up to protest the prosecutor's question, "Why did you steal the diamond ring?" so anyone confronted with a two-pronged question should insist that the implicit question be dealt with first. "Wait a minute. Let's determine first whether I ever beat my wife." A familiar legislative practice is to attach riders to an important bill. When the bill is brought up for a vote, legislators are faced with a dilemma. They may favor the main bill but object to the riders, or vice versa. But they are now placed in a situation where they have to accept or reject the whole package. In an argument, fortunately, we can insist that a complex question be dealt with part by part.

The Ethical Appeal

In the previous section we dealt at some length with the logical *pisteis,* the materials and methods of proof or persuasion that appeal to the reason. Ideally, people should be able to conduct a discussion or argument exclusively on the level of reason. But the rhetoricians were realistic enough to recognize that people are creatures of passion and of will as well as of intellect. We have to deal with people as they are, not as they should be. If we conceive of rhetoric as the art of discovering all the available means of persuasion, we will be disposed to make use of whatever effective (and, one would hope, legitimate) means lie open to us. As was pointed out earlier, Aristotle recognized a second means in the ethical appeal, the persuasive value of the speaker's or writer's character.

The ethical appeal can be the most effective kind of appeal; even the cleverest and soundest appeal to the reason could fall on deaf ears if the audience reacted unfavorably to the speaker's character. The ethical appeal is especially important in rhetorical discourse, because here we deal with matters about which absolute certainty is impossible and opinions are divided. Quintilian felt that of the three kinds of rhetorical discourse, deliberative oratory had the most need for the ethical appeal (he called it *auctoritas*). As Quintilian said, "For he who would have all men trust his judgment as to what is expedient and honourable, should possess and be regarded as possessing genuine wisdom and excellence of character."—*Institutio Oratoria,* III, viii, 13.

The ethical appeal is exerted, according to Aristotle, when the speech itself impresses the audience that the speaker is a person of sound sense (*phronēsis*), high moral character (*aretē*), and benevolence (*eunoia*). Notice that it is *the speech itself* that must create this impression. Thus a person wholly unknown to an audience (and this is often the case when we listen to a speech or read an article in a magazine) could by his or her words alone inspire this kind of confidence. Some people, of course, already have a reputation familiar to an audience, and this reputation, if it is a good one, will favorably dispose an audience toward them, even before they utter a word. In the last analysis, however, it is the discourse itself that must establish or maintain the ethical appeal, for what a person says in any particular discourse could weaken or destroy any previously established reputation.

How does one create the impression by a discourse that one is a person of sound sense, high moral character, and benevolence? The question is crucial; unfortunately, the answer must be couched in rather general terms. An obvious answer, of the general sort, is that a person must truly possess these qualities. "No one gives what he does not have," as the Latin maxim puts it. It is not the province of rhetoric, however, to form such a character—except perhaps in an indirect way. While it is true that the *whole* person is engaged in any communicative discourse, rhetoric can train only those faculties involved in the discovery, arrangement, and expression of ideas.

If we grant that a person strongly imbued with good sense, good moral fiber, and good will toward others will be disposed to conduct a discourse in a manner that will exert a strong ethical appeal, can we lay down any other positive precepts? Positive precepts, yes, but no more specific than the one just proposed. If a discourse is to exhibit a person's good sense, it must show that the speaker or writer has an adequate, if not a professionally erudite, grasp of the subject being talked about, that the speaker or writer knows and observes the principles of valid reasoning, is capable of viewing a situation in the proper perspective, has read widely, and has good taste and discriminating judgment. If a discourse is to reflect a person's moral character, it must display an abhorrence of unscrupulous tactics and specious reasoning, a respect for the commonly acknowledged virtues, and an adamant integrity. If the discourse is to manifest a person's good will, it must display a person's sincere interest in the welfare of the audience and a readiness to sacrifice any self-aggrandizement that conflicts with the benefit of others.

It will help too if the discourse displays a person's sound knowledge of human psychology and a nice sense of appropriate style. The speaker or writer must be aware of the kind of *ēthos* that Aristotle talked about in Book II, Chapters 12–17 of the *Rhetoric*—the nature of various forms of government and the character of different periods of life (youth, middle age, old age) and of different conditions of life (wealth, poverty, education, illiteracy, health, sickness). Aware of the disposition of people at various ages and in various conditions of life, the speaker or writer will adapt his or her tone and sentiments to fit the audience. Old people, for instance, do not think and act and view things in the same way that adolescents do. Young people are, by and large, quick-tempered, fickle, impetuous, idealistic; old people tend to be phlegmatic, conservative, deliberate, and pragmatic. Women react to certain things differently from men. Rich people and poor people view things in different ways. People accustomed to a democratic way of life respond to certain sentiments and arguments in a different way from people brought up in a dictatorship.

The *whole* discourse must maintain the "image" that the speaker or writer seeks to establish. The ethical appeal, in other words, must be pervasive throughout the discourse. The effect of the ethical appeal might very well be destroyed by a single lapse from good sense, good will, or moral integrity. A note of peevishness, a touch of malevolence, a flash of bad taste, a sudden display of inaccuracy or illogic could jeopardize a person's whole persuasive effort.

But although the ethical appeal must be maintained by the discourse as a whole, there may be places in the discourse where the author will make a special overt attempt to establish credit with the audience or to ingratiate himself or herself with the audience. The two places in the discourse where authors commonly make such explicit overtures are the introduction and the conclusion. The author does not explicitly call attention to the fact that he or she is seeking to impress or conciliate the audience, but the effort to impress the audience is nonetheless obvious and calculated. The following quotation, from the opening paragraph of one of Benjamin Franklin's speeches, exemplifies just such an overt attempt:

> It is with reluctance that I rise to express a disapprobation of any one article of the plan, for which we are so much obliged to the honorable gentleman who laid it before us. From its first reading, I have borne a good will to it, and, in general, wished it success. In this particular of salaries to the executive branch, I happen to differ; and, as my opinion may appear new and chimerical, it is only from a persuasion that it is right, and from a sense of duty, that I hazard it. The Committee will judge of my reasons when they have heard them, and their judgment may possibly change mine. I think I see inconvenience in the appointment of salaries; I see none in refusing them, but on the contrary great advantages.
>
> From Benjamin Franklin, *Speech in the Constitutional Convention on the Subject of Salaries,* June 2, 1787.

Franklin is about to argue against a proposal made to the Constitutional Convention, but he must dispose his audience to listen to his counterarguments. So he tries to show that he harbors no ill will toward the man who made the proposal ("for which we are so much obliged to the honorable gentleman who laid it before us"; "I have borne good will to it"); that he is motivated in his objection, not by partisan considerations but by principle ("from a persuasion that it is right, and from a sense of duty"); that he is not so cocksure of his own views that he is impervious to correction ("their judgment may possibly change mine"). The overall impression created by this brief overture is that of a modest, magnanimous, open-minded gentleman. Even his opponents in the assembly would be disposed to listen to his counterarguments.

Here is an example of a special attempt to exert an ethical appeal in the closing paragraph of a discourse:

> In this work, when it shall be found that much is omitted, let it not be forgotten that much likewise is performed; and though no book was ever spared out of tenderness to the author, and the world is little solicitous to know whence proceeded the faults of that which it condemns; yet it may gratify curiosity to inform it, that the *English Dictionary* was written with little assistance of the learned, and without any patronage of the great; not in the soft obscurities of retirement, or under the shelter of academic bowers, but amid inconvenience and distraction, in sickness and in sorrow. It may repress the triumph of malignant criticism to observe that if our language is not here fully displayed, I have only failed in an attempt which no human powers have hitherto completed. If the lexicons of ancient tongues, now immutably fixed, and comprised in a few volumes, be yet, after the toil of successive ages, inadequate and delusive; if the aggregated knowledge and cooperating diligence of the Italian academicians did not secure them from the censure of Beni; if the embodied critics of France, when fifty years had been spent upon their work, were obliged to change its economy and give their second edition another form, I may surely be contented without the praise of perfection, which, if I could obtain, in this gloom of solitude, what would it avail me? I have protracted my work till most of those whom I wished to please have sunk into the grave, and success and miscarriage are empty sounds: I therefore dismiss it with frigid tranquillity, having little to fear from censure or from praise.
>
> From Samuel Johnson, Preface to the *English Dictionary,* 1755.

Here a good deal of the ethical appeal is being exerted by the style, for this is certainly a magnificent piece of English prose. But Dr. Johnson is also making a deliberate effort to say those things about himself and his work that will leave his audience with a favorable opinion of him. Throughout the long discourse that preceded this final paragraph, Johnson had been explaining what he hoped to do in his *Dictionary,* what difficulties he faced in effecting his purpose, and what his successes and failures were. That elaborate exposition itself helped to create the impression of an intelligent, self-sacrificing, high-minded scholar. Here now in this final paragraph he makes an overt effort to reinforce the impression of himself. What comes through to the audience is a suitable blend of modesty and confidence, of regrets and self-gratulations, of animus and forgiveness.

It would be easy to find illustrations, in contemporary speeches, articles, and letters, of discourse that failed to create favorable impressions of the people who composed them. But since there is something uncharitable about publicly exposing someone, whether living or dead, as an example of an unprincipled, stupid, malevolent, or generally unprepossessing person, let us take as our example some fictitious person. Here is an excerpt from *Pride and Prejudice* in which Mr. Collins proposes marriage to Elizabeth Bennet:

> "My reasons for marrying are, first, that I think it a right thing for every clergyman in easy circumstances (like myself) to set the example of matrimony in his parish; secondly, that I am convinced it will add very greatly to my happiness; and thirdly—which perhaps I ought to have mentioned earlier—that it is the particular advice and recommendation of the very noble lady whom I have the honor of calling patroness. Twice has she condescended to give me her opinion (unasked too!) on this subject; and it was but the very Saturday night before I left Hunsford—between our pools at quadrille, while Mrs. Jenkinson was arranging Miss de Bourgh's footstool, that she said, 'Mr. Collins, you must marry. A clergyman like you must marry. Choose properly, choose a gentlewoman for *my* sake; and for your *own*, let her be an active, useful sort of person, not brought up high, but able to make a small income go a good way. This is my advice. Find such a woman as soon as you can, bring her to Hunsford, and I will visit her.' Allow me, by the way, to observe, my fair cousin, that I do not reckon the notice and kindness of Lady Catherine de Bourgh as among the least of the advantages in my power to offer. You will find her manners beyond anything I can describe; and your wit and vivacity, I think, must be acceptable to her, especially when tempered with the silence and respect which her rank will inevitably excite. Thus much for my general intention in favor of matrimony; it remains to be told why my views were directed to Longbourn instead of my own neighbourhood, where I assure you there are many amiable young women. But the fact is that being, as I am, to inherit this estate after the death of your honoured father (who, however, may live many years longer), I could not satisfy myself without resolving to choose a wife from among his daughters, that the loss to them might be as little as possible, when the melancholy event takes place—which, however, as I have already said, may not be for several years. This has been my motive, my fair cousin, and I flatter myself it will not sink me in your esteem. And now nothing remains for me but to assure you in the most animated language of the violence of my affection. To fortune I am perfectly indifferent, and shall make no demand of that nature on your father, since I am well aware that it could not be complied with; and that one thousand pounds in the four per cents, which will not be yours till after your

mother's decease, is all that you may ever be entitled to. On that head, therefore, I shall be uniformly silent; and you may assure yourself that no ungenerous reproach shall ever pass my lips when we are married."

From Jane Austen, Pride and Prejudice, Chapter 19.

There is certainly a rhetorical situation set up here in this scene from an early nineteenth-century novel: a man seeking to induce a young woman to marry him. Though an appeal to reason is hardly negligible at a time like this, emotions probably play a more important part in bringing two people to such a decision. And if there is ever a time when a man's ethical appeal must be strong, it is the moment when he proposes. Presumably, a man has been exerting an ethical appeal throughout the relationship, but when he comes to the moment of actually proposing marriage he can hardly wish to say anything that will destroy the woman's good opinion of him.

This speech provides a classic example of a man who intends to convey a favorable impression of himself but succeeds only in discrediting himself by what he says and the manner in which he says it. There are two audiences for Mr. Collins's speech: Elizabeth and the reader. Jane Austen clearly intends to reveal Mr. Collins for the pompous, self-righteous, egocentric timeserver that he is, but we cannot presume that Elizabeth will react in exactly the same way as we do to Mr. Collins's speech. We must make some allowances for the mores of the age and for the kind of person Elizabeth herself is. A young woman of that time would expect a man to propose to her in the highly formal language that Mr. Collins uses, and she would probably not have been as unfavorably impressed as we are by Mr. Collins's mercenary considerations.

But even when all these allowances are made for the differences in the reactions of the two audiences for the speech, we cannot believe that after this exposure of Mr. Collins's motives Elizabeth could regard him as a man of "good sense, good will, and high moral character." She had developed an antipathy for him before this moment that this display of rhetoric could do nothing but confirm. Hence, we are not at all surprised at the firmness and forthrightness of her rejection of Mr. Collins: "I am perfectly serious in my refusal. You could not make *me* happy, and I am convinced that I am the last woman in the world who would make you so." And if we the readers needed any further confirmation of our unfavorable impression of him we could turn to that delightfully obnoxious letter of condolence that he sends to the Bennet family in Chapter 48 upon the occasion of Lydia's elopement.

There is no denying the role that the ethical appeal plays in the persuasive process. In a sense, the ethical appeal is the "hidden persuader." In our world, such enterprises as public relations, motivational psychology, market research, and advertising, are engaged in searching for effective stimuli and in creating the proper "image." The groundwork for all of this activity was laid by Aristotle two thousand years ago.

Aristotle discussed the ethical appeal, not only because he recognized how vital it was in persuasion but also because he wanted to answer the enemies of rhetoric, like Socrates, who complained that rhetoricians sanctioned any kind of shallow knowledge, sophistical reasoning, and unscrupulous tactics that would gain the end of persuasion. If persuasion depends greatly, even pre-eminently, on ethical appeal, the persuader cannot afford to create the impression by the discourse that he or she is superficial, immoral, or malicious. Cicero and Quintilian, with their insistence on "the good man speaking," may have given greater emphasis to the importance of the ethical image than Aristotle did, but they were not supplying a note that Aristotle had entirely neglected.

The Emotional Appeal

The third mode of persuasion specified by Aristotle and recognized by all later rhetoricians is the appeal to the emotions of the audience. People are rather sheepish about acknowledging that their opinions can be affected by their emotions. They have the uneasy feeling that there is something undignified about being stirred to action through the emotions. And indeed, in some cases, there is something undignified about a rational creature being precipitated into action through the stimulus of aroused passions. All of us at one time or another have been ashamed of something we did under the pressure of strong emotion. The source of our shame was not so much that we had been prompted to action by our emotions as that we had done something regrettable. We are not ashamed of falling in love, even though the act of falling in love is prompted by strong emotion. But we are ashamed of hurling a vase against the wall in a fit of anger. What makes the difference here is the consequences of our emotional stress. Because falling in love was "good," we felt no compunction; because smashing the vase was "evil," we were ashamed of our impulsive act.

There is nothing necessarily reprehensible about being moved to action through our emotions; in fact, it is perfectly normal. Since it is our will ultimately that moves us to action and since the emotions have a powerful influence on the will, many of our actions are prompted by the stimulus of our emotions. When it is not pure emotion that prompts our will, it is a combination of reason and emotion. This fact has a great bearing on the strategies of rhetoric. George Campbell, the eighteenth-century Scottish rhetorician, made a strong claim for the important part that emotions play in the persuasive process: "So far, therefore, is it from being an unfair method of persuasion to move the passions, that there is no persuasion without moving them."—*Philosophy of Rhetoric,* Book I, Ch. VII.

Richard Whately, the nineteenth-century English rhetorician, analyzed the persuasive process this way: "For in order that the Will may be influenced, two things are requisite: (1) that the proposed Object should appear desirable; and (2) that the Means suggested should be proved to be conducive to the attainment of that object."—*Elements of Rhetoric,* Part II, Ch. I. It is argument (the appeal to the understanding) that produces conviction about the conduciveness of the means to the desired end; it is the appeal to the emotions that makes the end seem desirable. In order to whip up a people into a mood for war, one would have to do two things: (1) remind the people that the freedom and security of a nation is a desirable end; (2) convince them that going to war is the best means of securing this end. The order of these two activities can vary. Sometimes it will be better to excite the desire first and then show that there is some connection between the proposed action and the end; at other times, it will be more expedient to convince the understanding first and then stir up the emotions.

Do not some people play on other people's emotions for unscrupulous purposes? Of course they do. All of us could tick off a half dozen examples from history without much strain on the memory. The fact that some people exploit the emotions for unscrupulous purposes may constitute a caution about the use of emotional appeal, but it does not constitute a condemnation of emotional appeal. Some people use sophistical arguments, but we do not therefore condemn all argument as a means of effecting conviction.

An important consideration for rhetoric is that our emotions are not under the direct control of volition. We cannot *will* ourselves into being angry against someone. On the other hand, our intellectual faculties, reason and memory, are under the direct control of our will. We can, by an act of the will, force ourselves to recall historical facts, to engage in calculation, to analyze a whole, or to synthesize parts.

There are two consequences for rhetoric from the fact that our will does not have direct control of our emotions. The first consequence is that it is perilous to announce to an audience that we are going to play on the emotions. As soon as we apprize an audience of such an intention, we jeopardize, if we do not entirely destroy, the effectiveness of the emotional appeal. It is not so with appeals to the understanding. It is frequently advantageous to announce to an audience that we are about to embark upon a course of reasoning. Accordingly, we have no hesitation about calling attention to the conclusion we hope to establish, to the steps we will take in proving our point, or to our method of arguing.

The second consequence for rhetoric is that we must get at the emotions indirectly. We cannot arouse an emotion, either in ourselves or in others, by thinking about it. We arouse emotion by contemplating the object that stirs the emotion. So if we seek to arouse the anger of an audience, we must describe a person or a situation of a sort that will make the audience angry. The anger can be enkindled even when the description is quite dispassionate. Horace's precept that if you want me to feel an emotion, you must first feel that emotion yourself (*si vis me flere, dolendum est primum ipsi tibi*) is basically sound, but it is possible to feel an emotion without displaying it extravagantly. In fact, there will be times when the more dispassionate the emotion-provoking description is, the more intense will be the emotion aroused.

Here is a good example of how to stir an emotional response in the audience by describing a scene. Appealing to the patriotism of his English audience, Macaulay wants to arouse their righteous indignation against the arrogant, cruel, despotic Surajah Dowlah, so that he can subsequently justify the punitive expedition that Lord Clive led against the Indian colony. He might have described this same scene in such a way as to stir an Englishman's pride in the bravery of the colonial troops. But here he describes the scene in such a way as to arouse the audience's anger against the native troops and their commander. Here is Macaulay's account of the infamous episode of the Black Hole of Calcutta:

> Then was committed that great crime, memorable for its singular atrocity, memorable for the tremendous retribution by which it was followed. The English captives were left to the mercy of the guards, and the guards determined to secure them for the night in the prison of the garrison, a chamber known by the fearful name of the Black Hole. Even for a single European malefactor, that dungeon would, in such a climate, have been too close and narrow. The space was only twenty feet square. The air-holes were small and obstructed. It was the summer solstice, the season when the fierce heat of Bengal can scarcely be rendered tolerable to natives of England by lofty halls and by the constant waving of fans. The number of the prisoners was one hundred and forty-six. When they were ordered to enter the cell, they imagined that the soldiers were joking; and, being in high spirits on account of the promise of the Nabob to spare their lives, they laughed and jested at the absurdity of the notion. They soon discovered their mistake. They expostulated; they entreated; but in vain. The guards threatened to cut down all who hesitated. The captives were driven into the cell at the point of the sword, and the door was instantly shut and locked upon them.
>
> Nothing in history or fiction, not even the story which Ugolino told in the sea of everlasting ice, after he had wiped his bloody lips on the scalp of his murderer, approaches the horrors which were recounted by the few survivors of that night. They cried for mercy. They strove to

burst the door. Holwell, who, even in that extremity, retained some presence of mind, offered large bribes to the gaolers. But the answer was that nothing could be done without the Nabob's orders, that the Nabob was asleep, and that he would be angry if anybody woke him. Then the prisoners went mad with despair. They trampled each other down, fought for the places at the windows, fought for the pittance of water with which the cruel mercy of the murderers mocked their agonies, raved, prayed, blasphemed, implored the guards to fire among them. The gaolers in the meantime held lights to the bars, and shouted with laughter at the frantic struggles of their victims. At length the tumult died away in low gaspings and moanings. The day broke. The Nabob had slept off his debauch, and permitted the door to be opened. But it was some time before the soldiers could make a lane for the survivors, by piling up on each side the heaps of corpses on which the burning climate had already begun to do its loathsome work. When at length a passage was made, twenty-three ghastly figures, such as their own mothers would not have known, staggered one by one out of the charnel-house. A pit was instantly dug. The dead bodies, a hundred and twenty-three in number, were flung into it promiscuously and covered up.

From Thomas Babington Macaulay, "Lord Clive," Critical and
Historical Essays, 1843.

The kind of description calculated to stir emotion in the audience must appeal to the imagination, and the imagination can be seized in this kind of word-painting by the use of sensory, specific detail. Macaulay makes generous use of sensory detail in his description, and characteristically, he dramatizes the scene to increase its emotional impact. But unfortunately he is not content to let a vivid reporting of the scene create the desired emotional effect. He tries to excite an extra pulse of emotion by editorializing on the scene ("Nothing in history or fiction ...") and loading his description with hyperbolic, provocative words ("great crime," "singular atrocity," "loathsome work," "ghastly figures"). By contrast, note how Mark Antony speaking after Caesar's assassination arouses the anger of his audience:

> You all do know this mantle. I remember
> The first time ever Caesar put it on.
> 'Twas on a summer's evening, in his tent,
> That day he overcame the Nervii.
> Look, in this place ran Cassius' dagger through.
> See what a rent the envious Casca made.
> Through this the well-beloved Brutus stabbed,
> And as he plucked his cursed steel away,
> Mark how the blood of Caesar followed it,
> As rushing out of doors, to be resolved

If Brutus so unkindly knocked, or no.
For Brutus, as you know, was Caesar's angel.
Judge, O you gods, how dearly Caesar loved him!
This was the most unkindest cut of all,
For when the noble Caesar saw him stab,
Ingratitude, more strong than traitors' arms,
Quite vanquished him. Then burst his mighty heart,
And, in his mantle muffling up his face,
Even at the base of Pompey's statue,
Which all the while ran blood, great Caesar fell.

William Shakespeare, *Julius Caesar*, III, ii.

Mark Antony does not bid the mob, "Be angry, ye citizens of Rome!" Nor does he seek to arouse the anger of the mob by calling the assassins "scoundrels" and "traitors." Rather, he makes the people contemplate the bloody, dagger-rent mantle that Caesar wore the day he was killed. It is the sight of this object, dramatically displayed, its significance evoked by Antony's pathetic comments, and followed by Antony's incendiary comments on the brutality and ingratitude of the deed, that whips the people up into a frenzy of vindictive anger.

We have just seen two examples of how to arouse an emotional response in an audience by a vivid description of a scene. There's another method that speakers and writers use to stir emotions, which is not as dependable as the method we have been describing. This second method does not so much "earn" an emotional response as it "begs" for it. This is the method that relies for its effect mainly on the use of emotion-laden words. The author makes use of those honorific or pejorative terms, of those favorable or unfavorable connotations of words, that will touch an audience. Here is how Edmund Burke tried to stir his reader's resentment against the revolutionary mob that stormed the royal palace at Versailles at the beginning of the French Revolution in 1789 and seized the Queen, Marie Antoinette:

> It is now sixteen or seventeen years since I saw the queen of France, then the dauphiness, at Versailles; and surely never lighted on this orb, which she hardly seemed to touch, a more delightful vision. I saw her just above the horizon, decorating and cheering the elevated sphere she just began to move in—glittering like the morning-star, full of life, and splendor, and joy. Oh! what a revolution! and what a heart must I have, to contemplate without emotion that elevation and that fall! Little did I dream when she added titles of veneration to those of enthusiastic, distant, respectful love, that she should ever be obliged to carry the sharp antidote against disgrace concealed in that bosom; little did I dream that I should have lived to see such disasters fallen upon her in a nation of

gallant men, in a nation of men of honour and of cavaliers. I thought ten thousand swords must have leaped from their scabbards to avenge even a look that threatened her with insult.—But the age of chivalry is gone.—That of sophisters, economists, and calculators, has succeeded; and the glory of Europe is extinguished forever. Never, never more, shall we behold that generous loyalty to rank and sex, that proud submission, that dignified obedience, that subordination of the heart, which kept alive, even in servitude itself, the spirit of an exalted freedom. The unbought grace of life, the cheap defence of nations, the nurse of manly sentiment and heroic enterprise is gone! It is gone, that sensibility of principle, that chastity of honour, which felt a stain like a wound, which inspired courage whilst it mitigated ferocity, which ennobled whatever it touched, and under which vice itself lost half its evil, by losing all its grossness.

From Edmund Burke, *Reflections on the Revolution in France,* 1790.

Edmund Burke starts to picture the Queen so that the audience can contemplate her and feel the same emotion that he feels for her. But her picture never emerges through the blaze of Burke's "rhetoric." She glitters on the horizon "like the morning-star," but we never really get to see her. Instead, Burke takes over and stirs up our emotions with the grandiloquent rhythm of his prose and with his litany of honorific terms ("titles of veneration," "men of honour," "gallant men," "age of chivalry," "generous loyalty," "proud submission," "dignified obedience," "chastity of honor," etc.). It is somewhat unfair to pluck this purple patch out of its context, because when one sees it in its setting in the long pamphlet that Burke wrote, it does not strike the reader as being so blatantly sentimental as it appears in isolation. But the passage does illustrate very well what an individual skilled in the choice and manipulation of words can do to the emotions of an audience.

When Aristotle turns to a consideration of the emotions in Book II, Chapters 2-17 of the *Rhetoric,* he intends to supply the student of rhetoric with topics for an appeal to the emotions of an audience. Taking some of the common emotions, in pairs of opposites—e.g., anger and meekness, love and hatred, fear and boldness, shame and shamelessness—he analyzes these emotions from three angles: (1) their nature; (2) their object—that is, the kind of people toward whom we experience the emotion; (3) their exciting causes. Aristotle claims that we must know all three things about an emotion if we hope to arouse it in others.

This analysis is one of the earliest attempts at psychology. Admittedly, Aristotle's psychology is primitive and inchoate. John Locke and such eighteenth-century Scottish philosophers as David Hume, Thomas Reid, Francis Hutcheson, and Lord Kames made great advances over Aristotle's primitive psychology; and of course the major modern advances in psychology were begun by Sigmund Freud. But Aristotle's analysis of the emotions can be of value to the student who is not professionally trained in psychology, because his analysis was sound as far as it went and was based on the kind of commonsense observation of people that even the amateur is capable of making. From our knowledge of our own emotional mechanism and from our observation of the emotional reactions of others, we are familiar enough with the common emotions to be able to manipulate them for persuasive purposes.

The student should read Aristotle's analysis of the emotions in Book II of the *Rhetoric*. What we can do here is quote some excerpts from Aristotle's analysis of anger to show the elementary level and astuteness of Aristotle's nonprofessional observations about human emotions. As students read these excerpts, they should pause occasionally to ask themselves how well these observations accord with their own observations of angry people.

> Anger may be defined as an impulse, accompanied by pain, to a conspicuous revenge for a conspicuous slight directed without justification towards what concerns oneself or towards what concerns one's friends. If this is a proper definition of anger, it must always be felt towards some particular individual, e.g. Cleon, and not 'man' in general.... It must always be attended by a certain pleasure—that which arises from the expectation of revenge. For since nobody aims at what he thinks he cannot attain, the angry man is aiming at what he can attain, and the belief that you will attain your aim is pleasant.... It is also attended by a certain pleasure because the thoughts dwell upon the act of vengeance, and the images then called up cause pleasure, like the images called up in dreams.
>
> [A discussion of slighting follows, since it is the slight that excites anger.] Now slighting is the actively entertained opinion of something as obviously of no importance.... There are three kinds of slighting—contempt, spite, and insolence. (1) Contempt is one kind of slighting: you feel contempt for what you consider unimportant, and it is just such things that you slight. (2) Spite is another kind; it is a thwarting another man's wishes, not to get something yourself but to prevent his getting it.... (3) Insolence is also a form of slighting, since it consists in doing and saying things that cause shame to the victim, not in order that anything may happen to yourself, or because anything has happened to yourself, but simply for the pleasure involved.... The cause of the pleasure thus enjoyed by the insolent man is that he thinks himself greatly superior to others when ill-treating them.... A man expects to be specially respected by his inferiors in birth, in capacity, in goodness, and generally in anything in which he is much their superior: as where money is concerned, a wealthy man looks for respect from a poor man; where speaking is concerned, the man with a turn for oratory looks for respect from one who cannot speak: the ruler demands the respect of the ruled,

and the man who thinks he ought to be a ruler demands the respect of the man whom he thinks he ought to be ruling. . . .

. . . The persons with whom we get angry are those who laugh, mock, or jeer at us, for such conduct is insolent. Also those who inflict injuries upon us that are marks of insolence. . . . Also those who speak ill of us and show contempt for us, in connexion with the things we ourselves most care about: thus those who are eager to win fame as philosophers get angry with those who show contempt for their philosophy; those who pride themselves upon their appearance get angry with those who show contempt for their appearance; and so on in other cases. . . . Again, we are angrier with our friends than with other people, since we feel that our friends ought to treat us well and not badly. We are angry with those who have usually treated us with honour or regard, if a change comes and they behave to us otherwise: for we think that they feel contempt for us or they would still be behaving as they did before. . . . Further, with those who slight us before five classes of people: namely, (1) our rivals, (2) those whom we admire, (3) those whom we wish to admire us, (4) those for whom we feel reverence, (5) those who feel reverence for us: if anyone slights us before such persons, we feel particularly angry. . . .

The persons with whom we feel anger, the frame of mind in which we feel it, and the reasons why we feel it, have now all been set forth. Clearly the orator will have to speak so as to bring his hearers into a frame of mind that will dispose them to anger, and to represent his adversaries as open to such charges and possessed of such qualities as do make people angry.

Rhetoric, Book II, Chapter 2, trans. W. Rhys Roberts. Reprinted by permission of the Clarendon Press, from *The Works of Aristotle,* ed. W. D. Ross, Volume XI.

The point to make about Aristotle's analysis of the emotions—or any other analysis of emotions for that matter—is that after students have read the analysis they should "forget" about it. They should "forget" about it in the same sense that someone who has read a "how-to" book about batting should forget what he has read when he takes a bat in hand and starts swinging at the ball. Students will not really forget what they have read; they will unconsciously incorporate what they have learned about the emotions into their appeal. This is just another way of urging them to "be natural." All of us, to one degree or another, continually appeal to the emotions of others. From our dealings with other people and from our experience with our own emotional reactions, we develop certain instincts about the emotions. It is upon these instincts that we draw when we make an emotional appeal.

Some people's instincts along these lines are more fully developed than other people's. When we say of someone that he has "quite a line" or that she is a "smooth operator," we are probably paying tribute to that person's natural or developed talent for producing the right emotional touch at the right time.

Making a conscious study of the emotions and being aware that we are appealing to someone's emotions will not necessarily make us more adept at this kind of appeal. But a conscious knowledge of any art makes it more *likely* that we will practice the art skillfully. The person who learned to play the piano by ear will not be hurt by studying music; but that person might very well be helped to play better.

To sum up what we have said about the emotional appeal: Be aware that the emotional appeal plays a vital part in the persuasive process; intellectual conviction is often not enough to move people's will to act. Be alert for emotional appeals from others; don't allow your heart to prompt you to do something that your reason or conscience would later regret. Be natural; let the nature of the subject matter, the occasion, or the audience elicit the appropriate kind and the right amount of emotional appeal. Remember that you cannot command yourself or others to feel emotions; you must conjure up the scene or situation or person that will make people experience the emotions you want to rouse in them. Be aware—as will be pointed out again in the chapter on Arrangement—that people sometimes have to be put into the right emotional mood before they will listen to appeals to reason; at other times it is better to start out with appeals to reason and then rouse the audience to the proper emotional pitch in a grandiloquent peroration.

The Topics

Once students have a subject and have converted it into a sharply defined thesis, they are faced with the task of developing that subject. If they are engaged in persuasive discourse, they must find "arguments" to develop their subjects. In the preceding section we saw that anyone bent on persuading others makes use of one or more of the three modes of appeal—the appeal to reason, the appeal to emotions, the appeal of character. If one decides to make use of the appeal to reason, one will develop one's arguments inductively or deductively. If one argues deductively, one will resort to the syllogism or, more likely, the enthymeme. If one argues inductively, one will resort to full induction or the example. But for any of these modes of appeal, whether it be logical, emotional, or ethical, one must either *have* something to say or *find* something to say.

Sometimes, from their experience, their education, or their reading, students will already have something to say. On many of the subjects they are asked to write about in college classes, students are able to write a 500- to 800-word theme quite readily, for they have a sufficient stock of ideas on those subjects to be able to write, as it were, "off the top of the head." They are most likely to have a great deal to say when they feel very strongly about something, for then ideas seem to come to them unbidden.

In this chapter, however, we are concerned with the problems of writers who do not have, or think they do not have, something to say on some given subject. Writers can be said to have "nothing to say" when they have (1) no ideas at all on a subject, (2) only a few ideas or not enough ideas to develop a subject adequately, or (3) a mass of vague, jumbled, inaccurate, or untenable ideas. Those writers have to *find*, to *discover*, or, to use the rhetorical term, to *invent* their material. Some measure of *invention* will be involved in all four forms of discourse—exposition, argumentation, description, and narration. But invention figures most prominently in expository and argumentative discourse, because in description or narrative discourse the writer has more occasion to "create" the material than to "invent" it.

What are the writers' resources when they have to find their material? Their chief resources will always be the fruits of their education, their reading, their observation, and their reflection. Both Cicero and Quintilian maintained that the most valuable background for an orator was a liberal education, because they recognized that such a broad education was best calculated to aid a person faced with the necessity of inventing arguments on a wide variety of subjects.

But wide and varied experience, reflection, education, and reading come only with time and effort. What about those who have not yet reaped the benefits of experience and study? Are they condemned to be inarticulate? Is there some system that can supply the deficiencies of their resources? The rhetoricians thought that there was such a system in the *topics*.

As we saw in the section of Chapter I devoted to definitions of key terms, the topics were the general heads under which were grouped arguments for a particular subject or occasion. They were the "regions," the "haunts," the "places" where certain categories of arguments resided. There was some sense to the attempt by Peter Ramus and his followers in the seventeenth century to relegate the topics to the province of logic, for the system of the topics is really an outgrowth of the study of how the human mind thinks. The human mind, of course, does think about particular things, but its constant tendency is to rise above the particulars and to abstract, to generalize, to classify, to analyze, and to synthesize. The topics represented the system that the classical rhetoricians built upon this tendency of the human mind.

The rhetoricians saw, for instance, that one of the tendencies of the human mind is to seek out the nature of things. So they set up the topic of Definition. Another tendency of the human mind is to compare things, and when things are compared, one discovers similarities or differences—and the differences will be in kind or in degree. When one is presented with a subject, one then looks at it to find out whether, for one's specific purpose, it presents an opportunity for definition or comparison.

Perhaps writers will gain a clearer notion of the function of the topics if they will think of the topics as "suggesters," or "prompters," or "initiators," as a "checklist," of ideas on some subject. Being general heads or categories, the topics "prime the pump," as it were; by suggesting general strategies of development, they help to overcome inertia. Just as the starter on an automobile turns the motor over until the compression system takes over, so the topics initiate a line of thought, which then moves forward on its own momentum.

One of the terms we used in the previous paragraph to clarify the function of the topics was "checklist." The term "checklist" suggests that one goes through the list of topics, one by one, asking oneself whether this particular topic will turn up any material for the development of one's subject. In the beginning stages, the writers may very well have to do just this. He or she will eventually discover, however, that some of the many available topics will not be suitable for certain situations. The football coach does not go to his bench indiscriminately when he needs a substitute. He calls from the bench the player who has been trained for a particular position and who can best serve the particular situation that has developed on the field. As Quintilian said, "I would also have students of oratory consider that all forms of argument which I have just set forth cannot be found in every case and that when the subject on which we have to speak has been propounded, it is no use considering each separate type of argument and knocking at the door of each with a view to discovering whether they may chance to serve to prove our point, except while we are in the position of mere learners."—*Instit. Orat.*, V, x, 122. Quintilian envisioned the time when, as the result of study and practice, students would acquire that "innate penetration" and "power of rapid divination" which would lead them directly to those arguments suited to their particular case. Eventually, they would arrive at the happy condition in which the arguments would "spontaneously follow the thought."

In the remaining portion of this chapter, we are going to consider the aids to invention under three main heads: (1) the common topics; (2) the special topics; (3) external aids to invention. The common topics will provide students with a stock of general lines of argument that can be used in the development of any subject. The special topics will provide them with lines of argument especially pertinent to the particular kind of persuasive discourse in which they are engaged—deliberative, judicial, or ceremonial. The external aids to invention will direct students to some of the standard reference books which will provide them with the facts and figures they may need to substantiate their own arguments or to refute opposing arguments. These aids to invention, it will be noted, are arranged on an ascending scale of specialization: the common topics yield arguments on virtually any subject; the special topics yield arguments for a particular kind of discourse; and the external aids to invention yield data for a specific case. As Aristotle pointed out, the common topics are the aids belonging most properly to rhetoric; as we move up the scale and rely on more specialized knowledge for our arguments, we are moving out of the province of rhetoric and invading the provinces of other disciplines, such as law, history, ethics, politics, science.

The Common Topics

Before we consider the common topics in detail, let us set forth, in outline form, the common topics and their sub-topics:

DEFINITION
  A. Genus
  B. Division

COMPARISON
  A. Similarity
  B. Difference
  C. Degree

RELATIONSHIP
  A. Cause and Effect
  B. Antecedent and Consequence
  C. Contraries
  D. Contradictions

CIRCUMSTANCE
  A. Possible and Impossible
  B. Past Fact and Future Fact

TESTIMONY
  A. Authority
  B. Testimonial
  C. Statistics
  D. Maxims
  E. Law
  F. Precedents (Examples)

Definition

We have already discussed definition at some length in an earlier section of this chapter, where we were reviewing some of the basic principles of logic. Here we will confine our discussion to the uses that rhetoricians made of the topic. Definition is a way of unfolding what is wrapped up in a subject being examined. One of the rhetorical uses of this topic is to ascertain the specific issue to be discussed. Opponents in a dispute may be arguing at cross-purposes if they do not clearly establish just what the point at issue is. Therefore, after we have formulated our thesis, we may find it necessary to define the key terms in our thematic proposition so that our audience will clearly understand what we are talking about.

In law trials also, it is frequently necessary to define the point at issue. In the court trial, for instance, held in London's Old Bailey in October, 1960, against Penguin Books Ltd. for publishing D. H. Lawrence's *Lady Chatterley's Lover,* it was extremely important that both the prosecution and defense determine at the outset just what was the issue at stake. Was Penguin Books being prosecuted for violating the provisions of the Obscene Publications Act of 1959? If so, in what way specifically had Penguin Books offended against this law? Had it offended by publishing an obscene book? If so, what was to be the definition of "obscene book" used in this trial? If an obscene book is one that tends to "corrupt or deprave those who read it," what is the meaning of the terms "corrupt" and "deprave"? And should there not be some determination of *who* it is that is likely to be depraved or corrupted? And did *Lady Chatterley's Lover* fall under the provisions of Section 4 of the Act, which exempt from the charge of obscenity any book judged to be in the interests of "science, literature, art, or learning"? (For the transcript of this interesting trial, see *The Trial of Lady Chatterley: Regina v. Penguin Books Limited,* ed. C. H. Rolph. A Penguin Special, 1961.)

All these questions of definition were important in the trial and had to be posed and resolved at the outset. Students can well imagine how many words were expended to settle these questions. They can learn from this example how useful the topic of definition can be to them when they are faced with the problem of developing a subject. Judging from the frequency with which students begin their themes with a definition from the dictionary ("As Webster says, ..."), they would seem to realize instinctively the value of definition as a springboard for the development of a subject. The trouble with most "As Webster says" gambits in student themes, however, is that they serve no useful function. The definitions are there in the introduction because students do not know how to get into their subjects. They are a stalling tactic that students use while trying to work up momentum for the main push.

A definition becomes really functional when it is used as Matthew Arnold does in refutation of Thomas Henry Huxley's "Science and Culture," one of the essays reproduced among the readings at the end of this chapter.

> Let us, I say, be agreed about the meaning of the terms we are using. I talk of knowing the best which has been thought and uttered in the world; Professor Huxley says this means knowing *literature*. Literature is a large word; it may mean everything written with letters or printed in a book. Euclid's *Elements* and Newton's *Principia* are thus literature.

> All knowledge that reaches us through books is literature. But by litera-
> ture Professor Huxley means *belles lettres*. He means to make me say,
> that knowing the best which has been thought and said by the modern
> nations is knowing their *belles lettres* and no more. And this is no suffi-
> cient equipment, he argues, for a criticism of modern life. But as I do
> not mean, by knowing ancient Rome, knowing merely more or less of
> Latin *belles lettres,* and taking no account of Rome's military, and politi-
> cal, and legal, and administrative work in the world; and as, by knowing
> ancient Greece, I understand knowing her as the giver of Greek art, and
> the guide to a free and right use of reason and to scientific method, and
> the founder of our mathematics, and physics and astronomy and biology
> —I understand knowing her as all this, and not merely knowing certain
> Greek poems, and histories, and treatises, and speeches—so as to the
> knowledge of modern nations also.

When we are seeking to clarify some of the important terms in a discussion, we can quote definitions from a dictionary. But the dictionary definitions will suit our purpose only when these accepted definitions agree with
our notions. Sometimes, however, we have to devise our own definitions,
either because the accepted definitions are too vague or because we believe
them to be erroneous or inadequate. In such cases, we *stipulate* the meaning
we will attach to certain terms in our discussion. Because Coleridge found
that existing definitions of a poem did not accord with his notions of this
genre, he formulated a definition that he felt was accurate:

> The final definition then, so deduced, may be thus worded. A poem is
> that species of composition which is opposed to works of science by pro-
> posing for its *immediate* object pleasure, not truth; and from all other
> species (having *this* object in common with it) it is discriminated by
> proposing to itself such delight from the *whole* as is compatible with a
> distinct gratification from each component *part.*

> From Samuel Taylor Coleridge, *Biographia Literaria,* Chapter XIV, 1817.

Genus

The topic of definition can be used not only for clarifying the point at issue
but also for suggesting a line of argument. In the *Apology,* which is reproduced among the readings at the end of this chapter, we see Socrates using
the topic of definition to defend himself against the charge of being an atheist.
Asking what was meant by the "divine," Socrates proposed that it must refer
either to the gods or to the works or agencies of the gods. He then goes on
to argue from this definition that he could not be considered an atheist:

> But then you swear in the indictment that I teach and believe in divine
> or spiritual agencies (new or old, no matter for that); at any rate, I be-

lieve in spiritual agencies—so you swear in the affidavit; and yet if I believe in divine things, how can I help believing in spirits or demigods; —must I not? To be sure I must; and therefore I may assume that your silence gives consent. Now what are spirits or demigods? are they not either gods or the sons of gods?

In the last sentence of this quotation, Socrates is resorting to an argument based on the first sub-topic under definition—the sub-topic of genus. Whenever the predicate of a proposition puts the subject into a general class of things—"Americans are lovers of freedom," "Suicide is a crime against society"—the subject is, in a sense, being defined, because limits are being fixed to the term. But such propositions can also pose an argument. The rhetorical force of the topic of genus derives from the principle that what is true (or untrue) of the genus must be true (or untrue) of the species. If all men are mortal, then John Smith, if he is a man, must be mortal too. Cicero in his *Topica* gives this example of an argument from Genus. If a man, he says, bequeathed all the silver in his possession to his wife, a lawyer could argue that the man intended to leave his wife not only all his silver plates and statues and candlesticks but also all the coin in his coffers, for coin is just as much a species of silver as are plates and statues and candlesticks.

Simply predicating a genus of some subject term will constitute a "proof," however, only when the audience is disposed to grant the truth of the classification. The preacher who declares from the pulpit, "Murder is a grievous sin," can safely presume that his congregation will agree with him. Whenever speakers or writers cannot presume such ready assent, they must, of course, go on to justify their classifications.

Perhaps the commonest use of definitions in argument is as a premise for a further argument. One form of this is the proposal of a definition as a norm and then the demonstration that something else either conforms or does not conform to this standard. We see another form of this in *The Federalist, No. 10,* reproduced among the readings at the end of this chapter. In paragraph 13 of this discourse, James Madison defines "a pure democracy" as "a society consisting of a small number of citizens, who assemble and administer the government in person." After pointing out in the remainder of the paragraph the shortcomings of such a system of government, Madison goes on to indicate in the next two paragraphs the direction that his argument will take in the rest of the discourse:

A republic, by which I mean a government in which the scheme of representation takes place, opens a different prospect and promises the cure for which we are seeking. Let us examine the points in which it varies from pure democracy, and we shall comprehend both the nature of the cure and the efficacy which it must derive from the Union.

> The two great points of difference between a democracy and a republic are: first, the delegation of the government, in the latter, to a small number of citizens elected by the rest; secondly, the greater number of citizens, and greater sphere of country, over which the latter may be extended.

Madison is going to use the differences between the nature of a republic and the nature of a pure democracy as the means of proving his thesis that a confederation of states is the best way to control factions.

Division

We do in effect define something when we enumerate the parts that go to make it up and when we designate the species of a genus. We would be illuminating the nature of the state if we were to designate, as Socrates did in the early books of *The Republic,* the various occupations needed to make it function. So too the analysis of government into its various species—monarchy, democracy, oligarchy, tyranny, etc.—helps to throw some light on the concept.

One rhetorical use of the topic of division is to lay out the organization of the exposition or argument that is to follow. We see an example of this in the opening paragraphs of Francis Bacon's discourse on the Idols of the Mind:

> The idols and false notions which are now in possession of the human understanding and have taken deep root therein, not only beset men's minds that truth can hardly find entrance, but even after entrance obtained, they will again in the very instauration of the sciences meet and trouble us, unless men being forewarned of the danger fortify themselves as far as may be against their assaults.
>
> There are four classes of Idols which beset men's minds. To these for distinction's sake I have assigned names, calling the first class *Idols of the Tribe;* the second, *Idols of the Cave;* the third, *Idols of the Marketplace;* the fourth, *Idols of the Theatre.*
>
> From Francis Bacon, *Novum Organum,* 1620.

Bacon takes up each of these idols in turn, explains what they are, and shows how they inhibit clear thinking. For another example of this kind of division, see paragraph 6 of Martin Luther King's "Letter from Birmingham Jail," in which the author specifies the four basic steps in a nonviolent campaign. Subsequent paragraphs of the letter develop each of these basic steps in turn.

Besides this use of division as an organizing principle, it can also be used to establish the grounds for an argument. We see an example of this use in paragraph 13 of Matthew Arnold's essay reproduced among the readings at the end of this chapter:

> Deny the facts altogether, I think, he hardly can. He can hardly deny that when we set ourselves to enumerate the powers which go to the building up of human life, and say that they are the power of conduct, the power of intellect and knowledge, the power of beauty, and the power of social life and manners—he can hardly deny that this scheme, though drawn in rough and plain lines enough, and not pretending to scientific exactness, does yet give a fairly true representation of the matter. Human nature is built up by these powers; we have the need for them all. When we have rightly met and adjusted the claims of them all, we shall then be in a fair way for getting soberness and righteousness with wisdom. This is evident enough, and the friends of physical science would admit it.
>
> From Matthew Arnold, "Literature and Science."

Arnold then uses this division into four "powers" to argue that an education in the humanities is superior to an exclusively scientific education, because the humanities can administer to the development of all of these powers in man, whereas an education in the natural sciences alone cannot.

Division can also be used to set up an argument by elimination. One can set up alternatives—"A man is a citizen either by birth or by naturalization" —and then by proving (or disproving) one alternative, one disproves (or proves) the other. Or one can enumerate a series of possibilities and eliminate them one by one. For instance, a defense attorney might argue like this:

> A man in these circumstances might steal for any one of these reasons: (A). . . ; (B). . . ; (C). . . ; (D). . . . Now, we have firmly established that A and B could not possibly have been my client's motives. Furthermore, not even the prosecution has suggested in this trial that C or D could have been my client's motives. Since none of the possible motives are applicable in this case, it is clear that my client is innocent of the charge of stealing.

If the defense attorney has taken care to consider *all* the possible motives for this crime, a jury would find this to be a rather persuasive argument.

We have shown how division can be useful as a principle of organization and as the basis for an argument. In conclusion, we might point out that since explanation is sometimes managed by analysis of a whole into its parts, division can be as useful in expository writing as in argumentative discourse.

Comparison

The second common topic that we will consider is comparison. For the purposes of learning, explaining, or arguing, we frequently resort to the strategy of bringing two or more things together to study them for similarities, differences, superiority, or inferiority. This tendency to compare things is as natural for people as the tendency to define things. People in their most primitive states must early have turned to comparison in an attempt to fathom the bewildering world about them and to establish a scale of values. They discovered that the familiar often helped them to understand the unfamiliar, and they learned that by measuring one thing against another they could discriminate the "more" from the "less." In this section we will investigate some of the ways in which we can use the topic of comparison to discover something to say on a given subject.

Similarity

One possible result of comparing things is the detection of similarity, the likeness of two or more things. Similarity is the basic principle behind all inductive argument and all analogy. In induction, we note similarity among a number of instances and make an inference about a further unobserved or unconfirmed instance. Analogy argues that if two things are alike in one or two characteristics, they are probably alike in another characteristic. The rhetorical form of induction, as we have seen, is the example—drawing a probable conclusion from a single instance of similarity. Perhaps the simplest way to differentiate analogy from induction by example is to say that whereas analogy argues from the similarities of dissimilar things, example argues from the similarities of similar things.

The following is the simplest and commonest form of argument from similarity: "If self-control is a virtue, so is abstinence." Here, noting the similarity in kind between self-control and abstinence and observing that virtue can be predicated of self-control, one infers that abstinence too must be a virtue. The ordinary person resorts to this kind of argument every day: "The student who copies from a neighbor in an examination and the student who allows or encourages a neighbor to copy from her are equally culpable. Both actions are forms of cheating." "The last time we attempted prohibition of the sale of liquor all kinds of abuses resulted. If the present proposal to prohibit the sale of narcotics is passed, we'll experience the same kind of legal and moral chaos."

The student will find many arguments from similarity among the readings in this book. We will look at only one example—the one from paragraph 25 of Martin Luther King's "Letter from Birmingham Jail," in which Dr. King answers the charge that the demonstrations of his group should be proscribed because they tend to encourage violence:

> In your statement you assert that our actions, even though peaceful, must be condemned because they precipitate violence. But is this a logical assertion? Isn't this like condemning a robbed man because his possession of money precipitated the evil act of robbery? Isn't this like condemning Socrates because his unswerving commitment to truth and

his philosophical inquiries precipitated the act by the misguided populace in which they made him drink hemlock? Isn't this like condemning Jesus because his unique God-consciousness and never-ceasing devotion to God's will precipitated the evil act of crucifixion? We must come to see that, as the federal courts have consistently affirmed, it is wrong to urge an individual to cease his efforts to gain his basic constitutional rights because the quest may precipitate violence. Society must protect the robbed and punish the robber.

Here, in a series of rhetorical questions, Dr. King is arguing on the basis of the similarity in comparable situations existing in the *same* order of being. When, however, we draw our comparisons between similar things existing in *different* orders of being—as, for instance, when we compare the structure of a society to the organization of a beehive—we are moving over into the province of another variety of the topic of similarity, *analogy*.

We might have treated analogy along with some of the basic principles of logic, but analogy, like most rhetorical arguments, produces only probable proof. Hence we will give here some of the principles governing it. Analogy revolves around the principle that two things which resemble one another in a number of respects resemble one another in a further, unconfirmable respect. This principle might be graphically represented by this scheme:

$$A \quad 1\ 2\ 3\ 4 \longrightarrow \quad 5$$
$$B \quad 1\ 2\ 3\ 4 \longrightarrow \quad (5)$$

Two things, A and B, resemble one another in four known, confirmable respects. From these points of resemblance, we argue that B resembles A in a fifth respect (5 being known and confirmable in the case of A but not in the case of B). As in inductive argument, there is a leap from the known to the unknown. It is because of this inductive leap that analogy achieves probability rather than certainty.

Let us look at an example of argument by analogy:

> There is only one cure for the evils which newly acquired freedom produces; and that cure is freedom. When a prisoner first leaves his cell he cannot bear the light of day: he is unable to discriminate colours or recognise faces. But the remedy is, not to remand him into his dungeon, but to accustom him to the rays of the sun. The blaze of truth and liberty may at first dazzle and bewilder nations which have become half blind in the house of bondage. But let them gaze on, and they will soon be able to bear it. In a few years men learn to reason. The extreme violence of opinion subsides. Hostile theories correct each other. The scattered elements of truth cease to contend, and begin to coalesce. And at length a system of justice and order is educed out of the chaos.
>
> From Thomas Babington Macaulay, *Essay on Milton*, 1825.

Macaulay states his thesis in the first sentence of this passage: he contends that the cure for the evils that attend newly won emancipation is freedom. Noting similarities in the condition of a nation that has won its independence and that of a man who has just been released from prison, he elaborates that similarity to support his contention.

As we have already pointed out, an analogy does not really prove anything, but it can have persuasive value. Sometimes the nature of one's audience will determine how effective an argument by analogy will be. In most cases, however, the persuasiveness of the analogy will depend largely on adherence to these two principles:

1. The similarities between two things must concern pertinent, significant aspects of the two things.
2. The analogy must not ignore pertinent dissimilarities between the two things being compared.

For instance, an anthropologist might try to prove that a certain island in the Pacific was once inhabited by comparing it with another Pacific island known to have been inhabited. She might point out that both islands had palm trees, sandy beaches, placid lagoons, mild climate, and shelter from high winds. However, by ignoring the fact that the questionable island had a very low annual rainfall and that the island was too far from any mainlnad or other island to make it likely that people could have reached it by sailboat or canoe, the anthropologist would be ignoring factors that are important to the issue at hand—namely, could people have reached the island, and once they reached it, could they have survived? Most of the time when we say, "Your analogy doesn't hold," we are exposing an analogy that has avoided consideration of important differences. For instance, in the example quoted above, Macaulay has pointed out a number of similarities between the situation of a released prisoner and the situation of an emancipated nation. But are there not some relevant dissimilarities between the two situations? Is there not a significant difference between a nation of people and a single person—a difference that might justify a difference of treatment?

Analogy is often used too for purposes of exposition. By comparing something unfamiliar or abstruse with something familiar, one can facilitate the explanation. Here is an example of this use in an essay by Dr. J. Robert Oppenheimer, in which he uses the analogy of a tree to show how knowledge tends to ramify:

> How then does it go? In studying the different parts of nature, one explores with different instruments, explores different objects, and one gets a branching of what at one time had been common talk, common sense. Each branch develops new instruments, ideas, words suitable for

describing that part of the world of nature. This tree-like structure, all growing from the common trunk of man's common primordial experience, has branches no longer associated with the same question, nor the same words and techniques. The unity of science, apart from the fact that it all has a common origin in man's ordinary life, is not a unity of deriving one part from another, nor of finding an identity between one part and another, between let us say, genetics and topology, to take two impossible examples, where there is indeed some connection.

From J. Robert Oppenheimer, "On Science and Culture."

In paragraph 19 of Edmund Burke's "Letter to a Noble Lord," reproduced among the readings in this chapter, we see another use being made of analogy. By comparing his present situation with that of a fallen oak tree, Burke is seeking to stir the emotions of his audience:

But a Disposer whose power we are little able to resist and whose wisdom it behooves us not at all to dispute, has ordained it in another manner and (whatever my querulous weakness might suggest) a far better. The storm has gone over me; and I am like one of those old oaks which the late hurricane has scattered about me. I am stripped of all my honours, I am torn up by the roots and lie prostrate on the earth! There, and prostrate there, I most unfeignedly recognize the Divine justice and in some degree submit to it.

Difference

Another possible result of comparing two or more things is a detection of differences. At some time in their academic careers, students must have been asked to answer an essay-question that begins with the formula, "Compare and contrast...." The "compare" part of that formula is asking the students to set forth the similarities between things; the "contrast" part of the formula is asking them to note the differences between things. In the eighteenth century, it was common for those critics who were influenced by John Locke's psychology of knowledge to define *wit*, the imaginative faculty, as the faculty that saw resemblances between things and to define *judgment*, the rational faculty, as the faculty that saw differences between things. Wit, in other words, was the synthetic faculty, and judgment was the analytic faculty. It would be well to develop both judgment and wit.

Rhetoricians made use of the topic of difference to gather arguments for confirmation or refutation. Edmund Burke's essay at the end of this chapter, "Letter to a Noble Lord," is a good essay for the student to study for an illustration of the operation of the topic of difference. In this *apologia*, Burke bases most of his defense on difference. He spends a great deal of time, for instance, contrasting the pension that he has received from the government with the pension that the Duke of Bedford's family received many years ago. Here is just one example, from paragraph 3 of the essay, of Burke's argument from differences:

> I really am at a loss to draw any sort of parallel between the public merits of his Grace, by which he justifies the grants he holds, and these services of mine, on the favorable construction of which I have obtained what his Grace so much disapproves. In private life, I have not at all the honour of acquaintance with the noble Duke. But I ought to presume, and it costs me nothing to do so, that he abundantly deserves the esteem and love of all who live with him. But as to public service, why truly it would not be more ridiculous for me to compare myself in rank, in fortune, in splendid descent, in youth, strength, or figure, with the Duke of Bedford, than to make a parallel between his services and my attempts to be useful to my country. It would not be gross adulation, but uncivil irony, to say that he has any public merit of his own to keep alive the idea of the services by which his vast landed pensions were obtained. My merits, whatever they are, are original and personal; his are derivative. It is his ancestor, the original pensioner, that has laid up this inexhaustible fund of merit, which makes his Grace so very delicate and exceptious about the merit of all other grantees of the Crown. Had he permitted me to remain in quiet, I should have said, 'tis his estate; that's enough. It is his by law; what have I to do with it or its history? He would naturally have said on his side, 'tis this man's fortune.—He is as good now as my ancestor was two hundred and fifty years ago. I am a young man with very old pensions; he is an old man with very young pensions—that's all.

You can study the topic of difference as it occurs in the readings reproduced at the end of this chapter. In paragraph 15 of *The Federalist, No. 10,* for instance, James Madison, after defining the terms "pure democracy" and "republic," goes on to contrast the efficiency of these two forms of government. Matthew Arnold makes frequent use of the topic of difference in his essay "Literature and Science"; in paragraph 11, to pick out only one example, we see Arnold marking the differences between the physical sciences ("knowledge of things") and the humanities ("knowledge of words"). In paragraph 16 of "Letter from Birmingham Jail," Dr. King points out the crucial differences between a just law and an unjust law. A study of these and other examples should convince you of how common the topic of difference is in discourse and of how useful this topic can be for purposes of exposition or persuasion.

Degree

More and less—the topic to which we have attached the label "degree"—was one of the four common topics that Aristotle discussed in his *Rhetoric*. Aris-

totle perceived that in comparing things we sometimes discover, not a difference *in kind,* as in the previous topic, but a difference *in degree.* One thing
will be better than another; or it will be worse. The relevance of this fact
for rhetoric is that sometimes when we are seeking to persuade others to do
something or to accept something, we have to show our audience that the
choice before them is not between a good and an evil but between a greater
good and a lesser good—or between a greater evil and a lesser evil.

Questions of degree are not easy to settle, mainly because judgments about
such a difference are usually relative and subjective. To help orators find
arguments to decide questions of degree, Aristotle provided a set of criteria
in Book I, Chapter 7 of his *Rhetoric.* Here are some of his criteria:

> 1. A greater number of things can be considered more desirable
>   than a smaller number of the same things.

Deciding questions of degree by numerical superiority must be attended with
certain cautions. Numerical superiority, first of all, must be reckoned in regard to things of the same species. Ten one-dollar bills are obviously a greater
good than five one-dollar bills; but ten one-dollar bills are not a greater good
than five ten-dollar bills. Then too numerical superiority becomes a helpful
determinant of degree only when all other things are equal. A congressional
legislator might argue that a tax bill which will bring in four billion dollars
of revenue is a better proposal than the tax bill that will bring in only three
billion dollars. But the legislator's argument will persuade his or her colleagues only if a number of other considerations are equal: if both bills are
equally just; if both bills are equally enforceable; if both bills can be admin-
istered at relatively equal cost. Numerical superiority would also be qualified
by the quality of the things involved. It might be argued, for instance, that
the football coach who recruited twenty players had done a better job than
the coach who recruited only fifteen players. But the coach who had recruited
only fifteen players might actually have engaged a greater number of superior athletes or have recruited two or three players who are worth more to a
team than the entire twenty players hired by the other coach.

> 2. That which is an *end* is a greater good than that which is only
>   a *means.*

The principle underlying this criterion is that a *means* is desirable only for
the sake of something else; but an *end* is desirable for its own sake. Health,
for instance, is a greater good than exercise, because we indulge in exercise
for the sake of acquiring or maintaining health. Exercise is a means to a
good outside itself; but in relation to exercise, health is an end, something
which is desirable for its own sake.

3. What is scarce is greater than what is abundant.

This principle is the basis of most monetary systems. Silver coins are of greater value than copper coins because silver is a scarcer metal than copper; gold is more valuable than silver for the same reason. We should be aware, however, that in some circumstances the opposite principle could be used as a criterion of superior value. We could argue that what is abundant is a greater good than what is scarce because the abundant is more useful. Thus although water is more abundant than gold, in some circumstances water would be judged the greater good because it was more useful.

4. What men of practical wisdom would choose is a greater good than what ignorant men would choose.

Plato's many arguments about the "one" and the "many" were examples of the application of this criterion. What is involved here is the impressiveness of authority. As a practical matter, we all rely on the judgments of experts. Where judgments about value conflict, the antecedent probability is that the judgment of the expert is more reliable than that of the amateur. Under the fifth of the common topics, we shall discuss at some length the part that testimony or informed opinion plays in exposition and argument.

5. What the majority of men would choose is better than what the minority would choose.

This criterion, the opposite of the previous one, smacks very much of the nose-counting method of determining worth. "If you want to find out what the most worthwhile current novels are, consult the best-seller lists." "The better candidate is the one the people elect." This criterion will have persuasive value with people who conceive of the *good* in the Aristotelian sense of that which is desirable for its own sake. Desirability is a quite different thing from worth. We all know that what all people or most people desire is not always a good in the moral or aesthetic sense. But if, in any given discussion, people are thinking of good in terms of what is desirable, then the preference of the majority will be persuasive.

Advertisers make great use of this criterion. "More people drink Pepsi than any other cola." Sometimes of course what all people or most people choose *is* the worthiest good. There is a certain presumptive evidence that the product most people buy is the best product. Other factors, of course, influence the popularity of a product—its price, its prestige value, its advertising—but if there is any validity to the maxim "You can't fool all of the people all of the time," one is inclined to believe that it is the quality of the product that maintains sales at a high level.

6. What men would really like to possess is a greater good than what men would merely like to give the impression of possessing.

In *The Prince,* Machiavelli said that a reputation for virtue was so important to the image a ruler needs to create that if he was not *really* a virtuous man he must at least give the *appearance* of being a virtuous man. Tested by this sixth criterion, Machiavelli's view suggests that power is a greater good than virtue, because power is what the ruler really wants and in order to get it he is ready to assume a mask of virtue. Aristotle uses a similar example: one could argue that health is a greater good than justice, because while men can be content with the mere reputation for being just, men prefer being healthy to only seeming healthy.

7. If a thing does not exist where it is more likely to exist, it will not exist where it is less likely to exist.

This is a line of argument to which logicians commonly assign the Latin label *a fortiori* ("from the stronger"). John Donne, in the sonnet that depreciates the power and dreadfulness of death, used an *a fortiori* argument to develop his thesis. Here are the first six lines of that sonnet:

Death, be not proud, though some have called thee
Mighty and dreadful, for thou art not so,
For those, whom thou think'st thou dost overthrow,
Die not, poor Death, nor yet canst thou kill me.
From rest and sleep, which but thy pictures be,
Much pleasure, then from thee much more must flow,

A paraphrase of the elliptical syntax in lines 5 and 6 will clarify the *a fortiori* argument implicit in those lines. In line 5, Donne says that rest and sleep are like death, are "imitations" of death. We all know that we derive a great deal of pleasure from rest and sleep; therefore, we should derive even more pleasure from that which they imitate, from death. If so much pleasure from the *lesser* thing, how much more pleasure from the *greater* thing. Therefore death cannot be as dreadful as we have been led to believe.

An *a fortiori* argument can work in two directions: (1) from the greater to the lesser, or (2) from the lesser to the greater. Donne starts out with a consideration of the lesser and then makes an inference about the greater. An *a fortiori* argument that works in the other direction would take a form like this: "If a man would steal from a friend, he would steal from a stranger."

An *a fortiori* argument sets up two possibilities, one of which will be more probable than the other. Whatever can be affirmed about the less probable can be affirmed with even greater force about the more probable. Like most rhetorical arguments, an *a fortiori* argument does not lead to certainty; it leads to a more or less strong probability.

A number of arguments from the topic of degree are pointed out in the analyses of whole essays in this and the following chapter. Here are two leads to arguments from degree in some of the readings that are not analyzed:

> I have almost reached the regrettable conclusion that the Negro's great stumbling block in his strike toward freedom is not the White Citizen's Councilor or the Ku Klux Klanner, but the white moderate, who is more devoted to "order" than to justice; who prefers a negative peace which is the absence of tension to a positive peace which is the presence of justice; who constantly says: "I agree with you in the goal you seek, but I cannot agree with your methods of direct action"; who paternalistically believes he can set the timetable for another man's freedom; who lives by a mythical concept of time and who constantly advises the Negro to wait for a "more convenient season." Shallow understanding from people of good will is more frustrating than absolute misunderstanding from people of ill will. Lukewarm acceptance is much more bewildering than outright rejection.
>
> From paragraph 23 of Martin Luther King's "Letter from Birmingham Jail"

> If then there is to be separation and option between humane letters on the one hand and the natural sciences on the other, the great majority of mankind, all who have not exceptional and over-powering aptitudes for the study of nature, would do well, I cannot but think, to choose to be educated in humane letters rather than in the natural sciences. Letters will call out their being at more points, will make them live more.
>
> From final paragraph of Matthew Arnold's "Literature and Science."

Relationship

Cause and Effect

The first sub-topic that we will consider under the general head of relationship is cause and effect. Just as people have always exhibited a desire to know the nature of things and a curiosity about likenesses and differences, so they have always felt the urge to discover the "why" of something. A child exhibits the first glimerings of rationality when she passes from the stage of asking the question "what" about the world around her to the stage of asking the question "why." "What is that, Daddy?" "That's rain, dear. It's water that falls from those dark clouds." "Why, Daddy?" Having noted an effect, the child begins to ask questions about the cause.

People have traditionally accepted as axiomatic the principle that every effect must have a cause. Many of the arguments for the existence of God, for instance, have been based on this principle. Having observed the universe in its wonderful immensity, harmony, and complexity, people have postulated that this world had its beginnings in God, the Prime Mover, the Uncaused Cause.

Cause-and-effect relationships constitute one of the most fruitful sources of arguments. But before we explore the rhetorical uses of cause and effect, we should review a few principles governing this kind of reasoning.

First, we must recognize that an effect could have a number of possible causes. In the case of a broken window, for instance, we know that a number of things could account for that broken window. Someone could have thrown a rock at the window; the wind could have broken the window; tremors in the earth could have broken the window; a sonic boom from a passing jet airplane could have broken the window. Although these are all possible causes of the broken window, only one of these will be the cause of *this* broken window. The task is to determine *which* cause. Most detective stories start out with a murder. The detective must sort out, from all the possible or probable causes, *the* cause of this particular murder; he must discover the murderer.

Second, the cause that we assign for an effect must be capable of producing the effect. It must, in other words, be an *adequate* cause. If a detective discovers that a robust man was strangled to death, he immediately rules out as a suspect the elderly aunt, the twelve-year-old nephew of the deceased, and the 114-pound chambermaid. All of these people are capable of murdering someone, even by strangling a person, but they could not have strangled the powerful man stretched out on the carpet in the library. Now, there is the ju-jitsu artist who had been paying court to the victim's daughter....

Third, once we have a probable and adequate cause for something, we must consider whether there are other adequate causes for the effect. Yes, there was that ju-jitsu artist, but there was also that tall, gangly butler and that wiry, irascible gardener. They too could have strangled the man.

Fourth, we must consider whether the conditions or circumstances were such that the potential cause could operate. In a controlled experiment—like those that a chemist conducts in the laboratory—such conditions as time, temperature, humidity, proportions, can be stabilized or varied to test whether the hypothetical cause is the real cause. In the case of human beings acting as efficient causes, such conditions as opportunity and motivation must be considered.

Last, we must also consider whether the hypothetical cause always produces an effect and whether it invariably produces the same effect. In short, we must establish not only that a putative cause *could* produce a particular effect but also that it *would* produce the effect.

One of the commonest errors in cause-and-effect reasoning is the fallacy usually referred to by the Latin label *post hoc ergo propter hoc* ("after this, therefore because of this"). This is the error of supposing that where there is a time relationship between two events there is also a cause-and-effect relationship. A number of supersititons are built upon this fallacy. John Smith got hit by a car at the intersection of Fifth and Main Streets because five minutes before, he had walked under a painter's ladder. It is understandable, of course, why people tend to suppose that when one event chronologically follows another event the later event was caused by the earlier event. But we must *prove* the cause-and-effect relationship; we cannot *presume* relationship. Try proving that John Smith's having walked under a ladder resulted in his being hit by a car. On the face of it, the action does not seem to be a suitable or adequate cause for the effect. His walking under the ladder could indicate general carelessness, and that carelessness could explain why he was hit while crossing a busy intersection. But there was no direct relationship between the two events.

The principles we have been reviewing in connection with cause-and-effect relationships are the principles normally discussed in a logic class. Nevertheless, a conscientious rhetorician must be aware of these principles too and must observe them in his or her presentation of arguments. He or she must be especially careful to observe these principles when addressing a sophisticated audience that will not accept slipshod causal reasoning.

In persuasive discourse, arguments based on causal relationships work in two directions. We can argue from an effect back to a cause, or we can start with a cause and argue that it will produce a particular effect or effects. We see an instance of an argument from cause to effect in Jonathan Swift's *A Modest Proposal*. After making his "modest proposal" that the poor people of Ireland should sell their year-old infants as table fare for the wealthy, he points out that the implementation of his proposal would have these effects:

> I have too long digressed, and therefore shall return to my subject. I think the advantages by the proposal which I have made are obvious and many, as well as of the highest importance.
>
> For first, as I have already observed, it would greatly lessen the number of Papists, with whom we are yearly overrun, being the principal breeders of the nation, as well as our most dangerous enemies. . . .
>
> Secondly, the poorer tenants will have something valuable of their own, which by law may be made liable to distress and help to pay their landlords rent, their corn and cattle being seized, and *money a thing unknown.*
>
> Thirdly, Whereas the maintenance of an hundred thousand children, from two years old, and upwards, cannot be computed at less than ten shillings a piece *per annum,* the nation's stock will be thereby increased fifty thousand pounds *per annum,* besides the profit of a new dish, introduced to the tables of all gentlemen of fortune in the kingdom, who have

any refinement in taste, and the money will circulate among ourselves, the goods being entirely of our own growth and manufacture.

Swift goes on to name a fourth, fifth, and sixth effect of his proposal, but this is enough to illustrate our point. As any student knows who has read this famous ironical essay, Swift was not seriously offering a proposal that he expects the government to adopt, but the point is that he was using the terminology and the kind of argument that a hard-headed mercantilist of the eighteenth century might have used in trying to persuade others that "people represent the riches of a nation." If it is fairly self-evident, as in this instance, that the cause will produce the proposed effects and if the proposed effects seem desirable to the audience, the mere recital of the effects will be persuasive.

If, on the other hand, it is not self-evident that the proposed effects will follow from a particular cause, then one must prove one's claims. Before Dr. Jonas Salk, for instance, won approval from the U.S. Department of Health, Education, and Welfare to put his vaccine on the market, he had to present ample evidence that it would, as he claimed, prevent polio. With something as crucial as a vaccine, one would have to present proof sufficient to create virtual certainty about its effects. In many affairs of state, however, such as a proposal that a reduction in occupation taxes would attract dozens of new industries to a community, a legislator would have to produce only a high degree of probability in order to persuade his colleagues.

The other way to argue causally is from effect back to a cause. We see James Madison arguing from effect to cause in paragraph 7 of *The Federalist, No. 10:*

> But the most common and durable source of factions has been the various and unequal distribution of property. Those who hold and those who are without property have ever formed distinct interests in society. Those who are creditors and those who are debtors fall under a like discrimination. A landed interest, a manufacturing interest, a mercantile interest, a moneyed interest, with many lesser interests, grow up of necessity in civilized nations, and divide them into different classes, actuated by different sentiments and views. The regulation of these various and interfering interests forms the principal task of modern legislation and involves the spirit of party and faction in the necessary and ordinary operations of the government.

Again it may be well to point out that in human affairs it is not always necessary to demonstrate, with the same rigorous certainty that we expect in logic or science, that a particular effect was produced by a certain cause and no other. It is often sufficient that we produce a high degree of probability.

Antecedent and Consequence

Closely allied to the topic of cause and effect is the topic of antecedent and consequence. In fact, the latter may be regarded as merely a looser form of the cause-and-effect arguments practiced in logic. The etymology of the term *consequence* (the Latin verb *sequi,* to follow) is the key to an understanding of the way in which rhetoric used this topic. The persuader pursues this line of argument: given this situation (the antecedent), what follows (the consequence) from this? If he can detect a cause-and-effect relationship between the antecedent and consequence, he will avail himself of the relationship to strengthen his case. But he will also make use of less compelling kinds of consequences (things that follow). For instance, he might argue that since Jane Smith was not the legal wife of John Smith at the time of his death, it follows that she is not entitled to his possessions. Here there is no cause-and-effect relationship, but some judgment does follow from the existent situation.

We frequently use this kind of antecedent-consequence argument in our everyday affairs. "If women are admitted to the university as full-time students, they must be accorded the same rights and privileges as the male students." "If these students violated the university's regulations about drinking at school-sponsored gatherings, they must be suspended." "If this man is a natural-born citizen, he has the right to vote." Sometimes the consequence follows from the definition of the antecedent term. For example, "If this figure is a square, it has four right-angles" or "If this creature is a man, he is a rational animal."

Students should note that there is usually an implied premise whenever an argument takes this form. When we say, "If women are admitted to the university as full-time students, they must be accorded the same rights and privileges as the male students," we imply that all full-time students are entitled to the same rights and privileges. Oftentimes it is this unexpressed premise, this assumption, that is the vulnerable spot in an argument. So when one is looking for an opening to refute such an argument, one would do well to search for the assumption.

You may recall that in an earlier section of this chapter, where some of the main principles of logic were reviewed, the antecedent-consequence proposition often served as the major premise of the hypothetical syllogism. ("If this man is a natural-born citizen, he has the right to vote." "This man *is* a natural-born citizen." "Therefore, he has a right to vote.") You should review the rules governing the validity of such deductive reasoning so that you may be guided in formulating your own antecedent-consequence arguments and in detecting fallacies in the arguments that others present.

Here are a few examples of arguments from antecedent and consequence from the readings in this book:

> We cannot know all the best thoughts and sayings of the Greeks unless we know what they thought about natural phenomena. We cannot fully apprehend their criticism of life unless we understand the extent to which that criticism was affected by scientific conceptions. We falsely pretend to be the inheritors of their culture, unless we are penetrated, as the best minds among them were, with an unhesitating faith that the free employment of reason, in accordance with scientific method, is the sole method of reaching truth.
>
> From paragraph 30 of Thomas Henry Huxley, "Science and Culture."

> If one recognizes this vital urge that has engulfed the Negro community, one should readily understand why public demonstrations are taking place. The Negro has many pent-up resentments and latent frustrations, and he must release them. So let him march; let him make prayer pilgrimages to the city hall; let him go on freedom rides—and try to understand why he must do so. If his repressed emotions are not released in nonviolent ways, they will seek expression through violence; this is not a threat but a fact of history. So I have not said to my people: "Get rid of your discontent." Rather, I have tried to say that this normal and healthy discontent can be channeled into the creative outlet of nonviolent direct action. And now this approach is being termed extremist.
>
> From paragraph 23 of Martin Luther King's "Letter from Birmingham Jail."

Contraries

At first sight, the topic of contraries may seem very much like the topic of difference. But there is a subtle difference between the two topics. Difference involves unlike or dissimilar things, things that differ *in kind;* contraries on the other hand, involve opposite or incompatible things of the same kind. Differences become apparent when we compare things: contraries become apparent when we relate things. *Liberty* and *license* would be an example of difference; *liberty* and *slavery* would be an example of contraries.

Before discussing the rhetorical uses of the topic of contraries, we will briefly consider some of the logical principles governing contraries. Contrary terms are terms opposed to one another in the same order or genus. *Cold* and *loud* are different terms, but they are not contrary terms, because *cold* concerns the order of temperature, and *loud* the order of sound. *Cold* and *hot,* and *loud* and *quiet,* would be contrary terms. So if one person said, "This book is bad" and the other person said, "This book is good," we would say that the propositions are opposed as contraries.

These are the things we know about contrary propositions *a priori*—that is, before examination or analysis: (1) If one of the propositions is true, the other one is false; in other words, contrary propositions are incompatible; (2) If one of the propositions is false, the other one is not necessarily true; in other words, both of the propositions could be false. (See the "Square of Opposition" in the section on logic.)

In an argument, then, if it has been agreed upon that contrary assertions have been made about the same subject, one can discredit the other assertion by proving that one's own assertion is true; in that case, one doesn't have to *prove* that the other assertion is false (if I prove that the book is red, I don't have to prove that the book is not green). On the other hand, if one proves that the opponent's proposition is false, one's own proposition is not automatically true; one must go on to *prove* that one's own proposition is true. (If I prove that the book is not green, I cannot assume that the book is red; after all, the book might be blue.)

In rhetoric, arguments involving contraries or opposites sometimes take a form in which the subject terms and the predicate terms are both contrary. In Book II, Chapter 23, of the *Rhetoric,* Aristotle gives an example of an argument based on the topic of contraries: "Self-control is beneficial because licentiousness is harmful." Here the subject terms *self-control* and *licentiousness* are contraries; and the predicate terms *beneficial* and *harmful* are contraries too. We establish the truth of the first proposition ("Self-control is beneficial") by showing that the opposite of *beneficial* (namely, *harmful*) can be predicated of the opposite of *self-control* (namely, *licentiousness*). If we were to argue, "If war is the cause of our misery, peace is the way to promote our happiness," we would be advancing the same kind of argument, for we would in effect be saying, "Peace must be a good because war is an evil."

In the following excerpt, Henry David Thoreau argues from contraries— diligence (exertion) versus sloth (sluggishness), purity (chastity) versus impurity (sensuality), and wisdom versus ignorance—contending that whereas sloth makes a man ignorant and impure, diligence will make him wise and pure:

> All sensuality is one, though it takes many forms; all purity is one. It is the same whether a man eat, or drink, or cohabit, or sleep sensually. They are but one appetite, and we only need to see a person do any one of these things to know how great a sensualist he is. The impure can neither stand nor sit with purity. When the reptile is attacked at one mouth of his burrow, he shows himself at another. If you would be chaste, you must be temperate. What is chastity? How shall a man know if he is chaste? He shall not know it. We have heard of this virtue, but we know not what it is. We speak conformably to the rumor which we have heard. From exertion come wisdom and purity; from sloth, igno-

rance and sensuality. In the student, sensuality is a sluggish habit of mind. An unclean person is universally a slothful one, one who sits by a stove, whom the sun shines on prostrate, who reposes without being fatigued. If you would avoid uncleanness and all the sins, work earnestly, though it be at cleaning a stable.

From "Higher Laws," *Walden*, 1854.

Contradictions

In the previous discussion, we saw that propositions like "the water is hot" and "the water is cold" are contrary propositions. Contradictory propositions would be opposed this way: "the water is hot"; "the water is not hot." In studying the square of opposition in the section on logic, we saw also that A- and O-propositions are contradictory—"all fathers are members of the male species" and "some fathers are not members of the male species"—and that E- and I-propositions are contradictory—"no fathers are members of the male species" and "some fathers are members of the male species." Contradiction is built on the principle that a thing cannot at the same time and in the same respect be and not be.

As in the case of contraries, there are some things we know *a priori* about contradictory propositions: (1) one of the propositions must be true, and the other must be false; (2) if one of the propositions is true, the other is false; (3) if one of the propositions is false, the other is true. So if one group of medical experts says that cigarette-smoking causes lung cancer and another group says that it does not cause lung cancer, we know, before we ever investigate the facts, that one of these groups is right and the other is wrong. As we know from the heated controversy about this question in the press, it has been difficult for either group to prove conclusively that its claim is the correct one. But still we know that one of these groups has to be right, and someday scientists and doctors may be able to prove beyond doubt which group is right. Until such time, people will be guided in their decision about whether to smoke or not by the group that presents the most persuasive or probable arguments.

In preparing arguments, either for confirmation or for refutation, we will recognize contradictions as a helpful topic whenever we see two propositions related in such a way that the truth of one entails the falsity of the other. So we might begin a section of our discourse in this fashion: "Some people maintain that the Constitution guarantees the right of every citizen to vote; others maintain that the Constitution states no such right." From these two contradictory propositions, we could go on to argue for one or the other claim. Sometimes we will start out by setting up an either/or situation: "Either he is willing to take a loyalty oath, or he is not willing"; "One thing we know for certain is that this mysterious cousin of hers in Australia is either a man or a woman." And if the alternatives in the disjunctive proposition are indeed mutually exclusive, we know that if we can prove one of the alternatives to be true we will have proved that the other is necessarily false. Sometimes the contradiction between two related statements is implicit rather than explicit, and in that case our line of argument will be to point up the inconsistency or, as we say, "the contradiction in terms." So we might launch a refutation in this fashion: "My opponent claims that he is a fervent advocate of democracy. But has he not made it abundantly clear that he would deny the vote to certain citizens solely on the basis of color?" By showing that the two positions are incompatible, we would in effect be proving that our opponent is *not* a fervent advocate of democracy.

Circumstance

The Possible and the Impossible

The first sub-topic to be considered under the general head of circumstance is the possible and the impossible. Often when we are seeking to persuade others to do something, we have to show them that the proposed course of action is possible; likewise, when we are seeking to discourage others from doing something, we may want to show them that the proposed course of action is impossible. Even when people recognize that a course of action is desirable, they will sometimes hesitate to embark on it because they doubt that it is feasible.

A common way to inspire an audience with confidence in the practicality of a proposed course of action is to cite examples of people who have accomplished a similar or identical thing. The examples will be persuasive in proportion to the similarity of the actions and the circumstances.

One can also argue deductively about the possible. In his *Rhetoric*, Aristotle proposed some lines of arguments about the possible. He did not lay down another set of arguments for the impossible, but suggested at the end of the action on the possible, "As for the impossible, the speaker will obviously have his stock of arguments in the opposites of the foregoing." The student will recognize that in arguing the possible, one frequently employs some of the other topics that we have already discussed. Here are some of the lines of argument that Aristotle poses:

1. If one of a pair of contraries is possible, then the other is possible too.

The assumption here is that any two contraries, from their nature as contraries, are possible. For instance, if you can get well, you can fall sick. It should be pointed out, however, that in some cases the pair of contraries may not be *equally* possible. For instance, in some cases we may not be able to argue that if you can fall sick, you can get well, because you may be suffering from an incurable disease. As always in rhetoric, one must seize on the arguments that are available for the particular case in question.

2. If one of a pair of similar things is possible, the other thing is possible too.

For instance, if it is possible for a person to play an organ, it is possible for that person to play a piano. The fact that people have always argued for the possibility of one thing by pointing to the possibility of a similar instance suggests that the principle involved here is self-evident.

3. If the more difficult of two things is possible, then the easier is possible too.

For instance, a spokesperson for the National Aeronautic and Space Administration may one day be arguing before Congress that if it is possible to rocket a single astronaut to Mars, it is possible to rocket several astronauts to the moon. The student may recognize here the operation of the *a fortiori* argument that we discussed in connection with the topic of degree.

4. If something can have a beginning, it can have an end; and conversely, if something can have an end, it can have a beginning.

The principle upon which this argument is based is that no impossibility comes, or begins to come, into existence. Aristotle's classic example of an impossibility—of something that cannot have a beginning and therefore cannot have an end—is squaring a circle. Aristotle is not suggesting that everything that has a beginning will necessarily be finished. What he is suggesting is that every beginning implies an end and that every end implies a beginning. The person who uses this topic to win acceptance for a proposal is arguing for the feasibility or facility of the plan rather than for its mere possibility. That person argues, in effect, that "well begun is half done," that what has been begun can with faith, perseverance, and hard work be brought to fruition.

5. If the parts of a thing are possible, then the whole is possible; and conversely, if the whole is possible, the parts are possible.

One can imagine a group of space scientists once using this line of argument to convince members of Congress that it was possible to put a man into orbit. By showing that all the component parts of a launching vehicle had been manufactured or could be manufactured, they could argue that a rocket capable of putting a man into space could, if adequate appropriations were made by Congress, be constructed. The writers of the *Federalist* papers used an argument like this when they proposed that a confederation of states was possible because the components of such a confederation already existed. The persuasiveness of an argument in the other direction—from whole to part—is self-evident. If a functioning unit exists, then all the parts necessary for that functioning unit must exist.

> 6. If a thing can be produced without art or preparation, it certainly can be done with the help of art or planning.

This is a kind of *a fortiori* argument, but it differs slightly from the line of argument suggested in (3) above. Principle (3) is concerned with an argument about whether a thing can be done at all; (6) is concerned with whether a thing can be done well.

In paragraph 24 of his essay "Literature and Science," Matthew Arnold asks, "Have humane letters, then, have poetry and eloquence, the power here attributed to them of engaging the emotions?" To substantiate his claim that the humanities *can* engage the emotions, he refers to the common experience of people. "The appeal," Arnold says, "is to experience. Experience shows that for the vast majority of men, for mankind in general, they have the power." The assumption behind all appeals to experience or historical example is that if something *has* been done, it can be done again.

One of the advantages that James Madison attaches to a confederation of states is that there is less chance of unworthy individuals seizing control of the government. He does not say that it is *impossible* for unworthy people to seize power in a confederation of states, but he does say that it is *more difficult* for such people to seize power. He puts it this way in paragraph 8 of *The Federalist, No. 10:*

> In the next place, as each representative will be chosen by a greater number of citizens in the large than in the small republic, it will be more difficult for unworthy candidates to practise with success the vicious arts by which elections are too often carried; and the suffrages of the people being more free, will be more likely to center in men who possess the most attractive merit and the most diffusive and established characters.

Students will discover many other examples of arguments from the possible and impossible in the readings reproduced in this book.

Past Fact and Future Fact

The topic of past fact is concerned with whether something has or has not happened. In ancient rhetoric it played an important part in forensic oratory, since for the definition of the issue in a court trial it was important to determine whether an act had been done or not. Future fact—or, more accurately, future probability—was concerned with whether or not something would happen; this topic was used most often in deliberative oratory.

Wherever evidence or testimony is available to prove that something has happened, it should of course be presented to substantiate the claims that have been made about past events. But frequently in human affairs it is not easy, sometimes impossible, to discover the evidence or testimony that could confirm the occurrence of an event. In such cases, one must resort to arguing the *probability* of something having occurred. As we have said repeatedly, the *probable* is the main province in which the rhetorician operates; after all, there can be no room for argument about what is certain.

Where past fact cannot be established empirically, deductive reasoning takes over and, arguing from probable premises, draws more or less probable conclusions. Here are some lines of arguments that one can use to persuade others about a past fact:

> 1. If the less probable of two events has occurred, the more probable event is likely to have occurred too.

Here is the *a fortiori* argument again. Statisticians, among others, make use of this line of argument to establish the probability of past occurrences. If a number of triplets have been born, then a proportionate number of twins have been born too. Imagine a prosecuting lawyer using this line of argument to persuade a jury about the guilt of the defendant: "If, as has been admitted, this man has been guilty of stealing money from his father, do you find it too far-fetched to believe that he was capable of embezzling money from his employer?" The degree of probability would increase of course with the frequency of occurrence.

> 2. If something that naturally follows something else has occurred, then that something else has happened too; and conversely, if the antecedents were present, then the natural consequences occurred too.

People instinctively reason this way. If we hear thunder, we presume that lightning has flashed, even though we may never have seen the flash of lightning. Or if lightning flashed, then thunder followed. If someone has forgotten something, we presume that he or she once knew it. If a child has a fever, we suppose that the child has been seized by some illness. If a man shows up with a black eye and a swollen lip, the natural supposition is that he has been in a fight or walked into a door.

3. If someone had the power and the desire and the opportunity to do something, then he or she has done it.

The principle supporting the probability here is that people will gratify their desires when they have the chance, either through lack of self-control or through a natural appetite for what they perceive as a good. Prosecuting lawyers have employed this line of argument in trying to convince a jury that the defendant was guilty. Such arguments of course can legally establish nothing more than a strong suspicion of guilt, but combined with other incriminating evidence, they do have great persuasive power.

Arguments *against* the probability of something having occurred can be found in the opposites of the foregoing lines of argument.

One must more often rely on probable arguments to establish future fact than to establish past fact, because where something has occurred there is always the chance of discovering the proof that it has indeed occurred; but there is always a note of uncertainty about future events. Here are some suggestive lines of argument for persuading others about the likelihood of a future event:

1. If the power and the desire to do something are present, then that something will be done.

One of the strong arguments that have been advanced in support of nuclear disarmament is that the mere possession of atomic weapons poses a constant temptation to a nation to use them against an enemy. Some pacifists go so far as to argue that the use of the nuclear bomb is not only probable but inevitable.

2. If the antecedents of something are present, then the natural consequences will occur.

"If dark clouds have gathered, it is going to rain." (Even the weatherman will admit that this event is just a probability.) "If a raging mob has gathered in the public square, violence will follow." Some consequences, of course, occur so regularly, that high probability verges on virtual certainty. When a tightly closed room is filled with gas fumes, it is virtually certain that if someone strikes a match in that room an explosion will occur.

3. If the means are available, the end will be accomplished.

The odds-makers at Las Vegas are certainly going to pick as the winner of the World Series the baseball team that appears to be stronger on paper. But as everyone knows, the team with the "best means" does not always win the World Series. This line of argument is a familiar one in political debate. Now that we know how to manufacture a dependable electric car at a reasoable price, it appears likely that in the near future, we will be able to manufacture, on a large scale, automobiles that will not pollute the atmosphere with their effusions.

In paragraph 44 of "Letter from Birmingham Jail," Dr. King, making use of a skillful blend of the topic of future fact and the topic of past fact, supports his contention that the Negro will eventually triumph in his struggle for freedom and equality:

> I hope the church as a whole will meet the challenge of this decisive hour. But even if the church does not come to the aid of justice, I have no despair about the future. I have no fear about the outcome of our struggle in Birmingham, even if our motives are at present misunderstood. We will reach the goal of freedom in Birmingham and all over the nation, because the goal of America is freedom. Abused and scorned though we may be, our destiny is tied up with America's destiny. Before the pilgrims landed at Plymouth, we were here. Before the pen of Jefferson etched the majestic words of the Declaration of Independence across the pages of history, we were here. For more than two centuries our forebears labored in this country without wages; they made cotton king; they built the homes of their masters while suffering gross injustice and shameful humiliation—and yet out of a bottomless vitality they continued to thrive and develop. If the inexpressible cruelties of slavery could not stop us, the opposition we now face will surely fail. We will win our freedom because the sacred heritage of our nation and the eternal will of God are embodied in our echoing demands.

Testimony

Under the general head of testimony, we will consider six sub-topics—authority, testimonial, statistics, maxims, law, precedent. Unlike the other topics, which derive their material from the nature of the question under discussion, testimony derives its material from external sources. In the next section of this chapter, entitled "External Aids to Invention," the student will be advised about some of the standard reference works that can provide additional supporting material for exposition or argumentation.

Authority

The first sub-topic to be considered under the topic of testimony is authority. It is probably true that informed opinion or authority carries less weight today than it once did. In an age characterized by a scientific attitude and a democratic spirit, people are temperametally not as disposed as they once were to be impressed and swayed by the voice of authority and the pronouncements of people "in the know." In situations where facts are recoverable—and modern technology has greatly extended the realm of the empirical—people prefer facts to opinions. They are not as ready to accept something as true merely because someone says it is true. For them, it is "facts" which carry the persausive force.

Although people today are not as disposed to accept authority as their grandparents were, they are frequently forced by circumstances to rely on authority. Informed opinion does indeed still play a prominent part in the conduct of human affairs. For one thing, knowledge is so diversified and specialized in our age that no person can claim, as Francis Bacon once did, to take all knowledge for his or her province, and since the day-to-day affairs of a society cannot wait for all its citizens to catch up with the latest discoveries, people are obliged to take the "word" of some expert about the facts. For another thing, since people dispute mainly about uncertain, unpredictable matters, they frequently must turn to informed opinion to guide them in settling issues or making decisions.

Although informed opinion is not infallible, it has great persuasive force. We tend to grant more credence to the testimony of experts than to the testimony of amateurs; we place more faith in the opinions of those who pronounce on matters connected with their field of knowledge than in the opinions of those speaking outside their field of competence. A Congressional committee investigating the potential danger from nuclear fall-out will pay more attention to the renowned physicist than to the ordinary citizen, however interested and well-read the citizen may be. There have been instances, of course, where the expert turned out to be wrong and the amateur to be right, but there is always greater probability that the expert will be right.

Sometimes experts offer conflicting opinions. In evaluating conflicting testimony from equally competent experts, we must rely on other criteria in deciding which opinion to accept. In such cases, we ask questions like these:

1. Is there anything inconsistent, contradictory, or illogical in the expression of the opinion itself?
2. Do the experts harbor any prejudices that might influence or color the proffered opinion?
3. Do any of the experts have an axe to grind? an advantage to gain? a score to settle?
4. Is one expert's opinion based on more recent, more reliable information than the other's is?
5. Is one expert's opinion accepted by more experts? by the more authoritative experts?
6. What are the basic assumptions behind the expressions of opinion? Are any of these assumptions vulnerable? Does the exposure of these assumptions reveal that the conflict between the experts

is more apparent than real because they are viewing the same matter from different points of view?

Answers to probing questions like these will determine which of the conflicting opinions will have the greater persuasive force for a particular occasion and a particular audience.

Testimonial

Similar to the topic of authority is the strategy of the testimonial, which takes many forms: the letter of recommendation, the advertising "puff," the "blurb," the character-witness appraisal, the opinion-poll, the best-seller list, the audience-rating. All of these represent attempts to influence opinion, action, or acceptance. The testimonial does not have to come from an impartial, expert source to be persuasive. Sometimes the persuasive force of a testimonial stems from the esteem we have for the person or the achievements of the one offering the recommendation. "Jesse Lewis wears Adidas." An advertising slogan like that could influence thousands of people to buy Adidas shoes because Jesse Lewis is a renowned athlete. What a slogan like this attempts to do is to transfer the esteem we have for the person to the product that is recommended. In rhetorical terminology, the testimonial has "ethical appeal"—the kind of appeal that Aristotle says is often more effective in persuading an audience than appeals to reason or appeals to emotions. People tend to forget that Jesse Lewis's skill as a runner does not necessarily qualify him to be a good judge of running shoes; that Jesse Lewis is being paid to give his recommendation; that Jesse Lewis's testimonial does not necessarily prove anything about the quality of Adidas.

Two general observations can be made: (1) the testimonial can be remarkably persuasive in certain circumstances and with certain audiences; (2) the testimonial is remarkably vulnerable to refutation. Not every testimonial, of course, is to be discounted as dishonest, insincere, or irrelevant. The important caution is that the testimonial must not be used or accepted uncritically.

Statistics

Similar to the testimonial is the citation of statistics. "Five million people last year bought Humbug Products." "Fifty-eight percent of the new homes built last year were equipped with Leakproof Appliances." Sometimes this strategy is referred to as the "bandwagon technique." Everybody's doing it, so it must be good. Now, there is no denying that the preference for one product over another could be an indication that the preferred product is superior in quality to the other products. Most people have faith that superior quality, all other things being equal, will in the long run win out over the second-rate and the meretricious. So statistics can be a useful and an effective topic in many discussions.

What we must guard against in the use of statistics is making unwarranted inferences. Statistics, if accurate and if legitimately gathered, confirm a fact; but they do not always support an inference made from that fact. The fact that a book has been at the top of the best-seller list for twelve months or more supports the fact that many people have bought this book. That fact, however, will not necessarily justify the further assertion, "This best-selling novel is the best novel published last year" or "You too will thrill to the drama of this runaway best-seller."

In the previous paragraphs, we have been considering comparative statistics—pairs or groups of figures and percentages that help to decide questions of *more* and *less*. But statistics can be used in argument for purposes other than deciding superiority. Statistics can be used, for instance, to settle contrary and contradictory assertions. Suppose that one party in a dispute maintains, "Most Americans own their homes," and that the other party maintains, "Most Americans do not own their homes." If the two disputants agree upon the meaning of *own,* these two statements are directly contradictory. As we saw in the discussion of the topic of contradiction, one of these statements is true, and the other is false. An obvious way to determine which assertion is true is to cite statistics: "The 1960 Census reveals that (number) Americans or ———— percent of citizens over twenty-one years of age have completely paid off the mortgage on the house in which they dwell."

Statistics can be used to support or discredit all kinds of assertion. The chief caution to be observed in regard to the use of this topic is that one should not accept statistics uncritically. Statistics are always liable to the challenge of questions like these:

1. What is the source of these statistics?
2. Is this a qualified, unbiased source?
3. How were these figures arrived at?
4. Was the sampling a reliably representative survey?
5. When were these figures gathered?
6. Are these figures contradicted or superseded by figures from other sources?

Polls and surveys are playing an increasingly prominent role in modern life. The better polling agencies, by devising scientific formulas for extrapolating sample findings, have achieved an amazing record of accuracy. Electronic computing machines too have increased the reliability of the interpretations and predictions made from statistics. We should be aware, however, that polling techniques, especially those that depend for their findings on personal interviews with people, have certain built-in limitations. The wording of a question put to a person in the street influences the response. Any time a question-begging word gets into a question, the response will be biased. The responses to a question like "Do you favor the abolition of excessive taxes?" cannot be interpreted to mean that most people favor the abolition of taxes. Sometimes the juxtaposition of questions can bias the responses. If the question "Should subversive organizations be outlawed in America?" were followed by the question "Should the Communist Party be outlawed in America?" the response to the second question would undoubtedly be prejudiced by the response to the first question.

Another weakness inherent in the personal interview stems from two assumptions that pollsters make: (1) that people always know their own mind on questions put to them; (2) that people will give truthful answers to questions put to them. Do citizens in the street always know, at any given stage in a presidential campaign, which candidate they favor? If they are undecided or confused, they will sometimes give an answer, any answer, because they are ashamed to admit to the pollster that they do not really know which candidate they favor at the moment. When the question concerns a matter that is more complex, the likelihood increases that the interviewees do not know their own minds. Pollsters make provision for this uncertain state of mind by permitting the interviewee to answer "Undecided," but sometimes a person is undecided even about whether he or she is undecided. As for the other assumption, for one reason or another, some people deliberately mislead the questioner, by not giving a truthful answer. Recognizing this fact, pollsters include a discount-factor in their formulas for extrapolating the information they have gathered.

All of the above observations about the cogency and weaknesses of statistics suggest the ways in which we can use statistics to support our own arguments or to refute the arguments advanced by the opposition. Employed discreetly, statistics can be a valuable topic in expository and argumentative writing.

Maxims

We will use the term *maxims* (Greek, *gnomai;* Latin, *sententiae*) to cover precepts, proverbs, famous sayings, epigrammatic pronouncements, self-evident truths, sententious generalizations—all kinds of charismatic statements that people introduce into an argument. In the *Rhetoric,* Book II, Chapter 21, Aristotle treated maxims as a prelude to his discussion of the enthymeme, because, as he observed, maxims often constitute one of the premises of a syllogistic argument. For instance, in an argument about financial matters, one can imagine a disputant saying, "A fool and his money are soon parted." The full argument suggested by this proverb would run something like this:

> A fool and his money are soon parted.
> John Smith is undeniably a fool when it comes to money matters.
> John Smith is sure to lose out on his investment.

Maxims are statements, not about particular matters, but about universal matters. So the statement "Yon Cassius has a lean and hungry look" would not be a maxim, but it would take on the air of a maxim if it were changed to "One should be wary of lean and hungry men." It is not all general statements, however, that can be considered maxims. "A straight line is the shortest distance between two points" would not be one. Maxims are general statements about human actions, about things that are to be chosen or avoided in human action.

The value of maxims, according to Aristotle, is that they invest a discourse with "moral character," with that ethical appeal so important in persuading others. Because maxims touch upon universal truths about life, they win ready assent from the audience, and because of their air of hoary wisdom, they are endowed with a peculiar sanctity. Because maxims strike this note of ancient, sanctified wisdom, they are more appropriate, as Aristotle observed, when they come from the lips of older, experienced people. A maxim is just as true when uttered by a young person as when uttered by an older person, but, in certain circumstances, a maxim issuing from a callow youth will sound pretentious, even ridiculous. Alexander Pope was fortunate that many of his readers did not know that the author of the collection of wise and witty precepts in *The Essay on Criticism* was barely twenty-one years of age.

Maxims should not be avoided merely because they are well known. Their very familiarity may be an asset. The familiar often seems self-evident and for that reason wins an uncritical acceptance. Herein lies a danger however. The familiar quotation, the slogan, the platitude, the bromide have a way of acquiring immunity from criticism. For this reason, we often resort to the sanctified truism when we are seeking acceptance for our cause. Instead of earning assent, we bribe it. Besides running the danger of being unethical, such a practice can induce lazy habits. When the maxim upon which we are basing an argument is challenged, we may be unprepared to defend its truth. Sometimes too we wrongly concede an argument because we have not taken the trouble to question the apparently "truthful" premise.

These reminders are not intended to discourage the use of the topic of maxims; they are intended merely to alert us to the dangers of uncritical acceptance of "what oft was thought." The student should bear in mind Plato's salutary observation, "The unexamined life is not worth living."

Law

Under the topic of law will be included all statutes, contracts, testaments, records, and documents that can be drawn on to substantiate or refute a claim. Recorded evidence has a compelling force in any argument. An argument about the date of a person's birth, for instance, can usually be settled summarily by a birth certificate or a baptismal record. Producing a bona-fide will can silence rival claimants to an inheritance. When a critic adduces a statement from diaries or letters about an author's intention in a literary work, the critic does not necessarily clinch his or her interpretation, but certainly strengthens it.

People have a great awe of the written or printed word. How often we have heard the statement, "But it says so, right here in the book." Respect for the recorded word is in many ways a good thing. We could hardly conduct the affairs of daily life if society did not maintain respect for what is recorded "in black and white." Without deeds and contracts, all property rights, for one thing, would be tenuous. A verbal contract between a car-owner and a dealer will not stand up in court; but a written warranty, duly signed by both parties, gives a judge something concrete and definite upon which to decide a litigation.

What we must remember, however, is that documentary evidence does not necessarily foreclose all further debate; recorded words are open to challenge and to interpretation. We can protest, for instance, that a document produced in evidence is not an authentic document. Challenges like the following can also be brought forward to test the authenticity of a document:

1. There is no proof that the document in question actually issued from the hand of the alleged author.
2. The document was not duly witnessed.
3. This document is only a transcription or reproduction of an allegedly extant original.
4. In the process of transmission, the wording of the document was altered.
5. Those authorities who could attest to the authenticity of the document are not available.
6. Another or a later document invalidates this one.

Then too the wording of documents is always open to interpretation. The Constitution of the United States, for instance, is the bona fide document upon which our government is based. But one of the chief functions of the Supreme Court is to interpret the already authenticated wording of the Constitution. In our own time, we have seen what heated disputes have developed over the doctrine of separation of church and state in Article 1 of the Bill of Rights ("Congress shall make no law respecting an establishment of religion, or prohibiting the free exercise thereof") and over the doctrine of states' rights in Article 10 of the Bill of Rights ("The powers not delegated to the United States by the Constitution, nor prohibited by it to the States are reserved to the States respectively, or to the people."). The meaning of statute laws too is constantly being argued in courts.

Precedent (Example)

The last of the sub-topics to be considered under testimony is precedent or example. Etymologically, *precedent* stems from a Latin verb which meant "to go before"; hence the modern sense of "something that has happened before." In one of its modern senses, *precedent* is a technical term in law, designating a judicial decision in the past that can be used as a standard in making judgments about subsequent similar cases. Because judges are often guided by previous decisions, lawyers, in preparing briefs for a case, will search out decisions that other judges have made in similar cases. The task of the lawyer is to convince the judge that the case under consideration is indeed similar to the previous case. In effect, the lawyer's argument runs something like this:

> Your honor, I have shown that the case under consideration has a precedent in the case of New York vs. John Smith, No. 2435, tried on October 29, 1919 before Judge Mary Snodgrass. In that case, Judge Snodgrass returned a judgment that the defendant did not have to pay taxes to the plaintiff on property that had been confiscated before the due date of the tax payments. The judge ruled that although John Smith continued to occupy the property for three months, he ceased to be the owner of the property on the date that he signed the confiscation papers, and he was no longer liable for taxes once he transferred ownership, even though he continued, per agreement, to occupy the property rent-free for three months. Since the circumstances of this case are similar to those in the New York case and since the tax laws in this state are similar to those that prevailed in New York at that time, I respectfully propose that a similar ruling be made in this case.

The opposing lawyer, of course, will try to prove that the two cases are not similar or that an important difference has been overlooked or that an important consideration has been distorted. Or the lawyer will cite, if available, other precedents in which a quite different judgment was returned. When opposing precedents are presented, the lawyers will contend that one precedent should supersede the other. Each lawyer will try to show that his or her precedent is more relevant or more logical or more recent or more reliable (because it comes from a more reputable source) or more cogent (because there are more precedents of this kind than of the other kind).

So much for precedent in its legal sense. In a broader sense, precedent or example is the bringing to bear on a present case what has been done in a similar case in the past. Aristotle considered example to be the rhetorical equivalent of full induction in logic or in scientific demonstration, because in practical discourse the speaker or writer does not have the leisure to present, nor does the audience have the patience to listen to, the whole string of particulars that confirm a generalization arrived at through the inductive process; there is time and patience for the citation of only one or two examples. When there is a dispute, for instance, about how to finance the building of a bridge, the parties in the dispute will cite a few examples of how other states financed such a project and how successful the methods proved to be. The inference that the persuader hopes his audience will draw from the analogous case is that such-and-such a method of financing will be equally successful (or unsuccessful) in the case under consideration. The examples can be historical (and therefore verifiable by, or familiar to, an audience), or they can be, as in the case of the parables that Jesus Christ invented so frequently during his public ministry, fictional. The External Aids to Invention, discussed earlier in this chapter, are the resources to consult for apt historical examples, if such examples are not ready to hand.

It happens that the sub-topics we have considered under Testimony do not figure prominently in the readings reproduced at the end of this chapter. There are no uses, for instance, of Statistics in any of the readings in this chapter. But although there are not many examples of the use of Testimony in the readings in this chapter, such examples are not entirely absent. Students can consult the following places to observe how the various sub-topics of Testimony have yielded arguments for the authors:

> Authority: Huxley, ¶ 2, 20; Arnold, ¶ 11, 18, 21; King, ¶ 15, 32.
> Testimonial: Huxley, ¶ 14; Arnold, ¶ 5, 17, 19, 24; King, ¶ 31, 46.
> Maxims: Huxley, ¶ 39; King, ¶ 12, 16.
> Law: Burke, ¶ 6, 15; King, ¶ 18, 47.
> Precedents (Examples): Burke, ¶ 19; Arnold, ¶ 27, 28; King, ¶ 6, 7, 14, 21, 43, 45.

In our technological age, where knowledge is becoming more and more specialized and where the storage and retrieval of information have become highly sophisticated, the topic of Testimony is likely to be increasingly resorted to for both professional and popular discourse.

Special Topics

As pointed out in the introductory remarks of the previous section, rhetoricians commonly divided the topics into two general kinds—common topics and special topics. Common topics were depositories of general arguments that one could resort to when discussing virtually any subject. Special topics, on the other hand, were more particular lines of argument that one could resort to when discussing some particular subject. In the three main kinds of rhetorical activity—deliberative, judicial, and ceremonial—we tend to rely, fairly regularly, on certain topics that are more particular than common topics and yet more general than specialized knowledge. In a case at law, for instance, the teacher of rhetoric could not be expected to instruct students in all the points of law peculiar to this case; but the teacher could point out to students that most law cases turned on a limited number of recurring topics.

The value of the special topics in the composition process is that once writers have determined which of the three kinds of rhetorical discourse they are committed to, they know immediately what their general objective is and also the more or less special kinds of arguments that they must pursue to attain that objective. Their composition will not therefore write itself, but they have in the special topics a springboard to launch them in the right direction. And once they have their general direction fixed, they will more readily detect which of the common topics and what specialized knowledge are pertinent and therefore especially useful.

Let us look now at the special topics for each of the three kinds of persuasive discourse.

Special Topics for Deliberative Discourse

Are there some common denominators among the appeals that we use when we are engaged in exhorting someone to do or not to do something, to accept or to reject a particular view of things? There are indeed. When we are trying to persuade people to do something, we try to show them that what we want them to do is either good or advantageous. All of our appeals in this kind of discourse can be reduced to these two heads: (1) the worthy (*dignitas*) or the good (*bonum*) and (2) the advantageous or expedient or useful (*utilitas*). The English terms do not express fully and precisely what the Latin terms denoted, but perhaps the English terms do convey the general idea of "what is good in itself" (and therefore worthy of being pursued for its own sake) and "what is good for us" (a relative good, if you will, one that would be expedient for us to pursue because of what it can do for us or what we can do with it). John Henry Newman used somewhat the same distinctions in his *Idea of a University* when he was trying to show us the difference between "liberal knowledge" and "useful knowledge." There are some subjects or disciplines, Newman maintained, that we cultivate for their own sakes, irrespective of the power they give us or the use to which they can be put. There are other subjects or disciplines that we cultivate primarily, if not exclusively, for the use to which we can put them.

If we were trying to convince someone to study poetry, for instance, we might urge that the cultivation of poetry is a good in itself and therefore worthy of pursuit for its own sake and that it is no depreciation of the worth of poetry to admit that the study of poetry cannot be put to any practical uses. On the other hand, we might conduct our appeal on a less exalted level by showing that the study of poetry can produce practical results. The study of poetry can teach us, for instance, how to be more intensive readers, how to be more precise writers, how to be keener observers of the world about us.

Whether we lean heaviest on the topic of the worthy or the topic of the advantageous will depend largely on two considerations: (1) the nature of our subject, (2) the nature of our audience. It should be obvious that some things are intrinsically more worthy than others. It is easier to demonstrate, for instance, that the study of poetry is a good in itself than to demonstrate that the building of a bridge is a good in itself. In the latter case, it would be the wiser course—because it is the easier and more cogent course—to exploit the topic of the advantageous. When one is trying to convince a group of taxpayers that they should vote for a bond issue to finance the building of a bridge, one is more likely to impress the taxpayers by demonstrating the usefulness of such a bridge than by showing its aesthetic value.

So too the nature of our audience will influence our decision about the special topic to emphasize in a particular deliberative discourse. Because the audience is the chief determinant of the best means to effect a given end, we should have at least a general sense of the temper, interests, mores, and educational level of our audience. If we discern that our audience will be more impressed by appeals based on the topic of the worthy, then our knowledge of the audience will have to be a little fuller and a little more accurate, because now we must have, in addition to a general sense of the temper of the audience, some knowledge of just what things are regarded as "good" by this audience and what the hierarchy of good things is. People being what they are, however, it is probably true, as Cicero and the author of the *Ad Herennium* observed, that the topic of advantage will appeal more frequently to more people than will the topic of worth.

All deliberative discourses are concerned with what we should choose or what we should avoid. Aristotle observed that the end that determines what people choose and what they avoid is happiness and its constituents. Happiness then may be looked upon as the ultimate special topic in deliberative discourses, since we seek the worthy and the advantageous because they are conducive to our happiness. Unquestionably, people differ in their concept of happiness. Aristotle presented some of the commonly accepted definitions:

> We may define happiness as prosperity combined with virtue; or as independence of life; or as the secure enjoyment of the maximum of pleasure; or as a good condition of property and body, together with the power of guarding one's property and body and making use of them. That happiness is one or more of these things, pretty well everybody agrees.

> *Rhetoric,* I, 5.

Even today, most people, if asked, would say that happiness was one or other of these conditions or perhaps some combination or modification of these.

They would probably agree too with Aristotle's specifications of the constituent parts of happiness: "good birth, plenty of friends, good friends, wealth, good children, plenty of children, a happy old age, also such bodily excellences as health, beauty, strength, large stature, athletic powers, together with fame, honor, good luck, and virtue." One of the recurring themes in fantasies is the situation in which a good fairy allows a person three wishes. Presented with that opportunity, the person chooses the three things that will make him the happiest; and usually the choices will be some of those things enumerated in Aristotle's list. Students might ask themselves what *they* would specify if they were allowed three choices. Their choices would reveal not only a great deal about their scale of values but also how little their view of what constitutes happiness differs from the views that people have held down through the ages.

In summary then, let us say that when we are engaged in any kind of deliberative discourse, we are seeking to convince someone to adopt a certain course of action because it is conducive to happiness or to reject a certain course of action because it will lead to unhappiness. The two main special topics under the general head of happiness are the worthy and the advantageous. In developing these special topics, we will sometimes have occasion to use some of the common topics, such as the possible and the impossible (when urging the advantage, for instance, of a certain course of action, we may have to show that the course we are advocating is practicable or easy) and the topic of more and less (when seeking to direct a choice from among a number of goods, for instance, we have need of criteria to help us discriminate degrees of good). In developing the special topics, we will also need a fund of specialized knowledge pertinent to the subject we are debating. In discussing matters of public polity, for instance, we need a great deal of accurate and specific knowledge about kinds of government, the laws and constitution of a state, the mechanism of legislation. In addition, we must have at our fingertips, or know where to find, a sufficient number of facts, precedents, or statistics to support our assertions. It is not the special province of rhetoric to supply this specialized knowledge, but a rhetoric text like this can direct writers to the sources of such information. In a later section of this chapter, writers will be apprised of the standard reference works which can supply them with the specialized knowledge they may need to develop their discourse.

For an analysis of the special topics, as well as common topics, in a deliberative discourse, see the analysis of "The Obligation to Endure" at the end of this chapter.

Special Topics for Judicial Discourse

Anyone reading the classical rhetorics soon discovers that the branch of rhetoric that received the most attention was the judicial, the oratory of the courtroom. Litigations in court in Greece and Rome were an extremely common experience for even the ordinary free citizen—usually the male head of a household—and it was a rare citizen who did not go to court at least a half dozen times during the course of his adult life. Moreover, the ordinary citizen was often expected to serve as his own advocate before a judge or jury. The ordinary citizen did not possess the comprehensive knowledge of the law and its technicalities that the professional lawyer did, but it was greatly to his advantage to have a general knowledge of the strategies of defense and prosecution. As a result, the schools of rhetoric did a flourishing business in training the layperson to defend himself in court or to prosecute an offending neighbor. In defending the usefulness of the art of rhetoric, Aristotle said, "It is absurd to hold that a man ought to be ashamed of being unable to defend himself with his limbs, but not of being unable to defend himself with speech and reason, when the use of rational speech is more distinctive of a human being than the use of his limbs."—*Rhetoric,* I, 1.

In our time, the majority of citizens—except perhaps for traffic offenses—rarely if ever make an appearance in court. If they do have to go to court, they may, technically, serve as their own counsel, but usually they will hire a professional lawyer to serve them. Some of the students who are reading this text will become lawyers, and before they graduate from law school, they will have received an intensive training in the technicalities of the law and in the conduct of trials. For most people today, however, there is no need to become conversant with the subtleties of the law or to train themselves to become shrewd, eloquent pleaders before a judge or jury.

Training in this kind of rhetoric is, however, not entirely dispensable. All of us have occasion to indulge in this kind of persuasive discourse. We may never have to face the full panoply of the courtroom, but we do sometimes have to defend our actions or views, to impugn the actions of others, or to dispute the wording, interpretation, and application of texts of all kinds.

The special topics for judicial discourse developed from the efforts to ascertain the *status* of a case. As we saw in the initial section of this chapter devoted to the formulation of the thesis, the rhetoricians set up a useful formula for determining precisely the issue that was to be discussed. In order to pinpoint the issue or thesis, they asked three questions about the general subject: whether a thing is (*an sit*), what it is (*quid sit*), of what kind it is (*quale sit*).

Once the issue has been settled—and only then—the pleader, either for the defense or for the prosecution, can determine the special topics that will be pertinent to the development of the case. The ultimate special topics for all judicial discourse are justice and injustice. The terms *right* and *wrong* can serve as substitute terms if we take them in their legal, not moral, sense.

The sub-topics that can be used to develop the special topics of justice and injustice may be grouped under the three questions that serve to establish the issue:

A. Whether Something Happened

The major sub-topic here is *evidence*.

In developing this topic we pursue questions like these:
   1. What is the evidence?
   2. How, when, where, and by whom was the evidence gathered?
   3. What about the reliability of the evidence?
        a. Is it accurate?
        b. Is it relevant?
        c. Is it consequential?
        d. Is it merely circumstantial?
   4. What about the credibility of the witnesses adducing the evidence?
        a. Are they prejudiced?
        b. Are they reliable?
        c. Are they competent?
        d. Are they consistent?
   5. What about the conflicting evidence?

B. What It Is

The major sub-topic here is *definition*.

In developing this topic we pursue questions like these:
   1. What specifically is the charge being made?

2. What is the legal definition of the alleged injustice?
3. What law is supposedly violated?
   a. a written, promulgated law?
   b. an unwritten, natural law?
      (E.g. in Sophocles' play, Antigone pleads that although she had violated the written law of the community by burying her brother Polynices, she was thereby obeying a higher law.)
4. Who was harmed by the alleged injustice?
   a. an individual?
   b. the community?
5. Did the victim suffer the harm against his or her will?
6. What was the extent of the harm?

C. The Quality of What Happened

The major sub-topic here is *motives* or *causes of action*.

In developing this topic we pursue questions like these:

1. Was the alleged injustice done intentionally or unintentionally?
2. If unintentionally, what was the cause of action?
   a. chance?
   b. compulsion?
   c. natural inclination?
3. If intentionally, what was the cause of action?
   a. habit?
   b. deliberation?
   c. passion?
   d. appetite?
4. If intentionally, what was the wrongdoer's motive?
   a. profit?
   b. revenge?
   c. punishment?
   d. pleasure?
5. What kind of person was the doer of the act?
6. What kind of person was the victim of the alleged injustice?
7. Were there extenuating circumstances?

The topics we have just reviewed are the things that we invariably discuss when we are seeking to exculpate ourselves or to inculpate someone else. These topics are especially useful in courtroom trials, involving felonies and other violations of civil law. But they are useful also in discussions of the justice and injustice of human acts that are something less than crimes—misdemeanors, errors of judgment, incompetency, neglect of duties, malevolence, etc. The questions set down under the various sub-topics can serve as "suggesters" or "prompters" of the direction our discussion might take when we are engaged in this kind of persuasive activity. For the development of the special topics, pertinent common topics will present themselves as other resources. The nature of the case under consideration will in every instance determine which of the special topics and common topics are relevant.

For an analysis of the special topics, as well as the common topics, in a judicial discourse, see the analysis of Socrates' *Apology* at the end of this chapter.

Special Topics for Ceremonial Discourse

The nature of ceremonial discourse is perhaps easier to grasp than its distinction from the other two kinds. Ceremonial discourse sometimes shades off into deliberative discourse, sometimes into judicial discourse. Ceremonial orators seemed to be more intent on impressing an audience with the eloquence of their laudatory efforts than they were on persuading an audience to adopt a certain course of action. But in praising someone, they were suggesting, indirectly at least, that the audience go and do likewise; and in thus suggesting a course of action, they were moving over into the realm of deliberative discourse. Likewise, when they praised or censured someone, they encroached on the province of judicial discourse, because like the lawyer in the courtroom, they seemed to be engaged in exonerating or discrediting someone.

Despite this overlapping of kinds of discourse, however, ceremonial or epideictic discourse is a distinct type. It differs from deliberative discourse in that its *primary* object is to praise or censure someone, not to persuade others to do or not to do something. It differs from judicial discourse in that its *primary* object is not to convince judges or juries of the guilt or innocence of someone charged with crime or misconduct. Unless we recognize this distinct third category, we have no place to put such discourses as Fourth of July speeches, funeral orations, nominating speeches at political conventions, campaign commercials at election time, graduation speeches, obituaries, letters of reference, citations, and those remarks that masters of ceremony make in introducing a featured speaker. We must have a separate category for those discourses in which the primary object is to praise or depreciate the worth of an individual, a group of individuals, an institution, a nation, etc.

What then are the special topics relevant to this kind of discourse? All the rhetoricians agreed that the general aim of ceremonial discourse is to praise or censure a person or group of persons. This being the aim, the obvious special topics would be (1) virtues and vices and (2) personal assets and achievements. In praising someone, we stress the person's good qualities and notable accomplishments; in censuring someone, we stress his or her bad qualities and the absence of significant accomplishments. In assessing the worth of someone, we measure what the person *is* and what the person *does*. Some attributes represent natural endowments; others represent acquired habits. Although it seems unfair to praise someone for attributes that he or she is born with (health, good looks, strength), both natural endowments and acquired habits are commonly regarded as worthy of praise.

We are more likely to encounter discourses of praise than discourses of censure. Because of the laws governing libel and defamation of character, we rarely see in print discourses that discredit a person's character. There was a time—as recently as the eighteenth-century—when the laws protecting the public reputation of a person were so lax that vilifications of a person were often printed and circulated. It is difficult to imagine John Dryden being able to publish today his "MacFlecknoe," a clever but brutal discrediting of the Irish poet Flecknoe. We still have our scandal-mongering columnists, but they are usually careful about preserving the anonymity of the person whose affairs are being exposed.

We might look at some of the common virtues (or vices) and the common personal assets and achievements (or lack of them) that figure in discourses of praise (or censure). The point should be made that although some virtues, assets, and achievements are universally acknowledged and esteemed by all people in all ages, others enjoy a higher esteem in some civilizations or some periods than they do in other civilizations and periods. Humility, for instance, seemed not to have been a prized virtue in the civilization that Homer protrayed in the *Iliad* and the *Odyssey;* but in most Christian cultures, humility is regarded as one of the supreme virtues. So once again we are reminded of the importance of audience and context as determinants of what is said in a persuasive discourse. The age and sex of an audience, its economic and educational level, its political and religious affinities, its interests and values—all of these have a great influence on the types of virtues, assets, and achievements we tend to stress for a particular audience at a particular time in history. A man's gentleness might be the virtue to stress before an audience made up exclusively of women; a man's courage might be the virtue to stress before an audience of laboring men.

The following are some of the virtues that people commonly discuss when they are seeking to praise someone (in parentheses are the corresponding vices—those moral flaws that people mention when they are seeking to discredit someone):

1. *Courage (Cowardice)*: *bravery* and *fortitude* are commonly used as synonyms of this virtue, but *fortitude* is a somewhat broader term, signifying imperturbability in the face not only of dangerous situations but of all trying situations (we speak, for instance of a person's fortitude in enduring chronic bad health).

2. *Temperance (Indulgence)*: the virtue (and vice) connected with physical pleasures of all kinds—eating, drinking, smoking, sex. Moderation in satisfying these appetites is generally regarded as praiseworthy in most cultures.

3. *Justice (Injustice)*: these terms are to be taken in a somewhat narrower sense than they had as special topics in judicial discourse. Here, we might define justice as the virtue that respects the natural and legal rights of others.

4. *Liberality (Selfishness)*: *generosity* is another word for the virtue that disposes us to expend time, money, or effort for the good of others. *Altruism* is another close synonym.

5. *Prudence (Rashness)*: an intellectual virtue that disposes a person to make wise decisions about means and ends. This virtue is the underpinning of *commonsense* or *practical wisdom*.

6. *Gentleness (Brutality)*: *kindness,* because it is broader in its implications, might be a better term for this virtue.

7. *Loyalty (Disloyalty)*: faithfulness to a person, a group, an institution, a nation, an ideal is a universally admired quality in a person.

This list does not exhaust the virtues (and vices) by any means. It merely suggests the sort of qualities of character that people of most cultures and periods value in a man or a woman and that contribute to the esteem in which that person is held. In general, those virtues that produce benefits for others will be more highly regarded than the virtues that are good mainly for the person who possesses them. It is noteworthy that many of the Beatitudes that Christ mentioned in his famous Sermon on the Mount are social virtues—virtues that result in benefits for others. We do laud a person for personal saintliness (and personal sanctification must be each person's primary goal), but it is easier to praise a person whose virtues benefit others. For that reason, among others, St. Paul designated *charity* as the greatest of the virtues. But again, we need to emphasize that the particular circumstances or the particular audience may dictate whether it would be better to stress a person's personal virtues or a person's social virtues.

While virtue is one of the special topics that we resort to when we are engaged in composing a discourse of praise, there are other assets and achievements that we seek to discover. For instance, consider the following:

1. *Physical attributes:* agility, strength, good looks, health, stamina.
2. *External circumstances:* family background, education, economic status, political, social, and religious affiliations, friends ("Tell me who a person's friends are, and I'll tell you what kind of person he or she is.")

3. *Achievements:* work accomplished, services rendered, honors won, offices held, wise sayings, testimonials by others about the person.

Many of the resources that one uses in ceremonial discourse are the devices that novelists, dramatists, and short-story writers use to characterize the people in their fictions. The fiction writer uses dialogue (what a person says and how he or she says it), action (what a person does and how he or she does it), description of physical appearance, testimony of other characters in the story, and straight exposition of personality to give readers an idea of the characters that figure in a story. The writer of the ceremonial discourse tends to be more selective, however, than the fiction writer, concentrating on the most prominent and most favorable aspects of a person.

Aristotle observed that the common topic of *amplification* and *depreciation* plays a prominent role in ceremonial discourse, for when we seek to praise someone, we naturally try to magnify or amplify a person's virtues and to minimize or downplay a person's vices; and when we intend to censure someone, we do just the opposite: we magnify the vices and downplay the virtues. Aristotle pointed out some of the useful ways of magnifying or heightening the effect of praise:

1. Show that a person is the *first* one or the *only* one or almost the only one to do something.
2. Show that a person has done something *better* than anyone else, for superiority of any kind is thought to reveal excellence.
3. Show that a person has *often* achieved the same success, for frequency will indicate that the success was due not to chance but to the person's own powers.
4. Show the *circumstances* under which a person accomplished something, for it will redound more to a person's credit if it can be shown that he or she accomplished something under, for instance, adverse circumstances.
5. *Compare* the person to other famous people, for the praise of a person will be magnified if we can show that this person has equalled or surpassed other renowned people.

Variations of these points can be used to *depreciate* a person. If we can show, for instance, that many people have done the same thing, we can minimize a person's achievements.

In this section, we have reviewed the special topics that people commonly resort to when they are seeking to convince an audience that a person or group of persons is great or noble or virtuous or competent (or the opposite— that the person or group of persons is insignificant or base or vicious or inept). These special topics will not always yield material that can be incorporated into a discourse of praise (or censure). If a person does not possess a particular virtue or does not possess it to a pre-eminent degree, we cannot, obviously, extol that virtue in that person. If a particular virtue has no special appeal for a particular audience, it would be unwise for us to dwell on it. And if a particular virtue is not especially pertinent to the occasion, we do little to enhance the praise of a person by expatiating on that attribute.

Pericles, the author of one of the classic examples of ceremonial or epideictic discourse, his "Funeral Oration," which sings the praises of the Athenian soldiers who fought and died in the first campaign of the Peloponnesian War against Sparta, tells us in the third paragraph of that famous oration about the special difficulties that attend this kind of discourse:

> Then it is not easy to speak with a proper sense of balance, when a man's listeners find it difficult to believe the truth of what one is saying. The man who knows the facts and loves the dead may well think that an oration tells less than what he knows and what he would like to hear; others who do not know so much may feel envy for the dead, and think the orator over-praises them, when he speaks of exploits that are beyond their own capacities. Praise of other people is tolerable only up to a certain point, the point where one believes that one could do oneself some of the things one is hearing about. Once you get beyond this point, you will find people becoming jealous and incredulous.
>
> Rex Warner's translation from the Penguin edition of Thycydides's *The Peloponnesian War*, Bk. II, Ch. 4.

We might keep those judicious words in mind when we are composing our own, or analyzing someone else's, discourse of praise. Our praise will fall on deaf ears if we cannot make it sound sincere and credible and acceptable to our listeners or readers.

Manuel Bilsky, McCrea Hazlett, Robert E. Streeter, and Richard M. Weaver: Looking for an Argument

Up to this point, we have been discussing the topics abstractly, with occasional brief illustrations of the operation of the topics in actual discourse, and later in this chapter, we will provide analyses of the operation of the topics in whole discourses. Such illustrations and analyses provide evidence of how the topics have yielded matter for discourse that is already composed. But in ancient rhetoric, the topics were regarded as devices for generating matter for discourse that had yet to be composed. In the following article, the authors report how they made use of four of the topics in a composition class at the University of Chicago to help their students find something to say in their assigned themes.

I

1 It is widely believed that courses in composition should deal with argumentation; and few question that argumentation is related to logic. Many teachers of English stress the importance of "clear" or "straight" thinking and implement their convictions by giving their students more or less systematic training in the labyrinthine ways of the syllogism. This is clearly valuable. Because logic provides the form of good argument, it should be treated with some thoroughness.

2 However, most modern discussions of argumentation assume that the whole problem can be solved by means of logic. Students will be able to argue well, it is believed, if they are lectured on the principles of logic, trained in the detection of fallacies, and earnestly exhorted to think honestly. For the teaching of composition, such a point of view is not completely satisfactory, because logicians deliberately exclude subject matter. If this is not amply demonstrated by pointing to the complex sets of nonlinguistic symbols which they have concocted, it can be clearly established by a nonsense syllogism:

> If Gilbert and Sullivan wrote *Iolanthe,* then the fall of Napoleon was largely brought about by his invasion of Russia.
> Gilbert and Sullivan wrote *Iolanthe.*
> Therefore, the fall of Napoleon was largely brought about by his invasion of Russia.

This is formally a valid hypothetical syllogism. But it must be emphasized that it is unexceptionable only in a formal sense. A single reading reveals that the argument is ridiculous. Clearly, teachers and students of composition cannot stop where the logician does.

3 We are primarily concerned with teaching our students to write well. While the development of skill in logical analysis is a valuable means to this end, we need other techniques and tools which will assist in the process of creation. We need to discover ways to help students to find relevant and effective arguments. Because it is formal in its nature and analytic in its use, logic, though basic to the study of argumentation, cannot entirely fulfill this need. Recognizing this problem, the English Staff of the College of the Uni-

From *College English,* 14 (January 1953): 210–16. Copyright 1953 by the National Council of Teachers of English. Reprinted with permission.

versity of Chicago has recently been exploring one concrete solution. What follows is a summary account of the theory and practice of this experiment.

4 We may begin by recalling our implication that the student who is instructed in logic is only half-instructed in rhetoric. He has been told to write an argument, but the syllogism is only the frame of an argument. The sense of vague frustration over the syllogism not infrequently shown by students may be accounted for by the fact that the "argument" is still but a formula. In the argumentative process there is still wanting what the traditional rhetoricians call *invention*, and that means simply the discovery of content—of relevant supporting material.

5 All this points to the truth that, to have any power to move, an argument must say something intelligible about the actual world. Because real arguments are made up of such predications, we find most of our substance for argument by interpreting and classifying our experiences. The most fundamental of these categories of interpretation are being, cause, and similarity. To deny these is to deny all possibility of argument. But in actual practice no one denies them, for we no sooner begin to talk about the world than we find ourselves saying that such and such a thing exists as a member of such and such a class, or that it is the known cause of a certain effect (or the known effect of a certain cause), or that it has certain points of similarity with some other thing. These recognized aspects of phenomena provide examples of what the classical writers called the *topoi* or "regions," and what have come to be translated as the "topics."

6 They are so called because they constitute regions of experience from which the substance of an argument can be drawn. It is a matter of everyday observation that arguments are made by saying that X is a kind of thing, or that X has a known definite effect, or that X has important points of similarity with a thing better understood than itself. The "topics" represent only an analysis of these kinds of predicables that may appear in arguments. Let us suppose, for illustration, that you are accosted one night by a robber, who threatens you with a pistol and demands your money. Assuming that you could get him to listen to argument, you might find yourself ranging over the following "regions" or possibilities:

1. You could tell him that what he is attempting is a crime. This would be an argument from *genus*.
2. You could tell him that his act will result in his having to spend years in the penitentiary. This would be argument from *consequence*.
3. You could tell him that this is the sort of thing he would dislike if he were the victim of it himself. This would be argument from *similarity*.

4. You could tell him that this sort of thing is forbidden by the Bible. This would be argument from *authority*.

Although you may think that we have here overestimated the patience of our hypothetical gunman, you will have to admit that each of these arguments has a certain degree of force, which the abstract syllogism cannot have. That is why we say that we have now invented arguments. The areas from which they can be drawn here start to emerge with some distinctness, and so we have the beginning of a "topic."

7 In our teaching we have commonly referred to these topics as the "sources" of argument, which is another way of indicating their nature. To return to the classroom for illustration: suppose now the student is given the assignment of writing an argument about freedom of expression or democracy or world federation. With these sources outlined for him, he can begin to develop his case by consulting such recognized areas of experience and observation as genus, consequence, similarity, etc. Even the student of limited ability now finds that he has more to say about the subject than he had first supposed.

II

8 Naturally, introducing the topical approach into a college composition course calls for some practical decisions. One of the more important of these concerns the choice of specific topics to be presented. When we undertook to teach the topics as part of the Chicago composition course, we decided to deal with only a few topics but to choose them so that they could be related, sometimes explicitly but more often by implication, to a much longer list. This gives the teacher latitude; it enables him to emphasize one or another aspect of any one of the topics. Next we kept in mind that we wanted topics useful in the art of teaching composition. The result has been a relatively limited and pedagogically useful list, with a considerable degree of flexibility.

Genus

9 The argument from genus or definition comprises all arguments made from the nature of a thing. In presenting this type of argument, we merely take whatever fact or idea is the subject of our deliberation and refer it to its class. If our audience is sufficiently impressed with the actuality of that class (i.e., with its reality as a class containing this member among others), it will grant that whatever is true of that class is true of this fact or idea in question, which is the point we are seeking to make by our argument.

10   For example: suppose someone is seeking to argue that a certain fiscal policy of the government is undesirable. What he may do, if he is using the argument from genus, is to take this single policy and put it in the class "inflation." Now if he is successful in doing that, he transfers the significance of (presumably the feeling about) inflation to the fiscal policy of the government which he is attacking. We are assuming here that the speaker says no more than "This is inflation." If he goes into the consequences of inflation, he is leaving his argument from genus for a further argument from consequences. The same analysis holds for "This is treason," "This is a betrayal of the working class," "This is true Americanism," and for any other argument which seeks to find its motivation through a fixed predicable constituting a genus. It may be pointed out here, incidentally, that training in the critical and precise use of genera is the best possible safeguard against irresponsible "name-calling."

11   In teaching the topics, it may be necessary at some point to take into account the empirical fact that arguments employ two types of definition (and it may be possible to distinguish these as [1] *genus* and [2] *definition*). The first type employs a universally accepted convention for which the speaker does not feel that description, analysis, or "proof" is required. It is, so to speak, one of the established categories of the public mind, and one feels that nothing more is needed than to name it. Probably for a minister with a rather orthodox congregation, "sin" is such a term. Therefore, when he has categorized, either flatly or through extended exposition, such and such an action as "sin," he has made his argument. The genus is so well established that it would be superfluous for him to support it.

12   But there are many terms whose scope is by no means fixed, so that any successful employment of them requires a certain amount of explicit definition. One has to define them because one knows that their correct definitions are not perceived. A good example of this type of term is "liberty" in John Stuart Mill's famous essay of that name. Mill proposes to argue certain propositions about liberty and the individual, but before he can do this, he must go through a long process of defining. Only after that is completed, can he use "liberty" as a genus by which to approve or disapprove of certain actions. Anyone today predicating an argument upon "democracy" must do the same thing. "Democracy" is surrounded by so much nebulosity that one cannot, until this labor is performed, expect much similarity of conception. That is to say, it is not in the public mind now a clear genus.

13   The process of argument is, of course, the same in both instances, the difference being that in the first the genus is ready-made; in the second it has to be made. It is well to take notice of this because many arguments will be encountered by the students in their reading which devote most of their space to setting up the genera. Not until these are fixed is the writer prepared to make propositions with reference to special occurrences.

Consequence

14   In a consequence argument, one presents the casual relationships among experiences. As with arguments from genus and definition, these arguments may employ self-evident and widely accepted causal linkings, or the writer may seek to establish linkings which are less well recognized. Such arguments most frequently move directly from cause to effect or from effect to cause. The simple cause-to-effect argument is well illustrated in Burke's *Speech on American Taxation*, where the movement of the argument is from the cause (unjust treatment of the American Colonies) to the effect (discontent, disorder, disobedience). The classic argument from effect to cause is the proof of the existence of God from the existence of order in the universe. The argument here consists of observing the effect and then postulating a cause which will explain this effect.

15   A more complex argument is sometimes called the "argument from sign." Many causes have a multiplicity of effects. A cold snap not only will produce ice on ponds but will cause people to dress warmly. When one observes some of the effects and argues from them to the cause and thence to another effect, he is arguing from sign. The ice and the wearing of warm clothing are effects of the cause, coldness. By observing one effect, we can reason to the cause and thence to another effect, which, in this example, is a course of action.

16   All these arguments are in constant use in our civilization. The politician argues that, if he is elected (cause), there will be better government (effect); he argues that the present corruption in government (effect) must have been produced by a corrupt administration (cause); and that his happy home, successful career, and firm church and civic affiliations are clear signs that he will administer the office he seeks wisely and honestly.

Likeness and Difference

17   Likeness and difference are really two separate topics. But their structure as arguments is sufficiently similar to warrant their being grouped together. There is no significant difference between likeness and what we are more familiar with as analogy. Similarly, difference corresponds to what some logicans call "negative analogy." An important thing to remember in both is that they rest, as arguments, on two instances; that is, in using likeness or difference, we argue from one case to another, unlike the practice in induction, where we argue from a large number of particular cases to a general rule or law.

18 A distinction is sometimes drawn between two uses of likeness, or analogy. The rhetorician Whately, for example, suggests that it may be used, not only "to *prove* the proposition in question, but to make it more *clearly understood."* We must not mistake for argument, he goes on to tell us, what is used for clarification. When we reflect that "analogy" is sometimes used synonymously with "metaphor," we can see that the situation can become still further complicated. For our purposes, however, we can disregard such distinctions. Actually, it could be plausibly asserted that all comparisons are used, in varying degrees, for argument. Hence we will not go far wrong if we treat them as arguments.

Testimony and Authority

19 In that it seldom stands alone as the primary source of an extensive argument, testimony and authority differs from the other topics. It is an "external" source of argument, because its force is derived not from the immediate subject matter of the discourse but from consideration of the competence and integrity of the witness: if good and wise men believe this, it must be so. This topic may be directed toward the confirmation of either a general proposition or a specific circumstance. Testimony and authority involves also the writer's attempt to establish his own credibility as a witness or probity as a judge and, conversely, in some instances an effort to show that his opponent is careless with facts and unsound in judgment. Finally, style itself, through the use of terminology or even syntax associated with revered persons, ideas, or institutions, may constitute a subtle appeal to authority.

III

20 It may be objected that, although this approach to the teaching of argument has theoretical attractiveness, its relevance to the workaday job of writing a composition is somewhat tenuous. Some may feel, as some of us did during preliminary discussions of the idea, that, however plausible the introduction of the topics might appear when reflected upon in the teacher's study, it would only create confusion in the classroom by setting up another barrier of terminology between the student's thought and his written argument. However, on the basis of experience, we are now convinced that the topics can be intimately related to the student's problems in writing arguments, that they help the student to clarify the ideas which he wishes to set down on paper, and that, above all, they fulfill their primary purpose—the stimulation of the student's powers to discover relevant and effective arguments.

21 Perhaps the nature of this interplay between theory and practice may be suggested by a brief account of the way in which we familiarize our students with topical analysis. First, in order to make clear what a topic is and to exemplify the four topics chosen, we present a series of brief argumentative passages, classified according to the topic primarily employed in each. Thus, under genus, we show Tom Paine using a definition of a "true" constitution to support his argument that the British government is fundamentally lawless. As soon as the students show some ability to understand and recognize particular topics, they are asked to write a series of brief arguments in which they experiment with the appropriateness of various topical approaches. It should be noted that the students are *not* told to create an argument illustrating a particular topic but, instead, are instructed to write arguments supporting or attacking certain propositions which are chosen for their simplicity, closeness to students' interests, and capacity to stir controversy.

22 Obviously, in any reasonably complex argument, a skillful writer will draw upon a variety of topics, moving easily from one to another as he develops the full significance of his thought. Consequently, after introducing the topics through brief, categorized excerpts, we turn our attention to the examination of several substantial arguments—among them *The Federalist,* No. 10; Lincoln's First Inaugural Address; Thoreau's "Civil Disobedience"; Swift's "A Modest Proposal"; Bertrand Russell's "A Free Man's Worship"; Newman's "Knowledge Its Own End"—in which various topical approaches can be observed in the less artificial context of full, rich, and actual disputation. Accompanying the study of these texts is the writing of two or three fairly long arguments in which the student has an opportunity to practice not merely his ability to recognize relevant topics but also his skill in incorporating various topical arguments into a systematic and persuasive whole.

23 The most significant result traceable, we believe, to experimentation with the program outlined above has been a striking increase in the richness of students' arguments. With the topics providing a guide line, our writers show much less timidity about thrusting themselves into the heart of argumentative situations, instead of coyly and cautiously skirting the edges, as they have often done in the past. This fact has done much to strengthen our conviction that instruction in argumentation has a primary role in the composition course. In so far as familiarity with the rhetorical topics improves the young writer's ability to look for and recognize rational arguments which are appropriate to the line of thought or action he is advocating, the approach we have described makes it possible to deal seriously with argumentation. Placed in the posture of argument, students who know how to employ the topics are not so likely either to freeze or to foam. They have demonstrated that, given a technique to assist them in locating and evaluating arguments, they have something to say about controversial subjects.

Richard L. Larson: A Plan for Teaching Rhetorical Invention

One of the problems with the topics as a generating device for composition, especially when they are set forth, as they are earlier in this chapter and in the previous article, as categories or headings, like definition, similarity, difference, is that they tend to just "sit there," inert and unprovocative of ideas. Consequently, students are at a loss as to how to get the topics to turn up ideas for them on some subject or thesis. When the topics are posed in the form of questions, however, they seem to work better for students as generating devices, perhaps because a question, by its very nature, stimulates a response. The formula of one-word questions often taught in journalism schools as a guide to what must be included in the lead of a news story— who? what? when? where? how?—is a topical device of this kind. In the following selection, Richard L. Larson sets down a series of topical questions that can be productive of ideas when students are asked to write on subjects or propositions. In the first part of the article from which this list of questions was taken, Professor Larson says, "I propose, therefore, that in our teaching of 'invention' we make a persistent effort to force students to become as familiar as possible with the facts, and possible relationships among the facts, about experiences on which they might write, and also that we force them to experiences on which they might write, and also that we force them to examine the facts underlying concepts they consider important and the content of propositions on which they may want to write. . . . I propose that students come to this thorough knowledge of their experiences, concepts, and propositions through a process of systematic questioning—questioning which students engage in mostly by themselves, rather than questioning conducted for them by the teacher. . . . Not all the questions, of course, will produce useful answers for every subject, and the student should learn which questions provide valuable ideas on which subjects and which ones are comparatively fruitless on those subjects" (pp. 128–29).

I. "Topics" That Invite Comment
  A. *Writing about Single Items (in present existence)*
     What are its precise physical characteristics (shape, dimensions, composition, etc.)?

From "Discovery Through Questioning: A Plan for Teaching Rhetorical Invention," *College English,* 30 (November 1968): 126–34. Copyright 1968 by the National Council of Teachers of English. Reprinted with permission.

How does it differ from things that resemble it?

What is its "range of variation" (how much can we change it and still identify it as the thing we started with)?

Does it call to mind other objects we have observed earlier in our lives? why? in what respects?

From what points of view can it be examined?

What sort of structure does it have?

How do the parts of it work together?

How are the parts put together?

How are the parts proportioned in relation to each other?

To what structure (class or sequence of items) does it belong?

Who or what produced it in this form? Why?

Who needs it?

Who uses it? for what?

What purposes might it serve?

How can it be evaluated, for these purposes?

B. *Writing about Single Completed Events, or Parts of an Ongoing Process (These questions can apply to scenes and pictures, as well as to works of fiction and drama.)*

Exactly what happened? (Tell the precise sequence: who? what? when? how? why? Who did what to whom? why? What did what to what? how?)

What were the circumstances in which the event occurred? What did they contribute to its happening?

How was the event like or unlike similar events?

What were its causes?

What were its consequences?

What does its occurrence imply? What action (if any) is called for?

What was affected (indirectly) by it?

What, if anything, does it reveal or emphasize about some general condition?

To what group or class might it be assigned?

Is it (in general) good or bad? by what standard? How do we arrive at the standard?

How do we know about it? What is the authority for our information? How reliable is the authority? How do we know it to be reliable? (or unreliable?)

How might the event have been changed or avoided?

To what other events was it connected? how?

To what kinds of structure (if any) can it be assigned? On what basis?

C. *Writing about Abstract Concepts (e.g., "religion," "socialism")*
To what specific items, groups of items, events, or groups of events, does the word or words connect, in your experience or imagination?
What characteristics must an item or event have before the name of the concept can apply to it?
How do the referents of that concept differ from the things we name with similar concepts (e.g., "democracy" and "socialism")?
How has the term been used by writers whom you have read? How have they implicitly defined it?
Does the word have "persuasive" value? Does the use of it in connection with another concept seem to praise or condemn the other concept?
Are you favorably disposed to all things included in the concept? Why or why not?

D. *Writing about Collections of Items (in present existence)* [These questions are in addition to the questions about single items, which can presumably be asked of each item in the group.]
What, exactly, do the items have in common?
If they have features in common, how do they differ?
How are the items related to each other, if not by common characteristics? What is revealed about them by the possibility of grouping them in this way?
How may the group be divided? What bases for division can be found?
What correlations, if any, may be found among the various possible sub-groups? Is anything disclosed by the study of these correlations?
Into what class, if any, can the group as a whole be put?

E. *Writing about Groups of Completed Events, Including Processes* [These questions are in addition to questions about single completed events; such questions are applicable to each event in the group. These questions also apply to literary works, principally fiction and drama.]
What have the events in common?
If they have features in common, how do they differ?
How are the events related to each other (if they are not part of a chronological sequence)? What is revealed by the possibility of grouping them in this way (these ways)?
What is revealed by the events when taken as a group?
How can the group be divided? On what bases?
What possible correlations can be found among the several sub-groups?
Into what class, if any, can the events taken as a group fit?
Does the group belong to any other structures than simply a larger

group of similar events? (Is it part of a more inclusive chronological sequence? one more piece of evidence that may point toward a conclusion about history? and so on)

To what antecedents does the group of events look back? Where can they be found?

What implications, if any, does the group of events have? Does the group point to a need for some sort of action?

II. "Topics" with "Comments" Already Attached

A. *Writing about Propositions* (*statements set forth to be proved or disproved*)

What must be established for the readers before they will believe it?

Into what sub-propositions, if any, can it be broken down? (What smaller assertions does it contain?)

What are the meanings of key words in it?

To what line of reasoning is it apparently a conclusion?

How can we contrast it with other, similar, propositions? (How can we change it, if at all, and still have roughly the same proposition?)

To what class (or classes) of propositions does it belong?

How inclusive (or how limited) is it?

What is at issue, if one tries to prove the proposition?

How can it be illustrated?

How can it be proven (by what kinds of evidence)?

What will or can be said in opposition to it?

Is it true or false? How do we know? (direct observation, authority, deduction, statistics, other sources?)

Why might someone disbelieve it?

What does it assume? (What other propositions does it take for granted?)

What does it imply? (What follows from it?) Does it follow from the proposition that action of some sort must be taken?

What does it reveal (signify, if true)?

If it is a prediction, how probable is it? On what observations of past experience is it based?

If it is a call to action, what are the possibilities that action can be taken? (Is what is called for feasible?) What are the probabilities that the action, if taken, will do what it is supposed to do? (Will the action called for work?)

B. *Writing about Questions* (*interrogative sentences*)

Does the question refer to past, present, or future time?

What does the question assume (take for granted)?

In what data might answers be sought?

Why does the question arise?

What, fundamentally, is in doubt? How can it be tested? evaluated? What propositions might be advanced in answer to it?

Is each proposition true?

If it is true:

What will happen in the future? What follows from it? Which of these predictions are possible? probable? What action should be taken (avoided) in consequence? [Most of the other questions listed under "Propositions" also apply.]

External Aids to Invention

We have been considering the *topics,* those "places" to which the writer can resort for help in inventing or discovering arguments. The topics can be termed the "artistic means of persuasion" (*entechnoi pisteis*), because they are the means taught by the art of rhetoric. In addition to these, Aristotle spoke of the "nonartistic means of persuasion" (*atechnoi pisteis*)—"nonartistic" in the sense that these resources did not belong specifically to the art of rhetoric; they existed *outside* the art.

If reference books had been abundant in fourth-century Athens, Aristotle would certainly have encouraged his students to consult them as external aids to invention. Because of the need for a plentiful stock of special knowledge, Cicero and Quintilian maintained that a broad liberal education was the best background for an orator. Contemporary students can still get a broad liberal education, but, in addition, they have well-stocked libraries available to them to fill in the gaps in their fund of knowledge. They can also resort to the information stored in computers. But as yet, not all students have access to a computer, and so they will have to rely on the resources of a library. To take advantage of the rich resources of the library, however, they must gain some awareness of what the library has and must develop some strategy for getting at what the library has.

What will be proposed here will be a Search Strategy, a series of steps that can help you, in a systematic way, to gain access to those library resources that would be most relevant and useful for your purposes. In this sequence of steps, you move from the most general of the reference works to the successively more specific ones. Normally, you move linearly from step to step, but you can always loop back to previous steps if you find that you need to do so. For instance, dictionaries are the reference works to be consulted in the second step, but you may find it necessary to return to the dictionaries several times during the search. And in investigating some subjects, you may find that you can skip some of the steps in the sequence. After you have had considerable experience in working your way through the entire sequence, you will develop a sense for knowing which steps in the sequence might be skipped for a particular subject.

The steps in this Search Strategy are as follows:

1. Encyclopedias
2. Dictionaries
3. Handbooks
4. Bibliographies
5. Card Catalogue
6. Periodical, Newspaper, and Citation Indexes
7. *Essay and General Literature Index*
8. Biographical and Book-Review Indexes
9. Concordances and Books of Quotations
10. Statistical Sources and Government Documents

After consulting these categories of reference sources, you will, in most cases, accumulate a wealth of information on the subject you are researching. If you eventually have to make selections from the mound of information you collected, you may have to evaluate the information for its relevance, its accuracy, and its credibility. Judgments about the accuracy and the credibility of the information may depend on the expertness or the reputation of the author, and to find out about that expertness or reputation, you may have to consult one or more of the biographical reference works. To assess the reliability of the information, you could also consult reviews of the books in which you found the information (a reference work like the *Book Review Digest* could lead you to such reviews), or you could check the reliability of the newspapers or magazines in which you found the information by reading the characterizations of those periodicals in such reference works as Evan Ira Farber's *Classified List of Periodicals for the College Library,* 5th ed. (Westwood, Mass.: Faxon, 1972) and William A. Katz and Linda Sternberg Katz's *Magazines for Libraries: For the General Reader and School, Junior College, College University, and Public Libraries,* 4th ed. (New York: Bowker, 1982).

In the section that follows, some of the standard reference works that fit into one or other of the ten categories of the Search Strategy will be named and briefly described. For descriptions of other useful reference works that are not discussed here, you could consult Albert J. Walford's *Guide to Reference Materials,* 4th ed. (London: The Library Association, 1980), 3 vols. or Eugene P. Sheehy's *Guide to Reference Books,* 9th ed. (Chicago: American Library Association, 1976; Supplements in 1980 and 1984). Remember, too, that you can—and you should—ask members of the library staff for help.

After the selected reference works have been presented, Virginia M. Tiefel, Director of Library User Education at the Ohio State University Libraries, will take a sample topic through all ten steps of the Search Strategy to illustrate how the system works.

Biography

> **Dictionary of National Biography,** ed. Leslie Stephen and Sidney Lee. Originally published in 63 volumes by Smith, Elder & Co., 1885–1901; reissued in 21 volumes (combining three volumes in one) by Macmillan, 1908–09.

A cyclopedia of British biography on the plan and scope of some of the other European biographical collections (the French, 40 volumes, 1843–63; the Dutch, 24 volumes, 1852–78; the Austrian, 60 volumes, 1856–91; the German, 55 volumes, 1875–1900). On January 1, 1885, the first volume of the *Dictionary of National Biography* (abbreviated *DNB*) appeared, containing 505 biographies written by 87 contributors. Within fifteen years, this monumental 63-volume work, containing 29,120 biographies, was completed. In the autumn of 1901, three supplementary volumes were published, containing about 800 biographical sketches of noteworthy English people who had died while the work was in progress and about 200 memoirs of prominent people who had been overlooked in the original master-list. (These three volumes became Volume XXII of the Macmillan reissue.) In 1912, Macmillan published the 2nd supplement in three volumes to cover the years 1901–11. Since 1920, the Oxford University Press has been the publisher of the *DNB* and of the 2nd through the 7th supplement (1912–71), each covering a decade.

The value of the *DNB* is that it is often the only source of biographical information about British men and women who were prominent enough to have merited mention in newspapers and histories but not prominent enough to have merited a full-length biography or even a biographical sketch in an encyclopedia. The *DNB* is also helpful to someone seeking relatively brief but authoritative biographies of prominent statesmen, generals, clergy, scientists, writers, painters, etc. The longest biography in the *DNB* is the 49-page memoir that Sidney Lee wrote on Shakespeare. Although many of the biographees are given less than a page, most of the prominent ones receive an extended but compact treatment. Additional sources of biographical information, whenever available, are listed in the bibliography at the end of each article.

> **Dictionary of American Biography,** ed. Allen Johnson and others (New York: Charles Scribner's Sons, 1928–37), 20 volumes and Index; Supplements 1–4, Scribner's 1944–74.

This collection of American biographies, initiated by the American Council of Learned Societies in 1922, was patterned on the *Dictionary of National Biography*. The editorial committee set down these negative restrictions: (1) no living persons; (2) no persons who had not lived in the territory known as the United States; (3) no British officers serving in America after the colonies had declared their independence. The positive qualification for inclusion was stated in rather general terms: "those who have made some significant contribution to American life." These criteria permitted the admission into the *DAB* of people who are not, strictly speaking, Americans: Lafayette, for instance.

The original twenty volumes contained 13,633 biographical articles. Supplements 1–4 have added biographies of 2371 Americans who died in the period between 1935 and 1950.

Like the *DNB*, the *DAB* is often the only source of biographical information about deceased, relatively obscure Americans; but the *DAB* also provides compact biographical sketches of prominent deceased Americans. The memoir of Benjamin Franklin, for instance, occupies 25 full columns in Volume VI. James Franklin (1696/7–1735), his half-brother, rates only a column and a half in the same volume. The biographies are based on reliable, original sources of information, many of which are listed in the carefully selected bibliographies at the end of each article. The biographies are arranged alphabetically according to the last name of the subject.

> **Who's Who in America:** A Biographical Dictionary of Notable Living Men and Women (Chicago: A. N. Marquis Co., 1899–   ).

This is a valuable source of biographical data about prominent *living* Americans. Begun in 1899, this work is revised and reissued every two years. The introduction to Voume XXX gives the criteria for inclusion:

> The standards of admission divide the eligible into two classes: (1) those selected on account of special prominence in creditable lives of effort, making them the subjects of extensive interest, inquiry, or discussion; (2) those included arbitrarily on account of position—civil, military, religious, educational, corporate, or organizational.

Among those in the second category are all members of Congress and the Cabinet, federal judges, governors of states, heads of the larger universities, military officers above the rank of brigadier general, members of the National Academy, bishops and chief ecclesiastics of the larger religious denominations. Insisting that its biographees lead "creditable lives," the Marquis Company automatically drops from later volumes any biographee who has been convicted of a major crime or felony.

Most of the biographees supply their own biographical information. Although the *kinds* of information sought are fixed by the editors, the *amount* of information supplied is left largely up to the biographee. In Volume XXX, for instance, President Eisenhower has only 19 lines; his brother Milton, the president then of Johns Hopkins University, has 52 lines.

Students should remember that this is a reference source for *living Americans* only. When a person dies, he or she may then be relegated to another Marquis publication, *Who Was Who in America*. To find information about a particular person, students must consult a volume when that person is still alive and when that person is in the public eye or in a public office that automatically gains entry to *Who's Who in America*.

The Marquis Company also publishes periodically four regional biographical works: *Who's Who in the East; Who's Who in the Midwest; Who's Who in the West; Who's Who in the South and Southwest*. Whereas only three out of 10,000 living Americans are prominent enough to merit inclusion in the national *Who's Who in America*, an additional twelve out of 10,000 living Americans are included in one of the four regional volumes. So if students do not find a person in the national volume, they should consult the appropriate regional volume.

The Marquis Company also published biographical reference works about people associated with a profession or business—e.g., *Who's Who in Finance and Industry;* people associated with a Foreign-American group—e.g., *Italian-American Who's Who;* people associated with a particular religious or racial group—e.g., *American Catholic Who's Who* and *Who's Who in Colored America*.

> **Who's Who** (London: Adam and Charles Black; New York: St. Martin's, 1849– revised and reissued annually).

Who's Who, first published in Great Britain in 1848, served as the model for the American biographical dictionary of prominent, living citizens. It supplies biographical information about noteworthy, living British subjects, and its criteria of eligibility are much the same as those in the American equivalent. Each volume of *Who's Who* begins with an obituary of the prominent people who have died since the last volume appeared. Once deceased, these people appear in a later volume of a companion work called *Who Was Who*. Six volumes of *Who Was Who* have been published, each covering about a decade from 1897 through 1970.

The term "Who's Who" has become as much of a household word as "Webster's," and people often use the term indiscriminately to refer to both the American and the British works. Just remember that the American reference distinguishes itself from its British counterpart by its title, *Who's Who in America*.

> **International Who's Who** (London: Europa Publications, 1935–).

The biographies in this annual compilation are very brief, but a great many notable people throughout the world are covered in it. Many of the people covered in this work are included in the various national biographical dictionaries, but this is a convenient reference work for those people or those libraries that cannot afford to buy several of the national dictionaries. Another valuable feature of the work is that notable people from smaller countries whose biographies are not available in the usual sources are included.

Current Biography (New York: H. W. Wilson Company, 1940–   ).

Current Biography, published annually, is another valuable source of biographical information about prominent contemporary people. It is different in many ways from *Who's Who* and *Who's Who in America.* Each volume contains an average of only 300–350 new biographies, but its coverage is worldwide. The biographical sketches are composed by members of the editorial staff, not supplied by the biographees.

Here is the typical organization of a volume of *Current Biography:*

1. The biographical section, arranged alphabetically according to last names. This section comprises full biographies (usually two or three pages) of the prominent living persons in various countries selected for that particular year and also contains short obituary notices of some prominent world figures who have died that year.
2. A necrology—a list of *all* the prominent people who have died that year.
3. An index to biographies (in that particular volume) by profession.
4. A cumulative index of biographees who have been featured in one of the previous volumes. This section will refer the searcher to the particular volume and the exact page numbers where a particular person's biography appears—*if* that person has ever been featured in *Current Biography.*

Although each volume has an index of previously published biographies, searchers will save time in finding the volume and pages numbers if they consult the latest *Cumulative Index,* which lists all the people covered in all the volumes published to date.

Contemporary Authors (Detroit: Gale Research, 1962–   ).

Unlike the other biographical reference works mentioned so far, this one concentrates on the members of a single profession—active, living authors. Novelists, short-story writers, poets, playwrights, television writers, journalists, textbook writers, etc. are all eligible for inclusion—but the subjects must be published writers of some kind. An analysis once made of the listings in

Contemporary Authors revealed that over 75 percent of the authors were not covered in any other biographical source.

The biographical information in the many volumes of this source is presented in clearly marked-off sections, which follow this pattern: Personal (details about birth, education, marriage, children, religion, address); Career (positions held, honors and prizes won); Writings (a complete bibliography of all published books); Work in Progress; Sidelights (hobbies, avocations, comments about achievements and personality by others and sometimes by the authors themselves); Biographical and Critical Sources (if any have been published on the author). Some idea of the scope of this work can be gained from this statistic: with the publication of Volume 109 in 1983, biographical data about more than 74,000 writers and media people had appeared in *CA*.

> **Biography Index:** A Cumulative Index to Biographical Material in Books and Magazines (New York: H. W. Wilson Company, 1946–).

The *Biography Index* is a helpful guide to biographical material in currently published, English-language books and pamphlets, in over 1500 periodicals, in some legal and medical journals, and in the obituary notices of the *New York Times*. All types of biographical material are indexed: "pure biography, critical material of biographical significance, autobiography, letters, diaries, memoirs, journals, genealogies, fiction, drama, poetry, bibliographies, obituaries, pictorial works, and juvenile literature."

The *Biography Index* has two main parts: (1) the subject index, arranged alphabetically by last name; (2) the index to professions and occupations (large categories, like Authors, are listed by nationality—American, Australian, British, etc.). The value of the latter section is that it can direct the inquirer to all the biographical material written in some specific year about people associated with some profession. A person assigned to do a paper on, say, atomic physicists since World War II could collect a bibliography of biographical material about such people in short order by consulting this section.

As evidence of the amazing comprehensiveness of this work, the first bound volume of *Biography Index* (January 1946 to July 1949) contains the names of over 40,000 biographees, classified into some 1000 categories in the index to professions and occupations. Paperbound supplements are published quarterly and are bound in a separate volume each year, with a cumulative index. Subsequently, a three-year cumulation is published and bound in a separate volume.

Books of Quotations and Concordances

> **Bartlett's Familiar Quotations:** A Collection of Passages, Phrases, and Proverbs Traced to Their Sources in Ancient and Modern Literature by John Bartlett, 12th ed., rev. and enl. by Christopher Morley and Louella D. Everett (Boston: Little, Brown and Company, 1948); 13th ed. (Centennial, 1955); 14th ed., 1968.

Bartlett's Familiar Quotations is the best known and perhaps the most frequently used reference guide to quotations. John Bartlett, a New England publisher, compiled his first book of quotations in 1855 and continued to edit it through its ninth edition in 1891. In 1914, Nathan Haskell Dole edited the tenth edition. Christopher Morley and Louella D. Everett edited the book in its eleventh (1937) and twelfth (1948) editions; the thirteenth (1955) and fourteenth (1968) editions were compiled by the staff of Little, Brown under the direction of Emily Morison Beck.

All of us, at some time or another, have needed an apt quotation to illustrate, enhance, or substantiate something we have written or the exact wording of a quotation or the author of the quotation or the name of the work in which the quotation first appeared or the exact place in a work (e.g., the specific line-number in a poem) where the quotation appeared. If we can remember any key-word in the quotation, it is likely that we can find the answer to such questions in a reference work such as *Bartlett's Familiar Quotations.*

Let us suppose that we want to discover the source of the quotation, "Hope springs eternal in the human breast." Since quotations are not indexed under prepositions, pronouns, conjunctions, articles, and common words such as *is* and *was,* we can find this quotation indexed under any one of five keywords: *Hope, springs, eternal, human, breast.* If we look for this quotation under the word *springs,* we would probably find the quotation sooner than if we look for it under the word *human.* Looking under the word *springs* in the Index of the Thirteenth (Centennial) Edition of *Bartlett's,* we will find, four entries down in the list, this reference: "hope, eternal, 316a." Turning to the front half of *Bartlett's,* to the a-column (the left-hand column of the two-column page) on page 316, we will discover that "Hope springs eternal in the human breast" is the 95th line of Alexander Pope's *Essay on Man,* Epistle I.

The Fourteenth Edition of *Bartlett's* is a book of more than 1750 pages, carrying more than 20,000 quotations from 2250 authors; the Index has some 117,000 entries. Except for the quotations from anonymous sources and from such collective works as the Book of Common Prayer and the Bible, which are placed at the end of the text portion of the book, the quotations in *Bartlett's* are arranged chronologically according to the time in which the authors wrote. Occasionally, there are footnotes that explain, amplify, or correlate the quotations. Because later editions of *Bartlett's* drop some quotations and add new ones, we can sometimes find a quotation by looking at an earlier edition of *Bartlett's*.

When *Bartlett's* fails us, we can sometimes find the elusive quotation by consulting one of the other reference works of quotations:

> **Hoyt's New Cyclopedia of Practice Quotations,** ed. Jehiel Keeler Hoyt, new ed. (New York: Somerset Books, 1947).

> **Home Book of Quotations, Classical and Modern,** ed. Burton Egbert Stevenson, 10th ed. (New York: Dodd, Mead, 1967).

> **A New Dictionary of Quotations on Historical Principles from Ancient and Modern Sources,** ed. H. L. Mencken (New York: Knopf, 1942).

> **The Oxford Dictionary of Quotations,** ed. Bernard Darwin, 2nd ed. (London: Oxford University Press, 1953).

> **Dictionary of Quotations,** ed. Bergen Evans (New York: Delacorte Press, 1968).

H. L. Mencken's concordance contains many humorous, iconoclastic, or offbeat quotations that are not found in other concordances. A distinctive feature of *The Oxford Dictionary of Quotations* is that it carries quotations from Greek, Latin, French, German, and Italian authors in the original language (with English translations appended). The 791 pages of quotations in Bergen Evans's book are spiced with over 2000 witty historical and explanatory comments by the editor. Because the quotations in this concordance are arranged alphabetically according to topic or idea, it is easier to find an apt quotation for a certain subject in Evans's book than in the others mentioned.

> John Bartlett, **New and Complete Concordance or Verbal Index to Words, Phrases, and Passages in the Dramatic Works of Shakespeare with a Supplementary Concordance to the Poems** (London: Macmillan, 1894; reprinted New York: St. Martin's Press, 1953).

> Martin Spevack, **A Complete and Systematic Concordance to the Works of Shakespeare,** 6 volumes (Hildesheim: Georg Olms, 1969–70).

A concordance is available for all major English poets—Chaucer, Spenser, Milton, Pope, Wordsworth, Byron, Keats, Downing, Tennyson, and many other "greats." There are concordances available even for some of the lesser poets, such as Thomas Wyatt, Robert Herrick, Thomas Gray, Oliver Goldsmith, Robert Burns, and A. E. Houseman. Although handbooks are frequently prepared as helpful guides for the reading of famous prose writers, concordances to the works of prose writers are rare. Occasionally, however, as in the case of James Joyce, concordances are published for individual prose works.

As might be expected, many concordances have been prepared for Shakespeare's works. The best and the most comprehensive is the one compiled by the same John Bartlett who first published *Familiar Quotations*.

Concordances for the works of noted writers work much in the same way that dictionaries of quotations work. In Bartlett's concordance to England's greatest dramatist, all the lines in Shakespeare's poems and plays are indexed under all of the significant words in the line. Bartlett uses the act, scene, and line numbering as given in the 1891 Globe Edition of Shakespeare, and he always prints the entire line in his index, not just a portion of it.

In addition to using a concordance like this to find the exact location of a Shakespearean quotation, some people use it to gather data for a stylistic study of the author or, more specifically, for a study of the author's diction. Did Shakespeare ever use such-and-such a word? How many times did he use a particular word? What about the range and variety of his vocabulary? What's the total number of substantive words in his working vocabulary? A study of Shakespeare's imagery could also be worked out with the aid of a concordance.

The Martin Spevack concordance was done with the aid of an IBM computer and was based on the text of the *Riverside Shakespeare* by G. Blakemore Evans. This concordance can provide valuable data for all kinds of linguistic studies, because one of its features is that it records the frequency of each word and the relative frequency (expressed in a percentage) of each word in the play and in the speeches of each character.

Biblical Concordances

James Strong, **The Exhaustive Concordance of the Bible** (the Authorized and Revised versions of the King James text) (Nashville, Tenn.: Abingdon, 1894; reprinted 1947, 1963).

Newton Wayland Thompson and Raymond Stock, **Complete Concordance to the Bible** (Douay Version) (St. Louis: Herder, 1942; rev. ed. 1945).

Nelson's Complete Concordance of the Revised Standard Version of the Bible, Compiled by Univac under the supervision of John W. Ellison (New York: Thomas Nelson, 1957)

Only three of the many biblical concordances are listed above—one for the King James or Authorized Version of the Bible; one for the Revised Standard Version completed in 1952; one for the Douay or Roman Catholic version. Every college library and most public libraries of any size are sure to have one or more of the biblical concordances on the reference shelves. It took James Strong some thirty years to compile his concordance; it took Remington Rand's Univac computer only about 1000 hours to index more than 350,000 biblical contexts from the *RSVB*. All concordances for future translations of the Bible will undoubtedly be done on the computer.

The index system of a biblical concordance works in much the same way as it does in *Bartlett's Familiar Quotations,* but whereas *Bartlett's* reproduces the quotations it indexes, the biblical concordances do not include the text of the Bible; they merely indicate the book, chapter, and verse of the Bible where the quotation occurs. A complete concordance indexes *all* passages from the Bible, not just the familiar quotations from it. If you can remember any key-word in a quotation, you can find what you are looking for.

There are other uses for a concordance too. You could use the concordance, for instance, to find out whether the word *sacrament* ever occurred in the Old or the New Testament. You could find out when such a word as *bishop* became a part of ecclesiastical terminology, whether the Old Testament prophets ever used the word, whether Christ ever used the word in the Gospels, or whether it is found only in the Acts of the Apostles or in the Epistles. A concordance can serve too as a kind of *harmony*—that is, as a reference guide to various passages in the Bible where parallel or identical ideas or wordings occur.

Indexes to Periodicals

The Readers' Guide to Periodical Literature (New York: H. W. Wilson Company, 1900–).

Of all the periodical indexes, the *Readers' Guide* is the one that students have most likely used during their high-school years. It is an extremely useful reference guide to articles, stories, poems, and plays published in more than 100 American magazines during the twentieth century. Since March of 1935, it has been appearing twice a month. The indexing is cumulated, first in annual volumes and then in two-year volumes that contain in one alphabetical listing all entries for the period covered.

The *Readers' Guide* is primarily a subject and author index, but short stories, poems, plays, and motion pictures are listed by title as well as under the author's name. When entries appear under a person's name in two different listings, the first group of articles refers to articles *by* that person as an author; the second group of articles refers to articles *about* that person as a subject. Here are two examples, first of an author entry, then of a subject entry:

> WALKER, John S.
> Thermonuclear reactions: can they be used for man's benefit?
> For Affairs 33:605–14 Jl '55

The first thing that appears under the author's name is the title of the article (usually only the first word of the title is capitalized). Then appears the name of the magazine, in abbreviated form (the front of each volume gives a key to abbreviations). This article appeared in *Foreign Affairs*. Following the title of the magazine is a series of numbers specifying the issue of the magazine in which this article appeared. The number before the colon is the volume number of the periodical (the bound volume of the periodical in the library usually carries this same volume number). After the colon are the page numbers of the article. A plus sign ($+$) after a page number indicates that the article is continued on other pages toward the back of the magazine. Then the date of the issue is given in abbreviated form. If the magazine is a monthly, as in this case, only the month (July) and the year (1955) are given: if the magazine is a weekly (see below), the month (March), day (12), and year (1955) are given. Those compiling a list of articles for later investigation should be careful to record the exact volume number and date of the magazine, because they will need this information when they search for the bound volumes of the magazine on the library shelves or if they submit a call-slip to the librarian.

> CENSORSHIP
> Art censorship. H. Smith. Sat R 38:24 Mr 12 '55
> Light in San Diego. Nation 180: 389 My 7 '55
> Minnesota menaced by vigilante censors. Christian Cent 72: 468–9 Ap 20 '55

This second example of an entry is a subject heading (Censorship). All the articles published on that subject during the period covered by this particular volume will be listed, and often there will be "see also" references to other subject headings. In the subject entries, the titles of articles are given first. Then the name of the author is given (in subject entries, the author's first name is represented by the initial capital only). The absence of a name after the title of the article indicates an anonymous or unsigned article.

> **International Index** (New York: H. W. Wilson Company, 1907–65); between 1965–74 entitled **Social Sciences and Humanities Index;** since 1974 two works: **Humanities Index** and **Social Sciences Index.**

The *International Index* is a useful supplement to the *Readers' Guide*. During the first fifty years of its coverage, the *International Index* covered foreign-language periodicals as well as English-language periodicals, but foreign titles were dropped after World War II. The title of the volumes of this periodical guide appearing between June 1965 and March 1974 was changed to *Social Sciences and Humanities Index*. Starting in June of 1974, this reference source was split into two separate indexes: *Humanities Index* and *Social Sciences Index*. With these changes in title, the coverage of scientific and foreign-language periodicals was progressively curtailed in favor of concentration on the more scholarly English-language journals throughout the world that deal with the social sciences and the humanities. At present, this reference work indexes about 200 journals. As a subject and author index, it uses the same style of notation as the *Readers' Guide* does. Those seeking an extensive bibliography of magazine articles on some subject should consult this important periodical index in addition to the *Readers' Guide*. For certain subjects (e.g., topics of more scholarly interest), it is a more useful reference guide to periodical literature than the *Readers' Guide*.

> **The Nineteenth-Century Readers' Guide,** 1890–99, 2 volumes (New York: H. W. Wilson Co., 1944).

Whereas the *Readers' Guide* and the *International Index* cover the periodical literature of the twentieth century, the *Nineteenth-Century Guide* covers the last decade of the nineteenth century. Published in two volumes, this periodical guide indexes material in 57 English and American magazines that were being published late in the last century. In some cases, the indexing has been extended beyond the limits specified by the title. *The National Geographic Magazine,* for instance, is indexed from 1888, the year it began publication, to December 1908, when it begins to be indexed by the *Readers' Guide*. The British *Cornhill Magazine,* a periodical that published contributions from such distinguished writers as Thackeray, Ruskin, Arnold, and Trollope, is indexed from January 1890 to December 1922, when it was picked up by the *International Index*. *The Nineteenth-Century Guide* adopts the standard list of subject headings and cross-references used by the other periodical guides, has author entries, and gives title indexes to short stories, novels, plays, and poems.

> **Poole's Index to Periodical Literature,** ed. William Frederick Poole and William I. Fletcher, 6 volumes (New York: Houghton Mifflin, 1882–1907).

Poole's Index is the only index to English-language periodicals of the nineteenth century up to 1890. It was initiated by William F. Poole, librarian at the Mercantile Library of Boston, the public libraries in Cincinnati and Chicago, and, at the time of his death in 1894, the famous Newberry Library in Chicago. His colleague William Fletcher had a hand in the preparation of all the volumes and after Poole's death was assisted by Franklin O. Poole and Mary Poole. *Poole's Index* with its five supplements covered 479 different periodicals ranging across a period of 105 years and included more than 590,000 references.

Poole's Index is a subject index only. Writers are entered only when they are treated as subjects. Thus Thomas Babington Macaulay's contributions to the *Edinburgh Review* are entered not under Macaulay's name but under the subjects he wrote about—Milton, church and state, Clive, Machiavelli, etc. Critical articles on poetry, drama, and prose fiction appear under the name of the author whose work is being criticized. Hence a critical article on the Victorian novel *Dombey and Son* would appear under "Charles Dickens."

Poole did not supply the date of the magazine in his references. A typical reference following the title of an article looks like this: Fortn 29:816. The Table of Abbreviations in the front of the volume shows that "Fortn" is the abbreviation for the journal *Fortnightly Review*. The number before the colon is the volume number; the number after the colon is the first page of the article. By consulting the chronological conspectus at the front of the volume, the searcher would discover that volume 29 of the *Fortnightly Review* appeared in 1878. The chronological conspectus also indicates the volume numbers of the same date in other periodicals, so that from this table, the searcher could trace the discussion of a subject in several contemporary periodicals.

A paperbound volume, *Poole's Index: Date and Volume Key,* by Marion V. Bell and Jean C. Bacon (Chicago: Association of College and Reference Libraries, 1957), usually found on the shelves alongside *Poole's Index,* arranges the 479 periodical titles in a single alphabetical listing, with the year supplied for each volume of each periodical.

Other Periodical Indexes

Here is a list, with brief descriptions, of some other periodical indexes, which can usually be found on the reference shelves of public and college libraries. All of them, except the *Catholic Periodical Index,* are published by the H. W. Wilson Company of New York.

> **Agricultural Index** (1916–64); continued as **Biological and Agricultural Index,** 1964– . Published monthly. Subsequently published in bound volumes in annual and two-year cumulations. A subject index to anything connected with agriculture, biology, and related sciences in periodicals, pamphlets, and bulletins and in documents published by federal and state agricultural agencies.

Art Index (1929–). Published quarterly. Later, the separate issues are cumulated in a bound volume. A subject and author index to periodicals and museum bulletins in the fields of archaeology, architecture, ceramics, ornament, engraving, graphic arts, landscaping, painting, sculpture.

Education Index (1929–). Published monthly, except in July and August and later cumulated in annual and two-year bound volumes. Indexes about 240 periodicals, proceedings, monographs, bulletins, and reports on anything connected with education. Until 1961, books and articles were listed under both author and subject headings, but since 1961, there are subject headings only, and books on education are no longer indexed.

Industrial Arts Index (1913–57); continued since 1958 as two separate indexes: *Applied Science and Technology Index* (1958–) and *Business Periodicals Index* (1958–). Published monthly, except July, with subsequent annual cumulations. This is a subject index only to about 225 English-language periodicals. The *Applied Science and Technology Index* covers aeronautics, automation, chemistry, construction, electrical communication, engineering, geology, metallurgy, physics, and transportation. The *Business Periodicals Index* covers such fields as accounting, insurance, public administration, taxation, and allied subjects.

Catholic Periodical Index (New York: Catholic Library Association, 1939–67); continued as Catholic Periodical and Literature Index (1967–). This index covers about 200 periodicals published in the United States, Canada, England, and Ireland—some of which are not covered in such reference works as the *Readers' Guide* and the *International Index*. This author-subject index annually lists about 2500 books of interest to Catholic readers and also gives citations from book reviews at the end of the cumulative volumes.

Essay and General Literature Index, 1900–33 (New York: H. W. Wilson Co., 1934); kept up to date with a series of cumulated supplements (1934–69).

This is an author and a subject index (with title entries where needed) to collections of essays, articles, and miscellaneous works of some reference value. The basic volume, covering the years 1900–33, indexed over 40,000 essays and articles that were reprinted in some 2144 collections or miscellaneous works. The cumulated supplements, covering the year 1934–69, list more than 150,000 essays and articles reprinted in over 7000 collections.

The special value of the *Essay and General Literature Index* is that this reference work can guide researchers to collections that print essays, articles, stories, poems, etc. that have been long out of print or are not readily available in earlier editions or in bound periodicals. Sometimes researchers know of or discover through the periodical guides an essay or article that would be extremely useful for a paper they are writing, but in checking the library, they learn to their dismay that the library does not have the book or the bound periodical in which this piece originally appeared. However, they should not abandon hope of getting a copy of this piece. The *Essay and General Literature* may indicate that it has been printed in a collection or anthology, which the library has on its shelves. At the back of each bound volume is a list of all the books indexed in that volume, and many librarians put a checkmark opposite the titles that the library has on its shelves. The essays and articles reprinted in the "readers" that students may have bought for some of their courses are or will be indexed in this reference work.

New York Times Index (New York: New York Times, 1913–   ).

Times Official Index (London: Times Office, 1906–   ).

Some public and university libraries keep a file of the local newspapers and provide some kind of index to these newspapers. They are more likely, however, to maintain files of some of the great newspapers, like the London *Times* and the *New York Times,* both of which publish annual indexes to their copy. Formerly, libraries and newspaper "morgues" retained copies of the newspapers, but these stacks were awkward to store, difficult to handle, and susceptible to slow decay. Now, thanks to the microfilming process, an entire year's issue of a newspaper can be recorded on a few rolls of film or a few microfiche cards. Using a microfilm or microfiche reader, researchers can quickly turn to the particular issue and the particular feature they are interested in and can take notes from the enlarged reproduction of the newspaper type.

The *New York Times Index* is a subject index only to the Late City edition of each day's paper. Articles and features are not entered by the titles or headlines they had in the newspaper. Instead, the compilers supply a phrase or a sentence that concisely describes the substance of the piece. For each entry, the date, page number, and column are given (for Sunday issues the section-number of the paper is also supplied)—for example, Je 8, III, 3:4 June 8—the year is supplied by the particular annual volume being used—section 3, page 3, column 4).

Those tracing a news item that was covered over several days can, by turning the microfilm or microfiche reader to earlier or later issues, find additional material on the subject they are exploring. Either of these newspaper indexes can also serve as a guide to other newspapers, for major news events will most likely be covered in local newspapers on the same date as they were covered in these major world newspapers.

> **Science Citation Index** (Philadelphia: Institute for Scientific Information, 1961–).
>
> **Social Sciences Citation Index** (Philadelphia: Institute for Scientific Information, 1973–).
>
> **Arts and Humanities Citation Index** (Philadelphia: Institute for Scientific Information, 1978–).

By the time students come to college, most of them have never used a citation index, and many are not even aware that such a reference work exists. But these indexes can be very helpful to researchers, especially for contemporary subjects. They guide researchers to books and articles that discuss a particular subject by a particular author in a particular year. It may appear that citation indexes provide the same kind of service as the periodical indexes do, but they are different.

The best way for you to learn how to use this kind of reference work is to get your hands on one of the volumes of one of the three citation indexes listed above and to read the directions printed on the inside of the front and back covers and then to follow those directions in doing a literature search on some author or subject of your choosing. There are always several volumes of a citation index, even when it covers just one year, and those multiple volumes make it possible for you to conduct four basic types of literature search. For instance, although there are annual volumes of the *Social Sciences Citation Index,* there is a five-year cumulation that covers the years 1976–80. Volumes 1–9 of this cumulation are labelled Citation Index; Volume 10 is labelled Corporate Index; Volumes 11–19 are labelled Source Index; and Volumes 20–22 are labelled Permuterm Subject Index. Each of those four parts provides a different indexing system to related pieces of literature published during the five-year period.

If, for example, you knew of a single book or article dealing with a topic that you wanted to write a research paper on, you could consult one of the alphabetically arranged volumes of the Citation Index under the last name of the author of that book or article to see if any other books or articles are listed that mention or discuss that article or book. If that book or article has made a significant contribution to studies of the subject it deals with, there are likely to be a number of references to other subsequently published books or articles that mention or discuss the book or article that you have discovered. If those other books or articles mention the work you started with, it is likely that those books or articles are dealing with the same subject you are interested in writing about. Using the last name of the authors listed in the Citation Index, you can then get full bibliographical information about those related books or articles by consulting the appropriate alphabetically arranged volume of the Source Index. You can accumulate additional related works by consulting other years of the index, but you will not find references to a work until at least a year has elapsed since the work was first published.

If the book or article that you started with does not have an author's name attached to it, you can consult the Corporate Index to find references to a work that was published anonymously or that was produced by some organization, such as a university or a research foundation, or was produced in a particular location, such as a city in the United States.

If, however, you do not have a lead on even one book or article on the subject you want to write about, you can consult the Permuterm Subject Index volumes to collect a bibliography on the subject. For instance, say that you wanted to do a research paper on a subject indicated by a title such as The Effect of the Building of Nuclear-Power Plants on Unemployment in the Coal-Mining Industry in the Appalachian Section of the United States. You could begin to collect some pertinent books and articles by consulting the appropriate alphabetically arranged Permuterm Subject Index volume under one or other of the key-terms in that title—key-terms such as Unemployment, Nuclear-Power, Coal-Industry. Suppose that you looked at the volume that listed the key-word *Unemployment*. Under the word UNEMPLOYMENT, printed in boldfaced block-capital letters, you are likely to find listed in roman block-capital letters several Co-Terms—that is, other words that have appeared with the word UNEMPLOYMENT in the titles of books and articles published during the year covered by the volume you are consulting. The value of these Co-Terms is that they will help you to narrow your search from the broad topic of unemployment to a topic closer to the one you are interested in. You would want to look at books and articles that had in their titles, besides the word UNEMPLOYMENT, words such as NUCLEAR-POWER, COAL, APPALACHIA. You would not have much use for articles that dealt with the unemployment situation in the steel industry in and around South Chicago.

The citation indexes are relatively the newest kind of bibliographic reference tool, but they are so immensely rich with information about the related literature on particular topics that any serious researcher must become acquainted with them and learn how to use them. The main problem with the citation indexes as reference tools is that they are likely to provide you with leads to such a wealth of pertinent material that you will not know where to start your research. You will have to learn how to be judiciously selective when you use this research tool.

Handbooks

> **World Almanac and Book of Facts** (New York: New York World-Telegram and Sun Corporation, 1868–to date).

> **Information Please Almanac** (1947–to date; various publishers, currently Simon and Schuster, New York).

These almanacs are such rich storehouses of miscellaneous information that every student should buy one or the other. A large portion of each edition of the almanacs is reprinted every year without any changes, because certain kinds of data, like the names of the presidents and vice-presidents of the United States or the capitals of each state, are not subject to change. For that kind of information, a 1940 almanac is just as useful as a 1990 almanac. Other kinds of information, however, do change from year to year. Those seeking statistics on the federal tax revenues for 1980 must consult an almanac covering that year.

The World Almanac and Book of Facts is the most comprehensive of the American almanacs of miscellaneous information, but the *Information Please Almanac* contains more signed articles than does the *World Almanac,* and its coverage of foreign countries is more extensive. Because of the miscellaneous nature of the information, neither almanac arranges its material in alphabetical order. Instead, extremely detailed indexes to the material in each volume are provided. Frequent cross-references point to additional material. Almanacs like these supply such useful information in a wide variety of fields that one of them should be the first reference work, after a good desk dictionary, that everyone should buy for the library at home.

English Literature

> **The Oxford Companion to English Literature,** ed. Sir Paul Harvey, 4th ed. revised by Dorothy Eagle (Oxford: Clarendon Press, 1967).

> **The New Century Handbook of English Literature,** ed. Clarence L. Barnhart and William D. Halsey, rev. ed. (New York: Appleton-Century-Crofts, 1967).

American Literature

> **The Oxford Companion to American Literature,** ed. James D. Hart, 5th ed. (New York: Oxford University Press, 1984).

The Reader's Encyclopedia of American Literature, ed. Max J. Herzberg (New York: Thomas Y. Crowell, 1962).

World Drama

The Oxford Companion to the Theatre, ed. Phyllis Hartnoll, 4th ed. (New York: Oxford University Press, 1983).

The Reader's Encyclopedia of World Drama, ed. John Gassner and Edward Quinn (New York: Thomas Y. Crowell, 1969).

All of these handbooks supply the same kind of information about literature and the arts. Their scope is defined by their titles. Here are the kinds of information that can be found in these alphabetically arranged handbooks:

1. Short biographical sketches of poets, novelists, short-story writers, playwrights, essayists, artists, musicians.
2. Short biographical sketches of diplomats, scientists, philosophers, historians, actors, military officers—especially those who have some relation to literature.
3. Plot summaries of novels, plays, operas, and long narrative poems.
4. Résumés of major lyric, didactic, and satirical poems.
5. Identification of major characters in novels, plays, operas, and narrative poems.
6. Explanations of Biblical, classical, and mythological allusions.
7. Definitions of literary terms—e.g., heroic couplet, Shakespearean sonnet, pathetic fallacy.
8. Short essays on literary trends and movements—realism, existentialism, New Criticism, deconstructionism.
9. Explanations of historical and geographical references that have some pertinence to literature and the arts—e.g., Gunpowder Plot, Fleet Street, Waterloo.
10. Short essays on famous musical compositions and works of art that have had some influence on literature—e.g., Elgin Marbles, Mona Lisa, Mozart's *Don Giovanni.*

Some of this information could be found in any one of the six literature handbooks listed at the head of this section. But those seeking information about an American author or an American novel would probably find the most complete information in one of the handbooks devoted exclusively to American literature. For anything connected with the theater, the articles in the *Oxford Companion to the Theatre* are likely to be fuller and more satisfactory than those in the other handbooks. Students should understand, however, that all of these handbooks supply only essential facts; for studies in depth, students will have to turn to other sources.

Cassell's Encyclopaedia of World Literature, ed. J. Buchanan-Brown, rev. ed., 3 volumes (London: Cassell, 1973).

The Reader's Encyclopedia, ed. William Rose Benét, 2nd ed. (New York: Crowell, 1965).

Whereas the previously mentioned handbooks dealt with the literature and art of particular countries or a special art form, these two handbooks provide the same kinds of information about world literature and art. William Rose Benét's handbook covers the major world literatures—English, French, German, Italian, Russian, Greek, and Latin. *Cassell's* covers these literatures and, in addition, such minor ones as Armenian, Basque, Breton, Eskimo, Polynesian, Yiddish—cultures usually neglected by English-language reference works. The first volume of *Cassell's* deals with the histories of national literature, with various literary genres and movements, and with important literary terms. These articles range in length from two lines to the 10,000 words devoted to the treatment of the Bible. Volumes 2 and 3 present brief biographical sketches of literary figures and treatments of specific literary works. The majority of the articles include a selective bibliography for further reference.

The *Reader's Encyclopedia* is not as comprehensive as *Cassell's,* but it is a handy one-volume source of essential information about world literature and the arts.

The Oxford Companion to Classical Literature, ed. Sir Paul Harvey (Oxford: Clarendon Press, 1955).

The New Century Classical Handbook, ed. Catherine B. Avery (New York: Appleton-Century-Crofts, 1962).

Crowell's Handbook of Classical Literature, ed. Lillian Feder (New York: Thomas Y. Crowell, 1964).

These three handbooks are rich mines of classical lore. They (1) identify the figures of myth and legend; (2) provide biographies of dramatists, poets, sculptors, painters, philosophers, generals, and statesmen; (3) give résumés of such epics as the *Iliad, Odyssey,* and *Aeneid* and of the dramas of Aeschylus, Sophocles, Euripides, Aristophanes; (4) supply information about places of mythological, historical, and archaeological interest; (5) have articles on rivers, mountains, shrines, ancient works of art, ruins, and monuments; (6) define classical terms. *The New Century Classical Handbook* has a great many illustrations and photographs and spells out phonetically Anglicized pronunciations of classical proper names—an especially helpful feature. Some information about classical subjects can be found in the handbooks of English, American, and world literature, but since these handbooks concentrate on classical lore, their coverage is more extensive and expansive.

> **The New Grove Dictionary of Music and Musicians,** ed. Stanley Sadie, 20 volumes (London: Macmillan, 1980).

> **The Oxford Companion to Music,** ed. Percy A. Scholes, 10th ed. revised and edited by John Owen Ward (London: Oxford University Press, 1970).

Sir George Grove published the first edition of this famous reference work on music in 1879, contributing to it major articles on Beethoven, Mendelssohn, and Schubert. Those articles were carried over in subsequent editions until the Fifth Edition (1954), the edition that preceded the completely new version of the *Grove Dictionary* published in 1980, a hundred years after the first edition. The extent of the revision of the *New Grove* is indicated by the fact that the nine volumes of the Fifth Edition with its supplementary volume have been expanded into twenty volumes in the new version. Less than three percent of the material from the previous editions has been retained, and now there are entries on the music of virtually every country in the world. More than 2000 expert contributors have written articles on such subjects as these: (1) definitions of musical terms; (2) explanations of the forms and methods of musical composition; (3) studies of the origin, development, and structure of musical instruments; (4) histories of musical societies; (5) notices of the composition, production, and contents of important works of music; (6) lists of the principal published collections of music; (7) biographies of composers, singers, players, patrons, teachers, etc. Because of the increased attention to the folk music of several countries, you are now as likely to find an article on the Beatles as an article on Beethoven and to find an entry on the banjo as well as the bassoon.

The Oxford Companion to Music makes no pretense of rivaling the multivolume *New Grove,* but the 1189 double-column pages in the 1970 edition provide a wealth of information about music and musicians. Scattered throughout the text are over 1100 portraits and pictures, and, at the back of the book, there is a pronouncing glossary of some 7000 terms and names that appear in the articles.

> **An Encyclopedia of World History: Ancient, Medieval, and Modern, Chronologically Arranged,** ed. William L. Langer, 5th ed. (Cambridge, Mass.: Houghton Mifflin, 1972).

> **Encyclopedia of American History,** ed. Richard B. Morris, rev. ed. (New York: Harper & Row, 1970, 1976).

The Langer book is a reworking of the *Epitome of History* that the German professor Dr. Karl Ploetz prepared and that William H. Tillinghast translated into English in 1883. In this 5th edition, the coverage of this rich storehouse of historical facts has been brought down to the end of 1970, with some sections that discuss the exploration of space and recent scientific and technological advances. If students have trouble locating the information they are seeking by following the geographical and chronological indicators at the top of each page, they can consult the highly detailed index. The historical narrative is interspersed with many black-and-white maps and almost a hundred genealogical tables of the major ruling families, and the Appendix provides lists of the Roman and Byzantine emperors, the popes, and the British, French, and Italian ministries.

The Morris book is a comparable handbook for American history. It has three main divisions: Part I, chronologically arranged, which presents major political and military events of the nation from the pre-Columbian era to the inauguration of President John F. Kennedy in January 1961; Part II, topically organized, which presents such nonpolitical aspects of American history as constitutional developments, westward expansion, and economic, scientific, and cultural trends; Part III, alphabetically arranged, which presents brief biographical sketches of some 500 notable Americans. Scattered throughout the more than 1245 double-column pages of the greatly expanded "Bicentennial edition" of 1976 are charts, tables, and historical maps. An extremely detailed Index serves as a key to the wealth of information in this handbook.

Dictionaries

Every serious student should own a good desk dictionary. Such a dictionary provides useful information about the spelling, syllabification, pronunciation, and meanings of words but will also supply brief information about the proper names of persons, places, and institutions. Here are the titles of some of the authoritative desk dictionaries:

> **American College Dictionary,** ed. Clarence L. Barnhart (New York: Random House, 1962).

> **American Heritage Dictionary of the English Language,** ed. William Morris (New York: American Heritage, 1969).

> **Funk & Wagnalls Standard College Dictionary.** Text edition (New York: Harcourt Brace Jovanovich, 1963).

> **Random House Dictionary of the English Language.** Rev. ed. (New York: Random House, 1982).

> **Webster's New Collegiate Dictionary.** 9th ed. (Springfield, Mass.: G. & C. Merriam, 1981).

> **Webster's New World Dictionary of the American Language.** 2nd ed. Edited by David B. Guralnik (New York: World, 1970).

Although these desk dictionaries will supply helpful information about words, students should be familiar with some of the unabridged and other special dictionaries and be aware of the kinds of information that can be supplied by these dictionaries, which are usually available on the reference shelves of libraries. Here are some of those special dictionaries.

> **The Oxford English Dictionary on Historical Principles,** ed. James A. H. Murray, Henry Bradley, William A. Craigie, and C. T. Onions. 12 volumes. (Oxford: Clarendon Press, 1888–1928).

> **The Compact Edition of the Oxford English Dictionary.** 2 volumes. (Oxford: Clarendon Press, 1971).

> **The Oxford English Dictionary on Historical Principles,** 2nd ed., ed. John Simpson and Edmund Weiner. 20 volumes. (Oxford: Clarendon, 1989).

The greatest dictionary of the English language is the *New English Dictionary (NED)* or, as it has been referred to since about 1895, the *Oxford English Dictionary (OED)*. The idea for this comprehensive dictionary originated in a suggestion that Richard Chevenix Trench, then Dean of Westminster, made to the Philological Society of England in 1857. It was decided right from the start that this dictionary would provide a historical study of the language, and several hundred readers were engaged to select and transcribe quotations that would be the basis of the historical record of the language. Before the project was finished, some 1300 volunteer readers, most of them non-professional students of the language, culled more than a half million quotation slips from more than 5000 authors of all periods. When the final volume of the original dictionary was published in 1928, the *OED* had a total of 15,487 pages and carried definitions of 414,825 words and 1,827,306 illustrative quotations. Between 1933 and 1986, the Oxford University Press published four supplementary volumes to the dictionary, the last three of them under the editorship of R. W. Burchfield.

In the Preface to the first volume, the editors stated, "The aim of this Dictionary is to furnish an adequate account of the meaning, origin, and history of English words now in general use, or known to have been in use at any time during the last seven hundred years." In accordance with this objective, the *OED* supplies (1) the variant spellings a word has had down through the years; (2) the etymology of the word, established by the methods of modern philological science; (3) the pronunciation of the word (usually the pronunciation that prevailed at the time that particular volume was published); (4) the various meanings a word has had; (5) quotations illustrating the spellings and meanings, ranging from the first known occurrence of the word in printed works to the recent occurrences of the word in modern texts. Each illustrative quotation is preceded by the date of the occurrence, the name of the author, a short-title reference to the source, and the page number in the source. It should be emphasized that the earliest date supplied is not necessarily the date when the word was first used; this date indicates the earliest *discovered* written record of the use of the word.

The publication in two volumes of the *Compact Edition of the Oxford English Dictionary* has made it possible for individuals to add to their private libraries the contents of the multi-volume first edition of the *OED*. Through the miracle of a photo-reduction process, four pages of the original text were reproduced on one page in print so small that it has to be read with a magnifying glass. But now the ordinary person can afford to own a copy of this great treasure-house of English words. Then in 1988, the Oxford University Press published a CD—ROM (Compact Disk—Read Only Memory) version of the first edition of the *OED*. With this laser-disk version of the dictionary, users can more quickly turn to the word they are interested in, and with the eight indexes programmed into this computer version, users can readily compile lists of related words and quotations and authors.

In 1989, seventy-one years after the original publication of this great dictionary, the Clarendon Press at Oxford University brought out the Second Edition of the *Oxford English Dictionary*, already being referred to by the abbreviation *OED2*. Selling at a price of $2500, the 20-volume second edition contains 21,728 pages, defines 616,500 words and terms using almost 60 million words (34 percent more than the first *OED*), and reproduces 2,435,671 illustrative quotations. These 20 volumes contain the whole of the first edition (with some corrections and additions), the contents of the four supplements, and some 5000 new words or expressions that have come into the language since the early 1970s. Most of these new words come from the realms of science, business, medicine, and slang. But the longest entry in the *OED2* covers one of the oldest and the shortest words in the language—the verb *set*, an entry that contains over 60,000 words. Eventually a compact-disk version of the *OED2* will be available.

> **A Dictionary of American English on Historical Principles,** ed. Sir William A. Craigie and James R. Hulbert, 4 volumes (Chicago: University of Chicago Press, 1938–44).
>
> **A Dictionary of Americanisms on Historical Principles,** ed. Mitford M. Mathews, 2 volumes (Chicago: University of Chicago Press, 1951).

William A. Craigie, one of the editors of the *OED,* worked with Professor James R. Hulbert of the University of Chicago to produce a historical dictionary of American English. As the editors said in their Preface, this dictionary would include "not only words and phrases which are clearly or apparently of American origin or have greater currency here than elsewhere, but also every word denoting something which has a real connection with the development of the country and the history of its people." Using the historical principle that informed the *OED* and supplying the same kind of information, Craigie and Hulbert aimed to show how American English was distinguished from the languages of England and other English-speaking countries. The short-title references used in the citations are expanded in the 23-page bibliography. The end of the nineteenth century was arbitrarily chosen as the cut-off point for the admission of words to the lexicon, but many of the illustrative quotations are taken from works published during the first twenty-five years of the twentieth century.

In January 1944, the year in which the last volume of the *DAE* was published, Mitford M. Mathews and his staff began preparation for *A Dictionary of Americanisms* (abbreviated *DA*). The *DA* would seem to be superfluous, but Professor Mathews felt that the *DAE* had marked as Americanisms many terms that he had reasons to reject and that the *DAE* had omitted some terms that were clearly Americanisms. The narrower scope of the *DA* is due to Mathew's definition of "Americanism": "a word or expression that originated in the United States." This criterion admitted into the word-list "outright coinages," as *appendicitis, hydrant, tularemia;* such words as *adobe, campus, gorilla,* which first became English in the United States; and terms such as *faculty, fraternity, refrigerator,* when used in senses first given them in American usage." A 33-page bibliography gives the full titles of works cited in the illustrative quotations.

For many kinds of historical, cultural, and linguistic information about Americanisms, the student should consult one of these two dictionaries.

> **The Century Dictionary and Cyclopedia,** ed. William Dwight Whitney and Benjamin E. Smith, 12 volumes (New York: The Century Company, 1889–1914).

The Century Dictionary is generally regarded as the best multi-volume unabridged dictionary ever produced by a commercial publisher in America. Under the general editorship of William Dwight Whitney, the first edition appeared between 1889 and 1891. A cyclopedia of names appeared in 1894, an atlas in 1897, and two supplementary volumes in 1909. The final edition in 1914 was produced in a 12-volume set. The total number of words and names in the completed work was more than 500,000. Since about 1920, this great dictionary, which typographically is the most attractive and readable dictionary ever produced, has been out of print. Most college libraries, however, have a set on the reference shelves, and occasionally one can find a set in a secondhand bookstore.

This dictionary was designed to be as complete a record of *literary* English as possible. One of its values for the student of literature is the generous coverage given to obsolete words and forms, such as the Middle English of Chaucer's time. Moreover, the words and idioms of sixteenth- and seventeenth-century literature are more adequately covered than in any other American dictionary. The *Century Dictionary* gives illustrative quotations, presents full and accurate etymological information, lists synonyms for about 7000 words, and for many of the words adds a short informative essay.

The subtitle of the *Cyclopedia of Names* reveals the scope of this volume: *A Pronouncing and Etymological Dictionary of Names in Geography, Biography, Mythology, History, Ethnology, Art, Archaeology, Fiction, Etc.* This valuable dictionary of proper names has been made available in a separate publication: *The New Century Cyclopedia of Names,* in 3 volumes (New York: Appleton-Century-Crofts, 1954).

Among the 305 highly detailed colored maps in the world atlas are forty historical maps. There is an index, containing 170,000 names of towns, villages, cities, mountains, rivers, etc., with indications of where to locate them on the maps printed in the atlas.

Webster's Third New International Dictionary of the English Language, ed. Philip B. Gove (Springfield, Mass.: Merriam-Webster, 1961).

This edition represents a full-scale revision of the 1934 Second Edition of this famous American unabridged dictionary of the English language. More than 100,000 new entries were added to this edition, many of them being new meanings of old words or scientific and technical terms that had gained currency since the Second Edition, but because proper nouns and many obsolete and rare words were dropped, the total number of entries in this edition was reduced from the approximately 600,000 entries in the Second Edition to approximately 450,000. The geographical gazetteer and the biographical dictionary, which had been features of the Second Edition, were also dropped from this edition. Because of these omissions, most libraries have retained at least one copy of the Second Edition. But the *Webster's Third New International Dictionary,* with its rich store of living words and its hundreds of thousands of illustrative quotations (most of them culled from contemporary sources) remains the fullest record we have of the English language as it is used in the United States in the latter half of the twentieth century.

In 1976, the Merriam-Webster Company published **6,000 Words: A Supplement to Webster's Third New International Dictionary,** which presented some of the new words and new meanings that had entered the language during the fifteen years since the publication of the Third Edition. In the case of a vibrant language like English, a supplement like this may be necessary every fifteen years or so.

> **Origins: A Short Etymological Dictionary of Modern English,** ed.
> Eric Partridge, 4th ed. (London: Routledge and Paul, 1966).

Unlike the other dictionaries we have looked at in this section, *Origins* does not give the pronunciation or the meanings of words. It confines itself to the etymology or derivation of some 12,000 of the commonest words in modern English. But the 15-page section on prefixes, the 22-page section on suffixes, and the 100-page section on compound-forming elements will help students understand and remember hundreds of learned and technical words in the language. Medical students, for instance, who detect some form of the element *glosso-* (from the Greek word meaning "tongue") can guess at the meaning of words like *glossograph, glossology, glossotomy, glottioscope, glottogenic.*

Although a number of abbreviations are used, the etymoloiges in this dictionaries are traced in discursive prose that can be readily understood by the ordinary literate layperson. A valuable feature of the dictionary is that all cognates (words derived from the same root) are gathered under one heading and their etymologies traced in that section. Under the word *light,* for instance, more than fifty cognates are grouped—words like *leven, Lucy, enlighten, lucid, lucubration, luminary, lunatic, sublunary, luster, luxury, elucidate, illuminate, illustrate, leukemia.* The bonus for students from such an arrangement is that while looking up the etymology of the word *light*—or some other related word in that group—they are made aware of many other derivative words.

Any of the dictionaries mentioned in this section will supply etymological information about words, but for more extensive information about the history of words, students should turn to *Origins* or to one of the following:

> **The Oxford Dictionary of English Etymology,** ed. C. T. Onions with the assistance of W. W. S. Friedrichsen and R. W. Burchfield (Oxford: Clarendon Press, 1966).

> **An Etymological Dictionary of the English Language,** ed. Walter W. Skeat, rev. ed. (Oxford: Clarendon Press, 1956).

> **A Concise Etymological Dictionary of Modern English,** ed. Ernest Weekley, rev. ed. (London: Secker & Warburg, 1952).

Other Specialized Dictionaries

The titles of the following dictionaries indicate the nature and scope of their coverage:

> **A Dictionary of Slang and Unconventional English,** ed. Eric Partridge, 7th ed. (London: Macmillan, 1970).

Dictionary of American Slang, with a Supplement, ed. Harold Wentworth and Stuart Berg Flexner (New York: Thomas Y. Crowell, 1967).

A Dictionary of the Underworld, British and American, ed. Eric Partridge, 3rd ed. (New York and London: Macmillan, 1968).

English Dialect Dictionary, ed. Joseph Wright, 6 volumes (London: H. Frowde; New York: G. P. Putnam, 1898–1905).

A Pronouncing Dictionary of American English, ed. John S. Kenyon and Thomas A. Knott, 2nd ed. (Springfield, Mass.: G. &. C. Merriam Co., 1953).

Bibliographies

A bibliography is a list of books and articles on a certain subject or author. A bibliography of an author lists works *by* and/or *about* that author. Each field of study has standard reference works directing researchers to the published material in the discipline, and as researchers progress in their particular specialization, they will become familiar with the standard bibliographical guides in their field. Here we will review some general guides to bibliographies in all fields and then list a few of the principal bibliographical guides in some of the major fields of study.

A World Bibliography of Bibliographies, ed. Theodore Besterman, 4th ed. (Lausanne: Societas Bibliographica, 1965–66), 5 volumes.

This reference work, which was first published privately by its editor in 1939–40, is the most notable of the English-language bibliographies of bibliographies. The phrase "bibliography of bibliographies" may sound like double talk, but it is simply the term for a reference work that provides all the publication information about printed bibliographies on a variety of subjects. Someone assigned to do a term paper on witchcraft might want to find out whether a bibliography had ever been compiled on this subject. Besterman's work would not list the titles of works on witchcraft; it would simply give the titles of any bibliographies that had been compiled of such works. If the library had copies of those bibliographies, then the student would be able to assemble a list of books and articles pertinent to witchcraft. Besterman's work would be a logical starting place for anyone launching upon a major piece of research.

As its title suggests, Besterman's work is international in its scope. It covers bibliographies in the humanities, the sciences, and technology, but it is limited to separately published bibliographies—that is, to books, monographs, or pamphlets that are devoted exclusively or primarily to bibliography. Hence, the bibliographies given at the end of chapters or at the back of a book would not be listed in Besterman.

The bibliographies in Besterman are arranged alphabetically according to subject. An author index refers the student to the volume and pages of Besterman where a particular author's bibliography is listed. Since searchers for a bibliography usually do not know the name of compilers of bibliographies, they will probably have to consult the subject index. Frequent cross-references direct searchers to bibliographies on allied subjects.

> **Bibliographic Index: A Cumulative Bibliography of Bibliographies, 1937–** (New York: H. W. Wilson, 1938–).

The *Bibliographic Index* is a valuable complement or supplement to Besterman's *A World Bibliography of Bibliographies,* since it provides continuing coverage of bibliographies published since the time when Besterman's work was last published. It lists not only separately published bibliographies but also bibliographies included in books and periodicals. In searching for bibliographies, the compilers review somewhat between 1000 and 1900 periodicals every year, many of them written in foreign languages.

> **United States Catalog: Books in Print, January 1, 1928,** 4th ed. (New York: H. W. Wilson, 1928).

> **Cumulative Book Index, a World List of Books in the English Language, 1928/32–** (New York: H. W. Wilson, 1933–).

Together, the *United States Catalog* and the *Cumulative Book Index* (*CBI*) provide a comprehensive record of books published in the United States from 1898 to the present. Every published book is catalogued at least three times in a single alphabetical listing: once under the author's last name; once under the first significant word in the title; and at least once under a subject heading (there are frequent cross-references to other subject headings). The author entry supplies the fullest information about a book: (1) full name of the author (including pseudonym, if any); (2) complete title of the book; (3) name of the publisher (or source from which the book may be obtained); (4) date of publication; (5) paging; (6) price of the book; (7) the Library of Congress catalogue card number.

Students can use the *United States Catalog* and the *CBI* as a bibliographical aid by consulting the subject headings. For a paper dealing with "Linguistics in the Curriculum," they could consult the subject heading "Linguistics" or some subdivision of that heading in all the published volumes of both reference works and thereby collect a complete bibliography of all the English-language books published on linguistics in the United States since 1898. From that complete list, they could select the books that seem to be particularly pertinent to the subject of their paper.

Some Bibliographical Guides in Various Disciplines

> **Cambridge Bibliography of English Literature,** ed. F. W. Bateson (Cambridge: Cambridge University Press, 1940–57; New York: Macmillan, 1941–57), 5 volumes.

> **Literary History of the United States,** ed. Robert E. Spiller et al., 3d ed. (New York: Macmillan, 1963), volume 2 is the bibliography.

> **Harvard Guide to American History,** ed. Frank Freidel, rev. ed. (Cambridge, Mass.: Belknap Press of Harvard University, 1974), 2 volumes.

> **Bibliography of British History,** 2nd ed. (Oxford: Clarendon Press, 1928–70), 3 volumes.

> Lubomyr Roman Wynar, **Guide to Reference Materials in Political Science: A Selective Bibliography** (Denver, Colo.: Bibliographic Institute, 1966–68), 2 volumes.

> Lloyd H. Swift, **Botanical Bibliographies: A Guide to Bibliographic Materials Applicable to Botany** (Minneapolis, Minn.: Burgess, 1970).

> Charles Kenneth Moore and Kenneth John Spencer, **Electronics: A Bibliographical Guide** (London: MacDonald; New York: Plenum Press, 1961–65), 2 volumes.

> Rebecca Laurens Love Notz, **Legal Bibliography and Legal Research,** 3d ed. (Chicago: Callaghan, 1952).

> Vincent Harris Duckles, **Music Reference and Research Materials: An Annotated Bibliography,** 3rd ed. (New York: Free Press, 1974).

Annual Bibliographies

Any bibliography begins to date as soon as it is published. A bibliography continues to be useful, of course, as a record of the books and articles published during the period that it covers, but the record necessarily stops shortly before the date of publication. Several of the professional journals keep the scholar informed about all the important publications in a particular discipline during the previous year. When students adopt an undergraduate major and certainly when they go on to graduate school in their chosen field of study, they should become familiar not only with bibliographical guides like those discussed in the previous section but also with the annual bibliographies that are published in that field. Students can get guidance about the standard bibliographical guides and the annual bibliographies in their field by consulting the appropriate section of a reference work like Eugene P. Sheehy, *Guide to Reference Books,* 9th ed. (Chicago: American Library Association, 1976).

Syntopicon

> **The Great Ideas: A Syntopicon of Great Books of the Western World,** ed. Mortimer J. Adler and William Gorman, 2 vols. (Chicago: Encyclopaedia Britannica, Inc., 1952).

The Syntopicon, Volumes 2 and 3 of the 54-volume set of *The Great Books of the Western World,* is such a unique and valuable reference work that it merits a fuller exposition than is given to other reference works in this book. The term *syntopicon* is a coinage signifying "collection of topics." As a collection of topics, the *Syntopicon* is a reference resource that the ancient rhetoricians might have wished were available in their time as a guide to the relatively more specialized knowledge that speakers and writers need when they have to develop a particular subject. Mortimer Adler said of this extensive index that it is "the exact reverse of the giant comptometers which are fed data and do the thinking for the people; the *Syntopicon* feeds people the data—the issues and the various positions taken on them—and lets the human mind do its own thinking."

Some 443 works of seventy-four authors are printed in Volumes 4–54 of the Great Books, and Professor Adler had to decide on a basic list of great ideas that would serve as a detailed index to the topics discussed in the selected "great books" and in the Bible, the text of which is not presented in the set. He pared his list of great ideas down to a manageable 102, including such topics as aristocracy, beauty, democracy, evolution, fate, good and evil, love, nature, pleasure and pain, rhetoric, sign and symbol, time, wealth. A staff of indexers did a series of readings of the Great Books to gather references to discussions of these ideas by the great authors. Eventually, the basic ideas were subdivided into about 3000 topics.

Each of the 102 chapters of the *Syntopicon* consists of five parts:

1. *Introduction.* This is an essay summarizing the history of the discussion of the idea treated in that chapter. The various interpretations of the idea are reviewed, and the problems and controversies raised by the continual "conversation" about the idea are discussed.

2. *Outline of the Topics.* This section sets forth in outline form the

major themes of the discussion about the idea. Although there is an average of thirty topics to each chapter, the actual number varies from as few as six topics in a chapter to as many as seventy-six.

3. *References.* This section, arranged topically, is the heart of the *Syntopicon.* Under each topic, the exact location is indicated of all passages in the Great Books set related to that topic. Here is a typical entry:

35 Locke *Human Understanding* Bk. II, ch. xxi, 178a–200d

The inquirer is here referred to Volume 35 of the Great Books set, where John Lockes's *An Essay concerning Human Understanding* (1690) is reprinted in its entirety. The "Bk. II, ch. xxi" is a reference to the author's division of his treatise, a reference that enables an inquirer to find the relevant passage in some other edition of the author's work if the Great Books set is not readily available. The "178a–200d" cites the first and last pages, together with page section, of the relevant passage in Volume 35. The order in which the references are arranged enables the inquirer to pursue the discussion of some theme in a historical sequence or in a select group of authors or in a particular period. References to the Bible, if any, are always listed first.

4. *Cross-References.* This section directs the inquirer to other chapters in the *Syntopicon* where similar or related topics are treated. In addition to directing readers to allied material, the cross-references make them aware of the interrelationships among the great ideas.

5. *Additional Readings.* This section refers readers to other works not reprinted in the Great Books set. These bibliographies are divided into two sections: (1) works written by authors represented in Volumes 4–54 of *Great Books of the Western World;* (2) works by authors not included in the Great Books set. In this section, the additional readings are listed only by author and title, but in the Bibliography of Additional Readings at the back of the second volume of the *Syntopicon,* the full bibliographical information about each work is supplied.

Another valuable reference feature of the *Syntopicon* is the inventory of terms. This section serves as a kind of table of contents for the *Syntopicon.* Mortimer Adler remarks about this section in his introduction, "The person who wishes to use the *Syntopicon* as a reference book, in order to learn what the great books have to say on a particular subject, must be able to find that subject among the 3000 topics. The primary function of the Inventory of Terms is to enable him to find the topic or topics which either clearly express or approximately represent the subject of his inquiry."

For example, one of the terms that is likely to be involved in a discussion of Rhetoric is *persuasion*. Consulting the term *persuasion* in the Inventory of Terms, inquirers would find this notation:

> *Persuasion:* see RHETORIC, 1–5/b see also DIALECTIC 5; EMO-TION 5d; INDUCTION 4b; LANGUAGE 8; OPINION 2c; PLEA-SURE AND PAIN 10b; REASONING 5d.

The terms printed in block-capitals refer the inquirer to one of the 102 alpha-betically arranged chapters in the *Syntopicon;* the numbers and lowercase letters refer the inquirer to the particular subdivision of the references section of that chapter. This section will in turn direct the inquirer to the passages in the Great Books where the term *persuasion* is a major term of the discussion.

No exposition can adequately convey an idea of the wealth of information to be found in the pages of this unique reference work or make entirely clear how it works. Students should browse through it to discover for themselves the nature, scope, and method of this valuable guide to the wisdom of the ages.

Exercise

Since no amount of lecturing will do as much to acquaint you with reference works as will consulting the works to find answers to specific questions, this exercise is designed to get you to use the reference works discussed in the section on external aids to invention.

The answers to a few of the following questions could be found in one of the standard encyclopedias, the card catalogue in the library, or a desk dic-tionary. In every case, you should consult the reference work where you are *most likely* to find the information. For instance, if you wanted the date of publication of the novel *Vanity Fair,* you might find this information in a handbook of world literature, like William Rose Benét's *The Reader's En-cyclopedia;* but since William Makepeace Thackeray, the author of *Vanity Fair,* is an English novelist, it is *more likely* that you will find this informa-tion in a handbook devoted exclusively to English literature, like the *Oxford Companion to English Literature* or *The New Century Handbook of En-glish Literature.*

In doing this exercise, you should (1) write out the problem as it is stated below; (2) write out the answer to the problem (sometimes this will involve copying the answer as it appears in the reference work; in this case it should be copied exactly and put in quotation marks); (3) designate the source of the information—title of the reference work (underlined), edition of the work (if the work consulted is an edition later than the first—e.g., revised, second, etc.), the volume number (only in the case of a multi-volume reference work), the exact page number on which the answer was found. The following is a format that you might observe in doing this exercise:

Problem: Who established the American string quartet known as the Flonzaley Quartet?

Answer: Edward J. De Coppet of New York City established the Flonzaley Quartet.

Source: *Grove's Dictionary of Music and Musicians,* 3rd ed., II, 254.

You Want to Find:

1. When Sir Robert Peel, the man responsible for the repeal of the Corn Laws in 1842, became Lord Rector of the University of Glasgow.
2. In which of Frank Norris's novels the character Curtis Jadwin appeared.
3. Whether the *Dictionary of American English* and *The Dictionary of Americanisms* agree on the *date* when "O.K." or "okay" was first used as a verb in the sense of "to approve." (Give date and source of first occurrence as found in each dictionary.)
4. When and where Sir Harold Nicolson, the noted contemporary biographer, was born.
5. Whether the term *bishop* ever occurs in the New Testament (if so, cite the passages where the term occurs).
6. Some magazine articles on the subject of censorship of moving pictures that appeared in English-language publications published outside the United States during the years 1955–1958.
7. When and where Margaret Thatcher, Prime Minister of Great Britain, was born and in what field she took her university degree.
8. In what year John Hancock was elected to be the first governor of the state of Massachusetts.
9. During what years Ignazio Raimondi, the Neapolitan violinist and composer, served as director of concerts at Amsterdam.
10. At least six articles that appeared in American magazines in 1980–82 on the subject of foreign students in the United States.
11. Whether there is any collected edition of the works of Thomas Babington Macaulay.
12. Why Juan Luis Vives, the Spanish humanist and teacher of rhetoric, was imprisoned by Henry VIII.

13. A copy of Eileen Duggan's poem "Victory."

14. The meaning of the allusion, in a book about the Greeks, "battle of Leuctra."

15. Whether Frederick Jackson Turner's essay "The Frontier in American History" was reprinted in any collection or anthology published between 1948 and 1954.

16. In what novel by Dostoyevsky the character Nikolay Vsyevolodovich Stavrogin appeared.

17. At least three book-length biographical studies of the poet Emily Dickinson.

18. The earliest recorded use of the word *knight* as a designation of an order or rank and then the earliest recorded use of the word, in the same sense, spelled as we spell the word today.

19. The names of some contemporary puppeteers (like Burr Tillstrom) and then some biographical articles on these puppeteers in periodicals and newspapers between 1949 and 1952.

20. The source of the quotation, "There is no grievance that is a fit object of redress by mob law."

21. How many years Walter Paul Paepcke served as president of the Container Corporation of America.

22. What title Juan Bautista Diamante, the seventeenth-century Spanish dramatist, gave to his adaptation of Corneille's play *Le Cid*.

23. Whether the *Oxford English Dictionary* and the *Century Dictionary* agree that the word *romp,* as a noun meaning "a merry, lively girl who indulges in boisterous play," first came into use during the early years of the eighteenth century.

24. At least six articles on the Corn Laws that appeared at any time during the first seventy-five years of the nineteenth century.

25. Whether a bibliography has ever been compiled on the subject of witchcraft (if so, list two or three).

26. What the literary term "Spenserian stanza" means.

27. Whether Shakespeare ever used the word *rhetoric* in his plays (and if so, where).

28. The meaning of the term *astronaut*.

29. Six magazine articles that appeared in 1893 on the subject of the World's Columbian Exposition in Chicago.

30. When Pierre Lambert Goossens, Catholic archbishop of Mechlin in Belgium, was made a cardinal.

An Illustration of the Use of the Search Strategy*

Information is important because we live in an information society. The ability to find, evaluate, and use information will improve the quality of work for class assignments, and that ability will also enable you to make better decisions in selecting a career and may help you advance in the job market. Processing information quickly and efficiently will certainly increase your leisure time.

What is the best way to search for information? If you have only very specific needs, such as information about a particular person, you would go directly to the reference sources that provide that kind of information—for example, biographical indexes. If your needs, however, are broader, such as searching for a topic for a paper and turning up information on the topic you choose, a different approach is necessary. Devising a plan, as you would for almost any important undertaking, is the best approach. One such plan is what we have called the Search Strategy, a step-by-step method of finding information, moving from the most general information to progressively more relevant and useful material for your needs. By using this strategy, you not only will examine all the pertinent areas of the library but will make the most efficient use of your time.

As was pointed out earlier, a Search Strategy is a series of steps that, normally, are to be followed in order. But you can always loop back to previous steps as needed, and when you become more sophisticated in the use of the strategy, you will develop a sense for knowing when you can leap-frog some of the steps because they are not likely to yield useful information on the particular subject you are investigating. You will soon develop a sense for knowing which of the steps will turn up the greatest amount of information pertinent to your purposes. But in learning how to use the Search Strategy, you would be well advised to follow all the steps in the prescribed order: (1) encyclopedias, (2) dictionaries, (3) handbooks, (4) bibliographies, (5) card catalogue, (6) periodical and newspaper indexes, (7) *Essay and General Literature Index,* (8) biographical and book-review indexes, (9) concordances and books of quotations, (10) statistical sources and government documents. The section on External Aids to Invention gave you specific information about many specific reference books within those categories.

To illustrate the use of the Search Strategy, I will take a specific subject and run it through each of the ten steps in turn. Let us suppose that I have

* Developed and written by Virginia M. Tiefel, Director of Library User Education, Ohio State University Libraries.

to settle on a topic for a termpaper for a sociology class. For a long time, I have been mildly interested in the topic of mercy killing, but I have only a vague notion of what mercy killing is, and I have no idea where I might find useful information on the subject. So let me run that topic through each of the ten steps, starting with the most general sources of information and moving to progressively more specific sources of information.

Step One—Encyclopedias

Knowing that encyclopedias are good places to begin a search when one knows little about a topic, I look up mercy killing in the index of the *Encyclopedia Americana* and find this entry: "mercy killing: see euthanasia." Apparently, *euthanasia* is another term for mercy killing. So I turn to the volume of the encyclopedia that treats of subjects beginning with the letter *E,* and flipping the pages of that volume, I come to the article on *euthanasia.* There I learn that *euthanasia* is a Greek word meaning, literally, "good death"—or more precisely "easy death" or "peaceful death." The article goes on to give some historical and philosophical background on the subject, pointing out that "easy death" is an old, persistent topic of debate and that attitudes about it have varied over time and in different cultures. For additional information, I go next to another encyclopedia, the *Encyclopaedia Britannica.* The *Micropaedia* (the detailed index of this encyclopedia) defines the term and gives references to other sections of the encyclopedia that treat of the legal aspects of dying, on legislative actions and opposition on euthanasia, and on medical and ethical problems connected with the subject. It appears already that there is a lot of information on this subject, and so I need to narrow and refine the topic.

Step Two—Dictionaries

Since I want to understand the term better, I consult some of the special dictionaries discussed in External Aids to Invention. The annotation of the *Oxford English Dictionary* in that section stated that the *OED* is the most complete English dictionary ever compiled and that it traces the historical development of all English words in use between 1150 and 1933. Looking up *euthanasia* in the *OED,* I find that it meant "a gentle and easy death in the seventeenth century and that later it referred to a "means of bringing about a gentle and easy death." In the latter half of the nineteenth century, it took on its current meaning: "the action of inducing a gentle and easy death."

At this point, I am not very much interested in the medical, social, or historical aspects of euthanasia, but the legal aspects of "inducing a gentle and easy death" intrigue me and suggest that this may be the aspect of the subject that I will pursue for my term paper.

So now I see that I need to seek out some specifically legal definitions of *death* and *euthanasia*. Knowing that there are special dictionaries in most disciplines that cover topics and words in more detail than general dictionaries do, I find *Black's Law Dictionary* among the many special dictionaries in the Reference Room of the library. *Death* is defined in this legal dictionary as "the cessation of life," and *euthanasia* is defined as "the act or practice of painlessly putting to death persons suffering from incurable and distressing disease; an easy or agreeable death." *Murder* is here defined as "unlawful killing of a human being by another with malice aforethought, either expressed or implied ("malice aforethought is a predetermination to commit an act without legal justification or excuse").

Step Three—Handbooks

Because there seems to be some fuzziness about the legal definitions of some of the key terms connected with this subject, I need to gather more background information before extending my search. Handbooks are good sources for an overview of subjects, an overview, however, that provides more detailed information than is usually found in encyclopedias. Handbooks are, therefore, a good bridge between encyclopedias and the in-depth treatment found in books and journal articles on a subject.

I decide to do a subject search in the card catalogue to see if there is a handbook on my topic. Consulting the two-volume *Library of Congress Subject Headings* (*LCSH*), I find that "Euthanasia—Social Aspects" is an established subject-heading but that "Euthanasia—Handbooks" is not listed. But perhaps there is a handbook on the broader topic of "death." Looking under the word *death* in *LCSH,* I find the sub-topic "Death—Handbook manuals." A search in the card catalogue under that subject-heading turns up a handbook entitled *Sourcebook on Death and Dying,* which is shelved in the Reference Room of the library. After locating the book on the open shelves, I look at its table of contents. Under "Part I, Current Issues," there is a section titled "The Right to Die—Euthanasia." That section contains a lengthy overview of the legal aspects of euthanasia and a bibliography (not annotated) of books. The article cites many cases and their legal ramifications, defines "voluntary/involuntary euthanasia" and "active/passive" euthanasia," outlines the family's and the doctor's responsibilities in such cases, and notes the important issue of the right to privacy.

This handbook article, written by a doctor-lawyer, goes on to point out the differences among four forms of euthanasia: (1) voluntary/active (direct);

(2) voluntary/passive (indirect); (3) involuntary/active; and (4) involuntary/passive. "Voluntary euthanasia" denotes cases in which the patient or his or her representative gives consent to a death-resulting act; "involuntary euthanasia" applies when there has been no consent given to a death-resulting act. "Active" refers to an overt act resulting in death, such as giving someone poison; "passive" refers to withholding or discontinuing life-prolonging treatment so that the illness runs its course and the patient dies.

Since these differentiations help to clarify how euthanasia is categorized, I can now further narrow my topic to the legal aspects of voluntary/passive euthanasia. Continuing the discussion of the legal aspects of euthanasia, the chapter points out that nine states (in 1980) had passed carefully worded laws authorizing voluntary/passive euthanasia. Finally, this chapter cites the Karen Quinlan case as a classic example of voluntary/passive euthanasia. On the night of April 14, 1975, Karen swallowed a number of tranquilizers shortly before drinking several gin-and-tonics while she was out with some friends in a tavern. She fell into a coma and remained comatose for the next ten years, unable to speak or to see. Her parents, Joseph and Julia Quinlan, petitioned the courts early on to authorize the removal of all of Karen's life-supporting equipment, and the New Jersey state supreme court stated that the right to privacy made their action legal. But when the respirators were turned off, Karen remained alive, although a veritable "vegetable," for several years. Eventually, she died in June 1985. Since this case has become the classic instance in the twentieth century, I decided that I would further explore this case as part of my research project.

Step Four—Bibliographies

My next step was to consult bibliographies, which are often a fast way to find material on a specific subject. Encyclopedias and handbooks usually furnish bibliographies at the end of articles, and the handbook *Sourcebook on Death and Dying* has provided a lengthy list of titles, but most are not current, and because I had narrowed my topic, none of the titles in this bibliography are specific enough. A subject search in the card catalogue frequently yields bibliographies, as it did in my search for a handbook. Using the *Library of Congress Subject Headings* again, I find that "Euthanasia—Bibliography" is an accepted subject-heading, and the "sa" refers me to *Right to Die* as another heading. So when I go to my next step, the card catalogue, I will use these subject-headings to find some pertinent bibliographies.

Step Five—Card Catalogue

I copy down all the citation information that I find in the card catalogue and also write down the entire call-number for each citation. The call-number on a book is similar to the street address of a person: it tells you where the book is located in the library system. Recording the call-number carefully can save you time later on in obtaining library materials. One incorrect letter or number can put you in the wrong section of the collection, and the only way to correct such a mistake is to go back to the card catalogue and recopy the call-number.

Under the subject-heading "Euthanasia—Bibliography" in the card catalogue, I find *Euthanasia and the Right to Die,* which was published in 1977 by the government's Department of Health, Education, and Welfare. There is nothing under the subject heading "Right to Die—Bibliography," but the subject heading "Right to Die" has several titles listed under it, including *Karen Ann: The Quinlans Tell Their Story* by Joseph and Julia Quinlan, published in 1977. Because the bibliography listed in the card catalogue may be useful, I decide to check it out and also the book about Karen Quinlan.

Step Six—Periodical and Newspaper Indexes

The first decision I have to make is whether to consult the periodical index first or the newspaper index. In most cases, the periodical indexes are the most useful, and in some instances, there is no need to use newspaper indexes at all. You should be aware that newspapers usually do not contain intensive studies of subjects, that many topics are not prominent enough for inclusion in newspapers, and that time and space are important considerations for newspapers. Periodicals are less bound by time constraints than newspapers are, and often the periodicals—especially scholarly journals—will devote more space to a subject than newspapers do.

Since the Quinlan case was a prominent and recent story in the news, I decide to start with the newspaper indexes, and the one I chose to consult first was the *New York Times Index.* I know that this index often contains summaries of major stories, so I may be able to obtain a brief overview of the case from these summaries and then can pursue more details about the story by reading particular issues of the newspaper itself. Consulting the *Index* for 1975, I find that several articles and some summaries about the Quinlan case appeared in the newspaper that year. Just from the summaries alone I learned many of the facts about the case that I briefly listed at the end of Step Three—Handbooks, including the parents' fight in the New Jersey courts to gain the right to allow Karen to die peacefully. Many additional articles are listed in the 1976 *Index,* and a few articles are listed in the 1977 *Index.* Just from the *New York Times* I will be able to gather more than enough material on the Quinlan case for my term paper.

But I decide to look for further information in the bibliography that I check out of the library. I found notice of several articles on the Quinlan case in medical journals. Since those articles are likely to be very thoroughgoing, I copy down the citations to several of those medical articles for later consultation. I consult the *Readers' Guide to Periodical Literature* and *Social Sciences and Humanities Index,* but because those indexes lead you to popular magazines like *Time* and *Newsweek,* I decide that I am not going to get as much useful information from those indexes as I will get from the medical journals.

Step Seven—The Essay and General Literature Index

The Essay and General Literature Index (*EGLI*) indexes individual essays in books that are collections. For example, you may not be able to find an essay on euthanasia by looking in the card catalogue, because it carries the titles of books but usually does not list their content separately. Therefore, to find an individual essay that is published as one of many in a single book, you can consult the *EGLI,* where items are indexed by author and by subject. The 1975–79 volume of this reference work has a citation under the subject heading of *Quinlan, Karen.* The author of this essay is listed as "the New Jersey Superior Court," and the title of the essay is "In the matter of Karen Quinlan, an alleged incompetent," and the essay occurs on pages 271–77 of a book edited by Weir and entitled *Ethical Issues in Death and Dying.* Finding the book listed in the card catalogue, I check it out and discover that one whole section of the book consists of essays on euthanasia. But only the essay on Karen Quinlan is pertinent to my term paper. Since this essay was never published in a periodical, it would not be listed in one of the periodical indexes, and if I had not consulted the *EGLI,* I would never have discovered it. The essay provides valuable information for my purposes because it gives the details of the Quinlan court cases, first in the New Jersey Superior Court, where the judge ruled that turning off Karen's respirator would be tantamount to homicide, and then in the New Jersey Supreme Court, which ruled that the parents were authorized to remove all of Karen's life-supporting aids. The *EGLI* may not always yield leads to additional material on some subject, but students should be aware of its existence and of the kind of information it provides.

Step Eight—Biographical and Book-Review Indexes

Biographical indexes can lead us quickly to books, articles, and the kind of reference sources discussed in the biography section of the External Aids to Invention. For some research projects, finding biographical information about particular people—especially contemporary people who are not prominent enough to merit a book-length biography—is important. It happens that finding biographical information about Karen Quinlan was not as important for my research project as biographical information might be in other projects. *Biographical Index* did list the book I discovered in the card catalogue and checked out of the library, the book that Karen's parents Joseph and Julia Quinlan published in 1977, *Karen Ann: The Quinlans Tell Their Story*. If I had not found this work in one of the steps in the search strategy, the *Biographical Index* would have led me to it.

But another valuable use that can be made of the biographical and the book-review indexes is that they can lead you to works that can help you in evaluating the reputation and reliability of authors and the stature of particular books. If, for instance, the material we have found presents conflicting views on a particular issue, we could use these indexes to find biographies and book reviews that would help us evaluate the relative expertness of authors and the relative quality of books.

For instance, in assessing the credentials of two of the authors of articles that I may eventually use in my term paper, I consulted some biographical reference works that can give me quick and reliable information about living, professional people. An excellent starting place for information about scientists is the book *American Men and Women of Science*. In the 15th edition of that work, published in 1982, I found this pertinent information about Alexander Morgan Capron, the author of one of the articles I have on file: Capron took his law degree from Yale University and is currently a professor of law and an assistant dean at the University of Pennsylvania; among his prestigious appointments is the executive directorship of the President's Commission for the Study of Ethical Problems in Medicine, Bio-medicine, and Behavioral Research. In the 8th edition of the *Directory of American Scholars,* I found this pertinent information about Paul Ramsey, the author of another important article on the case of Karen Ann Quinlan: He has a Ph.D. degree in religion from Yale University and is an Emeritus Professor of Religion at Princeton University; he has a long list of institutions where he taught as well as a list of appointments to important boards and commissions. Information of that sort will help me make judgments about the qualifications of these authors to make pronouncements on the topics that they discuss in their articles.

I used the book *Magazines for Libraries* by William Katz and Linda Katz, which is mentioned in the introductory paragraphs of External Aids to Invention, to help me assess the reputation and reliability of two of the medical journals that published articles that I may use in my term paper. The Katzes declare that the *New England Journal of Medicine,* an organ of the Massachusetts Medical Society, is one of the "leading journals of medicine" in this country. They describe the *Hastings Center Report,* published by the Institute of Society, Ethics, and the Life Sciences, as a "scholarly but not technical" journal, which covers ethical issues in the biological and medical sciences as well as related issues in the social and behavioral sciences.

To help me evaluate the biographical book *Karen Ann: The Quinlans Tell Their Story* (1977), which I checked out of the library, I consulted the 1978 volume of *Book Review Digest*. This volume listed the location of several reviews of this book, reviews that I may later read to help me evaluate the account of Karen's life by her parents. This reference work also gives excerpts from reviews of the book that were published in two periodicals, *America* and *Library Journal*. Since the digest of reviews in this reference work usually include some favorable, semi-favorable, and negative reviews of a book, readers can frequently get a balanced view of the book just from these excerpts.

Step Nine—Concordances and Books of Quotations

Apt quotations may not be as important to my term paper as they might be in a paper on another subject—a paper, for instance, on a great historical event or a great historical personage—but a pithy quotation from some famous person or some famous literary work might be useful just as an epigraph for my paper on euthanasia and Karen Ann Quinlan. Perhaps the most famous of the reference works on famous quotations is John Barlett's *Familiar Quotations*. Under the word *death* in the index of the 1948 edition of this work, I find several quotations incorporating the notion of death. One that seems especially pertinent to my paper is suggested by this tag-line: "wish for, and not compass it." I turn to the page number that is attached to this tag-line and find this apt quotation from Sophocles's play *Electra*:

> Death is not the worst; rather, in vain
> To wish for death, and not to compass it.

This is an appropriate quotation for the euthanasia issue.

As explained in External Aids to Invention, a concordance provides an index to all or to most of the lines in a particular author's works. Two of the most often used concordances are the complete concordances to the Bible and to the works of Shakespeare. Under the word *death* in the index to the *Home Book of Shakespeare Quotations* (1937), I am referred to a page and section number of the book that contains an apt quotation from Act II, scene 2, lines 32–37 of Shakespeare's play *Julius Caesar*:

> Cowards die many times before their deaths;
> The valiant never taste of death but once.
> Of all the wonders that I yet have heard,
> It seems to me most strange that men should fear,
> Seeing that death, a necessary end,
> Will come when it will come.

That might prove to be a very moving quotation in connection with Karen Quinlan's tragic case.

Step Ten—Statistical Sources and Government Documents

The *Statistical Abstract of the United States,* which is published annually, is the best source for statistics about all aspects of the United States. In looking at a recent issue, I did not find euthanasia listed, but there was a detailed breakdown of statistics under the heading accidental deaths. Included are data on motor-vehicle deaths over the last fifteen years (declining steadily) and suicide (increasing). Some of the other causes of death that were listed are railway, air and space, falls, drowning, fire, and drugs and medicine. The "drugs and medicine" category has fluctuated from 1.2% of all accidental deaths in 1970 to 1.1% in 1980 to 1.5% in 1985, a fluctuation demonstrating a decline and then an overall increase. Accidental-death statistics are also broken down by sex, age, and resident state. These statistics, while not directly related to the topic I am concentrating on, can put euthanasia in the context of death and its causes.

Since the U.S. government is one of the largest publishers in the world, government publications can provide a wealth of information that should be considered when you are researching almost any topic. Government documents are indexed in the *Monthly Catalog of United States Government Publications.* To continue my search on euthanasia, I look in the cumulated subject-index of the *Monthly Catalog* under "Euthanasia—United States." I find a report entitled "Deciding to forego life—sustaining treatment: a report on the ethical, medical, and legal issues in treatment decisions." After recording the catalogue number (similar to the call-number of a book), I go to the *Monthly Catalog* and find that the document is a report from the President's Commission for the Study of Ethical Problems in Medicine and Biomedical and Behavioral Research. This report runs to 554 pages and has maps, a bibliography, and an index. This government report probably contains useful information that may not be available in its entirety anywhere else. I make careful notes of the document's title and number and go the library's government-document section to find this report.

As a final word on the Search Strategy, I might mention that technology has brought us new tools for retrieving information that are easier and faster to use than standard printed indexes. A variety of indexes are now available on compact disk, read-only-memory (CD-ROM). These are primarily bibliographies and indexes to magazines, journals, and newspapers and for that reason, should be considered when anyone is doing steps 3 and 6. These indexes on compact disk include such titles as *Art Index, Applied Science and Technology Index, Infotrac II-Academic Index* (similar to the *Readers' Guide* but covering a larger number of journals), the *Modern Language Association*

Bibliography, Sociofile (political sociology, social psychology, etc.), and *Medline* (medicine, nursing, psychiatry, etc.). One disadvantage of this research tool is that most indexes on CD-ROM cover only the most recent 4 to 6 years of publication. You will probably have to talk with a librarian about which materials are available on compact disk in the library where you are working. There seldom is any charge for the use of a CD-ROM.

Online (database) searching is another technological advance in information-seeking. It has certain advantages over the compact disk in that multiple indexes can be searched at the same time, and it usually covers more years than compact disks now cover. However, there is usually a charge for online searching. A librarian can advise you how best to meet your information needs, whether through the use of traditional print materials or of CD-ROM or of database searching.

Readings

The following readings have been provided to serve as texts for the study of the principles of logic and rhetoric that have been discussed in this chapter. Theory exemplifies and proves itself in these readings. Many of the authors represented here were aware of, if they were not thoroughly schooled in, rhetorical principles. Those authors who were not conscious of the rhetorical tradition confirm, by their practice, the soundness and workability of the principles that the rhetoricians had arrived at inductively.

While the readings can be used for the study of many of the things discussed in this chapter—inductive and deductive reasoning, the ethical appeal, the emotional appeal, the external aids to invention—they are designed primarily as working texts for the analysis of the common topics and the special topics. In the process of composition, the topics serve as the initiators of a line of development; in analyzing these texts for evidence of the operation of the topics, you are working backward from the finished text to what was, consciously or unconsciously, the beginning of the process. You may realize two benefits from this exercise: you will see that the topics are indeed aids to the discovery of "the available means of persuasion in any given case"; and you will develop another technique for the close reading of texts. Once you begin to approach a text from the point of view of the topics, it is surprising how soon you will develop an "eye" for the topics in any expository or argumentative prose that he reads.

The first three readings are examples of, respectively, deliberative discourse, judicial discourse, and ceremonial discourse. Extended analyses of these three readings have been provided to serve as models for your analyses of the other readings. You should begin the analysis by classifying the text according to type, since such a classification will alert you to the special topics that will be operating in the text. You will also find it useful to make an outline of the major divisions of the text you are analyzing.

In addition to your own analyses of the readings, another exercise can be worked off the selections. The sample analyses have made little or no attempt to assess the validity of the arguments and the effectiveness of the rhetoric. Taking up where these analyses leave off, you can evaluate these readings and the others that follow.

To facilitate reference to the parts of the texts, numbers have been placed before each paragraph.

Rachel Carson: The Obligation to Endure

Rachel Carson (1907-64) was a marine biologist who was employed for a good part of her adult life by the U.S. Fish and Wildlife Service. Her first three books were about the sea: Under the Sea Wind *(1941),* The Sea Around Us *(1951), and* Edge of the Sea *(1955). But early in the 1960s, she published a series of articles in* The New Yorker *magazine in which she gave warnings about the hazards to animal, plant, and human life from the irresponsible use of chemical insecticides. These articles, later published as a book under the title* The Silent Spring, *were among the first to raise the public consciousness in this country about the pollution of the environment by its human inhabitants, a situation that Thomas A. Sancton deals with in its crisis stage in a* Time *article that is reprinted and analyzed in the next chapter. In our analysis of this piece of deliberative discourse, we will concentrate on the topics yielding the arguments that Rachel Carson marshalled in her attempt to persuade her readers of their obligations in the face of this lethal danger.*

1   The history of life on earth has been a history of interaction between living things and their surroundings. To a large extent, the physical form and the habits of the earth's vegetation and its animal life have been molded by the environment. Considering the whole span of earthly time, the opposite effect, in which life actually modifies its surroundings, has been relatively slight. Only within the moment of time represented by the present century has one species—man—acquired significant power to alter the nature of his world.

2   During the past quarter century this power has not only increased to one of disturbing magnitude but it has changed in character. The most alarming

of all man's assaults upon the environment is the contamination of air, earth, rivers, and sea with dangerous and even lethal materials. This pollution is for the most part irrecoverable; the chain of evil it initiates not only in the world that must support life but in living tissues is for the most part irreversible. In this now universal contamination of the environment, chemicals are the sinister and little-recognized partners of radiation in changing the very nature of the world—the very nature of its life. Strontium 90, released through nuclear explosions into the air, comes to earth in rain or drifts down as fallout, lodges in soil, enters into the grass or corn or wheat grown there, and in time takes up its abode in the bones of a human being, there to remain until his death. Similarly, chemicals sprayed on croplands or forests or gardens lie long in soil, entering into living organisms, passing from one to another in a chain of poisoning and death. Or they pass mysteriously by underground streams until they emerge and, through the alchemy of air and sunlight, combine into new forms that kill vegetation, sicken cattle, and work unknown harm on those who drink from once-pure wells. As Albert Schweitzer has said, "Man can hardly even recognize the devils of his own creation."

3 It took hundreds of millions of years to produce the life that now inhabits the earth—eons of time in which that developing and evolving and diversifying life reached a state of adjustment and balance with its surroundings. The environment, rigorously shaping and directing the life it supported, contained elements that were hostile as well as supporting. Certain rocks gave out dangerous radiation; even within the light of the sun, from which all life draws its energy, there were short-wave radiations with power to injure. Given time—time not in years but in millennia—life adjusts, and a balance has been reached. For time is the essential ingredient; but in the modern world there is no time.

4 The rapidity of change and the speed with which new situations are created follow the impetuous and heedless pace of man rather than the deliberate pace of nature. Radiation is no longer merely the background radiation of rocks, the bombardment of cosmic rays, the ultraviolet of the sun that have existed before there was any life on earth; radiation is now the unnatural creation of man's tampering with the atom. The chemicals to which life is asked to make its adjustment are no longer merely the calcium and silica and copper and all the rest of the minerals washed out of the rocks and carried in rivers to the sea; they are the synthetic creations of man's inventive mind, brewed in his laboratories, and having no counterparts in nature.

5 To adjust to these chemicals would require time on the scale that is nature's; it would require not merely the years of a man's life but the life of generations. And even this, were it by some miracle possible, would be futile, for the new chemicals come from our laboratories in an endless stream; almost five hundred annually find their way into actual use in the United

States alone. The figure is staggering and its implications are not easily grasped—500 new chemicals to which the bodies of men and animals are required somehow to adapt each year, chemicals totally outside the limits of biologic experience.

6 Among them are many that are used in man's war against nature. Since the mid-1940s, over 200 basic chemicals have been created for use in killing insects, weeds, rodents, and other organisms described in the modern vernacular as "pests"; and they are sold under several thousand different brand names.

7 These sprays, dusts, and aerosols are now applied almost universally to farms, gardens, forests, and homes—nonselective chemicals that have the power to kill every insect, the "good" and the "bad," to still the song of birds and the leaping of fish in the streams, to coat the leaves with a deadly film, and to linger on in soil—all this though the intended target may be only a few weeds or insects. Can anyone believe it is possible to lay down such a barrage of poisons on the surface of the earth without making it unfit for all life? They should not be called "insecticides," but "biocides."

8 The whole process of spraying seems caught up in an endless spiral. Since DDT was released for civilian use, a process of escalation has been going on in which ever more toxic materials must be found. This has happened because insects, in a triumphant vindication of Darwin's principle of the survival of the fittest, have evolved super races immune to the particular insecticide used, hence a deadlier one has always to be developed—and then a deadlier one than that. It has happened also because, for reasons to be described later, destructive insects often undergo a "flareback," or resurgence, after spraying, in numbers greater than before. Thus the chemical war is never won, and all life is caught in its violent crossfire.

9 Along with the possibility of the extinction of mankind by nuclear war, the central problem of our age has therefore become the contamination of man's total environment with such substances of incredible potential for harm—substances that accumulate in the tissues of plants and animals and even penetrate the germ cells to shatter or alter the very material of heredity upon which the shape of the future depends.

10 Some would-be architects of our future look toward a time when it will be possible to alter the human germ plasm by design. But we may easily be doing so now by inadvertence, for many chemicals, like radiation, bring about gene mutations. It is ironic to think that man might determine his own future by something so seemingly trivial as the choice of an insect spray.

11 All this has been risked—for what? Future historians may well be amazed by our distorted sense of proportion. How could intelligent beings seek to control a few unwanted species by a method that contaminated the entire environment and brought the threat of disease and death even to

their own kind? Yet this is precisely what we have done. We have done it, moreover, for reasons that collapse the moment we examine them. We are told that the enormous and expanding use of pesticides is necessary to maintain farm production. Yet is our real problem not one of *overproduction?* Our farms, despite measures to remove acreages from production and to pay farmers *not* to produce, have yielded such a staggering excess of crops that the American taxpayer in 1962 is paying out more than one billion dollars a year as the total carrying cost of the surplus-food storage program. And is the situation helped when one branch of the Agriculture Department tries to reduce production while another states, as it did in 1958, "It is believed generally that reduction of crop acreages under provisions of the Soil Bank will stimulate interest in use of chemicals to obtain maximum production on the land retained in crops."

12 All this is not to say there is no insect problem and no need of control. I am saying, rather, that control must be geared to realities, not to mythical situations, and that the methods employed must be such that they do not destroy us along with the insects.

13 The problem whose attempted solution has brought such a train of disaster in its wake is an accompaniment of our modern way of life. Long before the age of man, insects inhabited the earth—a group of extraordinarily varied and adaptable beings. Over the course of time since man's advent, a small percentage of the more than half a million species of insects have come into conflict with human welfare in two principal ways: as competitors for the food supply and as carriers of human disease.

14 Disease-carrying insects become important where human beings are crowded together, especially under conditions where sanitation is poor, as in time of natural disaster or war or in situations of extreme poverty and deprivation. Then control of some sort becomes necessary. It is a sobering fact, however, as we shall presently see, that the method of massive chemical control has had only limited success, and also threatens to worsen the very conditions it is intended to curb.

15 Under primitive agricultural conditions the farmer had few insect problems. These arose with the intensification of agriculture—the devotion of immense acreages to a single crop. Such a system set the stage for explosive increases in specific insect populations. Single-crop farming does not take advantage of the principles by which nature works; it is agriculture as an engineer might conceive it to be. Nature has introduced great variety into the landscape, but man has displayed a passion for simplifying it. Thus he undoes the built-in checks and balances by which nature holds the species within bounds. One important natural check is a limit on the amount of suitable habitat for each species. Obviously then, an insect that lives on wheat can build up its population to much higher levels on a farm

devoted to wheat than on one in which wheat is intermingled with other crops to which the insect is not adapted.

16 The same thing happens in other situations. A generation or more ago, the towns of large areas of the United States lined their streets with the noble elm tree. Now the beauty they hopefully created is threatened with complete destruction as disease sweeps through the elms, carried by a beetle that would have only limited chance to build up large populations and to spread from tree to tree if the elms were only occasional trees in a richly diversified planting.

17 Another factor in the modern insect problem is one that must be viewed against a background of geologic and human history: the spreading of thousands of different kinds of organisms from their native homes to invade new territories. This worldwide migration has been studied and graphically described by the British ecologist Charles Elton in his recent book *The Ecology of Invasions.* During the Cretaceous Period, some hundred million years ago, flooding seas cut many land bridges between continents and living things found themselves confined in what Elton calls "colossal separate nature reserves." There, isolated from others of their kind, they developed many new species. When some of the land masses were joined again, about 15 million years ago, these species began to move out into new territories—a movement that is not only still in progress but is now receiving considerable assistance from man.

18 The importation of plants is the primary agent in the modern spread of species, for animals have almost invariably gone along with the plants, quarantine being a comparatively recent and not completely effective innovation. The United States Office of Plant Introduction alone has introduced almost 200,000 species and varieties of plants from all over the world. Nearly half of the 180 or so major insect enemies of plants in the United States are accidental imports from abroad, and most of them have come as hitchhikers on plants.

19 In new territory, out of reach of the restraining hand of the natural enemies that kept down its numbers in its native land, an invading plant or animal is able to become enormously abundant. Thus it is no accident that our most troublesome insects are introduced species.

20 These invasions, both the naturally occurring and those dependent on human assistance, are likely to continue indefinitely. Quarantine and massive chemical campaigns are only extremely expensive ways of buying time. We are faced, according to Dr. Elton, "with a life-and-death need not just to find new technological means of suppressing this plant or that animal"; instead we need the basic knowledge of animal populations and their relations to their surroundings that will "promote an even balance and damp down the explosive power of outbreaks and new invasions."

21 Much of the necessary knowledge is now available but we do not use it. We train ecologists in our universities and even employ them in our governmental agencies but we seldom take their advice. We allow the chemical death rain to fall as though there were no alternative, whereas in fact there are many, and our ingenuity could soon discover many more if given opportunity.

22 Have we fallen into a mesmerized state that makes us accept as inevitable that which is inferior or detrimental, as though having lost the will or the vision to demand that which is good? Such thinking, in the words of the ecologist Paul Shepard, "idealizes life with only its head out of water, inches above the limits of toleration of the corruption of its own environment . . . Why should we tolerate a diet of weak poisons, a home in insipid surroundings, a circle of acquaintances who are not quite our enemies, the noise of motors with just enough relief to prevent insanity? Who would want to live in a world which is just not quite fatal?"

23 Yet such a world is pressed upon us. The crusade to create a chemcially sterile, insect-free world seems to have engendered a fanatic zeal on the part of many specialists and most of the so-called control agencies. On every hand there is evidence that those engaged in spraying operations exercise a ruthless power. "The regulatory entomologists . . . function as prosecutor, judge and jury, tax assessor and collector and sheriff to enforce their own orders," said Connecticut entomologist Neely Turner. The most flagrant abuses go unchecked in both state and federal agencies.

24 It is not my contention that chemical insecticides must never be used. I do contend that we have put poisonous and biologically potent chemicals indiscriminately into the hands of persons largely or wholly ignorant of their potentials for harm. We have subjected enormous numbers of people to contact with these poisons, without their consent and often without their knowledge. If the Bill of Rights contains no guarantee that a citizen shall be secure against lethal poisons distributed either by private individuals or by public officials, it is surely only because our forefathers, despite their considerable wisdom and foresight, could conceive of no such problem.

25 I contend, furthermore, that we have allowed these chemicals to be used with little or no advance investigation of their effect on soil, water, wildlife, and man himself. Future generations are unlikely to condone our lack of prudent concern for the integrity of the natural world that supports all life.

26 There is still very limited awareness of the nature of the threat. This is an era of specialists, each of whom sees his own problem and is unaware of or intolerant of the larger frame into which it fits. It is also an era dominated by industry, in which the right to make a dollar at whatever cost is seldom challenged. When the public protests, confronted with some ob-

vious evidence of damaging results of pesticide applications, it is fed little tranquilizing pills of half truth. We urgently need an end to these false assurances, to the sugar-coating of unpalatable facts. It is the public that is being asked to assume the risks that the insect controllers calculate. The public must decide whether it wishes to continue on the present road, and it can do so only when in full possession of the facts. In the words of Jean Rostand, "The obligation to endure gives us the right to know."

Topical Analysis of Rachel Carson's "The Obligation to Endure"

In 1962, long before the pollution of our environment became a prominent public issue, Rachel Carson published her book *The Silent Spring,* an early warning about the dangerous contamination of the environment by the indiscriminate use of chemical insecticides. To assess her effectiveness as a persuader, one would have to examine the entire book, because it is her book as a whole that presents her case fully. But here we will examine only an excerpt from the book, Chapter 2, noting her rhetorical strategies in general and speculating about the topics that have yielded her arguments.

This excerpt is clearly an example of deliberative discourse, an attempt to change the attitudes and actions of the audience in regard to a matter of public concern. Like all deliberative discourse, this one deals, ultimately, with the future. Of course, it is talking about what is happening *now,* but that talk about the present situation is indulged in for the purpose of effecting a change in public policy in the future—the near future.

As we noted earlier in this chapter, the Special Topics that prevail in deliberative discourse are the Good/the Unworthy and the Advantageous/ the Disadvantageous. Of those two pairs of Special Topics, Rachel Carson is going to come down hard on the Advantageous/the Disadvantageous. To swing us away from our present practices, she has to persuade us that those practices are disadvantageous, that they are detrimental to the well-being of society, and that the practices she advocates are advantageous, that they will mitigate or eliminate the detrimental effects of our present policy.

Before we examine how Rachel Carson argues in this piece of deliberative discourse, we should get an overview of the main structure of this excerpt. In the next chapter, we will analyze in detail the arrangement or organization of a long essay and speculate about why the author chose to arrange the parts of the essay in a particular way. But here it will help if we simply outline the main divisions of Rachel Carson's discourse. Here are the main divisions of this second chapter of her book:

Introduction (paragraph 1)
I. Exposition of the situation in which people have developed an enormous capacity for contaminating the environment through nuclear radiation and chemical sprays (paragraphs 2–12)
II. Exposition of the situation in which the remedies invented to counteract disease-carrying and crop-destroying insects became worse than the problem (paragraphs 13–25)
Conclusion (paragraph 26)

As you can see from this overview, the author has devoted just about the same number of paragraphs to the two main, Roman-numeral parts of the discourse. The first part defines what the problem is; the second part explains how the problem developed. We might say that there is a cause-and-effect relationship between the two parts—Part I being the effect, Part II being the cause. And we will see later that the topics of Cause and Effect and Antecedent and Consequence have yielded many of Rachel Carson's arguments.

In the very first sentence of paragraph 1, which constitutes the Introduction to this excerpt, the author enunciates the premise upon which she bases her exposition of the development of the problem: "The history of life on earth has been a history of interaction between living things and their surroundings." Then she quickly points out a shift that has taken place in this basic relationship. Whereas for centuries, the environment held predominant power over living things, in the present century, one species of living things, human beings, have assumed predominant power over the environment.

In the next paragraph, which begins the body of her argument, the author argues that the Difference in the relationship of environment and living things is a difference not only in degree but in kind. Not only has the power of human beings over the environment increased at an accelerating rate, but that power is now exerting a lethal, irreversible influence on the environment. Mainly through the release of nuclear radiation and chemical sprays, people have pervasively contaminated the environment in which they live. At the end of this paragraph, there is a quotation from Albert Schweitzer, which constitutes an argument by Maxim: "Man can hardly even recognize the devils of his own creation."

In paragraph 3, the author points out another Difference in the situation that once prevailed and the one that now prevails. In the past, there was ample time for life to adjust to the natural changes in the environment, but today, the time needed for that kind of adjustment is not available. By contrasting the past with the present, Carson might be said to be exploiting the topics of the Possible and the Impossible for the future.

In the following sequence of paragraphs (4–8), the author explores the reasons we no longer have the necessary time for adjustments (and here the arguments are yielded mainly by the topic of Cause and Effect or the topic of Antecedent and Consequence): (1) the acceleration of the pace of contamination (paragraph 4); (2) the acceleration of the rate at which new chemicals are created (paragraphs 5–6); (3) the acceleration of the rate of indiscriminate destructiveness by insecticides (paragraph 7); (4) the acceleration of the degree of toxicity in the new sprays (paragraph 8).

In paragraph 9, we get a Definition of the "central problem of our age" (that is, a problem over and above the ever-present danger of the extinction of humanity by nuclear warfare): how to prevent the contamination of the whole environment with chemical sprays.

An argument from Future Fact is introduced rather incidentally in paragraph 10: not only can chemical sprays pollute our environment, but they also have the potential, like nuclear radiation, of causing gene mutations.

In paragraph 11, Rachel Carson raises the provocative question that was mainly responsible for her writing not only this chapter but the whole book: "Why, in seeking to control a few unwanted species, have we risked the contamination of our entire environment?" She then refutes *one* of the arguments commonly offered for the use of chemical sprays—namely, the argument that we must use insecticides to maintain our farm production. She exposes the weakness of that argument by pointing out that our present farm production is so high that we have to spend billions of dollars every year to store the excess.

In paragraph 12, the final paragraph in the first main division of the discourse, Rachel Carson enunciates her main contention, her thesis: not that we do not need to control the insect population but that the "control be geared to realities, not to mythical situations and that the methods employed must be such that they do not destroy us along with the insects." That is the policy she will be advocating farther on in the book, after she has convinced us of the "clear and present danger" of the prevailing situation. In the next major division of the essay (paragraphs 13–25), she will go on to point out for us what the "realities" are so that she can counteract the "mythical situations" that have dictated our practices so far.

In this first major division, we have seen that Rachel Carson's rhetorical strategy has been to start out with a rather general proposition and then gradually narrow down the discussion to the central problem that she is primarily concerned with. She starts out with the general premise that there is a natural interrelationship between living things and their environment. Then she points out that there has been a profound shift in the predominance of the two factors in this relationship. Then she focuses on just two of the ways in which people have assumed predominance over the environment—through nuclear radiation and through chemical sprays. By the time she reaches the end of this first major division, she has narrowed down the discussion to just one form of chemical sprays—insecticides. And for the remainder of this chapter, she will concentrate on insecticides.

In the second main division of the discourse, Rachel Carson is engaged primarily in presenting the historical and biological facts that account for the insect population becoming a threat to humanity. She will argue, however, that the method of control that people devised—spraying chemical insecticides into the atmosphere—has worsened the condition it was intended to correct. The topics that yield most of her arguments in this second section are Cause and Effect, Antecedent and Consequence, Testimony, and Statistics.

In paragraph 13, after making the point that insects inhabited the earth long before people did, Rachel Carson resorts to the topic of Division to make the point that eventually a small percentage of insects became a threat to humanity in two principal ways: as competitors for the food supply and as carriers of disease.

In paragraph 14, she deals briefly with one of these threats: disease-carrying insects. After picturing the situations that intensify the threat from disease-carrying insects, she concedes that some control of these insects is necessary, but she contends that the remedy people devised is worse than the disease. There is an element of the topic of Contraries in her argument here, an argument that runs something like the following: disease is *bad;* a remedy is supposed to be *good;* but the remedy in this case is *worse* than the disease.

From here to the end of the discourse, the author deals with the second of the threats: those insects that compete with human beings for the food supply. In paragraph 15, she resorts to Comparison to point out the Difference between the primitive agricultural situation and the agricultural situation today. Unlike the primitive agricultural situation, which had its own built-in system of checks and balances, single-crop farming today has intensified the growth of the insect population. In the next paragraph (16), she resorts to Comparison again to point out the analogous situation in which there was a wholesale planting of a single species of trees (elms) in many cities of the United States at the beginning of the twentieth century.

In paragraphs 17–19, Rachel Carson deals with another factor that has contributed to the intensification of the growth of the insect population in our time: the emigration of thousands of new species of insects from their native habitat to the United States. She cites the Authority of the British ecologist Charles Elton for an account of how this influx took place in the natural course of events as a result of the geological separation and then rejoining of masses of land by the action of the seas. In paragraph 18, she relates how this influx took place accidentally as the result of insects hitch-hiking on plants imported into this country. She cites the Statistic that almost half of the 180 major insect enemies of plants were introduced into the United States in this way. In paragraph 19, she resorts to an argument from Degree, saying that invading insects are often more devastating than native varieties because in their new environment, free of the natural checks and balances of their native habitat, they proliferate enormously.

In paragraph 20, she presents an argument from Antecedent and Consequence. Since these invasions are likely to continue indefinitely, we need to know more about animal populations and their relations to their environment. She quotes a Testimonial from Charles Elton's book again about this matter. In the next paragraph (21), she mentions the ironic fact that although much of this necessary knowledge is now available from entomologists and ecologists, most of us do not heed this Authority.

She raises the question, in paragraph 22, of why we have accepted as inevitable "that which is inferior or detrimental, as though having lost the will or the vision to demand that which is good." She quotes a Testimonial from the ecologist Paul Shepard about our inexplicable acceptance of an intolerable ecological situation.

In the next paragraph (23), she resorts again to an Antecedent-Consequence argument, maintaining that we have been so brainwashed about the need for a chemically sterile, insect-free world that we have enfranchised control agencies to exercise their powers ruthlessly and indiscriminately. She quotes the Authority of Neely Turner, a Connecticut entomologist, to the effect that the most flagrant abuses of the "regulatory entomologists" have gone unchecked by state and federal agencies.

In paragraphs 24–25, the final two paragraphs of the second major division, she repeats the thesis of this chapter and of the whole book: "we have put poisonous and biologically potent chemicals indiscriminately into the hands of persons largely or wholly ignorant of their potentials for harm." In repeating the thesis for the second time, she wants to make clear to her readers what she is advocating: not a categorical rejection of the use of chemical insecticides but a responsible and discriminating use of these lethal chemicals.

In the concluding paragraph (26), she winds down this section of her argument. What she mainly wants to do in this concluding paragraph is suggest a policy that the public should adopt in response to the menace of polluting insecticides: "The public must decide whether it wishes to continue on the present road, and it can do so only when in full possession of the facts." The quotation (almost a Maxim) from Jean Rostand with which she concludes the paragraph—"The obligation to endure gives us the right to know"—not only provides her with the title of this chapter but suggests that the decision that she is asking the public to make is not a matter of indifference but a matter of obligation. A Consequence of our obligation to endure is a right to know the facts. And in the rest of the book, she will be supplying her readers with the specific "facts" about chemical insecticides that will help the public make the obligated decision.

Throughout this chapter, she has been raising the apprehensions of her readers about the potential dangers of an indiscriminate and irresponsible use of chemical sprays. She has prepared them to receive the "damaging" facts that she will present in the rest of the book through Testimony of experts, through Examples and Statistics. We know from subsequent history that Rachel Carson succeeded in raising the consciousness of a large segment of the American public about the dangers of "fouling our own nest." Her arguments have been effective.

Socrates' Apology

Born in 469 B.C., Socrates was one of that remarkable group of poets, dramatists, philosophers, orators, statesmen, and generals who were responsible for Athens attaining its Golden Age in the fifth century B.C. He himself bequeathed no writing to posterity. His life, his philosophy, and his dialectical method are known to us only through the works of Plato and Xenophon. In 399 B.C., at the age of seventy, he was brought to trial in Athens, ostensibly on the charge that he was corrupting the youth and advocating the worship of new gods but really because he had become a troublesome citizen with his questioning of the policies and values of the Athenian Establishment. In the following instance of judicial rhetoric, we see him defending himself (the primary meaning of apology) against the charges leveled against him. Although Socrates speaks in the monologue form in the early part of the Apology, *his more usual method of conducting a discourse is illustrated in the question-and-answer dialogue with Meletus that begins with paragraph 13.*

1 How you, O Athenians, have been affected by my accusers, I cannot tell; but I know that they almost made me forget who I was—so persuasively did they speak; and yet they have hardly uttered a word of truth. But of the many falsehoods told by them, there was one which quite amazed me;—I mean when they said that you should be upon your guard and not allow

From *The Dialogues of Plato,* trans. Benjamin Jowett, 4th ed. (Oxford: Clarendon Press, 1953), Vol. I, pp. 341–53. Reprinted by permission of the publishers.

yourselves to be deceived by the force of my eloquence. To say this, when they were certain to be detected as soon as I opened my lips and proved myself to be anything but a great speaker, did indeed appear to me most shameless—unless by the force of eloquence they mean the force of truth; for if such is their meaning, I admit that I am eloquent. But in how different a way from theirs! Well, as I was saying, they have scarcely spoken the truth at all; from me you shall hear the whole truth, but not delivered after their manner in a set oration duly ornamented with fine words and phrases. No, by heaven! I shall use the words and arguments which occur to me at the moment, for I am confident in the justice of my cause;[1] at my time of life I ought not to be appearing before you, O men of Athens, in the character of a boy inventing falsehoods—let no one expect it of me. And I must particularly beg of you to grant me this favour:—If I defend myself in my accustomed manner, and you hear me using the words which many of you have heard me using habitually in the agora, at the tables of the money-changers, and elsewhere, I would ask you not to be surprised, and not to interrupt me on this account. For I am more than seventy years of age, and appearing now for the first time before a court of law, I am quite a stranger to the language of the place; and therefore I would have you regard me as if I were really a stranger, whom you would excuse if he spoke in his native tongue, and after the fashion of his country:—Am I making an unfair request of you? Never mind the manner, which may or may not be good; but think only of the truth of my words, and give heed to that: let the speaker speak truly and the judge decide justly.

2   And first, I have to reply to the older charges and to my first accusers, and then I will go on to the later ones. For of old I have had many accusers, who have accused me falsely to you during many years; and I am more afraid of them than of Anytus and his associates, who are dangerous, too, in their own way. But far more dangerous are the others, who began when most of you were children, and took possession of your minds with their falsehoods, telling of one Socrates, a wise man, who speculated about the heaven above, and searched into the earth beneath, and made the worse appear the better cause. The men who have besmeared me with this tale are the accusers whom I dread; for their hearers are apt to fancy that such inquirers do not believe in the existence of the gods. And they are many, and their charges against me are of ancient date, and they were made by them in the days when some of you were more impressible than you are now—in childhood, or it may have been in youth—and the cause went by default, for there was none to answer. And hardest of all, I do not know and cannot tell the names of my accusers; unless in the chance case of a comic poet. All who

---

[1] Or, I am certain that I am right in taking this course.

from envy and malice have persuaded you—some of them having first convinced themselves—all this class of men are most difficult to deal with; for I cannot have them up here, and cross-examine them, and therefore I must simply fight with shadows in my own defence, and argue when there is no one who answers. I will ask you then to take it from me that my opponents are of two kinds; one recent, the other ancient: and I hope that you will see the propriety of my answering the latter first, for these accusations you heard long before the others, and much oftener.

3 Well, then, I must make my defence, and endeavour to remove from your minds in a short time, a slander which you have had a long time to take in. May I succeed, if to succeed be for my good and yours, or likely to avail me in my cause! The task is not an easy one; I quite understand the nature of it. And so leaving the event with God, in obedience to the law I will now make my defence.

4 I will begin at the beginning, and ask what is the accusation which has given rise to the slander of me, and in fact has encouraged Meletus to prefer this charge against me. Well, what do the slanderers say? They shall be my prosecutors, and this is the information they swear against me: 'Socrates is an evil-doer; a meddler who searches into things under the earth and in heaven, and makes the worse appear the better cause, and teaches the aforesaid practices to others.' Such is the nature of the accusation: it is just what you have yourselves seen in the comedy of Aristophanes,[1] who has introduced a man whom he calls Socrates, swinging about and saying that he walks on air, and talking a deal of nonsense concerning matters of which I do not pretend to know either much or little—not that I mean to speak disparagingly of anyone who is a student of natural philosophy. May Meletus never bring so many charges against me as to make me do that! But the simple truth is, O Athenians, that I have nothing to do with physical speculations. Most of those here present are witnesses to the truth of this, and to them I appeal. Speak then, you who have heard me, and tell your neighbours whether any of you have ever known me hold forth in few words or in many upon such matters.... You hear their answer. And from what they say of this part of the charge you will be able to judge of the truth of the rest.

5 As little foundation is there for the report that I am a teacher, and take money; this accusation has no more truth in it than the other. Although, if a man were really able to instruct mankind, this too would, in my opinion, be an honour to him. There is Gorgias of Leontium, and Prodicus of Ceos, and Hippias of Elis, who go the round of the cities, and are able to persuade the young men to leave their own citizens by whom they might be taught for nothing, and come to them whom they not only pay, but are thankful if

[1] Aristoph. *Clouds,* 225 foll.

they may be allowed to pay them. There is at this time a Parian philosopher residing in Athens, of whom I have heard; and I came to hear of him in this way:—I came across a man who has spent more money on the sophists than the rest of the world put together, Callias, the son of Hipponicus, and knowing that he had sons, I asked him: 'Callias,' I said, 'if your two sons were foals or calves, there would be no difficulty in finding someone to put over them; we should hire a trainer of horses, or a farmer probably, who would improve and perfect them in the appropriate virtue and excellence; but as they are human beings, whom are you thinking of placing over them? Is there anyone who understands human and civic virtue? You must have thought about the matter, for you have sons; is there anyone?' 'There is,' he said. 'Who is he?' said I; 'and of what country? and what does he charge?' 'Evenus the Parian,' he replied; 'he is the man, and his charge is five minas.' Happy is Evenus, I said to myself, if he really has this wisdom, and teaches at such a moderate charge. Had I the same, I should have been very proud and conceited; but the truth is that I have no knowledge of the kind.

6 I dare say, Athenians, that someone among you will reply, 'Yes, Socrates, but what *is* your occupation? What is the origin of these accusations which are brought against you; there must have been something strange which you have been doing? All these rumours and this talk about you would never have arisen if you had been like other men: tell us, then, what is the cause of them, for we should be sorry to judge hastily of you.' Now I regard this as a fair challenge, and I will endeavour to explain to you the reason why I am called wise and have such an evil fame. Please to attend then. And although some of you may think I am joking, I declare that I will tell you the entire truth. Men of Athens, this reputation of mine has come of a certain sort of wisdom which I possess. If you ask me what kind of wisdom, I reply, wisdom such as may perhaps be attained by man, for to that extent I am inclined to believe that I am wise; whereas the persons of whom I was speaking have a kind of superhuman wisdom, which I know not how to describe, because I have it not myself; and he who says that I have, speaks falsely, and is taking away my character. And here, O men of Athens, I must beg you not to interrupt me, even if I seem to say something extravagant. For the word which I will speak is not mine. I will refer you to a witness who is worthy of credit; that witness shall be the god of Delphi—he will tell you about my wisdom, if I have any, and of what sort it is. You must have known Chaerephon; he was early a friend of mine, and also a friend of yours, for he shared in the recent exile of the people, and returned with you. Well, Chaerephon, as you know, was very impetuous in all his doings, and he went to Delphi and boldly asked the oracle to tell him whether—as I was saying, I must beg you not to interrupt—he actually asked the oracle to tell him whether anyone was wiser than I was, and the Pythian prophetess an-

swered that there was no man wiser. Chaerephon is dead himself; but his brother, who is in court, will confirm the truth of what I am saying.

7 Why do I mention this? Because I am going to explain to you why I have such an evil name. When I heard the answer, I said to myself, What can the god mean? and what is the interpretation of his riddle? for I know that I have no wisdom, small or great. What then can he mean when he says that I am the wisest of men? And yet he is a god, and cannot lie; that would be against his nature. After long perplexity, I thought of a method of trying the question. I reflected that if I could only find a man wiser than myself, then I might go to the god with a refutation in my hand. I should say to him, 'Here is a man who is wiser than I am; but you said that I was the wisest.' Accordingly I went to one who had the reputation of wisdom, and observed him—his name I need not mention, he was a politician; and in the process of examining him and talking with him, this, men of Athens, was what I found. I could not help thinking that he was not really wise, although he was thought wise by many, and still wiser by himself; and thereupon I tried to explain to him that he thought himself wise, but was not really wise; and the consequence was that he hated me, and his enmity was shared by several who were present and heard me. So I left him, saying to myself as I went away: Well, although I do not suppose that either of us knows anything really worth knowing, I am at least wiser than this fellow—for he knows nothing, and thinks that he knows; I neither know nor think that I know. In this one little point, then, I seem to have the advantage of him. Then I went to another who had still higher pretensions to wisdom, and my conclusion was exactly the same. Whereupon I made another enemy of him, and of many others besides him.

8 Then I went to one man after another, being not unconscious of the enmity which I provoked, and I lamented and feared this: but necessity was laid upon me,—the word of God, I thought, ought to be considered first. And I said to myself, Go I must to all who appear to know, and find out the meaning of the oracle. And I swear to you, Athenians,—for I must tell you the truth—the result of my mission was just this: I found that the men most in repute were nearly the most foolish; and that others less esteemed were really closer to wisdom. I will tell you the tale of my wanderings and of the 'Herculean' labours, as I may call them, which I endured only to find at last the oracle irrefutable. After the politicians, I went to the poets; tragic, dithyrambic, and all sorts. And there, I said to myself, you will be instantly detected; now you will find out that you are more ignorant than they are. Accordingly, I took them some of the most elaborate passages in their own writings, and asked what was the meaning of them—thinking that they would teach me something. Will you believe me? I am ashamed to confess the truth, but I must say that there is hardly a person present who would not

have talked better about their poetry than they did themselves. So I learnt that not by wisdom do poets write poetry, but by a sort of genius and inspiration; they are like diviners or soothsayers who also say many fine things, but do not understand the meaning of them. The poets appeared to me to be much in the same case; and I further observed that upon the strength of their poetry they believed themselves to be the wisest of men in other things in which they were not wise. So I departed, conceiving myself to be superior to them for the same reason that I was superior to the politicians.

9 At last I went to the artisans, for I was conscious that I knew nothing at all, as I may say, and I was sure that they knew many fine things; and here I was not mistaken, for they did know many things of which I was ignorant, and in this they certainly were wiser than I was. But I observed that even the good artisans fell into the same error as the poets;—because they were good workmen they thought that they also knew all sorts of high matters, and this defect in them overshadowed their wisdom; and therefore I asked myself on behalf of the oracle, whether I would like to be as I was, neither having their knowledge nor their ignorance, or like them in both; and I made answer to myself and to the oracle that I was better off as I was.

10 This inquisition has led to my having many enemies of the worst and most dangerous kind, and has given rise also to many imputations, including the name of 'wise'; for my hearers always imagine that I myself possess the wisdom which I find wanting in others. But the truth is, O men of Athens, that God only is wise; and by his answer he intends to show that the wisdom of men is worth little or nothing; although speaking of Socrates, he is only using my name by way of illustration, as if he said, He, O men, is the wisest, who, like Socrates, knows that his wisdom is in truth worth nothing. And so I go about the world, obedient to the god, and search and make inquiry into the wisdom of anyone, whether citizen or stranger, who appears to be wise; and if he is not wise, then in vindication of the oracle I show him that he is not wise; and my occupation quite absorbs me, and I have had no time to do anything useful either in public affairs or in any concern of my own, but I am in utter poverty by reason of my devotion to the god.

11 There is another thing:—young men of the richer classes, who have not much to do, come about me of their own accord; they like to hear people examined, and they often imitate me, and proceed to do some examining themselves; there are plenty of persons, as they quickly discover, who think that they know something, but really know little or nothing; and then those who are examined by them instead of being angry with themselves are angry with me: This confounded Socrates, they say; this villainous misleader of youth!—and then if somebody asks them, Why, what evil does he practise or teach? they do not know, and cannot tell; but in order that they may not appear to be at a loss, they repeat the ready-made charges which are used

against all philosophers about teaching things up in the clouds and under the earth, and having no gods, and making the worse appear the better cause; for they do not like to confess that their pretence of knowledge has been detected—which is the truth; and as they are numerous and ambitious and energetic, and speak vehemently with persuasive tongues, they have filled your ears with their loud and inveterate calumnies. And this is the reason why my three accusers, Meletus and Anytus and Lycon, have set upon me; Meletus, who has a quarrel with me on behalf of the poets; Anytus, on behalf of the craftsmen and politicians; Lycon, on behalf of the rhetoricians: and as I said at the beginning, I cannot expect to get rid of such a mass of calumny all in a moment. And this, O men of Athens, is the truth and the whole truth; I have concealed nothing, I have dissembled nothing. And yet, I feel sure that my plainness of speech is fanning their hatred of me, and what is their hatred but a proof that I am speaking the truth?—Hence has arisen the prejudice against me; and this is the reason of it, as you will find out either in this or in any future inquiry.

12   I have said enough in my defence against the first class of my accusers; I turn to the second class. They are headed by Meletus, that good man and true lover of his country, as he calls himself. Against these, too, I must try to make a defence:—Let their affidavit be read: it contains something of this kind: It says that Socrates is a doer of evil, inasmuch as he corrupts the youth, and does not receive the gods whom the state receives, but has a new religion of his own. Such is the charge; and now let us examine the particular counts. He says that I am a doer of evil, and corrupt the youth; but I say, O men of Athens, that Meletus is a doer of evil, in that he is playing a solemn farce, recklessly bringing men to trial from a pretended zeal and interest about matters in which he really never had the smallest interest. And the truth of this I will endeavour to prove to you.

13   Come hither, Meletus, and let me ask a question of you. You attach great importance to the improvement of youth?

14   Yes, I do.

15   Tell the judges, then, who is their improver; for you must know, as you take such interest in the subject, and have discovered their corrupter, and are citing and accusing me in this court. Speak, then, and tell the judges who is the improver of youth:—Observe, Meletus, that you are silent, and have nothing to say. But is this not rather disgraceful, and a very considerable proof of what I was saying, that you have no interest in the matter? Speak up, friend, and tell us who their improver is.

16   The laws.

17   But that, my good sir, is not my question: Can you not name some person—whose first qualification will be that he knows the laws?

18   The judges, Socrates who are present in court.

19 What, do you mean to say, Meletus, that they are able to instruct and improve youth?

20 Certainly they are.

21 What, all of them, or some only and not others?

22 All of them.

23 Truly, that is good news! There are plenty of improvers, then. And what do you say of the audience,—do they improve them?

24 Yes, they do.

25 And the senators?

26 Yes, the senators improve them.

27 But perhaps the members of the assembly corrupt them?—or do they too improve them?

28 They improve them.

29 Then every Athenian improves and elevates them; all with the exception of myself; and I alone am their corrupter? Is that what you affirm?

30 That is what I stoutly affirm.

31 I am very unfortunate if you are right. But suppose I ask you a question: Is it the same with horses? Does one man do them harm and all the world good? Is not the exact opposite the truth? One man is able to do them good, or at least very few;—the trainer of horses, that is to say, does them good, but the ordinary man does them harm if he has to do with them? Is not that true, Meletus, of horses, or of any other animals? Most assuredly it is; whether you and Anytus say yes or no. Happy indeed would be the condition of youth if they had one corrupter only, and all the rest of the world were their benefactors. But you, Meletus, have sufficiently shown that you never had a thought about the young: your carelessness is plainly seen in your not caring about the very things which you bring against me.

32 And now, Meletus, I adjure you to answer me another question: Which is better, to live among bad citizens, or among good ones? Answer, friend, I say; the question is one which may be easily answered. Do not the good do their neighbours good, and the bad do them evil?

33 Certainly.

34 And is there anyone who would rather be injured than benefited by those who live with him? Answer, my good friend, the law requires you to answer—does anyone like to be injured?

35 Certainly not.

36 And when you accuse me of corrupting and deteriorating the youth, do you allege that I corrupt them intentionally or unintentionally?

37 Intentionally, I say.

38 But you have just admitted that the good do their neighbours good, and the evil do them evil. Now, is that a truth which your superior wisdom has recognized thus early in life, and am I, at my age, in such darkness and ignorance as not to know that if a man with whom I have to live is corrupted by me, I am very likely to be harmed by him; and yet I corrupt him, and intentionally, too—so you say, although neither I nor any other human being is ever likely to be convinced by you. But either I do not corrupt them, or I corrupt them unintentionally; and on either view of the case you lie. If my offence is unintentional, the law has no cognizance of unintentional offences: you ought to have taken me privately, and warned and admonished me; for if I had had instruction, I should have left off doing what I only did unintentionally—beyond doubt I should; but you would have nothing to say to me and refused to teach me. And now you bring me up in this court, which is a place not of instruction, but of punishment.

39 It will be very clear to you, Athenians, as I was saying, that Meletus has never had any care, great or small, about the matter. But still I should like to know, Meletus, in what I am affirmed to corrupt the young. I suppose you mean, as I infer from your indictment, that I teach them not to acknowledge the gods which the state acknowledges, but some other new divinities or spiritual agencies in their stead. These are the lessons by which I corrupt the youth, as you say.

40 Yes, that I say emphatically.

41 Then, by the gods, Meletus, of whom we are speaking, tell me and the court, in somewhat plainer terms, what you mean! for I do not as yet understand whether you affirm that I teach other men to acknowledge some gods, and therefore that I do believe in gods, and am not an entire atheist—this you do not lay to my charge,—but only you say that they are not the same gods which the city recognizes—the charge is that they are different gods. Or, do you mean that I am an atheist simply, and a teacher of atheism?

42 I mean the latter—that you are a complete atheist.

43 What an extraordinary statement! Why do you think so, Meletus? Do you mean that I do not believe in the god-head of the sun or moon, like the rest of mankind?

44 I assure you, judges, that he does: for he says that the sun is stone, and the moon earth.

45 Friend Meletus, do you think that you are accusing Anaxagoras? Have you such a low opinion of the judges, that you fancy them so illiterate as not to know that these doctrines are found in the books of Anaxagoras the Clazomenian, which are full of them? And so, forsooth, the youth are said to be taught them by Socrates, when they can be bought in the book-market for one drachma at most; and they might pay their money, and laugh at Socrates if he pretends to father these extraordinary views. And so, Meletus, you really think that I do not believe in any god?

46 I swear by Zeus that you verily believe in none at all.

47 Nobody will believe you, Meletus, and I am pretty sure that you do not believe yourself. I cannot help thinking, men of Athens, that Meletus is reckless and impudent, and that he has brought this indictment in a spirit of mere wantonness and youthful bravado. Has he not compounded a riddle, thinking to try me? He said to himself:—I shall see whether the wise Socrates will discover my facetious self-contradiction, or whether I shall be able to deceive him and the rest of them. For he certainly does appear to me to contradict himself in the indictment as much as if he said that Socrates is guilty of not believing in the gods, and yet of believing in them—but this is not like a person who is in earnest.

48 I should like you, O men of Athens, to join me in examining what I conceive to be his inconsistency; and do you, Meletus, answer. And I must remind the audience of my request that they would not make a disturbance if I speak in my accustomed manner:

49 Did ever man, Meletus, believe in the existence of human things, and not of human beings? ... I wish, men of Athens, that he would answer, and not be always trying to get up an interruption. Did ever any man believe in horsemanship, and not in horses? or in flute-playing, and not in flute-players? My friend, no man ever did; I answer to you and to the court, as you refuse to answer for yourself. But now please to answer the next question: Can a man believe in the existence of things spiritual and divine, and not in spirits or demigods?

50 He cannot.

51 How lucky I am to have extracted that answer, by the assistance of the court! But then you swear in the indictment that I teach and believe in divine or spiritual things (new or old, no matter for that); at any rate, I believe in spiritual things,—so you say and swear in the affidavit; and yet if I believe in them, how can I help believing in spirits or demigods;—must I not? To be sure I must; your silence gives consent. Now what are spirits or demigods? are they not either gods or the sons of gods?

52 Certainly they are.

53 But this is what I call the facetious riddle invented by you: the demigods or spirits are gods, and you say first that I do not believe in gods, and then again that I do believe in gods; that is, if I believe in demigods. For if the demigods are the illegitimate sons of gods, whether by nymphs, or by other mothers, as some are said to be—what human being will ever believe that there are no gods when there are sons of gods? You might as well affirm the existence of mules, and deny that of horses and asses. Such nonsense, Meletus, could only have been intended by you to make trial of me. You have put this into the indictment because you could think of nothing real of which to accuse me. But no one who has a particle of understanding will ever be convinced by you that a man can believe in the existence of things divine and superhuman, and the same man refuse to believe in gods and demigods and heroes.

54 I have said enough in answer to the charge of Meletus: any elaborate defence is unnecessary. You know well the truth of my statement that I have incurred many violent enmities; and this is what will be my destruction if I am destroyed;—not Meletus, nor yet Anytus, but the envy and detraction of the world, which has been the death of many good men, and will probably be the death of many more; there is no danger of my being the last of them.

Analysis of the Topics in "Socrates' Apology"

Although only about half of Socrates' *Apology* is reproduced here, there is a fair enough sample for analysis of this classic example of judicial rhetoric. Judicial rhetoric is exercised most frequently in the courtroom, but this kind of persuasive discourse comprehends as well all extra-courtroom defenses of actions and character. If we understand the term *apologize* in its Greek sense of "to defend" and the term *categorize* in its Greek sense of "to accuse," we have two terms that most aptly describe the basic functions of judicial discourse. This term can comprehend works as various as Newman's *Apologia Pro Vita Sua*, Zola's *J'accuse*, Pope's *Epistle to Dr. Arbuthnot*, and the catalogue of charges against the king of England in the *Declaration of Independence*. If we are haled into court today we would probably entrust our defense to a lawyer. But there may be many occasions in life when we will be called upon to justify our conduct outside the courtroom.

Socrates' defense is a serious affair, for Socrates is liable to the death sentence if the jury returns a verdict of guilty. As every school child knows, Socrates lost his case and was made to drink the fatal "cup of hemlock." Almost everyone today who reads the *Apology* feels that Socrates had successfully answered the charges against him. The jury that heard Socrates' eloquent plea in the Athenian assembly was not more obtuse than modern readers; it happened that a number of extra-legal considerations played a part in their verdict. We will ignore here these extra-legal considerations that prejudiced the decision and concentrate on the speech itself.

As we have seen, the special topics that figure in judicial discourse are justice and injustice (or right and wrong, understood in their legal sense). In pursuing these special topics, the judicial speaker or writer is concerned primarily with one of these three questions: (1) whether the charge is so (*an sit*); (2) what the nature of the charge is (*quid sit*); (3) how serious the charge is (*quale sit*). In the course of a trial, the court may consider all three of these questions, but ultimately it must decide which one of these questions is at issue in a particular case. If *an sit* is the point at issue, evidence will be the main special topic; if *quid sit,* definition; if *quale sit,* motives or causes of action. In pursuit of the issue, the judicial pleader will pursue several of the common topics too. Let us see how the various topics operate in the *Apology.*

First of all, let us look at a general outline of the portion of the *Apology* that is reproduced here:

1. Socrates' introductory remarks to the assembly (paragraph 1).
2. *Narratio*—the statement of the charges (paragraph 2).
3. Refutation of the old charges (paragraphs 4–12).
4. Refutation of the recent charges—Socrates' cross-examination of Meletus (paragraphs 13–53).
5. Concluding remarks (paragraph 54).

In the opening paragraph, Socrates is setting the tone of the ethical appeal that he hopes his entire speech will exert. With typical ironic modesty, Socrates praises the eloquence of his accusers and depreciates his own skill as an orator. Lacking rhetorical skill, he will place his confidence in the justice of his cause, trusting that the recital of the truth and the whole truth will exonerate him. The reminder that he is seventy years old might be viewed as an emotional appeal for the sympathy or mercy of the court, but since Socrates nowhere else in the speech sounds this note, he seems to be reluctant to entrust his vindication to the emotional response of his hearers. Strategically, this avoidance of emotional appeal may have been a mistake, but distrust of emotion was typical of Socrates.

Resorting to the common topic of division in the second paragraph, Socrates divides the charges into two general classes, the ancient and the recent, and announces that he will answer the two groups of charges in turn. He does not specify the charges under these two general heads, being content here to indicate the general organization of his defense.

In paragraph 4 (after the transitional third paragraph) Socrates specifies the ancient charges. According to the "affidavit," he is charged with (1) being a student of natural philosophy; (2) making the worse appear the better cause; (3) being a teacher of these doctrines and taking money for his teaching. Pursuing the question of whether the first charge is true (*an sit*), Socrates denies the charge, maintaining that he has never engaged in speculations about physical matters. For confirmation of his claim, he calls for the testimony of those present. "Speak then," he says, "you who have heard me, and tell your neighbours whether any of you have ever known me hold forth in few words or in many upon such matters." This invitation meets with a stony silence from the audience. The implication of this silence is that there is no evidence to substantiate this ancient charge. It is simply not true. Since it is not true, Socrates does not have to go on to consider the nature of the offense and the seriousness of the offense.

Nor is there any evidence to substantiate the charge that he is a teacher and accepts money for his services. One wonders why no one in the assembly challenged Socrates' denial that he was a teacher. Socrates is certainly known to us, as he must have been to his contemporaries, as a teacher. Probably what is involved here is a matter of definition. What Socrates may be implying here—and he seems to be arguing this point in the next paragraph where he pursues the question of whether he is a wise man—is that technically he does not and cannot qualify as a teacher. After denying the charge, Socrates touches for a moment on the *quale sit* of the charge. Even if he were a qualified teacher who took money for his services, as do the sophists Gorgias and Prodicus and Hippias and Evenus, he would not consider this a crime. Resorting to analogy, Socrates reminds his audience that just as we would not consider it a crime if a trainer took a fee for improving foals or calves, so we should not consider it a crime if a teacher takes money for improving the minds of young people.

Socrates does not confront the charge that he makes the worse appear the better cause, but a denial of this charge seems to be implicit in his denial of the other two charges, and this charge is refuted really by some of the later arguments.

In paragraph 6, Socrates moves on to consider the reason why these false charges were levelled against him. Surely there must be some grounds for these charges. Their origin, Socrates thinks, lies in the pronouncement by the Delphic Oracle, "Socrates is the wisest man." When this Delphic pronouncement was reported to Socrates, he reasoned in the form of an enthymeme: "The god must be right, because a god cannot lie." But in what sense can the god be right in claiming that Socrates is the wisest of men?

In seeking an answer to this question, Socrates turns, in paragraph 7, to the common topic of definition. He recounts (in paragraphs 7, 8, 9) his experiences with politicians, poets, and artisans. He visited these men because they were supposedly wise and he wanted to find out why they were wise. But these so-called wise men disillusioned him. They were not really wise at all, and what was worse, they did not acknowledge or even recognize that they were ignorant. As a result of these inquiries, Socrates discovered the sense in which it could be said that he was the wisest of men: he alone knew that he did not know.

It is this rather paradoxical superiority that accounts for the animosity against Socrates. Moreover, the young people, who by nature relish the exposure of pretenders, began to imitate Socrates by examining charlatans. The pretenders to knowledge, disgruntled by their exposure, resorted to the standard but unproven charges made against all philosophers—that they teach things up in the clouds, that they have no gods, and that they make the worse appear the better cause. Prejudice, then, has motivated the wild, indiscriminate charges. Prejudice has prompted not only the old accusers but the recent accusers as well. Meletus is responding on behalf of the poets; Anytus, on behalf of the craftsmen and politicians; Lycon, on behalf of rhetoricians. Socrates concludes this part of his defense with an appeal to some rather dubious logic: "and what is their hatred but a proof that I am speaking the truth?" Socrates regards *hatred* as a sign. By the rules of strict logic, this sign cannot lead to an infallible conclusion. But the student may remember that Aristotle also recognized the effectiveness, for rhetorical purposes, of signs that lead only to probable conclusions. This kind of sign, as in the case of all probabilities, can produce only belief, not conviction.

In paragraph 12, Socrates specifies the charges made by the second group of accusers: (1) that I am a doer of evil; (2) that I corrupt the youth; (3) that I do not believe in the gods of the state; (4) that I set up other gods. Socrates reverses the first charge on Meletus; he will endeavor to show that it is *Meletus* who is the doer of evil, because he is not really serious about these matters. This reversing of the charge is a device recommended by all the classical rhetoricians. It puts the accuser on the defensive, and if the counter-charge can be substantiated, it takes the pressure off the defender.

In paragraphs 13–53, as we saw in the outline, Socrates cross-examines Meletus. Socrates shifts here from the discursive method of the early part of his defense to the question-and-answer style of dialectic. But although he has shifted his method, he does not abandon recourse to the special and common topics.

In paragraphs 18–38 of this section, Socrates examines the justice of the charge that he is a corrupter of the youth. At the outset of this cross-examination, Socrates resorts to the common topic of contraries. He says, in effect, "If I am a corrupter of youth, there must be some people whom Meletus regards as being improvers of youth." Who are these improvers of youth? Socrates gets Meletus to affirm that the judges, the audience, the senators, the members of the assembly—in fact, all Athenians except Socrates —improve the youth. Socrates proceeds to reduce this claim to absurdity by resorting to an analogy (the topic of similarity). Just as horses are improved, not by everyone but by the one person who is an excellent horse-trainer, so youth are improved not by the many but by the one. So Meletus' claim that Socrates alone corrupts the youth and that all others improve the youth is manifestly absurd. (Note that there is an implied *a fortiori* argument in Socrates' application of the analogy.)

In paragraphs 32–38, Socrates approaches the same charge from another tack. First of all, he prompts Meletus to agree to the truth of three propositions: (1) the good do good to their neighbors; the evil do evil; (2) everyone would rather be benefited than injured by another; (3) I corrupt the youth either intentionally or unintentionally. Having secured agreement on these three propositions, Socrates uses the third of them as the starting point of his refutation. As we saw in the exposition of contradiction under the common topic of comparison, contradictory propositions are incompatible—that is, they cannot both be true. And we saw also that if one proposition is proved to be false, the other is automatically true. Socrates' strategy is to show that the proposition "Socrates corrupts the youth intentionally" is false. Note how cleverly he makes use of the other two propositions that Meletus has agreed to:

> But how could I corrupt the youth intentionally? If I corrupt them, they become evil. Once they become evil, they are liable to harm me (because, as we agreed, the evil do evil). But since I—like everyone else—would rather be benefited than injured by my neighbor, it is not likely that I would intentionally produce the kind of person who would injure me. So we can dismiss the charge that I corrupt the youth intentionally.

The argument has been reduced now to two possibilities (and we can regard these as contraries): either I do not corrupt the youth, or I corrupt them *un*intentionally. Socrates now deals with these contraries in this fashion:

> Let's arbitrarily rule out the first possibility, since you have formally accused me of corrupting the youth. That leaves us with the possibility that I corrupt the youth unintentionally. But if I corrupt the youth *un*intentionally, I am not subject to the law, and I should not be in this courtroom at all.

By demonstrating the absurdity of Meletus' charge, Socrates has been indirectly proving what he said he would prove: that Meletus could not have made these charges seriously and that therefore he is the real doer of evil.

In paragraphs 39-53, Socrates demonstrates the inconsistency of the charge that he is an atheist. He detects in items 3 and 4 of this indictment a flagrant contradiction: item 3 claims that he does not believe in the gods; item 4 implies that he does believe in the gods. To prove that item 3 is untrue, Socrates makes use of the common topics of similarity and genus and species. He gets Meletus to admit that one cannot believe in humanity without believing in human beings, in horsemanship without believing in horses, in flute-playing without believing in flute-players; in other words, one cannot believe in the genus without believing in the species. Similarly, one cannot believe in divine agencies (as item 4 claims) without believing in spirits and demi-gods. So the charge that Socrates does not believe in the gods is utterly false. By the principle of contradiction, if one proposition in a contradictory opposition is false, the other proposition is true. Therefore Socrates *does* believe in the gods.

In paragraph 54, the last paragraph in the selection reproduced here, Socrates points out that he has successfully answered the charges levelled by Meletus and Anytus. He recognizes, however, that during his lifetime he has incurred the enmity of many people and that it is this enmity, rather than the indictments, that will eventually prove to be his undoing. Throughout this half of the *Apology*, Socrates has employed a negative strategy—the strategy of refutation—but from this point on Socrates will be advancing positive arguments for his innocence.

It might be pointed out finally that a great part of Socrates' strategy throughout this section was an effort to minimize Meletus' ethical appeal. At the same time that he is refuting Meletus' charges he is showing indirectly that Meletus is not a man of good sense, good character, and good will. Meletus' ethical appeal is further diminished by his frequent reluctance to answer Socrates' pointed questions. The crowning touch was the incremental irony of Socrates' repeated reference to Meletus as "my friend"—an irony that becomes as damaging as Mark Antony's use of the epithet "honorable men" in the famous "Friends, Romans, countrymen" speech in Shakespeare's *Julius Caesar*.

Obituary for Katharine Sergeant White

As we saw earlier, epideictic or ceremonial discourse concentrates on praising or blaming some person or group of people or institution or situation. Some of the common forms of this kind of discourse are funeral orations, apologias that people offer in defense of their conduct, graduation speeches, orations delivered on national holidays, and keynote speeches at nominating conventions. But next to the sermons delivered at funerals, perhaps the commonest form of ceremonial discourse in our society is the obituary that appears in local newspapers about prominent people. The following obituary appeared in The New Yorker *about a remarkable woman who was involved in the operations of that famous magazine from the first year of its founding. It will be analyzed for the rhetorical topics that yielded the "praise" that permeates this piece of discourse.*

1 For many of us, Katharine White was a monumental presence in the world. She was changeless amid change. She was a figure of order, composure, certainty, permanence. She was always there. Then, last week, the

event that we chose not to foresee took place: at the age of eighty-four, she died. Katharine White, as Mrs. Ernest Angell, came to work for *The New Yorker* in 1925, six months after the magazine was founded by Harold Ross. She started out as a manuscript reader, but she quickly became involved in everything else that went on in our office. Ross seized upon her intelligence, her energy, her aristocratic taste, her air of authority, and her awesome strength of character, and put them to work in the service of his young magazine. Within the routine chaos of a publication struggling to find itself, she had a stabilizing influence. Possessing an aesthetic of her own and some firm literary standards and judgments, she extended the range of Ross's ideas and interests by another full spectrum. When Ross knew what he wanted and didn't know how to get it, he began turning to Katharine. When he didn't know quite what he wanted, he turned to her to find out what it was. When he was unsure of himself, he was sure of her. Before long, she was his most valued collaborator. More than any other editor except Harold Ross himself, Katharine White gave *The New Yorker* its shape, and set it on its course.

2   As the years passed and the workings of the magazine grew more complicated and more compartmentalized, Mrs. White became the head of the Fiction Department, and she remained its head for about ten years, until she made an attempt to retire to a farm in North Brooklin, Maine, with her husband, Andy (E. B.) White. There, as a half-time editor, she continued to do considerably more than a normal full-time job. In the late nineteen-fifties, to meet an emergency, she came back to the city to put in two more years as Fiction Editor, and then she resumed her strenuous semi-retirement in Maine.

3   Katharine White's qualities as an editor were without parallel. She gave to every writer she worked with a seemingly limitless amount of attention. It was as if there were no other writers. Yet there were scores of writers, and she managed to devote herself to all of them. She talked with them for hours at a time, and carried on a prodigious correspondence with them. She took a genuine, nonprofessional interest in their personal lives; she encouraged them endlessly, reassured them, comforted them, counselled them, mothered them. She sent off hundreds of letters and notes to writers simply urging them to write, and they did. The history of American fiction in the last fifty years would not have been the same without Katharine White. Her standards and her taste had much to do with it, but there was something else. She had a mysterious ability to touch off the literary impulse, and could draw work even out of writers who were languishing or

thought they had run dry. No one can estimate how much good writing might have been less good if it had not been for Katharine White, or how much writing would not have been done at all if she had not been waiting, at her desk, to receive it. For many writers, she was the only muse they needed.

4   A calm, reserved, majestic, beautiful woman (as beautiful in her eighties as she was in her thirties), Katharine walked into her editorial career at *The New Yorker* as though that alone were what she was destined to do, and then, as though it were equally in the nature of things, she married the quintessential *New Yorker* writer. Somewhere along the line she found it possible to contribute to the magazine a definitive series of essays on children's books and, later, a series of erudite, poetic, humorous, ardent essays on gardening. In the last twenty years of her life, she had more than one person's share of illness—her afflictions crowded in on her without interruption, and three or four at a time—but she also had more than one person's share of courage, and she prevailed. Concentrating against pain, she wrote marvellously of the flower gardens she still tended, the gardens she remembered, and the gardens of her imagination. And she wrote letters. She was a torrential letter writer up to the last. Her letters to her friends, among them the writers who had worked with her, were long: page upon page filled with inquiries, thoughts, information—details, invariably fascinating, of the daily life she shared with Andy, and bulletins on the many other lives she kept track of. Her bits of domestic news were gifts to her friends, scattered about with a prodigal hand. The day before she died, she received a letter from one of the magazine's contributors saying, "To have your affectionate and warm letter made me feel nurtured as you did indeed always nurture me." A host of writers might have said the same.

5   Katharine White's loyalties were numerous, intense, and fixed: Brookline, Massachusetts, where she was raised; *St. Nicholas* magazine, to which she contributed as a child; Bryn Mawr, from which she graduated; the city of New York, no matter what happened to it; the state of Maine; the Boston Red Sox; her flowers; *The New Yorker* itself; her colleagues at the magazine; every writer she ever worked with; her adored Andy; her children, grandchildren, great-grandchildren, friends, neighbors; and the written word—particularly the word as written by E. B. White and by her son Roger Angell. It is E. B. White who, in an interview in the *Paris Review,* has described better than anyone else could what Katharine was like when she was in full editorial flight:

6   "She was one of the first editors to be hired, and I can't imagine what would have happened to the magazine if she hadn't turned up. . . . Katharine was soon sitting in on art sessions and planning sessions, editing fiction and poetry, cheering and steering authors and artists along the paths

they were eager to follow, learning makeup, learning pencil editing, heading the Fiction Department, sharing the personal woes and dilemmas of innumerable contributors and staff people who were in trouble or despair, and, in short, accepting the whole unruly business of a tottering magazine with the warmth and dedication of a broody hen. I had a bird's-eye view of all this because, in the midst of it, I became her husband. During the day, I saw her in operation at the office. At the end of the day, I watched her bring the whole mess home with her in a cheap and bulging portfolio. The light burned late, our bed was lumpy with page proofs, and our home was alive with laughter and the pervasive spirit of her dedication and her industry."

An Analysis of the Topics in Katharine Sergeant White's Obituary

The obituary is one of the commonest forms of ceremonial rhetoric. Even the most obscure citizens get a few lines of obituary in the local newspaper if their families pay to have the notice published. Prominent public figures, of course, have lengthy obituaries published about them in national magazines and in prestigious newspapers outside the city in which they lived and died. Katharine White's obituary was published in *The New Yorker,* the national magazine for which she worked for many years.

The death of loved ones, of prominent figures, of national heroes, invariably calls forth generous tributes, heartfelt sentiments, and noble resolutions. This most emotional of all human events usually manages to escape the blight of sentimentality, probably because we, the survivors, feel that no expression of sentiment, however extravagant, can be in excess of the occasion that prompts it. There is a chance, however, that when time removes us from emotional involvement with the occasion and the deceased, elegies will strike us as being maudlin. It is the perspective of time that separates the deathless prose from the perishable verbiage. Lincoln's *Gettysburg Address* and Pericles's *Funeral Oration,* two of the classic examples of epideictic utterance about soldiers from "our side" who died in battle, impress us as being as eloquent and genuine now as they were the day they were delivered from the podium.

The obituary for Katharine Sergeant White was written by an anonymous editor of the magazine, probably an editor who knew her for a long period of time. What this writer chooses to say in praise of the deceased represents his or her view about those facts and opinions that are likely to throw the most favorable light upon the deceased person's life and character. Each obituary-writer would probably choose some things to say about the deceased that others did not mention, but many things—especially the facts about a person's public career—would be mentioned in all the obituaries.

This obituary seems to be equally divided between details of Katharine White's professional career and her private life. It might be outlined in this fashion:

1. Her professional career (paragraphs 1-3)
   A. Her longtime connection with *The New Yorker* (paragraphs 1-2)
   B. Her merits as an editor (paragraph 3)
2. Her private life (paragraphs 4-6)
   A. Her domestic life (paragraph 4)
   B. Her many loyalties (paragraph 5)
   C. Testimony of her husband (paragraph 6)

The common topic that yields most of the material for obituaries is Testimony—matters of public record and the opinions and assessments of those who knew the person intimately. Most of the material in this obituary, too, comes from Testimony—testimony dealing with "facts" about her editorial career, her marriage, her writings, her loyalties, her birthplace, education, and residencies. The assessment of her career and her life comes largely from the Testimonial about her by the obituary-writer, but there is also the Testimonial of the author who wrote her shortly before her death (paragraph 4) and, in the last paragraph, the Testimonial of her husband, E. B. White.

The common topic of Comparison appears at least twice, yielding Differences of Degree: "More than any other editor except Harold Ross himself . . ." (paragraph 1) and "Katharine White's qualities as an editor were without parallel" (paragraph 2). The common topic of Cause and Effect figures in the discussion of the influence that her industrious nurturing of writers had on the course of writing in this country: "No one can estimate how much good writing might have been less good if it had not been for Katharine White" (paragraph 3) and "The history of American fiction in the last fifty years would not have been the same without Katharine White" (paragraph 3). The whole of the first paragraph might be regarded as a Definition of her role in the fortunes of the magazine.

But as usually happens in ceremonial discourse, the Special Topics have yielded a great deal of the substance of this obituary—the particular virtues, attributes, and achievements of the subject of this tribute. We might review, first of all, the particular virtues that the writer stresses about Katharine White. In paragraph 4, the writer mentions her extraordinary *courage* or *fortitude* in the face of protracted illness and pain. One of the pervasive notes in the tribute is the insistence on her *liberality* or *generosity* in expending time and effort to nurture writers and to write long letters to friends (paragraphs 3 and 4). Paragraph 1 emphasizes her *prudence,* that intellectual virtue of intelligence and taste, which made her such a valuable advisor and collaborator of Harold Ross, the founding editor of the magazine. There is a hint of her *gentleness* or *kindness* in the mention of two of her avocations: writing children's books and tending her flower gardens (paragraph 4). The note about her unswerving loyalty runs all through the obituary and comes to a crescendo in paragraph 5, where her many and varied loyalties are listed.

The designation of a number of her personal traits and achievements adds to the picture of her as a person. At least in a general way, we are given a picture of her physical bearing: "her air of authority" (paragraph 1); "a calm, reserved, majestic, beautiful woman (as beautiful in her eighties as she was in her thirties)" (paragraph 4). A number of detatils about her family background, education, domestic life, and friends are given: raised in Brookline, Massachusetts; educated at Bryn Mawr; her legion of friends; her marriage to "the quintessential *New Yorker* writer," E. B. White; mother of the noted sportswriter Roger Angell; her retirement in Maine; her devotion to flower-gardening. Besides her extraordinary achievement in shaping *The New Yorker* and fostering scores of writers, she published definitive essays on children's books and on gardening. If we were looking for passages that summed up her life and her character, we would find them in a sentence in the first paragraph ("She was a figure of order, composure, certainty, permanence") and in the final phrase of her husband's testimonial in the final paragraph ("the pervasive spirit of her dedication and her industry").

In the section on "Special Topics for Ceremonial Discourse," we saw the formulas that Aristotle proposed for heightening the effects of praise. The writer of this obituary has used at least three of those formulas: "Show that a person has done something *better* than anyone else" (next to Harold Ross himself, she did more to shape the magazine than anyone else; her qualities as an editor were beyond parallel); "Show that a person has *often* achieved the same success" (her ten-year success as fiction editor for the magazine, with a two-year additional stint after her retirement); "Show the *circumstances* under which a person accomplished something" (her faithful performance of her duties despite the pain of her illnesses during the last twenty years of her life).

This obituary exemplifies how one proceeds when one seeks to praise someone. One mentions or expatiates on those virtues, attributes, deeds, achievements, testimonies that reflect credit on the person being extolled. The same basic strategy is used when one seeks to discredit someone—although either because of considerations of charity or the sanctions of libel laws, we seldom see public displays of vilification of an individual. Satirists are more likely to paint unflattering pictures of *types* of people rather than of a particular individual or to disguise the target of the attack under a fictitious name. In ceremonial discourse, perhaps more than in the other two kinds, the nature of the subject will be the major factor determining what can be said, for the success of this kind of discourse depends mainly on the truth or credibility of what is said. Praise based upon fabricated or exaggerated details about a person's life and character will ultimately prove to be unconvincing.

James Madison: The Federalist, No. 10

On September 17, 1787, the Constitution of the United States was finally drafted and signed by the fifty-some members of the Constitutional Convention in Philadelphia. The newly drafted Constitution, however, still had to be ratified by the state conventions of at least nine of the original thirteen colonies. We who take our Constitution so much for granted find it difficult to believe that this incomparable document had to be "sold" to the people of the new confederacy of states. But the anti-Federalists soon marshalled their forces to defeat the ratification of the Constitution. They argued that the strong central government established by the Constitution was a threat to the autonomy of the states, that the Constitution gave too much power to the Chief Executive, that it instituted a dangerous system of federal courts, and that it opened the way to oppressive taxation. Five of the small states, however, quickly ratified the Constitution—Delaware, Maryland, New Jersey, Connecticut, and South Carolina. The most formidable opposition came from Pennsylvania, Massachusetts, Virginia, and New York. Because New York was a key state in the opposition, Alexander Hamilton, only thirty years old at the time, conceived the idea of publishing a series of articles refuting the objections to the Constitution and extolling its virtues, and he enlisted the help of James Madison of Virginia and John Jay of New York. In a series of eighty-five articles, published in various New York newspapers from October 1787 to April 1788, Publius—the pseudonym adopted for all the papers —exercised all the rhetorical skill at his command to persuade the New York convention to adopt the Constitution. James Madison, who wrote only about a third of the Federalist Papers (Jay wrote only five), was the author of No. 10, which appeared in the New York Packet *on Friday, November 23, 1787. It epitomizes the clear, eloquent style and the compelling logic with which Hamilton, Madison, and Jay argued their case. New York's eventual ratification by a narrow margin was inconsequential, because by that time the necessary nine states had adopted the Constitution. In the article that immediately follows "Federalist, No. 10," Mark Ashin provides a thoroughgoing topical analysis of Madison's argument.*

1 Among the numerous advantages promised by a well-constructed Union, none deserves to be more accurately developed than its tendency to break and control the violence of faction. The friend of popular governments never finds himself so much alarmed for their character and fate, as when he contemplates their propensity to this dangerous vice. He will not fail, therefore, to set a due value on any plan which, without violating the principles to which he is attached, provides a proper cure for it. The instability, injustice, and confusion introduced into the public councils, have, in truth, been the mortal diseases under which popular governments have everywhere perished; as they continue to be the favorite and fruitful topics from which the adversaries to liberty derive their most specious declamations. The valuable improvements made by the constitutions on the popular models, both ancient and modern, cannot certainly be too much admired; but it would be an unwarrantable partiality to contend that they have as effectually obviated the danger on this side, as was wished and expected. Complaints are everywhere heard from our most considerate and virtuous citizens, equally the friends of public and private faith, and of public and personal liberty, that our governments are too unstable, that the public good is disregarded in the conflicts of rival parties, and that measures are too often decided, not according to the rules of justice and the rights of the minor party, but by the superior force of an interested and overbearing majority. However anxiously we may wish that these complaints had no foundation, the evidence of known facts will not permit us to deny that they are in some degree true. It will be found, indeed, on a candid review of our situation, that some of the distresses under which we labor have been erroneously charged on the operations of our governments; but it will be found, at the same time, that other causes will not alone account for many of our heaviest misfortunes; and, particularly, for that prevailing and increasing distrust of public engagements and alarm for private rights, which are echoed from one end of the continent to the other. These must be chiefly, if not wholly, effects of the unsteadiness and injustice with which a factious spirit has tainted our public administrations.

2 By a faction, I understand a number of citizens, whether amounting to a majority or minority of the whole, who are united and actuated by some common impulse of passion, or of interest, adverse to the rights of other citizens or to the permanent and aggregate interests of the community.

3 There are two methods of curing the mischiefs of faction: the one, by removing its causes; the other, by controlling its effects.

4 There are again two methods of removing the causes of faction: the one, by destroying the liberty which is essential to its existence; the other, by giving to every citizen the same opinions, the same passions, and the same interests.

5 It could never be more truly said than of the first remedy, that it was worse than the disease. Liberty is to faction what air is to fire, an aliment without which it instantly expires. But it could not be less folly to abolish liberty, which is essential to political life, because it nourishes faction, than it would be to wish the annihilation of air, which is essential to animal life, because it imparts to fire its destructive agency.

6 The second expedient is as impracticable as the first would be unwise. As long as the reason of man continues fallible, and he is at liberty to exercise it, different opinions will be formed. As long as the connection subsists between his reason and his self-love, his opinions and his passions will have a reciprocal influence on each other; and the former will be objects to which the latter will attach themselves. The diversity in the faculties of men, from which the rights of property originate, is not less an insuperable obstacle to a uniformity of interests. The protection of these faculties is the first object of government. From the protection of different and unequal faculties of acquiring property, the possession of different degrees and kinds of property immediately results; and from the influence of these on the sentiments and views of the respective proprietors, ensues a division of the society into different interests and parties.

7 The latent causes of faction are thus sown in the nature of man; and we see them everywhere brought into different degrees of activity, according to the different circumstances of civil society. A zeal for different opinions concerning religion, concerning government, and many other points, as well of speculation as of practice; an attachment to different leaders ambitiously contending for pre-eminence and power; or to persons of other descriptions whose fortunes have been interesting to the human passions, have, in turn, divided mankind into parties, inflamed them with mutual animosity, and rendered them much more disposed to vex and oppress each other than to cooperate for their own common good. So strong is this propensity of mankind to fall into mutual animosities, that where no substantial occasion presents itself, the most frivolous and fanciful distinctions have been sufficient to kindle their unfriendly passions and excite their most violent conflicts. But the most common and durable source of factions has been the various and unequal distribution of property. Those who hold and those who are without property have ever formed distinct interests in society. Those who are creditors and those who are debtors fall under a like discrimination. A landed interest, a manufacturing interest, a mercantile interest, a moneyed interest, with many lesser interests, grow up of necessity in civilized nations, and divide them into different classes, actuated by different sentiments and views. The regulation of these various and interfering interests forms the principal task of modern legislation and involves the spirit of party and faction in the necessary and ordinary operations of the government.

8 No man is allowed to be a judge in his own cause, because his interest

would certainly bias his judgment, and, not improbably, corrupt his integrity. With equal, nay with greater reason, a body of men are unfit to be both judges and parties at the same time; yet what are many of the most important acts of legislation, but so many judicial determinations, not indeed concerning the rights of single persons, but concerning the rights of large bodies of citizens? And what are the different classes of legislators but advocates and parties to the causes which they determine? Is a law proposed concerning private debts? It is a question to which the creditors are parties on one side and the debtors on the other. Justice ought to hold the balance between them. Yet the parties are, and must be, themselves the judges; and the most numerous party, or, in other words, the most powerful faction must be expected to prevail. Shall domestic manufactures be encouraged, and in what degree, by restrictions on foreign manufactures? are questions which would be differently decided by the landed and the manufacturing classes, and probably by neither with a sole regard to justice and the public good. The apportionment of taxes on the various descriptions of property is an act which seems to require the most exact impartiality; yet there is, perhaps, no legislative act in which greater opportunity and temptation are given to a predominant party to trample on the rules of justice. Every shilling with which they overburden the inferior number, is a shilling saved to their own pockets.

9 It is in vain to say that enlightened statesmen will be able to adjust these clashing interests and render them all subservient to the public good. Enlightened statesmen will not always be at the helm. Nor, in many cases, can such an adjustment be made at all without taking into view indirect and remote considerations, which will rarely prevail over the immediate interest which one party may find in disregarding the rights of another or the good of the whole.

10 The inference to which we are brought is that the *causes* of faction cannot be removed and that relief is only to be sought in the means of controlling its *effects*.

11 If a faction consists of less than a majority, relief is supplied by the republican principle, which enables the majority to defeat its sinister views by regular vote. It may clog the administration, it may convulse the society; but it will be unable to execute and mask its violence under the forms of the Constitution. When a majority is included in a faction, the form of popular government, on the other hand, enables it to sacrifice to its ruling passion or interest both the public good and the rights of other citizens. To secure the public good and private rights against the danger of such a faction, and at the same time to preserve the spirit and the form of popular government, is then the great object to which our inquiries are directed. Let me add that it is the great desideratum by which this form of government can be rescued

from the opprobrium under which it has so long labored, and be recommended to the esteem and adoption of mankind.

12 By what means is this object attainable? Evidently by one of two only. Either the existence of the same passion or interest in a majority at the same time must be prevented, or the majority, having such coexistent passion or interest, must be rendered, by their number and local situation, unable to concert and carry into effect schemes of oppression. If the impulse and the opportunity be suffered to coincide, we well know that neither moral nor religious motives can be relied on as an adequate control. They are not found to be such on the injustice and violence of individuals, and lose their efficacy in proportion to the number combined together, that is, in proportion as their efficacy becomes needful.

13 From this view of the subject it may be concluded that a pure democracy, by which I mean a society consisting of a small number of citizens, who assemble and administer the government in person, can admit of no cure for the mischiefs of faction. A common passion or interest will, in almost every case, be felt by a majority of the whole; a communication and concert result from the form of government itself; and there is nothing to check the inducements to sacrifice the weaker party or an obnoxious individual. Hence it is that such democracies have ever been spectacles of turbulence and contention; have ever been found incompatible with personal security or the rights of property; and have in general been as short in their lives as they have been violent in their deaths. Theoretic politicians, who have patronized this species of government, have erroneously supposed that by reducing mankind to a perfect equality in their political rights, they would, at the same time, be perfectly equalized and assimilated in their possessions, their opinions, and their passions.

14 A republic, by which I mean a government in which the scheme of representation takes place, opens a different prospect and promises the cure for which we are seeking. Let us examine the points in which it varies from pure democracy, and we shall comprehend both the nature of the cure and the efficacy which it must derive from the Union.

15 The two great points of difference between a democracy and a republic are: first, the delegation of the government, in the latter, to a small number of citizens elected by the rest; secondly, the greater number of citizens, and greater sphere of country, over which the latter may be extended.

16 The effect of the first difference is, on the one hand, to refine and enlarge the public views, by passing them through the medium of a chosen body of citizens, whose wisdom may best discern the true interest of their country, and whose patriotism and love of justice will be least likely to sacrifice it to temporary or partial considerations. Under such a regulation, it may well happen that the public voice, pronounced by the representatives of the people, will be more consonant to the public good than if pronounced by the people themselves, convened for the purpose. On the other hand, the effect may be inverted. Men of factious tempers, of local prejudices, or of sinister designs, may, by intrigue, by corruption, or by other means, first obtain the suffrages, and then betray the interests, of the people. The question resulting is, whether small or extensive republics are more favorable to the election of proper guardians of the public weal; and it is clearly decided in favor of the latter by two obvious considerations:

17 In the first place, it is to be remarked that, however large it may be, they must be limited to a certain number, in order to guard against the confusion of a multitude. Hence, the number of representatives in the two cases not being in proportion to that of the two constituents and being proportionally greater in the small republic, it follows that, if the proportion of fit characters be not less in the large than in the small republic, the former will present a greater option, and consequently a greater probability of a fit choice.

18 In the next place, as each representative will be chosen by a greater number of citizens in the large than in the small republic, it will be more difficult for unworthy candidates to practice with success the vicious arts by which elections are too often carried; and the suffrages of the people being more free, will be more likely to center in men who possess the most attractive merit and the most diffusive and established characters.

19 It must be confessed that in this, as in most other cases, there is a mean, on both sides of which inconveniences will be found to lie. By enlarging too much the number of electors, you render the representative too little acquainted with all their local circumstances and lesser interests; as by reducing it too much, you render him unduly attached to these and too little fit to comprehend and pursue great national objects. The federal Constitution forms a happy combination in this respect; the great and aggregate interests being referred to the national, the local and particular to the State legislatures.

20 The other point of difference is the greater number of citizens and extent of territory which may be brought within the compass of republican than of democratic government; and it is this circumstance principally which renders factious combinations less to be dreaded in the former than in the latter. The smaller the society, the fewer probably will be the distinct parties and interests composing it; the fewer the distinct parties and interests, the more frequently will a majority be found of the same party; and the smaller the number of individuals composing a majority, and the smaller the compass within which they are placed, the more easily will they concert and execute their plans of oppression. Extend the sphere, and you take in a greater variety of parties and interests; you make it less probable that a majority of the whole will have a common motive to invade the rights of other citizens; or if such a common motive exists, it will be more difficult for all who feel

it to discover their own strength and to act in unison with each other. Besides other impediments, it may be remarked that, where there is a consciousness of unjust or dishonorable purposes, communication is always checked by distrust in proportion to the number whose concurrence is necessary.

21 Hence, it clearly appears, that the same advantage which a republic has over a democracy in controlling the effects of faction is enjoyed by a large over a small republic—is enjoyed by the Union over the States composing it. Does the advantage consist in the substitution of representatives whose enlightened views and virtuous sentiments render them superior to local prejudices and to schemes of injustice? It will not be denied that the representation of the Union will be most likely to possess these requisite endowments. Does it consist in the greater security afforded by a greater variety of parties, against the event of any one party being able to outnumber and oppress the rest? In an equal degree does the increased variety of parties comprised within the Union increase this security. Does it, in fine, consist in the greater obstacles opposed to the concert and accomplishment of the secret wishes of an unjust and interested majority? Here, again, the extent of the Union gives it the most palpable advantage.

22 The influence of factious leaders may kindle a flame within their particular States, but will be unable to spread a general conflagration through the other States. A religious sect may degenerate into a political faction in a part of the Confederacy; but the variety of sects dispersed over the entire face of it must secure the national councils against any danger from that source. A rage for paper money, for an abolition of debts, for an equal division of property, or for any other improper or wicked project, will be less apt to pervade the whole body of the Union than a particular member of it; in the same proportion as such a malady is more likely to taint a particular country or district than an entire State.

23 In the extent and proper structure of the Union, therefore, we behold a republican remedy for the diseases most incident to republican government. And according to the degree of pleasure and pride we feel in being republicans, ought to be our zeal in cherishing the spirit and supporting the character of Federalists.

PUBLIUS (1787)

Mark Ashin: The Argument of Madison's "Federalist," No. 10"

In the January issue of *College English,* some members of the English staff at the College of the University of Chicago questioned the value of trying to teach argument in a writing course by concentrating exclusively on the technique of formal logic. Their contention was that, while training in the inductive and deductive forms of logic would enable a student to judge the validity of arguments already constructed, such training does little or nothing to supply the young student's greatest need, some technique for discovering the material which makes up an argument. After an analysis of this problem, they recommended the introduction into courses in argument of an up-to-date system of rhetoric based upon what the classical rhetoricians called "the Topics," a term which can be translated as "the sources from which arguments are drawn." The four sources of argument which they described in detail and which the English staff at the College has tested in practice are the ideas of Genus or Definition, Consequence, Likeness and Difference, and Authority. Readers interested in the theory underlying this point of view are referred to the article in question.[1] However, even those who may be convinced that this new attack on the problem of teaching argument sounds promising in the abstract will certainly have many questions about how this rhetorical approach operates in the classroom. It is the aim of the present article to satisfy this curiosity, at least in part, by applying "topical" considerations to the analysis and interpretation of a classroom text, a recognized masterpiece of polemics, Madison's *Federalist*, No. 10.

This particular *Federalist* paper, on the control of faction in popular governments, has long since achieved political immortality as a classic defense of the theory of republicanism. Its usefulness as an instrument in teaching has been equally well demonstrated. It has been a required reading in civics and social science courses to give students an understanding of the theoretical bases of our Constitution. It has served the teacher of logic and argument as a cogent example of the controlling power of syllogistic reasoning. Practically every text in the social and intellectual history of the United States singles it out to illustrate the Federalist position during the political controversy surrounding the adoption of the Constitution. Even Vernon L. Parrington, whose great book is a crusade against Federalist conservatism, paid tribute to it as a worthy enemy by calling it "the remarkable tenth number, which compresses within a few pages pretty much the whole Federalist theory of political science." There is no denying that much can be and has been done with conventional modes of logical analysis to reveal the effectiveness of Madison's reasoning, since the essay is practically made-to-order as a sample of the syllogism in operation. However, I believe that to supplement a formal analysis with a consideration of the main sources from which the author draws the material for his arguments can immeasurably enrich the English teacher's handling of deduction, since it can present, on a level understand-

[1] Bilsky, Hazlett, Streeter, and Weaver, "Looking for an Argument," *College English,* XIV (January, 1953), 210–16. Copyright 1953 by the National Council of Teachers of English. Reprinted with permission.

able to all, the characteristic operation of Madison's mind as he proceeds with his demonstrations.

As will be seen, the major sources of argument for Madison are *definitions* and *consequences*. In any considered statement of political theory, careful definitions of key terms, used both as starting points (see the definition of "faction" in paragraph 2) and as stages in the argument (see the implied definition of "man" in paragraph 6), are required to clarify a position. In addition, to induce an audience to accept a recommended course of action, no more compelling motive can be invented than one which argues for the good consequences which will necessarily follow the adoption of your proposal and the evil consequences which will follow the adoption of any other.

The problem with which Madison was concerned and the direction of his reasoning are indicated in his opening sentences:

> Among the numerous advantages promised by a well constructed Union, none deserves to be more accurately developed than its tendency to break and control the violence of faction. The friend of popular governments never finds himself so much alarmed for their character and fate, as when he contemplates their propensity to this dangerous vice. He will not fail, therefore, to set a due value on any plan which, without violating the principles to which he is attached, provides a proper cure for it.

However, the explicit statement of his aim is reserved for paragraph 11, after he has disposed of the visionary thesis that the causes of faction can be removed, and has turned to the practical task of describing how to control its effects. First indicating that a majority rather than a minority faction is the main danger in popular government, he states:

> To secure the public good and private rights against the danger of such a faction, and at the same time to preserve the spirit and the form of popular government, is then the great object to which our inquiries are directed.

Madison thus sets himself the task of arguing for a particular design of government which will provide a "republican remedy" for the factional disturbances fostered by popular government, while, at the same time, preserving the spirit and the form of popular government. From a point high on the ladder of abstraction, this aim seems an impossible one, since it appears to call for the elimination of an effect while preserving the cause which leads to that effect. The very nature of this aim demands the careful discrimination of causes and effects which is characteristic of Madison's argument.

The formal pattern of Madison's logic is a series of "either-or" syllogisms, which, by eliminating the rejected alternatives, progressively narrow the inquiry down to the particular conclusion that a federal republic, such as that outlined in the proposed Constitution, can best control the effects of faction. In his first paragraph he presents a convincing rhetorical justification for his concern with the dangers of faction. From what general field of consideration of source of argument could he best derive the details which would make his readers equally concerned? The experiences of six years of government under the Articles of Confederation—experiences shared intimately and grievously by most of his audience—could be generalized into a statement of the *consequences* [2] which result from the operation of factions in an environment of freedom. So the indictment begins. Popular governments reveal a propensity to "this dangerous vice," factions. Once in existence, factions lead directly to instability, injustice, and confusion in the public councils. These, in turn, lead ultimately to the death of popular governments, "as they continue to be the favorite and fruitful topics [3] from which the adversaries to liberty derive their most specious declamation." Even though the various state constitutions of America are an improvement over popular models of the ancient and modern world, they have neither prevented the rise, nor effectively controlled the spread, of factional conflicts in the form of rival parties.

It is important to note that, in his introductory paragraph, Madison sets up the basic dichotomy which operates throughout his entire argument. The opposing terms are "justice," "the public good," and "minority rights," on the one hand, and, on the other, "majority faction."

> Complaints are everywhere heard from our most considerate and virtuous citizens, equally the friends of public and private faith, and of public and personal liberty, that our governments are too unstable, that the public good is disregarded in the conflicts of rival parties, and that measures are too often decided, not according to the rules of justice and the rights of the minor party, but by the superior force of an interested and overbearing majority.

The same dichotomy underlies the controlling *definition* of faction in paragraph 2:

> By a faction, I understand a number of citizens, whether amounting to a majority or minority of the whole, who are united and actuated by

[2] The terms "definition," "consequences," "likeness-difference," and "testimony-authority" have been italicized to call attention to Madison's uses of the sources of argument.
[3] Madison's use of the term "topics" in this quotation is in the same classical tradition which motivates the present article. "Instability," "injustice," and "confusion" are simply particularized *consequences* of faction in popular governments.

some common impulse of passion, or of interest, adverse to the rights of other citizens, or to the permanent and aggregate interests of the community.

Having demonstrated the disastrous consequences of faction in popular government and having defined his key term, Madison can proceed, in paragraph 3, to the logical development of his argument. The alternative syllogism set up there controls the movement of thought in the rest of the essay. "There are two methods of curing the mischiefs of faction: the one, by removing its causes; the other, by controlling its effects." This gives us a syllogism with the following form:

Either A [*we can remove causes*] or B [*we can control effects*].

The minor premise, which is developed in the first half of Madison's argument [paragraphs 3–10], is that we cannot remove the causes of faction, since they are grounded in the nature of man:

Not A [*we cannot remove causes*].

It follows that we must devote our efforts to controlling the effects:

Therefore, B [*we can control effects*].

An analysis of the argument for the minor premise reveals that A, the attempt to remove the causes of faction, is composed of two alternatives:

There are again two methods of removing the causes of faction: the one, by destroying the liberty which is essential to its existence; the other, by giving to every citizen the same opinions, the same passions, and the same interests.

These alternatives can be formally symbolized as A_1 and A_2.

A_1 [*destroying liberty*] is dismissed easily and speedily by means of an analogy or, in other words, by an argument based on *likenesses and differences:*

Liberty is to faction what air is to fire, an aliment without which it instantly expires. But it could not be less folly to abolish liberty, which is essential to political life, because it nourishes faction, than it would be to wish the annihilation of air, which is essential to animal life, because it imparts to fire its destructive agency.

The first analogical proportion [Liberty: Faction: : Air: Fire], which would logically lead to the inference that we ought to destroy liberty, since it causes faction, is immediately modified by changing the second and fourth terms in the proportion [Liberty: Political Life: : Air: Animal Life]. The folly of abolishing liberty as a cure for faction is self-evident. Madison does not need to devote time to this argument, since part of his fundamental aim was to preserve the spirit and form of popular government. Any measure which would cure faction by abolishing liberty is, as he says, a remedy worse than the disease.[4]

The argument against A$_2$ [*making all citizens alike in their passions, opinions, and interests*] is much more intricate and worthier of intensive study. Madison concludes that this alternative is impracticable, and his reasons for so deciding depend upon his view of human nature or, in other words, upon propositions drawn from the source of *definition*. In paragraphs 6–10, Madison uses the principles of Lockean psychology to prove that man, by nature, possesses faculties which operate to make factional conflicts inevitable. Men have a fallible reason which, in an environment of liberty, will lead to the formation of different opinions. There is a connection between reason and self-love which will direct the passions created by the latter to the support of the opinions resulting from the former. In addition to the fundamental characteristics—reason and self-love—men possess a diversity of other faculties which are the origin of different aptitudes for accumulating property. Since it is the first object of government to protect these diverse faculties and thus to protect the ensuing differences in degrees and kinds of property and since diverse property interests will inevitably influence the opinions and passions of the respective proprietors, society must always be divided into different interests and parties. As a result, "the latent causes of faction are thus sown in the nature of man."

In paragraph 7, Madison develops the *consequences* of the definition which he has established. Anything sown in the nature of man will spring up in everything he does. These latent causes reveal themselves in all aspects of civil society. Factions can result from a zeal for different opinions in religion, in government, and, indeed, in all the speculative and practical affairs of mankind; from an emotional attachment to ambitious leaders; or from conflicts over even frivolous and fanciful distinctions. However, "the most common and durable source of factions has been the various and unequal distribution of property." And here Madison expresses simply and directly a view of the economic basis of political government which derives from a tradition much older than that of Marx:

> Those who hold and those who are without property have ever formed distinct interests in society. Those who are creditors, and those who are debtors, fall under a like discrimination. A landed interest, a manufacturing interest, a mercantile interest, a moneyed interest, with many

---

[4] This analogy, simple as it seems, can open the way to a devastating refutation of the argument that the totalitarian or one-party state is better than a free government because it can eliminate factions.

lesser interests, grow up of necessity in civilized nations, and divide them into different classes, actuated by different sentiments and views. The regulation of these various and interfering interests forms the principal task of modern legislation, and involves the spirit of party and faction in the necessary and ordinary operations of the government.

The last proposition—that the spirit of faction is involved in the ordinary operations of government—requires an extension to another sphere of the *definition* of man previously presented. It is required in order to refute a possible objection. The counterargument might be raised that, since men's natures divide them into conflicting parties, it is the task of government somehow to stand above the conflicts and reconcile them in the interests of justice and the common good. This thesis would imply that legislators are superior to ordinary men in not being influenced by their own interests. To disprove this possible point of view, Madison continues in paragraph 8 with a *definition* of the two main factors in government—acts of legislation and legislators. Acts of legislation, such as laws concerning private debts, tariffs, and property taxes, are defined by Madison as judicial determinations concerning the rights of large bodies of citizens; and legislators are defined as advocates and parties to the causes which they determine. The self-love of the lawmakers will inevitably result in decisions which represent, not the principles of abstract justice, but their own party interests. Madison thinks it vain to depend upon the influence of "enlightened statesmen" to adjust the clash of diverse interests in the light of justice and the public good. Not only will such statesmen not always be at the helm, but in many cases the legislative questions will be so complex and pressing that it will be almost impossible for statesmen to act in an enlightened fashion.

Thus the first half of the paper, consisting of two powerful arguments based upon *definitions* of man and government, has led to the conclusion that all citizens cannot be made alike in their passions, opinions, and interests. As a result, "the inference to which we are brought is, that the *causes* of faction cannot be removed, and that relief is only to be sought in the means of controlling its *effects*." If we glance again at the controlling alternative syllogism:

Either A [*we can remove causes*] or B [*we can control effects*],
Not A,
Therefore, B,

we see that the argument from *likeness and difference* (directed against A_1) and the argument from *definition* (directed against A_2) have provided support for the minor premise: we cannot remove the causes of faction. The remainder of Madison's essay is devoted to substantiating the conclusion: therefore, we can control its effects.

The argument for B is much more complex than the argument against A. It is indicative of Madison's practical orientation as a political theorist that his main concern is with the control of effects rather than with the removal of causes. Removing the causes of something is a drastic but superficially simple alternative, whereas controlling effects usually involves a range of contingent methods whose varying degrees of success depend upon a multitude of factors which require careful analysis.

Before attacking the problem of the proper means for controlling the effects of faction, Madison further clarifies his problem by distinguishing between the dangers resulting from a minority and a majority faction. This key distinction, as we have seen, was set forth in the initial definition of "faction" in paragraph 2, "a number of citizens, whether amounting to a majority or minority of the whole. . . ." In paragraph 11, Madison uses another argument from *definition* to dismiss the dangers of a minority faction:

> If a faction consists of less than a majority, relief is supplied by the republican principle, which enables the majority to defeat its sinister views by regular vote.

Should this seem too cavalier a dismissal of a serious problem, one with which every state is plagued, Madison continues by revealing both his awareness of what a fanatical minority can do in a free society and the reason for his relative lack of concern. "It may clog the administration, it may convulse the society; but it will be unable to execute and mask its violence under the forms of the Constitution." The danger from a minority faction however serious, lies in the realm of practical administration and can, at the worst, be eliminated by the police power of the state. On the other hand, when a majority of the people coalesce into a faction, the very form of popular government enables such a faction to trample on the rights of other citizens and sacrifice the public good to its ruling passion. Here, exactly, was the concern of the Federalist theoreticians. How could the majority, operating in a mood of sudden and concerted aggression, be restrained from violating the rights of minorities and the over-all interests of the community?

The crucial importance of this question for Madison is indicated by the fact that, immediately after the distinction between minority and majority faction in paragraph 11, he makes explicit the aim of his essay:

> To secure the public good and private rights against the danger of such a faction [majority], and at the same time to preserve the spirit and form of popular government, is then the great object to which our inquiries are directed.

The argument in the second half of the essay involves the answer to two questions: (1) What, in theory, are the best means of controlling the effects of majority faction? and (2) Which form of popular government is best able to put these means into effect?

In form, the second main argument resembles the first, since it also starts with a division of alternatives. There are two means for controlling the effects of majority faction:

> Either the existence of the same passion or interest in a majority at the same time must be prevented, or the majority, having such coexistent passion or interest, must be rendered, by their number and local situation, unable to concert and carry into effect schemes of oppression.

These alternatives may be symbolized as B_1 and B_2. For a true picture of Madison's logical procedure, it is important to note that in the first argument both A_1 and A_2 were rejected, thus giving us a negative minor premise. However, the conclusion is a positive one. This means that both B_1 and B_2 are acceptable means of preventing majority oppression, with B_2 acting as an auxiliary method in case it is impossible to achieve B_1. Using these two methods as standards of judgment, Madison can turn his attention to the analysis of the two main forms of popular government—the pure democracy and the republic—to see which, by nature, can best control the effects of majority faction.

Again using the source of *definition,* Madison concludes that a pure democracy, "by which I mean a society consisting of a small number of citizens, who assemble and administer the government in person, can admit of no cure for the mischiefs of faction." Such a government, because its form permits both the creation and the immediate assertion of a majority passion or interest, will be able at will to sacrifice the rights of minorities or even of individuals obnoxious to the majority. Madison might have been thinking of the condemnation of Socrates by a majority of the Athenian citizens, since he supports his theoretical analysis at this point by a reference to history:

> Hence it is that such democracies have ever been spectacles of turbulence and contention; have ever been found incompatible with personal security or the rights of property; and have in general been as short in their lives as they have been violent in their deaths.

The general effect of this argument is similar to that in the first half of the essay, since pure democracy fails because it believes that, by making all men politically equal, it can equalize their possessions, their opinions, and their passions. Madison has already disposed of such a visionary hope.

By *definition,* a republic differs from a pure democracy in two important respects: in its form and in the magnitude of its possible operation. It is a form of popular government in which power is delegated to representatives elected by the people, and it can therefore be extended over a greater number of citizens and over a greater area than can a pure democracy. The definitions of these two forms of popular government prepare the way for the rather involved reasoning which starts at paragraph 16 and continues to the end. These paragraphs can be related to the rest of the argument by seeing them as detailed statements of the *consequences* resulting from the two main points of difference between a democracy and a republic. Paragraphs 16–19 deal with the effects of the difference in form, paragraph 20 with the difference in magnitude.

The formal difference—the principle of delegative power—does not by itself provide a guaranty that majority factions will be controlled. Acting as a cause, it may lead to opposite effects. When the opinions of the people are sifted through a body of representatives who may be influenced by patriotism and the love of justice, the process might result in refining and enlarging the public views and, probably, lead to decisions advancing the public good. However, the effect may as easily be inverted. As Madison puts it:

> Men of factious tempers, of local prejudices, or of sinister designs, may, by intrigue, by corruption, or by other means, first obtain the suffrages, and then betray the interests, of the people.

Since the delegative form of government alone provides no certainty that majority factions can be controlled, Madison then proceeds to the corollary question of whether small or large republics are best able to elect good legislators. Paragraphs 17 and 18 present two considerations which decide the question in favor of the large republic. Fundamentally, these two paragraphs present the probable *consequences* of the smaller ratio between representatives and constituents which characterizes the large republic by contrast with the small one. A hypothetical example will clarify the rather close reasoning of these paragraphs. Madison starts with the assumption that, regardless of the size of the republic, the representatives must be numerous enough to guard against the cabals of a few, and limited enough to avoid the confusion of a multitude. Let us suppose that the range for an efficient legislative body is from 100 to 500 representatives. If the smaller number, 100, is selected by the constituents of a small republic, say 10,000 voters, the ratio is 1 : 100. If the larger number, 500, is selected by 5,000,000 voters, the ratio is 1 : 10,000. Therefore, if it be granted that the proportion of good men is the same in both states, the large republic will present a much wider choice and, consequently, the greater probability of a fit choice. The second consideration in favor of a large republic is that, since each representative will be chosen by many more voters, there will be less chance for the voters to be fooled by unworthy candidates using the tricks of the demagogue. The argument in paragraph 17 depends for its force solely on numerical ratios. There will be more good men in a large republic from which to make a wise choice. Paragraph 18 adds the consideration that it will be harder to fool the many than to fool the few.

Madison then goes back to the second main difference between a democracy and a republic—the greater number of citizens and larger extent of territory which can be brought within the compass of the republican form. And here he sums up the *consequences* of his definitions in such a way as to re-emphasize the superiority of a republic over a democracy, on the one hand, and of a large republic over a small one, on the other:

> The smaller the society, the fewer probably will be the distinct parties and interests composing it; the fewer the distinct parties and interests, the more frequently will a majority be found of the same party; and the smaller the number of individuals composing a majority, and the smaller the compass within which they are placed, the more easily will they concert and execute their plans of oppression. Extend the sphere and you take in a greater variety of parties and interests; you make it less probable that a majority of the whole will have a common motive to invade the rights of other citizens; or if such a common motive exists, it will be more difficult for all who feel it to discover their own strength, and to act in unison with each other.

Thus a large republic can control the effects of faction better than any other form of popular government and "in the extent and proper structure of the Union, therefore, we behold a republican remedy for the diseases most incident to republican government." Madison concludes by identifying true republicanism with the Federalist advocacy of the proposed Constitution.

Madison's powerful plea for a federal republic can be felt most strongly when the sources of his argument are brought to light and his particular propositions are seen operating in the deductive form which moves relentlessly from assumptions and premises to conclusions. Many English teachers will be content to clarify the argumentative methods from which *The Federalist,* No. 10, derives its logical power. But others, perhaps those with an interest in political theory, will want to have their students examine the assumptions and challenge the conclusions of Madison's argument. Although possible refutations are beyond the scope of this article, an understanding of the sources can help in outlining some promising lines of attack. For instance, the fundamental dichotomy set up by Madison is that between the "public good," on the one hand, and "majority faction," on the other. Madison is careful to define what he opposes; but the term "the public good" remains an undefined ideal which controls his judgments but which is never pinned down. For those of us who, almost without thinking, identify the public good with the majority will, Madison's analysis seems shockingly undemocratic. The question could be asked: How can the public good be achieved or, for that matter, even known with certainty if majority faction is considered the main danger in a republic? Another point of possible refutation rests in Madison's cynical definition of man in paragraphs 6 and

7. Would a Jeffersonian or perhaps even a Christian definition of man lead to different conclusions? Finally, some question could be raised about whether large republics actually do produce a higher quality of legislators than small ones. Madison was arguing that national representatives would, in all probability, be better than those in a state legislature. However, we might ask whether our Congress today can compare in quality with the much smaller Constitutional Convention or, if that is unfair, even with the Congress of Madison's own day.

These questions, and others, would be directed toward awakening the student's interest not only in the vital subject matter of Madison's article but also in the intellectually exciting rigors of logical procedure. Through the step-by-step reconstruction of Madison's argument, the student can be led to see how a commanding piece of rhetoric came into being. By studying Madison's sources of argument and seeing how the forms of syllogistic reasoning are filled with material drawn from the realms of theory and experience, the student writer, faced with the challenge of supporting a proposition, can learn to use these directing ideas, the sources, to make his own arguments richer, more controlled, and, ultimately, more convincing.

Edmund Burke: Letter to a Noble Lord

In 1794, after the trial of Warren Hastings, in which he had been one of the relentless prosecutors, Edmund Burke (1729–97) retired from the House of Commons, where he had served for almost thirty years, and his son Richard was nominated to take his place. As a reward for his long service in the government, Burke was proposed for the peerage, with the title of Lord Beaconsfield, but upon the death of his son Richard in August of 1794, Burke lost all interest in any titular honors. King George III then bestowed a pension on Burke but failed to go through the formality of submitting the award to Parliament for approval. Francis Russell (1762–1802), the fifth Duke of Bedford, raised an objection to the pension in the House of Lords. As did Martin Luther King in his "Letter from Birmingham Jail," Burke attempted to vindicate himself in the form of an "open letter," which John Morley, the nineteenth-century critic, called "the most splendid repartee in the English language." Only about a third of the 1796 Letter is reproduced here; about twenty paragraphs have been omitted from the beginning of the Letter and about the same number of paragraphs from the end. In the paragraph immediately preceding the first paragraph printed here, Burke said, "The awful state of the time, and not myself or my own justification, is my true object in what I now write, or in what I shall ever write or say."

1   The Duke of Bedford conceives that he is obliged to call the attention of the House of Peers to his Majesty's grant to me, which he considers excessive and out of all bounds.

2   I know not how it has happened, but it really seems that, whilst his Grace was meditating his well-considered censure upon me, he fell into a sort of sleep. Homer nods; and the Duke of Bedford may dream; and as dreams (even his golden dreams) are apt to be ill-pieced and incongruously put together, his Grace preserved his idea of reproach to *me,* but took the subject-matter from the Crown grants *to his own family.* This is "the stuff of which his dreams are made." In that way of putting things together his Grace is perfectly in the right. The grants to the house of Russell were so enormous, as not only to outrage economy, but even to stagger credulity. The Duke of Bedford is the leviathan among all the creatures of the Crown. He tumbles about his unwieldy bulk; he plays and frolics in the ocean of the royal bounty. Huge as he is, and whilst "he lies floating many a rood," he is still a creature. His ribs, his fins, his whalebone, his blubber, the very spiracles through which he spouts a torrent of brine against his origin and covers me all over with the spray—everything of him and about him is from the throne. Is it for *him* to question the dispensation of the royal favour?

3   I really am at a loss to draw any sort of parallel between the public merits of his Grace, by which he justifies the grants he holds, and these services of mine, on the favourable construction of which I have obtained what his Grace so much disapproves. In private life, I have not at all the honour of acquaintance with the noble Duke. But I ought to presume, and it costs me nothing to do so, that he abundantly deserves the esteem and love of all who live with him. But as to public service, why truly it would not be more ridiculous for me to compare myself in rank, in fortune, in splendid descent, in youth, strength, or figure, with the Duke of Bedford, than to make a parallel between his services and my attempts to be useful to my country. It would not be gross adulation, but uncivil irony, to say that he has any public merit of his own to keep alive the idea of the services by which his vast landed pensions were obtained. My merits, whatever they are, are original and personal; his are derivative. It is his ancestor, the original pensioner, that has laid up this inexhaustible fund of merit, which makes his Grace so very delicate and exceptious about the merit of all other grantees of the Crown. Had he permitted me to remain in quiet, I should have said, 'tis his estate; that's enough. It is his by law; what have I to do with it or its history? He would naturally have said on his side, 'tis this man's fortune.—He is as good now as my ancestor was two hundred and fifty years ago. I am a young man with very old pensions; he is an old man with very young pensions,—that's all.

4   Why will his Grace, by attacking me, force me reluctantly to compare

my little merit with that which obtained from the Crown those prodigies of profuse donation, by which he tramples on the mediocrity of humble and laborious individuals? I would willingly leave him to the herald's college, which the philosophy of the *sans culottes* (prouder by far than all the Garters, and Norroys, and Clarencieux, and Rouge Dragons, that ever pranced in a procession of what his friends call aristocrats and despots) will abolish with contumely and scorn. These historians, recorders, and blazoners of virtues and arms, differ wholly from that other description of historians, who never assign any act of politicians to a good motive. These gentle historians, on the contrary, dip their pens in nothing but the milk of human kindness. They seek no further for merit than the preamble of a patent or the inscription on a tomb. With them every man created a peer is first a hero ready made. They judge of every man's capacity for office by the offices he has filled; and the more offices the more ability. Every general officer with them is a Marlborough; every statesman a Burleigh; every judge a Murray or a Yorke. They who, alive, were laughed at or pitied by all their acquaintance, make as good a figure as the best of them in the pages of Guillim, Edmondson, and Collins.

5   To these recorders, so full of good nature to the great and prosperous, I would willingly leave the first Baron Russell, and Earl of Bedford, and the merits of his grants. But the aulnager, the weigher, the meter of grants, will not suffer us to acquiesce in the judgment of the prince reigning at the time when they were made. They are never good to those who earn them. Well then; since the new grantees have war made on them by the old, and that the word of the sovereign is not to be taken, let us turn our eyes to history, in which great men have always a pleasure in contemplating the heroic origin of their house.

6   The first peer of the name, the first purchaser of the grants, was a Mr. Russell, a person of an ancient gentleman's family raised by being a minion of Henry the Eighth. As there generally is some resemblance of character to create these relations, the favourite was in all likelihood much such another as his master. The first of those immoderate grants was not taken from the ancient demesne of the Crown, but from the recent confiscation of the ancient nobility of the land. The lion having sucked the blood of his prey, threw the offal carcass to the jackal in waiting. Having tasted once the food of confiscation, the favourites became fierce and ravenous. This worthy favourite's first grant was from the lay nobility. The second, infinitely improving on the enormity of the first, was from the plunder of the church. In truth his Grace is somewhat excusable for his dislike to a grant like mine, not only in its quantity, but in its kind so different from his own.

7   Mine was from a mild and benevolent sovereign; his from Henry the Eighth.

8   Mine had not its fund in the murder of any innocent person of illustrious rank or in the pillage of any body of unoffending men. His grants were from the aggregate and consolidated funds of judgments iniquitously legal and from possessions voluntarily surrendered by the lawful proprietors, with the gibbet at their door.

9   The merit of the grantee whom he derives from was that of being a prompt and greedy instrument of a *levelling* tyrant, who oppressed all descriptions of his people, but who fell with particular fury on everything that was *great and noble*. Mine has been, in endeavouring to screen every man, in every class, from oppression, and particularly in defending the high and eminent, who in the bad times of confiscating princes, confiscating chief governors, or confiscating demagogues, are the most exposed to jealousy, avarice, and envy.

10   The merit of the original grantee of his Grace's pensions was in giving his hand to the work and partaking the spoil with a prince, who plundered a part of the national church of his time and country. Mine was in defending the whole of the national church of my own time and my own country, and the whole of the national churches of all countries, from the principles and the examples which lead to ecclesiastical pillage, thence to a contempt of *all* prescriptive titles, thence to the pillage of *all* property, and thence to universal desolation.

11   The merit of the origin of his Grace's fortune was in being a favourite and chief adviser to a prince, who left no liberty to their native country. My endeavour was to obtain liberty for the municipal country in which I was born and for all descriptions and denominations in it. Mine was to support with unrelaxing vigilance every right, every privilege, every franchise, in this my adopted, my dearer, and more comprehensive country; and not only to preserve those rights in this chief seat of empire, but in every nation, in every land, in every climate, language, and religion, in the vast domain that is still under the protection, and the larger that was once under the protection, of the British Crown.

12   His founder's merits were, by arts in which he served his master and made his fortune, to bring poverty, wretchedness, and depopulation on his country. Mine were, under a benevolent prince, in promoting the commerce, manufacture, and agriculture of his kingdom; in which his Majesty shows an eminent example, who even in his amusements is a patriot, and in hours of leisure an improver of his native soil.

13   His founder's merit was the merit of a gentleman raised by the arts of a court, and the protection of a Wolsey, to the eminence of a great and potent lord. His merit in that eminence was, by instigating a tyrant to injustice, to provoke a people to rebellion. My merit was, to awaken the sober part of the country, that they might put themselves on their guard against any one

potent lord, or any greater number of potent lords, or any combination of great leading men of any sort, if ever they should attempt to proceed in the same courses, but in the reverse order; that is, by instigating a corrupted populace to rebellion and, through that rebellion, introducing a tyranny yet worse than the tyranny which his Grace's ancestor supported and of which he profited in the manner we behold in the despotism of Henry the Eighth.

14 The political merit of the first pensioner of his Grace's house was that of being concerned as a counsellor of state in advising, and in his person executing, the conditions of a dishonourable peace with France; the surrendering the fortress of Boulogne, then our out-guard on the Continent. By that surrender, Calais, the key of France and the bridle in the mouth of that power, was, not many years afterwards, finally lost. My merit has been in resisting the power and pride of France, under any form of its rule; but in opposing it with the greatest zeal and earnestness, when that rule appeared in the worst form it could assume; the worst indeed which the prime cause and principle of all evil could possibly give it. It was my endeavour by every means to excite a spirit in the House where I had the honour of a seat, for carrying on, with early vigour and decision, the most clearly just and necessary war, that this or any nation ever carried on; in order to save my country from the iron yoke of its power and from the more dreadful contagion of its principles; to preserve, while they can be preserved, pure and untainted, the ancient, inbred integrity, piety, good nature, and good humour of the people of England, from the dreadful pestilence, which, beginning in France, threatens to lay waste the whole moral, and in a great degree the whole physical, world, having done both in the focus of its most intense malignity.

15 The labours of his Grace's founder merited the curses, not loud but deep, of the Commons of England, on whom *he* and his master had effected a *complete parliamentary reform,* by making them, in their slavery and humiliation, the true and adequate representatives of a debased, degraded, and undone people. My merits were, in having had an active, though not always an ostentatious, share, in every one act, without exception, of undisputed constitutional utility in my time, and in having supported, on all occasions, the authority, the efficiency, and the privileges of the Commons of Great Britain. I ended my services by a recorded and fully reasoned assertion on their own journals of their constitutional rights and a vindication of their constitutional conduct. I laboured in all things to merit their inward approbation, and (along with the assistance of the largest, the greatest, and best of my endeavours) I received their free, unbiased, public, and solemn thanks.

16 Thus stands the account of the comparative merits of the Crown grants which compose the Duke of Bedford's fortune as balanced against mine. In the name of common sense, why should the Duke of Bedford think that none but of the House of Russell are entitled to the favour of the Crown? Why should he imagine that no king of England has been capable of judging of merit but King Henry the Eighth? Indeed, he will pardon me; he is a little mistaken; all virtue did not end in the first Earl of Bedford. All discernment did not lose its vision when his Creator closed his eyes. Let him remit his rigour on the disproportion between merit and reward in others, and they will make no inquiry into the origin of his fortune. They will regard with much more satisfaction, as he will contemplate with infinitely more advantage, whatever in his pedigree has been dulcified by an exposure to the influence of heaven in a long flow of generations, from the hard, acidulous, metallic tincture of the spring. It is little to be doubted that several of his forefathers in that long series have degenerated into honour and virtue. Let the Duke of Bedford (I am sure he will) reject with scorn and horror the counsels of the lecturers, those wicked panders to avarice and ambition, who would tempt him, in the troubles of his country, to seek another enormous fortune from the forfeitures of another nobility and the plunder of another church. Let him (and I trust that yet he will) employ all the energy of his youth and all the resources of his wealth to crush rebellious principles which have no foundation in morals and rebellious movements that have no provocation in tyranny.

17 Then will be forgot the rebellions, which, by a doubtful priority in crime, his ancestor had provoked and extinguished. On such a conduct in the noble Duke, many of his countrymen might, and with some excuse might, give way to the enthusiasm of their gratitude and, in the dashing style of some of the old declaimers, cry out that if the fates had found no other way in which they could give a Duke of Bedford and his opulence as props to a tottering world, then the butchery of the Duke of Buckingham might be tolerated; it might be regarded even with complacency, whilst in the heir of confiscation they saw the sympathizing comforter of the martyrs who suffered under the cruel confiscation of this day; whilst they behold with admiration his zealous protection of the virtuous and loyal nobility of France and his manly support to his brethren, the yet standing nobility and gentry of his native land. Then his Grace's merit would be pure, and new, and sharp, as fresh from the mint of honour. As he pleased he might reflect honour on his predecessors or throw it forward on those who were to succeed him. He might be the propagator of the stock of honour, or the root of it, as he thought proper.

18 Had it pleased God to continue to me the hopes of succession, I should have been, according to my mediocrity and the mediocrity of the age I live in, a sort of founder of a family; I should have left a son, who, in all the points in which personal merit can be viewed, in science, in erudition, in genius, in taste, in honour, in generosity, in humanity, in every liberal sentiment and every liberal accomplishment, would not have shown himself inferior to the Duke of Bedford or to any of those whom he traces in his line.

His Grace very soon would have wanted all plausibility in his attack upon that provision which belonged more to mine than to me. He would soon have supplied every deficiency and symmetrized every disproportion. It would not have been for that successor to resort to any stagnant wasting reservoir of merit in me or in any ancestry. He had in himself a salient, living spring of generous and manly action. Every day he lived he would have re-purchased the bounty of the Crown and ten times more, if ten times more he had received. He was made a public creature; and had no enjoyment whatever but in the performance of some duty. At this exigent moment, the loss of a finished man is not easily supplied.

19 But a Disposer whose power we are little able to resist and whose wisdom it behooves us not at all to dispute, has ordained it in another manner and (whatever my querulous weakness might suggest) a far better. The storm has gone over me; and I lie like one of those old oaks which the late hurricane has scattered about me. I am stripped of all my honours, I am torn up by the roots and lie prostrate on the earth! There, and prostrate there, I most unfeignedly recognize the Divine justice and in some degree submit to it. But whilst I humble myself before God, I do not know that it is forbidden to repel the attacks of unjust and inconsiderate men. The patience of Job is proverbial. After some of the convulsive struggles of our irritable nature, he submitted himself and repented in dust and ashes. But even so, I do not find him blamed for reprehending, and with a considerable degree of verbal asperity, those ill-natured neighbours of his, who visited his dunghill to read moral, political, and economical lectures on his misery. I am alone. I have none to meet my enemies in the gate. Indeed, my Lord, I greatly deceive myself, if in this hard season I would give a peck of refuse wheat for all that is called fame and honour in the world. This is the appetite but of a few. It is a luxury, it is a privilege, it is an indulgence for those who are at their ease. But we are all of us made to shun disgrace, as we are made to shrink from pain and poverty and disease. It is an instinct; and under the direction of reason, instinct is always in the right. I live in an inverted order. They who ought to have succeeded me are gone before me. They who should have been to me as posterity are in the place of ancestors. I owe to the dearest relation (which ever must subsist in memory) that act of piety, which he would have performed to me; I owe it to him to show that he was not descended, as the Duke of Bedford would have it, from an unworthy parent.

20 The Crown has considered me after long service; the Crown has paid the Duke of Bedford by advance. He has had a long credit for any services which he may perform hereafter. He is secure, and long may he be secure, in his advance, whether he performs any services or not. But let him take

care how he endangers the safety of that constitution which secures his own utility or his own insignificance; or how he discourages those who take up, even puny arms, to defend an order of things which, like the sun of heaven, shines alike on the useful and the worthless. His grants are ingrafted on the public law of Europe, covered with the awful hoar of innumerable ages. They are guarded by the sacred rules of prescription, found in that full treasury of jurisprudence from which the jejuneness and penury of our municipal law has, by degrees, been enriched and strengthened. This prescription I had my share (a very full share) in bringing to its perfection. The Duke of Bedford will stand as long as prescriptive law endures; as long as the great stable laws of property, common to us with all civilized nations, are kept in their integrity and without the smallest intermixture of laws, maxims, principles, or precedents of the grand Revolution. They are secure against all changes but one. The whole revolutionary system, institutes, digest, code, novels, text, gloss, comment, are not only the same but they are the very reverse, and the reverse fundamentals, of all the laws on which civil life has hitherto been upheld in all the governments of the world. The learned professors of the rights of man regard prescription, not as a title to bar all claim, set up against all possession—but they look on prescription as itself a bar against the possessor and proprietor. They hold an immemorial possession to be no more than a long-continued and therefore an aggravated injustice.

21 Such are *their* ideas; such *their* religion, and such *their* law. But as to *our* country and *our* race, as long as the well-compacted structure of our church and state, the sanctuary, the holy of holies of that ancient law, defended by reverence, defended by power, a fortress at once and a temple, shall stand inviolate on the brow of the British Sion—as long as the British monarchy, not more limited than fenced by the orders of the state, shall, like the proud Keep of Windsor, rising in the majesty of proportion and girt with the double belt of its kindred and coeval towers, as long as this awful structure shall oversee and guard the subjected land—so long the mounds and dykes of the low, fat Bedford level will have nothing to fear from all the pickaxes of all the levellers of France. As long as our sovereign lord the king and his faithful subjects, the Lords and Commons of this realm—the triple cord which no man can break; the solemn, sworn, constitutional frank-pledge of this nation; the firm guarantees of each other's beings and each other's rights; the joint and several securities, each in its place and order, for every kind and every quality of property and of dignity; as long as these endure, so long the Duke of Bedford is safe: and we are all safe together—the high from the blights of envy and the spoliations of rapacity; the low from the iron hand of oppression and the insolent spurn of contempt....

Thomas Henry Huxley: Science and Culture

In the two selections that follow, we observe Thomas Henry Huxley (1825–95) and Matthew Arnold (1822–88) engaged in a vigorous debate on the relative merits of what C. P. Snow in our own time has called the "Two Cultures," the sciences and the humanities. Huxley was the most eloquent of the nineteenth-century spokesmen for the sciences. Having studied medicine as a young man, he became widely known for his research in comparative anatomy and embryology, for his courageous defense of Charles Darwin's theories of evolution, for his advocacy of higher education for women and Negroes, for his lectures at several working-men's colleges, and for his contributions to sociology and ethics. His "Science and Culture" was delivered as an address at the opening of Sir Josiah Mason's Science College in Birmingham, England, on October 1, 1880. His essay is presented here in an abbreviated version, fifteen paragraphs having been omitted from the beginning and four paragraphs at the end.

Along with John Henry Newman, Matthew Arnold stands as one of the dauntless nineteenth-century champions of liberal education. A son of the famous Dr. Thomas Arnold of Rugby, Arnold took only a second-class honors degree at Balliol College, Oxford, in 1844, but the following year he won a fellowship at Oriel College, Oxford. A distinguished poet, critic, and essayist in his own right, he was twice elected to the Chair of Poetry at Oxford. For thirty-five years of his life, he served as an Inspector of Schools in England, a job in which he exerted his influence to bring about compulsory education for young people of all social strata. His "Literature and Science" was first delivered as the Rede Lecture at Cambridge University and was subsequently published in the August 1882 issue of Nineteenth Century. *In a slightly revised version, it was again delivered during his American lecture tour of 1883–84. It too is reproduced here in an abbreviated version, but the section printed here is essentially the same lecture that he delivered at Cambridge and in America. It is instructive to observe these two formidable polemicists locking horns over a matter that both of them took very seriously.*

1   I hold very strongly by two convictions:—The first is that neither the discipline nor the subject-matter of classical education is of such direct value to the student of physical science as to justify the expenditure of valuable time upon either; and the second is that for the purpose of attaining

real culture, an exclusively scientific education is at least as effectual as an exclusively literary education.

2   I need hardly point out to you that these opinions, especially the latter, are diametrically opposed to those of the great majority of educated Englishmen, influenced as they are by school and university traditions. In their belief, culture is obtainable only by a liberal education; and a liberal education is synonymous, not merely with education and instruction in literature, but in one particular form of literature, namely, that of Greek and Roman antiquity. They hold that the man who has learned Latin and Greek, however little, is educated; while he who is versed in other branches of knowledge, however deeply, is a more or less respectable specialist, not admissible into the cultured caste. The stamp of the educated man, the University degree, is not for him.

3   I am too well acquainted with the generous catholicity of spirit, the true sympathy with scientific thought, which pervades the writings of our chief apostle of culture, to identify him with these opinions; and yet one may cull from one and another of those epistles to the Philistines, which so much delight all who do not answer to that name, sentences which lend them some support.

4   Mr. Arnold tells us that the meaning of culture is "to know the best that has been thought and said in the world." It is the criticism of life contained in literature. That criticism regards "Europe as being, for intellectual and spiritual purposes, one great confederation, bound to a joint action and working to a common result; and whose members have, for their common outfit, a knowledge of Greek, Roman, and Eastern antiquity, and of one another. Special, local, and temporary advantages being put out of account, that modern nation will in the intellectual and spiritual sphere make most progress, which most thoroughly carries out this programme. And what is that but saying that we too, all of us, as individuals, the more thoroughly we carry it out, shall make the more progress?"

5   We have here to deal with two distinct propositions. The first, that a criticism of life is the essence of culture; the second, that literature contains the materials which suffice for the construction of such a criticism.

6   I think that we must all assent to the first proposition. For culture certainly means something quite different from learning or technical skill. It implies the possession of an ideal and the habit of critically estimating the value of things by comparison with a theoretic standard. Perfect culture should supply a complete theory of life, based upon a clear knowledge alike of its possibilities and of its limitations.

7   But we may agree to all this and yet strongly dissent from the assumption that literature alone is competent to supply this knowledge. After having

learnt all that Greek, Roman, and Eastern antiquity have thought and said and all that modern literatures have to tell us, it is not self-evident that we have laid a sufficiently broad and deep foundation for that criticism of life which constitutes culture.

8 Indeed, to any one acquainted with the scope of physical science, it is not at all evident. Considering progress only in the "intellectual and spiritual sphere," I find myself wholly unable to admit that either nations or individuals will really advance, if their common outfit draws nothing from the stores of physical science. I should say that an army, without weapons of precision and with no particular base of operations, might more hopefully enter upon a campaign on the Rhine, than a man, devoid of a knowledge of what physical science has done in the last century, upon a criticism of life.

9 When a biologist meets with an anomaly, he instinctively turns to the study of development to clear it up. The rationale of contradictory opinions may with equal confidence be sought in history.

10 It is, happily, no new thing that Englishmen should employ their wealth in building and endowing institutions for educational purposes. But five or six hundred years ago, deeds of foundation expressed or implied conditions as nearly as possible contrary to those which have been thought expedient by Sir Josiah Mason. That is to say, physical science was practically ignored, while a certain literary training was enjoined as a means to the acquirement of knowledge which was essentially theological.

11 The reason of this singular contradiction between the actions of men alike animated by a strong and disinterested desire to promote the welfare of their fellows is easily discovered.

12 At that time, in fact, if any one desired knowledge beyond such as could be obtained by his own observation or by common conversation, his first necessity was to learn the Latin language, inasmuch as all the higher knowledge of the western world was contained in works written in that language. Hence, Latin grammar, with logic and rhetoric, studied through Latin, were the fundamentals of education. With respect to the substance of the knowledge imparted through this channel, the Jewish and Christian Scriptures, as interpreted and supplemented by the Romish Church, were held to contain a complete and infallibly true body of information.

13 Theological dicta were, to the thinkers of those days, that which the axioms and definitions of Euclid are to the geometers of these. The business of the philosophers of the middle ages was to deduce, from the data furnished by the theologians, conclusions in accordance with ecclesiastical degrees. They were allowed the high privilege of showing, by logical process, how and why that which the Church said was true, must be true. And if their

demonstrations fell short of or exceeded this limit, the Church was maternally ready to check their aberrations,—if need were, by the help of the secular arm.

14 Between the two, our ancestors were furnished with a compact and complete criticism of life. They were told how the world began and how it would end; they learned that all material existence was but a base and insignificant blot upon the fair face of the spiritual world and that nature was, to all intents and purposes, the playground of the devil; they learned that the earth is the centre of the visible universe and that man is the cynosure of things terrestrial; and more especially was it inculcated that the course of nature had no fixed order, but that it could be, and constantly was, altered by the agency of innumerable spiritual beings, good and bad, according as they were moved by the deeds and prayers of men. The sum and substance of the whole doctrine was to produce the conviction that the only thing really worth knowing in this world was how to secure that place in a better, which, under certain conditions, the Church promised.

15 Our ancestors had a living belief in this theory of life and acted upon it in their dealings with education, as in all other matters. Culture meant saintliness—after the fashion of the saints of those days; the education that led to it was, of necessity, theological; and the way to theology lay through Latin.

16 That the study of nature—further than was requisite for the satisfaction of everyday wants—should have any bearing on human life was far from the thoughts of men thus trained. Indeed, as nature had been cursed for man's sake, it was an obvious conclusion that those who meddled with nature were likely to come into pretty close contact with Satan. And if any born scientific investigator followed his instincts, he might safely reckon upon earning the reputation, and probably upon suffering the fate, of a sorcerer.

17 Had the western world been left to itself in Chinese isolation, there is no saying how long this state of things might have endured. But happily it was not left to itself. Even earlier than the thirteenth century, the development of Moorish civilization in Spain and the great movement of the Crusades had introduced the leaven which, from that day to this, has never ceased to work. At first, through the intermediation of Arabic translations, afterwards by the study of the originals, the western nations of Europe became acquainted with the writings of the ancient philosophers and poets and, in time, with the whole of the vast literature of antiquity.

18 Whatever there was of high intellectual aspiration or dominant capacity in Italy, France, Germany, and England, spent itself for centuries in taking possession of the rich inheritance left by the dead civilizations of Greece

and Rome. Marvelously aided by the invention of printing, classical learning spread and flourished. Those who possessed it prided themselves on having attained the highest culture then within the reach of mankind.

19 And justly. For, saving Dante on his solitary pinnacle, there was no figure in modern literature, at the time of the Renascence, to compare with the men of antiquity; there was no art to compete with their sculpture; there was no physical science but that which Greece had created. Above all, there was no other example of perfect intellectual freedom—of the unhesitating acceptance of reason as the sole guide to truth and the supreme arbiter of conduct.

20 The new learning necessarily soon exerted a profound influence upon education. The language of the monks and schoolmen seemed little better than gibberish to scholars fresh from Vergil and Cicero, and the study of Latin was placed upon a new foundation. Moreover, Latin itself ceased to afford the sole key to knowledge. The student who sought the highest thought of antiquity found only a second-hand reflection of it in Roman literature and turned his face to the full light of the Greeks. And after a battle, not altogether dissimilar to that which is at present being fought over the teaching of physical science, the study of Greek was recognized as an essential element of all higher education.

21 Thus the Humanists, as they were called, won the day; and the great reform which they effected was of incalculable service to mankind. But the Nemesis of all reformers is finality; and the reformers of education, like those of religion, fell into the profound, however common, error of mistaking the beginning for the end of the work of reformation.

22 The representatives of the Humanists, in the nineteenth century, take their stand upon classical education as the sole avenue to culture, as firmly as if we were still in the age of Renascence. Yet, surely, the present intellectual relations of the modern and the ancient worlds are profoundly different from those which obtained three centuries ago. Leaving aside the existence of a great and characteristically modern literature, of modern painting, and, especially, of modern music, there is one feature of the present state of the civilized world which separates it more widely from the Renascence than the Renascence was separated from the middle ages.

23 This distinctive character of our own times lies in the vast and constantly increasing part which is played by natural knowledge. Not only is our daily life shaped by it, not only does the prosperity of millions of men depend upon it, but our whole theory of life has long been influenced, consciously or unconsciously, by the general conceptions of the universe which have been forced upon us by physical science.

24 In fact, the most elementary acquaintance with the results of scientific investigation shows us that they offer a broad and striking contradiction to the opinion so implicitly credited and taught in the middle ages.

25 The notions of the beginning and the end of the world entertained by our forefathers are no longer credible. It is very certain that the earth is not the chief body in the universe and that the world is not subordinated to man's use. It is even more certain that nature is the expression of a definite order with which nothing interferes and that the chief business of mankind is to learn that order and govern themselves accordingly. Moreover, this scientific "criticism of life" presents itself to us with different credentials from any other. It appeals not to authority, nor to what anybody may have thought or said, but to nature. It admits that all our interpretations of natural fact are more or less imperfect and symbolic, and bids the learner seek for truth not among words but among things. It warns us that the assertion which outstrips evidence is not only a blunder but a crime.

26 The purely classical education advocated by the representatives of the Humanists in our day gives no inkling of all this. A man may be a better scholar than Erasmus and know no more of the chief causes of the present intellectual fermentation than Erasmus did. Scholarly and pious persons, worthy of all respect, favour us with allocutions upon the sadness of the antagonism of science to their mediaeval way of thinking, which betray an ignorance of the first principles of scientific investigation, an incapacity for understanding what a man of science means by veracity and an unconsciousness of the weight of established scientific truths, which is almost comical.

27 There is no great force in the *tu quoque* argument, or else the advocates of scientific education might fairly enough retort upon the modern Humanists that they may be learned specialists, but that they possess no such sound foundation for a criticism of life as deserves the name of culture. And, indeed, if we were disposed to be cruel, we might urge that the Humanists have brought this reproach upon themselves, not because they are too full of the spirit of the ancient Greek, but because they lack it.

28 The period of the Renascence is commonly called that of the "Revival of Letters," as if the influences then brought to bear upon the mind of Western Europe had been wholly exhausted in the field of literature. I think it is very commonly forgotten that the revival of science, effected by the same agency, although less conspicuous, was not less momentous.

29 In fact, the few and scattered students of nature of that day picked up the clue to her secrets exactly as it fell from the hands of the Greeks a thousand years before. The foundations of mathematics were so well laid by them that our children learn their geometry from a book written for the schools of Alexandria two thousand years ago. Modern astronomy is the natural continuation and development of the work of Hipparchus and of Ptolemy; modern physics of that of Democritus and of Archimedes; it was long before modern biological science outgrew the knowledge bequeathed to us by Aristotle, by Theophrastus, and by Galen.

30 We cannot know all the best thoughts and sayings of the Greeks unless we know what they thought about natural phenomena. We cannot fully apprehend their criticism of life unless we understand the extent to which that criticism was affected by scientific conceptions. We falsely pretend to be the inheritors of their culture, unless we are penetrated, as the best minds among them were, with an unhesitating faith that the free employment of reason, in accordance with scientific method, is the sole method of reaching truth.

31 Thus I venture to think that the pretensions of our modern Humanists to the possession of the monopoly of culture and to the exclusive inheritance of the spirit of antiquity must be abated, if not abandoned. But I should be very sorry that anything I have said should be taken to imply a desire on my part to depreciate the value of a classical education, as it might be and as it sometimes is. The native capacities of mankind vary no less than their opportunities; and while culture is one, the road by which one man may best reach it is widely different from that which is most advantageous to another. Again, while scientific education is yet inchoate and tentative, classical education is thoroughly well organized upon the practical experience of generations of teachers. So that, given ample time for learning and destination for ordinary life or for a literary career, I do not think that a young Englishman in search of culture can do better than follow the course usually marked out for him, supplementing its deficiencies by his own efforts.

32 But for those who mean to make science their serious occupation or who intend to follow the profession of medicine or who have to enter early upon the business of life,—for all these, in my opinion, classical education is a mistake; and it is for this reason that I am glad to see "mere literary education and instruction" shut out from the curriculum of Sir Josiah Mason's College, seeing that its inclusion would probably lead to the introduction of the ordinary smattering of Latin and Greek.

33 Nevertheless, I am the last person to question the importance of genuine literary education or to suppose that intellectual culture can be complete without it. An exclusively scientific training will bring about a mental twist as surely as an exclusively literary training. The value of the cargo does not compensate for a ship's being out of trim; and I should be very sorry to think that the Scientific College would turn out none but lopsided men.

34 There is no need, however, that such a catastrophe should happen. Instruction in English, French, and German is provided, and thus the three

greatest literatures of the modern world are made accessible to the student. French and German, and especially the latter language, are absolutely indispensable to those who desire full knowledge in any department of science. But even supposing that the knowledge of these languages acquired is not more than sufficient for purely scientific purposes, every Englishman has, in his native tongue, an almost perfect instrument of literary expression· and, in his own literature, models of every kind of literary excellence. If an Englishman cannot get literary culture out of his Bible, his Shakespeare, his Milton, neither, in my belief, will the profoundest study of Homer and Sophocles, Vergil and Horace, give it to him.

35 Thus, since the constitution of the College makes sufficient provision for literary as well as for scientific education and since artistic instruction is also contemplated, it seems to me that a fairly complete culture is offered to all who are willing to take advantage of it.

36 But I am not sure that at this point the "practical" man, scotched but not slain, may ask what all this talk about culture has to do with an Institution, the object of which is defined to be "to promote the prosperity of the manufactures and the industry of the country." He may suggest that what is wanted for this end is not culture, not even a purely scientific discipline, but simply a knowledge of applied science.

37 I often wish that this phrase, "applied science," had never been invented. For it suggests that there is a sort of scientific knowledge of direct practical use, which can be studied apart from another sort of scientific knowledge, which is of no practical utility and which is termed "pure science." But there is no more complete fallacy than this. What people call applied science is nothing but the application of pure science to particular classes of problems. It consists of deductions from those general principles, established by reasoning and observation, which constitute pure science. No one can safely make these deductions until he has a firm grasp of the principles; and he can obtain that grasp only by personal experience of the operations of observation and of reasoning on which they are founded.

38 Almost all the processes employed in the arts and manufactures fall within the range either of physics or of chemistry. In order to improve them, one must thoroughly understand them; and no one has a chance of really understanding them unless he has obtained that mastery of principles and that habit of dealing with facts, which is given by long-continued and well-directed purely scientific training in the physical and the chemical laboratory. So that there really is no question as to the necessity of purely scientific discipline, even if the work of the College were limited by the narrowest interpretation of its stated aims.

39 And as to the desirableness of a wider culture than that yielded by science alone, it is to be recollected that the improvement of manufacturing processes is only one of the conditions which contribute to the prosperity of industry. Industry is a means and not an end; and mankind work only to get something which they want. What that something is depends partly on their innate, and partly on their acquired, desires.

40 If the wealth resulting from prosperous industry is to be spent upon the gratification of unworthy desires, if the increasing perfection of manufacturing processes is to be accompanied by an increasing debasement of those who carry them on, I do not see the good of industry and prosperity.

41 Now it is perfectly true that men's views of what is desirable depend upon their characters and that the innate proclivities to which we give that name are not touched by any amount of instruction. But it does not follow that even mere intellectual education may not, to an indefinite extent, modify the practical manifestation of the characters of men in their actions, by supplying them with motives unknown to the ignorant. A pleasure-loving character will have pleasure of some sort; but, if you give him the choice, he may prefer pleasures which do not degrade him to those which do. And this choice is offered to every man who possesses in literary or artistic culture a never-failing source of pleasures, which are neither withered by age, nor staled by custom, nor embittered in the recollection by the pangs of self-reproach.

Matthew Arnold: Literature and Science

1 I am going to ask whether the present movement for ousting letters from their old predominance in education and for transferring the predominance in education to the natural sciences—whether this brisk and flourishing movement ought to prevail and whether it is likely that in the end it really will prevail. An objection may be raised which I will anticipate. My own studies have been almost wholly in letters, and my visits to the field of the natural sciences have been slight and inadequate, although those sciences have always strongly moved my curiosity. A man of letters, it will perhaps be said, is not competent to discuss the comparative merits of letters and natural science as means of education. To this objection I reply, first of all, that his incompetence, if he attempts the discussion but is really incompetent for it, will be abundantly visible; nobody will be taken in; he will have plenty of sharp observers and critics to save mankind from that danger. But the line I am going to follow is, as you will soon discover, so extremely simple, that perhaps it may be followed without failure even by one who for a more ambitious line of discussion would be quite incompetent.

2 Some of you may possibly remember a phrase of mine which has been the object of a good deal of comment; an observation to the effect that in our culture, the aim being *to know ourselves and the world,* we have, as the means to this end, *to know the best which has been thought and said in the world.* A man of science, who is also an excellent writer and the very prince of debaters, Professor Huxley, in a discourse at the opening of Sir Josiah Mason's college at Birmingham, laying hold of this phrase, expanded it by quoting some more words of mine, which are these: "The civilized world is to be regarded as now being, for intellectual and spiritual purposes, one great confederation, bound to a joint action and working to a common result; and whose members have for their proper outfit a knowledge of Greek, Roman, and Eastern antiquity, and of one another. Special local and temporary advantages being put out of account, that modern nation will in the intellectual and spiritual sphere make most progress which most thoroughly carries out this programme."

3 Now on my phrase, thus enlarged, Professor Huxley remarks that when I speak of the above-mentioned knowledge as enabling us to know ourselves and the world, I assert *literature* to contain the materials which suffice for thus making us know ourselves and the world. But it is not by any means clear, says he, that after having learnt all which ancient and modern literatures have to tell us, we have laid a sufficiently broad and deep foundation for the criticism of life, that knowledge of ourselves and the world, which constitutes culture. On the contrary, Professor Huxley declares that he finds himself "wholly unable to admit that either nations or individuals will really advance, if their outfit draws nothing from the stores of physical science. An army without weapons of precision, and with no particular base of operations, might more hopefully enter upon a campaign on the Rhine, than a man, devoid of a knowledge of what physical science has done in the last century, upon a criticism of life."

4 This shows how needful it is for those who are to discuss any matters together, to have a common understanding as to the sense of the terms they employ—how needful and how difficult. What Professor Huxley says, implies just the reproach which is so often brought against the study of *belles lettres,* as they are called: that the study is an elegant one, but slight and ineffectual; a smattering of Greek and Latin and other ornamental things, of little use for any one whose object is to get at truth and to be a practical man. So, too, M. Renan talks of the "superficial humanism" of a schoolcourse which treats us as if we were all going to be poets, writers, preachers, orators, and he opposes this humanism to positive science or the critical search after truth. And there is always a tendency in those who are remonstrating against the predominance of letters in education to understand by letters *belles lettres* and by *belles lettres* a superficial humanism, the opposite of science or true knowledge.

5 But when we talk of knowing Greek and Roman antiquity, for instance,

which is the knowledge people have called the humanities, I for my part mean a knowledge which is something more than a superficial humanism, mainly decorative. "I call all teaching *scientific*," says Wolf, the critic of Homer, "which is systematically laid out and followed up to its original sources. For example: a knowledge of classical antiquity is scientific when the remains of classical antiquity are correctly studied in the original languages." There can be no doubt that Wolf is perfectly right; that all learning is scientific which is systematically laid out and followed up to its original sources and that a genuine humanism is scientific.

6 When I speak of knowing Greek and Roman antiquity, therefore, as a help to knowing ourselves and the world, I mean more than a knowledge of so much vocabulary, so much grammar, so many portions of authors in the Greek and Latin languages—I mean knowing the Greeks and Romans, and their life and genius, and what they were and did in the world; what we get from them and what is its value. That, at least, is the ideal; and when we talk of endeavouring to know Greek and Roman antiquity, as a help to knowing ourselves and the world, we mean endeavouring so to know them as to satisfy this ideal, however much we may still fall short of it.

7 The same also as to knowing our own and other modern nations, with the like aim of getting to understand ourselves and the world. To know the best that has been thought and said by the modern nations is to know, says Professor Huxley, "only what modern *literatures* have to tell us; it is the criticism of life contained in modern literature." And yet "the distinctive character of our times," he urges, "lies in the vast and constantly increasing part which is played by natural knowledge." And how, therefore, can a man, devoid of knowledge of what physical science has done in the last century, enter hopefully upon a criticism of modern life?

8 Let us, I say, be agreed about the meaning of the terms we are using. I talk of knowing the best which has been thought and uttered in the world; Professor Huxley says this means knowing *literature*. Literature is a large word; it may mean everything written with letters or printed in a book. Euclid's *Elements* and Newton's *Principia* are thus literature. All knowledge that reaches us through books is literature. But by literature Professor Huxley means *belles lettres*. He means to make me say, that knowing the best which has been thought and said by the modern nations is knowing their *belles lettres* and no more. And this is no sufficient equipment, he argues, for a criticism of modern life. But as I do not mean, by knowing ancient Rome, knowing merely more or less of Latin *belles lettres* and taking no account of Rome's military and political and legal and administrative work in the world; and as, by knowing ancient Greece, I understand knowing her as the giver of Greek art and the guide to a free and right use of reason and to scientific method, and the founder of our mathematics and physics and

astronomy and biology—I understand knowing her as all this and not merely knowing certain Greek poems and histories and treatises and speeches—so as to the knowledge of modern nations also. By knowing modern nations, I mean not merely knowing their *belles lettres,* but knowing also what has been done by such men as Copernicus, Galileo, Newton, Darwin. "Our ancestors learned," says Professor Huxley, "that the earth is the centre of the visible universe and that man is the cynosure of things terrestrial; and more especially was it inculcated that the course of nature had no fixed order, but that it could be, and constantly was, altered." But for us now, continues Professor Huxley, "the notions of the beginning and the end of the world entertained by our forefathers are no longer credible. It is very certain that the earth is not the chief body in the material universe and that the world is not subordinated to man's use. It is even more certain that nature is the expression of a definite order, with which nothing interferes." "And yet," he cries, "the purely classical education advocated by the representatives of the humanists in our day gives no inkling of all this!"

9 In due place and time I will just touch upon that vexed question of classical education; but at present the question is as to what is meant by knowing the best which modern nations have thought and said. It is not knowing their *belles lettres* merely which is meant. To know Italian *belles lettres* is not to know Italy, and to know English *belles lettres* is not to know England. Into knowing Italy and England there comes a great deal more, Galileo and Newton amongst it. The reproach of being a superficial humanism, a tincture of *belles lettres,* may attach rightly enough to some other disciplines; but to the particular discipline recommended when I proposed knowing the best that has been thought and said in the world, it does not apply. In that best I certainly include what in modern times has been thought and said by the great observers and knowers of nature.

10 There is, therefore, really no question between Professor Huxley and me as to whether knowing the great results of the modern scientific study of nature is not required as a part of our culture, as well as knowing the products of literature and art. But to follow the processes by which those results are reached, ought, say the friends of physical science, to be made the staple of education for the bulk of mankind. And here there does arise a question between those whom Professor Huxley calls with playful sarcasm "the Levites of culture," and those whom the poor humanist is sometimes apt to regard as its Nebuchadnezzars.

11 The great results of the scientific investigation of nature we are agreed upon knowing, but how much of our study are we bound to give to the processes by which those results are reached? The results have their visible bearing on human life. But all the processes, too, all the items of fact, by which those results are reached and established, are interesting. All knowledge is

interesting to a wise man, and the knowledge of nature is interesting to all men. It is very interesting to know that from the albuminous white of the egg the chick in the egg gets the materials for its flesh, bones, blood, and feathers, while from the fatty yolk of the egg it gets the heat and energy which enable it at length to break its shell and begin the world. It is less interesting, perhaps, but still it is interesting, to know that when a taper burns, the wax is converted into carbonic acid and water. Moreover, it is quite true that the habit of dealing with facts, which is given by the study of nature, is, as the friends of physical science praise it for being, an excellent discipline. The appeal, in the study of nature, is constantly to observation and experiment; not only is it said that the thing is so, but we can be made to see that it is so. Not only does a man tell us that when a taper burns the wax is converted into carbonic acid and water, as a man may tell us, if he likes, that Charon is punting his ferry-boat on the river Styx, or that Victor Hugo is a sublime poet, or Mr. Gladstone the most admirable of statesmen; but we are made to see that the conversion into carbonic acid and water does actually happen. This reality of natural knowledge it is which makes the friends of physical science contrast it, as a knowledge of things, with the humanist's knowledge, which is, say they, a knowledge of words. And hence Professor Huxley is moved to lay it down that "for the purpose of attaining real culture, an exclusively scientific education is at least as effectual as an exclusively literary education." And a certain President of the Section for Mechanical Science in the British Association is, in Scripture phrase, "very bold," and declares that if a man, in his mental training, "has substituted literature and history for natural science, he has chosen the less useful alternative." But whether we go these lengths or not, we must admit that in natural science the habit gained of dealing with facts is a most valuable discipline and that everyone should have some experience of it.

12   More than this, however, is demanded by the reformers. It is proposed to make the training in natural science the main part of education, for the great majority of mankind at any rate. And here, I confess, I part company with the friends of physical science, with whom up to this point I have been agreeing. In differing from them, however, I wish to proceed with the utmost caution and diffidence. The smallness of my own acquaintance with the disciplines of natural science is ever before my mind, and I am fearful of doing these disciplines an injustice. The ability and pugnacity of the partisans of natural science make them formidable persons to contradict. The tone of tentative inquiry, which befits a being of dim faculties and bounded knowledge, is the tone I would wish to take and not to depart from. At present it seems to me that those who are for giving to natural knowledge, as they call it, the chief place in the education of the majority of mankind, leave one important thing out of their account: the constitution of human nature. But I

put this forward on the strength of some facts not at all recondite, very far from it; facts capable of being stated in the simplest possible fashion, and to which, if I so state them, the man of science will, I am sure, be willing to allow their due weight.

13   Deny the facts altogether, I think, he hardly can. He can hardly deny that when we set ourselves to enumerate the powers which go to the building up of human life, and say that they are the power of conduct, the power of intellect and knowledge, the power of beauty, and the power of social life and manners—he can hardly deny that this scheme, though drawn in rough and plain lines enough, and not pretending to scientific exactness, does yet give a fairly true representation of the matter. Human nature is built up by these powers; we have the need for them all. When we have rightly met and adjusted the claims of them all, we shall then be in a fair way for getting soberness and righteousness with wisdom. This is evident enough, and the friends of physical science would admit it.

14   But perhaps they may not have sufficiently observed another thing: namely, that the several powers just mentioned are not isolated, but there is, in the generality of mankind, a perpetual tendency to relate them one to another in divers ways. With one such way of relating them I am particularly concerned now. Following our instinct for intellect and knowledge, we acquire pieces of knowledge; and presently, in the generality of men, there arises the desire to relate these pieces of knowledge to our sense for conduct, to our sense for beauty—and there is weariness and dissatisfaction if the desire is balked. Now in this desire lies, I think, the strength of that hold which letters have upon us.

15   All knowledge is, as I said just now, interesting; and even items of knowledge which from the nature of the case cannot well be related, but must stand isolated in our thoughts, have their interest. Even lists of exceptions have their interest. If we are studying Greek accents, it is interesting to know that *pais* and *pas,* and some other monosyllables of the same form of declension, do not take the circumflex upon the last syllable of the genitive plural, but vary, in this respect, from the common rule. If we are studying physiology, it is interesting to know that the pulmonary artery carries dark blood and the pulmonary vein carries bright blood, departing in this respect from the common rule for the division of labour between the veins and the arteries. But every one knows how we seek naturally to combine the pieces of our knowledge together, to bring them under general rules, to relate them to principles; and how unsatisfactory and tiresome it would be to go on forever learning lists of exceptions or accumulating items of fact which must stand isolated.

16   Well, that same need of relating our knowledge, which operates here within the sphere of our knowledge itself, we shall find operating also outside that sphere. We experience, as we go on learning and knowing—the vast majority of us experience—the need of relating what we have learnt and known to the sense which we have in us for conduct, to the sense which we have in us for beauty.

17 A certain Greek prophetess of Mantineia in Arcadia, Diotima by name, once explained to the philosopher Socrates that love and impulse and bent of all kinds is, in fact, nothing else but the desire in men that good should forever be present to them. This desire for good, Diotima assured Socrates, is our fundamental desire, of which fundamental desire every impulse in us is only one particular form. And therefore this fundamental desire it is, I suppose—this desire in men that good should be forever present to them— which acts in us when we feel the impulse for relating our knowledge to our sense for conduct and to our sense for beauty. At any rate, with men in general the instinct exists. Such is human nature. And the instinct, it will be admitted, is innocent, and human nature is preserved by our following the lead of its innocent instincts. Therefore, in seeking to gratify this instinct in question, we are following the instinct of self-preservation in humanity.

18 But, no doubt, some kinds of knowledge cannot be made to directly serve the instinct in question, cannot be directly related to the sense of beauty, to the sense for conduct. These are instrument-knowledges; they lead on to other knowledges which can. A man who passes his life in instrument-knowledges is a specialist. They may be invaluable as instruments to do something beyond, for those who have the gift thus to employ them; and they may be disciplines in themselves wherein it is useful for everyone to have some schooling. But it is inconceivable that the generality of men should pass all their mental life with Greek accents or with formal logic. My friend Professor Sylvester, who is one of the first mathematicians in the world, holds transcendental doctrines as to the virtue of mathematics, but those doctrines are not for common men. In the very Senate House and heart of our English Cambridge I once ventured, though not without an apology for my profaneness, to hazard the opinion that for the majority of mankind a little of mathematics, even, goes a long way. Of course this is quite consistent with their being of immense importance as an instrument to something else; but it is the few who have the aptitude for using them, not the bulk of mankind.

19 The natural sciences do not, however, stand on the same footing with these instrument-knowledges. Experience shows us that the generality of men will find more interest in learning that, when a taper burns, the wax is converted into carbonic acid and water, or in learning the explanation of the phenomenon of dew, or in learning how the circulation of the blood is carried on, than they find in learning that the genitive plural of *pais* and *pas* does not take the circumflex on the termination. And one piece of natural knowledge is added to another, and others are added to that, and at last we come to propositions so interesting as Mr. Darwin's famous proposition that "our ancestor was a hairy quadruped furnished with a tail and pointed ears, probably arboreal in his habits." Or we come to propositions of such reach and magnitude as those which Professor Huxley delivers, when he says that the notions of our forefathers about the beginning and the end of the world were all wrong and that nature is the expression of a definite order with which nothing interferes.

20   Interesting indeed, these results of science are, important they are, and we should all of us be acquainted with them. But what I now wish you to mark is that we are still, when they are propounded to us and we receive them, we are still in the sphere of intellect and knowledge. And for the generality of men there will be found, I say, to arise, when they have duly taken in the proposition that their ancestor was "a hairy quadruped furnished with a tail and pointed ears, probably arboreal in his habits," there will be found to arise an invincible desire to relate this proposition to the sense in us for conduct and to the sense in us for beauty. But this the men of science will not do for us and will hardly even profess to do. They will give us other pieces of knowledge, other facts, about other animals and their ancestors, or about plants, or about stones, or about stars; and they may finally bring us to those great "general conceptions of the universe, which are forced upon us all," says Professor Huxley, "by the progress of physical science." But still it will be *knowledge* only which they give us; knowledge not put for us into relation with our sense for conduct, our sense for beauty, and touched with emotion by being so put; not thus put for us, and therefore, to the majority of mankind, after a certain while, unsatisfying, wearying.

21   Not to the born naturalist, I admit. But what do we mean by a born naturalist? We mean a man in whom the zeal for observing nature is so uncommonly strong and eminent that it marks him off from the bulk of mankind. Such a man will pass his life happily in collecting natural knowledge and reasoning upon it, and will ask for nothing, or hardly anything, more. I have heard it said that the sagacious and admirable naturalist whom we lost not very long ago, Mr. Darwin, once owned to a friend that for his part he did not experience the necessity for two things which most men find so necessary to them—religion and poetry; science and the domestic affections, he thought, were enough. To a born naturalist, I can well understand that this should seem so. So absorbing is his occupation with nature, so strong his love for his occupation, that he goes on acquiring natural knowledge and reasoning upon it, and has little time or inclination for thinking about getting it related to the desire in man for conduct, the desire in man for beauty. He relates it to them for himself as he goes along, so far as he feels the need; and he draws from the domestic affections all the additional solace necessary. But then Darwins are extremely rare. Another great and admirable master of natural knowledge, Faraday, was a Sandemanian. That is to say, he related his knowledge to his instinct for conduct and to his instinct for beauty by the aid of that respectable Scottish sectary, Robert Sandeman. And so strong, in general, is the demand of religion and poetry to have their share in a man, to associate themselves with his knowing, and to relieve and rejoice it, that, probably, for one man amongst us with the disposition to do as Darwin did in this respect, there are at least fifty with the disposition to do as Faraday.

22   Education lays hold upon us, in fact, by satisfying this demand. Professor Huxley holds up to scorn mediaeval education with its neglect of the knowledge of nature, its poverty even of literary studies, its formal logic devoted to "showing how and why that which the Church said was true must be true." But the great mediaeval Universities were not brought into being, we may be sure, by the zeal for giving a jejune and contemptible education. Kings have been their nursing fathers, and queens have been their nursing mothers, but not for this. The mediaeval Universities came into being because the supposed knowledge, delivered by Scripture and the Church, so deeply engaged men's hearts, by so simply, easily, and powerfully relating itself to their desire for conduct, their desire for beauty. All other knowledge was dominated by this supposed knowledge and was subordinated to it, because of the surpassing strength of the hold which it gained upon the affections of men, by allying itself profoundly with their sense for conduct, their sense for beauty.

23   But now, says Professor Huxley, conceptions of the universe fatal to the notions held by our forefathers have been forced upon us by physical science. Grant to him that they are thus fatal, that the new conceptions must and will soon become current everywhere, and that every one will finally perceive them to be fatal to the beliefs of our forefathers. The need of humane letters, as they are truly called, because they serve the paramount desire in men that good should be forever present to them—the need of humane letters, to establish a relation between the new conceptions and our instinct for beauty, our instinct for conduct, is only the more visible. The Middle Age could do without humane letters, as it could do without the study of nature, because its supposed knowledge was made to engage its emotions so powerfully. Grant that the supposed knowledge disappears, its power of being made to engage the emotions will of course disappear along with it—but the emotions themselves, and their claim to be engaged and satisfied, will remain. Now if we find by experience that humane letters have an undeniable power of engaging the emotions, the importance of humane letters in a man's training becomes not less, but greater, in proportion to the success of modern science in extirpating what it calls "mediaeval thinking."

24   Have humane letters, then, have poetry and eloquence, the power here attributed to them of engaging the emotions, and do they exercise it? And if

they have it and exercise it, *how* do they exercise it, so as to exert an influence upon man's sense for conduct, his sense for beauty? Finally, even if they both can and do exert an influence upon the senses in question, how are they to relate to them the results—the modern results—of natural science? All these questions may be asked. First, have poetry and eloquence the power of calling out the emotions? The appeal is to experience. Experience shows that for the vast majority of men, for mankind in general, they have the power. Next, do they exercise it? They do. But then, *how* do they exercise it so as to affect man's sense for conduct, his sense for beauty? And this is perhaps a case for applying the Preacher's words: "Though a man labour to seek it out, yet he shall not find it; yea, farther, though a wise man think to know it, yet shall he not be able to find it." Why should it be one thing, in its effect upon the emotions, to say, "Patience is a virtue," and quite another thing, in its effect upon the emotions, to say with Homer, *τλητὸν γὰρ Μοῖραι θυμὸν θέσαν ἀνθρώποισιν*—"for an enduring heart have the destinies appointed to the children of men"? Why should it be one thing, in its effect upon the emotions, to say with the philosopher Spinoza, *Felicitas in ea consistit quod homo suum esse conservare potest*—"Man's happiness consists in his being able to preserve his own essence," and quite another thing, in its effect upon the emotions, to say with the Gospel, "What is a man advantaged, if he gain the whole world, and lose himself, forfeit himself?" How does this difference of effect arise? I cannot tell, and I am not much concerned to know; the important thing is that it does arise and that we can profit by it. But how, finally, are poetry and eloquence to exercise the power of relating the modern results of natural science to man's instinct for conduct, his instinct for beauty? And here again I answer that I do not know *how* they will exercise it, but that they can and will exercise it I am sure. But I do not mean that modern philosophical poets and modern philosophical moralists are to come and relate for us, in express terms, the results of modern scientific research to our instinct for conduct, our instinct for beauty. But I mean that we shall find, as a matter of experience, if we know the best that has been thought and uttered in the world—we shall find that the art and poetry and eloquence of men who lived, perhaps long ago, who had the most limited natural knowledge, who had the most erroneous conceptions about many important matters—we shall find that this art, and poetry, and eloquence, have in fact not only the power of refreshing and delighting us; they have also the power—such is the strength and worth, in essentials, of their authors' criticism of life—they have a fortifying, and elevating, and quickening, and suggestive power, capable of wonderfully helping us to relate the results of modern science to our need for conduct, our need for beauty. Homer's conceptions of the physical universe were, I imagine, grotesque; but really, under the shock of hearing from modern science that "the world is not subordinated to man's use and that man is not the cynosure of things terrestrial," I could, for my own part, desire no better comfort than Homer's line which I quoted just now, τλητὸν γὰρ Μοῖραι θυμὸν θέσαν ἀνθρώποισιν—"for an enduring heart have the destinies appointed to the children of men"!

25 And the more that men's minds are cleared, the more that the results of science are frankly accepted, the more that poetry and eloquence come to be received and studied as what in truth they really are—the criticism of life by gifted men, alive and active with extraordinary power at an unusual number of points—so much the more will the value of humane letters, and of art also, which is an utterance having a like kind of power with theirs, be felt and acknowledged, and their place in education be secured.

26 Let us, therefore, all of us, avoid indeed as much as possible any invidious comparison between the merits of humane letters, as means of education, and the merits of the natural sciences. But when some President of a Section for Mechanical Science insists on making the comparison and tells us that "he who in his training has substituted literature and history for natural science has chosen the less useful alternative," let us make answer to him that the student of humane letters only, will, at least, know also the great conceptions brought in by modern physical science, for science, as Professor Huxley says, forces them upon us all. But the student of the natural sciences only, will, by our very hypothesis, know nothing of humane letters; not to mention that in setting himself to be perpetually accumulating natural knowledge, he sets himself to do what only specialists have in general the gift for doing genially. And so he will probably be unsatisfied, or at any rate incomplete, and even more incomplete than the student of humane letters only.

27 I once mentioned in a school-report how a young man in one of our English training colleges having to paraphrase the passage in *Macbeth* beginning,

> Can'st thou not minister to a mind diseased?

turned this line into, "Can you not wait upon the lunatic?" And I remarked what a curious state of things it would be if every pupil of our national schools knew, let us say, that the moon is two thousand one hundred and sixty miles in diameter, and thought at the same time that a good paraphrase for

> Can'st thou not minister to a mind diseased?

was, "Can you not wait upon the lunatic?" If one is driven to choose, I think I would rather have a young person ignorant about the moon's diameter, but aware that "Can you not wait upon the lunatic?" is bad, than a young person whose education had been such as to manage things the other way.

28 Or to go higher than the pupils of our national schools. I have in my

mind's eye a member of our British Parliament who comes to travel here in America, who afterwards relates his travels and who shows a really masterly knowledge of the geology of this great country and of its mining capabilities, but who ends by gravely suggesting that the United States should borrow a prince from our Royal Family, and should make him their king, and should create a House of Lords of great landed proprietors after the pattern of ours; and then America, he thinks, would have her future happily and perfectly secured. Surely, in this case, the President of the Section for Mechanical Science would himself hardly say that our member of Parliament, by concentrating himself upon geology and mineralogy and so on, and not attending to literature and history, had "chosen the more useful alternative."

29 If then there is to be separation and option between humane letters on the one hand and the natural sciences on the other, the great majority of mankind, all who have not exceptional over-powering aptitudes for the study of nature, would do well, I cannot but think, to choose to be educated in humane letters rather than in the natural sciences. Letters will call out their being at more points, will make them live more.

III / ARRANGEMENT OF MATERIAL

Once writers have discovered, through the process of invention, or discovery of material, something to say on a given subject, they are faced with the problem of selecting and marshalling the available material in order to effect their purpose. Since usually they cannot, and should not, use all the material available to them, they have to select what is most pertinent and cogent. This selected material must then be put in some order, for without order, the force of even the best material, though chosen with the keenest of discretion, will be weakened. The classical rhetoricians dealt with the problems of selection and arrangement under that part of rhetoric that the Greeks called *taxis* and the Latins called *dispositio;* we will use the term *arrangement.*

If we are to profit from the classical precepts about *dispositio,* we must come to a clear understanding of what *dispositio* meant for the ancients. For many people, disposition means simply the study of the several parts of a discourse: (1) the *exordium* or introduction; (2) the *narratio* or statement of facts or circumstances that need to be known about the subject of our discourse; (3) the *confirmatio* or proof of our case; (4) the *refutatio* or discrediting of the opposing views; (5) the *peroratio* or conclusion. Classical rhetoric did deal with those parts and in that sequence; but it was concerned with something more. It was concerned also with the strategic planning of the whole composition.

Quintilian hints at the more important concern of disposition when he says that it is to oratory what generalship is to war. It would be folly to hold a general to a fixed, predetermined disposition of his forces. He must be left free to distribute his troops in the order and proportion best suited to cope with the situation in which he may find himself at any particular moment. So he will mass some of his troops at one point on the battle line, thin them out at other points, keep other troops in reserve, and perhaps concentrate his crack troops at the most crucial area. Guided by judgment and imagination, the general stands ready to make whatever adjustments in strategy eventualities may dictate.

Cicero made explicit the twofold aspect of disposition when he said that the orator "ought first to find out what he should say; next to dispose and arrange his matter, not only in a certain order, but according to the weight of the matter and the judgment of the speaker" (*De Oratore,* I, 31). Those bent on persuasion will be guided in their decisions about the appropriate disposition of their resources by a number of considerations:

1. The kind of discourse in which they are engaged—whether deliberative, judicial, or ceremonial.
2. The nature of their subject—a consideration that in turn will determine the quantity and quality of the matter available to them.
3. Their own *ēthos*—their personality, their moral and philosophical bias, their limitations and capabilities.
4. The nature of the audience—their age, their social, political, economic, and educational level, their mood at the moment.

What all of this suggests is that disposition is what Aristotle meant by *techne:* an art by which one adapts means to an end.

What the classical rhetoricians seemed to be striving for under *dispositio* was that "subsuming form" which Ronald S. Crane spoke of when he described his own experience in composing an essay. The passage deserves to be quoted in full:

> The process of literary composition has often been rather crudely divided, especially by authors of textbooks on English writing, into two stages: a stage of preparatory reading, thinking, planning, incubation, and a stage of putting the materials thus assembled into words; and what happens in the second stage has usually been represented as a direct transference to paper of the ideas or imaginations which the writer has come into possession of in the first stage—as a simple matter, that is, of giving to an acquired content an appropriate verbal form. I have myself taught this easy doctrine to students; but never, I believe, since I began to meditate on the disturbing fact that all too frequently, when I have attempted to write an essay after a long and interested concentration on the subject, and the noting of many exciting ideas and patterns of key terms, and the construction of what looked like a perfect outline, I have found myself unable to compose the first sentence, or even to know what

it ought to be about, or, having forced myself to go on, to bring the thing to a satisfying conclusion, whereas, on other occasions, with no more complete preparation, no greater desire to write, and no better state of nerves, I have discovered, to my delight, that nearly everything fell speedily into place, the right words came (or at any rate words which I couldn't change later on), and the sentences and paragraphs followed one another with scarcely a hitch and in an order that still seemed to me the inevitable one when I came to reread the essay in cold blood.

I have had so many more experiences of the first sort than of the second that I have tried to isolate the reason for the difference. And the best way I can explain it is to say that what I failed to attain in the former cases and did somehow, at one moment or another of the total process, in the latter was a kind of intuitive glimpse of a possible subsuming form for the materials, or at least those I attached most importance to, which I had assembled in my mind and notes—a form sufficiently coherent and intelligible, as a form in my mind, so that I could know at once what I must or could do, and what I need not or ought not to do, in what order and with what emphasis in the various parts, in developing my arguments and putting them into words. I have never been able to write anything which seemed to me, in retrospect, to possess any quality of organic wholeness, however uninteresting or thin, except in response to such a synthesizing idea. It is more than a general intention, more than a "theme," and more than an outline in the usual sense of that word; it is, as I have said, a shaping or directing cause, involving at the same time, and in some sort of correlation, the particular conceptual form my subject is to take in my essay, the particular mode of argument or of rhetoric I am to use in discussing it, and the particular end my discussion is to serve: I must know, in some fashion, at least these three things before I can proceed with any ease or success.

From Ronald S. Crane, *The Languages of Criticism and the Structure of Poetry,* The Alexander Lectures, 1951–52. Reprinted by permission of the University of Toronto Press.

If Professor Crane's analysis of the writing process is accurate, composition would seem to exact from the writer a number of preliminary, as well as current, judgments and decisions. In Book VII, Chapter X of his *Institutio Oratoria,* Quintilian pointed out that disposition was concerned with judgments and decisions about questions like these:

1. When is an introduction necessary and when can it be omitted or abbreviated?
2. When should we make our statement of facts continuous and when should we break it up and insert it *passim?*
3. Under what circumstances can we omit the statement of facts altogether?

4. When should we begin by dealing with the arguments advanced by our opponents and when should we begin by proposing our own arguments?

5. When is it advisable to present our strongest arguments first and when is it best to begin with our weakest arguments and work up to our strongest?

6. Which of our arguments will our audience readily accept and which of them must they be induced to accept?

7. Should we attempt to refute our opponents' arguments as a whole or deal with them in detail?

8. How much ethical appeal must we exert in order to conciliate the audience?

9. Should we reserve our emotional appeals for the conclusion or distribute them throughout the discourse?

10. What evidence or documents should we make use of and where in the discourse will this kind of argument be most effective?

These and many other questions will confront writers when they sit down to plan their compositions and will call forth all their powers of discretion to decide. Their native good sense and intuition will be indispensable when they have to make crucial decisions about appropriate strategies, but rhetoric can lay down certain general principles to guide them at this stage. It remains for the writer, however, to discern where and how these principles are applicable to a particular situation.

It must be emphasized at this point that the disposition of one's material is not an indifferent matter. The importance of proper arrangement is pointed up by the incident in which the two great Athenian orators, Aeschines and Demosthenes, were engaged in an oratorical contest concerning Ctesiphon's proposal that Demosthenes be rewarded for his services with a golden crown. On that occasion, Aeschines proposed to the judges that Demosthenes be constrained to observe the same order of argument as he had followed in presenting his. But Demosthenes was quick to see that Aeschines' order would be disadvantageous to his own presentation. Accordingly, he pleaded with the judges to allow him to follow whatever order he saw fit. Demosthenes perceived that the arrangement of his arguments could be the decisive factor in the contest. The best of arguments could be weakened or nullified if inserted in the wrong place or if presented with inappropriate emphasis or proportion.

The Parts of a Discourse

Most rhetoricians recognized five parts for the usual argumentative discourse: *exordium, narratio, confirmatio* or *probatio, refutatio,* and *peroratio.* These terms were explained briefly in the introductory chapter of this book. In this text we will deal with four parts, using these labels: introduction, statement of fact, confirmation, and conclusion. This kind of partitioning of the discourse differs from the outlining system that the student may have learned. The outline is usually organized topically; this system of partitioning is determined by the *functions* of the various parts of a discourse.

We will use these four parts as the organizing principle of this chapter, but in accordance with the classical view of *dispositio,* we will be constantly pointing out the adjustments that one may have to make in sequence, proportion, emphasis, and coloring to fit a particular subject, occasion, purpose, or audience.

Introduction

Etymologically, *introduction* means "a leading into." The Greek and Latin rhetorical terms for this part carried the same suggestion. The Greek term *proemium* meant "before the song"; the Latin term *exordium* meant "beginning a web"—by mounting a woof or laying a warp. The basic function then of the introduction is to lead the audience into the discourse. Instinctively we feel that an abrupt, immediate entry into the body of our discourse would unsettle and confuse the audience. We sense that in most instances an audience must, as it were, be "eased into" the subject of the discourse.

Generally this preparation of the audience has a twofold aspect: (1) it informs the audience of the end or object of our discourse, and (2) it disposes the audience to be receptive to what we say. Conceivably, an audience could be well enough informed about a subject and sufficiently predisposed in our favor that the introduction could be made very brief or might be dispensed with entirely. Even under those conditions, however, most of us would feel that some kind of prelude was necessary—if nothing else a joke, an apt quotation, an entertaining anecdote, an ingratiating gesture toward the audience. Aristotle remarked that the introduction to some speeches was comparable to the preliminary flourishes that flute players made before their performance—an overture in which the musicians merely displayed what they could play best to gain the favor and attention of the audience for the main performance. Without this kind of "ornamental" introduction, the discourse would have an abrupt, negligent, unfinished air about it. So it is a rare discourse that plunges immediately into "the heart of the matter."

Informing the Audience

Granting then that most compositions require some kind of prelude, let us consider the first of the two main functions of the introduction—informing the audience of the end or subject of our discourse. In doing this, we are seeking to orient the audience, but, even more important, we are seeking to convince the audience that the subject of our discourse is worthy of their attention. We can render our subject attractive to the audience by showing that it is important, or momentous, or relevant to the interests of the audience, or startling, or pleasant. The nature of the subject that we have to deal with will determine, of course, which of these topics we will exploit. A subject that is trifling cannot, by any exercise of ingenuity, be made to appear important or momentous. But a trifling subject could be made to appear agreeable or exotic enough to warrant our attention.

Richard Whately in his *Elements of Rhetoric* invented a number of terms to designate the various kinds of introduction designed to arouse interest in our subject:

> 1. *Introduction Inquisitive*—to show that our subject is important, curious, or interesting.

In this example of the "introduction inquisitive," Arnold J. Toynbee asks a provocative question and then seeks to sustain the interest of the reader by suggesting the importance to the modern world of the answer to that question:

> Does history repeat itself? In our Western world in the eighteenth and nineteenth centuries, this question used to be debated as an academic exercise. The spell of well-being which our civilization was enjoying at the time had dazzled our grandfathers into the quaint pharisaical notion that they were "not as other men are"; they had come to believe that our Western society was exempt from the possibility of falling into those mistakes and mishaps that have been the ruin of certain other civilizations whose history, from beginning to end, is an open book. To us, in our generation, the old question has rather suddenly taken on a new and very practical significance. We have awakened to the truth (how, one wonders, could we ever have been blind to it?) that Western man and his works are no more invulnerable than the now extinct civilizations of the Aztecs and the Incas, the Sumerians and the Hittites. So to-day, with some anxiety, we are searching the scriptures of the past to find out whether they contain a lesson that we can decipher. Does history give us

any information about our own prospects? And, if it does, what is the burden of it? Does it spell out for us an inexorable doom, which we can merely await with folded hands—resigning ourselves, as best we may, to a fate that we cannot avert or even modify by our own efforts? Or does it inform us, not of certainties, but of probabilities, or bare possibilities, in our own future? The practical difference is vast, for, on this second alternative, so far from being stunned into passivity, we should be roused to action. On this second alternative, the lesson of history would not be like an astrologer's horoscope; it would be like a navigator's chart, which affords the seafarer who has the intelligence to use it a much greater hope of avoiding shipwreck than when he was sailing blind, because it gives him the means, if he has the skill and courage to use them, of steering a course between charted rocks and reefs.

From *Civilization on Trial* by Arnold J. Toynbee. Copyright 1948 by Oxford University Press, Inc.; renewed 1975 by Arnold Joseph Toynbee. Reprinted by permission of the publisher.

2. *Introduction Paradoxical*—to show that although the points we are trying to establish seem improbable, they must after all be admitted.

Here, from the pen of the British drama critic Kenneth Tynan, is an example of the "introduction paradoxical":

The most characteristic English play on the subject of physical love is Shakespeare's *Antony and Cleopatra*. It is characteristic because it has no love scenes. The English, as their drama represents them, are a nation endlessly communicative about love without ever enjoying it. Full-blooded physical relationships engaged in with mutual delight are theatrically tabu. Thwarted love is preferred, the kind Mr. Coward wrote about in *Brief Encounter,* where two married people (married, of course, to two other people) form a sad and meagre attachment without being able to follow it through. At the end of a play on some quite different subject—religion, perhaps, or politics—it is customary for the hero to say, as he does in *Robert's Wife:* "I was deeply in love with a fine woman," and for the wife to reply: "My dear, dear husband"; but there should be no hint elsewhere in the text that they have as much as brushed lips.

From *Curtains* by Kenneth Tynan. (Atheneum Publishers, 1961).

3. *Introduction Corrective*—to show that our subject has been neglected, misunderstood, or misrepresented.

In the first paragraph of the following "introduction corrective," George Orwell states that there is general agreement about the problem but that

there is widespread misunderstanding about the cause and the significance of the problem; then in the second paragraph Orwell suggests the "corrective" line that his essay will take:

> Most people who bother with the matter at all would admit that the English language is in a bad way, but it is generally assumed that we cannot by conscious action do anything about it. Our civilization is decadent and our language—so the argument runs—must inevitably share in the general collapse. It follows that any struggle against the abuse of language is a sentimental archaism, like preferring candles to electric light or hansom cabs to aeroplanes. Underneath this lies the half-conscious belief that language is a natural growth and not an instrument which we shape for our own purposes.
>
> Now, it is clear that the decline of a language must ultimately have political and economic causes: it is not due simply to the bad influence of this or that individual writer. But an effect can become a cause, reinforcing the original cause and producing the same effect in an intensified form, and so on indefinitely. A man may take to drink because he feels himself to be a failure, and then fail all the more completely because he drinks. It is rather the same thing that is happening to the English language. It becomes ugly and inaccurate because our thoughts are foolish, but the slovenliness of our language makes it easier for us to have foolish thoughts. The point is that the process is reversible. Modern English, especially written English, is full of bad habits which spread by imitation and which can be avoided if one is willing to take the necessary trouble. If one gets rid of these habits one can think more clearly, and to think clearly is a necessary first step toward political regeneration: so that the fight against bad English is not frivolous and is not the exclusive concern of professional writers. I will come back to this presently, and I hope that by that time the meaning of what I have said here will have become clearer. Meanwhile, here are five specimens of the English language as it is now habitually written.

4. *Introduction Preparatory*—to explain an unusual mode of developing our subject; or to forestall some misconception of our purpose; or to apologize for some deficiencies.

Here, in the first paragraph of Rachel Carson's *The Sea Around Us,* is an example of the "introduction preparatory," an introduction in which Miss Carson explains how she will proceed, lacking eye-witness accounts of the event, in tracing the history of the beginning of the ocean:

Beginnings are apt to be shadowy, and so it is with the beginnings of that great mother of life, the sea. Many people have debated how and when the earth got its ocean, and it is not surprising that their explanations do not always agree. For the plain and inescapable truth is that no one was there to see, and in the absence of eye-witness accounts there is bound to be a certain amount of disagreement. So if I tell here the story of how the young planet Earth acquired an ocean, it must be a story pieced together from many sources and containing many whole chapters the details of which we can only imagine. The story is founded on the testimony of the earth's most ancient rocks, which were young when the earth was young; on other evidence written on the face of the earth's satellite, the moon; and on hints contained in the history of the sun and the whole universe of star-filled space. For although no man was there to witness this cosmic birth, the stars and the moon and the rocks were there, and, indeed, had much to do with the fact that there is an ocean.

From *The Sea Around Us,* Revised Edition, by Rachel L. Carson. Copyright © 1950, 1951, 1961 by Rachel L. Carson; renewed 1979 by Roger Christie. Reprinted by permission of Oxford University Press, Inc.

5. *Introduction Narrative*—to rouse interest in our subject by adopting the anecdotal lead-in.

The anecdotal opening is one of the oldest and most effective gambits for seizing the attention of the reader. Here, from an article in *The Nation* about the mysterious murder of eight-year-old Melvin Dean Nimer's mother and father, is an example of the "introduction narrative":

A light flashed on the central switchboard of the New York Telephone Company office in Forest Avenue, West Brighton, S. I., at precisely 2:04 A.M., September 2, 1958. Mrs. Catherine B. Thompson, one of the operators on duty, plugged in on the line. She heard the sound of heavy breathing. "Hello," she said, "hello." There was no answer, just that heavy, breathing sound. Mrs. Thompson turned to another operator, Mrs. Florence Parkin, and asked her to trace the call. Mrs. Parkin quickly found that it was coming from a house at 242 Vanderbilt Avenue. Then she cut in on the line, holding it open, while Mrs. Thompson notified police that something appeared to be wrong.

Even as Mrs. Thompson was speaking to the desk sergeant at the St. George police station, Mrs. Parkin heard the labored breathing on the line turn into a voice. A woman gasped: "I've been stabbed."

The operator immediately cut the police in on the conversation, and both she and the desk officer heard the woman repeat: "I've been stabbed. I've been attacked with a knife." A second later, the voice added: "My husband has been stabbed, too."

Then there was silence. It lasted only a second. Then a new voice, a little boy's voice, came on the wire.

"My mother is bleeding," the voice said.

Mrs. Thompson told the boy police already were on the way.

"I'll wait for the police outside," he said.

"No," she told him, "you better stay with your mother."

Such was the beginning of a drama that was to shock the nation.

From Fred J. Cook and Gene Gleason, "He Never Had a Chance," first published in *The Nation*. Reprinted from *A View of The Nation: An Anthology, 1955–1959*, ed. H. M. Christman, pp. 152–53. Copyright © 1959 by The Nation Company, Inc. Reprinted by permission of *The Nation*, 72 Fifth Avenue, New York.

These are the common ways in which authors rouse interest in their subject at the same time that they are informing their readers of the object of their discourse. Obviously, there will be times when we do not have to rouse interest in the subject. The subject may be sufficiently interesting in itself (did Dr. Kinsey have to generate interest in his report about the sexual behavior of men and women?). Or the particular circumstances may make the subject interesting (did Winston Churchill have to fan interest in his subject when he got up in the House of Commons to deliver his "Blood, Toil, Tears, and Sweat" speech?). Or a subject will have its own interest for a particular kind of audience (did the speaker at a convention of geneticists have to whip up an interest in a report on DNA, the element that may hold the key to the creation of human life in a test tube?). Considerations of this sort will determine whether the speaker or writer will have to spend any time in the introduction rousing interest in his or her subject.

Ingratiating Oneself with the Audience

Even when we do not have to rouse interest in our subject, we may have to spend some time in the introduction establishing our credit with the audience. This function of the introduction, which the Latin rhetoricians called *insinuatio*, is closely tied up with the *ethical appeal* that a discourse must exert. Sometimes writers have to convince an audience that they are qualified to speak on some subject. At other times, they must counteract prejudices or misconceptions either about themselves or about the subject of their discourse. Or they must rouse hostility toward those whose point of view they are going to oppose in their discourse.

As the term *insinuation* suggests, authors must, in establishing their authority or counteracting prejudices, proceed with the utmost subtlety. To blatantly lay out their intellectual and moral qualifications—"to flaunt their clippings," as it were—could impress the audience as mere boasting and thereby nullify the intended effect of their recital. Good sense and good taste must guide the writer in presenting his credentials. An audience will usually accept a person's display of qualifying credentials if the facts are recited with due restraint and a becoming humility. The person who says, "I have spent fifteen years studying the problems of juvenile delinquency in such cities as New York, Chicago, and Los Angeles," will do more to establish his or her qualifications than the person who says, "My thoroughgoing studies of the problems of juvenile delinquency in many parts of the country have completely discredited the half-baked notions of those who have investigated the problems with more zeal than wisdom." The person who jingles his or her Phi Beta Kappa key usually stirs up more resentment than confidence.

In the following example, we observe C. P. Snow modestly presenting his qualifications to write about "the two cultures," the sciences and the humanities:

> It is about three years since I made a sketch in print of a problem which had been on my mind for some time. It was a problem I could not avoid just because of the circumstances of my life. The only credentials I had to ruminate on the subject at all came through those circumstances, through nothing more than a set of chances. Anyone with similar experience would have seen much the same things and I think made very much the same comments about them. It just happened to be an unusual experience. By training I was a scientist; by vocation I was a writer. That was all. It was a piece of luck, if you like, that arose through coming from a poor home.
>
> But my personal history isn't the point now. All that I need say is that I came to Cambridge and did a bit of research here at a time of major scientific activity. I was privileged to have a ringside view of one of the most wonderful creative periods in all physics. And it happened through the flukes of war—including meeting W. L. Bragg in the buffet on Kettering station on a very cold morning in 1939, which had a determining influence on my practical life—that I was able, and indeed morally forced, to keep that ringside view ever since. So for thirty years I have had to be in touch with scientists not only out of curiosity, but as a part of a working existence. During the same thirty years I was trying to shape the books I wanted to write, which in due course took me among writers.
>
> From *The Two Cultures: and a Second Look*, 1965. Reprinted by permission of Cambridge University Press.

Those who have to minimize prejudices against them must be equally discreet, but they can usually be more open-handed than the person who has to establish his or her qualifications. No one resents the person who openly strives to clear himself or herself of charges and misconceptions. An audience's natural sense of fair play stands ready to hear "the other side of the story."

In seeking to remove prejudices, a number of speakers or writers have several courses open to them. They can

1. deny the charges that have created the prejudices against them.
2. admit the charges but deny their alleged magnitude.
3. cite a compensating virtue or action.
4. attribute the discrediting action to an honest mistake on their part or to an accident or to an inescapable compulsion.
5. cite others who were guilty of the same thing but were not so charged.
6. substitute a different motive or cause for the one alleged.
7. inveigh against calumny and malicious insinuation in general.
8. cite the testimony of those who take a different view of the matter.

Here is a short example of a man seeking to remove a prejudice against him. Because of his sympathetic writings about the American colonists, Edmund Burke, the great British Parliamentarian, was suspected of pro-American tendencies and of grounding his sympathies not so much on abstract principles as on considerations of expediency. Note how he meets these charges:

> I am charged with being an American. If warm affection towards those over whom I claim any share of authority be a crime, I am guilty of this charge. But I do assure you (and they who know me publicly and privately will bear witness to me) that if ever one man lived more zealous than another for the supremacy of Parliament and the rights of this imperial crown, it was myself. Many others indeed might be more knowing in the extent or the foundation of these rights. I do not pretend to be an antiquary, a lawyer, or qualified for the chair of professor in metaphysics. I never ventured to put your solid interests upon speculative grounds. My having constantly declined to do so has been attributed to my incapacity for such disquisitions; and I am inclined to believe it is partly the cause. I never shall be ashamed to confess that where I am ignorant I am diffident. I am indeed not very solicitous to clear myself of this imputed incapacity, because men even less conversant than I am in this kind of subtleties and placed in stations to which I ought not to aspire, have, by the mere force of civil discretion, often conducted the affairs of great nations with distinguished felicity and glory.
>
> From *A Letter to John Farr and John Harris, Esqurs., Sheriffs of the City of Bristol, on the Affairs of America,* 1777.

Arousing hostility against one's opponent is usually more effective in the conclusion than in the introduction, for it is easier to discredit a person's *ethos* after one has demolished that person's arguments. But sometimes it is more expedient to stir up animosity in the introduction. If circumstances make it difficult or impossible to clear oneself of prejudices or suspicion, one might be able to gain a hearing by showing that one's opponent is a fool or a knave. And this strategy is best adopted in the introduction. We saw how Socrates early in the *Apology* sought to raise suspicions about Meletus's integrity. Socrates thereby "softened up" the audience for his subsequent refutation of Meletus's charges.

In these opening paragraphs of *The Rights of Man* (1791–92), Thomas Paine is seeking to prejudice the audience against Edmund Burke, the man whose political and social views Paine is going to attack in the main body of his book:

> Among the incivilities by which nations or individuals provoke and irritate each other, Mr. Burke's pamphlet on the French Revolution [Burke's *Reflections on the Revolution in France* (1790)] is an extraordinary instance. Neither the people of France nor the National Assembly were troubling themselves about the affairs of England or the English Parliament; and that Mr. Burke should commence an unprovoked attack upon them, both in Parliament and in public, is a conduct that cannot be pardoned on the score of manners, nor justified on that of policy.
>
> There is scarcely an epithet of abuse to be found in the English language with which Mr. Burke has not loaded the French nation and the National Assembly. Everything which rancor, prejudice, ignorance, or knowledge could suggest is poured forth in the copious fury of near four hundred pages. In the strain and on the plan Mr. Burke was writing, he might have written on to as many thousands. When the tongue or the pen is let loose in a frenzy of passion, it is the man, and not the subject, that becomes exhausted.
>
> Hitherto Mr. Burke has been mistaken and disappointed in the opinions he had formed of the affairs of France, but such is the ingenuity of his hope, or the malignancy of his despair, that it furnishes him with new pretenses to go on. There was a time when it was impossible to make Mr. Burke believe there would be any revolution in France. His opinion then was that the French had neither spirit to undertake it nor fortitude to support it; and now that there is one, he seeks an escape by condemning it.

What we have been saying about the content and strategy of the introduction adds up to this: the introduction seeks to render the audience *attentive, benevolent*—that is, well-disposed toward the writer and his or her cause, and *docile*—that is, ready to be instructed or persuaded. In order to determine what must be done in the introduction to effect these ends, we must consider (1) what we have to say, (2) before whom, (3) under what circumstances, (4) what the prepossessions of the audience are likely to be, (5) how much time or space has been allotted to us. An honest confrontation of those considerations will tell us not only what we must do in the introduction but how long it has to be. If we see that there is no need to render our audience attentive, benevolent, and docile, our introduction can be very brief—a few ingratiating flourishes and a brief statement of the thesis. But if the occasion demands that the audience be "conditioned," then our introduction may have to be more elaborate.

One caution needs to be stressed here: introductions tend to be disproportionately long. At some time or other, students have probably heard the classic advice, "Throw away the first page of your rough draft and begin your final draft at the top of page two." Obviously we cannot follow this advice in any mechanical fashion, but the principle here is fundamentally sound. Our first draft is often encumbered with excess fat. One of the reasons why a long "warming up" is so common is that there is a natural inertia to be overcome before we can get under way. Often it is the writers with little to say on an assigned topic who produce the top-heavy introduction. They have 800 words to write. If they can spend 400 of these words on preliminaries, they can put off that formidable moment when they have to get down to the subject . . . and then there are only 400 words to go! If the discipline of the topics can fill up the "dry wells," perhaps we can prevent this tendency to pad the introduction.

Allotted wordage is becoming more and more a major consideration in the determination of the length of introductions. Since space is at such a premium in modern newspapers and magazines, editors are insisting on strict observance of specified word limits. It may be that the nature of our subject or of our audience calls for a fairly elaborate introduction, but we have been asked to develop our thesis in 1200 words. So we will have to ignore the exigency and get into the body of our discourse as soon as possible. One's writing can profit from the discipline of observing word-limits: nothing serves better to trim the fat from one's prose. Anyone who has been required to write book reviews in 300 to 350 words soon learns many salutary lessons about economy of means.

No mention has been made so far of the kind of opening that immediately captures the reader's interest. In books on the technique of fiction or the feature story, this kind of opening is often called "the hook." A provocative question, a startling hyperbole, an intriguing paradox—these are some of the devices we are advised to use in order to buttonhole our reader. Norman Cousins uses the provocative question effectively in the opening paragraphs of his article "Don't Resign from the Human Race":

> Have you ever wondered what you would say if you were suddenly called upon to defend the human race?
> Suppose you were invited to participate in a great debate or, better still, a mock court trial called for the purpose of deciding whether the human species had justified its right to survive—whether, on the basis

of its virtues and weaknesses, it was actually entitled to the gift of life. Suppose your job was that of attorney for the defense. How would you go about collecting your evidence? What witnesses would you call? What arguments would you use?

From *Saturday Review*, August 7, 1948. Reprinted by permission.

There are a number of reasons why such an opening is an attention-getter. First, although the initial question is a *rhetorical question*—a type that does not require a direct and immediate answer from the audience or reader—it does challenge the audience, make them more alert. Another reason for the effectiveness of this particular question is that it is both an unusual question —imagine suggesting that the human race has to justify its right to existence! —and an important one—it may concern our very existence. So the elements of surprise and importance are contributing to the effectiveness of the gambit. The second paragraph further challenges us by posing a hypothetical situation: suppose you were called upon to be the defense attorney for the human race. The final three questions suggest some of the problems that would face us in that capacity. So these opening paragraphs both alert us and disconcert us. Challenged by the importance of the question asked and perhaps somewhat chagrined that we do not have a ready answer for this important question, we are now "set up" to listen to this person's answer.

Writers must exercise good taste and judgment when they search for an opening calculated to arrest attention. The overtly and excessively clever opening can repel readers rather than engage them. (*The New Yorker,* in one of its regular filler features, has a label for such brashly clever openings— Letters We Never Finished Reading.) As usual, the most reliable guide in regard to attractive openings is the nature and temper of the audience.

The closing lines of the introduction should be so managed that they lead easily and naturally into the next division of the discourse. The problem of transition is basically one of coherence. We want the parts of our discourse to "hang together," and while we would like the sutures to be as unobtrusive as possible, we nevertheless want our readers to be aware that they are passing over into another division of the discourse. Aristotle himself, that great master of exposition, is not at all hesitant about marking his transitions explicitly. For instance, at the end of Chapter 1 in Book I of the *Rhetoric* he says, "Let us now try to give some account of the systematic principles of rhetoric itself—of the right method and means of succeeding in the object set before us. We must make as it were a fresh start, and before going further define what rhetoric is." Throughout the *Rhetoric*—in fact, throughout most of his treatises—Aristotle carefully plants these transitional markers —often at the end of a chapter, sometimes at the beginning of a new chapter, occasionally at divisions of an especially long and involved exposition. Sometimes, just the logical development of our thought allows us to glide into the next division without our having to use "pointers." No rule-of-thumb can be laid down to tell us when it is best to mark our transitions explicitly and when we can rely on the logic of our thought development to carry the reader over into the next division. In this respect—as we have seen so often in the discussion of rhetorical strategies—the particular situation will dictate its own exigencies.

One final point about introductions. The things we strive to do in the introduction—to render the audience attentive, benevolent, and docile—have sometimes to be done at various points in the discourse, especially in long discourses. As some of the rhetoricians observed, it is sometimes more necessary to make a play for the attention of the audience at a later stage in the discourse than it is in the introduction. In fact, we can usually rely on a certain natural attentiveness in our audience at the beginning of our discourse, which may flag as we continue. In that case, we may have to pull our audience up again. Likewise, when we are about to launch forth into a particularly delicate argument, we may have to make another play for the good will of our audience.

Statement of Fact

We have used the term *statement of fact* to designate the second division of a discourse for want of a better term to translate the Latin *narratio. Narration* has taken on meanings for us that it did not have for the Romans. *Statement of fact* has its own ambiguities for us, but the term suggests more accurately than does *narration* what it is that we do in this part of expository and argumentative prose.

Statement of fact figured principally in forensic oratory. In this division of a forensic speech, the advocate set forth the essential facts of the case under consideration. "On the night of March 15," we can imagine the advocate saying, "Gaius Maximus was murdered in a back alley off the Forum. It has been alleged that my client, who was seen in the Forum that evening and who was known to be a political enemy of the deceased, was the murderer. Suspicion about my client has not been dispelled by the revelation that at the time of the murder my client was seen. . . ." If the prosecuting lawyer had previously set forth these facts, the defending lawyer might use this part in his or her speech to add pertinent facts or to correct details in the prosecution's statement. In a court trial, what often initiates this part of the trial is the reading of the formal indictment against the defendant—in other words, the defining of the issue in the case. For example, here was the indictment read by Attorney General A. T. Stewart on the second day of the "Monkey

Trial" in July 1925—a trial that became a *cause célèbre* partly because of the conflict that developed in the courtroom between William Jennings Bryan and Clarence Darrow:

> That John Thomas Scopes, heretofore on the 24th of April, 1925, in the county aforesaid, then and there, unlawfully did wilfully teach in the public schools of Rhea County, Tennessee, which said public schools are supported in part and in whole by the public school fund of the state, a certain theory and theories that deny the story of the divine creation of man as taught in the Bible, and did teach instead thereof that man has descended from a lower order of animals, he, the said John Thomas Scopes, being at the time, and prior thereto, a teacher in the public schools of Rhea County, Tennessee, aforesaid, against the peace and dignity of the State.
>
> From the official transcript of the trial *State of Tennessee vs. John Thomas Scopes,* Nos. 5231 and 5232, in the Circuit Court of Rhea County, Tennessee,
> p. 123.

Anyone familiar with the trial or with *Inherit the Wind,* the play based on the trial, knows that the argument frequently drifted far from the charge specified in that indictment. But despite all the pyrotechnic oratory about the larger issues involved in this case, the jury did eventually return a verdict of "guilty as charged."

Since the province of forensic discourse is the past, there is usually a set of facts or details to be recited for the benefit of the judge and jury. Ordinarily these "facts" have to be stated before they can be proved or refuted, and so *narratio* became a regular part of the oratory of the courtroom. Deliberative oratory, on the other hand, deals with the future, and consequently there are, strictly speaking, no "facts" to be recited. Because deliberative oratory argues about things that must be done, rather than things that have been done, *narratio* was regarded as an unnecessary, certainly as a dispensable, part of this kind of speech.

But the deliberative orator—and the ceremonial orator too—often felt the need to recite past events as a basis for recommendations about the future. As a result, *narratio* began to figure in deliberative and ceremonial oratory as well as in forensic. Whether or not statement of fact is a necessary part of deliberative or ceremonial discourse is debatable; but the fact of the matter is that most discourses, of whatever kind, *do* devote a section—the one immediately following the introduction—to a statement of fact. Recognizing that a *statement of fact* can often be dispensed with, let us go on to consider what is done and in what manner in this part of a discourse.

The statement of fact is fundamentally *expository.* In this section we are informing our readers of the circumstances that need to be known about our subject. If the readers are sufficiently informed about the subject under consideration, we can dispense with this part altogether. But most of the time, even well-informed readers will appreciate, even if they do not require, some recital of the circumstances, the details, the state of the question.

It is customary for authors of scholarly articles to summarize briefly the history of the idea they are going to discuss in their article. Here is an example of that kind of statement of fact from an article entitled "Charles Lamb's Contribution to the Theory of Dramatic Illusion." The final sentence of the author's introduction provides a transition to the statement of fact: "Before discussing Lamb's view, which was the product of numerous visits to the playhouse, it would be well to keep in mind the broad outlines of the main theories advanced before the Romantic period." The article continues:

> Neo-classical theory was committed, or thought it was committed, to advocating the dramatic unities of time, place, and action because it insisted upon the necessity of literal delusion. As might be expected, the late seventeenth century emphasized the rational aspect of the unities: it is unreasonable, the argument ran, to think that a spectator is able to pretend that the events of two days can be crowded into a few hours, or to demand that the audience, having transported itself to Asia, should be required to leap to Africa a few moments later. To make such demands is unfair, and to think that an audience can comply with them is, this view maintains, unreasonable. But in the eighteenth century a reply was evolved which gained increasing acceptance with audiences and with literary critics. Reasonable or not, this counterargument said, the mind can transport itself as easily to Africa from Asia as it can journey to Asia in the first place. The problem is not one of "reason" or "reasonableness," but of what, in fact (not in theory), the imagination is capable of doing. Dr. Johnson is somewhat in this second tradition, but he goes further than merely saying that the mind can hop about from place to place and condense time and space at its will. He insists that the playwright should not encumber himself with the unities (which at best might prevent a man from being a bad playwright, but could never make him a good one), but he denied that the spectator is literally deluded (by imagination or by reason) into believing he is watching a reality and not a play. Such is Johnson's broad theoretical generalization. We should perhaps keep in mind his practice—his reluctance, for example, to read *King Lear*, because Cordelia's death caused him such pain.

> From Sylvan Barnet, "Charles Lamb's Contribution to the Theory of Dramatic Illusion," *PMLA*, LXIX (Dec. 1954), 1150-59. Reprinted by permission of the Modern Language Association of America.

Because of the audience for which this article was written—mainly teachers of English on the university level—this summary of previous doctrines can be more abbreviated than it could be if the article were directed to a lay audience. This summary does not so much *inform* the audience as *remind* it.

As in this example from a scholarly article, we often will have occasion to present a summary of what others have thought or said on the theme we are going to develop in our composition. Closely allied to this kind of summary of relevant views advanced by others is the summary of views that we are going to support or refute in our essay. In the following example, Norman Podhoretz summarizes the main theses from Hannah Arendt's book *Eichmann in Jerusalem* that he is going to take issue with in his article. The final sentence of Mr. Podhoretz's introduction, which provides a transition to this statement of fact, read, "The point to begin with, then, is Miss Arendt's thesis, and the problem to settle is whether it justifies the distortions of perspective it creates and the cavalier treatment of evidence it impels." Then—

> According to Miss Arendt, the Nazis, in order to carry out their genocidal plan against the Jews, needed Jewish cooperation and in fact received it "to a truly extraordinary degree." This cooperation took the form of "administrative and police work," and it was extended by "the highly assimilated Jewish communities of Central and Western Europe" no less abundantly than by "the Yiddish-speaking masses of the East." In Amsterdam as in Warsaw, in Berlin as in Budapest, Miss Arendt writes,
>
>> Jewish officials could be trusted to compile the lists of persons and of their property, to secure money from the deportees to defray the expenses of their deportation and extermination, to keep track of vacated apartments, to supply police forces to help seize Jews and get them on trains, until, as a last gesture, they handed over the assets of the Jewish community in good order for final confiscation.
>
> All this has long been known. What is new is Miss Arendt's assertion that if the Jews (or rather, their leaders) had not cooperated in this fashion, "there would have been chaos and plenty of misery but the total number of victims would hardly have been between four and a half to six million people."
>
> So much for the Jews. As for the Nazis, carrying out the policy of genocide required neither that they be monsters nor pathological Jew-haters. On the contrary: since the murder of Jews was dictated by the law of the state, and since selfless loyalty to the law was regarded by the Germans under Hitler as the highest of virtues, it even called for a certain idealism to do what Eichmann and his cohorts did. Miss Arendt in this connection quotes the famous remark attributed to Himmler: "To have stuck it out and, apart from exceptions caused by human weakness, to have remained decent, that is what has made us hard." Eichmann, then, was telling the truth when he denied having been an anti-Semite: he did his duty to the best of his ability, and he would have performed with equal zeal even if he had loved the Jews. Thus, also, the Israeli prosecutor Gideon Hausner was absurdly off the point in portraying Eichmann as a brute and a sadist and a fiend: Eichmann was in actual fact a banal personality, a nonentity whose evil deeds flowed not from

anything in his own character, but rather from his position in the Nazi system.

This system is, of course, known as totalitarianism, and it is totalitarianism that brings the two halves of Miss Arendt's thesis together. Long ago, David Rousset, Bruno Bettelheim, and Miss Arendt herself taught us that securing the complicity of the victim is one of the distinguishing ambitions of totalitarian states, and her tale of Jewish complicity here is offered (at least on the surface) as yet another illustration of this point. Long ago, too, she and her colleagues taught us that totalitarian states aim at the destruction of common-sense reality and the creation of a new reality moulded to the lineaments of the official ideology, and her conception of Eichmann as an ordinary man whose conscience was made to function "the other way around" is similarly set forth in illustration of the more general point. Obviously, though, this ordinary man could not have been turned into so great and devoted a perpetrator of evil if the system had not been so tightly closed—if, that is to say, there had been voices to protest or gestures of resistance. Such voices as existed, however, were in Miss Arendt's judgment pathetically small and thin, and such gestures of resistance as were displayed she finds relatively insignificant. Not only did "good society everywhere" accept the Final Solution with "zeal and eagerness," but the Jews themselves acquiesced and even cooperated—as we have seen—"to a truly extraordinary degree." Here, then, is the finishing touch to Miss Arendt's reading of the Final Solution, and the explanation she gives for dwelling on Jewish complicity: this chapter of the story, she says, "offers the most striking insight into the totality of the moral collapse the Nazis caused in respectable European society—not only in Germany but in almost all countries, not only among the persecutors but also among the victims."

From Norman Podhoretz, "Hannah Arendt on Eichmann: A Study in the Perversity of Brilliance," *Commentary*, XXXVI (Sept. 1963), 201–8. Copyright 1963 by the American Jewish Committee and reprinted by permission of Norman Podhoretz.

The passage just quoted may strike the student as being an inordinately long statement of fact. But it is not really long when viewed in relation to the entire article, which covers eight double-column pages in the magazine. We quoted a fairly long passage to show what proportion a statement of fact might take in an extended discourse. In a shorter article, of course, the statement of fact, if one was needed, would have to be considerably condensed. As always, the importance and complexity of the subject matter and the depth of treatment we choose to give it will also dictate the proper length of the statement of fact. If Mr. Podhoretz had been writing a mere review of Miss Arendt's book he could not have given as much space as he does here to the *narratio*.

Quintilian advises that the instruction of the audience in the statement of fact be *lucid, brief,* and *plausible.* These three qualities are, of course, relative to the speech situation. An exposition that is lucid and plausible for one audience might not be either for another. Therefore, as in our discussion of the strategies of the introduction, we can lay down no hard-and-fast rules about the management of the statement of fact. We must adapt our means to the *ad hoc* situation. All we can do here is point to some of the ways that might be used to achieve the qualities that Quintilian mentions, and trust writers to choose those ways that will best fit the situation in which they find themselves.

Lucidity is largely a matter of style, a matter of so selecting and arranging words that we easily communicate our meaning to our audience. We will delay our discussion of this means of securing lucidity until the next chapter, on style. Lucidity, of course, should characterize all parts of the discourse. Here we will mention only those means of securing lucidity peculiar to the statement of fact. We will be clear if, first of all, we develop our exposition sufficiently to set forth all the facts that need to be known. A severe abridgement of the exposition could result in obscurity. On the other hand, an excessive elaboration could so clutter up the exposition that the main points are obscured. An *orderly* presentation of the facts will also aid lucidity. Sometimes *chronological order* will be the organizing principle of our exposition—first this happened, then this, then this, etc. At other times we will employ an order that moves *from the general to the particular* or *from the more familiar to the less familiar.*

Another aid to lucidity is the device that the Greeks called *enargeia* and that we may translate as *palpability* or *vividness. Enargeia* will be especially useful when our statement of fact lends itself more to a narrative treatment than to an expository treatment—as, for instance, in a recital of past events. Here if we can paint a word-picture of the scene instead of merely telling what happened we can produce that vividness—not to mention the emotional impact—which will etch the "facts" in the imaginations of our readers. One can imagine a prosecuting lawyer describing Raskolnikov's crime in words like these:

> He pulled the axe quite out, swung it with both arms, scarcely conscious of himself, and almost without effort, almost mechanically, brought the blunt side down on her head.... The old woman was as always bareheaded. Her thin, light hair, streaked with grey, thickly smeared with grease, was plaited in a rat's tail and fastened by a broken horn comb which stood out on the nape of her neck. As she was so short, the blow fell on the very top of her skull. She cried out, but very faintly, and suddenly sank all of a heap on the floor, raising her hands to her head.

> From Fyodor Dostoyevsky, *Crime and Punishment,* Part I, Chapter 7, translated by Constance Garnett.

In Dostoyevsky's novel, this vivid narrative is not part of a prosecuting lawyer's representation in a courtroom, but such a description could be, and often has been, the manner in which a lawyer manages the statement of fact in a case. There is no doubt about the clarity and effectiveness of such a presentation. And while *enargeia* can be employed in other parts of a discourse, it most often finds its opportunity in the statement of fact.

Before we leave the subject of lucidity, we should make the point that clarity of statement does not always serve our purpose. There may be occasions when it is expedient for us deliberately to obfuscate the exposition. If the facts tell against us, it might be best at this point to omit the statement of fact altogether or to render our exposition ambiguous. It might be that a frank, lucid recital of the facts would so alienate our audience that they would become indisposed to listen to our proofs later on. The particular situation will dictate when it is prudent to adopt the strategy of omission or obfuscation.

Brevity of statement, as we remarked in our comments on the passage quoted from Norman Podhoretz's article, will also be determined by the particular situation. Aristotle scoffed at the prescription that the statement of fact be brief. He asked why the statement of fact had to be short or long. Why couldn't it be just right? In this characteristic insistence on the *via media*, Aristotle is calling for the length that is appropriate to the needs of the moment. The principle of "just enough" is the only general prescript that has validity here. We will achieve this due brevity if (1) we start our recital at a point where it begins to concern our readers (comparable to Horace's precept that we begin a story *in medias res* instead of *ab ovo*); (2) we exclude all irrelevancies; (3) we excise anything, however relevant, which contributes little or nothing to our readers' understanding of our case or to their friendly disposition toward our cause.

The plausibility of the statement of fact will result partly from the ethical tone of the discourse itself or from the ethical image of the writer. Readers will believe that the situation is as it has been described if they trust the authority or the character of the writer. The ethical appeal, of course, is important in all parts of the discourse, but we must not minimize its importance in this part of the discourse, which is concerned with a bare recital of the facts.

We can further enhance the credibility of our statement of fact by being careful not to say anything contrary to nature or to historical fact, by assigning believable causes or reasons for events, by trusting more to understatement than to hyperbole. An audience is amazingly quick to detect that a writer "doth protest too much." If we alienate the credence of our readers at this state of the discourse, we jeopardize our chances of holding them when we come to the all-important stage of proof.

Confirmation

The use of the term *confirmation* to label this part may suggest that this division figures only in persuasive discourse. But if we regard *confirmation* or *proof* as the designation of that part where we get down to the main business of our discourse, this term can be extended to cover expository as well as argumentative prose. The previously discussed parts, the introduction and the statement of fact, certainly figure in both expository and argumentative discourse. If these two parts are regarded as the preliminaries, confirmation then may be regarded as the core, the central part, the main body, of our discourse—the part in which we do what we set out to do, whether that be to explain or to persuade. A good deal of what we say about confirmation is, of course, applicable only to argumentative discourse, but many of the precepts concerning this part of the discourse are equally applicable to expository prose. When we are talking about confirmation in the narrow sense of demonstrating or refuting an argument, this will be readily apparent to the student.

Because of the difficulty of illustrating the disposition of arguments by quoting short passages, such as we used in illustrating the previous two parts, we shall postpone exemplifying the points made until we come to consider whole essays in the readings at the end of this chapter.

It is in this part of the discourse principally that we use the material we have gathered in the process of invention. We must select and dispose this material for maximum effectiveness. The processes of invention and disposition are not really as independent of one another as we may have suggested by giving them separate treatments. In reading, the activity of evaluation can take place almost simultaneously with the activity of comprehension. Likewise, in composing, we are often engaged with the problems of selecting and arranging our material even while we are engaged in discovering our material. We have discussed invention and disposition separately partly because there is a sense in which we must *discover* before we can *arrange* and partly because there is a pedagogical convenience to a separate discussion of these two processes.

One of the main problems we face in this part of the discourse is the problem of sequence. What point do we take up first? Once we have dealt with that point, then what point do we take up? In expository discourse, we can sometimes organize our material according to a chronological scheme—as, for instance, in an explanation of a relatively simple process, like changing a tire. In the exposition of a more complicated subject, we may have to move from the general to the particular or from the familiar to the unknown.

Usually the nature of the thing to be explained will suggest the appropriate procedure.

In argumentative discourse, however, these organizing principles cannot always be relied on, for we are faced with questions like these: should I begin with my weakest arguments and build up to my strongest arguments? should I refute the opposing arguments first and then present my arguments, or should I establish my case first and then refute the opposition? As usual, the particular situation will dictate the appropriate strategy, and perhaps all that can be done here is to lay down some guidelines for the writer.

As a general rule, in presenting our own arguments we should not descend from our strongest arguments to our weakest. More often than not, such an anticlimactic order will considerably weaken the effectiveness of our suasive efforts. We want to leave our strongest argument ringing in the memory of our audience; hence we usually place it in the emphatic final position. If we present our strongest arguments first and then add a series of weaker arguments, we will diminish the effectiveness of the strong ones. The audience may get the impression that our case, solid at first sight, is beginning to unravel. The weaker arguments will strike the audience as being so many "after-thoughts." This suggests that we do not really have confidence in the cogency of our strong arguments, that we feel the need for adding some props. If we thus betray a lack of confidence, we will dispel the confidence of our readers.

If we have available a number of arguments of co-ordinate value, we can arrange these arguments in almost any order. But even here we might be guided by certain principles. Where our arguments are of relatively equal strength, it might be best to present first those arguments that are likely to have suggested themselves to our readers. If we gain concurrence for the familiar arguments, we condition our readers to receive the unfamiliar. We have confirmed what they suspected and then have added what they did not know before.

If we have available to us a number of relatively strong and weak arguments, we might find it best to start out with a strong argument, then slip in some of the weaker arguments, and then end up with the strongest argument. The initial strong argument conditions the audience to receive the weaker arguments; but then, just when the weaker arguments threaten to diminish the effectiveness of our opening argument, we come in with our strongest argument. The surprise that attends the introduction of a strong argument just when it seemed that we had "shot our bolt" will enhance the cogency of the final argument.

Refutation

So far we have been dealing only with the strategic sequence of arguments when we have merely to confirm our own case. Some additional problems present themselves when we have also to refute opposing views. In a public debate, involving an alternation of speakers, opposing views are actually voiced, and we have to decide which of the opposing arguments must be dealt with and whether we should refute the arguments first and then present our own arguments or present our own first and then refute the opposition. When we sit down to write an argumentative piece, there is no opponent whom we must confront and answer. Nevertheless, there usually is implicit in the issue we are discussing an opposing view that we must meet and dispose of. In such cases, it is not enough to establish our own case. However cogent our arguments may be, doubts will remain in the minds of our readers if we do not anticipate the objections to our thesis and answer those objections.

If the opposing views have been well received by the audience, it is usually advisable that we refute those views before we attempt to present our own arguments. People who are favorably disposed to the opposite point of view will not readily open their minds to our arguments, however valid and cogent they may be. The ground must be cleared, as it were, before we can parade our support.

It can never be an inflexible rule, however, that we must first refute the opposing arguments before we present our own. Where the opposing arguments are relatively weak, we can afford to delay answering them until after we have established our own case. In such instances, the cogency of our arguments will further dispose the audience to recognize the weakness of the opposing arguments. And even when the opposing arguments are strong and are favorably received by the audience, it will sometimes be expedient to delay refuting them. When an audience, for instance, is inordinately hostile to our view, the wisest strategy may be to keep the opposing arguments out of sight as long as possible. By reminding a hostile audience of opposing arguments at the outset, we could so confirm the audience in their prejudices that they would not lend an ear to our refutation of those arguments. Under those circumstances, presenting our own arguments first might dispose an audience at least to listen to our refutation.

As has been constantly emphasized so far in this chapter, no inflexible rules can be laid down dictating what must be done and in what sequence. Writers must be prepared to adapt their means to their end and to adjust their strategies to fit the particular situation. They must "feel" their way through any given situation. Because some writers have a natural sense, or develop a sense, for what are the "right" means in any given situation, they often succeed where others fail. Unfortunately, rhetoric cannot give rules-of-thumb that will cover every situation, but we can briefly review some of the available means of refuting opposing views.

Refutation by Appeal to Reason

There are two general ways in which we can refute a proposition: we can prove the contradictory of that proposition; we can demolish the arguments by which the proposition is supported. As we saw in the previous chapter, if we prove that one of a pair of contradictory propositions is true, we automatically prove that the other proposition is false. Proving a contradictory proposition can be the most compelling kind of refutation, since all people, because of their rational nature, readily recognize the principle that a thing cannot at the same time *be* and *not be*.

We are not always presented, however, with the convenience of contradictorily opposed arguments. More often we are faced with the challenge of refuting *contrary* propositions. One side maintains that a certain course of action is wise, and the other side maintains that it is foolish. In that case, we must knock out the props supporting the contrary assertion. We can do this (1) by denying the truth of one of the premises on which the argument rests and proving, perhaps through evidence or testimony, that the premise is false, or (2) by objecting to the inferences drawn from the premises. In rejecting the inferences, we say such things as, "I admit the principle, but I deny that it leads to such a consequence" or "I admit the principle but I deny that it applies in this case" or "Your assertion is true, but it has no force as an argument to support your conclusion."

These are ways of refuting arguments logically, but sometimes we have to deal with probabilities, which cannot be demolished by means of strict logic. In that case, we must draw on those enthymemes and examples which, if they do not refute the opposition conclusively, do have persuasive value. The emotional and ethical appeals, which we discussed in the previous chapter, will play their part in refutation too.

Refutation by Emotional Appeals

Knowledge of one's audience is perhaps nowhere more important than when one is using emotional appeals. A miscalculation about the temper of one's audience could destroy or reverse the intended effect. The wrong emotional appeal or an emotional appeal applied at an inappropriate place in the discourse or a disproportionate emotional appeal could not only render our refutation ineffectual but also diminish confidence in our previously established proof.

It should be obvious that emotional appeals will succeed better with some audiences than with others. One's problems with emotional appeals will increase in proportion to the heterogeneity of the audience. One can appreciate Senator Richard Nixon's dilemma in 1952 when he had to make decisions about the kind and degree of emotional appeal to employ in his address to a nationwide television audience in defense of his handling of campaign funds. Judging from the response to his speech, one would have to conclude that Mr. Nixon calculated wisely. His references to "the cloth coat" and to the "little dog Checkers" totally alienated one segment of the television audience. But for the majority of the audience, those references were the emotional touches that capped his apologia.

It would seem that when addressing a large, heterogeneous audience, one must estimate which emotional appeals are likely to succeed with the major portion of the audience. In other words, we may have to sacrifice the concurrence of one part of our audience in order to gain the assent of the major portion. The author who writes a piece for the *New Republic* or *Commonweal* or *The National Review* has, in many ways, an easier task than the author who writes an argumentative piece for *Life* or *TV Guide,* because the writer for magazines of limited circulation can presume more political, philosophical, or religious homogeneity in the audience than can the writer for the mass-circulation magazines.

Refutation by Ethical Appeal

The ethical appeal must pervade all parts of the discourse, but it is nowhere more important than in this part where we are seeking to prove our case or refute the opposition. So important is the ethical appeal in effecting persuasion that Aristotle said "it is more fitting for a good man to display himself as an honest fellow than as a subtle reasoner" (*Rhetoric,* III, 17). Sometimes when our case is weak, the ethical appeal, exerted either by the image of the writer or by the tone of the discourse, will carry the day. The effectiveness of the ethical appeal where one's case is weak was particularly evident in the speech that General Douglas MacArthur delivered before Congress in 1951 when he returned to this country after being relieved of his command in Korea. Old soldiers *do* die, but they sometimes achieve a kind of immortality in the minds of the people they have served.

Refutation by Wit

The Earl of Shaftesbury once claimed that "ridicule is the test of truth." Shaftesbury was suggesting that if what was alleged to be the truth could survive the onslaught of ridicule it must really be the truth. If Shaftesbury's claim can be accepted at all it must be accepted with reservations. A genuine truth might very well be reduced to absurdity by a witty rhetorician, but it would remain the truth despite its having been discredited in the minds of the audience.

Jests, sarcasm, and irony can be effective tools for refutation, but they must be used with the utmost discretion. The Greek rhetorician Gorgias advised that we should "kill our opponent's seriousness with our ridicule and his ridicule with our seriousness." Gorgias was shrewd enough to see that many times we cannot counteract the opposition by employing similar tactics. And since it is often difficult to "top" a display of wit, we might do well to avoid matching humorous sallies with our opponent and to adopt a becoming seriousness. On the other hand, we can sometimes destroy the effectiveness of a soberly presented argument by wittily reducing the argument to absurdity. Writers must be cautioned however; they risk the dissipation of their ethical appeal if their wit is merely a cloak for weak or specious arguments. Witty but empty retorts can fool some of the people some of the time, but the person who is scrupulous about his or her tactics will not sacrifice integrity for success.

A joke can be used simply to disarm an audience or to dispose an audience favorably. When a joke is employed for these purposes, it is most often found in the introduction, the most obvious place for those devices which are calculated to ingratiate the speaker or writer with the audience. But the disarming kind of joke can sometimes be used in the confirmation also—as, for instance, when we are about to launch into an argument that we suspect will not readily gain acceptance.

But the joke can also be used for purposes of refutation if it provides some kind of analogy to the point we are seeking to discredit. The analogous joke can induce an audience to take an objective view of the point being discussed. If we can get an audience laughing at a situation somewhat removed from the point being attacked, we will find it easier to make the audience perceive the absurdity when we make an application of the analogy.

With certain audiences, the more sophisticated varieties of humor will succeed best. One of the most effective kinds of sophisticated humor, especially for the purpose of disarming an audience, is the good-humored bantering in which speakers or writers make depreciatory remarks about themselves. Almost everyone responds favorably to those who take themselves down a peg or two, mainly because everyone likes to feel that a person, however exalted, is human after all and does not exaggerate his or her own importance or achievements. Although depreciation of others may sometimes backfire on us, belittling ourselves will never arouse anyone's resentment and rarely undercuts anyone's confidence in us.

The light touch resulting from an urbane finesse with words is another brand of humor that wears well with certain audiences, especially with the educated. As will be seen in the next chapter on style, many of the figures of speech can be used for this kind of beguiling verbal humor. Puns, for instance, have come to be regarded as a low form of humor, but most of the great writers, from Shakespeare to James Thurber, indulged in plays on words (the rhetoricians called it *paronomasia*) and felt no need to apologize for their verbal acrobatics. Irony is a subtle form of verbal ingenuity, and while irony comes naturally to most people ("My dear, it's a *beautiful* hat!"), we must exercise great care in using this trope. Because of its subtlety, irony can easily be misunderstood. There are college students even today who misread Swift's ironical *Modest Proposal*.

Sarcasm is another mode of humor that requires a master hand, for it can easily go wrong. Sarcasm seems to succeed best when it is directed at an individual; it is risky when it is directed at nationalities, classes, ranks, or vocations. That this should be so is rather curious, for of all modes of satirical wit, sarcasm is the one that most closely borders on uncharitableness. One might think that since the caustic gibe at an individual comes closer to violating the virtue of charity than the gibe at a group of people, personal sarcasm would be most likely to elicit unfavorable reactions in the audience. But human nature is so constituted that it will tolerate, even enjoy, the vituperation of an individual. The same London society that chuckled over Alexander Pope's vitriolic portrait of Lord John Hervey under the guise of "Sporus" would have been angered if his portrait had been directed at the class of aristocratic courtiers that Lord Hervey represented. The psychology behind this perverse pleasure is pointed up by La Rochefoucauld's famous maxim, "In the misfortune of our best friends, we often find something that pleases us."

Rhetoricians are unanimous in their condemnation of ribald jests in formal discourse. The "dirty story" may provoke laughter when told in small, intimate groups, but in a public discourse, it almost invariably offends and alienates a larger audience. Likewise, we usually react unfavorably to an obscene joke when we see it in print. It is difficult to imagine any situation when such a joke will serve our purpose. For rhetorical reasons, then, as well as for moral reasons, we should avoid the use of obscenity and a *double-entendre* in our discourses.

The type of literature that makes most use, for rhetorical purposes, of the varieties of humor that we have discussed—and of some that we have not discussed, like parody and burlesque—is satire. And it is notable that some of the greatest English satirists, like Ben Jonson, John Dryden, Alexander Pope, and Jonathan Swift, were thoroughly schooled in classical rhetoric. Students will learn their best lessons about the skillful uses of humor for rhetorical purposes from reading the great satirists. And they will acquire another method of reading and analyzing satiric literature if they will approach such literature as a manifestation of the kind of rhetoric we have been studying in this book.

Quintilian once said (*Instit. Orat.,* VI, iii, 26) that "there are no jests so insipid as those which parade the fact that they are intended to be witty." We might very well take these words as a general caution about the use of humor for rhetorical purposes. Humor that merely calls attention to our desire to be "funny" or to be "one of the boys" will alienate more people than it will win. Humor is an extremely difficult art, and if students do not have a natural gift or an acquired skill for humor, they would do best to avoid the use of this available means of persuasion. And they must also remember that there are many occasions when humor of any kind is wholly inappropriate. We round back finally to that cardinal principle of rhetoric: the subject, the occasion, the audience, and the personality of the speaker or writer will dictate the means we should employ to effect our purpose.

Conclusion

A look at the terms that the classical rhetoricians used to designate the conclusion will give us a hint of what the rhetoricians conceived the function of this part of a discourse to be. The most common Greek term was *epilogos,* from the verb *epilegein,* meaning "to say in addition." An even more instructive Greek term for this part was *anakephalaiōsis,* which is the equivalent of the Latin *recapitulatio,* from which we have the English "recapitulation." The common Latin term for this part was *peroratio,* a word which in the prefix *per-* suggested "a finishing off" of one's plea. What the Latins meant by "finishing off" is suggested by the two heads under which Quintilian treated of the peroration—*enumeratio* (an enumeration or summing-up) and *affectus* (producing the appropriate emotion in the audience).

While it is obvious that some discourses, because of the nature of the subject or situation or because of the limitations of time or allotted wordage, can dispense with an elaborate conclusion, the natural tendency for us, when we speak or write formally, is to "round off" what we have been molding in the earlier parts of the discourse. Without a conclusion, the discourse strikes us as merely *stopping* rather than *ending.* We are conscious too that because the conclusion stands in the final position in the discourse it is the part that is "left with" the audience, the part that lingers longest in the memory. Accordingly, this is the part where we feel the urge to pull out all the stops, where we tend to display the most conspicuous stylistic eloquence and emotional intensity. Because of this natural urge to sound the full diapason of our stylistic and emotional resources, we sometimes overdo these effects and thereby detract from the solid achievements of the earlier parts of the discourse. Discretion must be as alive here as it was in the earlier parts.

Aristotle taught that generally we strive to do four things in the conclusion:

1. to inspire the audience with a favorable opinion of ourselves and an unfavorable opinion of our opponents;
2. to amplify the force of the points we have made in the previous section and to extenuate the force of the points made by the opposition;
3. to rouse the appropriate emotions in the audience;
4. to restate in a summary way our facts and arguments.

Aristotle is suggesting that these are the things that we *may* do in the conclusion, not that we *must* do all of them in every discourse. Limitations of space may prevent our spinning out an elaborate conclusion. The nature of our subject or of our audience may make it inadvisable to attempt any kind of emotional appeal. When our arguments have been direct and uncomplicated, there may be no necessity to recapitulate or amplify them. The advice here, as in other parts of the discourse, is that we should do what needs to be done, not what convention says must be done.

Of the four things that Aristotle designates, *recapitulation* is the one that will most often figure in the conclusion. Normally when we come to the end of a discourse, we all feel the need to restate in general terms the points we have set forth in detail in the body of the discourse. This inclination is prompted perhaps by our feeling that we must refresh the memory of our audience. Then too there is the awareness that facts and arguments the force of which was blunted by details will gain in effect when set forth in capsule form at the end of the discourse.

Sometimes authors will explicitly signal that they are about to recapitulate the points they have made in the body of the essay. Here is an example of a formally announced recapitulation, together with the author's declaration of the reasons for the recapitulation, from the concluding paragraphs of an article, the thesis of which was set forth in the first sentence of the article: "I maintain that democratic manners—typified by the practice of calling the boss by his first name—have reached the point in our country where they conduce not to the preservation of personal dignity but to the abject submission of one man to another."

I have nearly finished. But I know that some fool—most likely, one with a Ph.D.—will read this article and forever after assert as a well-known fact that I yearn for a restoration of Tsardom, for a reinvigoration of the Hindu caste system and for a truly Chinese subjugation of women and children. So let me recapitulate, in the course of which I shall add one or two points that I forgot to mention earlier.

A sensible system of manners, sensibly formal, performs various services. Besides acting as a constant reminder of some important facts of life, it affords human beings the distinctly human satisfaction of symbolic expression. Besides making collective living possible, it provides a person, thanks to its formalities, with protective armor against collective pressures. For these formalities allow the individual to acquiesce in the social order while reserving his final judgment of it. They enable him to pledge his loyalty to men in authority without making those fine adjustments whose long-term results are the same as those of brainwashing.

Democratic manners in America are eating the heart out of American democracy. With no impressive way of saluting the system, and the position which a given official occupies in it, one must prostrate himself before the man. There is a country where such prostration is even more prostrate than in America. There the humblest citizen calls his mighty ruler *comrade.*

I suggest a prudent reform in American manners, not a revolution. If the only alternative to egalitarian manners is a nerveless society exhausted by protocol and ceremony, then this discussion is futile. But that is not the only alternative, except in the minds of latter-day Jacobins for whom the stratifications of the *ancien régime* are more real than the proletarianizations of their own time. There are in-between solutions, attuned to reality, however they resist simple and consistent formulation, as the English know, and as America, in her own fashion, can discover. Pedantic democrats presume to speak for wisdom, creative ability and service, as against mere money in the bank. But without a rectification of manners most men would rather achieve a Cadillac than such virtues, for these virtues, unacknowledged in any regular way, do not show on a man, at least not conspicuously, whereas a Cadillac shows on anyone, conspicuously.

From Morton J. Cronin, "The Tyranny of Democratic Manners," *The New Republic,* January 20, 1958. Reprinted by permission of the author and The New Republic, 1244 Nineteenth St., Washington, D.C.

To realize the value of such a recapitulation, the student would have to study this passage in conjunction with the body of the article, where the author developed his points at some length. And whereas the author here explicitly informs his readers that he is going to recapitulate the points he has made in the article and tells them why he feels the need to do so, most of the time, writers slip into recapitulation without explicitly alerting the reader. Most of the time it is fairly obvious that the author is summarizing points made earlier.

How important recapitulation can be is nowhere more dramatically demonstrated than in a court trial. The jury has spent days, sometimes weeks, listening to highly detailed testimony and cross-examination. Surely at the end of this period, the jury has all the material it needs to render a verdict. But, as anyone knows who has witnessed a real or a fictional trial, both the prosecuting and defending attorneys present a summary of their cases before the jury is sent out to deliberate its verdict. The prosecutor and defender spend most of their time in this summary reminding the jury of the main points established during the course of the trial. Not only are the issues and arguments sharpened by these summaries, but coming one upon the other in rapid succession, they gain a cumulative force.

Let us view a fictional example of such a summary. Because this summary is tightly controlled by the novelist, it is probably less rambling than the summaries lawyers present in actual trials. In this scene from the novel *To Kill a Mockingbird,* Atticus, the lawyer defending a black man falsely accused of raping a white girl, is making his final plea to the jury:

> "Gentlemen," he was saying, "I shall be brief, but I would like to use my remaining time with you to remind you that this case is not a difficult one, it requires no minute sifting of complicated facts, but it does require you to be sure beyond all reasonable doubt as to the guilt of the defendant. To begin with, this case should never have come to trial. This case is as simple as black and white.
>
> "The state has not produced one iota of medical evidence to the effect that the crime Tom Robinson is charged with ever took place. It has relied instead upon the testimony of two witnesses whose evidence has not only been called into serious question on cross-examination, but has been flatly contradicted by the defendant. The defendant is not guilty, but somebody in this courtroom is.
>
> "I have nothing but pity in my heart for the chief witness for the state, but my pity does not extend so far as to her putting a man's life at stake, which she has done in an effort to get rid of her own guilt.
>
> "I say guilt, gentlemen, because it was guilt that motivated her. She has committed no crime, she has merely broken a rigid and time-honored code of our society, a code so severe that whoever breaks it is hounded from our midst as unfit to live with. She is the victim of cruel poverty and ignorance, but I cannot pity her: she is white. She knew full well the enormity of her offense, but because her desires were stronger than the code she was breaking, she persisted in breaking it. She persisted, and her subsequent reaction is something that all of us have known at one time or another. She did something every child has done—she tried to put the evidence of her offense away from her. But in this case she was

no child hiding stolen contraband: she struck out at her victim—of necessity she must put him away from her—he must be removed from her presence, from this world. She must destroy the evidence of her offense.

"What was the evidence of her offense? Tom Robinson, a human being. She must put Tom Robinson away from her. Tom Robinson was her daily reminder of what she did. What did she do? She tempted a Negro.

"She was white, and she tempted a Negro. She did something that in our society is unspeakable: she kissed a black man. Not an old Uncle, but a strong young Negro man. No code mattered to her before she broke it, but it came crashing down on her afterwards.

"Her father saw it, and the defendant has testified as to his remarks. What did her father do? We don't know, but there is circumstantial evidence to indicate that Mayella Ewell was beaten savagely by someone who led almost exclusively with his left. We do know in part what Mr. Ewell did: he did what any God-fearing, persevering, respectable white man would do under the circumstances—he swore out a warrant, no doubt signing it with his left hand, and Tom Robinson now sits before you, having taken the oath with the only good hand he possesses—his right hand.

"And so a quiet, respectable, humble Negro who had the unmitigated temerity to 'feel sorry' for a white woman has had to put his word against two white people's. I need not remind you of their appearance and conduct on the stand—you saw them for yourselves. The witnesses for the state, with the exception of the sheriff of Maycomb County, have presented themselves to you gentlemen, to this court, in the cynical confidence that their testimony would not be doubted, confident that you gentlemen would go along with them on the assumption—the evil assumption—that *all* Negroes lie, that *all* Negroes are basically immoral beings, that *all* Negro men are not to be trusted around our women, an assumption one associates with minds of their caliber.

"Which, gentlemen, we know is in itself a lie as black as Tom Robinson's skin, a lie I do not have to point out to you. You know the truth, and the truth is this: some Negroes lie, some Negroes are immoral, some Negro men are not to be trusted around women—black or white. But this is a truth that applies to the human race and to no particular race of men. There is not a person in this courtroom who has never told a lie, who has never done an immoral thing, and there is no man living who has never looked upon a woman without desire."

Atticus goes on for three more paragraphs, appealing to the theme of equal justice for all in the courts. Anyone who has read *To Kill a Mockingbird* or has seen the movie based on the novel remembers how skillfully Atticus Finch had argued the points he is summarizing here and how necessary it was for him, considering the kind of jury he had to deal with, to remind the jury of the arguments in the case and to put the trial in its proper perspective. A summation like this does more, however, than merely remind the audience of the salient points; it continues and reinforces the persuasion that is the main object of the speech. So while Atticus's recapitulation is largely expository, it is argumentative, right down to the final period.

Closely allied to the kind of conclusion that recapitulates or summarizes, is the one that *generalizes*. This is the kind of conclusion that broadens and extends the view of the problem or issue that we have been considering in the body of the discourse, that considers the ultimate consequences of the views we have been arguing or refuting, that recommends an attitude to adopt or a course of action to follow. To put it another way, this is the kind of conclusion that presents the general conclusions we have arrived at as a result of considering our subject.

At the 1959 convention of the National Council of Teachers of English, Professor Warner G. Rice argued for the abolition of the Freshman English course in college. In rebuttal, Professor Albert R. Kitzhaber argued for a revision of the present English course. Here, in the concluding paragraph of his speech, Professor Kitzhaber generalizes on the points he had argued in the body of his speech:

> I can sum up very briefly my position with regard to the question we are discussing. I am dissatisfied with the present Freshman English course in its typical form; but I am convinced that any radical amelioration must wait on, not precede, changes in the English curriculum in high school. Attempted coercion of high school English teachers would get us nowhere. They would like to do a better job of teaching writing quite as much as we would like to have them do it; but we must help them, working with them as equals on a problem neither they nor we have so far been able to solve properly. If our combined efforts lead to the results we want, the need for this present Freshman course would disappear—but not the need for a new Freshman course that would take advantage of and build upon the revised high school courses. I would argue that such a course ought to be of at least as much value to the freshman as any other course he might take in that year—valuable because it would concentrate on trying to raise the level of his writing skill from competence to distinction, and valuable also because it would contribute significantly to his liberal education through the continued study of literature and language. Both of these are rightful concerns of an English department.
>
> Indeed, I think they are obligations.

From Albert R. Kitzhaber, "Death—or Transfiguration?" *College English,* 21 (April 1960): 367–73. Reprinted by permission of the author and the National Council of Teachers of English.

It is in the summarizing kind of conclusion that we have the best opportunity to engage in what the rhetoricians called *amplification* and *extenuation*. Amplification is the process by which we highlight, by which we make as "big as possible," the points we have made; amplification is a way of reminding audiences of the importance or cogency or superiority of our points. Extenuation does just the opposite: it insists that the points made by the opposition are insignificant, weak, or inferior. The common topics that we most resort to when we are seeking to amplify our own points or to minimize our opponent's points are the topic of size and the topic of degree. In other words, we try to emphasize or de-emphasize either the absolute or the relative magnitude of the points we have made. Of course we try to do this when we are presenting our arguments, but it can be helpful to our cause to engage in some amplifying and extenuating in a summary way in the conclusion.

One final caution about the recapitulation; let it be as brief as possible. Otherwise the conclusion will take on the proportions of a second discourse, and it will serve only to weary and alienate the audience. Nothing so exasperates an audience as speakers or writers who go "on and on" after announcing that they are about to conclude. A disproportionate conclusion is usually more damaging to the effect of an essay than a disproportionate introduction. A fresh audience may be disposed to forgive a treadmill introduction, but a weary audience will invariably resent the interminable conclusion.

Emotional appeals, as we have seen, are appropriate in any part of the discourse. Traditionally, however, the conclusion has been the part in which emotional appeals have figured most prominently. Present-day students have not been exposed very much to the Chautauqua style of oratory that was very popular in the early years of this century, but a look at the speeches of a flamboyant orator like William Jennings Bryan would show them how speakers once indulged the natural urge to pull out all the emotional stops in the peroration. Probably more familiar to modern students, Sir Winston Churchill was an orator in the grand old tradition. An example of the rousing kind of emotional appeal is found in the peroration of Sir Winston Churchill's famous speech to the House of Commons on May 13, 1940:

> I say to the House as I said to Ministers who have joined this government, I have nothing to offer but blood, toil, tears, and sweat. We have before us an ordeal of the most grievous kind. We have before us many, many months of struggle and suffering.
>
> You ask, what is our policy? I say it is to wage war by land, sea, and air. War with all our might and with all the strength God has given us, and to wage war against a monstrous tyranny never surpassed in the dark and lamentable catalogue of human crime. That is our policy.

> You ask, what is our aim? I can answer in one word. It is victory. Victory at all costs—victory in spite of all terrors—victory, however long and hard the road may be, for without victory there is no survival.
>
> Let that be realized. No survival for the British Empire, no survival for all that the British Empire has stood for, no survival for the urge, the impulse of the ages, that mankind shall move forward toward his goal.
>
> I take up my task in buoyancy and hope. I feel sure that our cause will not be suffered to fail among men.
>
> I feel entitled at this juncture, at this time, to claim the aid of all and to say, "Come then, let us go forward together with our united strength."

Even today most of us have a nostalgic fondness for this kind of oratory, and occasionally, such as at a nominating convention, we are treated to a display of this rousing brand of oratory. Generally, however, we profess to be suspicious of grandiloquent exploitations of our emotions. And while we have probably misjudged our susceptibility to emotional appeals, it is true that bombastic displays of emotion have largely passed out of fashion.

Today we are more likely to regard as fitting the temperate kind of emotional appeal that Abraham Lincoln exerted in his "Second Inaugural Address." In this example, a good deal of the emotional appeal is produced by the choice of diction and by the rhythm and structure of the sentences:

> The Almighty has His own purposes. "Woe unto the world because of offenses! for it must needs be that offenses come; but woe to that man by whom the offense cometh." If we shall suppose that American slavery is one of those offenses which, in the providence of God, must needs come, but which, having continued through His appointed time, He now wills to remove, and that He gives to both North and South this terrible war, as the woe due to those by whom the offense came, shall we discern therein any departure from those divine attributes which the believers in a living God always ascribe to Him? Fondly do we hope, fervently do we pray, that this mighty scourge of war may speedily pass away. Yet, if God wills that it continue until all the wealth piled by the bondman's two hundred and fifty years of unrequited toil shall be sunk, and until every drop of blood drawn with the lash shall be paid by another drawn with a sword, as was said three thousand years ago, so still it must be said, "The judgments of the Lord are true and righteous altogether."
>
> With malice towards none, with charity for all, with firmness in the right, as God gives us to see the right, let us strive on to finish the work we are in—to bind up the nation's wounds—to care for him who shall have borne the battle, and for his widow and his orphan—to do all which may achieve and cherish a just and lasting peace among ourselves and with all nations.

To note the passing of the bombastic style is not to admit that we have ceased to be responsive to emotional appeals or that we have ceased to employ emotional appeals. What has happened is that emotional appeals, especially as they appear in conclusions, tend to be more subtle and more restrained than they were in this country even fifty years ago. We seem to be relying less on direct emotional appeals and more on such indirect means as the graces of style. The rhythms of our sentences, for instance, exert an influence on the emotions that is no less real for being all but unnoticeable. We will consider these emotional effects at greater length in the chapter on style.

Whether we need to resort to emotional appeals in the conclusion and how hard we should come down on the emotional appeals will depend largely on the nature of our audience. It is extremely important that the speaker or writer gauge, as accurately as possible, the temper of the known or probable audience for the discourse. Some audiences will be less susceptible to emotional appeals than others. A professional group, for instance, inclined by temperament or training to accept or reject a proposal on its proven merits, may be impervious, even hostile, to any appeal to their emotions on matters of professional interest. An audience's susceptibility to emotional appeals could vary, of course, with the subject being discussed. A group of doctors, for instance, could be offended by any emotional appeal when they were being urged to adopt some new drug or technique; but on a subject like government sponsorship of medical insurance, this same group could be wide open to emotional appeals. Then too when the available means of logical persuasion on a given subject are weak—or at least weaker than those of the opposition—we may find it expedient to resort to emotional persuasion. Quintilian saw the effectiveness of emotional appeal in such a situation: "Proofs, it is true, may induce the judges to regard our case as superior to that of our opponent, but the appeal to the emotions will do more, for it will make them wish our case to be better. And what they wish, they will also believe."—*Instit. Orat.* VI, ii, 5. Quintilian went so far as to claim that "it is in its power over the emotions that the life and soul of oratory is to be found" (VI, ii, 7). The great Latin rhetorician may seem to be encouraging the use of any kind of unethical means to accomplish our purpose. But anyone who recalls Quintilian's view that the ideal orator is "the good man speaking" must reject this imputation. Quintilian is merely giving frank recognition to the fact that, people being what they are, emotional appeal will in some circumstances be the most effective of the available means of persuasion. This recognition is not the same as sanctioning any and all exploitations of emotion, for the classical rhetoricians did not regard emotional appeals as illegitimate *per se*. People sometimes abused this means of persuasion, but the fact that some people abused this power did not invalidate all uses of this resource.

The fourth thing we may do, and sometimes feel compelled to do, in the conclusion is to dispose the audience favorably toward ourselves. If we have not exerted an *ethical appeal* in the earlier parts of our discourse, it is probably too late to try to exert it in the conclusion. We have seen that as early as the introduction, we may have to ingratiate ourselves with a hostile audience or post our credentials with a skeptical audience, and in later parts of the discourse, we may frequently have to bolster the credit we have established with our audience. To delay establishing a favorable image of ourselves until the conclusion would usually jeopardize our chances of persuading an audience. So when we make an effort in the conclusion to dispose an audience favorably toward ourselves, we should be merely renewing and reinforcing the ethical appeal that has been working in earlier parts of the discourse.

The kinds of ethical appeal that seem to be most appropriate in the conclusion are the frank confession of our shortcomings, honest acknowledgment of the strength of the opposing case, and magnanimous gestures toward vindictive opponents. It is well to leave our audience with the impression that we have no illusions about ourselves or our position, that we have a respect for truth wherever we find it, and that we are capable of returning charity for malice. The audience gets the impression that the person capable of making frank confessions and generous concessions is not only a good person but a person so confident of the strength of his or her position that he or she can afford to concede points to the opposition.

We observed in the section on the introduction that if we feel it necessary to arouse hostility against our opponent, it is usually better to do this in the conclusion rather than in the introduction. It is easier, for one thing, to arouse hostility against an opponent *after* we have demolished his or her arguments. Circumstances, however, might dictate that it would be better to arouse this hostility early in the discourse. In the reading from *Apology* in the previous chapter, we saw that Socrates deemed it necessary to stir up animosity against Meletus quite early in his speech of defense.

Concluding Remarks on Arrangement

In this chapter, we have been reviewing the usual parts of an extensive discourse, noting what is normally done in each of these parts and remarking the adjustments that frequently have to be made to fit the particular situation. Almost no rule about arrangement is inflexible. Anything "bends" to the exigencies of the moment—to the demands, in other words, of the subject, or the kind of discourse, or the personality or ability of the writer, or the temper of the audience. Where so many adjustments may have to be made to the *ad hoc* situation, very few hard-and-fast precepts can be laid down. Some writers succeed better than others in making these strategic adjustments because they have been endowed with sound instincts for what is effective in any given situation. But other writers, not so gifted, can through experience and practice and guidance acquire a measure of this skill. Experience and practice writers must gain on their own; this text attempts to supply the general guidance that writers may need.

All that rhetoric can do is point out that given this subject or this purpose or this audience, this is what writers may have to do in some part of the discourse, and this is how they might do what they have to do. Disposition then becomes something more than the conventional system for organizing a discourse, something more than just a system of outlining the composition; it becomes a discipline that trains writers in the judicious selection and use of available means to the desired end.

Since so many decisions about arrangement depend upon the given situation, it would be well for writers to study now some readings to see how some authors have managed arrangement in their given situation.

Readings

Dorothy L. Sayers: "Are Women Human?"

Dorothy Leigh Sayers (1893–1957) was born in Oxford, England, the daughter of a clergyman. She was one of the first women in England to obtain an Oxford degree, when in 1915 she took first honors in medieval literature at Somerville College at Oxford. Dorothy Sayers is known to most readers primarily as a detective-story writer. Chambers' Biographical Dictionary *says of her that she is "perhaps the most celebrated detective-story writer since Conan Doyle." She and Agatha Christie are certainly the most celebrated women writers of detective stories. Her principal detective, Lord Peter Whimsey, made his first appearance in her first detective novel* Whose Body? *(1923). Her most noted detective novels were* Murder Must Advertise *(1933) and* The Nine Tailors *(1934). She stopped publishing detective fiction about the time of the outbreak of World War II. During the war years in England, she turned to writing religious dramas and essays on popular theology. A series of twelve radio plays on the life of Christ,* The Man Born To Be King, *was broadcast in England in 1943. Her major literary achievements in the later part of her life were her translations for Penguin Books of Dante's* Inferno *(1949) and* Purgatorio *(1955). The selection reprinted here was first delivered as an address to a Women's Society in 1938.*

1 When I was asked to come and speak to you, your Secretary made the suggestion that she thought I must be interested in the feminist movement. I replied—a little irritably, I am afraid—that I was not sure I wanted to "identify myself," as the phrase goes, with feminism, and that the time for "feminism," in the old-fashioned sense of the word, had gone past. In fact, I think I went so far as to say that, under present conditions, an aggressive feminism might do more harm than good. As a result I was, perhaps not unnaturally, invited to explain myself.

2 I do not know that it is very easy to explain, without offence or risk of misunderstanding, exactly what I do mean, but I will try.

3 The question of "sex-equality" is, like all questions affecting human relationships, delicate and complicated. It cannot be settled by loud slogans or hard-and-fast assertions like "a woman is as good as a man"—or "woman's place is the home"—or "women ought not to take men's jobs." The minute one makes such assertions, one finds one has to qualify them. "A woman is as good as a man" is as meaningless as to say, "a Kaffir is as good as a Frenchman" or "a poet is as good as an engineer" or "an elephant is as good as a racehorse"—it means nothing whatever until you add: "at doing what?" In a religious sense, no doubt, the Kaffir is as valuable in the eyes of God as a Frenchman—but the average Kaffir is probably less skilled in literary criticism than the average Frenchman, and the average Frenchman less skilled than the average Kaffir in tracing the spoor of big game. There might be exceptions on either side: it is largely a matter of heredity and education. When we balance the poet against the engineer, we are faced with a fundamental difference of temperament—so that here our question is complicated by the enormous social problem whether poetry or engineering is "better" for the State, or for humanity in general. There may be people who would like a world that was all engineers or all poets—but most of us would like to have a certain number of each; though here again, we should all differ about the desirable proportion of engineering to poetry. The only proviso we should make is that people with dreaming and poetical temperaments should not entangle themselves in engines, and that mechanically-minded persons should not issue booklets of bad verse. When we come to the elephant and the racehorse, we come down to bed-rock physical differences—the elephant would make a poor showing in the Derby, and the unbeaten Eclipse himself would be speedily eclipsed by an elephant when it came to hauling logs.

4 That is so obvious that it hardly seems worth saying. But it is the mark of all movements, however well-intentioned, that their pioneers tend, by

From Dorothy L. Sayers, *Are Women Human?* Grand Rapids, MI: William B. Eerdmans, 1971. Reprinted with permission of the Watkins/Loomis Agency, Inc. of New York.

much lashing of themselves into excitement, to lose sight of the obvious. In reaction against the age-old slogan, "woman is the weaker vessel," or the still more offensive, "woman is a divine creature," we have, I think, allowed ourselves to drift into asserting that "a woman is as good as a man," without always pausing to think what exactly we mean by that. What, I feel, we ought to mean is something so obvious that it is apt to escape attention altogether, viz: not that every woman is, in virtue of her sex, as strong, clever, artistic, level-headed, industrious and so forth as any man that can be mentioned; but, that a woman is just as much an ordinary human being as a man, with the same individual preferences, and with just as much right to the tastes and preferences of an individual. What is repugnant to every human being is to be reckoned always as a member of a class and not as an individual person. A certain amount of classification is, of course, necessary for practical purposes: there is no harm in saying that women, as a class, have smaller bones than men, wear lighter clothing, have more hair on their heads and less on their faces, go more pertinaciously to church or the cinema, or have more patience with small and noisy babies. In the same way, we may say that stout people of both sexes are commonly better-tempered than thin ones, or that university dons of both sexes are more pedantic in their speech than agricultural labourers, or that Communists of both sexes are more ferocious than Fascists—or the other way round. What is unreasonable and irritating is to assume that *all* one's tastes and preferences have to be conditioned by the class to which one belongs. That has been the very common error into which men have frequently fallen about women—and it is the error into which feminist women are, perhaps, a little inclined to fall about themselves.

5 Take, for example, the very usual reproach that women nowadays always want to "copy what men do." In that reproach there is a great deal of truth and a great deal of sheer, unmitigated and indeed quite wicked nonsense. There are a number of jobs and pleasures which men have in times past cornered for themselves. At one time, for instance, men had a monopoly of classical education. When the pioneers of university training for women demanded that women should be admitted to the universities, the cry went up at once: "Why should women want to know about Aristotle?" The answer is NOT that *all* women would be the better for knowing about Aristotle—still less, as Lord Tennyson seemed to think, that they would be more companionable wives for their husbands if they did know about Aristotle—but simply: "What women want as a class is irrelevant. *I* want to know about Aristotle. It is true that most women care nothing about him, and a great many male undergraduates turn pale and faint at the thought of him—but I, eccentric individual that I am, do want to know about Aristotle, and I submit that there is nothing in my shape or bodily functions which need prevent my knowing about him."

6 That battle was won, and rightly won, for women. But there is a sillier side to the university education of women. I have noticed lately, and with regret, a tendency on the part of the women's colleges to "copy the men" on the side of their failings and absurdities, and this is not so good. Because the constitution of the men's colleges is autocratic, old-fashioned and in many respects inefficient, the women are rather inclined to try and cramp their own collegiate constitutions—which were mapped out on freer democratic lines—into the mediaeval mould of the men's—and that is unsound. It contributes nothing to the university and it loses what might have been a very good thing. The women students, too, have a foolish trick of imitating and outdoing the absurdities of male undergraduates. To climb in drunk after hours and get gated is silly and harmless if done out of pure high spirits; if it is done "because the men do it," it is worse than silly, because it is not spontaneous and not even amusing.

7 Let me give one simple illustration of the difference between the right and the wrong kind of feminism. Let us take this terrible business—so distressing to the minds of bishops—of the women who go about in trousers. We are asked: "Why do you want to go about in trousers? They are extremely unbecoming to most of you. You only do it to copy the men." To this we may very properly reply: "It is true that they are unbecoming. Even on men they are remarkably unattractive. But, as you men have discovered for yourselves, they are comfortable, they do not get in the way of one's activities like skirts and they protect the wearer from draughts about the ankles. As a human being, I like comfort and dislike draughts. If the trousers do not attract you, so much the worse; for the moment I do not want to attract you. I want to enjoy myself as a human being, and why not? As for copying you, certainly you thought of trousers first and to that extent we must copy you. But we are not such abandoned copy-cats as to attach these useful garments to our bodies with braces. There we draw the line. These machines of leather and elastic are unnecessary and unsuited to the female form. They are, moreover, hideous beyond description. And as for indecency—of which you sometimes accuse the trousers—we at least can take our coats off without becoming the half-undressed, bedroom spectacle that a man presents in his shirt and braces."

8 So that when we hear that women have once more laid hands upon something which was previously a man's sole privilege, I think we have to ask ourselves: is this trousers or is it braces? Is it something useful, convenient and suitable to a human being as such? Or is it merely something unnecessary to us, ugly, and adopted merely for the sake of collaring the other fellow's property? These jobs and professions, now. It is ridiculous to take on a man's job just in order to be able to say that "a woman has done it—yah!" The only decent reason for tackling any job is that it is *your* job, and *you* want to do it.

9 At this point, somebody is likely to say: "Yes, that is all very well. But it *is* the woman who is always trying to ape the man. She *is* the inferior being. You don't as a rule find the men trying to take the women's jobs away from them. They don't force their way into the household and turn women out of their rightful occupations."

10 Of course they do not. They have done it already.

11 Let us accept the idea that women should stick to their own jobs—the jobs they did so well in the good old days before they started talking about votes and women's rights. Let us return to the Middle Ages and ask what we should get then in return for certain political and educational privileges which we should have to abandon.

12 It is a formidable list of jobs: the whole of the spinning industry, the whole of the dyeing industry, the whole of the weaving industry. The whole catering industry and—which would not please Lady Astor, perhaps—the whole of the nation's brewing and distilling. All the preserving, pickling and bottling industry, all the bacon-curing. And (since in those days a man was often absent from home for months together on war or business) a very large share in the management of landed estates. Here are the women's jobs—and what has become of them? They are all being handled by men. It is all very well to say that woman's place is the home—but modern civilisation has taken all these pleasant and profitable activities out of the home, where the women looked after them, and handed them over to big industry, to be directed and organised by men at the head of large factories. Even the dairy-maid in her simple bonnet has gone, to be replaced by a male mechanic in charge of a mechanical milking plant.

13 Now, it is very likely that men in big industries do these jobs better than the women did them at home. The fact remains that the home contains much less of interesting activity than it used to contain. What is more, the home has so shrunk to the size of a small flat that—even if we restrict woman's job to the bearing and rearing of families—there is no room for her to do even that. It is useless to urge the modern woman to have twelve children, like her grandmother. Where is she to put them when she has got them? And what modern man wants to be bothered with them? It is perfectly idiotic to take away women's traditional occupations and then complain because she looks for new ones. Every woman is a human being—one cannot repeat that too often—and a human being *must* have occupation, if he or she is not to become a nuisance to the world.

14 I am not complaining that the brewing and baking were taken over by the men. If they can brew and bake as well as women or better, then by all means let them do it. But they cannot have it both ways. If they are going to adopt the very sound principle that the job should be done by the person who does it best, then that rule must be applied universally. If the women make better office-workers than men, they must have the office work.

If any individual woman is able to make a first-class lawyer, doctor, archi-tect or engineer, then she must be allowed to try her hand at it. Once lay down the rule that the job comes first and you throw that job open to every individual, man or woman, fat or thin, tall or short, ugly or beautiful, who is able to do that job better than the rest of the world.

15 Now, it is frequently asserted that, with women, the job does not come first. What (people cry) are women doing with this liberty of theirs? What woman really prefers a job to a home and family? Very few, I admit. It is unfortunate that they should so often have to make the choice. A man does not, as a rule, have to choose. He gets both. In fact, if he wants the home and family, he usually has to take the job as well, if he can get it. Nevertheless, there have been women, such as Queen Elizabeth and Florence Nightingale, who had the choice, and chose the job and made a success of it. And there have been and are many men who have sacrificed their careers for women—sometimes, like Antony or Parnell, very disastrously. When it comes to a *choice,* then every man or woman has to choose as an individual human being, and, like a human being, take the consequences.

16 As human beings! I am always entertained—and also irritated—by the news-mongers who inform us, with a bright air of discovery, that they have questioned a number of female workers and been told by one and all that they are "sick of the office and would love to get out of it." In the name of God, what human being is *not,* from time to time, heartily sick of the office and would *not* love to get out of it? The time of female office-workers is daily wasted in sympathising with disgruntled male colleagues who yearn to get out of the office. No human being likes work—not day in and day out. Work is notoriously a curse—and if women *liked* everlasting work they would not be human beings at all. *Being* human beings, they like work just as much and just as little as anybody else. They dislike perpetual wash-ing and cooking just as much as perpetual typing and standing behind shop counters. Some of them prefer typing to scrubbing—but that does not mean that they are not, as human beings, entitled to damn and blast the type-writer when they feel that way. The number of men who daily damn and blast typewriters is incalculable; but that does not mean that they would be happier doing a little plain sewing. Nor would the women.

17 I have admitted that there are very few women who would put their job before every earthly consideration. I will go further and assert that there are very few men who would do it either. In fact, there is perhaps only one human being in a thousand who is passionately interested in his job for the job's sake. The difference is that if that one person in a thousand is a man, we say, simply, that he is passionately keen on his job; if she is a woman, we say she is a freak. It is extraordinarily entertaining to watch the historians of the past, for instance, entangling themselves in what they were pleased to call the "problem" of Queen Elizabeth. They invented the most complicated and astonishing reasons both for her success as a sovereign and for her tortuous matrimonial policy. She was the tool of Burleigh, she was the tool of Leicester, she was the tool of Essex; she was diseased, she was deformed, she was a man in disguise. She was a mystery, and must have some extraordinary solution. Only recently has it occurred to a few enlightened people that the solution might be quite simple after all. She might be one of the rare people who were born into the right job and put that job first. Whereupon a whole series of riddles cleared themselves up by magic. She was in love with Leicester—why didn't she marry him? Well, for the very same reason that numberless kings have not married their lovers—because it would have thrown a spanner into the wheels of the State machine. Why was she so bloodthirsty and unfeminine as to sign the death-warrant of Mary Queen of Scots? For much the same reasons that induced King George V to say that if the House of Lords did not pass the Parliament Bill he would create enough new peers to force it through— because she was, in the measure of her time, a constitutional sovereign, and knew that there was a point beyond which a sovereign could not defy Parliament. Being a rare human being with her eye to the job, she did what was necessary; being an ordinary human being, she hesitated a good deal before embarking on unsavoury measures—but as to feminine mystery, there is no such thing about it, and nobody, had she been a man, would have thought either her statesmanship or her humanity in any way mysterious. Remarkable they were—but she was a very remarkable person. Among her most remarkable achievements was that of showing that sovereignty was one of the jobs for which the right kind of woman was particularly well fitted.

18   Which brings us back to this question of what jobs, if any, are women's jobs. Few people would go so far as to say that all women are well fitted for all men's jobs. When people do say this, it is particularly exasperating. It is stupid to insist that there are as many female musicians and mathematicians as male—the facts are otherwise, and the most we can ask is that if a Dame Ethel Smyth or a Mary Somerville turns up, she shall be allowed to do her work without having aspersions cast either on her sex or her ability. What we ask is to be human individuals, however peculiar and unexpected. It is no good saying: "You are a little girl and therefore you ought to like dolls"; if the answer is, "But I don't," there is no more to be said. Few women happen to be natural born mechanics; but if there is one, it is useless to try and argue her into being something different. What we must *not* do is to argue that the occasional appearance of a female mechanical genius proves that all women would be mechanical geniuses if they were educated. They would not.

19   Where, I think, a great deal of confusion has arisen is in a failure to distinguish between special *knowledge* and special *ability*. There are certain questions on which what is called "the woman's point of view" is valuable,

because they involve special *knowledge*. Women should be consulted about such things as housing and domestic architecture because, under present circumstances, they have still to wrestle a good deal with houses and kitchen sinks and can bring special knowledge to the problem. Similarly, some of them (though not all) know more about children than the majority of men, and their opinion, *as women,* is of value. In the same way, the opinion of colliers is of value about coal-mining, and the opinion of doctors is valuable about disease. But there are other questions—as, for example, about literature or finance—on which the "woman's point of view" has no value at all. In fact, it does not exist. No special knowledge is involved, and a woman's opinion on literature or finance is valuable only as the judgment of an individual. I am occasionally desired by congenital imbeciles and the editors of magazines to say something about the writing of detective fiction "from the woman's point of view." To such demands, one can only say, "Go away and don't be silly. You might as well ask what is the female angle on an equilateral triangle."

20 In the old days it used to be said that women were unsuited to sit in Parliament, because they "would not be able to think imperially." That, if it meant anything, meant that their views would be cramped and domestic—in short, "the woman's point of view." Now that they *are* in Parliament, people complain that they are a disappointment: they vote like other people with their party and have contributed nothing to speak of from "the woman's point of view"—except on a few purely domestic questions, and even then they are not all agreed. It looks as though somebody was trying to have things both ways at once. Even critics must remember that women are human beings and obliged to think and behave as such. I can imagine a "woman's point of view" about town-planning, or the education of children, or divorce, or the employment of female shop-assistants, for here they have some special knowledge. But what in thunder is the "woman's point of view" about the devaluation of the franc or the abolition of the Danzig Corridor? Even where women have special knowledge, they may disagree among themselves like other specialists. Do doctors never quarrel or scientists disagree? Are women really *not human,* that they should be expected to toddle along all in a flock like sheep? I think that people should be allowed to drink as much wine and beer as they can afford and is good for them; Lady Astor thinks nobody should be allowed to drink anything of the sort. Where is the "woman's point of view"? Or is one or the other of us unsexed? If the unsexed one is myself, then I am unsexed in very good company. But I prefer to think that women are human and differ in opinion like other human beings. This does not mean that their opinions, as individual opinions, are valueless; on the contrary, the more able they are the more violently their opinions will be likely to differ. It only means that you cannot ask for "the woman's point of view," but only for the woman's special knowledge—and this, like all special knowledge, is valuable, though it is no guarantee of agreement.

21 "What," men have asked distractedly from the beginning of time, "what on earth do women want?" I do not know that women, *as* women, want anything in particular, but as human beings they want, my good men, exactly what you want yourselves: interesting occupation, reasonable freedom for their pleasures, and a sufficient emotional outlet. What form the occupation, the pleasures and the emotion may take, depends entirely upon the individual. You know that this is so with yourselves—why will you not believe that it is so with us? The late D. H. Lawrence, who certainly cannot be accused of underrating the importance of sex and talked a good deal of nonsense upon the subject, was yet occasionally visited with shattering glimpses of the obvious. He said in one of his *Assorted Articles:*

> "Man is willing to accept woman as an equal, as a man in skirts, as an angel, a devil, a baby-face, a machine, an instrument, a bosom, a womb, a pair of legs, a servant, an encyclopaedia, an ideal or an obscenity; the one thing he won't accept her as is a human being, a real human being of the feminine sex."

22 "Accepted as a human being!"—yes; not as an inferior class and not, I beg and pray all feminists, as a superior class—not, in fact, as a class at all, except in a useful context. We are much too much inclined in these days to divide people into permanent categories, forgetting that a category only exists for its special purpose and must be forgotten as soon as that purpose is served. There is a fundamental difference between men and women, but it is not the only fundamental difference in the world. There is a sense in which my charwoman and I have more in common than either of us has with, say, Mr. Bernard Shaw; on the other hand, in a discussion about art and literature, Mr. Shaw and I should probably find we had more fundamental interests in common than either of us had with my charwoman. I grant that, even so, he and I should disagree ferociously about the eating of meat—but that is not a difference between the sexes—on that point, the late Mr. G. K. Chesterton would have sided with me against the representative of his own sex. Then there are points on which I, and many of my own generation of both sexes, should find ourselves heartily in agreement; but on which the rising generation of young men and women would find us too incomprehensibly stupid for words. A difference of age is as fundamental as a difference of sex; and so is a difference of nationality. *All* categories, if they are insisted upon beyond the immediate purpose which they serve, breed class antagonism and disruption in the state, and that is why they are dangerous.

23 The other day, in the "Heart-to-Heart" columns of one of our popular newspapers, there appeared a letter from a pathetic gentleman about a little disruption threatening his married state. He wrote:

> "I have been married eleven years and think a great deal of the wedding anniversary. I remind my wife a month in advance and plan to make the evening a success. But she does not share my keenness, and, if I did not remind her, would let the day go by without a thought of its significance. I thought a wedding anniversary meant a lot to a woman. Can you explain this indifference?"

24 Poor little married gentleman, nourished upon generalisations—and convinced that if his wife does not fit into the category of "a woman" there must be something wrong! Perhaps she resents being dumped into the same category as all the typical women of the comic stories. If so, she has my sympathy. "A" woman—not an individual person, disliking perhaps to be reminded of the remorseless flowing-by of the years and the advance of old age—but "a" woman, displaying the conventional sentimentalities attributed to her unfortunate and ridiculous sex.

25 A man once asked me—it is true that it was at the end of a very good dinner, and the compliment conveyed may have been due to that circumstance—how I managed in my books to write such natural conversation between men when they were by themselves. Was I, by any chance, a member of a large, mixed family with a lot of male friends? I replied that, on the contrary, I was an only child and had practically never seen or spoken to any men of my own age till I was about twenty-five. "Well," said the man, "I shouldn't have expected a woman [meaning me] to have been able to make it so convincing." I replied that I had coped with this difficult problem by making my men talk, as far as possible, like ordinary human beings. This aspect of the matter seemed to surprise the other speaker; he said no more, but took it away to chew it over. One of these days it may quite likely occur to him that women, as well as men, when left to themselves, talk very much like human beings also.

26 Indeed, it is my experience that both men and women are fundamentally human, and that there is very little mystery about either sex, except the exasperating mysteriousness of human beings in general. And though for certain purposes it may still be necessary, as it undoubtedly was in the immediate past, for women to band themselves together, as women, to secure recognition of their requirements as a sex, I am sure that the time has now come to insist more strongly on each woman's—and indeed each man's—requirements as an individual person. It used to be said that women had no *esprit de corps;* we have proved that we have—do not let us run into the opposite error of insisting that there is an aggressively feminist "point of view" about everything. To oppose one class perpetually to another—young against old, manual labour against brain-worker, rich against poor, woman

against man—is to split the foundations of the State; and if the cleavage runs too deep, there remains no remedy but force and dictatorship. If you wish to preserve a free democracy, you must base it—not on classes and categories, for this will land you in the totalitarian State, where no one may act or think except as the member of a category. You must base it upon the individual Tom, Dick and Harry, and the individual Jack and Jill—in fact, upon you and me.

An Analysis of the Arrangement in Dorothy L. Sayers's "Are Women Human?"

The title of Dorothy Sayers's Address, "Are Women Human?," is arresting, even shocking. It must have been even more shocking to the group of women who first heard the address, especially back in 1938 when the general public consciousness about the feminist movement had not been raised as much as it has been in the last quarter of the twentieth century. To most of us today, the question "Are women human?" seems to be as impertinent as the question "Is the Pope Catholic?" But when we get into Dorothy Sayers's speech, we realize that the question she asks is crucial. One of the premises of her argument in this address is based on the answer to this question.

Sayers's basic argument here might be cast in the form of a syllogism—or at least in the form of an enthymeme. The full syllogism might be stated in this fashion:

> All human beings are equal.
> All men and women are human beings.
> Therefore all men and women are equal.

Dorothy Sayers does not explicitly argue in support of the major premise, "All human beings are equal"; in fact, she does not even enunciate that premise anywhere in the address. Knowing her audience—a group of upper-middle-class women living in a democratic country like England in the twentieth century—she can count on them to give their assent to that understood premise. But she several times enunciates the minor premise, "All men and women are human beings." Here are just three instances of that assertion, stated in words slightly different from the phraseology of the reconstructed premise: (paragraph 4) "a woman is just as much an ordinary human being as a man"; (paragraph 13) "every woman is a human being—one cannot repeat that too often"; (paragraph 26) "both men and women are fundamentally human." What she is arguing for in this address is that men and women are equal (the "therefore" proposition in our syllogism) and that consequently they should share equally in the rights and privileges due to all human beings. She adumbrates that conclusion in the first sentence of the third paragraph, when she uses the phrase "the question of sex-equality." Since Dorothy Sayers implies rather than asserts the major premise, we might formulate her basic argument in the form of this enthymeme:

Men and woman are equal because they are human beings.

Although in this analysis, we will be frequently noting and occasionally commenting on the arguments that Dorothy Sayers presents in her address, the emphasis here will be primarily on the arrangement, the organization, of the arguments. We want to trace out the sequence of her arguments and to see whether there is any logic or even method to the way in which she marshalls her arguments.

Since the address is fairly lengthy—it consists of 26 paragraphs—a broad outline of the speech might be helpful. Here is an overview of the organization of the speech:

> Introduction (paragraphs 1 and 2)
> Statement of Fact (paragraphs 3-4)
> Proof (paragraphs 4-25)
>   A. Refutation of three counter-arguments (paragraphs 5-20)
>   B. Confirmation of her own position on two issues (paragraphs 21-25)
> Conclusion (paragraph 26)

There may be differing views of where these divisions begin and end, but there will be general agreement about this organization.

What is revealed by this outline is that Sayers's major strategy is first of all to refute some of the arguments that are commonly offered for not granting women the same rights and privileges that men enjoy and then to present her own arguments. One wonders just who her audience is for this address. Ostensibly, she is addressing the members of a Women's Society, and surely she is aware that this audience does not need to be convinced that women are human beings and that women are morally and politically equal to men. But she may have other agendas: she may be intent (1) on providing these women with arguments that they might use in fighting for their rights and (2) on answering the counter-arguments that those outside the Society traditionally offer for not granting women their rights and privileges. In short, she may have a double audience in mind, and the secondary audience—the one outside the Society—may be the more important audience for her purposes.

Let us now examine more particularly the arrangement of her address in terms of the traditional parts of a persuasive discourse laid out by classical rhetoricians.

We learned earlier in this chapter that the two main functions of the *pro-emium* or the *exordium*—we have called this part the *introduction*—are

(1) to inform the audience about the end or the object of the discourse and (2) to dispose the audience to be receptive to the speaker's or writer's message. The introduction here is very short—just two brief paragraphs. The first paragraph, consisting of four sentences, introduces the general subject of her talk, the feminist movement, and then reveals the surprising position that she takes on the feminist movement: she does not want to be identified as a feminist, and she thinks that an aggressive feminism may do more harm than good. The one-sentence second paragraph then provides a transition into the next section, where she will explain what she means by the position she took in the first paragraph. She needs to explain her position because the stance that she enunciated here could damage her ethos with her immediate audience and thereby diminish her effectiveness with this audience.

Our general outline indicates that paragraphs 3 and 4 are given over to that part of a persuasive discourse that the classical rhetoricians called the *narratio* and that we have called the *statement of fact*. In these two paragraphs, Dorothy Sayers indicates what the main issue is in the controversy about the feminist movement and explains why she has taken a cautious position on the subject of the feminist movement. The main issue, as she indicates in the very first sentence of paragraph 3, is what she calls "sex-equality," and she has adopted a cautious position on this issue because it is "delicate and complicated." She gives several examples of general assertions about classes or categories of people and shows how these generalizations have to be qualified almost as soon as they are uttered. In paragraph 4 of the Statement of Fact, Dorothy Sayers lays out the general principle that will govern her argument in support of the equality of women in relation to men: that people should be characterized, not on the basis of the class to which they belong but on the basis of being individual human beings. And before the end of this paragraph, she asserts the minor premise of her main argument: a woman is just as much a human being as a man.

Beginning with paragraph 5, we get into the main body of the address or, in terms of persuasive discourse, into the proof section. The two main subdivisions of the proof section are the refutation section (paragraphs 5–17), where she responds to three assertions commonly made about women in comparison with men, and a confirmation section (paragraphs 18–25), where she presents her own arguments in support of her contention that because men and women are equal, they should both be accorded the same rights and privileges. Sayers felt that she should dispose of counter-arguments on this issue before she advanced her own arguments. This strategy is advisable whenever you sense that your opponents' position has more adherents in your immediate audience or among people in general than your own position does. You have to clear the ground before erecting your own edifice.

Without going very deeply into the substance of the arguments in the proof section—because here we are primarily interested in analyzing the organization of the discourse—we can take a closer look at the sequence of the arguments.

In paragraphs 5–8, she deals with the first assertion that women always want to copy what men do. Here she uses the homely example of women who are starting to wear trousers (we would call them slacks or pants today), a style of apparel that was quite shocking back in 1938, especially in Great Britain, where Sayers is speaking. In essence, her argument is "why not?" As human beings, women are just as much attracted to comfort and convenience as men are.

In paragraphs 9–14, she attempts to refute the second common assertion about women: that it is always women who try to ape men, never the other way around. People commonly say something like this: you never find men moving into the household and taking over women's jobs. The two-sentence tenth paragraph, provides a transition into what is perhaps her most impressive argument by saying, "Of course they do not. They have done it already." In paragraphs 10 and 11 then, she resorts to history and points out the kinds of jobs that women did in medieval households—jobs like spinning and dyeing and weaving and preserving and pickling and bottling. Now these jobs have all been appropriated by men, who do them, not in the house, as women once did, but in factories. In line with her insistence that men and women should be treated as equals, she asserts that the jobs—whatever they are—should go to those who do them best. That proposition would be difficult for anyone to discredit.

In paragraphs 15–17, she deals with the third assertion: that in the case of women, the job does not come first. Her main answer to this charge is that in the case of many men too, the job does not come first. Just as many men as women get sick of the tedium of work. But she points out that throughout history, there have been examples of women for whom the job did come first and who performed the job extraordinarily well. And the main example that she cites of a woman who gave priority to the job was Queen Elizabeth I.

Beginning with paragraph 18 and ending with paragraph 25, Sayers presents her own arguments in support of her position. And in this confirmation section, she focuses her arguments by concentrating on two questions: (1) what jobs, if any, are women's jobs? (2) what do women really want? Her answer to the first question is basically that women's jobs are those for which women, because of experience or temperament, have "special knowledge." Many women are especially suited for jobs involving the care and supervision of housing, children, and domestic architecture. But *some* women have a special aptitude for jobs that we commonly associate with men. Again, women, like men, should be judged primarily as individuals, not as members of a class.

Her answer to the second question, "What do women really want?" is encapsulated in this statement from paragraph 21: "I do not know that women, *as* women, want anything in particular, but as human beings they want, my good men, exactly what you want yourselves: interesting occupation, reasonable freedom for their pleasures, and a sufficient emotional outlet." She rounds back then to one of her general principles: women want to be treated as human beings, and she gives two examples of insensitive men who were inclined to treat women as stereotypes of a class and not as individual human beings.

Like her introduction, Dorothy Sayers's conclusion is relatively brief—one paragraph of six fairly lengthy sentences. What she mainly does in this final paragraph is recapitulate the general principles and main arguments advanced in the speech. However, she gives a more global perspective to her general principle that every man and woman should be treated as human individuals by saying the following in the last three sentences of her conclusion (or her peroration, as the classical rhetorician would dub this section):

> To oppose one class perpetually to another—young against old, manual labour against brain-worker, rich against poor, woman against man—is to split the foundations of the State; and if the cleavage runs too deep, there remains no remedy but force and dictatorship [remember that 1938 was the eve of Adolf Hitler's attempt to impose his fascist government on the whole of Western Europe]. If you wish to preserve a free democracy, you must base it—not on classes and categories, for this will land you in the totalitarian State, where no one may act or think except as the member of a category. You must base it upon the individual Tom, Dick, and Harry, and the individual Jack and Jill—in fact, upon you and me.

No one before or since has quite put the issue of the feminist movement in such global terms, and by thus universalizing the issue, she leaves her audience with the strong impression that resolving the feminist controversy is crucial for the welfare of the world community.

There is nothing either surprising or predictable about the organization of Dorothy Sayers's address. There is certainly nothing that is inevitable about that organization. It is *her* organization, just as it contains *her* arguments. On this issue, you may have used different arguments and a different organization. Sometimes the effectiveness of an organization is determined not by some pre-ordained ideal paradigm but by who is speaking or by the particular set of arguments that a speaker or writer chooses. We did note that either consciously or unconsciously, Dorothy Sayers decided to refute some opposing arguments before advancing her own arguments. That was *her* decision. That strategy might not have been your strategy if you were speaking on this topic. Different circumstances might dictate a different strategy for you.

But although one cannot always account for why Dorothy Sayers put a particular argument or a particular example in the position that she did, it would be difficult for us to demonstrate that she made tactical mistakes in the organization that she used. As a famed detective-story writer she is accustomed to putting sequences together in some kind of discernible and effective order. As a detective-story writer she is also used to devising rationalizations and inferences for her chief detective Lord Peter Whimsey. So we can presume that her instincts about effective arguments and effective organization are sound, if not infallible. And remember too that Dorothy Sayers's ethical appeal would have been very high with her immediate audience, not only because of the reasonableness that she displays in this discourse but because of her antecedent reputation, even in 1938, as a world-famous writer and Christian apologist. Dorothy Sayers was, along with Virginia Woolf, an early champion in Great Britain of the feminist movement. If we can judge by this discourse, she seems to have been a judicious and effective one.

Thomas A. Sancton: Planet of the Year

In the first issue of the new year, TIME magazine publishes its Man of the Year (or Woman of the Year) issue. In its January 2, 1989, issue, instead of naming a Person of the Year, TIME designated our endangered earth as Planet of the Year. (Once before, in 1982, TIME named the computer as the Machine of the Year.) Thomas A. Sancton's essay introduced a 33-page package, which included ten other essays and a poem entitled "Magnitudes" by Howard Nemerov, commonly regarded as the current poet laureate of the United States. Each of the essays following Sancton's treated in some depth one aspect of the deterioration of our planet. Here is a partial list of the titles of the subsequent essays:

> *"The Death of Birth" ("Man is recklessly wiping out life on earth.)*
> *"Deadly Danger in a Spray Can" ("Ozone-destroying CFCS [chlorofluorocarbons] should be banned.")*
> *"A Stinking Mess" ("Throwaway societies befoul their land and seas.")*
> *"Too Many Mouths" ("Swarms of people are running out of food and space.")*
> *"Preparing for the Worst" ("If the sun turns killer and the well runs dry, how will humanity cope?")*

In the February 13, 1989, issue of TIME, the editors reported that this Planet of the Year issue drew 1,687 letters, "the largest outpouring of mail for a

*Man of the Year issue since TIME selected the Ayatullah Khomeini in 1979."
Judging by that volume of letters to the editor, we would be safe in asserting
that the topic dealt with in this special issue touched an unusually sensitive
nerve in its readers. An analysis of the arrangement of Sancton's essay will
follow.*

> *One generation passeth away, and another generation cometh: but the
> earth abideth forever.*
>
> —*Eccelsiastes*

1   No, not forever. At the outside limit, the earth will probably last another
4 billion to 5 billion years. By that time, scientists predict, the sun will have
burned up so much of its own hydrogen fuel that it will expand and inciner-
ate the surrounding planets, including the earth. A nuclear cataclysm, on the
other hand, could destroy the earth tomorrow. Somewhere within those extremes lies the life expectancy of this wondrous, swirling globe. How long it
endures and the quality of life it can support do not depend alone on the immutable laws of physics. For man has reached a point in his evolution where
he has the power to affect, for better or worse, the present and future state of
the planet.

2   Through most of his 2 million years or so of existence, man has thrived
in earth's environment—perhaps too well. By 1800 there were 1 billion human beings bestriding the planet. That number had doubled by 1930 and
doubled again by 1975. If current birthrates hold, the world's present population of 5.1 billion will double again in 40 more years. The frightening irony
is that this exponential growth in the human population—the very sign of
homo sapiens' success as an organism—could doom the earth as a human
habitat.

3   The reason is not so much the sheer numbers, though 40,000 babies die of
starvation each day in Third World countries, but the reckless way in which
humanity has treated its planetary host. Like the evil genies that flew from
Pandora's box, technological advances have provided the means of upsetting
nature's equilibrium, that intricate set of biological, physical and chemical interactions that make up the web of life. Starting at the dawn of the Industrial
Revolution, smokestacks have disgorged noxious gases into the atmosphere,
factories have dumped toxic wastes into rivers and streams, automobiles have
guzzled irreplaceable fossil fuels and fouled the air with their detritus. In the
name of progress, forests have been denuded, lakes poisoned with pesticides,
underground aquifers pumped dry. For decades, scientists have warned of
the possible consequences of all this profligacy. No one paid much attention.

4 This year the earth spoke, like God warning Noah of the deluge. Its message was loud and clear, and suddenly people began to listen, to ponder what portents the message held. In the U.S., a three-month drought baked the soil from California to Georgia, reducing the country's grain harvest by 31% and killing thousands of head of livestock. A stubborn seven-week heat wave drove temperatures above 100° F across much of the country, raising fears that the dreaded "greenhouse effect"—global warming as a result of the buildup of carbon dioxide and other gases in the atmosphere—might already be under way. Parched by the lack of rain, the Western forests of the U.S., including Yellowstone National Park, went up in flames, also igniting a bitter conservationist controversy. And on many of the country's beaches, garbage, raw sewage and medical wastes washed up to spoil the fun of bathers and confront them personally with the growing despoliation of the oceans.

5 Similar pollution closed beaches on the Mediterranean, the North Sea and the English Channel. Killer hurricanes ripped through the Caribbean and floods devastated Bangladesh, reminders of nature's raw power. In Soviet Armenia a monstrous earthquake killed some 55,000 people. That too was a natural disaster, but its high casualty count, owing largely to the construction of cheap high-rise apartment blocks over a well-known fault area, illustrated the carelessness that has become humanity's habit in dealing with nature.

6 There were other forebodings of environmental disaster. In the U.S. it was revealed that federal weapons-making plants had recklessly and secretly littered large areas with radioactive waste. The further depletion of the atmosphere's ozone layer, which helps block cancer-causing ultraviolet rays, testified to the continued overuse of atmosphere-destroying chlorofluorocarbons emanating from such sources as spray cans and air-conditioners. Perhaps most ominous of all, the destruction of the tropical forests, home to at least half the earth's plant and animal species, continued at a rate equal to one football field a second.

7 Most of these evils had been going on for a long time, and some of the worst disasters apparently had nothing to do with human behavior. Yet this year's bout of freakish weather and environmental horror stories seemed to act as a powerful catalyst for worldwide public opinion. Everyone suddenly sensed that this gyrating globe, this precious repository of all the life that we know of, was in danger. No single individual, no event, no movement captured imaginations or dominated headlines more than the clump of rock and soil and water and air that is our common home. Thus in a rare but not unprecedented departure from its tradition of naming a Man of the Year, TIME has designated Endangered Earth as Planet of the Year for 1988.

8 To help focus its coverage, TIME invited 33 scientists, administrators and political leaders from ten countries to a three-day conference in Boulder in November. The group included experts in climate change, population, waste disposal and the preservation of species. In addition to explaining the complexities of these interlocking problems, the specialists advanced a wide range of practical ideas and suggestions that TIME has fashioned into an agenda for environmental action. That agenda, accompanied by stories on each of the major environmental problems, appears throughout the following pages.

9 What would happen if nothing were done about the earth's imperiled state? According to computer projections, the accumulation of CO_2 in the atmosphere could drive up the planet's average temperature 3° F to 9° F by the middle of the next century. That could cause the oceans to rise by several feet, flooding coastal areas and ruining huge tracts of farmland through salinization. Changing weather patterns could make huge areas infertile or uninhabitable, touching off refugee movements unprecedented in history.

10 Toxic waste and radioactive contamination could lead to shortages of safe drinking water, the sine qua non of human existence. And in a world that could house between 8 billion and 14 billion people by the mid–21st century, there is a strong likelihood of mass starvation. It is even possible to envision the world so wryly and chillingly prophesied by the typewriting cockroach in Donald Marquis' *archy and mehitabel:* "man is making deserts of the earth/ it wont be long now/ before man will have it used up/ so that nothing but ants/ and centipedes and scorpions/ can find a living on it."

11 There are those who believe the worst scenarios are alarming and ill founded. Some scientists contest the global-warming theory or predict that natural processes will counter its effects. Kenneth E. F. Watt, professor of environmental studies at the University of California at Davis, has gone so far as to call the greenhouse effect "the laugh of the century." S. Fred Singer, a geophysicist working for the U.S. Department of Transportation, predicts that any greenhouse warming will be balanced by an increase in heat-reflecting clouds. The skeptics could be right, but it is far too risky to do nothing while awaiting absolute proof of disaster.

12 Whatever the validity of this or that theory, the earth will not remain as it is now. From its beginnings as a chunk of molten rock and gas some 4.5 billion years ago, the planet has seen continents form, move together and drift apart like jigsaw-puzzle pieces. Successive ice ages have sent glaciers creeping down from the polar caps. Mountain ranges have jutted up from ocean beds, and landmasses have disappeared beneath the waves.

13 Previous shifts in the earth's climate or topology have been accompanied by waves of extinctions. The most spectacular example is the dying off of the great dinosaurs during the Cretaceous period (136 million to 65 million years ago). No one knows exactly what killed the dinosaurs, although a radical change in environmental conditions seems a likely answer. One popular theory is that a huge meteor crashed to earth and kicked up such vast clouds of dust that sunlight was obscured and plants destroyed. Result: the dinosaurs starved to death.

14 Whether or not that theory is correct, an event of no less magnitude is

taking place at this very moment, but this time its agent is man. The wholesale burning and cutting of forests in Brazil and other countries, as one major example, are destroying irreplaceable species every day. Says Harvard biologist E. O. Wilson: "The extinctions ongoing worldwide promise to be at least as great as the mass extinction that occurred at the end of the age of dinosaurs."

15 Humanity's current predatory relationship with nature reflects a man-centered world view that has evolved over the ages. Almost every society has had its myths about the earth and its origins. The ancient Chinese depicted Chaos as an enormous egg whose parts separated into earth and sky, yin and yang. The Greeks believed Gaia, the earth, was created immediately after Chaos and gave birth to the gods. In many pagan societies, the earth was seen as a mother, a fertile giver of life. Nature—the soil, forest, sea—was endowed with divinity, and mortals were subordinate to it.

16 The Judeo-Christian tradition introduced a radically different concept. The earth was the creation of a monotheistic God, who, after shaping it, ordered its inhabitants, in the words of *Genesis*. "Be fruitful and multiply, and replenish the earth and subdue it: and have dominion over the fish of the sea and over the fowl of the air and over every living thing that moveth upon the earth." The idea of dominion could be interpreted as an invitation to use nature as a convenience. Thus the spread of Christianity, which is generally considered to have paved the way for the development of technology, may at the same time have carried the seeds of the wanton exploitation of nature that often accompanied technical progress.

17 Those tendencies were compounded by the Enlightenment notion of a mechanistic universe that man could shape to his own ends through science. The exuberant optimism of that world view was behind some of the greatest achievements of modern times: the invention of laborsaving machines, the discovery of anesthetics and vaccines, the development of efficient transportation and communication systems. But, increasingly, technology has come up against the law of unexpected consequences. Advances in health care have lengthened life-spans, lowered infant-mortality rates and, thus, aggravated the population problem. The use of pesticides has increased crop yields but polluted water supplies. The invention of automobiles and jet planes has revolutionized travel but sullied the atmosphere.

18 Yet the advance of technology has never destroyed man's wonder and awe at the beauty of the earth. The coming of England's Industrial Revolution, with its "dark Satanic mills," coincided with the extraordinary flowering of Romantic poetry, much of it about the glory of nature. Many people in this century voiced the same tender feelings on seeing the first images of the earth as viewed from the moon. The sight of that shimmering, luminescent ball set against the black void inspired even normally prosaic astronauts to flights of eloquence. Edgar Mitchell, who flew to the moon aboard Apollo 14 in 1971, described the planet as "a sparkling blue-and-white jewel...laced with slowly swirling veils of white...like a small pearl in a thick sea of black mystery." Photos of the earth from space prompted geologist Preston Cloud to write, "Mother Earth will never seem the same again. No more can thinking people take this little planet...as an infinite theater of action and provider of resources for man, yielding new largesse to every demand without limit." That conclusion seems all the more imperative in the wake of the environmental shocks of 1988.

19 Let there be no illusions. Taking effective action to halt the massive injury to the earth's environment will require a mobilization of political will, international cooperation and sacrifice unknown except in wartime. Yet humanity is in a war right now, and it is not too Draconian to call it a war for survival. It is a war in which all nations must be allies. Both the causes and effects of the problems that threaten the earth are global, and they must be attacked globally. "All nations are tied together as to their common fate," observes Peter Raven, director of the Missouri Botanical Garden. "We are all facing a common problem, which is, How are we going to keep this single resource we have, namely the world, viable?"

20 As man heads into the last decade of the 20th century, he finds himself at a crucial turning point: the actions of those now living will determine the future, and possibly the very survival, of the species. "We do not have generations, we only have years, in which to attempt to turn things around," warns Lester Brown, president of the Washington-based Worldwatch Institute. Every individual on the planet must be made aware of its vulnerability and of the urgent need to preserve it. No attempt to protect the environment will be successful in the long run unless ordinary people—the California housewife, the Mexican peasant, the Soviet factory worker, the Chinese farmer—are willing to adjust their life-styles. Our wasteful, careless ways must become a thing of the past. We must recycle more, procreate less, turn off lights, use mass transit, do a thousand things differently in our everyday lives. We owe this not only to ourselves and our children but also to the unborn generations who will one day inherit the earth.

21 Mobilizing that sort of mass commitment will take extraordinary leadership, of the kind that has appeared before in times of crisis: Churchill's eloquence galvanizing his embattled countrymen to live "their finest hour," F.D.R.'s pragmatic idealism giving hope and jobs to Depression-ridden Americans. Now, more than ever, the world needs leaders who can inspire their fellow citizens with a fiery sense of mission, not a nationalistic or military campaign but a universal crusade to save the planet. Unless mankind embraces that cause totally, and without delay, it may have no alternative to the bang of nuclear holocaust or the whimper of slow extinction.

Analysis of the Arrangement in
Thomas A. Sancton's "Planet of the Year"

Thomas A. Sancton's essay "Planet of the Year" serves as a prelude or preface for a series of bylined articles, in the first issue of TIME magazine in 1989, on the general theme of our imperilled earth. Each of the articles deals with a particular threat to the welfare of our planet, such as overpopulation, the pollution of the environment, the heating up of the climate. Each article tries to alert readers to the threats by informing them about pertinent facts and demonstrating the consequences of those facts if we fail to do something about the situation. In this lead-off article, Thomas Sancton is giving readers an overview of the situation.

We could do an analysis of the cogency and the validity of the facts and the arguments that Sancton presents in this prefatory essay, but here we will concentrate on the arrangement, the organization, of his essay. There is no single, ideal way to organize an informative or an argumentative essay. The organization of almost any discourse represents a particular author's judgment about how to order the parts. We can analyze that organization and make our own judgments about the effectiveness or ineffectiveness of the order that the author has imposed on the parts. We may not often be able to say that the ordering of the parts of a particular essay was inevitable; but we may be able to say that the ordering was judicious or justifiable. We may be able to see why an author had to talk about *this* before *that:* or we might be able to show that it was a strategic mistake to talk about *this* before *that*. The sequence of arguments could be crucial to the success of an author's persuasive efforts, but the laws that govern the best sequence in a particular case or even a typical case are not laid out in heaven. Given the function of Sancton's essay, let us see how this author chose, either consciously or unconsciously, to organize this piece of discourse.

There are 21 paragraphs in Sancton's essay. What we have to do in outlining the essay is to see what groupings we can make of these 21 paragraphs. Where are the big chunks of paragraphs, and how are these chunks related to one another? There could be some differences of opinion among readers about just where a particular seam in the fabric of this essay occurs, but we probably could also get some consensus about the main divisions of the essay.

Whereas we laid out Dorothy Sayer's speech in terms of the Ciceronian parts of an oration—Introduction (*exordium*); Statement of Fact (*narratio*); Division (*divisio*); Proof (*confirmatio* and *refutatio*); Conclusion (*peroratio*)—let us here use another way of analyzing the structure of an essay—the Roman-numeral format of the traditional outline:

Introduction (paragraphs 1–3)
   I. Evidence of the deterioration of the planet (paragraphs 4–7)
  II. What TIME magazine did to alert us to our peril (paragraph 8)
 III. Answers to the question, "What would happen if we did nothing about the earth's imperilled state?" (paragraphs 9–11)
 IV. Past and present changes in the environment (paragraphs 12–14)
  V. Various myths about the origin of the world (paragraphs 15–18)
Conclusion (paragraphs 19–21)

Having laid out the groupings of the paragraphs in that Roman-numeral format, let us go back now and take a closer look at what the author is doing in each of those major divisions.

In the first paragraph of the Introduction, Thomas Sancton states his disagreement with the epigraph from the biblical text of Ecclesiastes—an epigraph which asserts that "the earth abideth forever." In contradicting that claim, Sancton enunciates the thesis of his essay: *How long the earth lasts will depend not only on the laws of physics but also on the behavior of the inhabitants of the planet.* In the second paragraph, he points out that human beings have thrived too well on this planet. Ironically, the phenomenal increase in the number of human inhabitants since 1800 could alone doom our planet. In the third paragraph of the Introduction, he points out that it is not just the increase in the number of inhabitants that dooms our planet; it is also the reckless way in which the inhabitants have treated our planet. Just our technological advances in the last two hundred years have dangerously polluted the atmosphere.

These three introductory paragraphs alert readers to what this essay and the subsequent essays are all about and states the thesis of this special issue of TIME. Then, starting with paragraph 4 and continuing through paragraph 7, the author launches into the body of his essay. In these four paragraphs, he cites some evidence of the ominous deterioration of our planet.

In paragraph 4, he talks about the deterioration that has taken place in the United States just in 1988 from such natural disasters as droughts, fires, earthquakes, hurricanes, and from the disposal of garbage and other wastes. In the next paragraph, he points out the similar disasters that have taken place in the same year in other countries of the world. In the sixth paragraph, the author points out some other recent man-made pollutions of our environment: contamination from radioactive wastes dumped by federal weapons-making plants, continued depletion of the ozone layer, wanton destruction of tropical forests. Paragraph 7, the last paragraph of the first major division of the essay, is a summary paragraph.

The second major division of the essay consists of a single paragraph, paragraph 8. Here the author tells us what the TIME corporation has done to alert people to the perils resulting from the destructive developments described in the previous major section. In conjunction with its plan to designate the earth as an Endangered Planet in its usual Man (or Woman) of the Year issue in January of 1989, TIME assembled 33 scientists, administrators, and political leaders from ten countries for a three-day conference in Boulder, Colorado, in November 1988. The results of that conference are represented in the series of articles in this issue on each of the major environmental problems dealt with by this august assembly.

The third Roman-numeral division of Thomas Sancton's essay provides four answers to the question "What would happen if we did nothing about the earth's imperilled state?" The first answer concerns the consequences of a substantial rise in the earth's temperature: rising temperatures would cause the oceans to rise, flooding coastal regions and ruining farmlands, and the changing weather patterns would make many regions "infertile and uninhabitable." The second answer concerns the consequences of toxic wastes: there would be a serious depletion in our supply of vital drinking water. The third answer concerns the consequences of a rampant increase in the population of our planet: the likelihood is that there would be mass starvation in all parts of the world. The fourth answer points to the general consequence of the deterioration of our planet: the whole earth would become inhospitable to life of any kind.

But in paragraph 11, the last paragraph in this third Roman-numeral division of the essay, the author remarks that many reputable scientists disagree with the alarmist views expressed in the previous two paragraphs of this section, and he quotes two of these demurring scientists, E. F. Watt and S. Fred Singer.

The fourth major division of the essay, consisting of paragraphs 12, 13, and 14, deals with some of the past and the present changes in the earth's environment. At the beginning of this section, in response to the conflicting views presented in the previous major division (paragraphs 9–11), the author says, "Whatever the validity of this or that theory, the earth will not remain as it is now." By pointing out the cataclysmic changes that have taken place and are taking place in the conditions of our environment, the author wants to make us aware that similar and maybe more disastrous changes will occur on our planet. The general consequence of these changes will be extensive extinctions of human, animal, and plant life.

The fifth and final major division of Sancton's essay, consisting of paragraphs 15–18, deals with the myths that human beings have created down through the ages about the origins of the world. This is the section where the reader may have great difficulty in discerning how the discussion here relates to the subject and the thesis of the essay as a whole. Even when the reader sees the author's review of some of the myths about the origin of the earth, he or she may continue to have difficulty in detecting the pertinence of this review to the general topic of the essay. A clue to how the author sees the relationship of this final section to what has gone before may be indicated in the first sentence of paragraph 15: "Humanity's current predatory relationship with nature reflects a man-centered world view that has evolved over the ages." By reviewing the myths about the origin of the world in the ancient Chinese, Greek, and Judeo-Christian cultures and then pursuing the development of a mechanistic view of the universe in the age of the Enlightenment, Sancton may intend to show us how the present "man-centered world view . . . evolved over the ages."

In any case, it is even more difficult to see how paragraph 18, the last paragraph of the body of the essay, relates to the rest of the essay. The first sentence of that paragraph seems to be the thesis sentence: "Yet the advance of technology has never destroyed man's wonder and awe at the beauty of the earth." But how does that thesis relate to what the author has been talking about in the rest of the essay?

Paragraphs 19, 20, and 21 constitute the Conclusion of the essay. The theme of this final section seems to be something like the following: Halting or reversing the massive deterioration of the earth's environment will require us to mobilize the political leadership of all nations. Thomas Sancton suggests that if we do not succeed in mobilizing that collective political will, there may be very few tomorrows left for any of us. The ticking of the clock is ominous.

We have seen how this author organized this essay, and we have reviewed what this author said in the successive parts of the essay. If we had written this essay on this topic, we might have used a different organization, but, most of the time, we can discern at least a plausible reason for the particular sequence of parts that this author adopted for his essay. Admittedly, it was somewhat difficult for us to determine how the final section (paragraphs 15–18) of the body of the essay related to the preceding parts, but even this section was not outrageously impertinent. The cumulative effect of the information and the arguments presented in the five major divisions of the body of the essay is that we are disposed, even compelled, to agree with what the author says in the Conclusion: it is imperative that all the nations of the world cooperate in an effort to arrest and reverse the rampant deterioration of our environment. We can make our own judgments about how much of our acceptance of the author's conclusion is due to the cogency of his arguments and how much is due to the effectiveness of his organization.

Martin Luther King, Jr.: Letter from Birmingham Jail *

*During the second half of the 1950s and most of the 1960s, the most charis-
matic figure in the civil-rights movement, especially in the passive-resistance,
nonviolent phase of it, was certainly the Rev. Martin Luther King, Jr. Born
in Atlanta, Georgia, January 15, 1929, he received his B.A. degree at Morehouse
College in Atlanta and his Ph.D. degree at Boston University in 1955. He
first came into public prominence when he led the successful bus boycott in
Montgomery, Alabama, following the arrest of Mrs. Rosa Parks, a Negro
seamstress, on December 1, 1955, when she refused to give up her seat in
the front of a bus on her way home from work. In 1957, he was elected
president of the Southern Christian Leadership Conference (SCLC), an
organization that sought to touch the conscience of the nation and to effect
the passage of social legislation by the strategies of civil-disobedience in-
herited from Mahatma Gandhi and ultimately from Henry David Thoreau.
In 1964, Dr. King was awarded the Nobel Peace Prize, the youngest man
ever to win that prize. On April 4, 1968, he was killed by an assassin's bullet
in Memphis, Tennessee. Dr. King exercised his influence mainly through his
eloquent oratory and through his participation in such physical demonstrations as marches and sit-ins. In the following selection, however, we find
him exerting his rhetorical talents in the written medium, largely of course
because at the time he was locked up in a Birmingham jail. ("Never before,"
he tells us in the letter itself, "have I written so long a letter.") The letter was
prompted by a public statement made on April 12, 1963, by the eight clergymen named in the author's footnote—a statement deploring the use of street
demonstrations and urging the white and Negro citizens of Alabama "to
observe the principles of law and order and common sense." This piece of
judicial rhetoric, cast in the form of an "open letter," has a double audience
—immediately the eight clergymen who signed the public statement but
ultimately the people of the nation and even the world.*

* AUTHOR'S NOTE: This response to a published statement by eight fellow clergymen
from Alabama (Bishop C. C. J. Carpenter, Bishop Joseph A. Durick, Rabbi Hilton L.
Grafman, Bishop Paul Hardin, Bishop Holan B. Harmon, the Reverend George M.
Murray, the Reverend Edward V. Ramage and the Reverend Earl Stallings) was composed under somewhat constricting circumstances. Begun on the margins of the newspaper in which the statement appeared while I was in jail, the letter was continued
on scraps of writing paper supplied by a friendly Negro trusty, and concluded on a
pad my attorneys were eventually permitted to leave me. Although the text remains in
substance unaltered, I have indulged in the author's prerogative of polishing it for
publication.

April 16, 1963

My Dear Fellow Clergymen:

1 While confined here in the Birmingham city jail, I came across your recent statement calling my present activities "unwise and untimely." Seldom do I pause to answer criticism of my work and ideas. If I sought to answer all the criticisms that cross my desk, my secretaries would have little time for anything other than such correspondence in the course of the day, and I would have no time for constructive work. But since I feel that you are men of genuine good will and that your criticisms are sincerely set forth, I want to try to answer your statement in what I hope will be patient and reasonable terms.

2 I think I should indicate why I am here in Birmingham, since you have been influenced by the view which argues against "outsiders coming in." I have the honor of serving as president of the Southern Christian Leadership Conference, an organization operating in every southern state, with headquarters in Atlanta, Georgia. We have some eighty-five affiliated organizations across the South, and one of them is the Alabama Christian Movement for Human Rights. Frequently we share staff, educational and financial resources with our affiliates. Several months ago the affiliate here in Birmingham asked us to be on call to engage in a nonviolent direct-action program if such were deemed necessary. We readily consented, and when the hour came we lived up to our promise. So I, along with several members of my staff, am here because I was invited here. I am here because I have organizational ties here.

3 But more basically, I am in Birmingham because injustice is here. Just as the prophets of the eighth century B.C. left their villages and carried their "thus saith the Lord" far beyond the boundaries of their home towns, and just as the Apostle Paul left his village of Tarsus and carried the gospel of Jesus Christ to the far corners of the Greco-Roman world, so am I compelled to carry the gospel of freedom beyond my own home town. Like Paul, I must constantly respond to the Macedonian call for aid.

4 Moreover, I am cognizant of the interrelatedness of all communities and states. I cannot sit idly by in Atlanta and not be concerned about what happens in Birmingham. Injustice anywhere is a threat to justice everywhere. We are caught in an inescapable network of mutuality, tied in a single garment of destiny. Whatever affects one directly, affects all indirectly. Never again can we afford to live with the narrow, provincial "outside

agitator" idea. Anyone who lives inside the United States can never be considered an outsider anywhere within its bounds.

5 You deplore the demonstrations taking place in Birmingham. But your statement, I am sorry to say, fails to express a similar concern for the conditions that brought about the demonstrations. I am sure that none of you would want to rest content with the superficial kind of social analysis that deals merely with effects and does not grapple with underlying causes. It is unfortunate that demonstrations are taking place in Birmingham, but it is even more unfortunate that the city's white power structure left the Negro community with no alternative.

6 In any nonviolent campaign there are four basic steps: collection of the facts to determine whether injustices exist; negotiation; self-purification; and direct action. We have gone through all these steps in Birmingham. There can be no gainsaying the fact that racial injustice engulfs this community. Birmingham is probably the most thoroughly segregated city in the United States. Its ugly record of brutality is widely known. Negroes have experienced grossly unjust treatment in the courts. There have been more unsolved bombings of Negro homes and churches in Birmingham than in any other city in the nation. These are the hard, brutal facts of the case. On the basis of these conditions, Negro leaders sought to negotiate with the city fathers. But the latter consistently refused to engage in good-faith negotiation.

7 Then, last September, came the opportunity to talk with leaders of Birmingham's economic community. In the course of the negotiations, certain promises were made by the merchants—for example, to remove the stores' humiliating racial signs. On the basis of these promises, the Reverend Fred Shuttlesworth and the leaders of the Alabama Christian Movement for Human Rights agreed to a moratorium on all demonstrations. As the weeks and months went by, we realized that we were the victims of a broken promise. A few signs, briefly removed, returned; the others remained.

8 As in so many past experiences, our hopes had been blasted, and the shadow of deep disappointment settled upon us. We had no alternative except to prepare for direct action, whereby we would present our very bodies as a means of laying our case before the conscience of the local and the national community. Mindful of the difficulties involved, we decided to undertake a process of self-purification. We began a series of workshops on nonviolence, and we repeatedly asked ourselves: "Are you able to accept blows without retaliating?" "Are you able to endure the ordeal of jail?" We decided to schedule our direct-action program for the Easter season, realizing that except for Christmas, this is the main shopping period of the year. Knowing that a strong economic-withdrawal program would be the by-product of direct action, we felt that this would be the best time to bring pressure to bear on the merchants for the needed change.

9 Then it occurred to us that Birmingham's mayoralty election was coming up in March, and we speedily decided to postpone action until after election day. When we discovered that the Commissioner of Public Safety, Eugene "Bull" Connor, had piled up enough votes to be in the run-off, we decided again to postpone action until the day after the run-off so that the demonstrations could not be used to cloud the issues. Like many others, we waited to see Mr. Connor defeated, and to this end we endured postponement after postponement. Having aided in this community need, we felt that our direct-action program could be delayed no longer.

10 You may well ask: "Why direct action? Why sit-ins, marches and so forth? Isn't negotiation a better path?" You are quite right in calling for negotiation. Indeed, this is the very purpose of direct action. Nonviolent direct action seeks to create such a crisis and foster such a tension that a community which has constantly refused to negotiate is forced to confront the issue. It seeks so to dramatize the issue that it can no longer be ignored. My citing the creation of tension as part of the work of the nonviolent-resister may sound rather shocking. But I must confess that I am not afraid of the word "tension." I have earnestly opposed violent tension, but there is a type of constructive, nonviolent tension which is necessary for growth. Just as Socrates felt that it was necessary to create a tension in the mind so that individuals could rise from the bondage of myths and half-truths to the unfettered realm of creative analysis and objective appraisal, so must we see the need for nonviolent gadflies to create the kind of tension in society that will help men rise from the dark depths of prejudice and racism to the majestic heights of understanding and brotherhood.

11 The purpose of our direct-action program is to create a situation so crisis-packed that it will inevitably open the door to negotiation. I therefore concur with you in your call for negotiation. Too long has our beloved Southland been bogged down in a tragic effort to live in monologue rather than dialogue.

12 One of the basic points in your statement is that the action that I and my associates have taken in Birmingham is untimely. Some have asked: "Why didn't you give the new city administration time to act?" The only answer that I can give to this query is that the new Birmingham administration must be prodded about as much as the outgoing one, before it will act. We are sadly mistaken if we feel that the election of Albert Boutwell as mayor will bring the millennium to Birmingham. While Mr. Boutwell is a much more gentle person than Mr. Connor, they are both segregationists, dedicated to maintenance of the status quo. I have hope that Mr. Boutwell will be reasonable enough to see the futility of massive resistance to desegregation. But he will not see this without pressure from devotees of civil rights. My friends, I must say to you that we have not made a single gain in civil

rights without determined legal and nonviolent pressure. Lamentably, it is an historical fact that privileged groups seldom give up their privileges voluntarily. Individuals may see the moral light and voluntarily give up their unjust posture; but, as Reinhold Niebuhr has reminded us, groups tend to be more immoral than individuals.

13 We know through painful experience that freedom is never voluntarily given by the oppressor; it must be demanded by the oppressed. Frankly, I have yet to engage in a direct-action campaign that was "well timed" in the view of those who have not suffered unduly from the disease of segregation. For years now I have heard the word "Wait!" It rings in the ear of every Negro with piercing familiarity. This "Wait" has almost always meant "Never." We must come to see, with one of our distinguished jurists, that "justice too long delayed is justice denied."

14 We have waited for more than 340 years for our constitutional and God-given rights. The nations of Asia and Africa are moving with jetlike speed toward gaining political independence, but we still creep at horse-and-buggy pace toward gaining a cup of coffee at a lunch counter. Perhaps it is easy for those who have never felt the stinging darts of segregation to say, "Wait." But when you have seen vicious mobs lynch your mothers and fathers at will and drown your sisters and brothers at whim; when you have seen hate-filled policemen curse, kick and even kill your black brothers and sisters; when you see the vast majority of your twenty million Negro brothers smothering in an airtight cage of poverty in the midst of an affluent society; when you suddenly find your tongue twisted and your speech stammering as you seek to explain to your six-year-old daughter why she can't go to the public amusement park that has just been advertised on television, and see tears welling up in her eyes when she is told that Funtown is closed to colored children, and see ominous clouds of inferiority beginning to form in her little mental sky, and see her beginning to distort her personality by developing an unconscious bitterness toward white people; when you have to concoct an answer for a five-year-old son who is asking: "Daddy, why do white people treat colored people so mean?"; when you take a cross-country drive and find it necessary to sleep night after night in the uncomfortable corners of your automobile because no motel will accept you; when you are humiliated day in and day out by nagging signs reading "white" and "colored"; when your first name becomes "nigger," your middle name becomes "boy" (however old you are) and your last name becomes "John," and your wife and mother are never given the respected title "Mrs."; when you are harried by day and haunted by night by the fact that you are a Negro, living constantly at tiptoe stance, never quite knowing what to expect next, and are plagued with inner fears and outer resentments; when you are for-

ever fighting a degenerating sense of "nobodiness"—then you will understand why we find it difficult to wait. There comes a time when the cup of endurance runs over, and men are no longer willing to be plunged into the abyss of despair. I hope, sirs, you can understand our legitimate and unavoidable impatience.

15 You express a great deal of anxiety over our willingness to break laws. This is certainly a legitimate concern. Since we so diligently urge people to obey the Supreme Court's decision of 1954 outlawing segregation in the public schools, at first glance it may seem rather paradoxical for us consciously to break laws. One may well ask: "How can you advocate breaking some laws and obeying others?" The answer lies in the fact that there are two types of laws: just and unjust. I would be the first to advocate obeying just laws. One has not only a legal but a moral responsibility to obey just laws. Conversely, one has a moral responsibility to disobey unjust laws. I would agree with St. Augustine that "an unjust law is no law at all."

16 Now, what is the difference between the two? How does one determine whether a law is just or unjust? A just law is a man-made code that squares with the moral law or the law of God. An unjust law is a code that is out of harmony with the moral law. To put it in the terms of St. Thomas Aquinas: An unjust law is a human law that is not rooted in eternal law and natural law. Any law that uplifts human personality is just. Any law that degrades human personality is unjust. All segregation statutes are unjust because segregation distorts the soul and damages the personality. It gives the segregator a false sense of superiority and the segregated a false sense of inferiority. Segregation, to use the terminology of the Jewish philosopher Martin Buber, substitutes an "I-it" relationship for an "I-thou" relationship and ends up relegating persons to the status of things. Hence segregation is not only politically, economically and sociologically unsound, it is morally wrong and sinful. Paul Tillich has said that sin is separation. Is not segregation an existential expression of man's tragic separation, his awful estrangement, his terrible sinfulness? Thus it is that I can urge men to obey the 1954 decision of the Supreme Court, for it is morally right; and I can urge them to disobey segregation ordinances, for they are morally wrong.

17 Let us consider a more concrete example of just and unjust laws. An unjust law is a code that a numerical or power majority group compels a minority group to obey but does not make binding on itself. This is *difference* made legal. By the same token, a just law is a code that a majority compels a minority to follow and that it is willing to follow itself. This is *sameness* made legal.

18 Let me give another explanation. A law is unjust if it inflicted on a minority that, as a result of being denied the right to vote, had no part in enacting or devising the law. Who can say that the legislature of Alabama which set up that state's segregation laws was democratically elected? Throughout Alabama all sorts of devious methods are used to prevent Negroes from becoming registered voters, and there are some counties in which, even though Negroes constitute a majority of the population, not a single Negro is registered. Can any law enacted under such circumstances be considered democratically structured?

19 Sometimes a law is just on its face and unjust in its application. For instance, I have been arrested on a charge of parading without a permit. Now, there is nothing wrong in having an ordinance which requires a permit for a parade. But such an ordinance becomes unjust when it is used to maintain segregation and to deny citizens the First-Amendment privilege of peaceful assembly and protest.

20 I hope you are able to see the distinction I am trying to point out. In no sense do I advocate evading or defying the law, as would the rabid segregationist. That would lead to anarchy. One who breaks an unjust law must do so openly, lovingly, and with a willingness to accept the penalty. I submit that an individual who breaks a law that conscience tells him is unjust, and who willingly accepts the penalty of imprisonment in order to arouse the conscience of the community over its injustice, is in reality expressing the highest respect for law.

21 Of course, there is nothing new about this kind of civil disobedience. It was evidenced sublimely in the refusal of Shadrach, Meshach and Abednego to obey the laws of Nebuchadnezzar, on the ground that a higher moral law was at stake. It was practiced superbly by the early Christians, who were willing to face hungry lions and the excruciating pain of chopping blocks rather than submit to certain unjust laws of the Roman Empire. To a degree, academic freedom is a reality today because Socrates practiced civil disobedience. In our own nation, the Boston Tea Party represented a massive act of civil disobedience.

22 We should never forget that everything Adolf Hitler did in Germany was "legal" and everything the Hungarian freedom fighters did in Hungary was "illegal." It was "illegal" to aid and comfort a Jew in Hitler's Germany. Even so, I am sure that, had I lived in Germany at the time, I would have aided and comforted my Jewish brothers. If today I lived in a Communist country where certain principles dear to the Christian faith are suppressed, I would openly advocate disobeying that country's antireligious laws.

23 I must make two honest confessions to you, my Christian and Jewish brothers. First, I must confess that over the past few years I have been gravely disappointed with the white moderate. I have almost reached the regrettable conclusion that the Negro's great stumbling block in his stride toward freedom is not the White Citizen's Counciler or the Ku Klux Klanner, but the white moderate, who is more devoted to "order" than to justice; who prefers a negative peace which is the absence of tension to a positive peace which is the presence of justice; who constantly says: "I agree with you in the goal you seek, but I cannot agree with your methods of direct action"; who paternalistically believes he can set the timetable for another man's freedom; who lives by a mythical concept of time and who constantly advises the Negro to wait for a "more convenient season." Shallow understanding from people of good will is more frustrating than absolute misunderstanding from people of ill will. Lukewarm acceptance is much more bewildering than outright rejection.

24 I had hoped that the white moderate would understand that law and order exist for the purpose of establishing justice and that when they fail in this purpose they become the dangerously structured dams that block the flow of social progress. I had hoped that the white moderate would understand that the present tension in the South is a necessary phase of the transition from an obnoxious negative peace, in which the Negro passively accepted his unjust plight, to a substantive and positive peace, in which all men will respect the dignity and worth of human personality. Actually, we who engage in nonviolent direct action are not the creators of tension. We merely bring to the surface the hidden tension that is already alive. We bring it out in the open, where it can be seen and dealt with. Like a boil that can never be cured so long as it is covered up but must be opened with all its ugliness to the natural medicines of air and light, injustice must be exposed, with all the tension its exposure creates, to the light of human conscience and the air of national opinion before it can be cured.

25 In your statement you assert that our actions, even though peaceful, must be condemned because they precipitate violence. But is this a logical assertion? Isn't this like condemning a robbed man because his possession of money precipitated the evil act of robbery? Isn't this like condemning Socrates because his unswerving commitment to truth and his philosophical inquiries precipitated the act by the misguided populace in which they made him drink hemlock? Isn't this like condemning Jesus because his unique God-consciousness and never-ceasing devotion to God's will precipitated the evil act of crucifixion? We must come to see that, as the federal courts have consistently affirmed, it is wrong to urge an individual to cease his efforts to gain his basic constitutional rights because the quest may precipitate violence. Society must protect the robbed and punish the robber.

26 I had also hoped that the white moderate would reject the myth concerning time in relation to the struggle for freedom. I have just received a letter from a white brother in Texas. He writes: "All Christians know that the colored people will receive equal rights eventually, but it is possible that you are in too great a religious hurry. It has taken Christianity almost two

thousand years to accomplish what it has. The teachings of Christ take time to come to earth." Such an attitude stems from a tragic misconception of time, from the strangely irrational notion that there is something in the very flow of time that will inevitably cure all ills. Actually, time itself is neutral; it can be used either destructively or constructively. More and more I feel that the people of ill will have used time much more effectively that have the people of good will. We will have to repent in this generation not merely for the hateful words and actions of the bad people but for the appalling silence of the good people. Human progress never rolls in on wheels of inevitability; it comes through the tireless efforts of men willing to be co-workers with God, and without this hard work, time itself becomes an ally of the forces of social stagnation. We must use time creatively, in the knowledge that the time is always ripe to do right. Now is the time to make real the promise of democracy and transform our pending national elegy into a creative psalm of brotherhood. Now is the time to lift our national policy from the quicksand of racial injustice to the solid rock of human dignity.

27 You speak of our activity in Birmingham as extreme. At first I was rather disappointed that fellow clergymen would see my nonviolent efforts as those of an extremist. I began thinking about the fact that I stand in the middle of two opposing forces in the Negro community. One is a force of complacency, made up in part of Negroes who, as a result of long years of oppression, are so drained of self-respect and a sense of "somebodiness" that they have adjusted to segregation; and in part of a few middle-class Negroes who, because of a degree of academic and economic security and because in some ways they profit by segregation, have become insensitive to the problems of the masses. The other force is one of bitterness and hatred, and it comes perilously close to advocating violence. It is expressed in the various black nationalist groups that are springing up across the nation, the largest and best-known being Elijah Muhammad's Muslim movement. Nourished by the Negro's frustration over the continued existence of racial discrimination, this movement is made up of people who have lost faith in America, who have absolutely repudiated Christianity, and who have concluded that the white man is an incorrigible "devil."

28 I have tried to stand between these two forces, saying that we need emulate neither the "do-nothingism" of the complacent nor the hatred and despair of the black nationalist. For there is the more excellent way of love and nonviolent protest. I am grateful to God that, through the influence of the Negro church, the way of nonviolence became an integral part of our struggle.

29 If this philosophy had not emerged, by now many streets of the South would, I am convinced, be flowing with blood. And I am further convinced that if our white brothers dismiss as "rabble-rousers" and "outside agitators" those of us who employ nonviolent direct action, and if they refuse to support our nonviolent efforts, millions of Negroes will, out of frustration and despair, seek solace and security in black-nationalist ideologies—a development that would inevitably lead to a frightening racial nightmare.

30 Oppressed people cannot remain oppressed forever. The yearning for freedom eventually manifests itself, and that is what has happened to the American Negro. Something within has reminded him of his birthright of freedom, and something without has reminded him that it can be gained. Consciously or unconsciously, he has been caught up by the *Zeitgeist,* and with his black brothers of Africa and his brown and yellow brothers of Asia, South America and the Caribbean, the United States Negro is moving with a sense of great urgency toward the promised land of racial justice. If one recognizes this vital urge that has engulfed the Negro community, one should readily understand why public demonstrations are taking place. The Negro has many pent-up resentments and latent frustrations, and he must release them. So let him march; let him make prayer pilgrimages to the city hall; let him go on freedom rides—and try to understand why he must do so. If his repressed emotions are not released in nonviolent ways, they will seek expression through violence; this is not a threat but a fact of history. So I have not said to my people: "Get rid of your discontent." Rather, I have the creative outlet of nonviolent direct action. And now this approach is tried to say that this normal and healthy discontent can be channeled into being termed extremist.

31 But though I was initially disappointed at being categorized as an extremist, as I continued to think about the matter I gradually gained a measure of satisfaction from the label. Was not Jesus an extremist for love: "Love your enemies, bless them that curse you, do good to them that hate you, and pray for them which despitefully use you, and persecute you." Was not Amos an extremist for justice: "Let justice roll down like waters and righteousness like an ever-flowing stream." Was not Paul an extremist for the Christian gospel: "I bear in my body the marks of the Lord Jesus." Was not Martin Luther an extremist: "Here I stand; I cannot do otherwise, so help me God." And John Bunyan: "I will stay in jail to the end of my days before I make a butchery of my conscience." And Abraham Lincoln: "This nation cannot survive half slave and half free." And Thomas Jefferson: "We hold these truths to be self-evident, that all men are created equal . . ." So the question is not whether we will be extremists, but what kind of extremists we will be. Will we be extremists for hate or for love? Will we be extremists for the preservation of injustice or for the extension of justice? In that dramatic scene on Calvary's hill three men were crucified. We must never forget that all three were crucified for the same crime—the crime of extremism. Two were extremists for immorality, and thus fell below their environment. The other, Jesus Christ, was an extremist for love, truth and goodness, and thereby rose above his environment. Perhaps the South, the nation and the world are in dire need of creative extremists.

32 I had hoped that the white moderate would see this need. Perhaps I was too optimistic; perhaps I expected too much. I suppose I should have realized that few members of the oppressor race can understand the deep groans and passionate yearnings of the oppressed race, and still fewer have the vision to see that injustice must be rooted out by strong, persistent and determined action. I am thankful, however, that some of our white brothers in the South have grasped the meaning of this social revolution and committed themselves to it. They are still all too few in quantity, but they are big in quality. Some—such as Ralph McGill, Lillian Smith, Harry Golden, James McBride Dabbs, Ann Braden and Sarah Patton Boyle—have written about our struggle in eloquent and prophetic terms. Others have marched with us down nameless streets of the South. They have languished in filthy, roach-infested jails, suffering the abuse and brutality of policemen who view them as "dirty nigger-lovers." Unlike so many of their moderate brothers and sisters, they have recognized the urgency of the moment and sensed the need for powerful "action" antidotes to combat the disease of segregation.

33 Let me take note of my other major disappointment. I have been so greatly disappointed with the white church and its leadership. Of course, there are some notable exceptions. I am not unmindful of the fact that each of you has taken some significant stands on this issue. I commend you, Reverend Stallings, for your Christian stand on this past Sunday, in welcoming Negroes to your worship service on a nonsegregated basis. I commend the Catholic leaders of this state for integrating Spring Hill College several years ago.

34 But despite these notable exceptions, I must honestly reiterate that I have been disappointed with the Church. I do not say this as one of those negative critics who can always find something wrong with the church. I say this as a minister of the gospel, who loves the church; who was nurtured in its bosom; who has been sustained by its spiritual blessings and who will remain true to it as long as the cord of life shall lengthen.

35 When I was suddenly catapulted into the leadership of the bus protest in Montgomery, Alabama, a few years ago, I felt we would be supported by the white church. I felt that the white ministers, priests and rabbis of the South would be among our strongest allies. Instead, some have been outright opponents, refusing to understand the freedom movement and misrepresenting its leaders; all too many others have been more cautious than courageous and have remained silent behind the anesthetizing security of stained-glass windows.

36 In spite of my shattered dreams, I came to Birmingham with the hope that the white religious leadership of this community would see the justice of our cause and, with deep moral concern, would serve as the channel through which our just grievances could reach the power structure. I had hoped that each of you would understand. But again I have been disappointed.

37 I have heard numerous southern religious leaders admonish their worshipers to comply with a desegregation decision because it is the law, but I have longed to hear white ministers declare: "Follow this decree because integration is morally right and because the Negro is your brother." In the midst of blatant injustices inflicted upon the Negro, I have watched white churchmen stand on the sideline and mouth pious irrelevancies and sanctimonious trivialities. In the midst of a mighty struggle to rid our nation of racial and economic injustice, I have heard many ministers say: "Those are social issues, with which the gospel has no real concern." And I have watched many churches commit themselves to a completely other-worldly religion which makes a strange, un-Biblical distinction between body and soul, between the sacred and the secular.

38 I have traveled the length and breadth of Alabama, Mississippi and all the other southern states. On sweltering summer days and crisp autumn mornings I have looked at the South's beautiful churches with their lofty spires pointing heavenward. I have beheld the impressive outlines of her massive religious-education buildings. Over and over I have found myself saying: "What kind of people worship here? Who is their God? Where were their voices when the lips of Governor Barnett dripped with words of interposition and nullification? Where were they when Governor Wallace gave a clarion call for defiance and hatred? Where were their voices of support when bruised and weary Negro men and women decided to rise from the dark dungeons of complacency to the bright hills of creative protest?"

39 Yes, these questions are still in my mind. In deep disappointment I have wept over the laxity of the church. But be assured that my tears have been tears of love. There can be no deep disappointment where there is not deep love. Yes, I love the church. How could I do otherwise? I am in the rather unique position of being the son, the grandson and the great-grandson of preachers. Yes, I see the church as the body of Christ. But, oh! How we have blemished and scarred that body through social neglect and through fear of being nonconformists.

40 There was a time when the church was very powerful—in the time when the early Christians rejoiced at being deemed worthy to suffer for what they believed. In those days the church was not merely a thermometer that recorded the ideas and principles of popular opinion; it was a thermostat that transformed the mores of society. Whenever the early Christians entered a town, the people in power became disturbed and immediately sought to convict the Christians for being "disturbers of the peace" and "outside agitators." But the Christians pressed on, in the conviction that they were "a colony of heaven," called to obey God rather than man. Small in number, they were big in commitment. They were too God-intoxicated to be "astronomically intimidated." By their effort and example they brought an end to such ancient evils as infanticide and gladiatorial contests.

41 Things are different now. So often the contemporary church is a weak, ineffectual voice with an uncertain sound. So often it is an archdefender of the status quo. Far from being disturbed by the presence of the church, the power structure of the average community is consoled by the church's silent —and often even vocal—sanction of things as they are.

42 But the judgment of God is upon the church as never before. If today's church does not recapture the sacrificial spirit of the early church, it will lose its authenticity, forfeit the loyalty of millions, and be dismissed as an irrelevant social club with no meaning for the twentieth century. Every day I meet young people whose disappointment with the church has turned into outright disgust.

43 Perhaps I have once again been too optimistic. Is organized religion too inextricably bound to the status quo to save our nation and the world? Perhaps I must turn my faith to the inner spiritual church, the church within the church, as the true *ekklesia* and the hope of the world. But again I am thankful to God that some noble souls from the ranks of organized religion have broken loose from the paralyzing chains of conformity and joined us as active partners in the struggle for freedom. They have left their secure congregations and walked the streets of Albany, Georgia, with us. They have gone down the highways of the South on tortuous rides for freedom. Yes, they have gone to jail with us. Some have been dismissed from their churches, have lost the support of their bishops and fellow ministers. But they have acted in the faith that right defeated is stronger than evil triumphant. Their witness has been the spiritual salt that has preserved the true meaning of the gospel in these troubled times. They have carved a tunnel of hope through the dark mountain of disappointment.

44 I hope the church as a whole will meet the challenge of this decisive hour. But even if the church does not come to the aid of justice, I have no despair about the future. I have no fear about the outcome of our struggle in Birmingham, even if our motives are at present misunderstood. We will reach the goal of freedom in Birmingham and all over the nation, because the goal of America is freedom. Abused and scorned though we may be, our destiny is tied up with America's destiny. Before the pilgrims landed at Plymouth, we were here. Before the pen of Jefferson etched the majestic words of the Declaration of Independence across the pages of history, we were here. For more than two centuries our forebears labored in this country without wages; they made cotton king; they built the homes of their masters while suffering gross injustice and shameful humiliation—and yet out of a bottomless vitality they continued to thrive and develop. If the inexpressible cruelties of slavery could not stop us, the opposition we now face will surely fail. We will win our freedom because the sacred heritage of our nation and the eternal will of God are embodied in our echoing demands.

45 Before closing I feel impelled to mention one other point in your statement that has troubled me profoundly. You warmly commended the Birmingham police force for keeping "order" and "preventing violence." I doubt that you would have so warmly commended the police force if you had seen its dogs sinking their teeth into unarmed, nonviolent Negroes. I doubt that you would so quickly commend the policemen if you were to observe their ugly and inhumane treatment of Negroes here in the city jail; if you were to watch them push and curse old Negro women and young Negro girls; if you were to see them slap and kick old Negro men and young boys; if you were to observe them, as they did on two occasions, refuse to give us food because we wanted to sing our grace together. I cannot join you in your praise of the Birmingham police department.

46 It is true that the police have exercised a degree of discipline in handling the demonstrators. In this sense they have conducted themselves rather "nonviolently" in public. But for what purpose? To preserve the evil system of segregation. Over the past few years I have consistently preached that nonviolence demands that the means we use must be as pure as the ends we seek. I have tried to make clear that it is wrong to use immoral means to attain moral ends. But now I must affirm that it is just as wrong, or perhaps even more so, to use moral means to preserve immoral ends. Perhaps Mr. Connor and his policemen have been rather nonviolent in public, as was Chief Pritchett in Albany, Georgia, but they have used the moral means of nonviolence to maintain the immoral end of racial injustice. As T. S. Eliot has said: "The last temptation is the greatest treason: To do the right deed for the wrong reason."

47 I wish you had commended the Negro sit-inners and demonstrators of Birmingham for their sublime courage, their willingness to suffer and their amazing discipline in the midst of great provocation. One day the South will recognize its real heroes. They will be the James Merediths, with the noble sense of purpose that enables them to face jeering and hostile mobs, and with the agonizing loneliness that characterizes the life of the pioneer. They will be old, oppressed, battered Negro women, symbolized in a seventy-two-year-old woman in Montgomery, Alabama, who rose up with a sense of dignity and with her people decided not to ride segregated buses, and who responded with ungrammatical profundity to one who inquired about her weariness: "My feets is tired, but my soul is at rest." They will be the young high school and college students, the young ministers of the gospel and a host of their elders, courageously and nonviolently sitting in at lunch counters and willingly going to jail for conscience' sake. One day the South will know that when these disinherited children of God sat down at lunch counters, they were in reality standing up for what is best in the American dream and for the most sacred values in our Judaeo-Christian heritage, thereby bringing our nation back to those great wells of democracy which were dug deep by the founding fathers in their formulation of the Constitution and the Declaration of Independence.

48 Never before have I written so long a letter. I'm afraid it is much too long to take your precious time. I can assure you that it would have been much shorter if I had been writing from a comfortable desk, but what else can one do when he is alone in a narrow jail cell, other than write long letters, think long thoughts and pray long prayers?

49 If I have said anything in this letter that overstates the truth and indicates an unreasonable impatience, I beg you to forgive me. If I have said anything that understates the truth and indicates my having a patience that allows me to settle for anything less than brotherhood, I beg God to forgive me.

50 I hope this letter finds you strong in the faith. I also hope that circumstances will soon make it possible for me to meet each of you, not as an integrationist or a civil-rights leader but as a fellow clergyman and a Christian brother. Let us all hope that the dark clouds of racial prejudice will soon pass away and the deep fog of misunderstanding will be lifted from our fear-drenched communities, and in some not too distant tomorrow the radiant stars of love and brotherhood will shine over our great nation with all their scintillating beauty.

Yours for the cause of Peace and Brotherhood,

Martin Luther King, Jr.

Analysis of the Arrangements of "Letter from Birmingham Jail"

Martin Luther King's "Letter from Birmingham Jail" is unusually long for an "open letter"—50 paragraphs totalling about 7000 words. Normally, an open letter intended for publication in the public press would be considerably shorter than this one is, and if the Reverend King had been writing a reply that would be delivered as a speech, he probably would have written a text that was about half as long as this one. (At a normal speaking rate, the present text would take at least an hour to deliver orally.) But under the circumstances of his incarceration for an act of civil disobedience, Reverend King had ample leisure—although very little comfort and convenience—to compose an expansive reply to the letter he had received from the eight clergymen. As King says toward the end of his letter (paragraph 48), where he confesses that this is the longest letter he has ever written, "I can assure you that it would have been much shorter if I had been writing from a comfortable desk, but what else can one do when he is alone in a narrow jail cell, other than write long letters, think long thoughts, and pray long prayers?"

In analyzing the arrangement of "Letter from Birmingham Jail," we are examining a piece that has already been written, trying to determine how many parts there are in the whole, where each part starts and ends, and how the parts are interrelated, and then speculating about why the author chose to organize the piece in the way that he did. We reverse this process, of course, when we write a document. Through the process of invention, we discover a number of things we could say on a particular topic, we make a selection from the list of things we could say, and then we make some decisions about the order in which we will dispose the parts. Sometimes, our plotting of the order of the parts takes the form of a formal or an informal outline. Our decisions about the organization of the discourse are governed by such considerations as the subject, the occasion, the audience, and the purpose. The decisions we make about organization could be crucial for the ultimate effectiveness of our communication.

"Letter from Birmingham Jail" is an instance of judicial rhetoric—a justification of one's actions. As we learn from the author's own note, the letter was written in response to a published statement by eight clergymen from Alabama, and in the very first sentence of the letter of response, Martin Luther King says, "While confined here in the Birmingham city jail, I came across your recent statement calling my present activities 'unwise and untimely,'" and in the last sentence of that first paragraph, he tells us, "I want to try to answer your statement in what I hope will be patient and reasonable terms." So this discourse is in the tradition of such noted "apologies" as Socrates's *Apology* and John Henry Newman's *Apologia Pro Vita Sua*.

The subject-matter of Martin Luther King's reply has been largely determined by the clergymen's published statement. The author will respond, in turn, to some or all of the clergymen's charges about his "unwise and untimely" actions. Although the substance of the various parts of the letter has been determined by the clergymen's published statement, the author has to make some decisions about how he is going to structure the parts of his reply. We can only speculate, of course, about the author's motives in making certain organizational decisions, but by examining this published letter, we can at least ascertain the decisions that he actually made. How deliberately he made those decisions is another matter that we can only speculate about.

Short of testimony from the author himself (and we will never be able to get that testimony now), the best we can do is point out what the parts are, where they seem to begin and end, and then offer some probable reasons for the parts being arranged in the order that they are.

The best way to start out is to look for the major divisions of the letter—for the parts that would be marked with Roman numerals in a formal outline. If we make any division at all of a whole, we must have at least two parts (in any subdivisions also, we must have at least two parts). But we should be suspicious of our division of this document if we end up with more than four or five major divisions. If we have more than five main divisions of a document of this length, we should suspect that we are not analyzing the structure of it in large enough chunks. We must look for the broadest possible categories under which to group the major parts.

One of the broad perspectives from which to view the structure of this, or any other, discourse is the traditional Introduction, Body, and Conclusion or, to use Aristotle's terms, the Beginning, the Middle, and the End. So we can start out by looking to see whether the discourse has an Introduction or a Beginning and determining how far that Introduction or Beginning runs. Then we can look to see whether the discourse has a Conclusion or an End and try to figure out where that Conclusion or End begins. If we discover that the discourse has an Introduction and a Conclusion and we determine where those parts begin and end, everything, presumably, between the Introduction and the Conclusion will constitute the Body or the Middle. The real challenge then will be to determine how many major, Roman-numeral divisions there are in the Body or Middle and where they begin and end. It is not always easy to determine the seams of an essay—especially of one as long as this one—and different readers will sometimes detect different seams* in the fabric of a piece of discourse. What follows in the rest of this analysis is *my* perception of the seams in Martin Luther King's letter.

The first paragraph constitutes the Introduction. Considering the length of the entire written document, this single paragraph of four sentences would seem to be an unusually brief introduction. But a single paragraph commonly serves as the introduction to a letter, and it might further be pointed out that the Author's Note, which appeared in all printed versions of the letter, might be considered part of the Introduction too. The four-sentence paragraph and the Author's Note do all that seems to be necessary under the circumstances: they inform us of the occasion for the letter, tell us about the circumstances

---

* In the chapter on Style, I have reproduced the stylistic analysis of King's letter from Richard Fulkerson's article "The Public Letter as a Rhetorical Form: Structure, Logic, and Style in King's 'Letter from Birmingham Jail,' " *Quarterly Journal of Speech*, 65 (1979), 121–36. In that section of his article where he treats of the structure of King's letter (a section not reproduced in this book), Fulkerson outlines the letter in terms of the traditional parts of a classical oration: *exordium, narratio, propositio, partitio, confirmatio, refutatio,* and *peroratio*.

in which the letter was written, indicate what the author intends to do in the rest of the letter, and hint at the author's ethos. We might expect the author to establish his credentials, but at this time, the author is so well known that he does not have to set forth his qualifications to speak on the subject dealt with in his letter.

But there are 49 more paragraphs in the letter. The next step is to determine whether the letter has a Conclusion.

The Conclusion of the letter consists of the last three paragraphs (48, 49, and 50). In those three paragraphs, the author is clearly winding down his discussion. There are subtle touches of emotion in these concluding paragraphs and clear attempts to further establish or reinforce his ethos—gestures of good will, humility, and ingratiation. After the vigor with which the author has argued his case, these concluding paragraphs leave us with a note of peacefulness and hopefulness.

Having determined where the Introduction and Conclusion begin and end, we can presume that the paragraphs that lie between those termini constitute the Body or the Middle of the discourse. Now the real challenge comes: to determine how many major divisions and first-level subdivisions there are in the Body and where those divisions begin and end.

The Body would seem to be made up of two major, Roman-numeral divisions: the section in which the author answers the specific questions asked by the clergymen in their public statement (paragraphs 2–22) and the section in which the author presents his more general arguments in defense of his actions (paragraphs 23–47). Before going on to consider the rhetorical effectiveness of this organization, we might take a look at a full outline of the letter, with the first-level (capital-letter) subdivisions:

> Introduction: the author indicates the occasion and the objective of his letter (para. 1 and Author's Note)
>
> I. Answering the specific questions asked by the clergymen in their public statement (paragraphs 2–22)
>   A. First question: Why did you come to Birmingham? (paragraphs 2–4)
>   B. Second question: Why did you resort to demonstrations instead of negotiations? (paragraphs 5–11)
>   C. Third question: Are not your actions untimely? (paragraphs 12–14)
>   D. Fourth question: How can you justify breaking the law? (paragraphs 15–22)
>
> II. Presenting the more general arguments in defense of his actions (paragraphs 23–47)
>   A. His grave disappointment with white moderates (paragraphs 23–32)

       B. His grave disappointment with the white church and its leadership (paragraphs 33-44)

       C. His grave disappointment with the eight clergymen for commending the restraint of the Birmingham police rather than the restraint of the demonstrators (paragraphs 45-47)

Conclusion: the author makes some conciliatory gestures toward his immediate audience and broadens the context of the discussion (paragraphs 48-50)

This outline neatly plots out the structure of the whole discourse. Some readers might detect other seams in the discourse or see the seams as occurring in different places, but essentially this outline does point out the main parts of the discourse and their arrangement. We must not suppose, of course, that Martin Luther King drew up any such formal outlines before he began to write his letter. In fact, given the circumstances in which the letter was composed, the author probably had only a rough idea of an organizational plan when he began to write. What we see in the finished product is the structure that the discourse ultimately took.

Although we cannot presume that Martin Luther King planned the organization of his letter in anything like the careful detail of the preceding outline, we can presume that he did make some choices, consciously or unconsciously, of a strategy of arrangement. Basically, the structure is one of refutation first and then of confirmation. He might have chosen the opposite order: presenting first the more general, positive arguments in defense of his actions and then refuting, point by point, the charges of the clergymen. Evidently, he decided that a more effective, more natural procedure would be to clear the ground first of the immediate questions raised by the disrupting events of the day and then go on to justify his actions on more global principles. If he can satisfy the readers' questions about the wisdom and timeliness of the demonstrators' actions on that particular day in a particular city, the audience will be more disposed to listen to arguments that justify civil-rights movements anywhere anytime.

Within each major part, some decisions had to be made about the order of the parts in the subdivision. In the first major section, for instance, the order in which the questions are raised and answered might have been dictated by the order in which the questions occurred in the clergymen's public statement. But whether or not Martin Luther King answered the questions in the order in which the clergymen asked them, the fact of the matter is that there is a discernibly natural sequence in which the questions are raised and answered. What are you, an outsider, doing in Birmingham in the first place? Okay, you have convinced us that you had a right, a need, to be in Birmingham at this time, but why did you not resort to negotiations with the city authorities instead of disrupting demonstrations? Okay, you have convinced us that demonstration was the only course of action open to you at this point, but wasn't this an inauspicious time to resort to demonstrations, just at the time when the city was undergoing a change of administration and possibly a change of heart? Okay, you have convinced us that you *had* to engage in an act of non-violent civil disobedience at this time, but can you really justify breaking the laws of a community to achieve your ends? Yes, indeed, the order that the Reverend King has adopted here does seem to be a natural sequence in which to present the questions and the answers.

In the subdivision in the second major part, there is also a discernible and explainable order to the parts. The order adopted in that subdivision is not the only possible order, but it is a justifiable one. The author first talks about his disappointment with white moderates in general, the one group that the blacks might have expected to get some support from for their cause. Then, mindful of the profession that his well-meaning accusers belong to, he talks about his disappointment with the white moderate church and its leaders. In the third part of this subdivision, he narrows the discussion further to a particular disappointing act by the eight representatives of the white moderate church: their act of praising the restraint of the Birmingham police. This sequence of steps shows that the whole civil-rights movement is all of a piece, whether viewed in a national or a local context.

We could descend to the next subdivision level (the level that is usually marked off with Arabic numbers in a formal outline) and could thereby get an even closer look at the ordering of particular arguments. But this examination of the main girders of the structure is sufficient to show us that this long letter, composed over several days in very adverse circumstances, has a discernible and justifiable order to it. The organization, however, is not as neatly compartmentalized as the outline makes it out to be. There are some digressions within the parts and some backing and filling and, occasionally, the lines between the parts seem to blur.

But in the main, Martin Luther King's classic apologia is not the rambling discourse that, given the circumstances under which it was composed, it might have been. Rather, it is a commendably ordered piece, which steadily moves forward instead of eddying chaotically. If we clearly get the message that Martin Luther King delivered to his immediate audience and also to his larger audience, the success of his act of communication is due almost as much to the way the message is organized as to the soundness of the arguments and the eloquence of the style. The events that occurred prior to the composition of this letter may have produced a measure of chaos in the city of Birmingham, but Martin Luther King has certainly imposed order on the potential chaos of the message that he wanted to convey to his double audience.

Henry David Thoreau: Civil Disobedience

The ultimate inspiration for the many manifestations of "body rhetoric"—marches, sit-ins, lie-ins, confrontations—that became so much a part of the world scene in the 1960s is generally acknowledged to be Henry David Thoreau's essay "Civil Disobedience." Mahatma Gandhi confessed that as a young man he took the name and the tactics of his passive-resistance movement from Thoreau's essay. The term civil disobedience, *he said, was the most suitable English equivalent of the Indian word* Satyagraha. *First delivered as a lecture, under the title "Resistance to Civil Government," the text was subsequently published in 1849 in* Aesthetic Papers. *Fresh from his famous sojourn at Walden Pond (1845–47), where he had gone, he tells us, "to front only the essential facts of life," Thoreau felt compelled to write this piece to arouse his fellow-citizens against the evils of the current Mexican War and the imminent Fugitive Slave Law. Thoreau had studied rhetoric at Harvard under Edward T. Channing, the third Boylston Professor of Rhetoric and Oratory. He once said, "The one great rule of composition—and if I were a professor of rhetoric I should insist on this—is to speak the truth." But there is more than just "speaking the truth" to Thoreau's effectiveness as a persuader. For one thing, he is noted for his vigorous, aphoristic, paradoxical style. The "ethical appeal" of the man himself also exercises a strong influence. And despite the apparently associational sequence of his prose there is a discernible order to the disposition of his arguments.*

1   I heartily accept the motto,—"That government is best which governs least"; and I should like to see it acted up to more rapidly and systematically. Carried out it finally amounts to this, which also I believe,—"That government is best which governs not at all"; and when men are prepared for it, that will be the kind of government which they will have. Government is at best but an expedient; but most governments are usually, and all governments are sometimes, inexpedient. The objections which have been brought against a standing army, and they are many and weighty, and deserve to prevail, may also at last be brought against a standing government. The standing army is only an arm of the standing government. The government itself, which is only the mode which the people have chosen to execute their will, is equally liable to be abused and perverted before the people can act through it. Witness the present Mexican war, the work of comparatively a few individuals using the standing government as their tool; for, in the outset, the people would not have consented to this measure.

2 This American government,—what is it but a tradition, though a recent one, endeavoring to transmit itself unimpaired to posterity, but each instant losing some of its integrity? It has not the vitality and force of a single living man; for a single man can bend it to his will. It is a sort of wooden gun to the people themselves. But it is not the less necessary for this; for the people must have some complicated machinery or other, and hear its din, to satisfy that idea of government which they have. Governments show thus how successfully men can be imposed on, even impose on themselves, for their own advantage. It is excellent, we must all allow. Yet this government never of itself furthered any enterprise, but by the alacrity with which it got out of its way. *It* does not keep the country free. *It* does not settle the West. *It* does not educate. The character inherent in the American people has done all that has been accomplished; and it would have done somewhat more, if the government had not sometimes got in its way. For government is an expedient by which men would fain succeed in letting one another alone; and, as has been said, when it is most expedient, the governed are most let alone by it. Trade and commerce, if they were not made of India-rubber, would never manage to bounce over the obstacles which legislators are continually putting in their way; and, if one were to judge these men wholly by the effects of their actions and not partly by their intentions, they would deserve to be classed and punished with those mischievous persons who put obstructions on the railroads.

3 But, to speak practically and as a citizen, unlike those who call themselves no-government men, I ask for, not at once no government, but *at once* a better government. Let every man make known what kind of government would command his respect, and that will be one step toward obtaining it.

4 After all, the practical reason why, when the power is once in the hands of the people, a majority are permitted, and for a long period continue, to rule is not because they are most likely to be in the right, nor because this seems fairest to the minority, but because they are physically the strongest. But a government in which the majority rule in all cases cannot be based on justice, even as far as men understand it. Can there not be a government in which majorities do not virtually decide right and wrong, but conscience? —in which majorities decide only those questions to which the rule of expediency is applicable? Must the citizen ever for a moment, or in the least degree, resign his conscience to the legislator? Why has every man a conscience, then? I think that we should be men first, and subjects afterward. It is not desirable to cultivate a respect for the law, so much as for the right. The only obligation which I have a right to assume is to do at any time what I think right. It is truly enough said, that a corporation has no conscience; but a corporation of conscientious men is a corporation *with* a conscience. Law never made men a whit more just; and, by means of their respect for it, even the well-disposed are daily made the agents of injustice. A common and natural result of an undue respect for law is, that you may see a file of soldiers, colonel, captain, corporal, privates, powder-monkeys, and all, marching in admirable order over hill and dale to the wars, against their wills, ay, against their common sense and consciences, which makes it very steep marching indeed, and produces a palpitation of the heart. They have no doubt that it is a damnable business in which they are concerned; they are all peaceably inclined. Now, what are they? Men at all? or small movable forts and magazines, at the service of some unscrupulous man in power? Visit the Navy-Yard, and behold a marine, such a man as an American government can make, or such as it can make a man with its black arts,—a mere shadow and reminiscence of humanity, a man laid out alive and standing, and already, as one may say, buried under arms with funeral accompaniments, though it may be,—

> "Not a drum was heard, not a funeral note,
>   As his corse to the rampart we hurried;
> Not a soldier discharged his farewell shot
>   O'er the grave where our hero we buried."

5 The mass of men serve the state thus, not as men mainly, but as machines, with their bodies. They are the standing army, and the militia, jailors, constables, posse comitatus, etc. In most cases there is no free exercise whatever of the judgment or of the moral sense; but they put themselves on a level with wood and earth and stones; and wooden men can perhaps be manufactured that will serve the purpose as well. Such command no more respect than men of straw or a lump of dirt. They have the same sort of worth only as horses and dogs. Yet such as these even are commonly esteemed good citizens. Others—as most legislators, politicians, lawyers, ministers, and office-holders—serve the state chiefly with their heads; and, as they rarely make any moral distinctions, they are as likely to serve the Devil, without *intending* it, as God. A very few, as heroes, patriots, martyrs, reformers in the great sense, and *men,* serve the state with their consciences also, and so necessarily resist it for the most part; and they are commonly treated as enemies by it. A wise man will only be useful as a man, and will not submit to be "clay," and "stop a hole to keep the wind away," but leave that office to his dust at least:—

> "I am too high-born to be propertied,
>   To be a secondary at control,
>   Or useful serving-man and instrument
>   To any sovereign state throughout the world."

6 He who gives himself entirely to his fellow-men appears to them useless and selfish; but he who gives himself partially to them is pronounced a benefactor and philanthropist.

7 How does it become a man to behave toward this American government to-day? I answer, that he cannot without disgrace be associated with it. I cannot for an instant recognize that political organization as *my* government which is the *slave's* government also.

8 All men recognize the right of revolution; that is, the right to refuse allegiance to, and to resist, the government, when its tyranny or its ineffi- ciency are great and unendurable. But almost all say that such is not the case now. But such was the case, they think, in the Revolution of '75. If one were to tell me that this was a bad government because it taxed certain foreign commodities brought to its ports, it is most probable that I should not make an ado about it, for I can do without them. All machines have their friction; and possibly this does enough good to counterbalance the evil. At any rate, it is a great evil to make a stir about it. But when the friction comes to have its machine, and oppression and robbery are organized, I say, let us not have such a machine any longer. In other words, when a sixth of the population of a nation which has undertaken to be the refuge of liberty are slaves, and a whole country is unjustly overrun and conquered by a foreign army, and subjected to military law, I think that it is not too soon for honest men to rebel and revolutionize. What makes this duty the more urgent is the fact that the country so overrun is not our own, but ours is the invading army.

9 Paley, a common authority with many on moral questions, in his chapter on the "Duty of Submission to Civil Government," resolves all civil obliga- tion into expediency; and he proceeds to say, "that so long as the interest of the whole society requires it, that is, so long as the established government cannot be resisted or changed without public inconveniency, it is the will of God that the established government be obeyed, and no longer. . . . This principle being admitted, the justice of every particular case of resistance is reduced to a computation of the quantity of the danger and grievance on the one side, and of the probability and expense of redressing it on the other." Of this, he says, every man shall judge for himself. But Paley appears never to have contemplated those cases to which the rule of expediency does not apply, in which a people, as well as an individual, must do justice, cost what it may. If I have unjustly wrested a plank from a drowning man, I must restore it to him though I drown myself. This, according to Paley, would be inconvenient. But he that would save his life, in such a case, shall lose it. This people must cease to hold slaves, and to make war on Mexico, though it cost them their existence as a people.

10 In their practice, nations agree with Paley; but does any one think that Massachusetts does exactly what is right at the present crisis?

> "A drab of state, a cloth-o'-silver slut,
>   To have her train borne up, and her soul trail in the dirt."

Practically speaking, the opponents to a reform in Massachusetts are not a hundred thousand politicians at the South, but a hundred thousand merchants and farmers here, who are more interested in commerce and agriculture than they are in humanity, and are not prepared to do justice to the slave and to Mexico, *cost what it may*. I quarrel not with far-off foes, but with those who, near at home, coöperate with, and do the bidding of, those far away, and without whom the latter would be harmless. We are accustomed to say, that the mass of men are unprepared; but improvement is slow, because the few are not materially wiser or better than the many. It is not so important that many should be as good as you, as that there be some absolute goodness somewhere; for that will leaven the whole lump. There are thousands who are *in opinion* opposed to slavery and to the war, who yet in effect do nothing to put an end to them; who, esteeming themselves children of Washington and Franklin, sit down with their hands in their pockets, and say that they know not what to do, and do nothing; who even postpone the question of freedom to the question of free-trade, and quietly read the prices-current along with the latest advices from Mexico, after dinner, and, it may be, fall asleep over them both. What is the price-current of an honest man and patriot to-day? They hesitate, and they regret, and sometimes they petition; but they do nothing in earnest and with effect. They will wait, well disposed, for others to remedy the evil, that they may no longer have it to regret. At most, they give only a cheap vote, and a feeble countenance and God-speed, to the right, as it goes by them. There are nine hundred and ninety-nine patrons of virtue to one virtuous man. But it is easier to deal with the real professor of a thing than with the temporary guardian of it.

11 All voting is a sort of gaming, like checkers or backgammon, with a slight moral tinge to it, a playing with right and wrong, with moral questions; and betting naturally accompanies it. The character of the voters is not staked. I cast my vote, perchance, as I think right; but I am not vitally concerned that that right should prevail. I am willing to leave it to the majority. Its obligation, therefore, never exceeds that of expediency. Even voting *for the right* is *doing* nothing for it. It is only expressing to men feebly your desire that it should prevail. A wise man will not leave the right to the mercy of chance, nor wish it to prevail through the power of the majority. There is but little virtue in the action of masses of men. When the majority shall at length vote for the abolition of slavery, it will be because they are indifferent to slavery, or because there is but little slavery left to be abolished by their vote. *They* will then be the only slaves. Only *his* vote can hasten the abolition of slavery who asserts his own freedom by his vote.

12 I hear of a convention to be held at Baltimore, or elsewhere, for the selection of a candidate for the Presidency, made up chiefly of editors, and men who are politicians by profession; but I think, what is it to any independent, intelligent, and respectable man what decision they may come to? Shall we not have the advantage of his wisdom and honesty, nevertheless? Can we not count upon some independent votes? Are there not many individuals in the country who do not attend conventions? But no: I find that the respectable man, so called, has immediately drifted from his position, and despairs of his country, when his country has more reason to despair of him. He forthwith adopts one of the candidates thus selected as the only *available* one, thus proving that he is himself *available* for any purposes of the demagogue. His vote is of no more worth than that of any unprincipled foreigner or hireling native, who may have been bought. O for a man who is a *man,* and, as my neighbor says, has a bone in his back which you cannot pass your hand through! Our statistics are at fault: the population has been returned too large. How many *men* are there to a square thousand miles in this country? Hardly one. Does not America offer any inducement for men to settle here? The American has dwindled into an Odd Fellow,—one who may be known by the development of his organ of gregariousness, and a manifest lack of intellect and cheerful self-reliance; whose first and chief concern, on coming into the world, is to see that the Almshouses are in good repair; and, before yet he has lawfully donned the virile garb, to collect a fund for the support of the widows and orphans that may be; who, in short, ventures to live only by the aid of the Mutual Insurance company, which has promised to bury him decently.

13 It is not a man's duty, as a matter of course, to devote himself to the eradication of any, even the most enormous wrong; he may still properly have other concerns to engage him; but it is his duty, at least, to wash his hands of it, and, if he gives it no thought longer, not to give it practically his support. If I devote myself to other pursuits and contemplations, I must first see, at least, that I do not pursue them sitting upon another man's shoulders. I must get off him first, that he may pursue his contemplations too. See what gross inconsistency is tolerated. I have heard some of my townsmen say, "I should like to have them order me out to help put down an insurrection of the slaves, or to march to Mexico;—see if I would go"; and yet these very men have each, directly by their allegiance, and so indirectly, at least, by their money, furnished a substitute. The soldier is applauded who refuses to serve in an unjust war by those who do not refuse

to sustain the unjust government which makes the war; is applauded by those whose own act and authority he disregards and sets at naught; as if the state were penitent to that degree that it hired one to scourge it while it sinned, but not to that degree that it left off sinning for a moment. Thus, under the name of Order and Civil Government, we are all made at last to pay homage to and support our own meanness. After the first blush of sin comes its indifference; and from immoral it becomes, as it were, *un-moral*, and not quite unnecessary to that life which we have made.

14 The broadest and most prevalent error requires the most disinterested virtue to sustain it. The slight reproach to which the virtue of patriotism is commonly liable, the noble are most likely to incur. Those who, while they disapprove of the character and measures of a government, yield to it their allegiance and support are undoubtedly its most conscientious supporters, and so frequently the most serious obstacles to reform. Some are petitioning the state to dissolve the Union, to disregard the requisitions of the President. Why do they not dissolve it themselves,—the union between themselves and the state,—and refuse to pay their quota into its treasury? Do not they stand in the same relation to the state that the state does to the Union? And have not the same reasons prevented the state from resisting the Union which have prevented them from resisting the state?

15 How can a man be satisfied to entertain an opinion merely, and enjoy *it?* Is there any enjoyment in it, if his opinion is that he is aggrieved? If you are cheated out of a single dollar by your neighbor, you do not rest satisfied with knowing that you are cheated, or with saying that you are cheated, or even with petitioning him to pay you your due; but you take effectual steps at once to obtain the full amount, and see that you are never cheated again. Action from principle, the perception and the performance of right, changes things and relations; it is essentially revolutionary, and does not consist wholly with anything which was. It not only divides states and churches, it divides families; ay, it divides the *individual,* separating the diabolical in him from the divine.

16 Unjust laws exist: shall we be content to obey them, or shall we endeavor to amend them, and obey them until we have succeeded, or shall we transgress them at once? Men generally, under such a government as this, think that they ought to wait until they have persuaded the majority to alter them. They think that, if they should resist, the remedy would be worse than the evil. But it is the fault of the government itself that the remedy *is* worse than the evil. *It* makes it worse. Why is it not more apt to anticipate and provide for reform? Why does it not cherish its wise minority? Why does it cry and resist before it is hurt? Why does it not encourage its citizens to be on the alert to point out its faults, and *do* better than *it* would have them? Why does it always crucify Christ, and excommunicate Copernicus and Luther, and pronounce Washington and Franklin rebels?

17 One would think, that a deliberate and practical denial of its authority was the only offense never contemplated by government; else, why has it not assigned its definite, its suitable and proportionate penalty? If a man who has no property refuses but once to earn nine shillings for the state, he is put in prison for a period unlimited by any law that I know, and determined only by the discretion of those who placed him there; but if he should steal ninety times nine shillings from the state, he is soon permitted to go at large again.

18 If the injustice is part of the necessary friction of the machine of government, let it go, let it go: perchance it will wear smooth,—certainly the machine will wear out. If the injustice has a spring, or a pulley, or a rope, or a crank, exclusively for itself, then perhaps you may consider whether the remedy will not be worse than the evil; but if it is of such a nature that it requires you to be the agent of injustice to another, then, I say, break the law. Let your life be a counter friction to stop the machine. What I have to do is to see, at any rate, that I do not lend myself to the wrong which I condemn.

19 As for adopting the ways which the state has provided for remedying the evil, I know not of such ways. They take too much time, and a man's life will be gone. I have other affairs to attend to. I came into this world, not chiefly to make this a good place to live in, but to live in it, be it good or bad. A man has not everything to do, but something; and because he cannot do *everything,* it is not necessary that he should do *something* wrong. It is not my business to be petitioning the Governor or the Legislature any more than it is theirs to petition me; and if they should not hear my petition, what should I do then? But in this case the state has provided no way: its very Constitution is the evil. This may seem to be harsh and stubborn and unconciliatory; but it is to treat with the utmost kindness and consideration the only spirit that can appreciate or deserve it. So is all change for the better, like birth and death, which convulse the body.

20 I do not hesitate to say, that those who call themselves Abolitionists should at once effectually withdraw their support, both in person and property, from the government of Massachusetts and not wait till they constitute a majority of one, before they suffer the right to prevail through them. I think that it is enough if they have God on their side, without waiting for that other one. Moreover, any man more right than his neighbors constitutes a majority of one already.

21 I meet this American government, or its representative, the state government, directly, and face to face, once a year—no more—in the person of its tax-gatherer; this is the only mode in which a man situated as I am necessarily meets it; and it then says distinctly, Recognize me; and the simplest, most effectual, and, in the present posture of affairs, the indispensablest mode of treating with it on this head, of expressing your little satisfaction with and love for it, is to deny it then. My civil neighbor, the taxgatherer, is the very man I have to deal with,—for it is, after all, with men and not with parchment that I quarrel,—and he has voluntarily chosen to be an agent of the government. How shall he ever know well what he is and does as an officer of the government, or as a man, until he is obliged to consider whether he shall treat me, his neighbor, for whom he has respect, as a neighbor and well-disposed man, or as a maniac and disturber of the peace, and see if he can get over this obstruction to his neighborliness without a ruder and more impetuous thought or speech corresponding with his action. I know this well, that if one thousand, if one hundred, if ten men whom I could name,—if ten *honest* men only,—if *one* HONEST man, in this State of Massachusetts, *ceasing to hold slaves,* were actually to withdraw from this copartnership, and be locked up in the county jail therefor, it would be the abolition of slavery in America. For it matters not how small the beginning may seem to be: what is once well done is done forever. But we love better to talk about it: that we say is our mission. Reform keeps many scores of newspapers in its service, but not one man. If my esteemed neighbor, the State's ambassador, who will devote his days to the settlement of the question of human rights in the Council Chamber, instead of being threatened with the prisons of Carolina, were to sit down the prisoner of Massachusetts, that State which is so anxious to foist the sin of slavery upon her sister,—though at present she can discover only an act of inhospitality to be the ground of a quarrel with her,—the Legislature would not wholly waive the subject the following winter.

22 Under a government which imprisons any unjustly, the true place for a just man is also a prison. The proper place to-day, the only place which Massachusetts has provided for her freer and less desponding spirits, is in her prisons, to be put out and locked out of the State by her own act, as they have already put themselves out by their principles. It is there that the fugitive slave, and the Mexican prisoner on parole, and the Indian come to plead the wrongs of his race should find them; on that separate, but more free and honorable ground, where the State places those who are not *with* her, but *against* her,—the only house in a slave State in which a free man can abide with honor. If any think that their influence would be lost there, and their voices no longer afflict the ear of the State, that they would not be as an enemy within its walls, they do not know by how much truth is stronger than error, nor how much more eloquently and effectively he can combat injustice who has experienced a little in his own person. Cast your whole vote, not a strip of paper merely, but your whole influence. A

minority is powerless while it conforms to the majority; it is not even a minority then; but it is irresistible when it clogs by its whole weight. If the alternative is to keep all just men in prison, or give up war and slavery, the State will not hesitate which to choose. If a thousand men were not to pay their tax-bills this year, that would not be a violent and bloody measure, as it would be to pay them, and enable the State to commit violence and shed innocent blood. This is, in fact, the definition of a peaceable revolution, if any such is possible. If the tax-gatherer, or any other public officer, asks me, as one has done, "But what shall I do?" my answer is, "If you really wish to do anything, resign your office." When the subject has refused allegiance, and the officer has resigned his office, then the revolution is accomplished. But even suppose blood should flow. Is there not a sort of blood shed when the conscience is wounded? Through this wound a man's real manhood and immortality flow out, and he bleeds to an everlasting death. I see this blood flowing now.

23 I have contemplated the imprisonment of the offender, rather than the seizure of his goods,—though both will serve the same purpose,—because they who assert the purest right, and consequently are most dangerous to a corrupt State, commonly have not spent much time in accumulating property. To such the State renders comparatively small service, and a slight tax is wont to appear exorbitant, particularly if they are obliged to earn it by special labor with their hands. If there were one who lived wholly without the use of money, the State itself would hesitate to demand it of him. But the rich man—not to make any invidious comparison—is always sold to the institution which makes him rich. Absolutely speaking, the more money, the less virtue; for money comes between a man and his objects, and obtains them for him; and it was certainly no great virtue to obtain it. It puts to rest many questions which he would otherwise be taxed to answer; while the only new question which it puts is the hard but superfluous one, how to spend it. Thus his moral ground is taken from under his feet. The opportunities of living are diminished in proportion as what are called the "means" are increased. The best thing a man can do for his culture when he is rich is to endeavor to carry out those schemes which he entertained when he was poor. Christ answered the Herodians according to their condition. "Show me the tribute-money," said he;—and one took a penny out of his pocket;—if you use the money which has the image of Cæsar on it and which he has made current and valuable, that is, *if you are men of the State,* and gladly enjoy the advantages of Cæsar's government, then pay him back some of his own when he demands it. "Render therefore to Cæsar that which is Cæsar's, and to God those things which are God's,"—leaving them no wiser than before as to which was which; for they did not wish to know.

24 When I converse with the freest of my neighbors, I perceive that, what-

ever they may say about the magnitude and seriousness of the question, and their regard for the public tranquility, the long and the short of the matter is, that they cannot spare the protection of the existing government, and they dread the consequences to their property and families of disobedience to it. For my own part, I should not like to think that I ever rely on the protection of the State. But, if I deny the authority of the State when it presents its tax-bill, it will soon take and waste all my property, and so harass me and my children without end. This is hard. This makes it impossible for a man to live honestly, and at the same time comfortably, in outward respects. It will not be worth the while to accumulate property; that would be sure to go again. You must hire or squat somewhere, and raise but a small crop, and eat that soon. You must live within yourself, and depend upon yourself always tucked up and ready for a start, and not have many affairs. A man may grow rich in Turkey even, if he will be in all respects a good subject of the Turkish government. Confucius said: "If a state is governed by the principles of reason, poverty and misery are subjects of shame; if a state is not governed by the principles of reason, riches and honors are the subjects of shame." No: until I want the protection of Massachusetts to be extended to me in some distant Southern port, where my liberty is endangered, or until I am bent solely on building up an estate at home by peaceful enterprise, I can afford to refuse allegiance to Massachusetts, and her right to my property and life. It costs me less in every sense to incur the penalty of disobedience to the State than it would to obey. I should feel as if I were worth less in that case.

25 Some years ago, the State met me in behalf of the Church, and commanded me to pay a certain sum toward the support of a clergyman whose preaching my father attended, but never I myself. "Pay," it said, "or be locked up in the jail." I declined to pay. But, unfortunately, another man saw fit to pay it. I did not see why the schoolmaster should be taxed to support the priest, and not the priest the schoolmaster; for I was not the State's schoolmaster, but I supported myself by voluntary subscription. I did not see why the lyceum should not present its tax-bill, and have the State to back its demand, as well as the Church. However, at the request of the selectmen, I condescended to make some such statement as this in writing: —"Know all men by these presents, that I, Henry Thoreau, do not wish to be regarded as a member of any incorporated society which I have not joined." This I gave to the town clerk; and he has it. The State, having thus learned that I did not wish to be regarded as a member of that church, has never made a like demand on me since; though it said that it must adhere to its original presumption that time. If I had known how to name them, I should then have signed off in detail from all the societies which I never signed on to; but I did not know where to find a complete list.

26 I have paid no poll-tax for six years. I was put into a jail once on this account, for one night; and, as I stood considering the walls of solid stone, two or three feet thick, the door of wood and iron, a foot thick, and the iron grating which strained the light, I could not help being struck with the foolishness of that institution which treated me as if I were mere flesh and blood and bones, to be locked up. I wondered that it should have concluded at length that this was the best use it could put me to, and had never thought to avail itself of my services in some way. I saw that, if there was a wall of stone between me and my townsmen, there was a still more difficult one to climb or break through before they could get to be as free as I was. I did not for a moment feel confined, and the walls seemed a great waste of stone and mortar. I felt as if I alone of all my townsmen had paid my tax. They plainly did not know how to treat me, but behaved like persons who are underbred. In every threat and in every compliment there was a blunder; for they thought that my chief desire was to stand the other side of that stone wall. I could not but smile to see how industriously they locked the door on my meditations, which followed them out again without let or hindrance, and *they* were really all that was dangerous. As they could not reach me, they had resolved to punish my body; just as boys, if they cannot come at some person against whom they have a spite, will abuse his dog. I saw that the State was half-witted, that it was timid as a lone woman with her silver spoons, and that it did not know its friends from its foes, and I lost all my remaining respect for it, and pitied it.

27 Thus the State never intentionally confronts a man's sense, intellectual or moral, but only his body, his senses. It is not armed with superior wit or honesty, but with superior physical strength. I was not born to be forced. I will breathe after my own fashion. Let us see who is the strongest. What force has a multitude? They only can force me who obey a higher law than I. They force me to become like themselves. I do not hear of *men* being *forced* to live this way or that by masses of men. What sort of life were that to live? When I meet a government which says to me, "Your money or your life," why should I be in haste to give it my money? It may be in a great strait, and not know what to do: I cannot help that. It must help itself; do as I do. It is not worth the while to snivel about it. I am not responsible for the successful working of the machinery of society. I am not the son of the engineer. I perceive that, when an acorn and a chestnut fall side by side, the one does not remain inert to make way for the other, but both obey their own laws, and spring and grow and flourish as best they can, till one, perchance, overshadows and destroys the other. If a plant cannot live according to its nature, it dies; and so a man.

28 The night in prison was novel and interesting enough. The prisoners in their shirt-sleeves were enjoying a chat and the evening air in the doorway, when I entered. But the jailer said, "Come, boys, it is time to lock up"; and so they dispersed, and I heard the sound of their steps returning into the hollow apartments. My roommate was introduced to me by the jailer as "a first-rate fellow and a clever man." When the door was locked, he showed me where to hang my hat, and how he managed matters there. The rooms were whitewashed once a month; and this one, at least, was the whitest, most simply furnished, and probably the neatest apartment in the town. He naturally wanted to know where I came from, and what brought me there; and, when I had told him, I asked him in my turn how he came there, presuming him to be an honest man, of course; and, as the world goes, I believe he was. "Why," said he, "they accuse me of burning a barn; but I never did it." As near as I could discover, he had probably gone to bed in a barn when drunk, and smoked his pipe there; and so a barn was burnt. He had the reputation of being a clever man, had been there some three months waiting for his trial to come on, and would have to wait as much longer; but he was quite domesticated and contented, since he got his board for nothing, and thought that he was well treated.

29 He occupied one window, and I the other; and I saw that if one stayed there long, his principal business would be to look out the window. I had soon read all the tracts that were left there, and examined where former prisoners had broken out, and where a grate had been sawed off, and heard the history of the various occupants of that room; for I found that even here there was a history and a gossip which never circulated beyond the walls of the jail. Probably this is the only house in the town where verses are composed, which are afterward printed in a circular form, but not published. I was shown quite a long list of verses which were composed by some young men who had been detected in an attempt to escape, who avenged themselves by singing them.

30 I pumped my fellow-prisoner as dry as I could, for fear I should never see him again; but at length he showed me which was my bed, and left me to blow out the lamp.

31 It was like traveling into a far country, such as I had never expected to behold, to lie there for one night. It seemed to me that I never had heard the town-clock strike before, nor the evening sounds of the village; for we slept with the windows open, which were inside the grating. It was to see my native village in the light of the Middle Ages, and our Concord was turned into a Rhine stream, and visions of knights and castles passed before me. They were the voices of old burghers that I heard in the streets. I was an involuntary spectator and auditor of whatever was done and said in the kitchen of the adjacent village-inn,—a wholly new and rare experience to me. It was a closer view of my native town. I was fairly inside of it. I never had seen its institutions before. This is one of its peculiar institutions; for it is a shire town. I began to comprehend what its inhabitants were about.

32 In the morning, our breakfasts were put through the hole in the door, in small oblong-square tin pans, made to fit, and holding a pint of chocolate, with brown bread, and an iron spoon. When they called for the vessels again, I was green enough to return what bread I had left; but my comrade seized it, and said that I should lay that up for lunch or dinner. Soon after he was let out to work at haying in a neighboring field, whither he went every day, and would not be back till noon; so he bade me good-day, saying that he doubted if he should see me again.

33 When I came out of prison,—for some one interfered, and paid that tax, —I did not perceive that great changes had taken place on the common, such as he observed who went in a youth and emerged a tottering and gray-headed man; and yet a change had to my eyes come over the scene,—the town, and State, and country,—greater than any that mere time could effect. I saw yet more distinctly the State in which I lived. I saw to what extent the people among whom I lived could be trusted as good neighbors and friends; that their friendship was for summer weather only; that they did not greatly propose to do right; that they were a distinct race from me by their prejudices and superstitions, as the Chinamen and Malays are; that in their sacrifices to humanity they ran no risks, not even to their property; that after all they were not so noble but they treated the thief as he had treated them, and hoped, by a certain outward observance and a few prayers, and by walking in a particular straight though useless path from time to time, to save their souls. This may be to judge my neighbors harshly; for I believe that many of them are not aware that they have such an institution as the jail in their village.

34 It was formerly the custom in our village, when a poor debtor came out of jail, for his acquaintances to salute him, looking through their fingers, which were crossed to represent the grating of a jail window, "How do ye do?" My neighbors did not thus salute me, but first looked at me, and then at one another, as if I had returned from a long journey. I was put into jail as I was going to the shoemaker's to get a shoe which was mended. When I was let out the next morning, I proceeded to finish my errand, and, having put on my mended shoe, joined a huckleberry party, who were impatient to put themselves under by conduct; and in half an hour,—for the horse was soon tackled,—was in the midst of a huckleberry field, on one of our highest hills, two miles off, and then the State was nowhere to be seen.

35 This is the whole history of "My Prisons."

36 I have never declined paying the highway tax, because I am as desirous of being a good neighbor as I am of being a bad subject; and as for supporting schools, I am doing my part to educate my fellow-countrymen now. It is for no particular item in the tax-bill that I refuse to pay it. I simply wish to refuse allegiance to the State, to withdraw and stand aloof from it effectually. I do not care to trace the course of my dollar, if I could, till it buys a man or a musket to shoot with,—the dollar is innocent,—but I am concerned to trace the effects of my allegiance. In fact, I quietly declare war with the State, after my fashion, though I will still make what use and get what advantage of her I can, as is usual in such cases.

37 If others pay the tax which is demanded of me, from a sympathy with the state, they do but what they have already done in their own case, or rather they abet injustice to a greater extent than the State requires. If they pay the tax from a mistaken interest in the individual taxed, to save his property, or prevent his going to jail, it is because they have not considered wisely how far they let their private feelings interfere with the public good.

38 This, then, is my position at present. But one cannot be too much on his guard in such a case, lest his action be biased by obstinacy or an undue regard for the opinions of men. Let him see that he does only what belongs to himself and to the hour.

39 I think sometimes, Why, this people mean well, they are only ignorant; they would do better if they knew how: why give your neighbors this pain to treat you as they are not inclined to? But I think again, This is no reason why I should do as they do, or permit others to suffer much greater pain of a different kind. Again, I sometimes say to myself, When may millions of men, without heat, without ill will, without personal feeling of any kind, demand of you a few shillings only, without the possibility, such is their constitution, of retracting or altering their present demand, and without the possibility, on your side, of appeal to any other millions, why expose yourself to this overwhelming brute force? You do not resist cold and hunger, the winds and the waves, thus obstinately; you quietly submit to a thousand similar necessities. You do not put your head into the fire. But just in proportion as I regard this as not wholly a brute force, but partly a human force, and consider that I have relations to those millions as to so many millions of men, and not of mere brute or inanimate things, I see that appeal is possible, first and instantaneously, from them to the Maker of them, and, secondly, from them to themselves. But if I put my head deliberately into the fire, there is no appeal to fire or to the Maker of fire, and I have only myself to blame. If I could convince myself that I have any right to be satisfied with men as they are, and to treat them accordingly, and not according, in some respects, to my requisitions and expectations of what they and I ought to be, then, like a good Mussulman and fatalist, I should endeavor to be satisfied with things as they are, and say it is the will of God. And, above all, there is this difference between resisting this and a purely brute or natural force, that I can resist this with some effect; but I cannot expect, like Orpheus, to change the nature of the rocks and trees and beasts.

40 I do not wish to quarrel with any man or nation. I do not wish to split hairs, to make fine distinctions, or set myself up as better than my neighbors. I seek rather, I may say, even an excuse for conforming to the laws of the land. I am but too ready to conform to them. Indeed, I have reason to suspect myself on this head; and each year, as the tax-gatherer comes round, I find myself disposed to review the acts and position of the general and State governments, and the spirit of the people, to discover a pretext for conformity.

"We must affect our country as our parents,
And if at any time we alienate
Our love or industry from doing it honor,
We must respect effects and teach the soul
Matter of conscience and religion,
And not desire of rule or benefit."

I believe that the State will soon be able to take all my work of this sort out of my hands, and then I shall be no better a patriot than my fellow-countrymen. Seen from a lower point of view, the Constitution, with all its faults, is very good; the law and the courts are very respectable; even this State and this American government are, in many respects, very admirable, and rare things, to be thankful for, such as a great many have described them; but seen from a point of view a little higher, they are what I have described them; seen from a higher still, and the highest, who shall say what they are, or that they are worth looking at or thinking of at all?

41 However, the government does not concern me much, and I shall bestow the fewest possible thoughts on it. It is not many moments that I live under a government, even in this world. If a man is thought-free, fancy-free, imagination-free, that which *is not* never for a long time appearing *to be* to him, unwise rulers or reformers cannot fatally interrupt him.

42 I know that most men think differently from myself; but those whose lives are by profession devoted to the study of these or kindred subjects content me as little as any. Statesmen and legislators, standing so completely within the institution, never distinctly and nakedly behold it. They speak of moving society, but have no resting-place without it. They may be men of a certain experience and discrimination, and have no doubt invented ingenious and even useful systems, for which we sincerely thank them; but all their wit and usefulness lie within certain not very wide limits. They are wont to forget that the world is not governed by policy and expediency. Webster never goes behind government, and so cannot speak with authority about it. His words are wisdom to those legislators who contemplate no essential reform in the existing government; but for thinkers, and those who legislate for all time, he never once glances at the subject. I know of those whose serene and wise speculations on this theme would soon reveal the limits of his mind's range and hospitality. Yet, compared with the cheap professions of most reformers, and the still cheaper wisdom and eloquence of politicians in general, his are almost the only sensible and valuable words, and we thank Heaven for him. Comparatively, he is always strong, original, and, above all, practical. Still, his quality is not wisdom, but prudence. The lawyer's truth is not Truth, but consistency or a consistent expediency. Truth is always in harmony with herself, and is not concerned chiefly to reveal the justice that may consist with wrong-doing. He well deserves to be called, as he has been called, the Defender of the Constitution. There are really no blows to be given by him but defensive ones. He is not a leader, but a follower. His leaders are the men of '87. "I have never made an effort," he says, "and never propose to make an effort; I have never countenanced an effort, and never mean to countenance an effort, to disturb the arrangement as originally made, by which the various States came into the Union." Still thinking of the sanction which the Constitution gives to slavery, he says, "Because it was a part of the original compact,—let it stand." Notwithstanding his special acuteness and ability, he is unable to take a fact out of its merely political relations, and behold it as it lies absolutely to be disposed of by the intellect, —what, for instance, it behooves a man to do here in America to-day with regard to slavery,—but ventures, or is driven to make some such desperate answer as the following, while professing to speak absolutely, and as a private man,—from which what new and singular code of social duties might be inferred? "The manner," says he, "in which the governments of those States where slavery exists are to regulate it is for their own consideration, under their responsibility to their constituents, to the general laws of propriety, humanity, and justice, and to God. Associations formed elsewhere, springing from a feeling of humanity, or other cause, have nothing whatever to do with it. They have never received any encouragement from me, and they never will."

43 They who know of no purer sources of truth, who have traced up its stream no higher, stand, and wisely stand, by the Bible and the Constitution, and drink at it there with reverence and humility; but they who behold where it comes trickling into this lake or that pool, gird up their loins once more, and continue their pilgrimage toward its fountain-head.

44 No man with a genius for legislation has appeared in America. They are rare in the history of the world. There are orators, politicians, and eloquent men, by the thousand; but the speaker has not yet opened his mouth to speak who is capable of settling the much-vexed questions of the day. We love eloquence for its own sake, and not for any truth which it may utter, or any heroism it may inspire. Our legislators have not yet learned the comparative value of free-trade and of freedom, of union, and of rectitude, to a nation. They have no genius or talent for comparatively humble ques-

tions of taxation and finance, commerce and manufacturers and agriculture. If we were left solely to the wordy wit of legislators in Congress for our guidance, uncorrected by the seasonable experience and the effectual complaints of the people, America would not long retain her rank among the nations. For eighteen hundred years, though perchance I have no right to say it, the New Testament has been written; yet where is the legislator who has wisdom and practical talent enough to avail himself of the light which it sheds on the science of legislation?

45 The authority of government, even such as I am willing to submit to,— for I will cheerfully obey those who know and can do better than I, and in many things even those who neither know nor can do so well,—is still an impure one: to be strictly just, it must have the sanction and consent of the governed. It can have no pure right over my person and property but what I concede to it. The progress from an absolute to a limited monarchy, from a limited monarchy to a democracy, is a progress toward a true respect for the individual. Even the Chinese philosopher was wise enough to regard the individual as the basis of the empire. Is a democracy, such as we know it, the last improvement possible in government? Is it not possible to take a step further towards recognizing and organizing the rights of man? There will never be a really free and enlightened State until the State comes to recognize the individual as a higher and independent power, from which all its own power and authority are derived, and treats him accordingly. I please myself with imagining a State at last which can afford to be just to all men, and to treat the individual with respect as a neighbor; which even would not think it inconsistent with its own repose if a few were to live aloof from it, not meddling with it, nor embraced by it, who fulfilled all the duties of neighbors and fellowmen. A State which bore this kind of fruit, and suffered it to drop off as fast as it ripened, would prepare the way for a still more perfect and glorious State, which also I have imagined, but not yet anywhere seen.

The third part of classical rhetoric was concerned with style. Once arguments had been discovered, selected, and arranged, they had to be put into words. Words—either the sound symbols or the graphic symbols—serve as the medium of communication between speakers or writers and their audience. *Elocutio,* the Latin word for style, carried this notion of "speaking out." *Lexis,* the usual Greek word for style, carried the triple notion of "thought" and "word" (both of these notions contained in the Greek word *logos*) and "speaking" (*legein*). The threefold implication of *lexis* indicates that the Greek rhetoricians conceived of style as that part of rhetoric in which we take the *thoughts* collected by invention and put them into *words* for the *speaking out* in delivery. Cardinal Newman's definition of style carried much the same idea: "Style is a thinking out into language."

It is this "thinking out into language" that presents the most formidable problem in composition for many students. The sight of a blank sheet of paper paralyzes them. It may be some comfort to such students to know that the transcription of words on a sheet of paper can be difficult even for professional writers. Writing never becomes easy; it just becomes easier. Alfred North Whitehead once said, "Style, in its finest sense, is the last acquirement of the educated mind; it is also the most useful." The difficulty that everyone has, in varying degrees, in putting thoughts into language stems partly from the inertia that must be overcome at the beginning of any task, partly from the lack of something to say, partly from indecisiveness about what to say first, and partly from the variety of possible ways to say something.

Inertia is a problem that can be overcome only by will power. One must simply sit down and resolve to write something on a piece of paper. Lack of things to say may be solved by the procedures discussed in the chapter on discovery of arguments. Indecisiveness about the order of the parts may be resolved by attention to the suggestions presented in the chapter on arrangement. The problems posed by the fact that thoughts and feelings can be worded in a variety of ways will be the principal concern of this chapter.

One notion about style that needs to be erased at the outset is that style is simply "the dress of thought." It is difficult to determine just which school of rhetoric gave currency to the notion that style was ornament or embellishment, like the tinsel draped over the bare branches of a Christmas tree, but it is certain that none of the prominent classical rhetoricians—Isocrates, Aristotle, Demetrius, Longinus, Cicero, Quintilian—ever preached such a doctrine. All of these taught that there is an integral and reciprocal relationship between matter and form. "Thought and speech are inseparable from each other"—those words of John Henry Newman express the view of style that all the best rhetoricians held. According to this view, matter must be fitted to the form, and form to the matter.

This notion of the integral relationship between matter and form is the basis for any true understanding of the rhetorical function of style. It precludes the view that style is merely the ornament of thought or that style is merely the vehicle for the expression of thought. Style does provide a vehicle for thought, and style can be ornamental; but style is something more than that. It is another of the "available means of persuasion," another of the means of arousing the appropriate emotional response in the audience, and of the means of establishing the proper ethical image.

If students adopt this functional notion of style, they will have gone part of the way toward solving some of their writing problems. They will begin to regard style in the way that Stendhal conceived of it: *Le style est ceci: Ajouter à une pensée donnée toutes les circonstances propres à produire tout l'effet que doit produire cette pensée* ("Style is this: to add to a given thought all the circumstances fitted to produce the whole effect which the thought is intended to produce"). Students will be guided in their choice of "the circumstances fitted to produce the whole effect" by a consideration of their subject matter, the occasion, their purpose, their own personality, and their audience. Jonathan Swift's definition of style as "proper words in proper places" is not much help to students until they have some criteria for deciding what is proper. The determination of what is proper can be arrived at only in relation to the above-named considerations.

Since *proper* is a relative term, there cannot be such a thing as an absolute "best style." A writer must be in command of a variety of styles, in order to draw on the style that is most appropriate to the situation. This is not to say that these several styles will differ radically from one another. Just as there is a common strain in the range of dialects that people command in their speech, so in their writing there will be a certain tenor that persists as they range from the most formal prose to the most relaxed prose. Each person, in other words, has an idiom—an idiom that is recognizable in all of his or her dialects and styles. The various styles will result from the variations that the writer or speaker works on this common tenor.

How do writers acquire the variety of styles needed for the variety of subject matter, occasion, and audience that they are bound to confront? The classical rhetoricians taught that a person acquired versatility of style in three ways: (1) through a study of precepts or principles (*ars*), (2) through practice in writing (*exercitato*), (3) through imitation of the practice of others (*imitatio*). Rhetoric textbooks are concerned mainly with laying down the principles that will guide the student in acquiring effective styles. Practice and imitation are exercises that the student usually performs outside the classroom. For homework, the student is required to write themes; or the student may be asked to read "good writers," or to write a stylistic analysis of some writer, or to imitate passages of good writing.

Although this chapter will deal mainly with the precepts of effective writing, specimens of prose will be presented later for observation, analysis, and imitation. Practice in writing will have to come from the writing assignments set by the instructor, but at this point it is important to remind the student that practice in writing is the most beneficial of the three means. Precepts and imitation can *teach* the student how to write, but it is only by writing that the student will *learn* how to write. *One learns to write by writing.* Once is enough to enunciate that truism; but its truth cannot be recalled often enough.

With these few general remarks about style, we are ready to consider some of the precepts about style.

Grammatical Competence

In the study of style, we should be clear about the provinces of grammar and rhetoric. Just as the confusion between *grammar* and *usage* produced a great deal of needless controversy, so the confusion between *grammar* and *rhetoric* could hamper an intelligent discussion of the effective use of language. There are times, of course, when considerations of grammar will shade over into considerations of rhetoric. But while it is generally true that we must possess grammatical competence before we can develop an effective style, "good grammar" does not invariably produce "good rhetoric." Nor does "bad grammar" invariably produce "bad rhetoric." In April 1927,

while awaiting execution in prison, Bartolomeo Vanzetti made this statement to a reporter:

> If it had not been for these thing, I might have live out my life, talking
> at street corners to scorning men. I might have die, unmarked, unknown,
> a failure. Now we are not a failure. This is our career and our triumph.
> Never in our full life can we hope to do such work for tolerance, for
> justice, for man's understanding of man, as now we do by an accident.

There are a number of errors in grammar and idiom in this utterance, but
the passage has such a moving eloquence about it that it has become the
most memorable statement to issue from the famous Sacco-Vanzetti case.
Translated into flawless English, the utterance loses a great deal of its
rhetorical effectiveness.

The smallest unit that falls within the province of rhetoric is the word.
Unlike grammar, rhetoric is not concerned with *parts* of words, such as
morphemes (the smallest segments that have meaning) and *phonemes* (those
contrasting sound segments which enable a native speaker of the language
to "hear" different words). It might be well at this point to set side by side
the provinces of grammar and rhetoric:

GRAMMAR: phoneme—syllable—word—phrase—clause
RHETORIC: word—phrase—clause—paragraph—division—whole composition

It is clear from this schema that grammar and rhetoric overlap in the areas
of the word, the phrase, and the clause. But although grammar and rhetoric
deal with these common elements, their concern with these elements is
not, strictly speaking, the same. Commonly we think of grammar as being
concerned with "correctness" and of rhetoric as being concerned with
"effectiveness." What we mean—or what we should mean—when we say
that grammar is concerned with "correctness" is that grammar is preoccupied
with how a particular language works—how words are formed and how
words can be put together in phrases and clauses. What we mean when we
say that rhetoric is concerned with "effectiveness" is that rhetoric deals with
the choice of the "best" from a number of *possible* expressions in a language.

We can illustrate the difference by looking at an English sentence:

> He already has forgive them for leaving, before the curtain fell, the
> theater.

What the grammarian would pounce on here would be the word *forgive*. He
or she would point out that modern English forms the perfect tense of the
third-person singular verb with the auxiliary verb *has* and the past participle
of the main verb. Once the grammarian had changed the verb in this

sentence to *has forgiven,* he or she would have no more grammatical errors to correct in the sentence—that is, the grammarian would have to make no further changes in word order, inflections, or function words. But if the grammarian were to assume the additional role of the rhetorician, he or she would probably recommend further changes in the sentence. Although it is grammatically possible to place the word *already* and the clause *before the curtain fell* in the positions they now occupy in the sentence, it would be rhetorically advisable to alter the word order. The rhetorician would recommend that, in normal circumstances, the sentence read this way:

> He has already forgiven them for leaving the theater before the curtain fell.

The rhetorician would probably justify the changes in word order on the grounds that the sentence reads more naturally, more euphoniously, that way. There might be a rhetorical situation that would justify placing the adverb clause where it was in the original sentence, but it is difficult to imagine what that situation would be. On the other hand, it is easy to imagine a situation that would justify putting *already* at the head of the sentence. If, for instance, we wanted to emphasize the time element, we might say, "Already he has forgiven them..."

Grammar would be concerned with the disposition of a word or clause only if the placement were impossible in English or would change the intended meaning of the sentence. English grammar would not permit this arrangement of words, for instance: *He has forgiven already them.* And if we were to say, "He had forgiven them before the curtain fell for leaving," the grammarian might ignore the awkward placement of the adverb clause but would have to point out that by such placement we have changed the meaning of the sentence: the adverb clause now modifies *had forgiven;* in the original sentence the adverb clause modified the gerund *leaving.*

Rhetoric and grammar are concerned, of course, with something more than just the placement of words, phrases, and clauses in a sentence, but this discussion of placement does illustrate the difference in the interest that grammar and rhetoric take in words.

Choice of Diction

An Adequate Vocabulary

Classical rhetoricians commonly considered style under two main heads: choice of diction, and composition of words in sentences. We will consider first the choice of diction.

In order to develop a good style, students must have, in addition to grammatical competence, an ample vocabulary. How do they acquire the rich vocabulary they need to develop a good style? There is no magic formula, certainly; the best advice that one can give students is to urge them to read at every opportunity. There is no doubt that persistent reading will add immeasurably to their vocabulary resources. Every English teacher is willing to testify that the best writing is usually done by those students who have been omnivorous readers. Not only do such students have more to say on any given subject, but they seem to have at their command the words they need to express what they have to say. We more easily remember the words that we encounter repeatedly in our reading. How we remember and recall words at the appropriate time is not known. But we do know that a person cannot give what he or she does not have. The person who reads a great deal is more likely to encounter new words than those who merely keep their ears open to the speech that is constantly swirling about them. The reason is that the vocabulary for impromptu talk and conversation is considerably more limited than the vocabulary for written prose.

Writers who have words ready when they need them are in a happy condition indeed. When apt words come readily, they know that they have gained command over words. They must feel something of the assurance displayed by the centurion in the New Testament: "I say to one, 'Go,' and he goes, and to another, 'Come,' and he comes." What is especially fortunate about such a verbal facility is that words that present themselves readily are likely to be the "proper words in proper places." When we have to strain for the *mot juste,* there is always the danger that the word finally chosen will be slightly awry.

So students who want to acquire an adequate vocabulary should heed the advice to read, read, read. But let them not trust solely to unconscious acquisition. Although they will absorb many new words merely by meeting them frequently, they will accelerate the assimilation of new words if they will take the trouble to look up the meaning of unfamiliar words as they meet them. As Henry James said, "Try to be one of the people on whom nothing is lost!" Students will be amazed at how quickly and solidly their vocabulary grows if they take the trouble to consult their dictionary every time they meet a new word.

Consulting the meaning of new words as one meets them is the best of the *conscious* methods of increasing one's vocabulary. It is best because it is functional: one is pursuing the meanings of words that one needs to know in order to understand what one reads.

There are other conscious ways to accelerate the acquisition of a rich vocabulary. One of these is to study lists of "new," "unusual," or "useful" words. We can add rapidly to our stock of words by such a systematic study of word-lists, and those who feel themselves to be notably deficient in vocabulary can expedite the catching-up process by learning and constantly reviewing a recommended list of words. There are many vocabulary exercises available, which students who want to add quickly to their knowledge of words would be well advised to consult.

Students should be warned, however, that this is the least satisfactory of the methods of vocabulary study. For one thing, they are studying words in isolation, not in a context. Studying words out of context can have a number of unfortunate consequences. First, knowledge of words tends to become an end in itself instead of a means. For another thing, the meanings of words studied out of context tend not to "stick" with the student as readily as they do when words are seen in the context of the reading that the student does. Any teacher who has subjected students to the study of selected word-lists knows how often he or she has been disappointed by seeing few of these words appear in the students' writing. The third consequence of studying words out of context is that students often use these words ineptly or unidiomatically. The student who writes, "George ate his chicken with hedonistic gusto," seems to be aware that *hedonistic* has some connection with sensuous pleasure but also reveals that he or she has not yet acquired the fine sense of knowing when words "fit." Nor does it help much to insist that students should compose a sentence using the word they have just looked up, because if they have not seen or heard the word used aptly they have no guide to its use. Students should not be discouraged, of course, from investigating the meanings of words that they find in some recommended list, because there is always some profit in such a pursuit, but students should be aware of the limitations of such an approach to words.

If writers have any reference tools on their desks, they are most likely to have a dictionary and a thesaurus. Writers often resort to their dictionary for spelling, for syllabication of words, for meanings of words. They do not resort to a thesaurus as often as they do to a dictionary, but it is the rare writer who has not sometime felt the need to consult a thesaurus. A thesaurus is indeed a valuable vocabulary-aid when the exact word that we need does not come to us readily.

The most famous thesaurus—the one that has become as much associated with synonymy as Webster is with lexicography and Bulfinch with mythology—is *Roget's Thesaurus of English Words and Phrases,* compiled originally by an English physician, Peter Mark Roget, and first published in London in 1852. Roget arranged his "treasury of words" under topical headings. Subsequent editors have revised the original *Thesaurus,* adding new words and removing some that had become obsolete, and the most recent editors have arranged the entries in alphabetical order to facilitate use. There are many inexpensive editions of *Roget's* available today, as well as other thesauruses prepared by modern editors. Students will find enough use for a thesaurus to warrant their buying a copy.

A thesaurus merely lists synonyms (and some antonyms) for the entry word, with cross-references to other entries. Since synonyms seldom if ever are identical in meaning, students need considerable knowledge of words and a fine discrimination to use a thesaurus intelligently. Suppose that a student is composing a paragraph describing the people who attended the opening of an opera season. In one of the sentences, she wants to convey the idea that the women who attended this event displayed a lack of taste and moderation in the way they dressed. She has written the sentence this way:

> The ladies ostentatiously showed off their silks and satins and diamonds.

But she is not satisfied with the sentence. For one thing, she does not like the awkwardness of *showed off*. For another thing, she senses that there is something repetitious about *ostentatiously showed off* (doesn't *ostentation* mean "a show"?) Well, she will have to reword, perhaps recast, the sentence. If the new words or new phrases do not come to her immediately, she may find help in a thesaurus. But where does she start in the thesaurus?

Part of the difficulty in using a thesaurus is knowing just which entry one should consult. If one merely wants a substitute for a word, one has only to consult the entry for that word in the thesaurus. But sometimes one has an idea that one wants to convey, but no word for that idea suggests itself. In that case, one must conjure up some word or some concept (and it was here that Roget's original topical categories were helpful) that is close to the notion one wants to convey. Even a remote word will give the writer a starting point in the thesaurus. Synonyms for that word and cross-references to other words will move the writer closer to the exact word.

The student in our example is not sure, however, whether she needs just a substitute word or whether she needs an entirely new way of phrasing what she means to say. But since "showing off" is the general idea that she wants to convey with this sentence, she decides to start by consulting the entry *ostentation*. In *Roget's* she finds, as she will in most thesauruses, that the synonyms are grouped under part-of-speech headings—noun, verb, adjective, adverb. Looking at the list of synonyms under each part-of-speech heading may suggest to the student how to reword or revise her sentence. She would like to keep, if she can, the "silks and satins and diamonds" of her present sentence because these words are concrete and sensory. (Perhaps without knowing it, the student has produced the figure of synecdoche—the material here standing for the thing made from it.) From the nouns listed under *ostentation*, she experiments with various combinations:

> The ladies made a *display* (or *show, flourish, parade*) of their silks and satins and diamonds.

Perhaps adding the adjective *vulgar* (or *garish, gaudy, glittering*) would reveal her value judgment on the scene—would, in other words, reveal her attitude toward the scene:

> The ladies made a vulgar display of their silks and satins and diamonds.

Then she experiments with some verb combinations suggested by the synonyms listed under *ostentation: to exhibit, to display, to parade, to flaunt, to prink, to primp.* She finally settles on the verb *flaunt*—

> The ladies flaunted their silks and satins and diamonds.

—because *flaunt* combines all the notions and attitudes that she tried to convey in her original sentence; and *flaunt*, being concrete and picturesque, fits well with the figure of speech that follows it.

A thesaurus can be a valuable aid when "the proper word in the proper place" does not immediately present itself. But students should be on their guard against the temptations offered by such a treasury. Those who have gone through a period of serious effort to improve their style may recall how difficult it was at times to resist the temptation to replace all the drab, ordinary words with some of the resplendent, polysyllabic words discovered in a thesaurus. A student, for instance, might compose a sentence like this:

> After the fire had been put out, the police roped off the street and prevented all sightseers from strolling past the charred ruins.

But that is too lackluster, he tells himself. So mining his lexicographical lode for some sesquipedalian nuggets, he bedizens his humdrum sentence in this fashion:

> After the conflagration had been extinguished, the police obstructed the thoroughfare and forefended all inquisitive spectators from perambulating before the incinerated residue of the pyrogenic catastrophe.

Fortunately, students who persist in their efforts to improve their style eventually outgrow their penchant for such polysyllabic anfractuosities. Perhaps the price that one has to pay for an enriched vocabulary is a period of addiction to "big" words. The ordeal will inflict no permanent damage if the student can "kick the habit" in its early stages.

Purity, Propriety, and Precision of Diction

So far in our discussion of diction we have touched on two qualifications that students must have if they are to improve their style: they must know the grammar of the language, and they must have an adequate vocabulary. Our concern from this point on will be mainly with the *rhetorical* competence that students must have to make wise choices among words. George Campbell pointed up the distinction between grammatical and rhetorical competence in this way: "the grammatical art bears much the same relation to the rhetorical which the art of the mason bears to that of the architect."

The prime quality of prose style is *clarity*—or, to use the sonorous Latinate term, *perspicuity*. Since the object of rhetorical prose is persuasion, it follows that such prose must communicate with those who are to be persuaded. And if rhetorical prose must communicate, it follows that it must, above all, be clear. As one might expect from the person who viewed rhetoric as an activity that always involved an audience, Aristotle held that "language which does not convey a clear meaning fails to perform the very function of language." Lord Macaulay, one of the masters of the limpid prose style, put it this way: "The first rule of all writing—that rule to which every other is subordinate —is that the words used by the writer shall be such as most fully and precisely convey his meaning to the great body of his readers."

Clarity comes from selecting words carefully and arranging them well. Leaving aside the problem of arrangement for now, how can writers learn to select the proper words? They will be helped in making the selection by keeping three criteria in mind—purity, propriety, and precision. While some judgments about whether language is pure, appropriate, and precise can be made only when writers see words in a sentence and when they view them in relation to their subject, purpose, and audience, it is still possible to say something about the purity, propriety, and precision of isolated words.

The discussion of *purity of diction* involves us, willy-nilly, in a consideration of those much-maligned criteria that George Campbell set forth in the eighteenth century to determine "good usage." In order to merit the stamp of approval, words must be, according to Campbell, in *reputable* use, in *national* use, and in *present* use. Despite the relativity of these criteria, there would seem to be little practical difficulty in using at least two of the criteria —national use and present use—to help us determine whether our diction is "pure" and therefore clear. If we are to communicate with a contemporary audience, it stands to reason that we must use current words and idioms— that is, words and idioms, however "old" they may be, that are understood by people today. Likewise, we must use the words that have a national currency. This criterion demands that we avoid dialectical words, technical words, coinages, and foreign words. But this second criterion immediately calls for some qualification. If we view words in relation to an audience, for instance, we see that there are some situations that call for localisms, technical jargon, neologisms, and even foreign words.

When we try the third criterion, reputable use, we run into more difficulty. Campbell proposed this standard for judging reputable locutions: "whatever modes of speech are authorized as good by the writings of a great number, if not the majority, of celebrated authors." But is it conceivable that in a modern pluralistic society we could ever arrive at any consensus about who our "celebrated authors" are? Moreover, if two "celebrated authors" are in conflict on a matter of usage, which author do we follow?—the one who is *more* celebrated? And is it possible for the ordinary educated person to determine in every case, or even in many cases, whether a certain locution is sanctioned by a "great number" or "the majority" of celebrated authors?

These practical difficulties lead many people to rely on some arbiter of usage. The best source of such guidance is a reference work that boldly claims to be an arbiter. Fortunately, there are a few esteemed dictionaries of usage available. These dictionaries offer reliable guidance because the men or women who prepared them had good taste in language to start with and refined their taste with a close study of actual usage.

The most famous of these reference words is H. W. Fowler's *A Dictionary of Modern English Usage,* first published in 1926 but many times reprinted. This book has become a bible of usage for many famous writers and editors. Fowler was himself a lexicographer, having compiled, with the help of his brother Francis George Fowler, *The Concise Oxford Dictionary.* To his sound knowledge of the English language, Fowler added a discriminating taste, and he wrote with such grace and wit that he was himself an exemplar of the "good English" that he advocated. It was Fowler who assured us, once and for all, that it was permissible at times, even advisable, to split an infinitive or to end a sentence with a preposition. And he made household words of some of the headings in his alphabetically arranged dictionary—tags like Battered Ornaments, Cannibalism, Elegant Variation, Out of the Frying Pan, Sturdy Indefensibles.

Students will have to consult *A Dictionary of Modern English Usage* to discover for themselves the value and flavor of this admirable reference work. But here is a taste of Fowler's wit and judgment, taken from his article on the subject we have just been discussing—purity of diction:

> PURISM. Now & then a person may be heard to 'confess', in the pride that apes humility, to being 'a bit of a purist'; but *purist* & *purism* are for the most part missile words, which we all of us fling at anyone who insults us by finding not good enough for him some manner of speech that is good enough for us. It is in that disparaging sense that the words are used in this book; by *purism* is to be understood a needless & irritat-

ing insistence on purity or correctness of speech. Pure English, however, even apart from the great numbers of elements (vocabulary, grammar, idiom, pronunciation, & so forth) that go to make it up, is so relative a term that almost every man is potentially a purist & a sloven at once to persons looking at him from a lower & a higher position in the scale than his own. The words have therefore not been very freely used; that they should be renounced altogether would be too much to expect considering the subject of the book. But readers who find a usage stigmatized as purism have a right to know the stigmatizer's place in the purist scale, if his stigma is not to be valueless. Accordingly, under headings of various matters with which purism is concerned, a few articles are now mentioned illustrating the kind of view that may be expected in other articles of a similar nature: ...

From H. W. Fowler, *Dictionary of Modern English Usage,* Oxford University Press, pp. 474–75. Copyright © 1965 by the Clarendon Press, Oxford University Press. Reprinted by permission.

With the passage of time, Fowler's dictionary was bound to become outdated—at least on some matters of usage. And as the gap between British English and American English widened, American writers began to see that Fowler was not relevant to some of the locutions that had developed in the United States.

To fill the need for an up-to-date dictionary of usage that would pay special attention to American English, the Oxford University Press in 1957 published Margaret Nicholson's *A Dictionary of American-English Usage.* In her Preface, Miss Nicholson announces that her book is an adaptation of, not a replacement for, Fowler's *MEU.* She has retained many of Fowler's long articles, has abridged others, and has added a number of her own entries on modern Americanisms.

In 1965, the Clarendon Press published a revised edition of *A Dictionary of Modern English Usage* by Sir Ernest Gower. Now the Clarendon Press at Oxford has in the works a completely new edition of Fowler's *A Dictionary of Modern English Usage.*

In 1957, Bergen Evans and Cornelia Evans published a completely new dictionary of American usage, *A Dictionary of Contemporary American Usage* (Random House). Writers who are loyal to Fowler will continue to use *due to* only in adjectival structures (*His absence was due to sickness,* but not, *The government failed due to widespread discontent with its policies*). But those writers who have come to trust the painstaking study that the Evanses have made of actual usage will probably be guided by this statement about the present status of *due to:*

> *due to* may be used to qualify a noun, as in *a mistake due to carelessness.* This use of *due to* was listed by Dr. Johnson as "proper, but not usual." Since then it has become a familiar form of speech and no one

thinks of objecting to it. But the words are also used today to qualify a verb, as in *he failed, due to carelessness.* This construction is relatively new and is condemned by some grammarians.

In both cases the words *due to* are being used as *owing to* might be used. It is claimed that *due to* is acceptable in the first case but not in the second, and that only the form *owing to* may be used with a verb. This distinction cannot be defended on theoretical grounds, since *due to* and *owing to* are grammatically alike. The critics usually content themselves with saying that *"due to* cannot be used to qualify a verb." But it is used to qualify a verb, millions of times every day. And it is used in this way in very respectable places. A tablet in front of the Old State House in Philadelphia reads: *Here the Continental Congress sat from the date it convened, May 10, 1775, until the close of the Revolution, except when, in 1776-77, it sat in Baltimore, and in 1777-78, in Lancaster and York, due to the temporary occupation of Philadelphia by the British army.* (See also *owe.*)

From Bergen Evans and Cornelia Evans, *A Dictionary of Contemporary American Usage.* Copyright © 1957. Reprinted by permission of Random House Inc.

Any of the three dictionaries of usage we have discussed would be a valuable addition to your library. If your dictionary does not settle your doubts about the "purity" of a certain expression, a dictionary of usage can be of real help to you. You should be cautioned, however, not to develop a neurotic concern about usage. If American schools had been as much concerned with grammar, logic, and rhetoric, as they have been with "good usage," the quality of student writing today might be better than it generally is.

The principal point to be emphasized about purity of diction is that one's language must be intelligible and acceptable to an audience. There will always be a certain level of diction below which a speaker or writer will never slip, however crude and unlettered the audience may be. There is a large stock of words, a reservoir of "basic English," that will always be intelligible and acceptable to any audience. Deviations from this basic stock of ordinary words will be governed mainly by the nature of the audience addressed.

Propriety or appropriateness is the quality of diction that can least be judged in isolation; it always implies a judgment made in relation to something else. Conceivably, we could look at isolated words and make some judgment about whether they were current or national or reputable, but it is impossible to judge the appropriateness of isolated words.

Diction is appropriate when it suits our subject matter, our purpose, the occasion, and the audience. Unfortunately, there are no handbooks that can help you make judgments about the appropriateness of your diction. Everyone seems to be endowed with a certain minimal sense of appropriateness—a sense absorbed from the experience of living in a society. Instinctively, we "tone up" our everyday language when we shift from a situation in which we are addressing our peers and intimates to a situation in which we are addressing, say, the dean of the college. We make similar adjustments in our diction as our subject matter, occasion, and purpose change.

The refinements of this minimal sense of appropriateness will come naturally, as our experience deepens and our education advances, and will develop in proportion to our native intelligence and our conscious efforts to improve this sense. Just as certain people seem to inherit and develop a superior ability to get along with other people, so some of them develop a keener sense than others for the appropriateness of their language.

Involved in this matter of appropriateness are the connotations of words. When we are concerned with the purity or precision of diction, we are concerned mainly with the denotations of words—with the dictionary meanings of verbal symbols. But in our choice of appropriate diction we must also take into consideration the connotations of words—those emotional and tonal qualities that come to be associated with words. We cannot control the connotations that cluster around a word; we can only be aware of those connotations and take advantage of them. It makes a great difference whether we call a person a "politician" or a "diplomat." Because of the connotations that attend these words, the first word will tend, with most audiences, to dishonor the person, while the second word will tend to honor him or her.

The connotations of words have great rhetorical value—for example, in promoting the emotional appeal of a discourse. Robert H. Thouless has ably demonstrated the emotional value of connotations in his analysis of the diction in two verses by John Keats:

> In *The Eve of St. Agnes*, Keats has written:
>
>> Full on this casement shone the wintry moon,
>> And threw warm gules on Madeline's fair breast.
>
> These are beautiful lines. Let us notice how much of their beauty follows from the proper choice of emotionally colored words and how completely it is lost if these words are replaced by neutral ones. The words with strikingly emotional meanings are *casement, gules, Madeline, fair,* and *breast. Casement* means simply a kind of window with emotional and romantic associations. *Gules* is the heraldic name for red, with the suggestion of romance which accompanies all heraldry. *Madeline* is simply a girl's name, but one calling out favorable emotions absent from a relatively plain and straightforward name. *Fair* simply means, in objective fact, that her skin was white or uncolored—a necessary condition for the colors of the window to show—but also fair implies warm emotional preference for an uncolored skin rather than one which is yellow, purple, black, or any of the other colors which skin might be. *Breast* has also

similar emotional meanings, and the aim of scientific description might have been equally well attained if it had been replaced by such a neutral word as *chest*.

Let us now try the experiment of keeping these two lines in a metrical form, but replacing all the emotionally colored words by neutral ones, while making as few other changes as possible. We may write:

> Full on this window shone the wintry moon
> Making red marks on Jane's uncolored chest.

No one will doubt that all of its poetic value has been knocked out of the passage by these changes. Yet the lines still mean the same in external fact; they still have the same objective meaning. It is only the emotional meaning which has been destroyed.

From Robert H. Thouless, *How To Think Straight,* Hodder and Stoughton Ltd., Copyright 1932 by Robert H. Thouless.

You are probably well aware by now that poets exploit the emotional values of words, but you may not always be alert to the subtle emotional effects exerted by connotation in a prose text. Faced with the evidence of H. L. Mencken's scholarly three-volume study of American English, you would have to concede that he had a profound knowledge of his native language, but perhaps you would not be sufficiently aware of how he manipulated the connotations of words to effect his rhetorical purpose. Consider this example, in which Mencken is seeking to influence our attitude toward a certain kind of teacher:

> Such idiots, despite the rise of "scientific" pedagogy, have not died out in the world. I believe that our schools are full of them, both in pantaloons and in skirts. There are fanatics who love and venerate spelling as a tom-cat loves and venerates catnip. There are grammatomaniacs; school-marms who would rather parse than eat; specialists in an objective case that doesn't exist in English; strange beings, otherwise sane and even intelligent and comely, who suffer under a split infinitive as you or I would suffer under gastro-enteritis. There are geography cranks, able to bound Mesopotamia and Baluchistan. There are zealots for long division, experts in the multiplication table, lunatic worshipers of the binomial theorem. But the system has them in its grip. It combats their natural enthusiasm diligently and mercilessly. It tries to convert them into mere technicians, clumsy machines.

> From H. L. Mencken, "Pedagogy," *A Mencken Chrestomathy,* New York: Alfred A. Knopf, 1949, p. 305. Reprinted by permission of the publisher.

We cannot examine all the techniques that Mencken uses in his satirical writings, but we can note here the subtle way in which he influences our reactions simply by his choice of words. A good deal of the effect of this passage is produced by Mencken's "name-calling." The "names" that Mencken used here are heavily freighted with emotional overtones—*idiots, fanatics, schoolmarms* (one of Mencken's favorite derogatory epithets), *cranks, zealots, lunatic worshipers*. All of these words carry the discrediting connotation of extreme, irrational commitment to a cause—the taint of "enthusiasm" that many critics ascribed to the evangelical sects in eighteenth- and nineteenth-century England. Where Mencken fails to find an emotional epithet to suit his purpose, he invents one—*grammatomaniacs*. Most readers do not know what *gastro-enteritis* means; but they do not have to know—the word just *sounds* awful. Notice how Mencken, in the second sentence of this passage, indicates that he is talking about both men and women teachers—"in pantaloons and in skirts." *Pantaloons* was an especially clever choice. *Pants* would have been the word that most of us would have chosen as the counterpart of *skirts*. But Mencken detected the extra connotative value of the word *pantaloons,* suggesting to a modern audience something archaic, slightly feminine. Note too how Mencken uses a simile in the third sentence to depreciate the object of his satire, comparing devotees of correct spelling to the lowly, back-alley *tom-cat*. One of the deadliest words in the English language is the word *mere*. Mencken uses this word with devastating effectiveness at the end of this passage, where he begins to shift his ground of attack, warning us that these "enthusiastic" pedagogues are now in danger of being turned into dispassionate machines as a result of their exposure to "teachers' college" bunkum. What is more chilling than to be called a "mere technician"?

We see then that the connotations of words must be considered in any judgment about the appropriateness of diction. Sensitivity to the connotations of words cannot be taught; it must be learned. What is even harder for the student to acquire is a fine sense for knowing how far to go in exploiting the emotional force of connotations. Mencken perhaps goes too far in the passage we have just considered. In most of his satirical writings, he relied too heavily on the shock technique that derived from the use of hyperbolic, simplistic diction. Many people are alienated rather than persuaded by his intemperate language. Clever writers can sometimes be too clever for their own good. It does not take a sledge-hammer to drive a nail.

We turn now to the third quality, precision. The word *precision* has its roots in the Latin verb *praecidere,* "to cut off." A precise word is a word shorn of all superfluous and irrelevant notions, a word that signifies neither more nor less than we intend to say. Words may be dubbed "imprecise" (1) when they do not express exactly what we intended to say; (2) when they express the idea but not quite fully (3) when they express the idea but with something more than we intended.

If we write, "I was pleased by his fulsome praise," we may not have said what we intended to say. If we consult the dictionary meaning of *fulsome* ("disgusting or offensive, mainly because of its excessiveness or insincerity"), we will see how wide of the mark we have come. If we write, "I thought it was a tremendous performance," we convey the general idea that we approved of the performance, but we convey no exact notion of the particular way in which this performance was "tremendous." If we write, "As a result of examining the basic flaws in the situation, he came up with a radical solution to the problem," we choose an apt word in *radical* (a solution that gets at the *root* of the problem), but unwittingly we suggest an additional meaning that we did not intend (a solution that is *wild* or *subversive*). A word then will be inexact if it expresses *too little* or *too much* or if it is *too general.*

It is perhaps better to discuss faulty idiom here than under the head of pure diction, because, like the diction cited in the previous paragraph, faulty idiom "misses the mark." The reason why lapses in idiom constitute one of the commonest faults in student writing is that idiom, like connotation, is one of the tricky aspects of language. Dictionaries and handbooks of usage will more often be helpful to you in matters of idiom than in matters of connotation, but your most reliable guide to correct idiom is your own awareness of how your native language is spoken. Those who have not read very much or who have not kept their ears open to the turns of phrase are the ones most likely to violate the idiom of the language.

The "turns of phrase" in the previous sentence suggests an important observation about idiom. No single word, considered in isolation, can be declared unidiomatic. If we say of a certain word, "Native speakers of the language do not use that word," we are saying simply that such a word does not exist in the English language. A word can be classified as unidiomatic only in relation to some other word or words. No one could say of the word *for* that it is unidiomatic; either it is an English word or it is not. *For* can become unidiomatic only when it is used in conjunction with another word, as with the word *unequal,* in the sentence, "The judge proved to be unequal for the task." Then we can point out that native speakers of the language do not use the preposition *for* with *unequal;* they say "unequal *to* the task."

What complicates the difficulty is that grammar is of no help to the student in deciding matters of idiom. There is nothing ungrammatical in the locution "unequal for the task." Idiom is a matter of usage rather than of grammar: native speakers just do not say "unequal for." Neither is logic of much help to the student in regard to idiom. When we say, for instance, "He *looked up* the word in the dictionary," we are, in a sense, violating logic, because when we consult a word in the dictionary, we are more likely to *look down* the page to find the word than to *look up* the page. But "look up a word" is the correct idiom simply because that is the way people say it.

Sometimes the prefixes of words will provide a clue to the idiomatic preposition that goes with those words. So we say, "he *de*parted *from* the scene," "the crowd *e*merged *from* the stadium," "he *is ad*verse *to* the proposal," "they *com*pared it *with* the first version," "the station-wagon *col*lided *with* the motorcycle," "he *ab*stained *from* all alcoholic beverages." But the lexical meaning of these Latin prefixes is not always a clue to the proper preposition, for we also say, "in *con*trast *to*" (as well as "in *con*trast *with*"), "he *de*parted *for* the station," "she *com*pared him *to* an overgrown bear."

Since neither grammar nor logic is a reliable guide to proper idiom, we must develop our own awareness of the peculiar way in which native speakers of the language say certain things. Perhaps the last proficiency we acquire in learning a foreign language is a sense for the idioms of the language. It is a commonplace that the best way to attune our ear to the idioms of a foreign language is to live for a time in a community where that language is spoken exclusively. So in learning the idioms of our own language, we must *listen* to the speech that is all about us, and we must carefully observe the turns of phrase in the contemporary prose we read. Teachers can point out lapses in idiom and can correct the faulty idiom in your writing, but in the absence of any "rules" about idiom, you must develop your own sense for the idiosyncrasies of expression. You must become aware not only of the proper idiom but of the subtle changes of meaning and tone affected by idiom. In an article on the idiomatic preposition, John Nist has illustrated some of the vagaries of idiom:

> Doting grandparents may indulge in loving pride and make *over* a favorite one-toothed blue-eyed darling. But a pouting lover had better make *up with* his sweetheart first; his chances of making *out* are otherwise very slim. An imbiber can conceivably be sleeping *in* while sleeping *out* for the sole sake of sleeping it *off*. How many a long-suffering son-in-law has had a run *in* with her whose kiss is colder than a mackerel because he intended to *run out* on his wife by running *off with* the understanding secretary? One of the favorite maxims of chilly age for flaming youth goes like this: Be careful how you live it *up;* you may never live it *down!* A philosopher chews *upon* a difficult thought; an able prosecutor chews *up* the defense attorney's arguments; a catcher chews *over* the signals with his pitcher; a diner chews *around* the bone; and an angry man chews *out* his offensive neighbor. A cut*up* at the party may cut *out* from the stag line and cut *in* on the belle of the ball. And he who goes all *out* in tracking down the tricky idiomatic preposition will undoubtedly find himself all *in*.

> From John Nist, "The Idiomatic Preposition." By permission. From a December issue of Word Study © 1963 by Merriam-Webster Inc., publisher of the Merriam-Webster dictionaries®.

Many other observations might be made about diction, such as that diction should be "natural," "vigorous," "concrete," "graceful," "harmonious," but these epithets merely represent alternate ways of saying that diction should be *pure, appropriate,* and *precise.* Besides, our judgments about the naturalness, vigor, concreteness, gracefulness, and harmony of diction—or, to use our own terms, the purity, propriety, and precision of diction—can best be made when we view diction in the context of a sentence and in relation to our rhetorical purpose. There will be times, for instance, when it might suit our purpose to make our diction awkward or insipid or abstract or ugly or unmusical.

In summary: Since words are the building-blocks of our sentences, it is obvious that we must have an adequate supply of words to erect the kind of edifice we have planned. When our supply of words is low, we will have to make some effort to add to our stock. Our working vocabulary will naturally expand as our experience and education expand, but we can accelerate the expansion by reading a great deal and by consulting dictionaries and thesauruses. Since we seek to communicate with others, it stands to reason that our diction must first of all be intelligible—intelligible, that is, to a particular audience. It will be mainly the audience that will determine whether we can use learned words or technical terms or foreign words or slang. The audience, the subject matter, the occasion, and our purpose constitute the criteria for judging the appropriateness of our diction. In addition to choosing intelligible and appropriate diction, we must choose diction that is as precise as the situation permits and demands. Dictionaries and handbooks of usage will help solve some of our problems with usage, idiom, and connotation, but we will have to depend mainly on the development of our own sensitivity to these aspects of language.

Composition of the Sentence

Words are symbols of ideas, but they do not begin to "say" anything until we put them together. Sentences, which are syntactical units composed of words, "say" something, partly because of the *lexical content* (the meaning) of the words and partly because of the *grammatical forms* that govern words put together in patterns. Up to this point, we have been speaking mainly about the lexical aspect of words. As we move now to a discussion of the composition of the sentence, we must begin to be concerned with syntax. Eventually, we will be led into a discussion of another aspect of language: how the *rhetorical forms* of sentences, the schemes, constitute a third carrier of meaning.

As we pointed out in the previous section on choice of diction, no one can begin to develop a style until he or she has a basic competence in the grammar of the language. We presume that the student has this basic competence and is thus ready to develop the rhetorical competence he or she needs to compose effective sentences.

Rhetorical competence plays its part in the writing process when there are choices to be made from among two or more grammatical possibilities. Stylistic variations in the syntax of the sentence cannot ignore the grammar of the language. Any changes we make must be grammatical.

As a starting point for our discussion of the rhetoric of the sentence, let us take this minimal sentence:

> The boy loves the girl.

Native speakers of the language recognize this as a pattern of words that make a statement. They know the meanings of the words, and they are familiar with the grammar of the sentence: the function word *the,* the inflectional concordance between the subject and predicate, and the word order. Anyone who wanted to make a statement, in the English language, about a young male of the human species having a certain emotional attitude toward a young female of the human species would be limited in the words that could be chosen to express this idea and even more severely limited in the way these words could be put together to say what was intended. As far as *rhetoric* goes, there is very little we could do with this sentence. We might make some different choice of words—proper nouns to replace the *boy* and *girl* or a synonymous verb to replace *loves*—to make the sentence rhetorically more effective. But there is almost nothing we could do to alter the grammar of the sentence. We cannot say "Boy love girl" or "Loves the boy the girl." No, we must dispose whatever words we choose in the usual pattern for a statement—subject–verb–complement (S–V–C)—and use the proper inflectional forms.

It is when we begin to expand this minimal sentence pattern that rhetoric has a bearing. There are a number of ways in which we can expand this sentence, and within each of the various ways there are often alternatives. Once there are alternatives, there are choices to be made; and once choices are to be made, rhetoric comes into the picture.

One of the ways in which we can expand our minimal sentence is by adding single-word, phrasal, or clausal modifiers to the *head word* in the S or V or C. For instance:

> The tall, handsome boy sincerely loves the short, homely girl.

Can we alter the order of any of these modifiers? Yes, we can make *some* changes—changes that are grammatically and idiomatically possible but not always stylistically advisable. For example, we could make these changes:

> The boy, tall and handsome, loves sincerely the short, homely girl.

Rarely does one see adjectival single-word modifiers placed *after* the head word in the complement: ... *sincerely loves the girl, short and homely.* The following order is also possible in English:

> Tall and handsome, the boy loves the short, homely girl sincerely.

We might choose this order, for instance, if we wanted to emphasize the boy's tallness and handsomeness and the sincerity of his love for the girl.

Another way to expand the minimal sentence is to use prepositional phrases as modifiers of any one or all of the head words in the S–V–C pattern:

> The boy from Montana loves, with uncommon fervor, the girl from Missouri.

Prepositional phrases used as adjectival modifiers are almost always placed *after* the noun or pronoun they modify. There are some instances, however, when the prepositional phrase used adjectivally will be placed *before* the noun that it modifies. For example,

> About this development, he had been given no advance warning.

(Here the phrase *about this development* modifies *warning*.)

Prepositional phrases used adverbially have more freedom of movement than do prepositional phrases used adjectivally. There are three other places where the phrase *with uncommon fervor* could be placed in our sentence:

> With uncommon fervor, the boy from Montana loves the girl from Missouri.
> The boy from Montana loves the girl from Missouri with uncommon fervor.
> The boy from Montana with uncommon fervor loves the girl from Missouri.

There are a number of other ways in which we could expand our minimal sentence:

1. compounding the head words in the S–V–C pattern;
2. juxtaposing appositives to the head words in the S–V–C pattern;
3. using verbals or verbal phrases (participles, gerunds, and infinitives) in the S–V–C pattern;
4. using noun clauses to serve as the S or the C in the S–V–C pattern;
5. using adjective clauses to modify the S or C head word in the S–V–C pattern;
6. using adverb clauses to modify the V in the S–V–C pattern.

We could go on to illstrate these methods of expanding the sentence and to investigate the alternatives (if any) in word order of each of these methods, but we can pursue these matters in the structural and transformational grammars now available. This brief excursion into the syntax of the English sentence serves to give a general idea of what we mean by the rhetoric of the sentence.

When we are presented with a number of syntactical choices, all of them grammatically and idiomatically possible, we will elect the possibility that best serves our purpose at the moment. If, for instance, one of the possibilities allows us to put a word or phrase in an emphatic position and if emphasis of that word or phrase is what we want at that point, then we should take advantage of that possibility. There are times when we want to de-emphasize a word or phrase, and in that case we should elect that possibility which would bury the word or phrase somewhere in the interior of the sentence. We might elect another grammatical possibility on the grounds that this disposition of words improved the rhythm of the sentence. Sometimes we might reject a grammatical possibility because it lends itself to ambiguity. (Such a case would be the "squinting modifier" in the sentence "The bandmaster strutted along *boldly* twirling a baton.") And of course we sometimes elect a grammatical possibility for no other reason than that we want to avoid monotony of sentence structure.

There is another point to be made here about the rhetoric of the sentence. Style, like grammar, is part of the expressive system of a language. Just as grammatical devices, like word order and inflections, are carriers of meaning, so the forms of sentence—the *schemes,* as the Renaissance rhetoricians called them—are expressive of meaning too. For example, let us consider the rhetorical device of parallelism. When we have to express a series of similar or equivalent "meanings," we usually resort to the grammatical device of compounding, and we reinforce the co-ordinate value of the compounded elements with the rhetorical device of parallelism.

We can illustrate how parallelism can be expressive of meaning by looking at a sentence in which it is a pronounced feature:

> He [the president of a large, complex university] is expected to be a friend of the students, a colleague of the faculty, a good fellow with the alumni, a sound administrator with the trustees, a good speaker with the public, an astute bargainer with the foundations and the federal agencies, a politician with the state legislatures, a friend of industry, labor, and agriculture, a persuasive diplomat with donors, a champion of education generally, a supporter of the professions (particularly law and medicine), a spokesman to the press, a scholar in his own right, a public servant at the state and national levels, a devotee of opera and football equally, a decent human being, a good husband and father, an active member of a church.

> From Clark Kerr, *The Uses of the University.* Copyright © 1963. Reprinted by permission of Harvard University Press.

This is an unusually long sentence, but it is so well articulated that it conveys its meaning clearly. The expansion, all of which takes place in the complement part of the sentence, is managed with a series of parallel structures.

The student could learn the whole art of parallelism from a close study of this remarkable sentence. An analysis of the sentence reveals several levels of parallelism and enough variation in the basic pattern to break an otherwise monotonous rhythm. The basic pattern is this:

indefinite article	noun	prepositional phrase
a	friend	of the students
a	colleague	of the faculty

Dr. Kerr varies the rhythm of this basic pattern in several ways: (1) by introducing an adjective before the noun ("a good fellow with the alumni"); (2) by throwing in an adverb ("a champion generally"); (3) by inserting a parenthesis ("particularly law and medicine"); (4) by compounding the objects of the preposition ("a friend of industry, labor, and agriculture") or by compounding the adjectives modifying the object of the preposition ("a public servant at the state and national levels").

The main point that we want to make about this sentence, however, is that the rhetorical form is one of the carriers of meaning. The theme of Dr. Kerr's essay is that the modern university has become so huge and complex that it can no longer be regarded as a *uni*-versity but must be regarded now as a *multi*-versity. The point he is making in the section of the essay from which the above sentence was taken is that the president of such a multiversity must wear many hats, must be many things to many people. In this sentence he is enumerating some of the capacities in which the president is expected to serve, using a series of phrases. This compounding (without conjunctions, for the most part) is one of the expressive devices for indicating the variety of roles the president must play. But because Dr. Kerr also wants to indicate that the president is expected to play each of these roles equally well he uses the device of parallelism, which serves to reinforce the co-ordinate value of these several capacities. Dr. Kerr does not expect his reader to remember all these roles; he wants only to convey the general impression of the heavy burden that the president carries. Incidentally, the *length* of the sentence has a rhetorical function too: the long cataloguing is weighty and exhausting to the reader, as the job is to the president.

In the next sentence but one, Dr. Kerr makes use of antithesis, another rhetorical device, to convey the notion of the contrary qualities that the president must combine in his personality. Here is that sentence of 114 words:

> He should be firm, yet gentle; sensitive to others, insensitive to himself; look to the past and the future, yet be firmly planted in the present; both visionary and sound; affable, yet reflective; know the value of a dollar and realize that ideas cannot be bought; inspiring in his visions yet cautious in what he does; a man of principle yet able to make a deal;

a man with broad perspective who will follow the details conscientiously; a good American but ready to criticize the status quo fearlessly; a seeker of truth where the truth may not hurt too much; a source of public pronouncements when they do not reflect on his own institution.

From Clark Kerr, *The Uses of the University.* Copyright © 1963. Reprinted by permission of Harvard University Press.

The various levels of parallelism and antithesis in this sentence look like this when laid out schematically:

```
He   should be  firm  /  yet gentle
                 sensitive     /        insensitive
                      to others              to himself
     look                      /  yet be firmly planted
         to the past and the future                    in the present
                 both visionary / and sound
                 affable / yet reflective
     know the value of a dollar / and realize the ideas cannot be bought
                 inspiring          /  yet cautious
                     in his visions         in what he does

                 a man           /  yet able
                    of principle         to make a deal
```

(antithesis persists, but parallelism is violated: a noun, *man,* yoked with an adjective, *able; man* modified by prepositional phrase but *able* modified by infinitive phrase)

a man
   with broad perspective
   who will follow the details conscientiously

(again the antithesis is in the words—*broad perspective / details*—rather than in the structure)

a good American / but ready
                      to criticize the status quo fearlessly

(departure from parallelism again)

a seeker
   of truth
      where the truth may not hurt too much

a source
   of public pronouncements
      when they do not reflect on his own institution

As we will make clear when we come to discuss the figures of speech, the rhetoricians commonly associated the various schemes and tropes with the topics of *logos, pathos,* and *ēthos*. Antithesis, for instance, was tied up with the topic of dissimilarity or with the topic of contraries. In the third book of his *Rhetoric*, Aristotle pointed out the value of antithesis in discourse: "Such a form of speech is satisfying, because of the significance of contrasted ideas is easily felt, especially when they are thus put side by side." Whether Dr. Kerr was aware of the theory of antithesis is immaterial. What is important is that by putting his "contrasted ideas" in juxtaposition, he has assisted the communication of his meaning.

Up to this point we have been concentrating on only a few stylistic features —word order, methods of expansion, parallelism, antithesis. It is time now to consider a broader range of stylistic features, not only so that we can get to know what these various features are and how they function but so that we can derive the maximum benefit from the exercises in imitation later on in the chapter and can incorporate some of these features into our own style.

Study of Style

Before you can benefit from a close observation of stylistic features, you must have some technique for analyzing prose style. Because you have spent little or no time analyzing prose style, you may not know what to look for in sentences and paragraphs. You have undoubtedly been impressed by the style of certain prose writers, but you are almost tongue-tied when asked to point out what it is you particularly admire about their style. The best you can do is to characterize various styles with such general, subjective epithets as "clear," "crisp," "urbane," "orotund," "whimsical," "heavy," "flowing," "staccato." The New Criticism gave students a technique and a terminology for analyzing poetry, but most students do not know where to begin if they are asked to analyze the style of a piece of prose.

First, let us set down, in outline form a list of features that you can look for when analyzing prose style.

A. Kind of diction ⟶ *word choice*
1. general or specific
2. abstract or concrete
3. formal or informal
4. Latinate (usually polysyllabic) or Anglo-Saxon (usually monosyllabic)
5. common words or jargon
6. referential (denotative) or emotive (connotative)

B. Length of sentences (measured in number of words)
C. Kinds of sentences
   1. grammatical: simple, compound, complex, compound-complex
   2. rhetorical: loose, periodic, balanced, antithetical (antithesis)
   3. functional: statement, question, command, exclamation
D. Variety of sentence patterns
   1. inversions
   2. sentence openers
   3. method and location of expansion
F. Means of articulating sentences (coherence devices)
G. Use of figures of speech
H. Paragraphing
   1. length (measured in number of words and number of sentences)
   2. kind of movement or development in paragraphs
   3. use of transitional devices

Most of the items in this outline represent features that lend themselves to objective study. Some of the either/or combinations under "Kind of diction" are relative, and opinions about them could vary. But most of the features lend themselves to objective study in the same way that grammatical features (word order, inflections, function words) do. There are a number of incalculable features of style about which we might never be able to secure general agreement, but if we are to develop any system for analyzing prose style we must start with those features that are objectively observable.

Kind of Diction

The kind of diction that a writer habitually uses can tell us a great deal about the quality of the writer's mind and style. We made the point earlier that a writer must be in command of several styles, so that he or she can accommodate his or her manner to various subject matters, occasions, purposes, and audiences. But even within this range of styles, there will be a certain persistent level of style associated with that author. Dr. Johnson and Oliver Goldsmith displayed their versatility by trying their hands at several literary genres, but whether they were writing poems or plays or novels or familiar essays or critical essays, they maintained a certain note that identified the style as their own and no one else's. That peculiar note was achieved partly by the kind of diction they used: Johnson's philosophical, polysyllabic, Latinate diction; Goldsmith's concrete, familiar, colloquial diction. The "weight" of a person's style can be measured partly by the syllabic composition of the words. The "tone" of a person's style can be measured partly by the texture of the words—their phonic values, their relative abstractness or concreteness, their level of usage. Judgments about the formality or informality of a person's style are made largely on the basis of the level of diction used.

Length of Sentences

The average length of sentences also can lead to some valid generalizations about a person's style. Modern prose style is characterized by sentences that are generally shorter than those of earlier centuries. (The narrow columns into which journalistic prose is fitted undoubtedly had some influence on the shortening of the sentence.) But we still discover remarkable variations in sentence-length in modern writers. We can arrive at a tenable generalization about a writer's characteristic sentence-length by counting the words in, say, five hundred consecutive sentences and then dividing the total number of words by the number of sentences. Having determined this average sentence-length, we would have to pursue the more important consideration: what relation does this characteristic sentence-length have to the rhetorical situation?

Kinds of Sentences

Some very interesting observations can be made about a person's style and habits of thought by studying the kinds of sentences used and the proportions in which the various kinds are used. W. K. Wimsatt, for instance, in his valuable study *The Prose Style of Samuel Johnson,* saw in Dr. Johnson's persistent use of parallel and antithetical clauses a reflection of the bent of his mind: "Johnson's prose style is a formal exaggeration—in places a caricature—of a certain pair of complementary drives, the drive to assimilate ideas, and the drive to distinguish them—to collect and to separate." And so Dr. Johnson disposed his collection of ideas in parallel structures; he reinforced the distinctions in ideas by juxtaposing them in antithetical structures.

The history of the prose style of most Western languages reveals a gradual evolution from a paratactic syntax—stringing together a series of co-ordinate structures without conjunctions—to the most sophisticated of sentence patterns, subordination. In Anglo-Saxon, for instance—the earliest extant record of the English language—we note the lack of the relative pronoun and the subordinating conjunction, two of the grammatical devices by which Modern English renders clauses dependent. When we catalogue the kinds of grammatical sentences found in modern professional prose, we find surprisingly few compound sentences. Modern writers expand their sentences more by subordination and apposition than by compounding. Observation of the grammatical kinds of sentences can tell us a great deal about someone's prose style and can point up significant deficiencies in our own prose style.

Variety of Sentence Patterns

A study of variety in sentence patterns also has some valuable lessons to teach us about style. For one thing, such a study can dispel many of the myths about prose style. It is true that professional writers command a greater variety of lexical and syntactical resources than unpracticed writers do, but they do not make a fetish of variety for its own sake. Professor Francis Christensen made a study, for instance, of sentence-openers in the first 200 sentences of some narrative and expository works written by modern American writers. Here are the results of his findings in the expository pieces:

Expository	Sentence Openers	Adverbial	Verbal	Inverted	Co-ord. Conj.
Carson, *Sea Around Us*	79	74	4	1	29
M. Chute, *Shakespeare of London*	64	63	0	1	4
De Voto, *Easy Chair*	51	50	1	0	16
Edman, *Arts and the Man*	37	33	2	2	14
Highet, *Art of Teaching*	47	45	2	0	22
Mencken, *Vintage Mencken*	72	67	5	0	9
Lloyd & Warfel, *American English*	77	72	4	1	4
Trilling, *Liberal Imagination* (pp. 216-34)	60	57	3	0	34
Van Doren, *Shakespeare: Four Tragedies*	32	32	0	0	29
Wilson, *Literary Chronicle: 1920-1950* (pp. 9-29, 422-27)	56	51	3	2	14
TOTAL	575	544	24	7	175
PERCENTAGE	28.75	27.20	1.15	0.40	8.75

From Francis Christensen, "Notes Toward a New Rhetoric: I. Sentence Openers," *College English,* 25 (October 1963): 9. Copyright 1963 by the National Council of Teachers of English. Reprinted with permission.

The numbers in the first column indicate the number of sentences, among the 200 studied in each piece, that had sentence openers (words, phrases, or clauses which are not part of the subject cluster); the numbers under the next four columns mark the various kinds of sentence openers. Rachel Carson had the highest percentage of sentence openers (39.5 percent); Mark Van Doren had the lowest percentage (16 percent). But the combined percentages show that almost three-quarters of the sentences written by these authors started out with the subject cluster rather than the sentence openers and that almost 95 percent of the 575 sentence openers were of the adverbial type.

These figures would seem to indicate that some of our esteemed modern writers do not, contrary to common opinion and to the advice given in some writing texts, strive for a notable variety in the ways they begin their sentences. And the figures also invalidate the prescription about not beginning a sentence with a co-ordinating conjunction. Descriptive studies of other aspects of prose as it is actually written would probably destroy some additional illusions about how professional writers create their effects.

Sentence Euphony

Prose rhythm is one of the most difficult aspects of style to analyze. Perhaps the closest thing we have to the elaborate prosody that the Greeks and Romans devised for their quantitative languages is the system for scanning the English sentence that George Saintsbury worked out in his *A History of English Prose Rhythm* (Edinburgh, 1912). The euphony and rhythm of sentences undoubtedly play a part in the communicative and persuasive process—especially in producing emotional effects—but students would be ill advised to spend a great deal of time learning a system for scanning prose sentences. Euphony and rhythm are largely a matter for the ear, and students would do just as well to read their prose aloud to catch awkward rhythms, clashing vowel and consonant combinations (as in that five-word phrase), and distracting jingles. If, for instance, the student who wrote the following sentence had read it aloud, he or she might have caught the distracting repetition of the *ect* sound: "I will show how the testimony affected some people indirectly connected with the selection of the jurors." It is probably more important to apply this test when one is preparing a discourse for oral delivery, but most good writers apply this test also to prose that they know will be read silently. The sentence that is difficult to enunciate is often a grammatically or rhetorically defective sentence.

But if writers are not confident about relying on their ears for testing the rhythm of their sentences, they can resort to the fairly simple method of marking the stresses in series of words. With a little more ingenuity, they might be able to group the stressed and unstressed syllables into feet. In scanning poetry, we can get by with knowing the five most common feet in classical prosody: iambic ($\smile$ —), trochaic (— $\smile$), anapaestic ($\smile$ $\smile$ —), dactylic

$(- \smile \smile)$, and spondaic $(- -)$. To scan prose, however, we need a great many more combinations. In her book, *The Anatomy of Prose,* Marjorie Boulton defines 23 different combinations, which constitute, she says, "all the possible feet used in English prose." (Students who want to pursue these technicalities can consult pp. 55–57 of her book.) To illustrate this system of scansion, here is the way that Miss Boulton scanned the first nine verses of Psalm 90 in the Authorized Version of the Bible:

Lord, thou/ has been/ our dwelling place/ in all generations./

Before/ the mountains/ were brought forth,/ or ever/ thou hadst formed/ the earth/ and the world,/ even/ from everlasting/ to everlasting,/ thou art God./

Thou turnest man/ to destruction;/ and sayest,/ Return,/ ye children/ of men./

For a thousand/ years in/ thy sight/ are but/ as yesterday/ when it is past,/ and as a watch/ in the night./

Thou carriest/ them away/ as with a flood;/ they are as a sleep:/ in the morning/ they are like grass/ which groweth up./

In the morning/ it flourisheth,/ and groweth up;/ in the evening/ it is cut down,/ and withereth./

For we are consumed/ by thine anger,/ and by thy wrath/ are we troubled./

Thou hast set/ our iniquities/ before thee,/ our secret sins/ in the light/ of thy countenance./

For all/ our days/ are passed/ away/ in thy wrath;/ we spend/ our years/ as a tale/ that is told./

Miss Boulton goes on to say about this passage: "My stresses will not, I think, be disputed much, though even on this point some ears might object; many readers will probably disagree with the division into feet at some point. However, we can now see the contrast of stressed, monosyllabic endings and lighter endings, with the finality of the stress at the end on a heavy monosyllable. We see how the important words are also placed where, with their own strong stresses, they are surrounded by weak stresses to make them stronger by contrast. We may also notice, if we are beginners, that the four-syllable and five-syllable feet are needed to describe prose accurately."

Articulation of Sentences

An investigation of the ways in which writers articulate their sentences can be one of the most fruitful exercises for students who want to improve the quality of their own prose. Coherence is a troublesome problem for most students. They usually develop a sense for unity and emphasis long before they master coherence. Cultivating the habit of thinking in an orderly, logical fashion is the best way to insure that they will express their thoughts coherently. But practiced writers use a number of linguistic devices to assist the coherent display of their thoughts. Let us see how an accomplished writer like Matthew Arnold makes his prose "hang together." Some of the verbal devices he uses to promote coherence are italicized; others will be pointed out in the commentary afterward.

> The critical power is of lower rank than the creative. *True;* but in assenting to *this proposition, one or two things* are to be kept in mind. It is undeniable that the exercise of a *creative* power, that a free *creative* activity, is the highest function of man; *it* is *so* by man's finding in it his true happiness. *But* it is undeniable, *also,* that men may have the sense of exercising *this free creative activity* in *other* ways than in producing great works of literature or art; if it were not *so,* all but a very few men would be shut out from the *true happiness* of all men. *They may have it* in well-doing, *they may have it* in learning, *they may have it* even in criticising. *This* is *one thing* to be kept in mind. *Another* is that the exercise of the *creative* power in the production of *great works of literature or art,* however high *this* exercise of *it* may rank, is not at all epochs and under all conditions possible; *and* that *therefore* labour may be vainly spent in attempting *it, which* might with more fruit be used in preparing for *it,* in rendering *it* possible. *This creative power* works with elements, with materials; what if *it* has not *those materials,* those *elements,* ready for *its* use? *In that case, it* must surely wait till *they* are ready.
>
> From Matthew Arnold, "The Function of Criticism at the Present Time,"
> *Essays in Criticism,* First Series, 1865.

Most coherence devices (pronouns, demonstrative adjectives, repeated words and phrases, and some of the conjunctions) point backwards to what has just been said, thus connecting what has been said with what is about to be said. One of the commonest devices in Matthew Arnold's prose—so common, in fact, that it has become a distinctive mark of his style—is the frequent repetition of key words and phrases. Arnold was a great phrase-maker, and once he had coined a phrase that carried the theme of an essay, he repeated that phrase time and time again in the essay. So conspicuous was this mannerism in his prose that one is inclined to believe that the cardinal principle of his expository technique was the famous pedagogical maxim, "Repetition is the mother of studies." The most obtrusive repetition in this selection is the word *creative*—the key word of this paragraph and one of the two key words in the entire essay. The repetition then of substantive words is one of the linguistic means of stitching our sentences together.

Arnold also frequently uses demonstrative pronouns and demonstrative adjectives (*this, that; these, those*) and personal pronouns. The original meaning of the word *demonstrate* is "to show, to point." Demonstrative pronouns and adjectives usually point backwards, tying what follows to what has gone before. By their very nature, all pronouns (except indefinite pronouns, like *anyone* and *someone*) point to a referent. Because of the close relationship between the pronoun and its referent, it is extremely important to be sure the referent is clear. When it is vague or, worse yet, when the referent is not there at all, the coherence of our writing is bound to suffer.

Good writers also make liberal use of conjunctions and conjunctive adverbs for stitching sentences together. The chief grammatical function of co-ordinating conjunctions is to splice together words, phrases, and clauses. But when co-ordinating conjunctions are placed at the beginning of the sentence (and Professor Christensen's chart reveals how often modern writers use sentence-openers), these conjunctions assume the rhetorical function of providing a logical bridge between sentences. Conjunctive adverbs—words like *however, nevertheless, moreover, also, indeed, therefore*—are even more common devices for aiding coherence. One can point up the logical relationship between sentences simply by inserting the appropriate conjunctive word.

We will note only two additional devices that Arnold uses to connect his sentences. Fragmentary sentences can sometimes strengthen coherence. We have an instance of this in the second sentence of Arnold's paragraph. The single word *True* constitutes an elliptical sentence. Filled out, the ellipsis would read something like this: "That proposition is true." The single word here conveys a meaning only because of its juxtaposition to the previous sentence; since it has to look backward to the previous sentence in order to become meaningful, it is "tied" to that sentence. This same principle of "dependent meaning" prevails in conversation, where we often talk in fragmentary sentences ("Where are you going tonight?" "The movies." "With whom?" "Charlotte.").

Another device that Arnold uses in this paragraph is parallelism, which is reinforced by the figure of anaphora (repetition of identical words at the beginning of successive phrases). Three independent clauses are set **down,** one after the other ("They may have it in well-doing, they may have it in learning, they may have it even in criticising"). Although there are no conjunctions (asyndeton) to tie the clauses together grammatically, the clauses are connected by parallel structure and identical words. In addition to the functions that we noted in the analysis of Clark Kerr's two sentences, parallelism can also be used for coherence.

The passage quoted from Matthew Arnold exemplifies most of the verbal devices that good writers use to articulate their sentences. Good writers use such devices so unobtrusively that the sutures hardly show. A study of how an author uses them will help to account for the clarity of one person's prose and the fuzziness of another's.

Figures of Speech

Since we are going to devote a long section of this chapter to a discussion of figures of speech, this is not the place to discuss them in detail. Suffice it to say here that they constitute one of the most revealing features of a person's prose style. If they are apt and fresh, they can contribute greatly to the clarity, liveliness, and interest of one's style. But they must not be cultivated for their own sake. The excessive, strained use of figures proved to be detrimental to the "gracefulness" for which the Euphuistic writers of the sixteenth century were striving in their prose. On the other hand, the absence or scarcity of figurative language can have a deadening effect on style. Although it is not true that Jonathan Swift excluded all figurative language from his prose, it is true that he used figurative language sparingly. That rarity of metaphorical language may have been what Dr. Johnson had in mind when he made his famous comment on Swift's style: "For purposes merely didactic, when something is to be told that was not known before, [his style] is in the highest degree proper, but against that inattention by which known truths are suffered to lie neglected, it makes no provision; it instructs, but does not persuade."

Paragraphing

There is a style of paragraphing as well as a style of sentence structure. Paragraphing, like punctuation, is a feature only of the written language. As a matter of fact, we can regard paragraphing as a typographical device for punctuating units of thought larger than the thought conveyed by a single sentence. We are so accustomed to seeing, in the print we read, indentations of segments of thought that we come to take paragraphing as much for granted as we do the left-to-right movement of printed words.

And because the indentations are always there on the printed page, we do not realize how much the marking off of thought-units facilitates our reading. Perhaps the best way to show how typographical devices contribute to the readability of printed prose is to reproduce a passage of prose with no punctuation, capitalization, or paragraphing:

> it seems to me that it was far from right for the professor of english in yale the professor of english literature in columbia and wilkie collins to deliver opinions on cooper's literature without having read some of it it would have been much more decorous to keep silent and let persons talk who have read cooper cooper's art has some defects in one place in deerslayer and in the restricted space of two thirds of a page cooper has scored 114 offenses against literary art out of a possible 115 it breaks the record there are nineteen rules governing literary art in the domain of romantic fiction some say twenty two in deerslayer cooper violated eighteen of them these eighteen require that a tale shall accomplish something and arrive somewhere but the deerslayer tale accomplishes nothing and arrives in the air they require that the episodes of a tale shall be necessary parts of the tale and shall help to develop it but as the deerslayer tale is not a tale and accomplishes nothing and arrives nowhere the episodes have no rightful place in the work since there was nothing for them to develop they require that the personages in a tale shall be alive except in the case of corpses and that always the reader shall be able to tell the corpses from the others but this detail has often been overlooked in the deerslayer tale

If we have difficulty making sense out of this river of words, we should be grateful to those printers and grammarians who invented typographical devices to mark off meaningful segments of thought. After trying out various combinations, we might eventually be able to make sense of this passage, especially in those sections where there are enough grammatical signals to tell us what words are related. We will probably make faster progress in deciphering the passage if we read it aloud, because the voice will add another grammatical element, intonation, which is the vocal equivalent of the graphic marks of punctuation. But there will be spots in this passage that will remain ambiguous, because grammar will allow in those places two or more combinations of words, each of which would make sense.

Now let us reproduce the passage as Mark Twain wrote it, restoring his punctuation, capitalization, and paragraphing:

> It seems to me that it was far from right for the Professor of English in Yale, the Professor of English Literature in Columbia, and Wilkie Collins to deliver opinions on Cooper's literature without having read

some of it. It would have been much more decorous to keep silent and let persons talk who have read Cooper.

Cooper's art has some defects. In one place in *Deerslayer,* and in the restricted space of two-thirds of a page, Cooper has scored 114 offenses against literary art out of a possible 115. It breaks the record.

There are nineteen rules governing literary art in the domain of romantic fiction—some say twenty-two. In *Deerslayer* Cooper violated eighteen of them. These eighteen require:

1. That a tale shall accomplish something and arrive somewhere. But the *Deerslayer* tale accomplishes nothing and arrives in the air.

2. They require that the episodes of a tale shall be necessary parts of the tale and shall help to develop it. But as the *Deerslayer* tale is not a tale, and accomplishes nothing and arrives nowhere, the episodes have no rightful place in the work, since there was nothing for them to develop.

3. They require that the personages in a tale shall be alive, except in the case of corpses, and that always the reader shall be able to tell the corpses from the others. But this detail has often been overlooked in the *Deerslayer* tale.... [Twain goes on to designate, in a series of short, numbered paragraphs, the remaining fifteen "rules."]

From Mark Twain, "Fenimore Cooper's Literary Offenses," 1895.

The typographical device that contributes most, of course, to clarifying the syntax of a succession of words is the device for marking off sentences— an initial capital letter and end-punctuation (period, question mark, exclamation point). We underestimate, perhaps, how much of a contribution to clarity is made by other typographical devices—such simple things as commas, capital letters, italics, hyphens, quotation marks. Nor should we overlook the contribution that indentation of paragraphs makes to ease of reading. The value of paragraphing is evident in the Mark Twain passage. Indentation marks the shifts in the development of thought and indicates the relationship of the parts. Simply by setting off the violated rules in separate paragraphs and further marking them with numbers, Mark Twain makes it clear that he is specifying a series of parts.

A study of the density of an author's paragraph tells us a great deal about the "weight" of his or her style. Many considerations, of course, dictate whether paragraphs will be long or short—the subject matter, the occasion, the audience. Narrative, for instance, especially when it is dealing with rapid action, often moves along in a series of short paragraphs. In dialogue, too, each shift of speaker is indicated by a new paragraph. For purposes of transition or emphasis, an author will insert a one- or two-sentence paragraph. And if we are writing copy for the narrow columns of a newspaper, we will rather arbitrarily chop up our prose into very short paragraphs.

But when all allowances have been made for such conventions and for various rhetorical situations, it remains true that professional writers generally write longer paragraphs than unpracticed writers do. Many of the one- and two-sentence paragraphs that students write have no rhetorical justification whatever. Such short paragraphs simply reveal that the students have not developed their thoughts adequately. They have nothing more to say, or think they have nothing more to say, on the idea presented in that paragraph. Perhaps by resorting to the topics to find something to say, students will be able to put some meat on the bare bones of their paragraphs.

A Student Report on a Study of Style

We have devoted several pages to a discussion of the objectively observable features of style because it is by this kind of close analysis that one learns why the style of an author produces its effects and learns also how to go about improving one's own style. To illustrate the profit to be derived from such a close study, we will present the results of a student project.*

Two sections of an Honors Freshman class were set the task of making a comparative analysis of the length of sentences and paragraphs in a specified number of paragraphs in F. L. Lucas's essay "What Is Style?" and in all the paragraphs of one of their expository themes. For the purposes of this study, a sentence was defined as "a group of words beginning with a capital letter and ending with some mark of end-punctuation." The students were told that in choosing eight paragraphs from the Lucas essay they should avoid short transitional paragraphs and any paragraphs containing two or more sentences of quoted material. The students were presented with a mimeographed sheet containing the following items to be filled in:

EVALUATION	PROFESSIONAL	STUDENT
A. Total number of words in the piece studied	————	————
B. Total number of sentences in the piece studied	————	————
C. Longest sentence (in no. of words)	————	————
D. Shortest sentence (in no. of words)	————	————
E. Average sentence (in no. of words)	————	————
F. Number of sentences that contain more than 10 words *over* the average sentence	————	————
G. Percentage of sentences that contain more than 10 words over the average	————	————

* For an account of similar projects devised for an Advanced Composition course at the University of Nebraska, see Margaret E. Ashida and Leslie T. Whipp, "A Slide-Rule Composition Course," *College English*, XXV (October, 1963), 18-22.

EVALUATION	PROFESSIONAL	STUDENT
H. Number of sentences that contain 5 words or more *below* the average	————	————
I. Percentage of sentences that contain 5 words or more below the average	————	————
J. Paragraph length		
longest paragraph (in no. of sentences)	————	————
shortest paragraph (in no. of sentences)	————	————
average paragraph (in no. of sentences)	————	————

The numbers that the students entered in the first column differed according to the paragraphs they chose to study, but we can give some mean figures for four of the items in the list:

1. The average length of Lucas's sentences was 20.8 words.
2. About 17 percent of Lucas's sentences were ten words or more over the average.
3. About 40 percent of Lucas's sentences were five words or more below the average.
4. Lucas averaged 7.6 sentences per paragraph—a fairly well-developed paragraph.

Most of the students found that their average sentence matched the length of Lucas's average sentence. Many of the students were surprised to learn, however, that they had a higher percentage of above-average sentences and a strikingly lower percentage of below-average sentences. Perhaps the most dramatic difference that the students noted was in paragraph development. At least half of the students found that they were averaging between three and four sentences in their paragraphs.

In addition to filling out the mimeographed sheet, the students submitted an essay in which they commented on what they had learned about style from this exercise. Excerpts from their essays are reproduced below.

First of all, here are some of the students' comments about sentence length and sentence variety:

> I found that the percentage of sentences in Lucas's essay that contained more than ten words over the average sentence was 17%, while mine was a mere 3%. But the percentage of his sentences that contained five words or more below the average was 39% compared to my 16%. I see now that I must strive for greater variety of sentence structure and length in my themes in order for the pieces to be more effective.

. . . . .

My average sentence length is very close to that of Mr. Lucas. I think this is misleading, however, since in my high school newspaper work I acquired the habit of gathering more than one thought in a single sentence. My sentence length is good, but my sentence content could be improved. Another factor that was evident is that I tend to use fewer short sentences than professional writers do. I think I can explain this lack of short sentences by considering the subject matter of the themes I write. I have noticed that in the past I would use longer, more involved (and less clear) sentences to write about things I didn't feel completely at ease in writing about. I use short sentences to present ideas that are very lucid to me.

. . . . .

One thing I found is that good prose doesn't necessarily imply long verbose sentences and polysyllabic words.

. . . . .

There is not quite enough variety in length or pattern in my sentences. Even my longer sentences tend to be of the compound variety rather than the complex or compound-complex type.

Now for some excerpts from students' comments on paragraphing:

This paragraph analysis revealed some drastic differences in style. My paragraphs, surprisingly, are considerably longer than Lucas's. The average number of sentences per paragraph in my work is twelve, whereas Mr. Lucas's average is about eight. My longest paragraph has sixteen sentences, twice the professional's average. This could indicate poor paragraph planning and division on my part. My extended paragraphs seem much like run-on sentences and probably have a tiring effect on my reader.

. . . . .

My longest paragraph is 17 sentences, almost 10 sentences over my average paragraph length; Lucas's longest paragraph has 10 sentences, less than 3 sentences over his average paragraph length. Also, in this long paragraph the average length of sentences is 14 words, which is 7 words per sentence below the average for the whole theme. And in this same paragraph of mine there are 12 out of the total 17 sentences which contain 5 words or more below the average sentence. The reason for this paragraph being strikingly different from my average paragraph is that I used a different style of writing in this paragraph. I tried to make an emotional appeal to back up my arguments, using short questions and terse statements. In trying to give the effect of an impassioned speech, I departed from my usual prose style; thus this paragraph is not representative of my usual style of paragraphing.

. . . . .

In Lucas's piece there is an average of 126 words per paragraph, while I have an average of only 70 words per paragraph. I probably should use more words to develop my ideas, not for the sake of wordiness but for the sake of being more fully understood. I leave out examples and explanations which may be vital to the clarity of the theme.

．　．　．　．　．

In the paragraphs I chose to study, Mr. Lucas used a total of fifty-six sentences. I used a total of fifty-four sentences in my theme. This averages to approximately seven sentences per paragraph in both essays. However, this similarity is slightly invalid. In choosing the Lucas paragraphs, I was careful to choose only those which were of an "average" length; I purposely skipped those paragraphs which seemed short. One of the paragraphs in my theme contained only three sentences, but I had to count it. This tended to lower my average number of sentences per paragraph, whereas Mr. Lucas's average was slightly inflated because only "average" paragraphs were studied.

．　．　．　．　．

Another thing that I realized when doing this stylistic study is that in the professional writers' work the paragraphs fit together like the pieces in a jigsaw puzzle. Each paragraph develops a separate thought but becomes an integral part of the whole. I have trouble tying my ideas together. Although all my ideas relate to the theme topic, often I find that they do not follow in a logical pattern.

In addition to commenting on sentences and paragraphs, several students commented on other features of style that they had noted in doing this study. Here are some excerpts from those comments:

I see now that enlarging my vocabulary is necessary to improve my style. I don't mean necessarily that I must start using bigger words; I mean rather that I must learn when certain words should be used. I must learn to use big words only when they fall naturally into place and when they can be fully understood by the intended audience. Professional writers do not always use big words, but their knowledge of words enables them to use the proper word at the proper time.

．　．　．　．　．

One characteristic of Lucas's style which I don't like and which I think I avoided in my writing is the excessive use of parentheses and dashes. I certainly feel that a parenthesis or a dash is appropriate at times, and, in fact, I used a dash four times in my writing. But I believe that Mr. Lucas overworked parentheses and dashes. I feel that the reader's train of thought is broken when the writing contains many dashes or parentheses.

．　．　．　．　．

Lucas brings his writing to life by the use of figures of speech. When he says, "Men are often taken, like rabbits, by the ears," his writing becomes vivid and distinctive. Another of Mr. Lucas's figures of speech, "There are blustering signatures that swish across the page like cornstalks bowed before a tempest," shows that he avoids the trite, overworked figures. He searches for new and fresh expressions. I noticed that in my piece of writing there wasn't a single simile, metaphor, or personification.

. . . . .

Although Lucas's longest sentence is twice as long as my longest sentence, my sentence is harder to follow. This difference in readability can be attributed partly to the number of syllables. Although syllable-count was not included on the study sheet, it has a great bearing on the clarity of one's prose. The majority of words in Lucas's sentences are monosyllabic. Because of the monosyllabic diction, the interest of the reader is not bogged down by heavy words.

. . . . .

This study also confirmed something I was already suspicious of—I don't write really long sentences. This, I believe, is due to the fact that I am afraid of the punctuation a long sentence may require. It is much simpler to write two short sentences correctly than to write one long sentence correctly. Since we were graded in high school more on correctness than on style, I formed the habit of writing two shorter sentences rather than one long one. I guess I'll have to start worrying about style as well as correctness if I want to become a good writer.

. . . . .

I noticed how well the parts of Mr. Lucas's essay were proportioned and how mine seemed rather top-heavy. A closer look showed me that I overdevelop the beginnings of my essays, often leaving the middle thinly developed.

. . . . .

I have noticed that sometimes my sentences sound artificial and stiff because I place adverb clauses and verbal phrases where they do not fit naturally. . . . Good professional writers have mastered the art of appropriateness. I have found that most professional writers' long sentences are surprisingly easy to follow, while my long sentences are frequently too involved to be understood.

. . . . .

Here are a few excerpts from the students' comments on the general value of a close study like this. What is particularly notable is that the students retained their sense of perspective. They saw no merit in cultivating any feature of style for its own sake; a stylistic device became a virtue only when it contributed to the effectiveness of the passage in which it occurred:

> I know that this study of sentence and paragraph length has been beneficial to me, but I would like to consider the choice and arrangement of words used by professional authors. I may be wrong, but to me an author's word choice and word arrangement is more important than the length of his sentences and paragraphs.

> . . . . .

> I believe, however, that this comparison between my prose and Lucas's reveals simply a difference in style and that no definite decisions can be made about what I should do with my prose style. In order to make such a decision, I would have to compare my vocabulary and sentence structure with Mr. Lucas's when both of us were writing on the same subject-matter.

> . . . . .

> In general, style depends on a person's individuality and his basic knowledge of English grammar. It doesn't depend on how long the sentences are or how short they are. Mr. Lucas has successfully combined English grammar with his own personal touch to produce a good piece of prose. My own style suffers from the fact that my knowledge of English grammar has not yet developed enough to aid my individuality of expression.

> . . . . .

> Although this study cannot definitely determine whether my style is good or bad (since there is no entirely good or bad style), it can show the major similarities and differences between my style and a typical modern style.

> . . . . .

> The style of a professional—in this case, F. L. Lucas—shouldn't be slavishly copied, for it is only by evolving his own style that a student gains enough command over the language to become an effective writer.

> . . . . .

Here are three additional charts for the tabulation of other stylistic features. Students may devise their own charts for the quantitative study of objectively observable stylistic features not included here.

Stylistic Study—II
(Grammatical Types of Sentence)

A *simple* sentence is a sentence beginning with a capital letter, containing one independent clause, and ending with terminal punctuation.

A *compound* sentence is a sentence beginning with a capital letter, containing two or more independent clauses, and ending with terminal punctuation.

A *complex* sentence is a sentence beginning with a capital letter, containing one independent clause and one or more dependent clauses, and ending with terminal punctuation.

A *compound-complex* sentence is a sentence beginning with a capital letter, containing two or more independent clauses and one or more dependent clauses, and ending with terminal punctuation.

Title of professional essay _____

Author _____

	PROFESSIONAL	STUDENT
A. Total number of sentences in essay	———	———
B. Total number of simple sentences	———	———
C. Percentage of simple sentences	———	———
D. Total number of compound sentences	———	———
E. Percentage of compound sentences	———	———
F. Total number of complex sentences	———	———
G. Percentage of complex sentences	———	———
H. Total number of compound-complex sentences	———	———
I. Percentage of compound-complex sentences	———	———

Sequence of Grammatical Types

Set down the sequence of grammatical types in paragraphs ——— and ———, using these abbreviations: S, Cp, Cx, Cp-Cx.

In ——— paragraph: _____

In ——— paragraph: _____

Stylistic Study—III

(Sentence Openers)

Title of professional essay _____

Author _____

For this study, use only *declarative* sentences. No interrogative or imperative sentences.

Total number of declarative sentences: Professional_____   Student_____

SENTENCES BEGINNING WITH	PROFESSIONAL		STUDENT	
	No.	%	No.	%
A. Subject (e.g., *John* broke the window. *The high cost* of living will offset . . .)	—	—	—	—
B. Expletive (e.g., *It* is plain that . . . *There* are ten Indians. Exclamations: *Alas, Oh*)	—	—	—	—
C. Coordinating conjunction (e.g., *and, but, or, nor, for, yet, so*)	—	—	—	—
D. Adverb word (e.g., *first, thus, moreover, nevertheless, namely*)	—	—	—	—
E. Conjunctive phrase (e.g., *on the other hand, as a consequence*)	—	—	—	—
F. Prepositional phrase (e.g., *after the game, in the morning*)	—	—	—	—
G. Verbal phrase (e.g., participial, gerundive, or infinitive phrase)	—	—	—	—
H. Adjective phrase (e.g., *Tired but happy*, we . . .)	—	—	—	—
I. Absolute phrase (e.g., *The ship having arrived safely*, we . . .)	—	—	—	—
J. Adverb clause (e.g., *When the ship arrived safely*, we . . .)	—	—	—	—
K. Front-Shift (e.g., inverted word order: The expense we could not bear. Gone was the wind. Happy were they to be alive.)	—	—	—	—

Stylistic Study—IV

(Diction)

Title of professional essay_____
Author_____

For this investigation, confine yourself to this range of paragraphs: paragraph ___ through ___. For the investigation of your own prose, confine yourself to a comparable number of paragraphs.

In A, B, and C, below, count only *substantive words*—nouns, pronouns, verbs, verbals, adjectives, and adverbs.

	PROFESSIONAL	STUDENT
A. Total number of substantive words in the passage	——	——
B. Total number of monosyllabic substantive words	——	——
C. Percentage of monosyllabic substantive words	——	——
D. Total number of nouns and pronouns in the passage	——	——
E. Total number of *concrete* nouns and pronouns	——	——
F. Percentage of concrete nouns and pronouns	——	——
G. Total number of *finite verbs* in all dependent and independent clauses in the passage	——	——
H. What percentage does G represent of A?	——	——
I. Total number of linking verbs	——	——
J. Percentage of linking verbs (using A)	——	——
K. Total number of active verbs (do not count linking verbs)	——	——
L. Percentage of active verbs (using A)	——	——
M. Total number of passive verbs (do not count linking verbs)	——	——
N. Percentage of passive verbs (using A)	——	——
O. Total number of adjectives in the passage (do not count participles or articles)	——	——
P. Average number of adjectives per sentence (divide by the total number of sentences in the passage)	——	——

So much for this discussion of what to look for when you analyze prose style. You will be further aided in developing your own style and in developing a technique for analyzing style by practicing some of the imitation exercises recommended in a later section of this chapter. You are also urged to read the stylistic analyses of Addison's *Spectator* essay and of President Kennedy's Inaugural Address at the end of this chapter.

Figures of Speech

We come now to a consideration of figures of speech. It is fair enough to regard figures of speech as the "graces of language," as the "dressing of thought," as "embellishments," for indeed they do "decorate" our prose and give it "style," in the couturier's sense. But it would be a mistake to regard embellishment as the chief or sole function of figures. The classical rhetoricians certainly did not look upon them as decorative devices primarily. Metaphor, according to Aristotle, did give "charm and distinction" to our expression; but even more than that, metaphor was another way to *give* "clearness" and "liveliness" to the expression of our thoughts. Figures, in his view, provided one of the best ways to strike that happy balance between "the obvious and the obscure," so that our audience could grasp our ideas promptly and thereby be disposed to accept our arguments.

"What, then, can oratorical imagery effect?" Longinus asked. He was even more explicit than Aristotle in pointing out the rhetorical function of figures: "Well, it is able in many ways to infuse vehemence and passion into spoken words, while more particularly when it is combined with the argumentative passages it not only persuades the hearer but actually makes him its slave." —*On the Sublime*, XV, 9.

It was Quintilian who most explicitly related the figures to the *logos, pathos,* and *ēthos* of argument. Quintilian looked upon the figures as another means of lending "credibility to our arguments," of "exciting the emotions," and of winning "approval for our characters as pleaders" (*Instit. Orat.,* IX, i). This view of the function of figures of speech is perhaps the most reliable attitude to adopt toward these devices of style. Because figures can render our thoughts vividly concrete, they help us to communicate with our audience clearly and effectively; because they stir emotional responses, they can carry truth, in Wordsworth's phrase, "alive into the heart by passion"; and because they elicit admiration for the eloquence of the speaker or writer, they can exert a powerful ethical appeal.

Sister Miriam Joseph in her book *Shakespeare's Use of the Arts of Language* reclassified the more than 200 figures distinguished by the Tudor rhetoricians according to the four categories: grammar, logos, pathos, and ethos. By classifying the figures in this way, she was able to demonstrate, quite convincingly, that the three "schools" of rhetoric during the Renaissance (the Ramists, the traditionalists, and the figurists) saw the figures as being intimately connected with the topics of invention. Metaphor, for instance, involving comparison of like things, is tied up with the topic of similarity;

antithesis, involving the juxtaposition of opposites, is tied up with the topic of dissimilarity or of contraries. Then there were figures, like apostrophe, that were calculated to work directly on the emotions, and figures, like *comprobatio,* that were calculated to establish the ethical image of the speaker or writer. In our exposition, we will frequently point out the relationship of the figures either with grammar or with the three modes of persuasive appeal.

The mention of two hundred figures of speech in the previous paragraph may have appalled you. If pressed, you could name—even if you could not define or illustrate—a half dozen figures of speech. But where did those *other* figures come from? and what are they? In their passion for anatomizing and categorizing knowledge, the humanists of the Renaissance delighted in classifying and sub-classifying the figures. Admittedly, they were being overly subtle in distinguishing such a multitude of figures. The most widely used classical handbook in the Renaissance schools, *Rhetorica ad Herennium,* required the students to learn only 65 figures. Susenbrotus, in his popular *Epitome troporum ac schematum* (1540), distinguished 132 figures. But Henry Peacham, in his 1577 edition of *The Garden of Eloquence,* pushed the number up to 184. Pity the poor Tudor school children who were expected to define and illustrate and to use in their own compositions a goodly number of these figures.

We are not going to plague you with a long catalogue of figures, but we are going to introduce more figures than you have met with in your previous study of style. If nothing else, you should become aware, through this exposure, that your language has more figurative resources than you were conscious of. And you may discover that you have been using many of the figures of speech all your life. For people did not begin to use figures of speech only after academicians had classified and defined them; rather, the figures were classified and defined after people had been using them for centuries. Like the principles of grammar, poetics, and rhetoric, the doctrine of the figures was arrived at inductively. Rhetoricians merely gave "names" to the verbal practices of human beings.

What do we mean by the term "figures of speech"? We mean the same thing that Quintilian meant when he used the term *figura:* "any deviation, either in thought or expression, from the ordinary and simple method of speaking, a change analogous to the different positions our bodies assume when we sit down, lie down, or look back.... Let the definition of a figure, therefore, be *a form of speech artfully varied from common usage* (Ergo figura sit arte aliqua novata forma dicendi)"—*Instit. Orat.,* IX, i, 11.

We will use "figures of speech" as the generic term for any artful deviations from the ordinary mode of speaking or writing. But we will divide the figures of speech into two main groups—the *schemes* and the *tropes.* A scheme (Greek *schēma,* form, shape) involves a deviation from the ordinary pattern or arrangement of words. A trope (Greek *tropein,* to turn) involves a deviation from the ordinary and principal signification of a word.

Both types of figures involve a *transference* of some kind: a trope, a transference of meaning; a scheme, a transference of order. When Shakespeare's Mark Antony said, "Brutus is an honorable man," he was using the trope called irony, because he was "transferring" the ordinary meaning of the word *honorable* to convey a different meaning to his audience. If Mark Antony had said, "Honorable is the man who gives his life for his country," he would have been using a species of the scheme hyperbaton, because he would be "transferring" the usual order of words. In a sense, of course, both schemes and tropes involve a change of "meaning," since both result in effects that are different from the ordinary mode of expression. But for all practical purposes, our distinction is clear enough to enable you to distinguish between a scheme and a trope.

The terms used to label the various figures appear formidable—strange, polysyllabic words, most of them merely transliterated from the Greek. But technical terms, in any discipline, are always difficult at first sight; they are difficult, however, mainly because they are unfamiliar. Whenever we study a new discipline we have to learn the "names" of things peculiar to that discipline. Inevitably these specialized terms will be puzzling, but they will remain puzzling only until we learn to connect the *sign* with the concept or thing for which it stands. The word *tree* is difficult for the child only until he or she learns to associate the sound or the graphic mark of this word with the thing that it designates. The term *prosopopeia* may frighten you at first, but once you get to the point where you can immediately associate the term with its significance, *prosopopeia* will be no more frightening to you than the familiar terms *metaphor* and *simile.* We could, as the Renaissance rhetorician George Puttenham tried to do, invent English terms for the various figures, but since they would have to be coined terms, they would not necessarily be any easier to learn than the classical terms. However, wherever a familiar Anglicized term exists for a figure, we will use that term instead of the classical one.

In any case, we must not look upon terminology as an end in itself. Just as we can speak and write our native language without knowing the names of the parts of speech, so we can use and respond to figurative language without knowing the names of the figures. Nomenclature, in any study, is a convenience for purposes of classification and discussion. But an awareness of the various figures of speech can increase our verbal resources, and if we make a conscious effort to learn the figures of speech, it is likely that we will resort to them more often.

The Schemes

Schemes of Words

We shall not dwell very long on schemes of words because while they occur frequently in poetry—especially in the poetry of earlier centuries—they rarely occur in prose. The schemes of words (sometimes called *orthographical schemes,* because they involve changes in the spelling or sound of words) are formed (1) by adding or subtracting a letter or a syllable at the beginning, middle, or end of a word, or (2) by exchanging sounds. Terms like the following are of more concern to the grammarian and the prosodist than to the rhetorician:

> *prosthesis*—adding a syllable in front of word—e.g. *beloved* for *loved*
>
> *epenthesis*—adding a syllable in the middle of word—e.g. *visitating* for *visiting*
>
> *proparalepsis*—adding a syllable at the end of word—e.g. *climature* for *climate*
>
> *aphaeresis*—subtracting a syllable from the beginning of word—e.g. *'neath* for *beneath*
>
> *syncope*—subtracting a syllable from the middle of word—e.g. *prosprous* for *prosperous*
>
> *apocope*—subtracting a syllable from the end of word—e.g. *even* for *evening*
>
> *metathesis*—transposition of letters in a word—e.g. *clapse* for *clasp*
>
> *antisthecon*—change of sound—e.g. *wrang* for *wrong*

One can easily see that all of these involve a change in the shape or configuration of words. Poets used to employ such schemes to accommodate the rhyme or the rhythm of a line of verse. And because such changes are associated primarily with poetry, it is customary to regard such altered words as "poetic diction." Perhaps the situation in modern prose where we are most likely to use schemes of words would be the dialogue in a story. If a character in a story habitually clipped syllables from his words or mispronounced certain words, we might try to indicate those speech habits with spelling changes. Readers of *Finnegan's Wake* could supply numerous examples of other uses that James Joyce made of orthographical schemes in his remarkably ingenious prose.

Schemes of Construction

1. *Schemes of Balance*

Parallelism—similarity of structure in a pair or series of related words, phrases, or clauses.

Examples: He tried to make the law clear, precise, and equitable.

> . . . for the support of this declaration, with a firm reliance on the protection of Divine Protection, we mutually pledge to each other our Lives, our Fortunes, and our sacred Honor.—The Declaration of Independence

> We must now hope that Mr. Moynahan will devote his next decade to those four or five more novels which will banish his vacillations and uncertainties, purge his unneeded influences, and perfect his native gifts for language, landscape, and portraiture.—L. E. Sissman, *The New Yorker*

> It is certain that if you were to behold the whole woman, there is that dignity in her aspect, that composure in her motion, that complacency in her manner, that if her form makes you hope, her merit makes you fear.—Richard Steele, *Spectator,* No. 113

> I am a simple citizen who wants to live in peace and not be taxed out of existence or poisoned out of oxygen or sonically boomed out of my sanity and my home by all the things you do to help me, to defend me, to better provide me speed, electricity, national prestige, and freedom from bugs.—Talk of the Town, *The New Yorker*

> It is rather for us to be here dedicated to the great task remaining before us—that from those honored dead we take increased devotion to that cause for which they gave the last full measure of devotion; that we here highly resolve that these dead shall not have died in vain; that this nation, under God, shall have a new birth of freedom; and that government of the people, by the people, for the people, shall not perish from the earth.—Abraham Lincoln

Parallelism is one of the basic principles of grammar and rhetoric. The principle demands that equivalent things be set forth in co-ordinate grammatical structures. So nouns must be yoked with nouns, prepositional phrases with prepositional phrases, adverb clauses with adverb clauses. When this principle is ignored, not only is the grammar of co-ordination violated, but the rhetoric of coherence is wrenched. Students must be made to realize that violations of parallelism are serious, not only because they impair communication but because they reflect disorderly thinking. Whenever you see a coordinating conjunction in one of your sentences, you should check to make sure that the elements joined by the conjunction are of the same grammatical kind. Such a check might prevent you from writing sentences like these, all taken from student papers:

> Teenagers who dance the frug or the jerk are either wild or juvenile delinquents or both.

> Other common complaints are the failure of *Webster's Third* to include encyclopedic matter and for its technique of definition.

> Was this act rational and premeditated, or was it irrational and a spur-of-the-moment?

> He sounds like a nobleman threatened with revolution and who fears liberation of the masses.

> This situation not only is a problem for the fan, but it also affects the athletes. (A common violation of parallelism when correlative conjunctions are used.)

When the parallel elements are similar not only in structure but in length (that is, the same number of words, even the same number of syllables), the scheme is called **isocolon** (ī-sō-cō′-lon). For example: His purpose was *to impress the ignorant, to perplex the dubious,* and *to confound the scrupulous.* The addition of symmetry of length to similarity of structure contributes greatly to the rhythm of sentences. Obviously, you should not strive for isocolon every time you produce parallel structure. Such regularity of rhythm would approach the recurrent beat of verse.

Since parallelism is a device that we resort to when we are specifying or enumerating pairs or series of like things, it is easy to see the intimate relationship between this device of form and the topic of similarity. See the analysis of the rhetorical effect of parallelism in Clark Kerr's sentence in the previous section.

Antithesis (an-tith′-ə-sis)—the juxtaposition of contrasting ideas, often in parallel structure.

Examples: Though studious, he was popular; though argumentative, he was modest; though inflexible, he was candid; and though metaphysical, yet orthodox.—Dr. Samuel Johnson on the character of the Reverend Zacariah Mudge, in the *London Chronicle,* May 2, 1769

Essex thought him wanting in zeal as a friend; Elizabeth thought him wanting in duty as a subject.—Thomas Babington Macaulay, "Francis Bacon" (1837)

Our knowledge separates as well as it unites; our orders disintegrate as well as bind; our art brings us together and sets us apart.— J. Robert Oppenheimer, *The Open Mind* (1955)

Those who have been left out, we will try to bring in. Those left behind, we will help to catch up.—Richard M. Nixon, Inaugural Address, January 20, 1969

That's one small step for a man, one giant leap for mankind.—Neil Armstrong, as he stepped on the moon, Sunday, July 20, 1969

It is the best of times, yet the worst of times: we live in unparalleled prosperity, yet have starvation; modern science can perform miracles to save lives, yet we have war; we balance ourselves delicately on the moon, yet destroy the delicate balance of the earth. Young people search for meaning in life, yet are confused, demoralized, frustrated.—Jesse E. Hobson and Martin E. Robbins, from an article in *America*, December 27, 1969

By the time it's empty, life will be full.—Caption for a magazine ad picturing a bottle of Canoe, a men's cologne by Dana.

It was the unknown author of *Rhetorica ad Alexandrum* who most clearly pointed up the fact that the opposition in an *antithesis* can reside either in the words or in the ideas or in both:

> An antithesis occurs when both the wording and the sense, or one or other of them, are opposed in a contrast. The following would be an antithesis both of wording and sense: "It is not fair that my opponent should become rich by possessing what belongs to me, while I sacrifice my property and become a mere beggar." In the following sentence we have a merely verbal antithesis: "Let the rich and prosperous give to the poor and needy"; and an antithesis of sense only in the following: "I tended him when he was sick, but he has been the cause of very great misfortune to me." Here there is no verbal antithesis, but the two actions are contrasted. The double antithesis (that is, both of sense and of wording) would be the best to use; but the other two kinds are also true antitheses. (From *Rhetorica ad Alexandrum*, Ch. 26, trans. E. S. Forster.)

Nicely managed, antithesis can produce the effect of aphoristic neatness and can win for the author a reputation for wit. Antithesis is obviously related to the topic of dissimilarity and the topic of contraries. (See the analysis of antithesis in Clark Kerr's sentence.)

2. *Schemes of unusual or inverted word order* (hyperbaton)

Anastrophe (a-năs'-trō-fē)—Inversion of the natural or usual word order.

Examples: Backward run the sentences, till reels the mind. (From a parody
of the style of *Time* Magazine.)

> The question between preaching extempore and from a written
> discourse, it does not properly fall within the province of this treatise
> to discuss on any but what may be called rhetorical principles.—
> Richard Whately, *Elements of Rhetoric* (1828)

> The emotional isolation, the preoccupation with God and them-
> selves, the struggles for freedom, which seem to have possessed many
> of my friends at the same age, I knew almost nothing of.—
> C. P. Snow, *The Search*

> Puffed-up asses Arcangeli and Bottini unquestionably are.—Richard
> D. Altick and James F. Loucks, *Browning's Roman Murder Story*
> (1968)

> I got, so far as the immediate moment was concerned, away.—
> Henry James, *The Turn of the Screw*

> Rich, famous, proud, a ruling despot Pope might be—but he *was*
> middle class!—V. S. Pritchett, from a review in the *New York Re-
> view of Books,* February 27, 1969

> Good musicians of their type they are. Clean and neat in appearance
> they are. Needed, we might say, they are.—Student paper

> People that he had known all his life he didn't really know.—Student
> paper

> One ad does not a survey make.—Caption from an ad for Peugeot
> automobiles

Perfectly does *anastrophe* conform to our definition of a scheme as "an
artful deviation from the ordinary pattern or arrangement of words." Because such deviation surprises expectation, anastrophe can be an effective
device for gaining attention. But its chief function is to secure emphasis.
It is a commonplace that the beginning and end of a clause are the positions
of greatest emphasis. Words placed in those positions draw special attention,
and when those initial or terminal words are not normally found in those
positions, they receive extraordinary emphasis.

Parenthesis (pə-ren'-thə-sis)—insertion of some verbal unit in a position that
interrupts the normal syntactical flow of the sentence.

Examples: But wherein any man is bold—I am speaking foolishly—I also am bold. . . . Are they ministers of Christ? I—to speak as a fool —am more.—St. Paul, 2 Cor. 11, 21 and 23

But when Savage was provoked, and very small offences were sufficient to provoke him, he would prosecute his revenge with the utmost acrimony till his passion had subsided.—Samuel Johnson, *Life of Richard Savage*

All that remained for the moment was to decide where I would go to graduate school, and that question was settled—the "snobs" had been right—by a Kellett Fellowship and then a Fulbright Scholarship to boot.—Norman Podhoretz, *Making It* (1967)

Any theory of post-historical society—our sense of being "in history" is largely determined by the pressure of political and social conflicts —will have to consider the dilemma of human motivations in the just city.—George Steiner, *Language and Silence* (1967)

However far the interpreters alter the text (another notorious example is the Rabbinic and Christian "spiritual" interpretations of the clearly erotic Song of Songs), they must claim to be reading off a sense that is already there.—Susan Sontag, *Against Interpretation* (1966)

He said he supervised ten editors—another euphemism—in his department, which clears 90% of NBC's entertainment programming, including movies.—Joan Barthel, from an article in *Life*, August 1, 1969

There is even, and it is the achievement of this book, a curious sense of happiness running through its paragraphs.—Norman Mailer, from a book review in *Cannibals and Christians* (1966)

The distinguishing mark of *parenthesis* is that the interpolated member is "cut off" from the syntax of the rest of the sentence. A parenthesis abruptly —and usually briefly—sends the thought off on a tangent. Although the parenthetical matter is not necessary for the grammatical completeness of the sentence, it does have a pronounced rhetorical effect. For a brief moment, we hear the author's voice, commenting, editorializing, and, for that reason, the sentence gets an emotional charge that it would otherwise not have. Note, for instance, the difference in effect if the parenthetical element in St. Paul's first sentence is synactically integrated with the rest of the sentence: "But I am speaking foolishly if I claim that wherein any man is bold, I also am bold."

Apposition (ap-ə-zish'-en)—placing side by side two co-ordinate elements, the second of which serves as an explanation or modification of the first.

Examples: John Morgan, the president of the Sons of the Republic, could not be reached by phone.

Men of this kind—soldiers of fortune, pool-hall habitués, gigolos, beachcombers—expend their talents on trivialities.—Student paper

Apart from the association of Latin with rhetoric as an art, this last mentioned fact, that Latin was totally controlled by writing no matter how much it was used for speech, produced other special kinds of drives toward the oral within the academic world.—Walter J. Ong, from an article in *PMLA,* June 1965

So we would have gone together, the Orthodox and I.—George Steiner, from an article in *Commentary,* February, 1965

A miscellaneous list, this, but all of the items on it are characterized by the same misunderstandings and misconceptions of the nature of American power; and all have this in common, that they defy solution so long as the energies and resources of the nation are monopolized by the war in Vietnam.—Henry Steele Commager, from a book review in the *New York Review of Books,* December 5, 1968

Apposition is such a common method of expansion in modern prose that it hardly seems to conform to our definition of a scheme as "an artful deviation from the ordinary patterns of speech." But if we reflect upon our own experience, we will have to acknowledge that appositional structures seldom occur in impromptu speech. Apposition may not be the exclusive property of written prose, but it certainly occurs most frequently in written prose—in a situation, in other words, where we have time to make a conscious choice of our arrangement of words. So there is something *artful* about the use of the appositive. And there is something out-of-the-ordinary about the appositive, too. Although the appositive does not disturb the natural flow of the sentence as violently as parenthetical expressions do (mainly because the appositive is grammatically co-ordinate with the unit that it follows), it does interrupt the flow of the sentence, interrupts the flow to supply some gratuitous information or explanation.

3. *Schemes of Omission*

Ellipsis (ē-lip'-sis)—deliberate omission of a word or of words which are readily implied by the context.

Examples: And he to England shall along with you.—*Hamlet*, III, iii, 4

> Kant, we may suppose, was more startled by Hume's apparent destruction of all basis for philosophical certainty; Reid, by the remoter consequences to morality and theology.—Sir Leslie Stephen, *History of English Thought in the Eighteenth Century* (1876)

> So singularly clear was the water that when it was only twenty or thirty feet deep the bottom seemed floating in the air! Yes, where it was even *eighty* feet deep. Every little pebble was distinct, every speckled trout, every hand's-breadth of sand.—Mark Twain, *Roughing It*

> As with religion, so with education. In colonial New England, education was broad-based, but nevertheless elitist; and in its basic assumptions, intellectualist.—David Marquand, from an article in *Encounter*, March 1964

> Rape is the sexual sin of the mob, adultery of the bourgeoisie, and incest of the aristocracy.—John Updike, from a book review in the *New Yorker*, August 2, 1969

> So let the class invent its own assignments. If it wants more sophistication, fine.—Peter Elbow, from an article in *College English*, November 1968

> The Master's degree is awarded by seventy-four departments, and the Ph.D. by sixty.—Student paper

Ellipsis can be an artful and arresting means of securing economy of expression. We must see to it, however, that the understood words are grammatically compatible. If we wrote, "The ringleader was hanged, and his accomplices imprisoned," we would be guilty of a solecism, because the understood *was* is not grammatically compatible with the plural subject (*accomplices*) of the second clause. And we produce a "howler" if we say, "While in the fourth grade, my father took me to the zoo."

Asyndeton (a-sin′-də-ton)—deliberate omission of conjunctions between a series of related clauses.

Examples: I came, I saw, I conquered.

> They may have it in well-doing, they may have it in learning, they may have it even in criticism.—Matthew Arnold

The infantry plodded forward, the tanks rattled into position, the big guns swung their snouts toward the rim of the hills, the planes raked the underbrush with gunfire.

The Tudor rhetoricians had a special name for the omission of conjunctions between single words or phrases. They would have labelled the following as instances of **brachylogia** (brak-ə-lo′-jē-a):

> . . . and that government of the people, by the people, for the people, shall not perish from the earth.—Abraham Lincoln

> . . . that we shall pay any price, bear any burden, meet any hardship, support any friend, oppose any foe to assure the survival and the success of liberty.—John F. Kennedy

But there seems to be no good reason why we cannot use the single term *asyndeton* for all these instances of omission of conjunctions. The principal effect of asyndeton is to produce a hurried rhythm in the sentence. Aristotle observed that asyndeton was especially appropriate for the conclusion of a discourse, because there, perhaps more than in other places in the discourse, we may want to produce the emotional reaction that can be stirred by, among other means, rhythm. And Aristotle concluded his *Rhetoric* with an instance of asyndeton that is noticeable even in translation: "I have done. You have heard me. The facts are before you. I ask for your judgment."

The opposite scheme is **polysyndeton** (pol-ē-sin′-də-ton) (deliberate use of many conjunctions). Note how the proliferation of conjunctions in the following quotation slows up the rhythm of the prose and produces an impressively solemn note:

> And God said, "Let the earth bring forth living creatures according to their kinds: cattle and creeping things and beasts of the earth according to their kinds." And it was so. And God made the beasts of the earth according to their kinds and the cattle according to their kinds and everything that creeps upon the ground according to its kind. And God saw that it was good.—Genesis, 1:24-25

Ernest Hemingway uses polysyndeton to create another effect. Note how the repeated *and*'s in the following passage suggest the flow and continuity of experience:

> I said, "Who killed him?" and he said, "I don't know who killed him but he's dead all right," and it was dark and there was water standing in the street and no lights and windows broke and boats all up in the town and trees blown down and everything all blown and I got a skiff and went out and found my boat where I had her inside Mango Key and she was all right only she was full of water.—Hemingway, "After the Storm"

Polysyndeton can also be used to produce special emphasis. Note the difference in effect of these two sentences:

> This semester I am taking English, history, biology, mathematics, sociology, and physical education.

> This semester I am taking English and history and biology and mathematics and sociology and physical education.

4. Schemes of Repetition

Alliteration (ə-lit-er-ā′-shən)—repetition of initial or medial consonants in two or more adjacent words.

Examples: A sable, silent, solemn forest stood.
                           —James Thomson, "The Castle of Indolence," l. 38

> Progress is not proclamation nor palaver. It is not pretense nor play on prejudice. It is not the perturbation of a people passion-wrought nor a promise proposed.—Warren G. Harding nominating William Howard Taft in 1912

> Already American vessels had been searched, seized, and sunk.— John F. Kennedy, *Profiles in Courage*

> A moist young moon hung above the mist of a neighboring meadow.—Vladimir Nabokov, *Conclusive Evidence*

> I should hear him fly with the high fields
> And wake to the farm forever fled from the childless land.
>   —Dylan Thomas, "Fern Hill," ll. 50–51

> Tart, tingling, and even ticklish.—Caption from an ad for Sprite

> We double-distill a dram at a time, instead of taking the faster big batch away.—Caption from an ad for Old Grand-Dad bourbon

In Anglo-Saxon poetry, *alliteration* rather than rhyme was the device to bind verses together. Because it contributes to the euphony of verse or prose, alliteration became a conspicuous feature of Euphuistic prose and Romantic poetry. Because it is such an obvious mannerism, alliteration is rarely used in modern prose. It is sometimes used today, however, for special effects—as a mnemonic device for slogans (Better Business Builds Bigger Bankrolls) and advertising catch-lines (Spark*l*ing . . . F*l*avorful . . . Mi*l*ler High Life . . . The Champagne of Bott*l*e Beer . . . Brewed on*l*y in Mi*l*waukee. Sometimes alliteration is deliberately used for humorous effect: He was a preposterously pompous proponent of precious pedantry.

Assonance (as'-ə-nəns)—the repetition of similar vowel sounds, preceded and followed by different consonants, in the stressed syllables of adjacent words.

Examples: An old, mad, blind, despised, and dying king—
Princes, the dregs of their dull race, who flow
Through public scorn—mud from a muddy spring—
—Shelley, "Sonnet: England in 1819"

Had Gray written often thus, it had been vain to blame and useless to praise him.—Samuel Johnson, *Life of Thomas Gray*

Under a juniper-tree the bones sang, scattered and shining
We were glad to be scattered, we did little good to each other
Under a tree in the cool of the day, with the shining sand
—T. S. Eliot, "Ash Wednesday"

Whales in the wake like capes and Alps
Quaked the sick sea and snouted deep
—Dylan Thomas, "Ballad of the Long-Legged Bait"

Refresh your zest for living
—Caption from an ad for French Line Ships

Assonance, a device of sound, like alliteration, is used mainly in poetry. A prose writer might deliberately use assonance to produce certain onomatopoetic or humorous effects. The danger for the prose writer, however, lies in the careless repetition of similar vowel-sounds, producing awkward jingles like this: "He tries to revise the evidence supplied by his eyes."

Anaphora (ə-naf'-ə-rə)—repetition of the same word or group of words at the beginnings of successive clauses.

Examples: The Lord sitteth above the water floods. The Lord remaineth a King forever. The Lord shall give strength unto his people. The Lord shall give his people the blessing of peace.—Psalm 29

We shall fight on the beaches, we shall fight on the landing-grounds, we shall fight in the fields and in the streets, we shall fight in the hills.—Winston Churchill, speech in the House of Commons, June 4, 1940

We are moving to the land of freedom. Let us march to the realization of the American dream. Let us march on segregated housing. Let us march on segregated schools. Let us march on poverty. Let us march on ballot boxes, march on ballot boxes until race baiters disappear from the political arena, until the Wallaces of our nation tremble away in silence.—Martin Luther King, Jr., on a civil-rights march from Selma to Montgomery, Alabama, 1965

They are common just as theft, cheating, perjury, adultery have always been common. They were common, not because people did not know what was right, but because people liked to do what was wrong. They were common, though prohibited by law. They were common, though condemned by public opinion. They were common, because in that age law and public opinion united had not sufficient force to restrain the greediness of powerful and unprincipled magistrates.—Thomas Babington Macaulay, "Francis Bacon," 1837

Why should white people be running all the stores in our community? Why should white people be running the banks of our community? Why should the economy of our community be in the hands of the white man? Why?—Speech by Malcolm X

It is a luxury, it is a privilege, it is an indulgence for those who are at their ease.—Edmund Burke, "Letter to a Noble Lord," 1796

It is 1969 already, and 1965 seems almost like a childhood memory. Then we were the conquerors of the world. No one could stop us. We were going to end the war. We were going to wipe out racism. We were going to mobilize the poor. We were going to take over the universities.—Jerry Rubin, from an article in the *New York Review of Books,* February 13, 1969

Whenever anaphora occurs, we can be sure that the author has used it deliberately. Since the repetition of the words helps to establish a marked rhythm in the sequence of clauses, this scheme is usually reserved for those passages where the author wants to produce a strong emotional effect. Note how Reinhold Niebuhr combines anaphora with plays on words to produce this neat aphorism: "Man's capacity for justice makes democracy possible; but man's inclination to injustice makes democracy necessary."

Epistrophe (ə-pis′-trō-fē)—repetition of the same word or group of words at the ends of successive clauses.

Examples: Shylock: I'll have my bond! Speak not against my bond!
I have sworn an oath that I will have my bond!
—*The Merchant of Venice,* III, iii, 3–4

To the good American many subjects are sacred: sex is sacred, women are sacred, children are sacred, business is sacred, America is sacred, Mason lodges and college clubs are sacred.—George Santayana, *Character and Opinion in the United States*

But to all those who would be tempted by weakness, let us leave no doubt that we will be as strong as we need to be for as long as we need to be. . . . We cannot learn from one another until we stop shouting at one another.—Richard M. Nixon, Inaugural Address, January 20, 1969

Perhaps this is the most important thing for me to take back from beach-living: simply the memory that each cycle of the tide is valid, each cycle of the wave is valid, each cycle of a relationship is valid.
    —Anne Lindbergh, *Gift from the Sea*

As long as the white man sent you to Korea, you bled. He sent you to Germany, you bled. He sent you to the South Pacific to fight the Japanese, you bled.—Speech by Malcolm X

In a cake, nothing tastes like real butter, nothing moistens like real butter, nothing enriches like real butter, nothing satisfies like real butter.—Caption from a Pillsbury ad

He's learning fast. Are you earning fast?—Caption from an ad for Aetna Life Insurance

Epistrophe not only sets up a pronounced rhythm but secures a special emphasis, both by repeating the word and by putting the word in the final position in the sentence.

Epanalepsis (ə-pon-ə-lep′-sis)—repetition at the end of a clause of the word that occurred at the beginning of the clause.

Examples: Blood hath bought blood, and blows have answer'd blows:
        Strength match'd with strength, and power confronted power.
            —Shakespeare, *King John*, II, i, 329–30

Year chases year, decay pursues decay.—Samuel Johnson, "The Vanity of Human Wishes"

Possessing what we still were unpossessed by,
Possessed by what we now no more possessed.
            —Robert Frost, "The Gift Outright"

> And when the shadow fades and is no more, the light that lingers becomes a shadow to another light.—Kahlil Gibran, *The Prophet*

> A nut nut is a person who is nuts about the fun of eating nuts.
> —Caption from an ad for Skippy Peanut Butter

> Business forms are as various as people forms.—Caption from an ad for Nekoosa Paper Company

Epanalepsis is rare in prose, probably because when the emotional situation arises that can make such a scheme appropriate, poetry seems to be the only form that can adequately express the emotion. It would seem perfectly natural for a father to express his grief over the death of a beloved son in this fashion: "He was flesh of my flesh, bone of my bone, blood of my blood." But would the father be speaking prose or poetry? Perhaps the only answer we could give is that it is heightened language of some sort, the kind of language which, despite its appearance of contrivance, springs spontaneously from intense emotion. Repetition, we know, is one of the characteristics of highly emotional language. And in this instance what better way for the father to express the intimacy of the relationship with his son than by the repetition of words at the beginning and end of successive groups of words?

Perhaps the best general advice about the use of epanalepsis—in fact of all those schemes that are appropriate only to extraordinary circumstances—would be, If you find yourself consciously deciding to use epanalepsis, don't use it." When the time is appropriate, the scheme will present itself unbidden.

Anadiplosis (an-ə-di-plō′-sis)—repetition of the last word of one clause at the beginning of the following clause.

Examples: Labor and care are rewarded with success, success produces confidence, confidence relaxes industry, and negligence ruins the reputation which diligence had raised.—Dr. Johnson, *Rambler* No. 21

> They point out what is perfectly obvious, yet seldom realized: That if you have a lot of things you cannot move about a lot, that furniture requires dusting, dusters require servants, servants require insurance stamps. . . . It [property] produces men of weight. Men of weight cannot, by definition, move like the lightning from the East unto the West.—E. M. Forster, "My Wood," *Abinger Harvest*

> The crime was common, common be the pain.—Alexander Pope, "Eloisa to Abelard"

The laughter had to be gross or it would turn to sobs, and to sob would be to realize, and to realize would be to despair.—John Howard Griffin, *Black Like Me*

Having power makes it [totalitarian leadership] isolated; isolation breeds insecurity; insecurity breeds suspicion and fear; suspicion and fear breed violence.—Zbigniew K. Brzezinski, *The Permanent Purge, Politics in Soviet Totalitarianism*

Queeg: "Aboard my ship, excellent performance is standard. Standard performance is sub-standard. Sub-standard performance is not permitted to exist."—Herman Wouk, *The Caine Mutiny*

Climax (klī'-maks)—arrangement of words, phrases, or clauses in an order of increasing importance.

Examples: More than that, we rejoice in our sufferings, knowing that suffering produces endurance, endurance produces character, and character produces hope, and hope does not disappoint us, because God's love has been poured into our hearts through the Holy Spirit which has been given to us.—St. Paul, Romans, 5, 3–5

Let a man acknowledge obligations to his family, his country, and his God.—Student paper

Renounce my love, my life, myself—and you.—Alexander Pope, "Eloisa to Abelard"

I think we've reached a point of great decision, not just for our nation, not only for all humanity, but for life upon the earth.—George Wald, "A Generation in Search of a Future," speech delivered at MIT on March 4, 1969

When a boy lays aside his tops, his marbles, and his bike in favor of a girl, another girl, and still another girl, he becomes a youth. When the youth discards his first girl and his second girl for *the* girl, he becomes a bachelor. And when the bachelor can stand it no longer, he turns into a husband.—Alan Beck, from an article in *Good Housekeeping*, July 1957

It shreds the nerves, it vivisects the psyche—and it may even scare the living daylights out of more than a few playgoers.—A review in *Time*, January 7, 1966

Climax can be considered a scheme of repetition only when, as in the first example quoted above, it is a continued *anadiplosis* involving three or more members. Otherwise, as in the second and third examples, it is simply a scheme which arranges a series in an order of gradually rising importance. This latter variety of climax can be looked upon as a scheme related to the topic of degree, and it is the kind of climax that you will most often find in modern prose and that you will probably find occasion to use in your own prose.

Antimetabole (an-tē-mə-tab'-ō-lē)—repetition of words, in successive clauses, in reverse grammatical order.

Examples: One should eat to live, not live to eat.—Molière, *L'Avare*

> It ought to be the first endeavor of a writer to distinguish nature from custom, or that which is established because it is right from that which is right only because it is established.—Samuel Johnson, *Rambler* #156

> This man [Lord Chesterfield] I thought had been a lord among wits; but, I find, he is only a wit among lords.—Samuel Johnson, as quoted in Boswell's *Life of Johnson*

> Mankind must put an end to war—or war will put an end to mankind.—John F. Kennedy, United Nations Speech, 1961

> Ask not what your country can do for you; ask what you can do for your country.—John F. Kennedy, Inaugural Address

> The Negro needs the white man to free him from his fears. The white man needs the Negro to free him from his guilt.—Martin Luther King, Jr., from a speech delivered in 1966

> You can take Salem out of the country. But you can't take the country out of Salem.—Caption from a Salem cigarette ad

> You like it, it likes you.—Advertising slogan for Seven-Up

All of these examples have the air of the "neatly turned phrase"—the kind of phrasing that figures in most memorable aphorisms. Would the sentence from President Kennedy's Inaugural Address be so often quoted if it had read something like this: "Do not ask what America can do for you. You would do better to ask whether your country stands in need of *your* services"? The "magic" has now gone out of the appeal. It would be a profitable exercise for the student to take several of the schemes presented in this section and convert them into ordinary prose. Such an exercise would undoubtedly reveal what the schemes add to the expression of the thought.

Chiasmus (kī-əz'-mus) ("the criss-cross")—reversal of grammatical structures in successive phrases or clauses.

Examples: By day the frolic, and the dance by night.—Samuel Johnson, "The Vanity of Human Wishes"

His time a moment, and a point his space.—Alexander Pope, *Essay on Man,* Epistle I

Exalts his enemies, his friends destroys.—John Dryden, "Absalom and Achitophel"

It is hard to make money, but to spend it is easy.—Student paper

Language changes. So should your dictionary.—Caption from ad for *Webster's Seventh New Collegiate Dictionary*

Chiasmus is similar to *antimetabole* in that it too involves a reversal of grammatical structures in successive phrases or clauses, but it is unlike *antimetabole* in that it does not involve a repetition of words. Both *chiasmus* and *antimetabole* can be used to reinforce *antithesis.*

Polyptoton (pō-lip'-tə-tahn)—repetition of words derived from the same root.

Examples: The Greeks are *strong,* and *skilful* to their *strength.*
Fierce to their *skill,* and to their *fierceness* valiant;
—Shakespeare, *Troilus and Cressida,* I, i, 7–8

But alas . . . the gate is narrow, the threshold high, few are *chosen* because few *choose* to be *chosen.*—Aldous Huxley, from *Collected Essays* (1955)

Let me assert my firm belief that the only thing we have to *fear* is *fear* itself.—Franklin Delano Roosevelt, First Inaugural Address, March 1933

But in this desert country they may see the land being rendered *useless* by *overuse.*—Joseph Wood Krutch, *The Voice of the Desert* (1955)

We would like to *contain* the *uncontainable* future in a glass.—Loren Eiseley, from an article in *Harper's,* March 1964

Not as a call to *battle,* though *embattled* we are.—John F. Kennedy, Inaugural Address

Their *blood bleeds* the nation of its sanguine assurance.—Student paper

Please, Please Me.—Title of a Beatles' song

Polyptoton is very much akin to those plays on words that we will investigate in the next section on tropes.

The Tropes

Metaphor and Simile

Metaphor (met′-ə-for)—an implied comparison between two things of unlike nature that yet have something in common.
Simile (sim′-ə-lē)—an explicit comparison between two things of unlike nature that yet have something in common.

Examples (all from student themes):

> He had a posture like a question-mark. (simile)
>
> On the final examination, several students went down in flames. (metaphor)
>
> Like an arrow, the prosecutor went directly to the point. (simile)
>
> The question of federal aid to parochial schools is a bramble patch. (metaphor)
>
> Silence settled down over the audience like a block of granite. (simile)
>
> Birmingham lighted a runaway fuse, and as fast as the headlines could record them, demonstrations exploded all over the country. (metaphor)

We will treat metaphor and simile together because they are so much alike. The difference between metaphor and simile lies mainly in the manner of expressing the comparison. Whereas metaphor says, "David was a lion in battle," simile says, "David was *like* a lion in battle." Both of these tropes are related to the topic of similarity, for although the comparison is made between two things of unlike nature (*David* and *lion*), there is some respect in which they are similar (e.g., they are courageous, or they fight ferociously, or they are unconquerable in a fight). The thing with which the first thing is compared is to be understood in some "transferred sense": *David* is not literally a *lion*, but he is a lion in some "other sense."

An extended or continued metaphor is known as an *allegory*. We see one of these sustained metaphors in *The Battle of the Books*, where Jonathan Swift compares the classical writers, not to the spider, which spins its web out of its own entrails, but to the far-ranging bee:

> As for us the ancients, we are content with the bee to pretend to nothing of our own, beyond our wings and our voices, that is to say, our flights and our language. For the rest, whatever we have got has been by infinite labor and search, and ranging through every corner of nature; the difference is that instead of dirt and poison, we have chosen to fill our hives with honey and wax, thus furnishing mankind with the two noblest of things, which are sweetness and light.

Closely allied to this form of extended metaphor is *parable,* an anecdotal narrative designed to teach a moral lesson. The most famous examples of parable are those found in the New Testament. In the parable of the sower of seeds, for instance, our interest is not so much in the tale of a man who went out to sow some seeds as in what each detail of the anecdote "stands for," in what the details "mean." Whenever the disciples were puzzled about what a particular parable meant, they asked Christ to interpret it for them.

And while we are talking about these analogical tropes, we should warn writers to be on their guard against the "mixed metaphor," which results when they lose sight of the terms of their comparisons. When Joseph Addison said, "There is not a single view of human nature which is not sufficient to extinguish the seeds of pride," it is obvious that he is mixing two different metaphors. We could say "to extinguish the *flames* of pride" or "to *water* the seeds of pride," but we cannot mix the notion of extinguishing with that of seeds. The rhetoricians sometimes called such "wrenching of words" **catachresis** (kat-ə-krē'-sis).

Synecdoche (si-nek'-də-kē)—a figure of speech in which a part stands for the whole.

Examples:

> genus substituted for the species:
> *vessel* for *ship, weapon* for *sword, creature* for *man, arms* for *rifles, vehicle* for *bicycle*
>
> species substituted for the genus:
> *bread* for *food, cutthroat* for *assassin*
>
> part substituted for the whole:
> *sail* for *ship, hands* for *helpers, roofs* for *houses*
>
> matter for what is made from it:
> *silver* for *money, canvas* for *sail, steel* for *sword*

In general, we have an instance of *synecdoche* when the part or genus or adjunct that is mentioned suggests something else. It is an *oblique* manner of speaking. All of the following illustrate this trope: "Give us this day our daily *bread.*" "All *hands* were summoned to the quarter-deck." "Not *marble,* nor the gilded monuments of princes, shall outlive this powerful *rhyme.*" "They braved the *waves* to protect their fatherland." "Brandish your *steel*, men." "Are there no *roofs* in this town that will harbor an honorable man?" "It is pleasing to contemplate a *manufacture* rising gradually from its first mean state by the successive *labors* of innumerable *minds.*"—Johnson, *Rambler* No. 9. "The door closed upon the extempore surgeon and midwife, and *Roaring Camp* sat down outside, smoked its pipe, and awaited the issue."—Bret Harte, "The Luck of Roaring Camp."

Metonymy (mə-tahn′-ə-mē)—substitution of some attributive or suggestive word for what is actually meant.

Examples: crown for *royalty, mitre* for *bishop, wealth* for *rich people, brass* for *military officers, bottle* for *wine, pen* for *writers*

Metonymy and synecdoche are so close to being the same trope that George Campbell, the eighteenth-century rhetorician, wondered whether we should make any great effort to distinguish them. Those rhetoricians who did make the effort to discriminate these tropes would label the following as examples of metonymy:

> If the nearness of our last necessity brought a nearer conformity into it, there were happiness in *hoary hairs* and no calamity in *half senses.* . . . and Charles the Fifth can never hope to live within two *Methuselahs* of Hector.—Sir Thomas Browne, *Urn-Burial* (1658)

> I have nothing to offer but *blood, toil, tears,* and *sweat.*—Sir Winston Churchill, speech in the House of Commons May 13, 1940

> . . . and with firm confidence in justice, freedom, and peace on earth that will raise the hearts and the hopes of mankind for that distant day when no one *rattles a saber* and no one *drags a chain.* —Adlai Stevenson, acceptance speech, July 21, 1952

> In Europe, we gave the *cold shoulder* to De Gaulle, and now he gives the *warm hand* to Mao Tse-tung.—Richard M. Nixon, campaign speech, 1960

> You can't read the history of the United States, my friends, without learning the great story of those thousands of unnamed women. And if it's ever told straight, you'll know it's the *sunbonnet* and not the *sombrero* that has settled the country.—Edna Ferber, *Cimarron* (1930)

Capital has learned to sit down and talk with *labor*.—George Meany, speech in 1966

Breaching the *White Wall* of Southern Justice.—Title of article in *Time*, April 15, 1966

In another song written by [Bob] Dylan and sung by the Turtles, he lectures *clinging vines* who only want a *strong shoulder* to lean on.—Review in *Time*, September 17, 1966

Puns—generic name for those figures which make a play on words.

    (1) **Antanaclasis** (an-ta-nak'-la-sis)—repetition of a word in two different senses.

But lest I should be condemned of introducing *license*, when I oppose *licensing*, . . . —John Milton, *Areopagitica* (1644)

If we don't *hang* together, we'll *hang* separately.—Benjamin Franklin

Your argument is *sound*, nothing but *sound*.—Benjamin Franklin

Although we're *apart*, you're still *a part* of me.—Lyrics of the song "On Blueberry Hill"

Nothing is closer to the supreme *commonplace* of our *commonplace* age than its preoccupation with *Nothing*.—Robert Martin Adams, *Nil* (1966)

You may not find this *Scotch* as smooth as Barrymore, of course, but then Barrymore wasn't *Scotch*.—Ad for Seagram's Scotch Whiskey

The *long* cigarette that's *long* on flavor.—Ad for Pall Mall cigarettes

We make the traveler's *lot* a *lot* easier.—Ad for Overseas National Airways

    (2) **Paronomasia** (par-ə-nō-mā'-zha)—use of words alike in sound but different in meaning.

Neither hide nor hair of him had been seen since the day that Kwame Nkrumah had been *ostrichized,* accused of being the biggest *cheetah* in Ghana, but *safaris* anyone knew, no *fowl* play was involved.—Article in *Time*, April 8, 1966

The Bustle: A *Deceitful Seatful.*—Vladimir Nabokov, *Lolita*

Casting my *perils* before *swains*.—Marshall McLuhan

Fran [Elizabeth Taylor] is a chorine waiting for her paramour to obtain a divorce and *altar* her situation.—Movie review in *Time,* March 9, 1970

The end of the *plain plane, explained.*—Ad for Braniff International

One's metaphoric *retch* exceeds one's metaphoric *gasp.*—John Leonard, column in *Esquire,* February 1969

Independence is what a boy feels when all he wants from father is to be left *a loan.*—Minneapolis *Star,* April 26, 1966

The "in" idea in business travel—Hilton Inns.—Ad for Hilton Inns

(3) **Syllepsis** (si-lep′-sis)—use of a word understood differently in relation to two or more other words, which it modifies or governs.

> Here thou, great Anna! whom three realms obey
> Dost sometimes counsel *take*—and sometimes tea.
> —Alexander Pope, *The Rape of the Lock*

The play is armed with irascible wit, and Nicol Williamson's whiplash acting *raises* laughs as well as welts.—Review in *Time,* April 1, 1966

There is a certain type of woman who'd rather *press* grapes than clothes.—Ad for Peck & Peck suits

Lights are as likely to *attract* a Viet Cong bullet as a mosquito.—Article in *Time,* September 10, 1966

Who was the first to *wrap up* a case: Scotland Yard or Alexander Gordon?—Ad for Gordon's Whiskey

The ink, like our pig, keeps *running* out of the pen.—Student paper

The figure of **zeugma** (zōōg′-mə) is somewhat like syllepsis, but whereas in *syllepsis* the single word is grammatically and idiomatically compatible with both of the other words that it governs, in a *zeugma* the single word does not fit grammatically or idiomatically with one member of the pair. If we say, "Jane *has murdered* her father, and may you too" or "He maintained a *flourishing* business and racehorse," we would be producing an instance of *zeugma,* because in both sentences the *italicized* word is either grammatically or idiomatically incongruous with one member (in these examples, the second member) of the pair it governs. Those two lines from Pope's *Rape of the Lock* that are often classified as *zeugma*—"Or stain her honour, or her new brocade" and "Or lose her heart, or necklace, at a ball"—would, according to our definition, be examples of *syllepsis. Syllepsis* is the only one of these two figures that can be considered a form of pun. *Zeugma,* if skillfully managed, could be impressive as a display of wit, but often enough, *zeugma* is nothing more than a faulty use of the scheme of *ellipsis.*

Anthimeria (an-thə-mer'-ē-a)—the substitution of one part of speech for another.

Examples: I'll *unhair* thy head.—Shakespeare, *Antony and Cleopatra* II, v, 64

> A mile before his tent fall down, and *knee*
> The way into his mercy.—Shakespeare, *Coriolanus,* V, i, 5

> The thunder would not *peace* at my bidding.—Shakespeare, *King Lear,* IV, vi, 103

> That ghastly thought would drink up all your joy,
> And quite *unparadise* the realms of light.
> —Edward Young, *Complaint, or Night Thoughts*

> George Rogers Clark may have camped under that tree; buffalo may have *nooned* in its shade, switching flies.—Aldo Leopold, *A Sand County Almanac* (1949)

> They whack-whacked the white horse on the legs and he *kneed* himself up.—Ernest Hemingway, *in our time*

> Me, *dictionary-ing* heavily, "Where was the one they were watching?"—Ernest Hemingway, *Green Hills of Africa*

> *Gift* him with *Playboy.*—Promotional letter for *Playboy* magazine

Dozens of other examples of anthimeria could be quoted from Shakespeare's plays. If a word was not available for what he wanted to express, Shakespeare either coined a word or used an old word in a new way. Writers today must use *anthimeria* seldom and with great discretion unless they are truly masters of the existing English language. On the other hand, an apt creation can be pungent, evocative, witty, or memorable. English today is a rich, flexible language, because words have been borrowed, changed, and created. Think of all the ways in which a word like *smoke* has been used since it first came into the language:

> The smoke rose from the chimney.
> The chimney smokes.
> He smoked the ham.
> He smokes.
> She asked for a smoke.
> He objected to the smoke nuisance.

> She noticed the smoky atmosphere.
> He tried smoking on the sly.
> She smoked out the thief.
> His dreams went up in smoke.
> The Ferrari smoked along the wet track.

Someday someone will say, if it hasn't been said already, "He looked at her smokily."

Periphrasis (pə-rif'-ə-sis)—substitution of a descriptive word or phrase for a proper name or of a proper name for a quality associated with the name.

Examples: The *Splendid Splinter* hit two more *round-trippers* today.

> In his later years he became in fact the most scarifying of his own creatures: a *Quixote* of the Cotswolds who abdicated his century and thereafter lived in quasi-medieval delusions that degenerated at last into melancholia.—Article on Evelyn Waugh in *Time*, April 22, 1966

> They do not escape *Jim Crow;* they merely encounter another, not less deadly variety.—James Baldwin, *Nobody Knows My Name*

> Disney's *Pollyanna* is looking more like an aging *Lolita* now, but it's perfectly all right.—Article in *Time*, April 1, 1966

> Pale young men with larded and *Valentino-black* side whiskers.—Dylan Thomas, "Memoirs of an August Bank Holiday"

> When you're out of *Schlitz,* you're out of beer.—Advertising slogan for Schlitz beer

> She may not have been a *Penelope,* but she was not as unfaithful as the gossips made her out to be.—Student paper

The frequency with which we meet this trope, even in modern prose, is evidence of the urge in man to express familiar ideas in uncommon ways. Circumlocutions and tags can become tiresome clichés (as they often do on the sports page), but when they display a fresh, decorous inventiveness, they can add grace to our writing. It is the trite or overly ingenious oblique expression that wearies the reader.

Personification or **Prosopopoeia** (prə-sō-pō-pe'-ə)—investing abstractions or inanimate objects with human qualities or abilities.

Examples: The ground thirsts for rain.—Student paper

He glanced at the dew-covered grass, and it winked back at him.—
Student paper

A tree whose hungry mouth is prest
Against the earth's sweet-flowing breast.

—Joyce Kilmer, "Trees"

And indeed there will be time
For the yellow smoke that slides along the street,
Rubbing its back upon the window panes.
T. S. Eliot, "The Love Song of J. Alfred Prufrock"
—T. S. Eliot, "The Love Song of J. Alfred Prufrock"

Mother Tongue is a self-reliant female.—Charlton Laird, *The
Miracle of Language*

The handsome houses on the street to the college were not fully
awake, but they looked very friendly.—Lionel Trilling, "Of This
Time, Of That Place"

Personification is such a familiar figure that there is no need to multiply examples of it. This is one of the figures that should be reserved for passages
designed to stir the emotions. Another emotional figure, closely allied to personification, is *apostrophe* (ə-pos′-trə-fē) (addressing an absent person or a
personified abstraction). Here is an example of *apostrophe* from Sir Walter
Raleigh's *History of the World:*

> O eloquent, just, and mighty Death! whom none could advise, thou hast
> persuaded; what none hath dared, thou hast done; and whom all the
> world has flattered, thou only hast cast out of the world and despised.
> Thou hast drawn together all the far-stretched greatness, all the pride,
> cruelty, and ambition of man, and covered it all with these two narrow
> words, *Hic jacet.*

Hyperbole (hī-pur′-bə-lē)—the use of exaggerated terms for the purpose of
emphasis or heightened effect.

Examples: His eloquence would split rocks.

> It's really ironical . . . I have gray hair. I really do. The one side of
> my head—the right side—is full of millions of gray hairs.—Holden
> Caulfield in *Catcher in the Rye*

> My left leg weighs three tons. It is embalmed in spices like a
> mummy. I can't move. I haven't moved for five thousand years. I'm
> of the time of Pharaoh.—Thomas Bailey Aldrich, "Marjorie Daw"

"Rozelle's right," pitched in the only man in New York still wearing a 1951 crew cut.—Rex Reed, article in *Esquire,* October 1969

What he does not like is the press, which he tells us misrepresents him ninety percent of the time, by which we must understand, in a world of hyperbole which so naturally accentuates in a world of sport (how excruciating it must be for the sportswriter who cannot report that Joe Namath ran two hundred yards for a touchdown!) that occasionally we have got him wrong.—William F. Buckley, Jr., article in *Esquire,* October 1969

I will buy anything—ANYTHING—that has been reduced to one third its original price.—Jean Kerr, *The Snake Has All the Lines*

We walked along a road in Cumberland and stooped, because the sky hung so low.—Thomas Wolfe, *Look Homeward, Angel*

Hyperbole is so steadily droned into our ears that most of us have ceased to think of it as a figure of speech. Advertisers and teenagers can hardly talk without using superlatives. Perhaps we would not be so much amused by the Oriental greeting, "We welcome you, most honorable sir, to our miserable abode," if we stopped to consider how exaggerated many of our forms of greeting, address, and compliment are.

Hyperbole can be a serviceable figure of speech if we learn to use it with restraint and for a calculated effect. Under the stress of emotion, it will slip out naturally and will then seem appropriate. If we can learn to invent fresh hyperboles, we will be able to produce the right note of emphasis (as in the first example above) or humor (as in the quotation from Aldrich).

Being related to the topic of degree, hyperbole is like the figure called **auxesis** (awk-ses'-is) (magnifying the importance or gravity of something by referring to it with a disproportionate name). So a lawyer will try to impress a jury by referring to a scratch on the arm as "a wound" or to pilfering from the petty-cash box as "embezzlement." We can accept Mark Antony's reference to the wound that Brutus inflicted on Caesar as "the most unkindest cut of all," but the occasion seemed not to warrant Senator Joseph McCarthy's classic remark, "That's the most unheard of thing I ever heard of."

Litotes (lī'-tə-tēz)—deliberate use of understatement, not to deceive someone but to enhance the impressiveness of what we say.

Examples: I am a citizen of no mean city.—St. Paul

To write is, indeed, no unpleasing employment.—Samuel Johnson, *Adventurer,* No. 138

Last week I saw a woman flayed, and you will hardly believe how much it altered her appearance for the worse.—Jonathan Swift, *A Tale of a Tub*

With its oratorical blast, the session filled more than 33,250 pages of the *Congressional Record,* another record which cost the taxpayers only some $3,000,000.—Article in *Time,* October 29, 1965

Dick was awake. He was rather more than that; he and Inez were making love.—Truman Capote, *In Cold Blood*

Entertainer Frank Sinatra isn't the slow-burn type.—Article in *Newsweek,* November 15, 1965

It isn't very serious. I have this tiny little tumor on the brain.—J. D. Salinger, *The Catcher in the Rye*

For four generations we've been making medicines as if people's lives depended on them.—Ad for Eli Lilly Drug Company

Litotes is a form of **meiosis** (mī-ō′-sis) (a lessening). The same lawyer whom we saw in the previous section using *auxesis* might represent another client by referring to a case of vandalism as "teenage highjinks." A rose by any other name will smell as sweet, but a crime, if referred to by a name that is not too patently disproportionate, may lose some of its heinousness.

Rhetorical Question (erotema) (er-ot′-ə-ma)—asking a question, not for the purpose of eliciting an answer but for the purpose of asserting or denying something obliquely.

Examples: What! Gentlemen, was I not to foresee, or foreseeing was I not to endeavor to save you from all these multiplied mischiefs and disgraces? . . . Was I an Irishman on that day that I boldly withstood our pride? or on the day that I hung down my head and wept in shame and silence over the humiliation of Great Britain? I became unpopular in England for the one, and in Ireland for the other. What then? What obligation lay on me to be popular? —Edmund Burke, *Speech in the Electors of Bristol*

Wasn't the cult of James a revealing symbol and symbol of an age and society which wanted to dwell like him in some false world of false art and false culture?—Maxwell Geismar, *Henry James and His Cult*

How can the poor feel they have a stake in a system which says that the rich may have due process but the poor may not? How can the uneducated have faith in a system which says that it will take advantage of them in every possible way? How can people have hope when we tell them that they have no recourse if they run afoul of the state justice system?—Senator Edward Kennedy, Senate debate on the Omnibus Crime Control and Safe Streets Act, 1968

A good student-body is perhaps the most important factor in a great university. How can you possibly make good wine from poor grapes?—Student paper

The *rhetorical question* is a common device in impassioned speeches, but it can be used too in written prose. It can be an effective persuasive device, subtly influencing the kind of response one wants to get from an audience. The manner in which the question is phrased can determine either a negative or an affirmative response. If we say, "Was this an act of heroism?" the audience will respond, in the proper context, with a negative answer. By inducing the audience to make the appropriate response, the rhetorical question can often be more effective as a persuasive device than a direct assertion would be.

Irony (ī′-rə-nē)—use of a word in such a way as to convey a meaning opposite to the literal meaning of the word.

Examples: For Brutus is an *honourable* man;
So are they all, *honourable* men.—Shakespeare, *Julius Caesar,* III, ii, 88-9

It is again objected, as a very absurd, ridiculous custom that a set of men should be suffered, much less employed and hired, to bawl one day in seven against the *lawfulness* of those methods most in use toward the pursuit of greatness, riches, and pleasure, which are the constant practice of all men alive on the other six. But this objection is, I think, a little unworthy of *so refined* an age as ours.—Swift, *Argument Against the Abolishing of Christianity*

By Spring, if God was good, all the *proud privileges* of trench lice, mustard gas, spattered brains, punctured lungs, ripped guts, asphyxiation, mud, and gangrene, might be his.—Thomas Wolfe, *Look Homeward, Angel*

Fielder smiled. "I like the English," he said. "That gives me a *nice warm* feeling," Leamas retorted.—John Le Carré, *The Spy Who Came in from the Cold*

Neither the union nor anyone else could persuade a single soul to move into this "model facility."—John Barron, article on the FHA in *Reader's Digest,* April 1966

I was simply *overjoyed* at the thought of having to leave my guy and return to school for finals.—Student paper

Sure you could live without Yellow Pages (or without newspapers or automobiles or clocks).—Bell Telephone ad

As a trope that quite definitely conveys a "transferred meaning," *irony* is related to the topic of contraries or the topic of contradiction. A highly sophisticated device, irony must be used with great caution. If you misjudge the intelligence of your audience, you may find that your audience is taking your words in their ostensible sense rather than in the intended opposite sense.

The Tudor rhetoricians had a special name for the kind of irony in which one proposed to pass over some matter, yet managed subtly to reveal the matter anyway. They called this kind of irony **paralipsis** (par-ə-lip'-sis). A notable example of *paralipsis* is found in Mark Antony's famous "Friends, Romans, countrymen" speech in *Julius Caesar:*

> Let but the commons hear this testament,
> Which (pardon me) I do not mean to read,
> And they would go and kiss dead Caesar's wounds . . .
> Have patience, gentle friends; I must not read it.
> It is not meet you know how Caesar lov'd you. . . .
> 'Tis good you know not that you are his heirs.
>
> (III, ii, 136-51)

A look at the entire speech will show how Antony, despite his disclaimers, managed to let the mob know what was in Caesar's last will.

Onomatopoeia (on-ə-mot-ə-pe'-a)—use of words whose sound echoes the sense.

Examples: 'Tis not enough no harshness gives offense,
  The sound must seem an echo to the sense:
  Soft is the strain when Zephyr gently blows,
  And the smooth stream in smoother numbers flows;
  But when loud surges lash the sounding shore,
  The hoarse, rough verse should like the torrent roar:
  When Ajax strives some rock's vast weight to throw,
  The line too labors, and the words move slow;
  Not so, when swift Camilla scours the plain,
  Flies o'er the unbending corn, and skims along the main.
    —Pope, *Essay on Criticism,* II, 364-73

> Over the cobbles he clattered and clashed in the dark innyard.—Alfred Noyes, "The Highwayman"

> Strong gongs groaning as the guns boom far.—G. K. Chesterton, *Lepanto*

> My days have crackled and gone up in smoke.—Francis Thompson, "The Hound of Heaven"

> A talking twitter all they had to sing.—Robert Frost, "Our Singing Strength"

> The birds chirped away. Fweet, Fweet, Bootchee-Fweet.—Saul Bellow, "Masby's Memoirs," *The New Yorker,* July 20, 1968

In the passage quoted above from Pope, some of the onomatopoetic effects are produced by the rhythm of the lines as well as by the sounds of words. Since *onomatopoeia* seeks to match sound with sense, it is easy to see why this figure was commonly associated with the topic of similarity. *Onomatopoeia* will be used much less frequently in prose than in poetry, yet it still has its appropriate uses in prose. Wherever sound-effects can be used to set the emotional or ethical tone of a passage, *onomatopoeia* can make a contribution. In seeking to discredit a person or an act, we could reinforce the effect of pejorative diction with cacophony. In a phrase like "a dastardly episode," we reveal our attitude toward the event not only by the unpleasant connotations of the word *dastardly* but also by the harsh sound of the word.

Oxymoron (ok-sē-mor′-on)—the yoking of two terms that are ordinarily contradictory.

> *Examples:* expressions like *sweet pain, cheerful pessimist, conspicuous by her absence, cruel kindness, thunderous silence, luxurious poverty, abject arrogance, make haste slowly, jumbo shrimp.*

By thus combining contradictories, writers produce a startling effect, and they may, if their *oxymorons* are fresh and apt, win for themselves a reputation for wit. There is displayed in this figure, as in most metaphorical language, what Aristotle considered a special mark of genius: the ability to see similarities. Here are some examples of *oxymoron:*

> Here's much to do with hate, but more with love.
> Why then, O *brawling love!* O *loving hate!*
> O *anything* of *nothing* first create!
> O *heavy lightness, serious vanity!*
> *Misshapen* chaos of *well-seeming* forms!

Feather of lead, bright smoke, cold fire, sick health!
Still-waking sleep, that is not what it is!
This love I feel, that feel no love in this
> —William Shakespeare, *Romeo and Juliet,* I, i

O *miserable abundance,* O *beggarly riches!*
> —John Donne, *Devotions Upon Emergent Occasions*

A soul immortal, spending all her fires
Wasting her strength in *strenuous idleness.*
> —Edward Young, *The Complaint, or Night Thoughts*

There is a sort of *dead-alive* hackneyed people about, who are scarcely conscious of living except in the exercise of some conventional occupation.—Robert Louis Stevenson, "An Apology for Idlers"

The new show at the Museum of Modern Art somehow manages to avoid *visual din.*—Aline Saarinen, a report on a showing of advertising posters on the Huntley-Brinkley show, January 24, 1968

. . . or, possibly, to a draft of Edward Kennedy, whose *absent presence* constituted one of the few phenomena here that were not familiar to those who had seen the Early Show at Miami Beach.—Richard H. Rovere, "Letter from Chicago," *The New Yorker,* September 7, 1968

The *relaxed tenseness* of the Beatles' music reflects the restlessness of the teenage generation.—Student paper

These devices were calculated to stir his audience into a *rational hysteria.*—Student paper

Closely allied to oxymoron is **paradox** (par'-ə-doks) an apparently contradictory statement that nevertheless contains a measure of truth. *Paradox* is like oxymoron in that both are built on contradictories, but paradox may not be a trope at all, because it involves not so much a "turn" of meaning in juxtaposed words as a "turn" of meaning in the whole statement. Here are some examples of *paradox:*

Art is a form of lying in order to tell the truth.—Pablo Picasso

The less we copy the renowned ancients, the more we shall resemble them.—Edward Young, *Conjectures on Original Composition*

Portnoy's Complaint, a novel in the form of a psychoanalytic monologue carried on by a guilt-ridden bachelor, is too funny not to be taken seriously.—Book review in *Time,* February 21, 1969

Professor [Harry] Levin has always in a sense suffered from the weakness of this strength.—Book review in the London *Times Literary Supplement*, September 1, 1966

He [Joseph K. in Kafka's *The Trial*] is guilty of being innocent.—J. Mitchell Morse, article in *College English*, May, 1969

But the essence of that ugliness is the thing which will always make it beautiful.—Gertrude Stein, "How Writing Is Written"

We know too much for one man to know much.—J. Robert Oppenheimer, *The Open Mind*

The past is the prologue.—Paul Newman, an NBC special "From Here to the Seventies," October 7, 1969

Concluding Remarks on the Figures of Speech

A knowledge of the figures that have been presented in this chapter will not insure that you will be able to invent your own figures or that when you use figures you will use them aptly and efficaciously. The benefit from such an investigation is rather that having been made aware of the various schemes and tropes you may make a conscious effort to use figures when you see that they will suit your purpose. In acquiring any skill, we must at first do consciously what experts do automatically; or, as Dr. Johnson said, "What we hope ever to do with ease, we must learn first to do with diligence." And during this period of apprenticeship, we can expect to do awkwardly what experts do smoothly. With practice, however, we will arrive at that happy state of naturalness that Longinus spoke of in *On the Sublime:*

> Wherefore a figure is at its best when the very fact that it is a figure escapes attention. . . . For art is perfect when it seems to be nature, and nature hits the mark when she contains art hidden within her.

Exercise

Directions: Find illustrations in twentieth-century prose or poetry of the following: (Page numbers refer to section in *Classical Rhetoric for the Modern Student* where the figure is discussed and illustrated.)

Schemes

Parallelism—similarity of structure in a pair of series of related words, phrases, or clauses (p. 428)

Isocolon—similarity not only of structure but of length (p. 429)

Antithesis—the juxtaposition of contrasting ideas, often in parallel structure (p. 429)

Anastrophe—inversion of the natural or usual word order (p. 431)

Parenthesis—insertion of some verbal unit in a position that interrupts the normal syntactical flow of the sentence (p. 431)

Apposition—placing side by side two co-ordinate elements, the second of which serves as an explanation or modification of the first (p. 433)

Ellipsis—the deliberate omission of a word or of words readily implied by the context (p. 433)

Asyndeton—deliberate omission of conjunctions between a series (p. 434)

Polysyndeton—deliberate use of many conjunctions (p. 435)

Alliteration—repetition of initial or medial consonants in two or more adjacent words (p. 436)

Assonance—the repetition of similar vowel forms, preceded and followed by different consonants, in the stressed syllables of adjacent words (p. 437)

Anaphora—repetition of the same word or group of words at the beginning of successive clauses (p. 437)

Epistrophe—repetition of the same word or group of words at the ends of successive clauses (p. 438)

Epanalepsis—repetition at the end of a clause of the word that occurred at the beginning of the clause (p. 439)

Anadiplosis—repetition of the last word of one clause at the beginning of the following clause (p. 440)

Climax—arrangement of words, phrases, or clauses in an order of increasing importance (p. 441)

Antimetabole—repetition of words, in successive clauses, in reverse grammatical order (p. 442)

Chiasmus—reversal of grammatical structures in a successive clauses (but no repetition of words) (p. 443)

Polyptoton—repetition of words derived from the same root (p. 443)

Tropes

Metaphor—implied comparison between two things of unlike nature (p. 444)

Simile—explicit comparison between two things of unlike nature (p. 444)

Synecdoche—figure of speech in which a part stands for the whole (p. 445)

Metonymy—substitution of some attributive or suggestive word for what is actually meant (p. 446)

Antanaclasis—repetition of a word in two different senses (p. 447)

Paronomasis—use of words alike in sound but different in meaning (p. 447)

Syllepsis—use of a word understood differently in relation to two or more other words, which it modifies or governs (p. 448)

Anthimeria—the substitution of one part of speech for another (p. 449)

Periphrasis (antonomasia)—substitution of a descriptive word or phrase for a proper name or of a proper name for a quality associated with the name (p. 450)

Personification (prosopopoeia)—investing abstractions for inanimate objects with human qualities or abilities (p. 450)

Hyperbole—the use of exaggerated terms for the purpose of emphasis or heightened effect (p. 451)

Litotes—deliberate use of understatement (p. 452)

Rhetorical question—asking a question, not for the purpose of eliciting an answer but for the purpose of asserting or denying something obliquely (p. 453)

Irony—use of a word in such a way as to convey a meaning opposite to the literal meaning of the word (p. 454)

Onomatapoeia—use of words whose sound echoes the sense (p. 455)

Oxymoron—the yoking of two terms which are ordinarily contradictory (p. 456)

Paradox—an apparently contradictory statement that nevertheless contains a measure of truth (p. 457)

Imitation

Up to this point we have been dealing with the precepts of style. Now we will move on to the second of the ways in which one learns to write or to improve one's writing—imitation. Classical rhetoric books are filled with testimonies about the value of imitation for the refinement of the many skills involved in effective speaking or writing. Style is, after all, the most imitable of the skills that cooperate to produce effective discourse.

Rhetoricians recommended a variety of exercises to promote conscious imitation. Roman schoolchildren, for example, were regularly set the task of translating Greek passages into Latin and vice versa. In some of the Renaissance schools in England, students worked back and forth between Greek and Latin and English. Schoolmasters—the better ones anyway—were aware that grammatical differences among these three languages necessitated certain stylistic adjustments in the translation from one language to another. Despite these differences, however, students did learn from this exercise many valuable lessons about sentence structure.

Another exercise was the practice of paraphrasing poetry into prose. Here again many adjustments in style had to be made. Besides teaching students the salient differences between the poetic medium and the prose medium, this exercise made students pay close attention to the potentialities of precise, concrete diction, of emphatic disposition of words, and of figures of speech. Even today there are those who maintain that the best way to improve one's prose style is to study or write poetry.

Another common practice was to set the students the task of saying something in a variety of ways. This process usually started out with a model sentence, which had to be converted into a variety of forms each retaining the basic thought of the original. Erasmus, for instance, in Chapter 33 of his widely-used little book, *De duplici copia verborum ac rerum,* showed the students 150 ways of phrasing the Latin sentence, *Tuae literae me magnopere delectarunt* (Your letter has delighted me very much). This variety was achieved partly by the choice of different words, partly by different collocations of words. Here, in English, is a sampling of Erasmus's reworkings:

> Your epistle has cheered me greatly.
>
> Your note has been the occasion of unusual pleasure for me.
>
> When your letter came, I was seized with an extraordinary pleasure.
>
> What you wrote to me was most delightful.
>
> On reading your letter, I was filled with joy.
>
> Your letter provided me with no little pleasure.

Obviously, not all of the 150 sentences were equally satisfactory or appropriate; in fact, some were monstrosities. But by artificially experimenting with various forms, students became aware of the flexibility of the language in which they were working and learned to extend their own range. Ultimately they learned that although there is a variety of ways of saying something, there is a "best way" for their particular subject matter, occasion, or audience. What was "best" for one occasion or audience, they discovered, is not "best" for another occasion or audience.

This text will give you the opportunity to practice two kinds of imitation—copying passages of prose and imitating various sentence patterns. But before we get into those exercises, we will present the testimony of some famous writers about how they learned to write. You will see as you read these testimonies how basic imitation is to the formation of style.

Testimonies about the Value of Imitation

Malcolm X

I saw that the best thing I could do was get hold of a dictionary—to study, to learn some words. I was lucky enough to reason also that I should try to improve my penmanship. It was sad. I couldn't even write in a straight line. It was both ideas together that moved me to request a dictionary along with some tablets and pencils from the Norfolk Prison Colony school.

I spent two days just riffling uncertainly through the dictionary's pages. I'd never realized so many words existed! I didn't know *which* words I needed to learn. Finally, just to start some kind of action, I began copying.

In my slow, painstaking, ragged handwriting, I copied into my tablet everything printed on that first page, down to the punctuation marks.

I believe it took me a day. Then, aloud, I read back, to myself, everything I'd written on the tablet. Over and over, aloud, to myself, I read my own handwriting.

I woke up the next morning, thinking about those words—immensely proud to realize that not only had I written so much at one time, but I'd written words that I never knew were in the world. Moreover, with a little effort, I also could remember what many of these words meant. I reviewed the words whose meanings I didn't remember. Funny thing, from the dictionary first page right now, that "aardvark" springs to my mind. The dictionary had a picture of it, a long-tailed, long-eared, burrowing African mammal, which lives off termites caught by sticking out its tongue as an anteater does for ants.

I was so fascinated that I went on—I copied the dictionary's next page. And the same experience came when I studied that. With every succeeding page, I also learned of people and places and events from history. Actually the dictionary is like a miniature encyclopedia. Finally the dictionary's A section had filled a whole tablet—and I went on into the B's. That was the way I started copying what eventually became the entire dictionary. It went a lot faster after so much practice helped me to pick up handwriting speed. Between what I wrote in my tablet, and writing letters, during the rest of my time in prison I would guess I wrote a million words.

Benjamin Franklin

About this time I met with an odd volume of the *Spectator*. It was the third. I had never before see. any of them. I bought it, read it over and over, and was much delighted with it. I thought the writing excellent, and wished, if possible, to imitate it. With this view I took some of the papers, and, making short hints of the sentiment in each sentence, laid them by a few days, and then, without looking at the book, try'd to compleat the papers again, by expressing each hinted sentiment at length, and as fully as it had been expressed before, in any suitable words that should come to hand. Then I compared my *Spectator* with the original, discovered some of my faults, and corrected them. But I found I wanted a stock of words, or a readiness in recollecting and using them, which I thought I should have acquired before that time if I had gone on making verses; since the continual occasion for words of the same import, but of different length, to suit the measure, or of different sound for the rhyme, would have laid me under a constant necessity of searching for variety, and also have tended to fix that variety in my mind, and make me master of it. Therefore I took some of the tales and turned them into verse; and, after a time, when I had pretty well forgotten the prose, turned them back again. I also sometimes jumbled my collections of hints into confusion, and after some weeks endeavored to reduce them into the best order, before I began to form the full sentences and compleat the paper. This was to teach me method in the arrangement of thoughts. By comparing my work afterwards with the original, I discovered many faults and amended them; but I sometimes had the pleasure of fancying that, in certain particulars of small import, I had been lucky enough to improve the method or the language, and this encouraged me to think I might possibly in time come to be a tolerable English writer, of which I was extreamly ambitious.

From *The Autobiography of Benjamin Franklin*, 1771.

Winston S. Churchill

I continued in this unpretentious situation for nearly a year. However, by being so long in the lowest form [at Harrow] I gained an immense advantage over the cleverer boys. They all went on to learn Latin and Greek and splendid things like that. But I was taught English. We were considered such dunces that we could learn only English. Mr. Somervell—a most delightful man, to whom my debt is great—was charged with the duty of teaching the stupidest boys the most disregarded thing—namely, to write mere English. He knew how to do it. He taught it as no one else has ever taught it. Not only did we learn English parsing thoroughly, but we also practised continually English analysis. Mr. Somervell had a system of his own. He took a fairly long sentence and broke it up into its components by means of black, red, blue, and green inks. Subject, verb, object: Relative Clauses, Conditional Clauses, Conjunctive and Disjunctive Clauses! Each had its colour and its bracket. It was a kind of drill. We did it almost daily. As I remained in the Third Form (β) three times as long as anyone else, I had three times as much of it. I learned it thoroughly. Thus I got into my bones the essential structure of the ordinary British sentence—which is a noble thing. And when in after years my schoolfellows who had won prizes and distinction for writing such beautiful Latin poetry and pithy Greek epigrams had to come down again to common English, to earn their living or make their way, I did not feel myself at any disadvantage. Naturally I am biased in favour of boys learning English. I would make them all learn English: and then I would let the clever ones learn Latin as an honour, and Greek as a treat. But the only thing I would whip them for is not knowing English, I would whip them hard for that.

Somerset Maugham

IX

As it is, I have had to teach myself. I have looked at the stories I wrote when I was very young in order to discover what natural aptitude I had, my original stock-in-trade, before I developed it by taking thought. The manner had a superciliousness that perhaps my years excused and an irascibility that was a defect of nature; but I am speaking now only of the way in which I expressed myself. It seems to me that I had a natural lucidity and a knack for writing easy dialogue.

When Henry Arthur Jones, then a well-known playwright, read my first novel, he told a friend that in due course I should be one of the most successful dramatists of the day. I suppose he saw in it directness and an effective way of presenting a scene that suggested a sense of the theatre. My language was commonplace, my vocabulary limited, my grammar shaky and my phrases hackneyed. But to write was an instinct that seemed as natural to me as to breathe, and I did not stop to consider if I wrote well or badly. It was not till some years later that it dawned upon me that it was a delicate art that must be painfully acquired. The discovery was forced upon me by the difficulty I found in getting my meaning down on paper. I wrote dialogue fluently, but when it came to a page of description I found myself entangled in all sorts of quandaries. I would struggle for a couple of hours over two or three sentences that I could in no way manage to straighten out. I made up my mind to teach myself how to write. Unfortunately I had no one to help me. I made many mistakes. If I had had someone to guide me like the charming don of whom I spoke just now I might have been saved much time. Such a one might have told me that such gifts as I had lay in one direction and that they must be cultivated in that direction; it was useless to try to do something for which I had no aptitude. But at that time a florid prose was admired. Richness of texture was sought by means of a jewelled phrase and sentences stiff with exotic epithets: the ideal was a brocade so heavy with gold that it stood up by itself. The intelligent young read Walter Pater with enthusiasm. My common sense suggested to me that it was anaemic stuff; behind those elaborate, gracious periods I was conscious of a tired, wan personality. I was young, lusty and energetic; I wanted fresh air, action, violence, and I found it hard to breathe that dead, heavily scented atmosphere and sit in those hushed rooms in which it was indecorous to speak above a whisper. But I would not listen to my common sense. I persuaded myself that this was the height of culture and turned a scornful shoulder on the outside world where men shouted and swore, played the fool, wenched and got drunk. I read *Intentions* and *The Picture of Dorian Gray*. I was intoxicated by the colour and rareness of the fantastic words that thickly stud the pages of *Salome*. Shocked by the poverty of my own vocabulary, I went to the British Museum with pencil and paper and noted down the names of curious jewels, the Byzantine hues of old enamels, the sensual feel of textiles, and made elaborate sentences to bring them in. Fortunately I could never find an opportunity to use them, and they lie there yet in an old notebook ready for anyone who has a mind to write nonsense. It was generally thought then that the Authorized Version of the Bible was the greatest piece of prose that the English language has produced. I read it diligently, especially the Song of Solomon, jotting down for future use turns of phrase that struck me and making lists of unusual or beautiful words. I studied Jeremy Taylor's *Holy Dying*. In order to assimilate his style I copied out passages and then tried to write them down from memory.

The first fruit of this labour was a little book about Andalusia called *The Land of the Blessed Virgin*. I had occasion to read parts of it the other day. I know Andalusia a great deal better now than I knew it then, and I have changed my mind about a good many things of which I wrote. Since it has continued in America to have a small sale it occurred to me that it might be worth while to revise it. I soon saw that this was impossible. The book was written by someone I have completely forgotten. It bored me to distraction. But what I am concerned with is the prose, for it was as an exercise in style that I wrote it. It is wistful, allusive and elaborate. It has neither ease nor spontaneity. It smells of hothouse plants and Sunday dinner like the air in the greenhouse that leads out of the dining-room of a big house in Bayswater. There are a great many melodious adjectives. The vocabulary is sentimental. It does not remind one of an Italian brocade, with its rich pattern of gold, but of a curtain material designed by Burne-Jones and reproduced by Morris.

x

I do not know whether it was a subconscious feeling that this sort of writing was contrary to my bent or a naturally methodical cast of mind that led me then to turn my attention to the writers of the Augustan Period. The prose of Swift enchanted me. I made up my mind that this was a perfect way to write, and I started to work on him in the same way as I had done with Jeremy Taylor. I chose *The Tale of a Tub*. It is said that when the Dean re-read it in his old age he cried: 'What genius I had then!' To my mind his genius was better shown in other works. It is a tiresome allegory, and the irony is facile. But the style is admirable. I cannot imagine that English can be better written. Here are no flowery periods, fantastic turns of phrase or high-flown images. It is a civilized prose, natural, discreet and pointed. There is no attempt to surprise by an extravagant vocabulary. It looks as though Swift made do with the first word that came to hand, but since he had an acute and logical brain it was always the right one, and he put it in the right place. The strength and balance of his sentences are due to an exquisite taste. As I had done before, I copied passages and then tried to write them out again from memory. I tried altering words or the order in which they were set. I found that the only possible words were those Swift had used and that the order in which he had placed them was the only possible order. It is an impeccable prose.

But perfection has one grave defect: it is apt to be dull. Swift's prose is like a French canal, bordered with poplars, that runs through a gracious and undulating country. Its tranquil charm fills you with satisfaction, but it neither excites the emotions nor stimulates the imagination. You go on and on and presently you are a trifle bored. So, much as you may admire Swift's wonderful lucidity, his terseness, his naturalness, his lack of affectation, you find your attention wandering after a while unless his matter peculiarly interests you. I think if I had my time over again I would give to the prose of Dryden the close study I gave to that of Swift. I did not come across it till I had lost the inclination to take so much pains. The prose of Dryden is delicious. It has not the perfection of Swift nor the easy elegance of Addison, but it has a springtime gaiety, a conversational ease, a blithe spontaneousness that are enchanting. Dryden was a very good poet, but it is not the general opinion that he had a lyrical quality; it is strange that it is just this that sings in his softly sparkling prose. Prose had never been written in England like that before; it has seldom been written like that since. Dryden flourished at a happy moment. He had in his bones the sonorous periods and the baroque massiveness of Jacobean language, and under the influence of the nimble and well-bred felicity that he learnt from the French he turned it into an instrument that was fit not only for solemn themes but also to express the light thought of the passing moment. He was the first of the rococo artists. If Swift reminds you of a French canal Dryden recalls an English river winding its cheerful way round hills, through quietly busy towns and by nestling villages, pausing now in a noble reach and then running powerfully through a woodland country. It is alive, varied, windswept; and it has the pleasant open-air smell of England.

The work I did was certainly very good for me. I began to write better; I did not write well. I wrote stiffly and self-consciously. I tried to get a pattern into my sentences, but did not see that the pattern was evident. I took care how I placed my words, but did not reflect that an order that was natural at the beginning of the eighteenth century was most unnatural at the beginning of ours. My attempt to write in the manner of Swift made it impossible for me to achieve the effect of inevitable rightness that was just what I so much admired in him. I then wrote a number of plays and ceased to occupy myself with anything but dialogue. It was not till five years had passed that I set out again to write a novel. By then I no longer had any ambition to be a stylist; I put aside all thought of fine writing. I wanted to write without any frills of language, in as bare and unaffected a manner as I could. I had so much to say that I could afford to waste no words. I wanted merely to set down the facts. I began with the impossible aim of using no adjectives at all. I thought that if you could find the exact term a qualifying epithet could be dispensed with. As I saw it in my mind's eye my book would have the appearance of an immensely long telegram in which for economy's sake you had left out every word that was not necessary to make the sense clear. I have not read it since I corrected the proofs and do not know how near I came to doing what I tried. My impression is that it is written at least more naturally than anything I had written before; but I am sure that it is often slipshod, and I daresay there are in it a good many mistakes in grammar.

Since then I have written many other books; and though ceasing my methodical study of the old masters (for though the spirit is willing, the flesh is weak), I have continued with increasing assiduity to try to write better. I discovered my limitations, and it seemed to me that the only sensible thing was to aim at what excellence I could within them. I knew that I had no lyrical quality. I had a small vocabulary, and no efforts that I could make to enlarge it much availed me. I had little gift of metaphor; the original and striking simile seldom occurred to me. Poetic flights and the great imaginative sweep were beyond my powers. I could admire them in others as I could admire their far-fetched tropes and the unusual but suggestive language in which they clothed their thoughts, but my own invention never presented me with such embellishments; and I was tired of trying to do what did not come easily to me. On the other hand, I had an acute power of observation, and it seemed to me that I could see a great many things that other people missed. I could put down in clear terms what I saw. I had a logical sense, and if not great feeling for the richness and strangeness of words, at all events a lively appreciation of their sound. I knew that I should never write as well as I could wish, but I thought with pains I could arrive at writing a well as my natural defects allowed. On taking thought it seemed to me that I must aim at lucidity, simplicity, and euphony. I have put these three qualities in the order of the importance I assigned to them.

Rollo Walter Brown: How the French Boy Learns to Write

As soon as an American teacher comes into direct contact with the French educational system, he marvels at the large place writing holds in the schools and their routine life. First, it matters not in what classroom a small boy may be seen, he is never without his general notebook, in which he records all assignments, all problems, all experiments, all quotations to be learned, all geographical and historical notes and maps, as well as many special exercises; and the language he employs in this work is carefully marked and graded by the teacher. In the second place, compositions are numerous. From the time the boy is regarded as mature enough to think consecutively, he prepares compositions at regular intervals. In some classes he writes two short exercises every three or five days. In the elementary primary schools, even up to the time the boy is thirteen or fourteen years old, the shorter themes once or twice a week seem to stand in great favor. These vary in length, usually, from a hundred and fifty to four hundred words—they are rather longer than the average American daily theme—and the less frequent, longer compositions range ordinarily from six hundred to fifteen hundred words. Then, in the upper grades, there are, in addition, many papers in history, civics, philosophy, and literature. So it may be seen that a boy is provided with much opportunity to write. It is, in fact, scarcely an exaggeration to say that he writes all the time. In any event, his practice is so continuous that he sooner or later comes to do the work in a perfectly normal frame of mind, just as he performs his other schoolday labors.

The volume of required writing, however, is regarded as less important than its quality. If a boy thinks and writes poorly, he is looked upon as an unfortunate who deserves either pity or contempt. If, on the other hand, he is able to think and write skillfully, he is held in great honor by his teachers and his classmates. And this interest in ability to write is evident outside the recitation-room. Authors of books and articles discuss the perils of the pure mother tongue as seriously as if they were dealing with a question of ethics or of grave national policy. Parents, I found when I was securing compositions for the purposes of this book, are usually desirous of preserving the written work of their children. Moreover, when pupils distinguish themselves in examinations—which in France are always largely a matter of composition—they receive prizes and public mention very much as if they were the winners of athletic trophies. Now I would not have anyone make the hasty inference that intellectual contests are substituted for athletics. The French boy loves the open just as much as the American boy does, and outdoor sports are steadily taking a larger place in school life. But the ideal of writing well has been held up before the schoolboy so long, and with such seriousness, that he attaches more importance to ability of this kind than the average American boy could at present be led to comprehend.

When so much importance is everywhere attached to ability to write, it is not surprising to find that in both the primary and secondary school systems the course in the mother tongue gives large place to systematic training in composition. It is the conviction of the great body of teachers, as well as the Ministry, that work in grammar, rhetoric, and literature is in most respects lost unless it contributes to the pupil's ability to give full, intelligent expression to his thought. Moreover, theories of teaching, and all the proposed changes in the course of study, seem to be considered first in respect to their influence on this ability of the pupil. Expression is not the sole end, but in all the lower schools it is the primary end. And, taking the other point of view, the chief responsibility for the pupil's manner of expression rests upon the teacher of the mother tongue. As we shall see later, the writing that the boy does in history, geometry, and his other subjects is made to contribute its full share to his skill; yet upon the teacher of the native language rests the largest responsibility and the greatest burden of labor. He accepts his task as difficult, very expensive in time and energy, but extremely important. Without going into any examination of exceptional aims or of intricate personal devices, let us see what he attempts to accomplish and how he pursues his way.

Two groups of exercises are everywhere regarded as essential preliminaries to work in original composition. Those in the first group are intended to enlarge and organize the pupil's vocabulary. Now, I am aware that when one stands apart and looks at exercises designed to improve the vocabulary, they are likely to appear very artificial and ineffective. And, in truth, they may be. In the hands of a poorly trained teacher, or one who lacks the all-important teaching instinct, it would be difficult to imagine an exercise that could be more dismally futile. But this possibility seems to be disregarded by French educators. They are ready to admit that the lessons may become valueless, or even harmful, when directed by a poor teacher—and what exercise may not?—but they do not spring to the conclusion that such lessons should for that reason be cast aside. They have taken the good teacher as the norm, and have given themselves earnestly to the task of obviating the dangers and developing the advantages of a kind of instruction which at its best appears to them to have unquestioned value.

The theory upon which this instruction is based is not the individual opinion of the occasional teacher; it is accepted doctrine throughout the country. In the volume of *Instructions* issued by the Minister to teachers in the secondary school system, it is summarized as follows: "The preceding exercises [in grammar] help the pupil to understand his native language and to enrich his vocabulary; but for this latter purpose, one ought not to rely solely upon them or even upon conversation, dictations, reading, or the explication of texts. The pupil must learn words, though never apart from things; he must be able to seize their signification and the exact shade of their meaning; and he must become accustomed to finding the words quickly when he stands in need. Hence the value of exercises devoted especially to the study of the vocabulary."

The teaching of the vocabulary I found, then, falls readily into three parts: (1) enlarging; (2) sharpening; (3) quickening. To be sure, the instruction is not divided into three separate processes, but the teacher has a threefold aim that determines his method. One will not see every aspect of the method in one recitation or in several. Yet the principles emphasized in the *Instruc-*

tions to secondary teachers, in textbooks for primary schools, in classes in the mother tongue in both school systems, and even in many classes in English, serve to give outline to the varying details of the work.

In the exercise designed to enlarge the vocabulary, it is held to be absolutely essential that the pupil relate the word unmistakably to the object or idea which it represents. Although it is much more difficult to have a word in mind without relating it to some idea than we generally suppose, the French teacher seems to take no risk. He guides the pupil to feel the uselessness of words unless they are symbols of something physically or mentally real. Secondly, the pupil is required to relate a new word to other words already in his working vocabulary, so that it will remain firmly fixed in his mind. The new word may be linked to a synonym that is known to the pupil, it may be contrasted with words already known to him, or it simply may be linked to a group of ideas that by circumstances are brought to his mind frequently; but in some manner he is led to associate it with words which he knows well. Thirdly, the word is put into normal contexts—sometimes before its meanings are explained—so that the pupil may develop a feeling for its idiomatic use. And finally, in the definition or explanation that a word or a group of words may require, the beginning is specific rather than general, concrete rather than abstract. In theory at least, a teacher would establish the meaning of *sincere* in a boy's mind before he discussed the abstract quality, *sincerity*. He would show the boy that many things are *rich* before he explained *richness;* or *noble,* before he explained *nobility.* Moreover, if a word has many definitions, the simplest one, the one most easily understood, the one that would most readily associate itself with the boy's stock of concrete ideas and images is explained before those that are predominantly abstract or figurative. It is taken for granted that if a word is to be of much value to a boy, it must represent an idea clearly established in his mind, and it must have its individual flavor.

.   .   .

In the exercises designed primarily to sharpen feeling for words, one is sure to be impressed with the many means by which a word is brought into the pupil's life. He defines it, he finds examples of its accepted uses, he learns its original significance—its literal meaning when the word is predominantly figurative—he compares it with other words of similar meaning, and above all, he contrasts it with words that are essentially its opposite. It is scarcely too much to say that the basis of all word-teaching is contrast rather than likeness. If a given word is used chiefly as a noun, the teacher does not let the pupil form the notion that synonymous adjectives may be attached to it indiscriminately, but helps him to learn what adjectives are or may be used appropriately with it. If the word is an adjective or verb, he shows how it normally takes certain adverbs, and how others, as soon as they are brought into close relation with it, seem awkward and unidiomatic. In a similar manner he guides the pupil to see the distinctions that usage has established between nouns which in general meaning are the same. To take a very simple example, if the word *stem* appeared in a lesson, he would be extremely careful to bring out the difference between *stem* and *stalk,* *stem* and *trunk,* and *stalk* and *trunk,* so that the pupil would never fall into the error of using them as if they were convertible terms. Through numerous exercises of this kind the pupil is made to see that words do not have the same value, and that the choosing of them is not merely a question of finding approved dictionary definitions when occasion arises, but of possessing a word sense.

Concerning the exercises in calling words to mind quickly, little need be said. Their character has already been suggested. They usually consist of rapid-fire questions about the word itself, its use, its likes and opposites, and of oral or written practice in composition on subjects likely to call words of a given class into use. I saw no turning of verse into prose, but I did see many exercises that required the pupils to turn one kind of prose into another. In most instances the teacher simply read a story or an essay to the class and then called upon pupils to repeat it in language of their own. After a little practice of this kind, a boy unconsciously adopts many words that he has well understood but has not made a part of his working vocabulary. He does not surrender his individuality, as he must do—momentarily, at least—in writing imitations, yet he is in a state of open-mindedness that encourages a definite impression of what he reads or hears read.

The scope of the lessons in vocabulary is wide. By the time a boy has reached the age of twelve he not only has had practice in calling simple objects by their right names, but he has reached out into the world around him and made acquaintance with words belonging to a great variety of activities. He can speak intelligently about the professions, the occupations of workingmen, the farm, social life, political life; he can discuss the more familiar phenomena of the atmosphere, the physical qualities of his friends, their moral virtues and their moral faults; he can use accurately the words that spring from such relations as commerce, war, colonization, life in the city or the small village; and he can talk or write about such means of communication as railways, steamships, street-railways, and the telegraph and telephone. This ability he gains not by sporadic or blind plunging about, but by means of orderly, systematic study. The instruction is not overrigid or mechanical; one might visit classrooms for months without feeling that the instruction was organized in any large way. Yet it is the careful organization that makes the wide scope of the work possible. The simplicity is not that of isolated, individual effort, but of well-designed plan.

.   .   .

The second of the preliminary exercises universally employed by the French teacher of the mother tongue is dictation. In America, dictation seems to have been put aside to make way for something new. French teachers, however, do not hesitate to use an old-fashioned method or device if they believe it is good. Instead, therefore, of dropping dictation from the programme of studies, they have emphasized it and developed it until it is now a very important and thoroughly established part of their educational procedure. It is based on the conviction that a child can acquire skill before he develops the power of profound or sustained thought. He has much practice, then, in writing the thoughts of others while he is yet too young to write his own. Teachers admit that dictation has its dangers, but since they regard these as incomparable to its possible value, they employ it, just as they employ exercises in vocabulary, with the confidence that though they are risking small dangers, they are following the direction of a larger common sense.

French teachers usually dwell upon four or five specific values of dictation. It gives the pupil much practice in the handling of the sentence; it directs his attention to grammatical constructions; it helps him to learn to spell, to punctuate, and to capitalize; it enlarges his vocabulary and gives him practice in the use of words already known to him; and it fills his mind with good standards of speech. To these should be added one value that the thoughtful teacher must regard as greatest of all; namely, that dictation prevents the pupil from separating spoken language and writing. One of the objections almost invariably made by the young pupil to practice in original composition is that writing seems an artificial process quite unlike anything he has ever before attempted. In making this objection, he is, of course, merely giving expression to the fact that language is naturally a matter of speech rather than writing, and the additional fact that he has not felt a close relation between what he says by word of mouth and what he writes on paper. If then, before he begins composition, and later while he is practicing it in an elementary manner, he has drill in writing down what he hears, the relation between speech and writing is much less likely to be weakened. While he is listening carefully to his teacher's reading, catching the words in their natural thought groups, and putting them down one by one in his exercise-book, he is not only learning much about the mechanics of composition, but he is saving himself from the error of looking upon theme-writing as something far removed from normal existence.

In giving dictations, the teacher exercises great care. After the very earliest classes, where the work must of necessity be simple, he does not give isolated or detached sentences, but instead, a complete, interesting paragraph. Moreover, he always explains the paragraph fully before he asks the pupil to write it down. This precaution is regarded as so important that a teacher is prohibited from requiring a pupil to write down anything that is meaningless or vague. Again, he reads a paragraph that contains material suited to keep the pupil's attention. That is to say, the ideas and the words in which they are expressed must be just within the pupil's reach. And finally, the teacher guards against letting the exercise become monotonous. It is never long—usually it is a short, crisp paragraph—the corrections are made immediately while interest is warm, and the pupil is not asked to rewrite the dictation unless he has been exceedingly careless. The ten or fifteen minutes are so full of pleasant activity that the time passes quickly, and the boy seems never to dream that he is doing something that might, under a thoughtless teacher, become a dreary, useless punishment.

.   .   .

Summary

The attention, then, that the actual business of writing receives in the French schools is a matter not only of adequate instruction, but of full and definite practice under stimulating circumstances. Composition is held up as a very important part—in fact, the most important part—of the course in the mother tongue. Studies in vocabulary and practice in dictation are carried on constantly in the lower grades in order that the boy may express himself without hindrance when he is once old enough to have something of his own to say in organized compositions. The material assigned is regarded as a matter of great moment. It is intended to develop, in order, the powers of attention and observation, the imagination, and habits of reflection. This material, moreover, is almost invariably discussed in the classroom until the pupil is awakened and interested; and when he writes upon it, he must give the most thoughtful care to organization and general good form. In the criticism of themes, oral discussion holds a large place. Furthermore, the teacher makes his critical suggestions distinctly constructive; that is, he emphasizes the difference between poor work and good, and he leads the pupils to reflect upon the possibilities that the subject-matter possesses, rather than upon the magnitude of their own shortcomings. And finally, the training that pupils receive in the study of the mother tongue is re-enforced to no small degree by the work in other subjects.

Exercises in Imitation

Copying Passages

The first exercise in imitation that we will recommend to you consists of copying passages, word for word, from admired authors. This may strike you as being a rather brainless exercise, but it can teach you a great deal about the niceties of style. Earlier in this chapter, we pointed out a number of features one looks for when one makes a close study of style. These features will strike you as you carefully transcribe the passage.

If you are to derive any benefit from this exercise, you must observe a few simple rules:

1. You must not spend more than fifteen or twenty minutes copying at any one time. If you extend this exercise much beyond twenty minutes at any one sitting, your attention will begin to wander, and you will find yourself merely copying words.

2. You must do this copying with a pencil or pen. Typing is so fast and so mechanical that you can copy off whole passages without paying any attention to the features of an author's style. Copying by hand, you transcribe the passage at such a pace that you have time to observe the choice and disposition of words, the patterns of sentences, and the length and variety of sentences.

3. You must not spend too much time with any one author. If you concentrate on a single author's style, you may find yourself falling into that "servile imitation" that rhetoricians warned of. The aim of this exercise is not to acquire someone else's style but to lay the groundwork for developing your own style by getting the "feel" of a variety of styles.

4. You must read the entire passage before starting to copy it so that you can capture the thought and the manner of the passage as a whole. When you are copying, it is advisable to read each sentence through before transcribing it. After you have finished copying the passage, you should read your transcription so that you once again get a sense of the passage as a whole.

5. You must copy the passage slowly and accurately. If you are going to dash through this exercise, you might as well not do it at all. A mechanical way of insuring accuracy and the proper pace is to make your handwriting as legible as you can.

You will derive the maximum benefit from this copying exercise if you practice it over an extended period of time. Transcribing a single different passage every day for a month will prove more beneficial to you than transcribing several different passages every day for a week. You must have time to absorb what you have been observing in this exercise; and you will not have time to absorb the many lessons to be learned from this exercise if you cram it into a short period.

Specimen Passages for Imitation

The Bible

I returned and saw under the sun that the race is not to the swift, nor the battle to the strong, neither yet bread to the wise, nor yet riches to men of understanding, nor yet favour to men of skill; but time and chance happeneth to them all. For man also knoweth not his time: as the fishes that are taken in an evil net, and as the birds that are caught in the snare; so are the sons of men snared in an evil time, when it falleth suddenly upon them. This wisdom have I seen also under the sun, and it seemed great unto me. There was a little city, and few men within it; and there came a great king against it, and besieged it, and built great bulwarks against it. Now there was found in it a poor wise man, and he by his wisdom delivered the city; yet no man remembered that same poor man. Then said I, Wisdom is better than strength: nevertheless the poor man's wisdom is despised, and his words are not heard. The words of wise men are heard in quiet more than the cry of him that ruleth among fools. Wisdom is better than weapons of war: but one sinner destroyeth much good.

(From Ecclesiastes, IX, 11–18, King James Version, 1611.)

And so it was, that, while they were there, the days were accomplished that she should be delivered. And she brought forth her firstborn son and wrapped him in swaddling clothes and laid him in a manger; because there was no room for them in the inn. And there were in the same country shepherds abiding in the field, keeping watch over their flock by night. And, lo, the angel of the Lord came upon them, and the glory of the Lord shone round about them: and they were sore afraid. And the angel said unto them, Fear not: for, behold, I bring you good tidings of great joy, which shall be to all people. For unto you is born this day in the city of David a Saviour, which is Christ the Lord. And this shall be a sign unto you; Ye shall find the babe wrapped in swaddling clothes, lying in a manger. And suddenly there was with the angel a multitude of the heavenly host praising God and saying, Glory to God in the highest, and on earth peace, good will toward men.

(From St. Luke, II, 6–14, King James Version, 1611.)

Sir Thomas Browne

If the nearness of our last necessity brought a nearer conformity into it, there were a happiness in hoary hairs, and no calamity in half-senses. But the long habit of living indisposeth us for dying; when avarice makes us the sport of death, when even David grew politicly cruel, and Solomon could hardly be said to be the wisest of men. But many are too early old, and before the date of age. Adversity stretcheth our days, misery makes Alcmena's nights, and time hath no wings unto it. But the most tedious being is that which can unwish itself, content to be nothing, or never to have been, which was beyond the malcontent of Job, who cursed not the day of his life, but his nativity; content to have so far been, as to have a title to future being, although he had lived here but in an hidden state of life, and as it were an abortion.

(From *Hydriotaphia, Urn-Burial,* 1658.)

Handwritten annotations: periphrasis · alliteration · polyptoton · death · antithesis · focuses at center · adversation · (frosty Gray) Old age · death to a person who's never born

John Dryden

'Tis a vanity common to all writers, to overvalue their own productions; and 'tis better for me to own this failing in myself, than the world to do it for me. For what other reason have I spent my life in so unprofitable a study? why am I grown old in seeking so barren a reward as fame? The same parts and application which have made me a poet might have raised me to any honours of the gown, which are often given to men of as little learning and less honesty than myself. No Government has ever been, or ever can be, wherein time-servers and blockheads will not be uppermost. The persons are only changed, but the same jugglings in State, the same hypocrisy in religion, the same self-interest and mismanagement, will remain for ever. Blood and money will be lavished in all ages, only for the preferment of new faces, with old consciences. There is too often a jaundice in the eyes of great men; they see not those whom they raise in the same colours with other men. All whom they affect look golden to them, when the gilding is only in their own distempered sight. These considerations have given me a kind of contempt for those who have risen by unworthy ways. I am not ashamed to be little, when I see them so infamously great; neither do I know why the name of poet should be dishonourable to me, if I am truly one, as I hope I am; for I will never do anything that shall dishonour it.

(From the Dedication to *Examen Poeticum,* 1693.)

Daniel Defoe

I must confess myself to have been very much dejected just before this happened; for the prodigious number that were taken sick the week or two before, besides those that died, was such, and the lamentations were so great everywhere, that a man must have seemed to have acted even against his reason if he had so much as expected to escape; and as there was hardly a house but mine in all my neighbourhood but what was infected, so had it gone on it would not have been long that there would have been any more neighbours to be infected. Indeed it is hardly credible what dreadful havoc the last three weeks had made, for if I might believe the person whose calculations I always found very well grounded, there were not less than 30,000 people dead and near 100,000 fallen sick in the three weeks I speak of; for the number that sickened was surprising; indeed it was astonishing, and those whose courage upheld them all the time before, sank under it now.

In the middle of their distress, when the condition of the City of London was so truly calamitous, just then it pleased God, as it were, by His immediate hand to disarm this enemy; the poison was taken out of the sting. It was wonderful; even the physicians themselves were surprised at it. Wherever they visited they found their patients better; either they had sweated kindly, or the tumors were broke, or the carbuncles went down, and the inflammations round them changed color, or the fever was gone, or the violent headache was assuaged, or some good symptom was in the case; so that in a few days everybody was recovering, whole families that were infected and down, that had ministers praying with them, and expected death every hour, were revived and healed, and none died at all out of them.

(From *A Journal of the Plague Year*, 1722.)

Lady Mary Wortley Montagu

This little digression has interrupted my telling you we passed over the fields of Carlowitz, where the last great victory was obtained by Prince Eugene over the Turks. The marks of that glorious bloody day are yet recent, the field being strewed with the skulls and carcases of unburied men, horses, and camels. I could not look without horror, on such numbers of mangled human bodies, and reflect on the injustice of war, that makes murder not only necessary but meritorious. Nothing seems to me a plainer proof of the irrationality of mankind (whatever fine claims we pretend to reason) than the rage with which they contest for a small spot of ground, when such vast parts of fruitful earth lie quite uninhabited. It is true, custom has now made it unavoidable; but can there be a greater demonstration of want of reason, than a custom being firmly established, so plainly contrary to the interest of man in general? I am a good deal inclined to believe Mr. Hobbes, that the state of nature is a state of war; but thence I conclude human nature is not rational, if the word reason means common sense, as I suppose it does. I have a great many admirable arguments to support this reflection; but I won't trouble you with them, but return, in a plain style, to the history of my travels.

(From a letter to Alexander Pope on February 12, 1717, Old Style, from Belgrade.)

Edward Gibbon

The renewal, or perhaps the improvement, of my English life was embittered by the alteration of my own feelings. At the age of twenty-one I was, in my proper station of a youth, delivered from the yoke of education, and delighted with the comparative state of liberty and affluence. My filial obedience was natural and easy; and in the gay prospect of futurity, my ambition did not extend beyond the enjoyment of my books, my leisure, and my patrimonial estate, undisturbed by the cares of a family and the duties of a profession. But in the militia I was armed with power; in my travels, I was exempt from control; and as I approached, as I gradually passed, my thirtieth year, I began to feel the desire of being master in my own house. The most gentle authority will sometimes frown without reason, the most cheerful submission will sometimes murmur without cause; and such is the law of our imperfect nature that we must either command or obey; that our personal liberty is supported by the obsequiousness of our own dependents. While so many of my acquaintances were married or in parliament, or advancing with a rapid step in the various roads of honour and fortune, I stood alone, immovable and insignificant; for after the monthly meeting of 1770, I had even withdrawn myself from the militia, by the resignation of an empty and barren commission. My temper is not susceptible of envy, and the view of successful merit has always excited my warmest applause. The miseries of a vacant life were never known to a man whose hours were insufficient for the inexhaustible pleasures of study. But I lamented that at the proper age I had not embraced the lucrative pursuits of the law or of trade, the chances of civil office or India adventure, or even the fat slumbers of the church; and my repentance became more lively as the loss of time was more irretrievable.

(From *Memoirs of My Life and Writings*, 1796.)

Fanny Burney

He had put the pistol upon a table, and had his hand in his pocket, whence, in a few moments, he took out another: he then emptied something on the table from a small leather bag; after which, taking up both the pistols, one in each hand, he dropt hastily upon his knees, and called out, "O God!—forgive me!"

In a moment, strength and courage seemed lent me as by inspiration: I started, and rushing precipitately into the room, just caught his arm, and then, overcome by my own fears, I fell down at his side, breathless and senseless. My recovery, however, was, I believe, almost instantaneous; and then the sight of this unhappy man, regarding me with a look of unutterable astonishment, mixed with concern, presently restored to me my recollection. I arose, though with difficulty; he did the same; the pistols, as I soon saw, were both on the floor.

Unwilling to leave them, and indeed, too weak to move, I lent one hand on the table, and then stood perfectly still: while he, his eyes cast wildly towards me, seemed too infinitely amazed to be capable of either speech or action.

(From *Evelina*, 1778.)

Mary Wollstonecraft

I may be accused of arrogance; still I must declare what I firmly believe, that all the writers who have written on the subject of female education and manners, from Rousseau to Dr. Gregory, have contributed to render women more artificial, weak characters, than they would otherwise have been and consequently, more useless members of society. I might have expressed this conviction in a lower key, but I am afraid it would have been the whine of affectation, and not the faithful expression of my feelings, of the clear result which experience and reflection have led me to draw. When I come to that division of the subject, I shall advert to the passages that I more particularly disapprove of, in the works of the authors I have just alluded to; but it is first necessary to observe that my objection extends to the whole purport of those books, which tend, in my opinion, to degrade one-half of the human species, and render women pleasing at the expense of every solid virtue.

(From *Vindication of the Rights of Woman*, 1792.)

Washington Irving

The dominant spirit, however, that haunts this enchanted region and seems to be commander-in-chief of all powers of the air, is the apparition of a figure on horseback without a head. It is said by some to be the ghost of a Hessian trooper, whose head had been carried away by a cannon-ball, in some nameless battle during the revolutionary war; and who is ever and anon seen by the country folk, hurrying along in the gloom of night, as if on the wings of the wind. His haunts are not confined to the valley, but extend at times to the adjacent roads, and especially to the vicinity of a church at no great distance. Indeed, certain of the most authentic historians of those parts, who have been careful in collecting and collating the floating facts concerning this spectre, allege that the body of the trooper having been buried in the churchyard, the ghost rides forth to the scene of battle in nightly quest of his head; and that the rushing speed with which he sometimes passes along the Hollow, like a midnight blast, is owing to his being belated and in a hurry to get back to the churchyard before daybreak.

(From "The Legend of Sleepy Hollow," *The Sketch-Book*, 1819–20.)

William Hazlitt

Any one may mouth out a passage with a theatrical cadence, or get upon stilts to tell his thoughts; but to write or speak with propriety and simplicity is a more difficult task. Thus it is easy to affect a pompous style, to use a word twice as big as the thing you want to express: it is not so easy to pitch upon the very word that exactly fits it. Out of eight or ten words equally common, equally intelligible, with nearly equal pretensions, it is a matter of some nicety and discrimination to pick out the very one, the preferableness of which is scarcely perceptible, but decisive. The reason why I object to Dr. Johnson's style is that there is no discrimination, no selection, no variety in it. He uses none but "tall, opaque words," taken from the "first row of the rubric"—words with the greatest number of syllables, or Latin phrases with merely English terminations. If a fine style depended on this sort of arbitrary pretension, it would be fair to judge of an author's elegance by the measurement of his words, and the substitution of foreign circumlocutions (with no precise associations) for the mother-tongue. How simple it is to be dignified without ease, to be pompous without meaning! Surely, it is but a mechanical rule for avoiding what is low to be always pedantic and affected. It is clear you cannot use a vulgar English word, if you never use a common English word at all. A fine tact is shewn in adhering to those which are perfectly common, and yet never falling into any expressions which are debased by disgusting circumstances, or which owe their significance and point to technical or professional allusions. A truly natural or familiar style can never be quaint or vulgar, for this reason, that it is of universal force and applicability, and that quaintness and vulgarity arise out of the immediate connection of certain words with coarse and disagreeable, or with confined, ideas.

(From "On Familiar Style," 1821.)

Jane Austen

Mr. Bingley had soon made himself acquainted with all the principal people in the room; he was lively and unreserved, danced every dance, was angry that the ball closed so early, and talked of giving one himself at Nether-field. Such amiable qualities must speak for themselves. What a contrast between him and his friend! Mr. Darcy danced only once with Mrs. Hurst and once with Miss Bingley, declined being introduced to any other lady, and spent the rest of the evening in walking about the room, speaking occasionally to one of his own party. His character was decided. He was the proudest, most disagreeable man in the world, and everybody hoped that he would never come there again. Amongst the most violent against him was Mrs. Bennet, whose dislike of his general behavior was sharpened into particular resentment by his having slighted one of her daughters.

(From *Pride and Prejudice,* 1813.)

Charles Lamb

I am by nature extremely susceptible of street affronts; the jeers and taunts of the populace; the low-bred triumph they display over the casual trip, or splashed stocking, of a gentleman. Yet can I endure the jocularity of a young sweep with something more than forgiveness. In the last winter but one, pacing along Cheapside with my accustomed precipitation when I walk westward, a treacherous slide brought me upon my back in an instant. I scrambled up with pain and shame enough—yet outwardly trying to face it down, as if nothing had happened—when the roguish grin of one of these young wits encountered me. There he stood, pointing me out with his dusky finger to the mob, and to a poor woman (I suppose his mother) in particular, till the tears for the exquisiteness of the fun (so he thought it) worked themselves out at the corners of his poor red eyes, red from many a previous weeping, and soot-inflamed, yet twinkling through all with such a joy, snatched out of desolation that Hogarth—but Hogarth has got him already (how could he miss him?) in "The March to Finchley," grinning at the pie-man—there he stood, as he stands in the picture, irremovable, as if the jest was to last for ever—with such a maximum of glee, and minimum of mischief, in his mirth—for the grin of a genuine sweep hath absolutely no malice in it—that I could have been content, if the honour of a gentleman might endure it, to have remained his butt and his mockery till midnight.

(From "The Praise of Chimney-Sweepers," 1822.)

George Eliot (Mary Ann Cross)

She was naturally the subject of many observations this evening, for the dinner-party was large and rather more miscellaneous as to the male portion than any which had been held at the Grange since Mr. Brooke's nieces had resided with him, so that the talking was done in duos and trios more or less inharmonious. There was the newly-elected mayor of Middlemarch, who happened to be a manufacturer; the philanthropic banker his brother-in-law, who predominated so much in the town that some called him a Methodist, others a hypocrite, according to the resources of their vocabulary; and there were various professional men. In fact, Mrs. Cadwallader said that Brooke was beginning to treat the Middlemarchers, and that she preferred the farmers at the tithe-dinner, who drank her health unpretentiously, and were not ashamed of their grandfathers' furniture. For in that part of the country, before Reform had done its notable part in developing the political consciousness, there was a clearer distinction of ranks and a dimmer distinction of parties; so that Mr. Brooke's miscellaneous invitations seemed to belong to that general laxity which came from his inordinate travel and habit of taking too much in the form of ideas.

(From *Middlemarch*, 1871–72.)

Abraham Lincoln

Fourscore and seven years ago our fathers brought forth on this continent a new nation, conceived in liberty and dedicated to the proposition that all men are created equal.

Now we are engaged in a great civil war, testing whether that nation, or any nation so conceived and so dedicated, can long endure. We are met on a great battle-field of that war. We have come to dedicate a portion of that field as a final resting-place for those who here gave their lives that that nation might live. It is altogether fitting and proper that we should do this.

But, in a larger sense, we cannot dedicate—we cannot consecrate—we cannot hallow—this ground. The brave men, living and dead, who struggled here, have consecrated it far above our poor power to add or detract. The world will little note nor long remember what we say here, but it can never forget what they did here. It is for us, the living, rather, to be dedicated here to the unfinished work which they who fought here have thus far so nobly advanced. It is rather for us to be here dedicated to the great task remaining before us—that from these honored dead we take increased devotion to that cause for which they gave the last full measure of devotion; that we here highly resolve that these dead shall not have died in vain; that this nation, under God, shall have a new birth of freedom; and that government of the people, by the people, for the people, shall not perish from the earth.

epic

employs harmony & unity to

(From *The Gettysburg Address*, 1863.)

Mark Twain

Once a day a cheap, gaudy packet arrived upward from St. Louis, and another downward from Keokuk. Before these events, the day was glorious with expectancy; after them, the day was a dead and empty thing. Not only the boys, but the whole village, felt this. After all these years I can picture that old time to myself now, just as it was then: the white town drowsing in the sunshine of a summer's morning; the streets empty, or pretty nearly so; one or two clerks sitting in front of the Water Street stores, with their splint-bottomed chairs tilted back against the walls, chins on breasts, hats slouched over their faces, asleep—with shingle-shavings enough around to show what broke them down; a sow and a litter of pigs loafing along the sidewalk, doing a good business in watermelon rinds and seeds; two or three lonely little freight piles scattered about the "levee"; a pile of "skids" on the slope of the stone-paved wharf, and the fragrant town drunkard asleep in the shadow of them; two or three wood flats at the head of the wharf, but nobody to listen to the peaceful lapping of the wavelets against them; the great Mississippi, the majestic, the magnificent Mississippi, rolling its mile-wide tide along, shining in the sun; the dense forest away on the other side; the "point" above the town, and the "point" below, bounding the river-glimpse and turning it into a sort of sea, and withal a very still and brilliant and lonely one. Presently a film of dark smoke appears above one of those remote "points"; instantly a negro drayman, famous for his quick eye and prodigious voice, lifts up the cry, "S-t-e-a-m-boat a-comin'!" and the scene changes! The town drunkard stirs, the clerks wake up, a furious clatter of drays follows, every house and store pours out a human contribution, and all in a twinkling the dead town is alive and moving. Drays, carts, men, boys, all go hurrying from many quarters to a common center, the wharf. Assembled there, the people fasten their eyes upon the coming boat as upon a wonder they are seeing for the first time.

(From *Life on the Mississippi*, 1883.)

Henry James

The house of fiction has in short not one window, but a million—a number of possible windows not to be reckoned, rather; every one of which has been pierced, or is still pierceable, in its vast front, by the need of the individual vision and by the pressure of the individual will. These apertures, of dissimilar shape and size, hang so, all together, over the human scene that we might have expected of them a greater sameness of report than we find. They are but windows at the best, mere holes in a dead wall, disconnected, perched aloft; they are not hinged doors opening straight upon life. But they have this mark of their own that at each of them stands a figure with a pair of eyes, or at least with a field-glass, which forms, again and again, for observation, a unique instrument, insuring to the person making use of it an impression distinct from every other. He and his neighbours are watching the same show, but one seeing more where the other sees less, one seeing black where the other sees white, one seeing big where the other sees small, one seeing coarse where the other sees fine. And so on, and so on; there is fortunately no saying on what, for the particular pair of eyes, the window may *not* open; "fortunately" by reason, precisely, of this incalculability of range. The spreading field, the human scene, is the "choice of subject"; the pierced aperture, either broad or balconied or slit-like and low-browed, is the "literary form"; but they are, singly or together, as nothing without the posted presence of the watcher—without, in other words, the consciousness of the artist. Tell me what the artist is, and I will tell you of what he has *been* conscious. Thereby I shall express to you at once his boundless freedom and his "moral" reference.

(From the Preface to *The Portrait of a Lady*, 1915.)

Ernest Hemingway

Sometimes in the dark we heard the troops marching under the window and the guns going past pulled by motor-tractors. There was much traffic at night and many mules on the roads with boxes of ammunition on each side of their packsaddles and gray motor-trucks that carried men, and other trucks with loads covered with canvas that moved slower in the traffic. There were big guns too that passed in the day drawn by tractors, the long barrels of the guns covered with green branches and green leafy branches and vines laid over the tractors. To the north we could look across a valley and see a forest of chestnut trees and behind it another mountain on this side of the river. There was fighting for that mountain too, but it was not successful, and in the fall when the rains came the leaves all fell from the chestnut trees and the branches were bare and the trunks black with rain. The vineyards were thin and bare-branched too and all the country wet and brown and dead with the autumn. There were mists over the river and clouds on the mountain and the trucks splashed mud on the road and the troops were muddy and wet in their capes; their rifles were wet and under their capes the two leather cartridge-boxes on the front of the belts, gray leather boxes heavy with the packs of clips of thin, long 6.5 mm. cartridges, bulged forward under the capes so that the men, passing on the road, marched as though they were six months gone with child.

Jean Shepherd

When we got the ham home, my mother immediately stripped off the white paper and the string in the middle of our chipped white-enamel kitchen table. There it lay, exuding heavenly perfumes—proud, arrogant, regal. It had a dark, smoked, leathery skin, which my mother carefully peeled off with her sharpened bread knife. Then the old man, the only one who could lift the ham without straining a gut, placed it in the big dark-blue oval pot that was used only for hams. My mother then covered the ham with water, pushed it onto the big burner and turned up the gas until it boiled. It just sat there on the stove and bubbled away for maybe two hours, filling the house with a smell that was so luscious, so powerful as to have erotic overtones. The old man paced back and forth, occasionally lifting the lid and prodding the ham with a fork, inhaling deeply. The ham frenzy was upon him.

N. Scott Momaday

Although my grandmother lived out her long life in the shadow of Rainy Mountain, the immense landscape of the continental interior lay like memory in her blood. She could tell of the Crows, whom she had never seen, and of the Black Hills, where she had never been. I wanted to see in reality what she had seen more perfectly in the mind's eye, and travelled fifteen hundred miles to begin my pilgrimage.

Yellowstone, it seemed to me, was the top of the world, a region of deep lakes and dark timber, canyons and waterfalls. But, beautiful as it is, one might have the sense of confinement there. The skyline in all directions is close at hand, the high wall of the woods and deep cleavages of shade. There is a perfect freedom in the mountains, but it belongs to the eagle and the elk, the badger and the bear. The Kiowas reckoned their stature by the distance they could see, and they were bent and blind in the wilderness.

> From N. Scott Momaday, *The Way to Rainy Mountain*. First published in *The Reporter*, 26 January 1967. Reprinted from *The Way to Rainy Mountain*, © 1969, The University of New Mexico Press.

E. B. White

I had marked Apathy's hatching date on my desk calendar. On the night before the goslings were due to arrive, when I made my rounds before going to bed, I looked in on her. She hissed, as usual, and ran her neck out. When I shone my light at her, two tiny green heads were visible, thrusting their way through her feathers. The goslings were here—a few hours ahead of schedule. My heart leapt up. Outside, in the barnyard, both ganders stood vigil. They knew very well what was up: ganders take an enormous interest in family affairs and are deeply impressed by the miracle of the egg-that-becomes-goose. I shut the door against them and went to bed.

> (From E. B. White, "Geese." In *Essays of E. B. White*. New York: Harper & Row, 1971. Reprinted by permission of Harper & Row.)

James Baldwin

Negroes want to be treated like men: a perfectly straightforward statement, containing only seven words. People who have mastered Kant, Hegel, Shakespeare, Marx, Freud, and the Bible find this statement utterly impenetrable. The idea seems to threaten profound, barely conscious assumptions. A kind of panic paralyzes their features, as though they found themselves trapped on the edge of a steep place. I once tried to describe to a very well-known American intellectual the conditions among Negroes in the South. My recital disturbed him and made him indignant; and he asked me in perfect innocence, "Why don't all the Negroes in the South move North?" I tried to explain what *has* happened, unfailingly, whenever a significant body of Negroes move North. They do not escape Jim Crow: they merely encounter another, not-less-deadly variety. They do not move to Chicago, they move to the South Side; they do not move to New York, they move to Harlem. The pressure within the ghetto causes the ghetto walls to expand, and this expansion is always violent. White people hold the line as long as they can, and in as many ways as they can, from verbal intimidation to physical violence. But inevitably the border which has divided the ghetto from the rest of the world falls back bitterly before the black horde; the landlords make a tidy profit by raising the rent, chopping up the rooms, and all but dispensing with the upkeep; and what has once been a neighborhood turns into a "turf." This is precisely what happened when the Puerto Ricans arrived in their thousands—and the bitterness thus caused is, as I write, being fought out all up and down those streets.

Susan Sontag

This is why so many of the objects prized by Camp taste are old-fashioned, out-of-date, *démodé*. It's not a love of the old as such. It's simply that the process of aging or deterioration provides the necessary detachment—or arouses a necessary sympathy. When the theme is important, and contemporary, the failure of a work of art may make us indignant. Time can change that. Time liberates the work of art from moral relevance, delivering it over to the Camp sensibility. . . . Another effect: time contracts the sphere of banality. (Banality is, strictly speaking, always a category of the contemporary.) What was banal can, with the passage of time, become fantastic. Many people who listen with delight to the style of Rudy Vallee revived by the English pop group The Temperance Seven, would have been driven up the wall by Rudy Vallee in his heyday.

Thus, things are campy, not when they become old—but when we become less involved in them, and can enjoy, instead of be frustrated by, the failure of the attempt. But the effect of time is unpredictable. Maybe "Method" Acting (James Dean, Rod Steiger, Warren Beatty) will seem as Camp some day as Ruby Keeler's does now—or as Sarah Bernhardt's does in the films she made at the end of her career. And maybe not.

Tom Wolfe

The first good look I had at customized cars was at an event called a "Teen Fair," held in Burbank, a suburb of Los Angeles beyond Hollywood. This was a wild place to be taking a look at art objects—eventually, I should say, you have to reach the conclusion that these customized cars *are* art objects, at least if you use the standards applied in a civilized society. But I will get to that in a moment. Anyway, about noon you drive up to a place that looks like an outdoor amusement park, and there are three serious-looking kids, like the cafeteria committee in high school, taking tickets, but the scene inside is quite mad. Inside, two things hit you. The first is a huge platform a good seven feet off the ground with a hully-gully band—everything is electrified, the bass, the guitars, the saxophones—and then behind the band, on the platform, about two hundred kids are doing fantastic dances called the hully-gully, the bird, and the shampoo. As I said, it's noontime. The dances the kids are doing are very jerky. The boys and girls don't touch, not even with their hands. They just ricochet around. Then you notice that all the girls are dressed exactly alike. They have bouffant hairdos—all of them—and slacks that are, well, skin-tight does not get the idea across; it's more the conformation than how tight the slacks are. It's as if some lecherous old tailor with a gluteous-maximus fixation designed them, striation by striation. About the time you've managed to focus on this, you notice that out in the middle of the park is a huge, perfectly round swimming pool; really rather enormous. And there is a Chris-Craft cabin cruiser in the pool, going around and around, sending up big waves, with more of these bouffant babies bunched in the back of it. In the water, suspended like plankton, are kids in Skuba-diving outfits; others are tooling around underwater, breathing through a snorkel. And all over the place are booths, put up by shoe companies and guitar companies and God knows who else, and there are kids dancing in all of them—dancing the bird, the hully-gully, and the shampoo —with the music of the hully-gully band piped all over the park through loudspeakers.

James Dickey

(*The man described in these paragraphs has just been shot through the breast with an arrow*)

I got up with the gun and the power, wrapping the string around my right hand. I swung the barrel back and forth to cover everything, the woods and the world. There was nothing in the clearing but Bobby and the shot man and me. Bobby was still on the ground, though now he was lifting his head. I could understand that much, but something kept blurring the clear idea of Bobby and myself and the leaves and the river. The shot man was still standing. He wouldn't concentrate in my vision; I couldn't believe him. He was like a film over the scene, gray and vague, with the force gone out of him; I was amazed at how he did everything. He touched the arrow experimentally, and I could tell that it was set in him as solidly as his breastbone. It was in him tight and unwobbling, coming out front and back. He took hold of it with both hands, but compared to the arrow's strength his hands were weak; they weakened more as I looked, and began to melt. He was on his knees, and then fell to his side, pulling his legs up. He rolled back and forth like a man with the wind knocked out of him, all the time making a bubbling, gritting sound. His lips turned red, but from his convulsions—in which there was something comical and unspeakable—he seemed to gain strength. He got up on one knee and then to his feet again while I stood with the shotgun at port arms. He took a couple of strides toward the woods and then seemed to change his mind and danced back to me, lurching and clog-stepping in a secret circle. He held out a hand to me, like a prophet, and I pointed the shotgun straight at the head of the arrow, ice coming into my teeth. I was ready to put it all behind me with one act, with one pull of a string.

But there was no need. He crouched and fell forward with his face on my white tennis shoe tops, trembled away into his legs and shook down to stillness. He opened his mouth and it was full of blood like an apple. A clear bubble formed on his lips and stayed there.

Barbara Tuchman

In the excitement at St. Paul's the matter of Wyclif had not been tested. The English prelates, caught between clerical interest and national sentiment, might have been content to let the matter drop, but the papacy was not. In May, Gregory XI issued five Bulls addressed to the English epicopacy and to the king and the University of Oxford, condemning Wyclif's errors and demanding his arrest. All discussion of his heretical doctrines was to be suppressed and all who supported them removed from office. An issue full of danger was added to all the other sources of strife. The new Parliament was strongly anti-papal; the king, babbling of hawks and hunting instead of attending to the urgent needs of his soul, was dying. For the moment, while England waited uneasily for the change of reign, the bishops held the proceedings against Wyclif in abeyance.

Frances Fitzgerald

After 1900, a new distinction appears in American history textbooks: there are "we Americans," and there are "the immigrants." The textbook discovery of "the immigrants" was actually somewhat belated, since the great wave of European immigration to the United States had been under way for some time. Europeans—and particularly Irish and Germans—had been crossing the Atlantic in large numbers since the eighteen-forties, but between 1881 and 1890 more than five million immigrants came to the United States, and by 1910 the total had risen to more than sixteen million. The newcomers not only increased the American population significantly but altered its ethnic composition. After 1900, immigrants from the southern and eastern countries of Europe vastly outnumbered those from the northern and western ones. The schools were particularly affected, since they were the only public agencies that offered special services for the immigrants. Having been charged with the "Americanization" of the newcomers, they naturally had to take on the task of defining what "an American" was and was not.

(From Frances FitzGerald, *America Revised: History Schoolbooks in the Twentieth Century*. Copyright © 1979 by Frances FitzGerald. Reprinted by permission of Little, Brown and Company.)

Alice Walker

Corinne's mother was a dedicated housewife and mother who disliked her more adventurous sister. But she never prevented Corrine from visiting. And when Corrine was old enough, she sent her to Spelman Seminary where Aunt Theodosia had gone. This was a very interesting place. It was started by two white missionaries from New England who used to wear identical dresses. Started in a church basement, it soon moved up to Army barracks. Eventually these two ladies were able to get large sums of money from some of the richest men in America, and so the place grew. Buildings and trees. Girls were taught everything: Reading, Writing, Arithmetic, sewing, cleaning, cooking. But more than anything else, they were taught to serve God and the colored community. Their official motto was OUR WHOLE SCHOOL FOR CHRIST. But I always thought their unofficial motto should have been OUR COMMUNITY COVERS THE WORLD, because no sooner had a young woman got through Spelman Seminary than she began to put her hand to whatever work she could do for her people, anywhere in the world. It was truly astonishing. These very polite and proper young women, some of them never having set foot outside their own small country towns, except to come to the Seminary, thought nothing of packing up for India, Africa, the Orient. Or for Philadelphia or New York.

Richard Rodriquez

It saddened my mother to learn about Mexican-American parents who wanted their children to start working after finishing high school. In schooling she recognized the key to job advancement. And she remembered her past. As a girl, new to America, she had been awarded a diploma by high school teachers too busy or careless to notice that she hardly spoke English. On her own she determined to learn to type. That skill got her clean office jobs and encouraged an optimism about the possibility of advancement. (Each morning when her sisters put on uniforms for work, she chose a bright-colored dress.) She became an excellent speller—of words she mispronounced. ("And I've never been to college," she would say smiling when her children asked about a word they didn't want to look up in a dictionary.)

Joan Didion

It is time for the baby's birthday party: a white cake, strawberry-marshmallow ice cream, a bottle of champagne saved from another party. In the evening, after she has gone to sleep, I kneel beside the crib and touch her face, where it is pressed against the slats, with mine. She is an open and trusting child, unprepared for and unaccustomed to the ambushes of family life, and perhaps it is just as well that I can offer her little of that life. I would like to give her more. I would like to promise her that she will grow up with a sense of her cousins and of rivers and of her great-grandmother's teacups, would like to pledge her a picnic on a river with fried chicken and her hair uncombed, would like to give her *home* for her birthday, but we live differently now and I can promise her nothing like that. I give her a xylophone and a sundress from Madeira, and promise to tell her a funny story.

Shirley Brice Heath

The environment of both boy and girl babies during their first year of life is a very human one. They sleep with family members, are held, carried, and cuddled by family members, and by all residents of the community as well. For all community members of Trackton, not only older brothers and sisters, babies are playthings. When they cry, they are fed, tended, held, and fondled by anyone nearby. Since bottle-feeding is the norm, anyone can take on feeding responsibilities. Babies are restrained from exploring beyond the human interactions which surround them. They have little occasion to coo and babble by themselves or in quiet situations where their babbling sounds can be heard above the general talk which seems to go on around them most of the time. They sleep and eat at will; they are fed when they seem hungry if food is available, and they go to sleep whenever or wherever they become sleepy. They are often waked up to be played with when children come home from school or a visitor comes in, and they are often awake late into the night in the living room where a television or record player blares, or loud conversation is going on. Their inclusion as part of the family is continuous. If they fall asleep in the midst of a lively story-telling session or a family argument, they continue to be held until the person holding them needs to move about. Then someone else takes over. The child is almost never alone and very rarely in the company of only one other person.

(From Shirley Brice Heath, *Ways with Words*. Cambridge and New York: Cambridge University Press, 1983.)

Garrison Keillor

School started the day after Labor Day, Tuesday, the Tuesday when my grandfather went, and in 1918 my father, and in 1948 me. It was the same day, in the same brick schoolhouse, the former New Albion Academy, now named Nelson school. The same misty painting of George Washington looked down on us all from above the blackboard, next to his closest friend, Abraham Lincoln. Lincoln was kind and patient, and we looked to him for sympathy. Washington looked as if he had a headache. His mouth was set in a prim pained expression of disapproval. Maybe people made fun of him for his long frizzy hair, which resembled our teacher's, Mrs. Meiers', and that had soured his disposition. She said he had bad teeth—a good lesson for us to remember: to brush after every meal, up and down, thirty times. The great men held the room in their gaze, even the back corner by the windows. I bent over my desk, trying to make fat vowels sit on the line like fruit, the tails of consonants hang below, and colored maps of English and French empires, and memorized arithmetic tables and state capitals and major exports of many lands, and when I was stumped, looked up to see George Washington's sour look and Lincoln's pity and friendship, an old married couple on the wall. School, their old home, smelled of powerful floor wax and disinfectant, the smell of patriotism.

Toni Morrison

All forty-six men woke to a rifle shot. All forty-six. Three whitemen walked along the trench unlocking the doors one by one. No one stepped through. When the last lock was opened, the three returned and lifted the bars, one by one. And one by one the blackmen emerged—promptly and without the poke of a rifle butt if they had been there more than a day; promptly with the butt if, like Paul D, they had just arrived. When all forty-six were standing in a line in the trench, another rifle shot signaled the climb out and up to the ground above, where one thousand feet of the best hand-forged chain in Georgia stretched. Each man bent and waited. The first man picked up the end and threaded it through the loop in his leg iron. He stood up then, and, shuffling a little, brought the chain tip to the next prisoner, who did likewise. As the chain was passed on and each man stood in the other's place, the line of men turned around, facing the boxes they had come out of. Not one spoke to the other. At least not with words. The eyes had to tell what there was to tell: "Help me this mornin; 's bad"; "I'm a make it"; "New man"; "Steady now steady."

Eudora Welty

She's not the only teacher who has influenced me, but Miss Duling, in some fictional shape or form, has stridden into a larger part of my work than I'd realized until now. She emerges in my perhaps inordinate number of schoolteacher characters. I loved those characters in the writing. But I did not, in life, love Miss Duling. I was afraid of her high-arched bony nose, her eyebrows lifted in half-circles above her hooded, brilliant eyes, and of the Kentucky R's in her speech, and the long steps she took in her hightop shoes. I did nothing but fear her bearing-down authority, and did not connect this (as of course we were meant to) with our own need or desire to learn, perhaps because I already had this wish, and did not need to be driven.

Imitating Sentence Patterns

After you have spent some time merely copying passages, you might attempt another kind of imitation. You can take individual sentences as patterns on which to devise sentences of your own. This is a more difficult exercise than the verbatim copying, but it pays high dividends to those who use it conscientiously.

How closely should you follow the model? As closely as you care to, is the most sensible answer. But you will find this exercise most fruitful if you will observe at least the same *kind, number,* and *order* of clauses and phrases. If the model sentence has an adverb clause, you should write an adverb clause. If the model sentence is introduced by a participial phrase, you should put a participial phrase in the lead-off position. If the model sentence has three noun clauses arranged in parallel structure, you should write a sentence containing three noun clauses in a similar structure.

The aim of this exercise is not to achieve a word-for-word correspondence with the model but rather to achieve an awareness of the variety of sentence structures of which the English language is capable. The reason why many students never venture outside their puerile, monotonous sentence structure is that they have never attempted sophisticated sentence patterns. Writing such patterns according to models will increase their syntactical resources. And with more resources at their command, they will acquire more confidence in their writing ability.

No one, of course, says while he or she is writing, "I just wrote a compound sentence interspersed with gerund phrases. This time I think I'll begin my sentence with an adverb clause and use a series of noun clauses as the object of the main verb." Such a self-conscious approach to writing would undoubtedly result in some monstrous prose.

No, our prose must come as naturally as—to use Keats's words—"the leaves to the trees." The kind of prose we write cannot be arbitrary; it is governed by the subject matter, the occasion, the purpose, the audience, and the personality of the writer. If it is true that matter and form are intimately related, then there must be one best way in which to say a particular thing for a given audience and purpose. But as a practical matter, what we manage to achieve most of the time is one of a number of *better* ways to say something. Coleridge once said that the infallible test of a perfect style was "its *untranslatableness* in words of the same language without injury to the meaning." Only seldom, perhaps, do we achieve this kind of "inevitable prose." What we achieve most of the time is, at best, an adequate prose.

A great deal of the writing you may be called upon to do in the future will be impromptu, spur-of-the-moment writing. While you are still in school, you will have to write essay-type examinations, where you have little time for reflection and almost no time for revision. In your job someday, you will have to dash off memos, directives, and letters. As a private citizen, you will have to scribble off notes to send to school with your children, pen a hurried letter to your parents, pound out a letter to the editor of the local newspaper. The more practice you have had in writing, the better will be this one-draft prose.

But you may also be called upon at times to do some writing that entails a great deal of reflection, research, organization, and revision. You may have to write a report to be read to the board of governors or prepare a speech to be delivered before the Chamber of Commerce. It is this kind of deliberate writing that will call upon all the inventive and stylistic resources at your command. This will necessarily be slow writing, but it does not have to be labored writing for being slow. Someone once said that "hard writing makes for easy reading." And Quintilian once said, "Write quickly and you will never write well; write well and you will soon write quickly."

So with these cautions and objectives in mind, now try your hand at imitating the sentence patterns of practiced writers. You may never in your life have occasion to write a sentence like some of those that you have mechanically imitated in this exercise, but you will be none the worse for having gone through the paces.

As examples of how to imitate sentence patterns, a few samples of the method are printed below. For models, you can select sentences from your favorite authors, or you can use sentences from the specimen passages reproduced in this chapter.

Sample Imitations

MODEL SENTENCE: The gallows stood in a small yard, separate from the main grounds of the prison and overgrown with tall prickly weeds.— George Orwell, *Burmese Days*

(Write a sentence according to the pattern of the model sentence.)

IMITATION: The dog shivered in the background, wet from nosing his way through the early-morning grasses and covered with damp cockle-spurs.

MODEL SENTENCE: He went through the narrow alley of Temple Bar quickly, muttering to himself that they could all go to hell because he was going to have a good night of it.—James Joyce, "Counterparts"

IMITATION: They stood outside on the wet pavement of the terrace, pretending that they had not heard us when we called to them from the library.

MODEL SENTENCE: To regain the stage in its own character, not as a mere emulation of prose, poetry must find its own poetic way to the mastery the stage demands—the mastery of action. Archibald MacLeish, "The Poet as Playwright"

IMITATION: To discover our own natures, not the personalities imposed on us by others, we must honestly assess the values we cherish—in short, our "philosophy of life."

MODEL SENTENCE: If one must worship a bully, it is better that he should be a policeman than a gangster.—George Orwell, "Raffles and Miss Blandish"

IMITATION: Since he continued to be belligerent, it was plain that cajoling would prove more effective than scolding.

MODEL SENTENCE: I went to the woods because I wished to live deliberately, to front only the essential facts of life, and see if I could learn what it had to teach, and not, when I came to die, discover that I had not lived.—Henry David Thoreau, *Walden*

IMITATION: I greeted him politely, although I planned to challenge him repeatedly, to assess his erudition, to test whether he could discriminate what was expedient in each situation, and, after I had probed him thoroughly, to announce that we had no place for him in our organization.

MODEL SENTENCE: To have even a portion of this illuminated reason and true philosophy is the highest state to which nature can aspire, in the way of intellect.—John Henry Newman, *The Idea of a University*

IMITATION: To win a measure of his affection and esteem was the most difficult task that I had ever assigned myself.

MODEL SENTENCE: As most of these old Custom House officers had good traits and as my position in reference to them, being paternal and protective, was favorable to the growth of friendly sentiments, I soon grew to like them all.—Nathaniel Hawthorne, *Scarlet Letter*

IMITATION: When he offered me the gift and when his classmates, perceiving his embarrassment, discreetly withheld their applause, I gratefully accepted his gesture of friendship.

MODEL SENTENCE: The real art that dealt with life directly was that of the first men who told their stories round the savage camp-fire.—Robert Louis Stevenson, "A Humble Remonstrance"

IMITATION: The man who insists on perfection in others is the man who is most tolerant of imperfection in himself.

MODEL SENTENCE: The most important Indian grouping on the continent, north of Mexico, from the very beginning of European conquest on through and after the American Revolution was the Confederacy of the Iroquois.—John Collier, *Indians of the Americas*
IMITATION: The foremost alliance in Europe, amenable to expansion, during the eighteenth century and again after the collapse of the three-nation concordat, was the pact among the Big Four.

MODEL SENTENCE: This brings us to that growing army of "publicity men" and women who sometimes do not—but frequently do—give the best of their years and their vitality to pushing causes in which they have no faith and to becoming personalities whom privately they designate as stuffed shirts.—Stuart Chase, "The Luxury of Integrity"
IMITATION: He presented a startling conglomeration of statistics and testimonies that confirmed—or allegedly confirmed—the general's capacity for subverting causes of which he was suspicious and toward minimizing faults that he considered "politically innocent."

Another exercise that can be worked off this concentration on a single sentence is to vary the pattern of the model sentence or to devise an alternate way of expressing it. At the beginning of this section on imitation, we mentioned the 150 variations that Erasmus worked off a single Latin sentence. Besides making you aware that style is the result of choices that a writer makes from among the available lexical and syntactical resources, such an exercise forces you to discover the options that are available to you. Varying the sentence pattern usually calls for nothing more than a reordering of the words in the original sentence. Devising an alternate expression, however, often involves the choice of different words and different syntactical structures. Let us take the first three model sentences that we worked with earlier and show how they might be varied and altered.

MODEL SENTENCE: The gallows stood in a small yard, separate from the main grounds and overgrown with tall prickly weeds.—George Orwell, *Burmese Days*
VARIATION OF THE PATTERN: In a small yard, separate from the main grounds and overgrown with tall prickly weeds, stood the gallows.
ALTERNATE EXPRESSIONS: Located in a small yard, which was overgrown with tall prickly weeds, the gallows was separated from the main grounds.

The gallows was situated outside the main grounds, in a small yard that was overgrown with tall prickly weeds.

(Transformational grammar can be a help in suggesting alternate ways of phrasing a sentence. Reducing the model sentence to its "kernel sentences" can reveal how the "deep structure" was transformed into the "surface structure" that the author actually wrote. These are some of the "kernel sentences" of Orwell's sentence:

> The gallows stood in a yard.
> The yard was small.
> The yard was separate from the main grounds.
> Or: The gallows was separate from the main grounds.
> The yard was overgrown with weeds.
> Or: The gallows was overgrown with weeds.
> The weeds were tall.
> The weeds were prickly.

There is some ambiguity of structure in the Orwell sentence, because the two adjectival phrases "separate from . . ." and "overgrown with . . ." could modify *gallows* or *yard*. By reducing the original sentence to its kernels, however, you can see how Orwell transformed them into different grammatical combinations and can see what other combinations are possible.)

MODEL SENTENCE: He went through the narrow alley of Temple Bar quickly, muttering to himself that they could all go to hell because he was going to have a good night of it.—James Joyce, "Counterparts"

VARIATION OF THE PATTERN: Muttering to himself that they could all go to hell because he was going to have a good night of it, he went quickly through the narrow alley of Temple Bar.

ALTERNATE EXPRESSIONS: As he went quickly through the narrow alley of Temple Bar, he muttered to himself that they could all go to hell, for he was going to have a good night of it.

"You can all go to hell," he muttered to himself as he went quickly through the narrow alley of Temple Bar. "I am going to have a good night of it."

MODEL SENTENCE: To regain the stage in its own character, not as a mere emulation of prose, poetry must find its own poetic way to the mastery the stage demands—the mastery of action.—Archibald MacLeish, "The Poet as Playwright"

VARIATION OF THE PATTERN: Poetry must find its own poetic way to the mastery the stage demands—the mastery of action—if it is to regain the stage in its own character, not as a mere emulator of prose.

ALTERNATE EXPRESSIONS: Poetry can regain the stage in its own character, not as a mere emulator of prose, only if it can master the kind of action that the stage peculiarly demands.

> If poetry is to regain the stage in its own character, it must master the kind of action that the stage peculiarly demands; otherwise it will remain a mere emulator of prose.

All of these exercises in imitation—copying passages, writing original sentences according to pattern, varying the pattern of a model sentence, and devising alternate expressions for the same thought—can teach you a number of valuable lessons: (1) they can make you aware of the variety of lexical and syntactical resources which your language offers; (2) they can afford you practice in choosing apt words and collocating them in various ways; (3) they can teach you that not every variation is equally clear, graceful, or appropriate; (4) they can teach you that variation of the pattern of the sentence often results in a different *effect* and that an alternate expression often results in a different *meaning*. The ultimate goal of all imitation exercises, however, is eventually to cut you loose from your models, equipped with the competence and resources to go it on your own.

Readings

Hugh Blair: Critical Examination of the Style of Mr. Addison in No. 411 of "The Spectator" *

In 1759, Dr. Hugh Blair began teaching rhetoric at the University of Edinburgh, and in 1762, he was appointed the first Regius Professor of Rhetoric and Belles Lettres at Edinburgh. In 1783, upon his retirement from this post, Blair published the forty-seven lectures on rhetoric and literature that he had presented for twenty-four years to packed classrooms. This text Lectures on Rhetoric and Belles Lettres *became a widely used book in the English and American schools in the late eighteenth and early nineteenth century.*

Midway in the course of lectures Blair presented detailed stylistic analyses of four of Addison's Spectator *essays (Nos. 411–14) and an analysis of Jonathan Swift's "A Proposal for Correcting, Improving, and Ascertaining the English Tongue." These analyses represent one of the few instances in English of a stylistic analysis of an entire essay.*

Blair comments on points of grammar, usage, and style in Addison's essays. From the reprinting of Blair's first analysis, students will learn one technique of analyzing, pointedly and concretely, English prose sentences and may become more conscious of their own prose style. Some of Blair's stric-

---

* Lecture XX of Blair's *Lectures on Rhetoric and Belles Lettres,* first published in 1783.

tures on Addison's style, such as his views on the relative pronouns which *and* that, *are delivered from the standpoint of eighteenth-century usage. And while some of Blair's comments may strike a modern audience as being somewhat picky, most students will find Blair's criticism judicious. In almost every case where Blair has rewritten Addison's sentences, students will notice an improvement in the neatness and clarity of the prose.*

Occasionally, Blair's style of punctuation has been silently changed.

I have insisted fully on the subject of language and style, both because it is, in itself, of great importance and because it is more capable of being ascertained by precise rule, than several other parts of composition. A critical analysis of the style of some good author will tend further to illustrate the subject, as it will suggest observations which I have not had occasion to make and will show, in the most practical light, the use of those which I have made.

Mr. Addison is the author whom I have chosen for this purpose. *The Spectator,* of which his papers are the chief ornament, is a book which is in the hands of every one and which cannot be praised too highly. The good sense and good writing, the useful morality and the admirable vein of humour which abound in it, render it one of those standard books which have done the greatest honour to the English nation. I have formerly given the general character of Mr. Addison's style and manner as natural and unaffected, easy and polite, and full of those graces which a flowery imagination diffuses over writing. At the same time, though one of the most beautiful writers in the language, he is not the most correct; a circumstance which renders his composition the more proper to be the subject of our present criticism. The free and flowing manner of this amiable writer sometimes led him into inaccuracies which the more studied circumspection and care of far inferior writers have taught them to avoid. Remarking his beauties, therefore, which I shall have frequent occasion to do, as I proceed, I must also point out his negligences and defects. Without a free, impartial discussion, of both the faults and beauties which occur in his composition, it is evident this piece of criticism would be of no service; and from the freedom which I use in criticising Mr. Addison's style, none can imagine that I mean to depreciate his writings, after having repeatedly declared the high opinion which I entertain of them. The beauties of this author are so many and the general character of his style is so elegant and estimable that the minute imperfections I shall have occasion to point out are but like those spots in the sun, which may be discovered by the assistance of art but which have no effect in obscuring its lustre. It is, indeed, my judgment that what Quintilian applies to Cicero, *"Ille se profecisse sciat, cui Cicero valde placebit,"* may, with justice, be applied to Mr. Addison: that to be highly pleased with his manner of writing is the criterion of one's having acquired a good taste in English style. The paper on which we are now to enter is No. 411, the first of his celebrated Essays on the Pleasures of the Imagination in the sixth volume of *The Spectator*. It begins thus:

(1) Our sight is the most perfect and most delightful of all our senses.

This is an excellent introductory sentence. It is clear, precise, and simple. The author lays down, in a few plain words, the proposition which he is going to illustrate throughout the rest of the paragraph. In this manner, we should always set out. A first sentence should seldom be a long, and never an intricate, one.

He might have said, *"Our sight is the most perfect and the most delightful."* But he has judged better in omitting to repeat the article *the*. For the repetition of it is proper, chiefly when we intend to point out the objects of which we speak, as distinguished from, or contrasted with, each other; and when we want that the reader's attention should rest on that distinction. For instance, had Mr. Addison intended to say that our sight is at once the most *delightful* and the most *useful* of all our senses, the article might then have been repeated with propriety, as a clear and strong distinction would have been conveyed. But as between *perfect* and *delightful* there is less contrast, there was no occasion for such repetition. It would have had no other effect but to add a word unnecessarily to the sentence. He proceeds:

(2) It fills the mind with the largest variety of ideas, converses with its objects at the greatest distance, and continues the longest in action, without being tired or satiated with its proper enjoyments.

This sentence deserves attention, as remarkably harmonious and well constructed. It possesses, indeed, almost all the properties of a perfect sentence. It is entirely perspicuous. It is loaded with no superfluous or unnecessary words. For *tired or satiated* towards the end of the sentence are not used for synonymous terms. They convey distinct ideas and refer to different members of the period: that this sense *continues the longest in action without being tired,* that is, without being fatigued with its action; and also, without being *satiated with its proper enjoyments*. That quality of a good sentence which I termed its unity is here perfectly preserved. It is *our sight* of which he speaks. This is the object carried through the sentence and presented to us, in every member of it, by those verbs, *fills, converses, continues,* to each of which it is clearly the nominative. Those capital words are disposed of in the most proper places; and that uniformity is maintained in the construction of the sentence which suits the unity of the object.

Observe, too, the music of the period; consisting of three members, each of which, agreeable to a rule I formerly mentioned, grows and rises above the other in sound, till the sentence is conducted, at last, to one of the most melodious closes which our language admits—*without being tired or satiated with its proper enjoyments. Enjoyments* is a word of length and dignity, exceedingly proper for a close which is designed to be a musical one. The harmony is the more happy, as this disposition of the members of the period which suits the sound so well is no less just and proper with respect to the sense. It follows the order of nature. First, we have the variety of objects mentioned, which sight furnishes to the mind; next, we have the action of sight on those objects; and lastly, we have the time and continuance of its action. No order could be more natural and happy.

This sentence has still another beauty. It is figurative, without being too much so for the subject. A metaphor runs through it. The sense of sight is, in some degree, personified. We are told of its *conversing* with its objects; and of its not being *tired or satiated* with its *enjoyments;* all which expressions are plain allusions to the actions and feelings of men. This is that slight sort of personification which, without any appearance of boldness and without elevating the fancy much above its ordinary state, renders discourse picturesque and leads us to conceive the author's meaning more distinctly, by clothing abstract ideas, in some degree, with sensible colours. Mr. Addison abounds with this beauty of style beyond most authors; and the sentence which we have been considering is very expressive of his manner of writing. There is no blemish in it whatever, unless that a strict critic might perhaps object that the epithet *large,* which he applies to *variety—the largest variety of ideas*—is an epithet more commonly applied to extent than to number. It is plain that he here employed it to avoid the repetition of the word *great,* which occurs immediately afterwards.

> (3) The sense of feeling can, indeed, give us a notion of extension, shape, and all other ideas that enter at the eye, except colours; but, at the same time, it is very much straitened and confined in its operations to the number, bulk, and distance of its particular objects.

This sentence is by no means so happy as the former. It is, indeed, neither clear nor elegant. *Extension* and *shape* can, with no propriety, be called *ideas;* they are properties of matter. Neither is it accurate, even according to Mr. Locke's philosophy (with which our author seems here to have puzzled himself), to speak of any sense *giving us a notion of ideas;* our senses give us the ideas themselves. The meaning would have been much more clear if the author had expressed himself thus: "The sense of feeling can, indeed, give us the idea of extension, figure, and all the other properties of matter which are perceived by the eye, except colours."

The latter part of the sentence is still more embarrassed. For what meaning can we make of the sense of feeling being *confined in its operation to the number, bulk, and distance, of its particular objects?* Surely, every sense is confined, as much as the sense of feeling, to the number, bulk, and distance of its own objects. Sight and feeling are, in this respect, perfectly on a level; neither of them can extend beyond its own objects. The turn of expression is so inaccurate here that one would be apt to suspect two words to have been omitted in the printing, which were originally in Mr. Addison's manuscript, because the insertion of them would render the sense much more intelligible and clear. These two words are *with regard—it is very much straitened and confined in its operations, with regard to the number, bulk, and distance of its particular objects.* The meaning then would be that feeling is more limited than sight *in this respect—*that it is confined to a narrower circle, to a smaller number of objects.

The epithet *particular,* applied to *objects,* in the conclusion of the sentence, is redundant and conveys no meaning whatever. Mr. Addison seems to have used it in place of *peculiar,* as indeed he does often in other passages of his writings. But *particular* and *peculiar,* though they are too often confounded, are words of different import from each other. *Particular* stands opposed to *general; peculiar* stands opposed to what is possessed in *common with others. Particular* expresses what, in the logical style, is called *species; peculiar,* what is called *differentia. Its peculiar objects* would have signified, in this place, the objects of the sense of feeling, as distinguished from the objects of any other sense and would have had more meaning than *its particular objects,* though, in truth, neither the one nor the other epithet was requisite. It was sufficient to have said simply, *its objects.*

> (4) Our sight seems designed to supply all these defects, and may be considered as a more delicate and diffusive kind of touch, that spreads itself over an infinite multitude of bodies, comprehends the largest figures, and brings into our reach some of the most remote parts of the universe.

Here again the author's style returns upon us in all its beauty. This is a sentence distinct, graceful, well arranged, and highly musical. In the latter part of it, it is constructed with three members, which are formed much in the same manner with those of the second sentence, on which I bestowed so much praise. The construction is so similar that if it had followed immediately after it, we should have been sensible of a faulty monotony. But the interposition of another sentence between them prevents this effect.

> (5) It is this sense which furnishes the imagination with its ideas; so that by the pleasures of the imagination or fancy (which I shall use

promiscuously) I here mean such as arise from visible objects, either when we have them actually in our view or when we call up their ideas into our minds by paintings, statues, descriptions, or any the like occasion.

In place of, *It is this sense which furnishes,* the author might have said more shortly, *This sense furnishes.* But the mode of expression which he has used is here more proper. This sort of full and ample assertion, *it is this which,* is fit to be used when a proposition of importance is laid down to which we seek to call the reader's attention. It is like pointing with the hand at the object of which we speak. The parenthesis in the middle of the sentence, *which I shall use promiscuously,* is not clear. He ought to have said, *terms which I shall use promiscuously;* as the verb *use* relates not to the pleasures of the imagination but to the terms of fancy and imagination, which he was to employ as synonymous. *Any the like occasion.* To call a painting or a statue *an occasion* is not a happy expression, nor is it very proper to speak of *calling up ideas by occasions.* The common phrase, *any such means,* would have been more natural.

> (6) We cannot indeed have a single image in the fancy that did not make its first entrance through the sight; but we have the power of re-taining, altering, and compounding those images which we have once received into all the varieties of picture and vision that are most agree-able to the imagination; for, by this faculty, a man in a dungeon is capa-ble of entertaining himself with scenes and landscapes more beautiful than any that can be found in the whole compass of nature.

It may be of use to remark that in one member of this sentence, there is an inaccuracy in syntax. It is very proper to say, *altering and compounding those images which we have once received into all the varieties of picture and vision.* But we can with no propriety say, *retaining them into all the varieties;* and yet, according to the manner in which the words are ranged, this construction is unavoidable. For *retaining, altering,* and *compounding* are participles, each of which equally refers to, and governs, the subsequent noun, *those images;* and that noun again is necessarily connected with the following preposition, *into.* This instance shows the importance of carefully attending to the rules of grammar and syntax; when so pure a writer as Mr. Addison could, through inadvertence, be guilty of such an error. The construction might easily have been rectified by disjoining the participle *retaining* from the other two participles in this way: "We have the power of retaining, altering, and compounding those images which we have once received and of forming them into all the varieties of picture and vision." The latter part of the sentence is clear and elegant.

> (7) There are few words in the English language which are employed
> in a more loose and uncircumscribed sense than those of the fancy and
> the imagination.

There are few words—which are employed. It had been better if our
author here had said more simply, *few words in the English language are
employed.* Mr. Addison, whose style is of the free and full, rather than the
nervous, kind, deals, on all occasions, in this extended sort of phraseology.
But it is proper only when some assertion of consequence is advanced, and
which can bear an emphasis, such as that in the first sentence of the former
paragraph. On other occasions, these little words, *it is,* and *there are,* ought
to be avoided as redundant and enfeebling. *Those of the fancy and the
imagination.* The article ought to have been omitted here. As he does not
mean the powers of *the fancy and the imagination* but the words only, the
article certainly had no proper place; neither, indeed, was there any occasion
for the other two words, *those of.* Better if the sentence had run thus: "Few
words in the English language are employed in a more loose and uncircumscribed sense than fancy and imagination."

> (8) I therefore thought it necessary to fix and determine the notion of
> these two words, as I intend to make use of them in the thread of my
> following speculations, that the reader may conceive rightly what is the
> subject which I proceed upon.

Though *fix* and *determine* may appear synonymous words, yet a difference
between them may be remarked, and they may be viewed, as applied here,
with peculiar delicacy. The author had just said that the words of which
he is speaking were *loose* and *uncircumscribed.* *Fix* relates to the first of
these, *determine* to the last. We *fix* what is *loose;* that is, we confine the
word to its proper place that it may not fluctuate in our imagination and
pass from one idea to another; and we *determine* what is *uncircumscribed;*
that is, we ascertain its *termini* or limits, we draw the circle round it that
we may see its boundaries. For we cannot conceive the meaning of a word,
or indeed of any other thing, clearly, till we see its limits and know how
far it extends. These two words, therefore, have grace and beauty as they
are here applied, though a writer more frugal of words than Mr. Addison
would have preferred the single word *ascertain,* which conveys, without
any metaphor, the import of them both.

The *notion of these words* is somewhat of a harsh phrase, at least not so
commonly used as the *meaning of these words.* *As I intend to make use
of them in the thread of my speculations.* This is plainly faulty. A sort of
metaphor is improperly mixed with words in the literal sense. He might
very well have said, *as I intend to make use of them in my following speculations.* This was plain language; but if he chose to borrow an allusion from

thread, that allusion ought to have been supported; for there is no consistency in *making use of them in the thread of speculations;* and indeed, in expressing anything so simple and familiar as this is, plain language is always to be preferred to metaphorical. *The subject which I proceed upon* is an ungraceful close of a sentence; better, *the subject upon which I proceed.*

> (9) I must therefore desire him to remember that, by the pleasures of the imagination, I mean only such pleasures as arise originally from sight, and that I divide these pleasures into two kinds.

As the last sentence began with, *I therefore thought it necessary to fix,* it is careless to begin this sentence in a manner so very similar, *I must therefore desire him to remember*—especially as the small variation of using, *on this account* or *for this reason,* in place of *therefore* would have amended the style. When he says, *I mean only such pleasures,* it may be remarked that the adverb *only* is not in its proper place. It is not intended here to qualify the word *mean* but *such pleasures,* and therefore should have been placed in as close a connexion as possible with the word which it limits or qualifies. The style becomes more clear and neat when the words are arranged thus: "By the pleasures of the imagination, I mean such pleasures only as arise from sight."

> (10) My design, being first of all to discourse of those primary pleasures of the imagination, which entirely proceed from such objects as are before our eyes; and, in the next place, to speak of those secondary pleasures of the imagination, which flow from the ideas of visible objects, when the objects are not actually before the eye but are called up into our memories or formed into agreeable visions of things that are either absent or fictitious.

It is a great rule in laying down the division of a subject to study neatness and brevity as much as possible. The divisions are then more distinctly apprehended and more easily remembered. This sentence is not perfectly happy in that respect. It is somewhat clogged by a tedious phraseology. *My design being first of all, to discourse—in the next place, to speak of—such objects as are before our eyes—things that are either absent or fictitious.* Several words might have been spared here; and the style made more neat and compact.

> (11) The pleasures of the imagination, taken in their full extent, are not so gross as those of sense, nor so refined as those of the understanding.

This sentence is distinct and elegant.

> (12) The last are indeed more preferable, because they are founded on some new knowledge or improvement in the mind of man; yet it must

be confessed that those of the imagination are as great and as transporting as the other.

In the beginning of this sentence, the phrase *more preferable* is such a
plain inaccuracy that one wonders how Mr. Addison should have fallen
into it, seeing *preferable,* of itself, expresses the comparative degree and is
the same with "more eligible" or "more excellent."

I must observe farther that the proposition contained in the last member
of this sentence is neither clear nor neatly expressed—*it must be confessed
that those of the imagination are as great and as transporting as the other.*
In the former sentence, he had compared three things together—the pleasures
of the imagination, those of sense, and those of the understanding. In the
beginning of this sentence, he had called the pleasures of the understanding
the last; and he ends the sentence with observing that those of the imagination are as great and transporting *as the other.* Now, besides that *the other*
makes not a proper contrast with *the last,* he leaves it ambiguous whether,
by *the other,* he meant the pleasures of the understanding or the pleasures
of the sense; for it may refer to either, by the construction; though, undoubtedly, he intended that it should refer to the pleasures of the understanding only. The proposition reduced to perspicuous language runs thus:
"Yet it must be confessed that the pleasures of the imagination, when compared with those of the understanding, are no less great and transporting."

> (13) A beautiful prospect delights the soul as much as a demonstration;
> and a description in Homer has charmed more readers than a chapter in
> Aristotle.

This is a good illustration of what he had been asserting and is expressed
with that happy and elegant turn, for which our author is very remarkable.

> (14) Besides, the pleasures of the imagination have this advantage above
> those of the understanding, that they are more obvious and more easy
> to be acquired.

This is also an unexceptionable sentence.

> (15) It is but opening the eye, and the scene enters.

This sentence is lively and picturesque. By the gayety and briskness which
it gives the style, it shows the advantage of intermixing such a short sentence
as this amidst a run of longer ones, which never fails to have a happy
effect. I must remark, however, a small inaccuracy. A *scene* cannot be said
to *enter;* an *actor* enters, but a scene *appears* or *presents itself.*

> (16) The colours paint themselves on the fancy, with very little attention
> of thought or application of mind in the beholder.

This is still beautiful illustration, carried on with that agreeable floweriness of fancy and style which is so well suited to those pleasures of the imagination of which the author is treating.

> (17) We are struck, we know not how, with the symmetry of anything we see, and immediately assent to the beauty of an object, without inquiring into the particular causes and occasions of it.

There is a falling off here from the elegance of the former sentences. *We assent* to the truth of a proposition but cannot so well be said *to assent to the beauty of an object. Acknowledge* would have expressed the sense with more propriety. The close of the sentence too is heavy and ungraceful—*the particular causes and occasions of it;* both *particular* and *occasions* are words quite superfluous; and the pronoun *it* is in some measure ambiguous, whether it refers to beauty or to object. It would have been some amendment to the style to have run thus: "We immediately acknowledge the beauty of an object, without inquiring into the cause of that beauty."

> (18) A man of polite imagination is let into a great many pleasures that the vulgar are not capable of receiving.

Polite is a term more commonly applied to manners or behaviour than to the mind or imagination. There is nothing farther to be observed on this sentence, unless the use of *that* for a relative pronoun, instead of *which*—an usage which is too frequent with Mr. Addison. *Which* is a much more definitive word than *that,* being never employed in any other way than as a relative, whereas *that* is a word of many senses—sometimes a demonstrative pronoun, often a conjunction. In some cases we are indeed obliged to use *that* for a relative, in order to avoid the ungraceful repetition of *which* in the same sentence. But when we are laid under no necessity of this kind, *which* is always the preferable word and certainly was so in this sentence. *Pleasures which the vulgar are not capable of receiving* is much better than *pleasures that the vulgar etc.*

> (19) He can converse with a picture and find an agreeable companion in a statue. He meets with a secret refreshment in a description; and often feels a greater satisfaction in the prospect of fields and meadows than another does in the possession. It gives him, indeed, a kind of property in every thing he sees; and makes the most rude, uncultivated parts of nature administer to his pleasures: so that he looks upon the world, as it were, in another light and discovers in it a multitude of charms that conceal themselves from the generality of mankind.

All this is very beautiful. The illustration is happy and the style runs with the greatest ease and harmony. We see no labour, no stiffness or affectation;

but an author writing from the native flow of a gay and pleasing imagination. This predominant character of Mr. Addison's manner, far more than compensates all those little negligences which we are now remarking. Two of these occur in this paragraph. The first, in the sentence which begins with *it gives him indeed a kind of property*. To this *it* there is no proper antecedent in the whole paragraph. In order to gather the meaning, we must look back as far as to the third sentence before, the first of the paragraph, which begins with *a man of a polite imagination*. This phrase, *polite* imagination, is the only antecedent to which this *it* can refer; and even that is an improper antecedent, as it stands in the genitive case, as the qualification only of *a man*.

The other instance of negligence is towards the end of the paragraph, *so that he looks upon the world, as it were in another light*. By *another* light, Mr. Addison means a light different from that in which other men view the world. But though this expression clearly conveyed this meaning to himself when writing, it conveys it very indistinctly to others and is an instance of that sort of inaccuracy, into which, in the warmth of composition, every writer of a lively imagination is apt to fall and which can only be remedied by a cool, subsequent review. *As it were* is upon most occasions no more than an ungraceful palliative; and here there was not the least occasion for it, as he was not about to say anything which required a softening of this kind. To say the truth, this last sentence, *so that he looks upon the world,* and what follows had better been wanting altogether. It is no more than an unnecessary recapitulation of what had gone before—a feeble adjection to the lively picture he had given of the pleasures of the imagination. The paragraph would have ended with more spirit as the words immediately preceding—*the uncultivated parts of nature administer to his pleasures*.

> (20) There are, indeed, but very few who know how to be idle and innocent, or have a relish of any pleasures that are not criminal; every diversion they take is at the expense of some one virtue or another, and their very first step out of business is into vice or folly.

Nothing can be more elegant or more finely turned than this sentence. It is neat, clear, and musical. We could hardly alter one word or disarrange one member without spoiling it. Few sentences are to be found more finished or more happy.

> (21) A man should endeavour, therefore, to make the sphere of his innocent pleasures as wide as possible that he may retire into them with safety and find in them such a satisfaction as a wise man would not blush to take.

This is also a good sentence and gives occasion to no material remark.

(22) Of this nature are those of the imagination, which do not require such a bent of thought as is necessary to our more serious employments, nor, at the same time, suffer the mind to sink into that indolence and remissness, which are apt to accompany our more sensual delights; but like a gentle exercise to the faculties awaken them from sloth and idleness, without putting them upon any labour or difficulty.

The beginning of this sentence is not correct and affords an instance of a period too loosely connected with the preceding one. *Of this nature,* says he, *are those of the imagination.* We might ask, of what nature? For it had not been the scope of the preceding sentence to describe the nature of any set of pleasures. He had said that it was every man's duty to make the sphere of his innocent pleasures as wide as possible, in order that, within that sphere, he might find a safe retreat and a laudable satisfaction. The transition is loosely made by beginning the next sentence with saying, *of this nature are those of the imagination.* It had been better if, keeping in view the governing object of the preceding sentence, he had said, "This advantage we gain" or "This satisfaction we enjoy by means of the pleasures of imagination." The rest of the sentence is abundantly correct.

(23) We might here add that the pleasures of the fancy are more conducive to health than those of the understanding, which are worked out by dint of thinking and attended with too violent a labour of the brain.

On this sentence, nothing occurs deserving of remark, except that *worked out by dint of thinking* is a phrase which borders too much on vulgar and colloquial language to be proper for being employed in a polished composition.

(24) Delightful scenes, whether in nature, painting, or poetry, have a kindly influence on the body, as well as the mind, and not only serve to clear and brighten the imagination but are able to disperse grief and melancholy and to set the animal spirits in pleasing and agreeable motions. For this reason, Sir Francis Bacon, in his Essay upon Health, has not thought it improper to prescribe to his reader a poem or a prospect, where he particularly dissuades him from knotty and subtile disquisitions and advises him to pursue studies that fill the mind with splendid and illustrious objects, as histories, fables, and contemplations of nature.

In the latter of these two sentences, a member of the period is altogether out of its place—which gives the whole sentence a harsh and disjointed cast and serves to illustrate the rules I formerly gave concerning arrangement. The wrong-placed member which I point at is this: *where he particularly dissuades him from knotty and subtile disquisitions;* these words should undoubtedly have been placed not where they stand but thus: *Sir Francis Bacon, in his Essay upon Health, where he particularly dissuades the reader from knotty and subtile speculations, has not thought it improper to prescribe to him etc.* This arrangement reduces every thing into proper order.

> (25) I have in this paper, by way of introduction, settled the motion of those pleasures of the imagination, which are the subject of my present undertaking, and endeavoured, by several considerations, to recommend to my readers the pursuit of those pleasures; I shall, in my next paper, examine the several sources from whence these pleasures are derived.

These two concluding sentences afford examples of the proper collocation of circumstances in a period. I formerly showed that it is often a matter of difficulty to dispose of them in such a manner as that they shall not embarrass the principal subject of the sentence. In the sentences before us, several of these incidental circumstances necessarily come in—*By way of introduction—by several considerations—in this paper—in the next paper.* All which are with great propriety managed by our author. It will be found, upon trial, that there were no other parts of the sentence, in which they could have been placed to equal advantage. Had he said, for instance, "I have settled the notion (rather, *the meaning*) of those pleasures of the imagination, which are the subject of my present undertaking, by way of introduction, in this paper, and endeavoured to recommend the pursuit of those pleasures to my readers, by several considerations," we must be sensible that the sentence, thus clogged with circumstances in the wrong place, would neither have been so neat nor so clear, as it is by the present construction.

John F. Kennedy: Inaugural Address

(January 20, 1961)

1 We observe today not a victory of party but a celebration of freedom, symbolizing an end as well as a beginning, signifying renewal as well as change. For I have sworn before you and Almighty God the same solemn oath our forebears prescribed nearly a century and three-quarters ago.

2 The world is very different now. For man holds in his mortal hands the power to abolish all forms of human poverty and all forms of human life. And yet the same revolutionary belief for which our forebears fought is still at issue around the globe, the belief that the rights of man come not from the generosity of the state but from the hand of God.

3 We dare not forget today that we are the heirs of that first revolution. Let the word go forth from this time and place, to friend and foe alike, that the torch has been passed to a new generation of Americans, born in

this century, tempered by war, disciplined by a hard and bitter peace, proud of our ancient heritage, and unwilling to witness or permit the slow undoing of those human rights to which this nation has always been committed, and to which we are committed today at home and around the world.

4 Let every nation know, whether it wishes us well or ill, that we shall pay any price, bear any burden, meet any hardship, support any friend, oppose any foe to assure the survival and the success of liberty.

5 This much we pledge—and more.

6 To those old allies whose cultural and spiritual origins we share, we pledge the loyalty of faithful friends. United, there is little we cannot do in a host of co-operative ventures. Divided, there is little we can do, for we dare not meet a powerful challenge at odds and split asunder.

7 To those new states whom we welcome to the ranks of the free, we pledge our word that one form of colonial control shall not have passed away merely to be replaced by a far more iron tyranny. We shall not always expect to find them supporting our view. But we shall always hope to find them strongly supporting their own freedom, and to remember that, in the past, those who foolishly sought power by riding the back of the tiger ended up inside.

8 To those peoples in the huts and villages of half the globe struggling to break the bonds of mass misery, we pledge our best efforts to help them help themselves, for whatever period is required, not because the Communists may be doing it, not because we seek their votes, but because it is right. If a free society cannot help the many who are poor, it cannot save the few who are rich.

9 To our sister republics south of our border, we offer a special pledge: to convert our good words into good deeds, in a new alliance for progress, to assist free men and free governments in casting off the chains of poverty. But this peaceful revolution of hope cannot become the prey of hostile powers. Let all our neighbors know that we shall join with them to oppose aggression or subversion anywhere in the Americas. And let every other power know that this hemisphere intends to remain the master of its own house.

10 To that world assembly of sovereign states, the United Nations, our last best hope in an age where the instruments of war have far outpaced the instruments of peace, we renew our pledge of support: to prevent it from becoming merely a forum for invective, to strengthen its shield of the new and the weak, and to enlarge the area in which its writ may run.

11 Finally, to those nations who would make themselves our adversary, we offer not a pledge but a request: that both sides begin anew the quest for peace, before the dark powers of destruction unleashed by science engulf all humanity in planned or accidental self-destruction.

12 We dare not tempt them with weakness. For only when our arms are

sufficient beyond doubt can we be certain beyond doubt that they will never be employed.

13 But neither can two great and powerful groups of nations take comfort from our present course—both sides over-burdened by the cost of modern weapons, both rightly alarmed by the steady spread of the deadly atom, yet both racing to alter that uncertain balance of terror that stays the hand of mankind's final war.

14 So let us begin anew, remembering on both sides that civility is not a sign of weakness, and sincerity is always subject to proof. Let us never negotiate out of fear, but let us never fear to negotiate.

15 Let both sides explore what problems unite us instead of belaboring those problems which divide us.

16 Let both sides, for the first time, formulate serious and precise proposals for the inspection and control of arms, and bring the absolute power to destroy other nations under the absolute control of all nations.

17 Let both sides seek to invoke the wonders of science instead of its terrors. Together let us explore the stars, conquer the deserts, eradicate disease, tap the ocean depths and encourage the arts and commerce.

18 Let both sides unite to heed in all corners of the earth the command of Isaiah to "undo the heavy burdens...[and] let the oppressed go free."

19 And if a beachhead of co-operation may push back the jungle of suspicion, let both sides join in creating a new endeavor, not a new balance of power, but a new world of law, where the strong are just and the weak secure and the peace preserved.

20 All this will not be finished in the first one hundred days. Nor will it be finished in the first one thousand days, nor in the life of this Administration, nor even perhaps in our lifetime on this planet. But let us begin.

21 In your hands, my fellow citizens, more than mine, will rest the final success or failure of our course. Since this country was founded, each generation of Americans has been summoned to give testimony to its national loyalty. The graves of young Americans who answered the call to service surround the globe.

22 Now the trumpet summons us again—not as a call to bear arms, though arms we need; not as a call to battle, though embattled we are; but a call to bear the burden of a long twilight struggle, year in and year out, "rejoicing in hope, patient in tribulation," a struggle against the common enemies of man: tyranny, poverty, disease and war itself.

23 Can we forge against these enemies a grand and global alliance, North and South, East and West, that can assure a more fruitful life for all mankind? Will you join in that historic effort?

24 In the long history of the world, only a few generations have been granted the role of defending freedom in its hour of maximum danger. I

do not shrink from this responsibility; I welcome it. I do not believe that any of us would exchange places with any other people or any other generation. The energy, the faith, the devotion which we bring to this endeavor will light our country and all who serve it, and the glow from that fire can truly light the world.

25 And so, my fellow Americans, ask not what your country can do for you; ask what you can do for your country.

26 My fellow citizens of the world, ask not what America will do for you, but what together we can do for the freedom of man.

27 Finally, whether you are citizens of America or citizens of the world, ask of us here the same high standards of strength and sacrifice which we ask of you. With a good conscience our only sure reward, with history the final judge of our deeds, let us go forth to lead the land we love, asking His blessing and His help, but knowing that here on earth God's work must truly be our own.

The Editors of *The New Yorker:* John F. Kennedy's Inaugural Address

As rhetoric has become an increasingly dispensable member of the liberal arts, people have abandoned the idea, held so firmly by the ancient Greeks and Romans, that eloquence is indispensable to politics. Perhaps President Kennedy's achievements in both spheres will revive a taste for good oratory —a taste that has been alternately frustrated by inarticulateness and dulled by bombast. There have been a few notable orators in our day—most recently Adlai Stevenson—but they have been the exceptions, and it has taken Mr. Kennedy's success as a politician to suggest that the power to "enchant souls through words" (Socrates) may soon be at a premium once more. Whatever the impact of the Inaugural Address on contemporary New Frontiersmen, we find it hard to believe that an Athenian or Roman citizen could have listened to it unmoved, or that Cicero, however jealous of his own reputation, would have found reason to object to it.

We are all familiar by now with the generally high praise the President received for his first speech, but before the responsibility for a final judgment is yielded to Time it would be a shame not to seek the opinion of a couple of true professionals. Both Aristotle and Cicero, the one a theorist and the other a theorizing orator, believed that rhetoric could be an art to the extent that the orator was, first, a logician and, second, a psychologist with an appreciation and understanding of words. Cicero felt further, that the ideal orator was the thoroughly educated man. (He would be pleased by Mr. Kennedy's background, with its strong emphasis on affairs of state: the philosopher-orator-statesman.) Of the three types of oratory defined by the ancients—political, forensic, and display (in which audience participation was limited to a judgment of style)—the political was esteemed most highly, because it dealt with the loftiest of issues; namely, the fate of peoples, rather than of individuals. ("Now the trumpet summons us again...against the common enemies of man....") The ideal speech was thought to be one in which three kinds of persuasion were used by the speaker: logical, to present the facts of the case and construct an argument based on them; emotional, to reach the audience psychologically; and "ethical," to appeal to the audience by establishing one's own integrity and sincerity. The Inaugural Address, being a variation on the single theme of man's rights and obligations, is not primarily logical, although it contains no illogic; it is an appeal to men's souls rather than to their minds. During the Presidential campaign, Mr. Kennedy tested and patented an exercise in American psychology that proved to be all the emotional appeal he required for the inaugural speech: "And so, my fellow-Americans, ask not what your country can do for you, ask what you can do for your country." His ethical persuasion, or indication of his personal probity, consisted of an extension of that appeal: "...ask of us here the same high standards of strength and sacrifice which we ask of you."

Aristotle recognized only one (good) style, while Cicero thought that there were three styles—the plain, the middle, and the grand. To Aristotle, who considered it sufficient for a style to be clear and appropriate, avoiding undue elevation (whence bombast) and excessive lowliness, it would have seemed that Mr. Kennedy had achieved the Golden Mean. The formality of the Inaugural Address ("To that world assembly of sovereign states, the United Nations...") is appropriate to the subject; the language ("In your hands, my fellow-citizens, more than mine, will rest the final success or failure of our course") is clear and direct. Cicero's ideal orator was able to speak in all three styles, in accordance with the demands of his subject, and in that respect Mr. Kennedy filled the role by speaking plainly on the practical ("All this will not be finished in the first one hundred days"), by speaking formally but directly on the purpose of national defense ("For only when our arms are sufficient beyond doubt can we be certain beyond doubt that they will never be employed"), and by speaking grandly on the potential accomplishments of the movement toward the New Frontier ("The energy, the faith, the devotion which we bring to this endeavor will light our country and all who serve it—and the glow from that fire can truly light the world").

The address, however, is largely in the grand style, which is characterized by Cicero as the ultimate source of emotional persuasion, through figures of speech and a certain degree of dignified periodic rhythm, not iambic ("The world is very different now. For man holds in his mortal hands the power to abolish all forms of human poverty, and all forms of human life"). The oration is so rich in figures of speech—the many metaphors include a torch, a beachhead, jungles, a trumpet, a tiger—that we can imagine students of the future studying it for examples of antithesis ("If a free society cannot help the many who are poor, it cannot save the few who are rich"), personification ("...the hand of mankind's final war"), and anaphora ("Not as a call to bear arms, though arms we need; not as a call to battle, though embattled we are..."). "Battle" and "embattled"—an excellent example of paronomasia.

And so we leave the speech to the students of rhetoric, having invoked for Mr. Kennedy the blessings of Aristotle and Cicero, and for ourself the hope that he has re-established the tradition of political eloquence.

Analysis of the Style of John F. Kennedy's Inaugural Address

"If, in the effective use of language, style is the man, style is the nation too; men, countries, and entire civilizations have been tested and judged by their literary tone."—John F. Kennedy

General Situation for the Speech

If we are to relate the style of the Inaugural Address to its content, we must take into account the subject matter, the occasion, the audience, and the ethos of the speaker. An inauguration is a solemn, ceremonial event, attended by certain traditions and rituals. A speech delivered on such an occasion is usually of the ceremonial variety, although there may be deliberative elements in it. What the people have come to expect is not so much a speech that lays down a specific program as a speech that sets a mood. In striking the keynote of the coming administration, the speaker will try to heal the wounds that may have been inflicted during the campaign, to remind the audience of a common heritage and a common purpose, to set forth, in a general way, the policies and objectives of the new administration, and to reassure the international community of the continuity and determination of the nation.

Since a ceremonial speech like this deals in generalities rather than in particulars, it can very easily slip off into platitude and pious cant. In seeking to please everyone with a "safe" speech, the speaker runs the risk of pleasing no one. In striving for that happy mean between the general and the specific, between the trite and the bizarre, and between the offensive and the fulsome, the speaker will have to draw on all his or her ingenuity to come up with a content and a form that will impress the audience without boring them.

Having characterized the kind of speech that is usually delivered at an inauguration, we might consider now the special situation that faced President Kennedy on that January morning in 1961. John Fitzgerald Kennedy was the youngest man and the first Catholic to be elected to the highest office in America, and he had been elected by a narrow margin of votes. His youth, his religious affiliation, and his narrow victory at the polls—all these combined to establish some doubts about him in the minds of his own people and the people of other countries. Having created an image, during the campaign, of enormous vitality and considerable political shrewdness, this leader of the New Frontier had to fulfill his promise to push the country forward. Clearly, this was an occasion when a powerful ethical appeal would have to be exerted if the confidence and initiative of the people were to be aroused.

What about the audience for this address? There would be the immediate audience—the high dignitaries on the platform and the thousands of people gathered in the plaza in front of the Capitol building. Then there were the millions of people who would see and hear the speaker through the medium of television. And finally there would be the millions of people in foreign lands who would read accounts of the speech in their newspapers the next day. Taken together, this was a vast, heterogeneous audience, posing special problems for the speaker. As we have remarked before, the larger and more heterogeneous the audience is, the more difficult it is to adjust the discourse to fit the audience. In his content and his style, the President must strike some common denominator—but a common denominator that does not fall below the dignity that the occasion demands.

Having looked at the general situation that prevailed for the speech, let us now see how the President accommodated his means to his end. In this analysis, of course, we are going to investigate only the way in which the President accommodated his *style* to the subject matter, occasion, audience, and his own personality.

The Speech as a Whole

One of the first things that strikes the reader is the relative brevity of the speech—1343 words, which at the normal rate for public address would take between nine and ten minutes to deliver. When the President wrote this speech he could not have known that the "live" audience for the speech would be standing in the biting cold that followed a heavy snowstorm in the Washington area on the day before the inauguration. So the President had not made his speech brief out of consideration for his wind-chilled audience.

In preparing the speech, however, he might have taken into consideration that it would be delivered at the end of some lengthy preliminary speech-making. But perhaps the consideration that mainly determined the brevity of the speech was the traditional nature of inaugural addresses. As we have observed, inaugural addresses usually deal in broad, undeveloped generalities. Principles, policies, and promises are enunciated without elaboration.

Paragraphs

The relative brevity of the speech is reflected in the paragraph and sentence structure. A glance at the printed text of the speech reveals a succession of short paragraphs. Of the twenty-seven paragraphs in the speech, ten have only one sentence; seven paragraphs are two sentences long; and another seven are three sentences long. The longest paragraphs (9 and 24) contain only four sentences. In terms of averages, there are 49.3 words per paragraph and 1.92 sentences per paragraph.

The President is trying to cover a lot of ground in this short speech. In order to do this, he enunciates his principles, promises, and policies in a litany of capsule paragraphs. The effect of these unelaborated paragraphs would have been slight if the President had not rendered many of those paragraphs memorable by the brilliance of his style.

Sentences: Length

Descending to the next smallest unit of discourse, the sentence, we note some interesting facts about the length and kinds of sentences. The two extremes of sentence length are represented by the sentence of eighty words (second sentence of paragraph 3) and the sentence of four words (third sentence of paragraph 20). The average length of the President's sentences is 25.8 words. But what is more revealing about the President's style is the variation above and below this average. Fourteen of the fifty-two sentences (27 percent) in the speech are ten words or more *above* the average; but twenty-three sentences (44 percent) are five words or more *below* the average. Although the President has a number of unusually long sentences—66 words (paragraph 10), 64 words (paragraph 22), 54 words (paragraphs 8 and 13) —an unusually high proportion of his sentences are composed of twenty words or less. Even by modern journalistic standards, a twenty-word sentence is short. This high proportion of short sentences matches the over-all brevity of the speech and the short paragraphs. Although the President displays an admirable variety in sentence-length, his heavy use of the short sentence does suggest that he had his *listening* audience in mind when he composed his speech. Another consideration that may have influenced the

President in the use of short sentences is that short sentences help to create the effect of sententiousness that is appropriate for a ceremonial speech.

Sentences: Grammatical Types

Having noted a high proportion of relatively short sentences, we might expect that a majority of the sentences would be of the simple or compound type. But a close investigation of the grammatical types reveals that this is not so. Twenty (38.4 percent) of the sentences are simple; only six (11.6 percent) sentences are compound. But twenty-six sentences (exactly 50 percent) are complex. Taken together, the simple and compound sentences constitute 50 percent of the whole, but the predominant grammatical type is the complex sentence. What this reveals is that the President manages the expansion of his sentences mainly through the sophisticated pattern of subordination. A study of the sequence of sentences, however, shows how well the President has mixed the grammatical types in order to avoid monotony of structure. Only in a half dozen or so places in the speech does he string together two or more sentences of the same grammatical type.

Sentences: Rhetorical Types

When we study the rhetorical patterns of the speech, we note another interesting feature of President Kennedy's style. The predominant rhetorical structure is antithesis. This recurring structure was perhaps dictated by the fact that the speech deals mainly with comparisons of opposites (end–beginning, old–new, rich–poor, friend–enemy). He strikes the theme of the speech and the antithetical keynote in the first sentence: "We observe today *not a victory of party/ but a celebration of freedom*—symbolizing *an end/* as well as *a beginning*—signifying *renewal/* as well as *change.*" Additional examples of antithesis are not hard to find:

> to friend and foe alike (paragraph 3)
>
> United . . . Divided (paragraph 6)
>
> To those old allies . . . To those new states (paragraphs 6, 7)
>
> If a free society cannot help the many who are poor, it cannot save the few who are rich. (paragraph 8)
>
> What problems unite us . . . those problems which divide us (paragraph 15)

And the most memorable line of the speech is cast in the form of an antithesis:

> . . . Ask not what your country can do for you—ask what you can do for your country.

Most of these antitheses of thought are laid out in parallel grammatical structure. The recurring parallelism is appropriate here because although the President is pointing up opposites by his antitheses he wants to suggest that these opposites can be reconciled. Opposites can be reconciled only if they are co-ordinate, and one way to emphasize the co-ordinate value of opposites is to juxtapose them in a parallel grammatical structure.

The other use that the President makes of parallelism is for the purpose of specification or enumeration, as in these three examples:

> born in this century, tempered by war, disciplined by a hard and bitter peace, proud of our ancient heritage (paragraph 3)
>
> pay any price, bear any burden, meet any hardship, support any friend, oppose any foe (paragraph 4)
>
> Together let us explore the stars, conquer the deserts, eradicate disease, and encourage the arts and commerce (paragraph 17)

As we shall see when we come to study the figures of speech, there are additional schemes intertwined in many of these parallel and antithetical patterns.

Before concluding this section on rhetorical patterns, we shall point out some other features of style. If students needed any evidence to justify their use of a co-ordinating conjunction at the beginning of the sentence, they could cite this speech. The President begins fourteen of his sentences (over 25 percent) with a co-ordinating conjunction. There is, of course, ample precedent for this usage in modern prose and the prose of earlier centuries. But it is interesting to note how effective rhetorically this means of articulating sentences is in the President's speech. Let us look at just one example of this usage:

> We dare not tempt them with weakness. For only when our arms are sufficient beyond doubt can we be certain beyond doubt that they will never be employed. (paragraph 12)

Contrast the effect of this with the following:

> We dare not tempt them with weakness, for only when our arms are sufficient beyond doubt can we be certain beyond doubt that they will never be employed.

The content and rhetorical scheme of both sentences is exactly the same, and perhaps if one were *reading* the second sentence aloud, one could produce the same effect as the first sentence has. But on the printed page, a special emphasis is achieved by setting off the second clause in a sentence by itself and by signaling the syllogistic relationship of the two clauses by the capitalized initial *For*. If you analyze the other uses of initial co-ordinating conjunctions, you will usually find some rhetorical purpose being served.

Sentences: Functional Types

The overwhelming majority of the sentences are declarative. This proportion is appropriate in a speech that is designed to inform and reassure the world about the objectives of the new administration. Occasionally, however, the President uses some other functional types of sentence. In paragraph 23, he uses two rhetorical questions ("Can we forge against these enemies a grand and global alliance, North and South, East and West, that can assure a more fruitful life for all mankind? Will you join in that historic effort?"). These questions occur at the point in the speech when the President is about to launch into his peroration. Up to this point the President has been declaring what he will do, what the American people will do. Now he wants to suggest what the international community can do to support his program of peace and prosperity. But he can only suggest—he cannot dictate or predict —what other countries will do. The rhetorical questions are phrased in such a way, however, that the natural answer to them is a resounding *Yes*.

The President groups together two other types of functional sentences— imperatives and hortatives. In paragraphs 25, 26, 27 (the concluding paragraphs of the speech), we see three sharp imperatives, using the verb *to ask*, which leave the citizens with a call to action. Up to this point, the audience have been mere listeners to this ceremonial discourse. Now the audience must be engaged actively. The imperatives point to the general line of action that they must take.

The series of fourteen hortative sentences ("Let us...Let both sides...") in paragraphs 14 through 20 also lays down a program of action, but the directives are softened by being cast in a hortatory form. (The Latin and Greek languages would have used the subjunctive mood of the verb to create this effect.) The President here is seeking to induce action, not command it In other words, he wants to persuade rather than coerce.

Diction

The diction of the speech unobtrusively but unmistakably exerts an influence on the effect of the speech. The simplicity of the diction is perhaps not immediately noticeable, but when one studies it, one notes that there is almost no word that a moderately intelligent high-school graduate would have to look up in a dictionary. A closer study of the diction reveals a high proportion of monosyllabic words: some 951 words in the speech (71 percent) are monosyllabic. In paragraphs 19 and 20, the proportion of monosyllabic words is as high as 80 per cent. Even in the peroration of the speech, where one might expect the orator to make use of the sonorous cadence that can be achieved with polysyllabic diction, one finds a high proportion of one-syllable words. This monosyllabism helps to account not only for the impression of simplicity but also for the note of strength in the speech—a note that people had come to associate with the vigor of this youthful public figure. In working over the drafts of the speech, the President must consciously have sought out simple, Anglo-Saxon words.

Having noted the high proportion of monosyllabic words, one might expect to find also a high proportion of concrete words. But this is not the case. Investigation of the nouns in the speech turns up many abstract words—words like *freedom, poverty, tyranny, loyalty, devotion, responsibility, aggression, subversion*. And most of this abstract diction is Latinate and polysyllabic. Aside from the figures of speech—which we will investigate later—there are surprisingly few concrete words—*huts, villages, stars, deserts, graves*. Whatever air of concreteness the speech has is created by the figures of speech. Perhaps the high proportion of abstract words is the natural consequence of the brief, unelaborated character of the speech. Once the President had decided to enunciate only the broad, general policy of his administration, it was almost inevitable that most of his substantive words would be abstract. What we have in this short speech really is a series of undeveloped topic sentences.

Another thing that accounts for the formal quality of this ceremonial speech is the occasional use of slightly archaic diction. We find the President using such words as *forebears* (twice), *host, anew, asunder, foe, adversary, writ*. Besides echoing the tone of Lincoln's *Gettysburg Address* ("Fourscore and seven years ago," "our fathers," "final resting-place," "hallow"), this quaint diction has Biblical overtones and a certain appropriateness to the old-new motif. The President reinforced the effect of this kind of diction by two quotations from the Old Testament and the folksy adage about riding the back of the tiger. The repetition of certain honorific key terms, like *pledge, citizens, peace* also helps to reinforce the reverential tone of the speech.

Figures of Speech: Schemes

First of all, let us look at some of the schemes—those patternings of words which represent departures from the ordinary way of speaking. Since we have already remarked about the pervasive parallelism and antithesis in the speech, we will concentrate here on some of the other schemes.

There are a number of schemes of repetition. The most notable of these is anaphora—repetition of the same words at the beginning of successive clauses. Anaphora is conspicuous in two key passages in the speech: the section (paragraphs 6-11) in which the President is making a series of pledges ("To those ..."); and the section (paragraphs 15-18) in which the President is suggesting a course of action ("Let both sides ..."). We have previously observed that these two sections make use of parallelism. The addition of *anaphora* to these passages performs two functions: it combines with the parallelism to mark off and emphasize the co-ordinateness of the series, and it helps to establish the rhythm of the passages. The speech has no example of the opposite scheme, epistrophe (repetition of the same word at the end of successive clauses), but it does have two examples of repetition of similar words in a medial position: "bear *any* burden, meet *any* hardship, support *any* friend, oppose *any* foe" (paragraph 4); "sufficient *beyond doubt* ... certain *beyond doubt*" (paragraph 12).

The most remembered sentence in the speech—"ask not what your country can do for you—ask what you can do for your country"—contains a figure of repetition known as antimetabole (repetition of words in converse order). Another memorable utterance—"Let us never negotiate out of fear. But never fear to negotiate"—appears to be another example of antimetabole, but it is more accurately classified as polyptoton (repetition of words derived from the same root). Here we have different conjugates of the word *fear*—serving as a noun in the first clause and as an infinitive in the second clause. There is another example of polyptoton in paragraph 22 ("Not as a call to *battle,* though *embattled* we are")—although, as the editors of *The New Yorker* observed, there is a suggestion here too of the trope called paronomasia (play on words).

President Kennedy made sparing use of the scheme of repetition known as alliteration. There are only two instances of noticeable alliteration in the speech—"the *a*rea in which its *w*rit may *r*un" (paragraph 10); "to *l*ead the *l*and we *l*ove" (paragraph 27). Perhaps in accord with his personality, the President avoided frequent use of alliteration because of the soft, effeminate sound-effect often produced by this figure; the President was striving for a note of strength and vigor. One wonders, though, whether the President did not intend some sound-effect of appropriate harshness in the succession of *s* and *d* sounds in "before the dark powers of destruction unleashed by science engulf all humanity in planned or accidental self-destruction" (paragraph 11).

Let us look briefly at a few more schemes. In most of his parallel series, the President shows a preference for the hurried rhythms that can be achieved with asyndeton (omission of conjunctions)—e.g. "born in this century, tempered by war, disciplined by a hard and bitter peace, proud of our ancient heritage" (paragraph 3). The President makes little use of the scheme called anastrophe (unusual word order). In the entire speech, there is only one structure that is inverted: *"United,* there is little we cannot do in a host of co-operative ventures. *Divided,* there is little we can do" (paragraph 6). It is easy to see the special emphasis the President achieves here by placing the past participles in the initial position, even though these participles do not modify, as they normally do in this position, the subject of the main clause. One could regard this structure, however, as ellipsis rather than anastrophe. The closest the President comes to the figure known as climax is in paragraphs 25, 26, 27; but even here we have to strain a bit to find any element of rising importance in the series.

Figures of Speech: Tropes

Although the President makes rather skillful use of the schemes, he is less satisfactory in his use of tropes. There are a number of metaphors in the speech, and those metaphors represent, as we remarked earlier, the chief way in which the President introduces concreteness into the speech. But many of these metaphors—"the torch," "bonds of mass misery," "the chains of poverty," "corners of the earth," "the trumpet," "the glow from that fire"—are rather hackneyed. He achieves a little more freshness in some of his more subtle metaphors, like "iron tyranny," "destruction unleashed," "twilight struggle," "forge." Perhaps his most successful metaphor is the one in paragraph 19—"And if a beachhead of co-operation may push back the jungle of suspicion." By themselves, *beachhead* and *jungle* are rather shopworn metaphors, but they acquire a certain freshness by being combined in a complex metaphor.

The several uses of "hands" (part for the whole) and "arms" (genus for the species) can be looked upon as examples of synecdoche, but those tropes too are fairly trite. The use of "hand" in paragraph 13—"that uncertain balance of terror that stays the hand of mankind's final war"—should be classified as an instance of personification rather than of synecdoche. Perhaps the only other expression in the speech which might be read as an instance of personification is found in the last paragraph—"with history the final judge of our deeds."

Style of Delivery

Undoubtedly, a good deal of the effect of this speech was produced by the "style" of delivery. Those who watched the inauguration ceremonies on television may recall the President's clear, crisp voice, the distinctive Bostonian accent, the mannerisms of the jabbing finger, the pauses, the inflections, the stresses. All of these features of voice and gesture helped to put the speech across; combined with the carefully worked-out style, they helped to communicate the President's message to the electorate and to the world. And perhaps it would be well for the student who has read this close analysis of the style to put the speech together again by listening to it on one of the many memorial records that were issued shortly after the President's assassination. Listening to a recording of the speech will make the student aware that this was a discourse designed for oral delivery, and it might prove interesting to note how much of the highly refined style of the speech comes through to the student once he or she has had the devices of style pointed out.

Concluding Remarks

The various stylistic devices we have been observing may be looked upon by some people as the ornamentation of the speech. These devices do "dress up" the speech, but if they are regarded as no more than ornamentation, they have failed to perform the functions that rhetoricians traditionally assigned to them. These formal devices should be one of the carriers of meaning. If the diction, the composition of words, and the figures of speech are not functioning to clarify, enliven, and emphasize the thought, if they are not exerting an ethical, emotional, or logical appeal, then indeed the style of a piece is so much sounding brass and tinkling cymbals, so much sound and fury signifying nothing.

It is not so important that the style of the speech be recognizable as the "Kennedy style" as it is that the style be seen as appropriate to the subject matter, the occasion, the purpose, and the audience. Just as Lincoln's *Gettysburg Address* was not particularly impressive to the audience who heard it in the National Cemetery on November 19, 1863, so Kennedy's Inaugural Address was not—if we may judge from the restrained applause that greeted it while it was being delivered—notably impressive to the audience who heard it in the snow-packed Capitol Plaza on January 20, 1961. It is only when we get a chance to read and reread Lincoln's and Kennedy's speeches that we realize what splendid performances they were. Only a close analysis such as we have engaged in can make us aware of the great care and deliberation President Kennedy devoted to the "expression" of his speech. So much eloquence did not come by chance. It had to come from calculated choices from among a number of possibilities.

We should now be in a better position to judge whether the President's choices were judicious. And we should be in a better position to predict whether future generations will judge this Inaugural Address to be one of the noblest utterances to issue from the lips of an American statesman.

A Paragraph by Virginia Woolf
To Be Analyzed for Style

The selection here is the final paragraph of a speech that Virginia Woolf gave to the London/National Society for Women's Service on January 21, 1931. The address was later printed under the title "Professions for Women" in a collection of Woolf's essays The Death of the Moth and Other Essays *(1942). In this address, Virginia Woolf is talking about a theme that she talked about in an earlier speech in 1928, a speech that was subsequently published under the title* A Room of One's Own *(1929). In the latter half of the paragraph reprinted here, Woolf picks up on the metaphor of "a room of one's own" and carries it through to the end of the paragraph. Woolf was unquestionably in the vanguard of the feminist movement in English-speaking countries. Barbara Hill Rigney, in her article "'A Wreath Upon the Grave': The Influence of Virginia Woolf on Feminist Critical Theory" (1984), said, "She [Woolf] was the first woman writer who is also readily identifiable as a feminist critic, and her methods as well as the ideology which informed those methods, her questions and self-contradictions, still constitute the methods, the questions, and the contradictions which are the central concerns of feminist theorists today." This paragraph will be analyzed for its style. Readers might ask themselves how much of the style of this piece was prompted by the fact that this is the wind-up paragraph of a discourse that is being orally delivered to a live audience of educated women. The selection here is reprinted from* Women and Writing. Ed. Michele Barrett. New York and London: Harcourt Brace Jovanovich, 1980, pp. 62–63.

(1) Those are the questions that I should like, had I time, to ask you. (2) And indeed, if I have laid stress upon these professional experiences of mine, it is because I believe that they are, though in different forms, yours also. (3) Even when the path is nominally open—when there is nothing to prevent a woman from being a doctor, a lawyer, a civil servant—there are many phantoms and obstacles, as I believe, looming in her way. (4) To discuss and define them is I think of great value and importance; for thus only can the labor be shared, the difficulties be solved. (5) But besides this, it is necessary also to discuss the ends and the aims for which we are fighting, for which we are doing battle with these formidable obstacles. (6) Those aims cannot be taken for granted; they must be perpetually questioned and examined. (7) The whole position, as I see it—here in this hall surrounded by women practising for the

first time in history I know not how many different professions—is one of extraordinary interest and importance. (8) You have won rooms of your own in the house hitherto exclusively owned by men. (9) You are able, though not without great labor and effort, to pay the rent. (10) You are earning your five hundred pounds a year. (11) But this freedom is only a beginning; the room is your own, but it is still bare. (12) It has to be furnished; it has to be decorated; it has to be shared. (13) How are you going to furnish it, how are you going to decorate it? (14) With whom are you going to share it, and upon what terms? (15) These, I think, are questions of the utmost importance and interest. (16) For the first time in history you are able to ask them; for the first time you are able to decide for yourselves what the answers should be. (17) Willingly would I stay and discuss those questions and answers—but not tonight. (18) My time is up; and I must cease.

An Analysis of the Style of the Paragraph by Virginia Woolf

You have just seen an analysis of a complete discourse, President John F. Kennedy's "Inaugural Address," and subsequently you will see Richard Fulkerson's analysis of another complete discourse, Martin Luther King's "Letter from Birmingham Jail." But here we will analyze a small segment of a full discourse, the final paragraph of Virginia Woolf's address to a group of women in Great Britain.

Earlier in this chapter, there is a series of Specimen Passages for Imitation, segments of longer discourses by a variety of English and American authors. You were invited to copy some of these paragraphs verbatim, just to observe and perhaps appropriate some stylistic features of professional writers' prose. You can learn a great deal simply by copying passages that others have written. But you could learn much more about style if after copying a passage, you were to write out what you had observed about the author's style while copying it.

In the analysis that follows, we will record our observations about the style of Virginia Woolf. But we must be careful about the generalizations we make from our observation of this small segment of Virginia Woolf's published writing. We can say that the features we observed are characteristic of *this* paragraph, but we would not be justified in saying that these features were characteristic of Woolf's style as a whole. Some of the features *might* be characteristic of her overall style, but we would have to analyze a much larger portion of her prose, written over a long period of time, to be justified in declaring that some salient feature that we observed in the paragraph was characteristic of her style as a whole. But even if we would not be justified in making generalizations about Woolf's style as a whole from our study of just one paragraph of her prose, we still might observe some unusual choice of diction or arrangement of words that we could adopt for our own style. And so there would be some profit for us in writing out our observations about someone's style after copying a short passage.

In preparation for your reading of this analysis, you might want to copy Virginia Woolf's paragraph so that you could observe it more closely than you can by just reading the passage and so that you could compare *your* observations with the observations recorded in the following analysis.

At the end of the analysis, there is a statistical summary of some of the features of the Virginia Woolf passage. Some of those statistics you could not come up with simply from reading the passage or even from copying it. For instance, in reading or copying the passage, you might have observed that there is a great variety in the length of Woolf's sentences, but until you had actually done some close counting you would not be able to come up with such statistics as the average number of words per sentence in this paragraph or the actual word-count for each of the eighteen sentences in this paragraph. But if you did sense that Virginia Woolf achieves an exemplary variety in the length of her sentences, you might be prompted to count the words in each sentence to confirm what you sensed. And if you were aware that one of the weaknesses of your style was a lack of variety in the length of your sentences, you might be prompted to make a conscious effort to achieve a variety in the length of your sentences. Your compilation of statistical information about other features of Woolf's style might likewise prompt you to resolve to incorporate some of those features into your own style. But don't feel that you have to adopt all features of her style. Some features may not suit your purposes or your personality.

One observation we might make about Virginia Woolf's style in this paragraph is that she seems to have a penchant for doublets—pairs of words, phrases, or clauses. For instance, here are the pairs of *words* found in this paragraph (with the number of the sentence in parentheses following the pair): "value and importance" (4); "the ends and the aims" (5); "questioned and examined" (6); "interest and importance" (7); "labor and effort" (9); "importance and interest" (15); "stay and discuss" and "questions and answers" (17). If you look closely at these pairs, you will see that in most cases, the two words are more synonymous than different in meaning. For instance, in sentence 17, "stay and discuss" and "questions and answers" are doublets in which the two words in both pairs are different in meaning; but in all the other doublets, the words in the pairings are roughly or closely synonymous—"value and importance," "the ends and the aims," "labor and effort." What these synonymous pairings indicate is that Woolf seems to use doublets more for rhythmical purposes than for discriminatory purposes.

Moreover, of the seven compound (Cp) and compound-complex (CC) sentences in this paragraph, four of them (6, 13, 16, and 18) are bipartite—that is, they are made up of two independent clauses. (The other three compounded sentences (4, 11, 12) are tripartite—made up of three independent clauses.) Closely allied to this tendency to structure words and clauses in doublets is Woolf's predilection for parallelism (balanced clauses) and anaphora (the scheme in which the beginnings of successive clauses begin with the same words). There are three examples of these stylistic features in the paragraph: *"It has to be* furnished; *it has to be* decorated; *it has to be* shared" (12); *"How are you going to* furnish it, *how are you going to* decorate it?* (13); *"For the first time* in history you are able to ask them; *for the first time* you are able to decide for yourselves what the answers should be" (16). Here again, the parallelism and especially the anaphora seem to be used primarily for the rhythms they set up.

Another prominent feature of the style of this paragraph is the split construction. The very first sentence of the paragraph has one of these split constructions: ". . . that I should like, had I time, to ask you." Here, it would be natural to keep the syntax in this order: "that I should like to ask you, had I time." Instead, Woolf starts the structure, then interrupts the normal syntax with the intervening clause "had I time," and then completes the initial structure. The effect of this splitting is to give due emphasis to the phrase "to ask you." In the natural order—see above—the clause "had I time" gets the chief emphasis.

After this first sentence, there are seven other instances of split construction: 2, 3, 4, 5, 7, 9, 15. The shortest interrupting splitter is the "I think" in 4 and 15; the longest interrupting splitters are found in 7 and 9. Sometimes—especially when the interrupters are long—the reader has difficulty in processing the suspended syntax; so you should be cautioned about overusing split constructions or about using those that involve unusually long interrupters.

Another stylistic feature that Woolf is fond of is the elliptical structure. Here are three examples of elliptical structure from this paragraph—with the understood words enclosed with brackets:

> ". . . for thus only can the labor be shared, [can] the difficulties be solved" (4)

> "With whom are you going to share it, and upon what terms [are you going to share it]" (14)

> "Willingly would I stay and discuss those questions and answers—but not tonight [will I stay and discuss those questions and answers] (17)

Ellipsis is a highly sophisticated structure, and you may want to add it to your stylistic repertory. But you should be cautioned that ellipsis is a tricky syntactical structure and that if it is not handled skillfully, readers may not be able to supply the missing words.

Some of the less prominent features of the style of this paragraph are the three sentences that begin with a coordinating conjunction (2, 5, 11) (how many of you have been told by your English teacher never to start a sentence with a coordinating conjunction?); the slightly archaic adverb *hitherto* in 8 and the "had I time" in 1, an alternative way of phrasing the subordinate clause "if I had time"; the expletive structures, which some teachers discourage students from using: "it is" (2), "there is" and "there are" (3), "it is necessary" (5); the number of monosyllabic words and of metaphors in the paragraph (see the statistical data at the end of this analysis).

Perhaps the least noticeable stylistic feature is the subtle way in which Virginia Woolf shifts from the first-person pronoun *I*, which predominates in the first half of the paragraph, to the second-person pronoun *you/your* in the second half. Starting with sentence 8, the focus is on *you*, the audience, and not until the last two sentences of the paragraph does Woolf revert to the pronoun *I* again. It was a clever move by Woolf to put the emphasis on the audience in the second half of the paragraph, and she achieves that emphasis simply by shifting pronouns. Another clever device was the short final sentence—the shortest sentence (eight words) in the paragraph. It was appropriate to end with that short sentence, because with her time on the podium having run out, she must abruptly cease talking.

What additional stylistic features did you notice?

Statistics on the Virginia Woolf Passage

A paragraph of 337 words and 18 sentences. Average sentence—18.72 words. Longest sentence: #3 (37 words). Shortest sentence: #18 (8 words). Number of sentences 5 words or more *below* the average—9 (50 percent). Number of sentences 10 words or more *above* the average—4 (22 percent). Number of predicate verbs in all the clauses—44:

> *to be* verbs—19 (43 percent)
> Active verbs—17 (38.6 percent)
> Transitive verbs—13 (29.5 percent)
> Intransitive verbs—4 (9.1 percent)
> Passive verbs—8 (18.4 percent)

Sentence	1	2	3	4	5	6	7	8	9	10	11	12	13	14	15	16	17	18
Grammatical Type	Cx	Cx	Cx	CC	Cx	Cp	Cx	S	S	S	Cp	Cp	Cp	S	Cx	CC	S	Cp
No. of words	14	27	37	25	29	14	35	15	14	9	17	15	14	12	11	28	13	8
No. of mono-syllables	13	20	22	18	20	8	24	13	10	7	14	13	10	10	7	22	8	8

> 247 (73%) of the 337 words are monosyllabic (not a single sentence in which the majority of the words are not monosyllabic)

Split constructions: #1, 2, 3, 4, 5, 7, 9, 15

Parallelism and anaphora: #12, 13, and 16 (is #13 a comma splice?)

Ellipsis: #4, 14, and 17

Repeated words: #4 great value and importance
                   #7 extraordinary interest and importance
                   #11 utmost importance and interest
                   #1 questions
                   #6 questioned and examined
                   #13 [asks two questions]
                   #14 [asks two questions]
                   #15 questions
                   #16 them [questions]; answers
                   #17 questions and answers

Metaphors: #3 path, phantoms and obstacles looming
              #5 doing battle with obstacles [mixed metaphor?]
              #8 rooms in house
              #9 pay the rent
              #11 room
              #12 furnished, decorated, shared
              #13 furnish, decorate
              #14 share

Analysis of Style as Persuasion in the "Letter from Birmingham Jail" by Richard P. Fulkerson

In the previous chapter, we looked at the arrangement of Martin Luther King's "Letter from Birmingham Jail." Here Richard P. Fulkerson analyzes the style of that letter. Earlier in the article from which this excerpt was taken, Fulkerson analyzed the structure and the arguments of the letter. In this section, he points out some salient features of the style and shows how the style contributes to King's persuasive intent. The text of the letter begins on p. 342. (From Richard P. Fulkerson, "The Public Letter as a Rhetorical Form: Structure, Logic, and Style in King's 'Letter from Birmingham Jail.'" Quarterly Journal of Speech 65 (April 1979): 121–136. This excerpt occupied pp. 130–135. Reprinted with the permission of the Speech Communication Association and the author.)

The positive ethical image does not result only from the chosen audience conceptualization and refutative strategies discussed above, however. It also results from the essay's style. Although this is not the place for a complete descriptive analysis of King's stylistic versatility in "Letter from Birmingham Jail," I would like to highlight some of its more striking stylistic features and to speculate on the ways they reinforce the total persuasive effort. The essay's style is supple and sophisticated yet readable. An audience is likely to be favorably impressed, without being overwhelmed. The stylistic manipulations both create an image of competence and sincerity and operate on the reader's emotions.

Like all rhetorical choices, stylistic decisions have multiple effects. But to clarify the relation between stylistic choice and persuasion, it may be useful to assert that an effective stylistic choice will work in one or more of the following three ways. It may adapt the style in order to carry meaning more effectively to the audience as fictionalized by the rhetor, such as a decision to use a simpler synonym in place of a more elaborate equivalent. This is the *adaptive* dimension of style. Or the choice may operate on the reader's emotions in a less than obvious way, such as in a decision to use words that alliterate. This is the *affective* dimension of style, as I hope to clarify below. Finally, the stylistic choice may be effective primarily because it helps enhance the rhetor's image and thus the rhetor's credibility. This is the *ethical* dimension of style. These three varieties of stylistic impact correspond closely to the three classical modes of persuasion; the adaptive choice is a rational technique (*logos*), the affective choice works on the emotions (*pathos*), and the ethical choice is a technique for enhancing *ethos*.

To illustrate these three persuasive dimensions of King's style, it may be well to start with an obvious and relatively simple feature of the essay. A reader can scarcely help noticing how often King refers to other famous men whom he expects his readers to recognize. These allusions are directly effective in their adaptive and affective appeals to both the limited and broader audiences and indirectly effective in the image of him they help create.

King unabashedly puts himself into a great tradition of protest beginning with Socrates, referred to three times, and extending down through primarily Christian history, from the early prophets to Christ himself, to Paul, to Aquinas, Augustine, Martin Luther, and Bunyan. In addition to such historical allusions, King also buttresses his argument by quoting or paraphrasing Reinhold Niebuhr, Martin Buber, and Paul Tillich, leading modern spokesmen from both Christian and Jewish faiths and thus presumably adaptive references for all of the eight clergymen at one time or another as well as to virtually all of King's broader audience. He even manages to quote an unidentified justice of the United States Supreme Court and T. S. Eliot. This man, who is potentially suspect as an outsider, a rabble-rouser, even a criminal, reveals himself to be educated, wise, and widely read. At least that is the impression such allusions make in discourse. They have multiplicative ethical impact, since an auditor assumes they are a carefully chosen sample drawn from a much larger store of information.

King's style in the essay is also marked by the extensive use of metaphors drawn from contemporary technology. Two archetypal patterns are dominant, that of depth versus height and dark versus light. The present system and segregation are repeatedly characterized as being *down* and *dark,* while the hope for the future involves rising and coming into the *light.* The Negroes live in a "dark shadow" and must "rise from the dark depths." They are "plunged into an abyss of injustice where they experience the bleakness of corroding despair." Policy must be lifted from "quicksand" to "rock," and "we have fallen below our environment"; Negroes are in a "dark dungeon"; in the emphatic and optimistic final paragraph (quoted below), America now suffers under the "dark clouds of racial prejudice" in a "deep fog of misunderstanding," but "tomorrow the radiant stars of love and brotherhood will shine."

As Osborn has argued, "Because of their strong positive and negative associations with survival and developmental motives, such metaphors express intense value judgments and may thus be expected to elicit significant value responses." Such "argument by archetype" also appeals to an audience's desire for simplification through its built-in, two-valued orientation.

Other metaphors come from modern technology. The nations of Africa are moving forward with "jet-like speed" while we go at "a horse and buggy pace"; and the church stands "as a tail light behind other community agencies rather than a headlight leading men to higher levels of justice." The church is now merely a "thermometer" recording popular opinion instead of what it once was, "a thermostat that transformed the mores of society."

Specifically medical metaphors unite the technological imagery with the archetypal metaphor of disease and health. Segregation is a disease and later a boil that must be exposed to the healing sun. The liberal argument to wait has "been a tranquilizing thalidomide, relieving the emotional stress for a moment, only to give birth to an ill-formed infant of frustration." Some whites have sensed the need for "antidotes" to segregation, but others have remained silent "behind the anesthetizing security of stained glass windows." All told, I count seventy-two metaphors, including both explicit and suppressed forms. Almost none are presented through clichés (common verbal formulas). They share several stylistic functions. On the adaptive level they are memorable for their ingenuity, and they help make an abstract philosophical argument vividly concrete. On the affective level, the archetypal metaphors speak to fundamental urges in us all and thus enhance the message indirectly. Finally, like all rhetorical choices, the stylistic decision to use metaphors also affects King's image. The archetypal references create the image of a sincere man of deep feeling who is fundamentally like the reader and who has confidence both in his own moral judgment and in the inevitability of a better tomorrow. The technological images help build an identification between King and his readers; both speaker and listener inhabit the same world of jet planes, thermometers, and wonder drugs, a world of rapid change in which only one element—the status of blacks—has not kept up.

This same identity of rhetor and reader is also enhanced by a series of stylistic choices which, taken together, constitute the conciliatory tone that characterizes the essay and serves to unite a variety of other tones. From the salutation onward, King is not out to criticize or belittle, but merely to explain patiently and sadly to those who do not (yet) see the light of the truth. Throughout the essay, King may be righteous, hurt, disappointed, ironic, sorry that he must say some unavoidably critical things, but neither angry nor despairing. He has "almost reached the regrettable conclusion that the Negroes' great stumbling block in the stride toward freedom is not the White Citizens' 'Counciler' or the Ku Klux Klanner, but the white moderate": almost but not quite. And he has paid his clerical audience the compliment of having listened carefully to their views. His essay thus fulfills Carl Rogers' demand that one must first hear a position and be able to repeat it with understanding and clarity before real communication can occur. Throughout the essay, King shows his respect for his reader. He knows that his clerical audience is composed of sincere and devout men, men who share his basic religious values and whom he can call "My dear Fellow Clergymen" and "My Christian brothers." King even praises some by name for their own (limited) efforts to move toward integration. He can criticize such men only with regret. Echoing through the essay are phrases such as "I must say" and "I feel impelled to mention." Such a stylistic stance flatters him as well as his addressees. It serves the positive image he wants; this writer is not a shouting, belligerent, trouble-maker, but a sincere and understanding human being whose views are forced out of him by his concern for their misguided positions.

The identification with the audience and the conciliatory tone are further created by one of the most subtle stylistic elements in the "Letter," the use of personal pronouns. Since the "Letter" is a deeply personal apologia, it is not surprising that *I* occurs regularly—139 times to be exact, 100 times as the subject of a main clause. Similarly, King often addresses his ostensible audience directly: in rephrasing their arguments ("you stated"), in asking for understanding ("I hope that you can see"), in direct address ("Each of you has taken some significant stands"), and in personal appeal ("I beg you to forgive me." "I hope this letter finds you strong in the faith."). There are forty uses of *you* to refer to the clergymen, not to mention other generic uses of the word, which also carry personal overtones. The net effect is an impression of informality as well as personal commitment on the part of the the *I*.

More subtle still is King's manipulation of ambiguous first-person plural pronouns. Often *we* and *our* and *us* in the essay refer clearly to some or all of the Birmingham protesters: "Several months ago our local affiliate here . . . invited us to be on call . . . We readily consented." In other places, the *we* is more general, as in "Never again can we afford to live with the narrow, provincial 'outside agitator' idea." Yet frequently a *we, our,* or *us* seems to refer to the protesters but may also include the audience, in effect reinforcing the frequent direct addresses by gathering King and his opponents into a unit sharing a single outlook. Consider this sentence: "I have tried to stand between these two forces saying that we need not follow the 'do-nothingism' of the complacent or the hatred and despair of the black nationalist." *We* here at first seems to mean "we the moderate protesters," but it may equally well mean "we who recognize the problem and want to see it solved." We, all of us, you clergymen as well as my followers, may take this middle road. The union is subtle, but is at least subconsciously forced on the reader by King's choice of pronouns.

A similar movement from "I-you" to *we* operates in the closing paragraph of the essay in conjunction with extended archetypal imagery:

> *I* hope this letter finds *you* strong in the faith. *I* also hope that circumstance will soon make it possible for *me* to meet each of *you,* not as an integrationist or a civil-rights leader, but as a fellow clergyman and a Christian brother. Let *us* all hope that the dark clouds of racial prejudice will soon pass away and the deep fog of misunderstanding will be lifted from *our* fear-drenched communities and in some not too distant tomorrow the radiant stars of love and brotherhood will shine over *our* great nation with all their scintillating beauty [italics added].

In the first two sentences, the current separation between *I* and *you* is both stated and reinforced by the pronouns, but after the conciliatory "fellow clergyman," in the second sentence, both groups merge in a vision of future unity in "our communities" and "our great nation" under the scintillating beauty of the high, bright stars.

King's style in the "Letter," as Larson has pointed out, is primarily characterized by variety. It shows in the allusions and metaphors already discussed and in the range of tones united by the dominant conciliatory stance, but it is nowhere more obvious than in the essay's syntactic structures.

The original published text of King's "Letter" consisted of 48 paragraphs, 325 sentences, and 7,110 words, with a moderate average sentence of 22 words and an average paragraph of almost 7 sentences or 149 words. The average sentence, not so long as that of normal American intellectual prose, is consequently appropriate for King's extensive audience. But such statistics mask the variety of King's syntax. Of the 325 sentences, many are short: 62 have 10 or fewer words. Some are aphoristic, such as "We are caught in an inescapable network of mutuality tied in a single garment of destiny. Whatever affects one directly affects all indirectly." Thus parts of the essay are quite easy to read and eminently quotable. On the other hand, 18 sentences are more than 50 words long and 2 exceed 100 words. I know of no other modern public prose including sentences of such length. Although some readers are likely to stumble over such sentences, my impression is that overall, the style is clear and vivid and relatively easy to read but with no hint of condescension. The extreme variations in sentence length as well as similar variety in clausal construction and levels of formality seem primarily to work on the ethical level. That is, they dramatize for the readers a rhetor who is a master manipulator of language.

The one syntactic feature that emerges as common within the variation is elaborate parallelism. In it, as in the metaphors, it is easy to hear the cadences of the evangelist, another dimension of King's self-dramatization through style. Sometimes King's parallelism is tight and aphoristic as in "Shallow understanding from people of good will is more frustrating than absolue misunderstanding from people of ill will," or "Whatever affects one directly affects all indirectly." More often, however, it is spread out and rhythmic: "I say it as a minister of the gospel, who loves the Church; who was nurtured in its bosom; who has been sustained by its spiritual blessings and who will remain true to it as long as the cord of life shall lengthen." Or,

> I have almost reached the regrettable conclusion that the Negroes' great stumbling block in the stride toward freedom is not the White Citizens' "Counciler" or the Ku Klux Klanner, but the white moderate who is more devoted to "order" than to justice; who prefers a negative peace which is the absence of tension to a positive peace which is the presence of justice; who constantly says "I agree with you in the goal you seek, but I can't agree with your methods of direct action"; who paternalistically feels that he can set the time-table for another man's freedom; who lives by the myth of time and who constantly advises the Negro to wait until a "more convenient season."

Frequently this extended parallelism continues through several sentences:

> They have left their secure congregations and walked the streets of Albany, Georgia, with us. They have gone through the highways of the South on torturous rides for freedom. Yes, they have gone to jail with us. Some have been kicked out of their churches and lost the support of their bishops and fellow ministers. But they have gone with the faith that right defeated is stronger than evil triumphant.

In all, I count 15 instances of sustained parallelism, some involving as many as 6 sentences and one (discussed below) a single sentence of more than 300 words.

The effects of such parallelism must be largely conjectural, but it is difficult to imagine that they can lie in the adaptive domain. That is, there seems to be no reason to think that parallel syntax is any more clear or easy to follow than are other syntactic structures. On the other hand, the rhythms and balance created by parallelism, especially when a series of parallel constructions is used to build to a climax, probably have an affective impact, much as they would in oral discourse but to a lesser degree. The major effect is ethical, portraying the rhetor as a man who can balance various views and who has his ideas under complete control.

The "Letter's" most impressive stylistic feat is its longest sentence. Unique form serves to emphasize unique content since it is the one place in the essay where the evil of segregation, rather than the necessity of protest, is delineated. Because it contains in miniature so much that is syntactically and metaphorically characteristic of the essay, I quote it in full. It occurs within the refutation of the argument that now is not the proper time for protest. It opens, as do many of the sentences, with a conjunctive turn:

> But when you have seen vicious mobs lynch your mothers and fathers at will and drown your sisters and brothers at whim; when you have seen hate-filled policemen curse, kick, brutalize, and even kill your black brothers and sisters with impunity; . . . [for the continuation of this long periodic sentence, see paragraph 14 of King's "Letter" as reproduced on p. 346 of this text] . . . then you will understand why we find it difficult to wait.

This most impressive periodic sentence of 331 words is highlighted through contrast with the preceding sentence of 19 words and succeeding sentences of 33, 11, 13, and 6 words. Its nine major subordinate clauses are each addressed directly to the audience with "when you," and they comprise an elaborate catalogue, frequently with metaphor, of the injustices suffered daily by the Negro in America. The sentence builds to a climax after detail is piled on detail, only to end with the one main clause of magnificently understated direct address: "then you will understand why we find it difficult to wait." Here the pronouns create no union: *you* are distinctly not *we*. It is appropriate that this single indictment of American racism, the only point in the essay at which pathos is used as a major suasive mode, should be the longest sentence. But it is also appropriate that it not be dominant. For the subject of the essay is not racial injustice. That is, except here, a given.

The history of classical rhetoric covers more than two thousand years, from the fifth century B.C. until the first quarter of the nineteenth century. During most of that time, rhetoric was a prominent, and for long stretches the dominant, discipline in the schools, and some of the most famous people in history were involved in either the teaching or the practice of rhetoric. In view of this long and honorable tradition, it is presumptuous of anyone to think that he or she could present a satisfactory, not to speak of an adequate, survey of rhetoric in a few dozen pages. The article that R. C. Jebb wrote for the Ninth Edition of the *Encyclopaedia Britannica* was devoted almost entirely to Aristotle. Because of the formidableness of the task, most historians of rhetoric have sensibly confined themselves to a coverage of individual rhetoricians or to limited periods. The Bibliography appended to this survey directs the student's attention to some of the best of these limited histories. But, to date, no one has attempted to write a history of rhetoric on the scale of George Saintsbury's *History of Criticism and Literary Taste in Europe* or even of René Wellek's *A History of Modern Criticism, 1750–1950.*

Despite the impossibility of presenting an adequate survey of rhetoric in a few pages, an attempt will be made here to introduce the student to at least some of the key figures and some of the significant developments in rhetoric. Occasionally, authors and rhetoric texts will be mentioned, not because of their enduring worth or influence, but because they were historically important (the first of a kind, for instance) or representative of an especially important type.

539

Classical Rhetorics

The "art" or "science" of any discipline is almost always formulated inductively from a study of the long-standing practice of that discipline. This is certainly true of all the verbal arts—grammar, logic, poetics, and rhetoric. In the case of these language arts, the codification of principles did not come until several centuries after the practice had become a conspicuous feature of a national culture. There is ample evidence in extant Greek literature that rhetoric, conceived of as persuasive oratory, figured prominently in Hellenic society many hundreds of years before the first handbook of rhetorical precepts was compiled. One has only to note the prominence of speeches and debates in the Homeric epics, in the plays of the Greek dramatists, in the histories of Herodotus and Thucydides, and in the philosophical treatises of Hesiod, to be convinced that persuasive discourse exerted a continuing influence upon the ancient Greeks almost from the dawn of their civilization.

Although the practice of an art antedates its codification, there comes a time when people feel the urge to derive a set of "rules" from the study of accepted practice. The art of rhetoric was first formulated, in Sicily, during the second quarter of the fifth century B.C. Corax of Syracuse is commonly designated as the first formulator of the art of rhetoric. Certain political and social changes taking place at the time prompted him to establish some system of rhetoric. When Thrasybulus, the tyrant of Syracuse, was deposed and a form of democracy established, the newly enfranchised citizens flooded the courts with litigations to recover property that had been confiscated during the reign of the despot. The "art" that Corax formulated was designed to help ordinary citizens plead their claims in court. Since, understandably enough, no documentary evidence was available to prove their claims, they had to rely on inferential reasoning and on the general topic of probability (*eikos*) to establish their proprietary rights. Perhaps the chief contribution that Corax made to the art of rhetoric was the formula he proposed for the parts of a judicial speech—proem, narration, arguments (both confirmation and refutation), and peroration—the arrangement that becomes a staple of all later rhetorical theory.

There are references in Plato, Aristotle, Cicero, and Quintilian to the part that Corax and his pupil Tisias played in formulating rhetorical theory, but none of their handbooks survive. All we know of Tisias from the scattered references to him is that his theory was concerned exclusively with the rhetoric of the courtroom, that he wrote some judicial speeches for others to deliver, and that he may have been one of the teachers of at least two of the Attic orators—Lysias and Isocrates.

If modern students have heard the name of Gorgias at all, it is probably in connection with the Platonic dialogue that bears his name. In the history of rhetoric, however, Gorgias of Leotini is notable, first of all, for having stirred up interest in oratorical theory and practice among the Athenians. As an ambassador from Sicily to Athens in 427 B.C., he dazzled the Athenians with the brilliance of his speech-making. Thereafter he was, for several years, the most successful teacher and practitioner of oratory in Athens. Although he was one of the first rhetoricians to recognize the persuasiveness of emotional appeals, he distinguished himself mainly by the attention he paid to the cultivation of an ornate style. He placed great emphasis on the value of figures of speech, especially antithesis and parallelism. All the later rhetoricians who concentrated on the cultivation of a highly literary style of address could, for the sake of convenience, be placed in the Gorgianic school, but it is unfair to blame Gorgias for all the excesses of those rhetoricians who were concerned more with the flowers of style than with the substance. If some of Gorgias' speeches had survived, we would be better able to judge just how much the gaudy, mannered style known in Renaissance England as "Euphuism" owed to his influence.

Gorgias may well lay claim to being the *first* of the successful Sophists in Athens, but Isocrates competes with Aristotle for the title of the most influential of the Greek rhetoricians. Judging from the length of his reign as a renowned teacher of rhetoric (he lived to be 98 years old) and from the number of skillful orators who emerged from his school, it would probably be safe to say that Isocrates was the most influential Greek rhetorician among his contemporaries. Aristotle, with his more philosophical treatise on rhetoric, wins the title for long-range influence.

A word needs to be said here about the term *Sophist,* since it applies to men like Gorgias and Isocrates and since it figures in the views that Plato and Aristotle entertained toward the art of rhetoric. Among the Athenians of the fifth century B.C., the term *Sophist* carried no invidious connotations. It was a rather neutral term applied to professors who lectured on the "new learning" in literature, science, philosophy, and especially oratory. The Sophists set up small private schools and charged their pupils a fee for what amounted in many cases to tutoring. These schools eventually proved to be so lucrative that they attracted a number of charlatans into the teaching profession, and it was men like these who eventually gave Sophists an unsavory reputation and made "sophistry" a synonym for deceitful reasoning.

But men like Isocrates were highly ethical, with noble ideals and unimpeachable standards of intellectual integrity. We have already mentioned that he may have studied under Tisias, and there are hints in some of the early histories of rhetoric that he also studied under Gorgias and Socrates. He began his professional career as a *logographos,* the Greek term for a hired writer of courtroom speeches—a beginning that he later wanted to forget. About 392, he set up a school of oratory, and although he charged unusually high fees, he soon had more students than any other Sophists. During his lifetime he amassed a considerable fortune from his teaching.

Although some twenty-one discourses and nine letters of Isocrates have survived, the *Art of Rhetoric* that Isocrates is said to have compiled has been lost; hence we are forced to abstract his rhetorical theory from such autobiographical works as his *Antidosis* or his educational works like *Against the Sophists.* One of his major contributions to rhetoric was his development of an artistic prose style. He took the rather artificial style of Gorgias, tempered it, refined it, and made it an elegant vehicle for both written and spoken discourse. Whereas the structural units that Gorgias was most interested in were antithesis and parallelism, Isocrates, with his great interest in the rhythm of prose, centered his attention on the sonority of the periodic sentence—certainly one of Cicero's debts to him. His concept of the proper training for the ideal orator also had a marked influence on Cicero and Quintilian. He preached that the whole man must be brought to bear in the persuasive process, and so it behooved the aspiring orator to be broadly trained in the liberal arts and securely grounded in good moral habits. In all his discourses, he stressed the Greek ideals of freedom and autonomy, and perhaps as much as any other ancient humanist, he preached the value of the supreme Greek virtue, *sophrosyne* (that we may translate as "self-control," for want of a more adequate English equivalent).

Despite the high ideals that Isocrates set for his pupils and the exemplary eloquence of his discourses, he did not succeed in allaying Plato's suspicions of rhetoric. We should look briefly at what Plato (through his spokesman Socrates) had to say about rhetoric, because all the derogatory things that men have said about this art down through the ages have their roots in Plato's strictures.

Remarks about rhetoric are scattered through several of Plato's dialogues, but the two dialogues in which he concentrated his attacks were the *Gorgias* and the *Phaedrus.* Ironically, in the very act of depreciating rhetoric, Plato shows himself to be a masterful rhetorician; and equally ironic is the fact that some of the charges he made against the Sophists (e.g. that they corrupted young people and accepted fees for their teaching) were indictments later made against Socrates—as we see in the *Apology.* Students who read *The Republic* are often shocked to find that Plato would exclude poets from his ideal commonwealth. Basically, Plato's objections to poets are the same as those he made against the teachers of rhetoric. For one thing, rhetoric could not be considered a true art because it did not rest on universal principles. Moreover, rhetoricians, like poets, were more interested in opinions, in appearances, even in lies, than in the transcendental truth that the philosopher sought. They made the "worse appear the better reason." They were mere enchanters of the soul, more interested in dazzling their audience than in instructing it. Rhetoric—to bring it down to its lowest terms—was a form of flattery, like cosmetics.

Toward the end of the *Phaedrus,* Plato concedes the possibility of a true art of rhetoric. But it could be a true art only if the speaker made an effort to learn the truth about the subject he was going to talk about; if he would seek out essential definitions of key terms in his discourse; if he learned to make the proper divisions of his subject; and if he made an effort to fashion his speech to suit the nature of his audience. There are a lot of *if*'s here, and it is apparent that Plato does not have much confidence that rhetoricians, in their great eagerness to please the ignorant multitudes, will devise and teach such a rhetoric.

Certainly one of Aristotle's purposes in composing his *Rhetoric* was to counteract his former teacher's low estimate of the persuasive art. Even while he was still a pupil at Plato's Academy, he opened a school of rhetoric in competition with Isocrates. It is not known precisely when Aristotle first started to write his *Rhetoric,* but it is known that his treatise was not published until the second period of Aristotle's residence in Athens, sometime around 333 B.C. From internal evidence alone, we know that he completed his *Poetics* before he wrote Book Three of his *Rhetoric.* The late composition of Book Three, which deals mainly with style and arrangement, may suggest that this book was an afterthought, a concession to the interest taken in style by the other schools of rhetoric. But we must remember that he devoted several chapters of his *Poetics* to a discussion of language and style, and it is believed that the *Theodectea,* one of his lost rhetorical works, treated in great detail the subject matter of Book Three of the *Rhetoric.* Nevertheless, it is true that Aristotle was not as much interested in style as he was in the invention of arguments. And it is this primary interest in invention that indicates how he sought to counteract the bad opinion that many of his contemporaries had of rhetoric.

By concentrating in the first two books of his *Rhetoric* on the discovery of arguments, Aristotle sought to answer those who accused rhetoricians of being more concerned with words than with matter. And by abstracting first principles from the practice of oratory, he hoped to show that rhetoric was not, as Plato had accused it of being, a mere "knack," but was a true art, a teachable and systematic discipline that could guide men in adapting means to an end. With his philosophic treatise, Aristotle became the fountainhead of all later rhetorical theory. As Lane Cooper has said, "...the Rhetoric not only of Cicero and Quintilian, but of the Middle Ages, of the

Renaissance, and of modern times, is, in its best elements, essentially Aristotelian."

Perhaps the key to understanding Aristotle's approach to rhetoric is the recognition that *probability* is the basis of the persuasive art. Orators often based their arguments on opinions, on what people *believed* to be true rather than on what was demonstrably and universally true. But whereas Plato found this reliance to be a defect in the art, Aristotle saw it as a necessity. Discoverable, verifiable truth fell within the province of science or logic. But in dealing with contingent human affairs, people soon learned that universal truths were not always discoverable or verifiable. It was in this area that dialectic and rhetoric had a part to play. "Rhetoric is the counterpart of Dialectic," Aristotle said in the very first sentence of his *Rhetoric*. It is significant that the Greek word that Aristotle used for rhetorical proofs was *pisteis,* which has its roots in the word *pistis,* "belief." *Belief,* Aristotle perceived, is often the highest degree of certainty to which we can attain in dealing with the everyday affairs of human beings.

This recognition of probability as the essence of the persuasive art lies behind most of Aristotle's contributions to rhetorical theory: the three modes of proof—the appeal to reason (*logos*), the appeal to emotion (*pathos*), the ethical appeal (*ēthos*); the enthymeme as the rhetorical equivalent of the syllogism, the example as the rhetorical equivalent of logical induction; the topics as a system of discovering available arguments; his stress on the audience as the chief informing principle in persuasive discourse. Another of his contributions was the removal of the success-at-any-price emphasis that had brought rhetoric into bad repute. By stressing the notion of "the available means of persuasion in any given case," he emphasized the virtuosity of the effort rather than the success of the results. This stress also tended to make rhetoric a morally indifferent activity. Another of his unique contributions was his analysis, in Book Two, of the more common emotions or passions. One of the three modes of appeal that Aristotle explores is the emotional, and he was trying to show his students how to evoke the appropriate emotional response. This mode was the beginning, admittedly primitive but amazingly perceptive, of psychology.

There is a great temptation to follow out all the ramifications of Aristotle's rhetorical theory, but this brief survey will not permit such an intriguing excursion. In fact, this textbook is so much indebted to Aristotle's theory that it can be regarded as a mere restatement, with some modifications and extensions, of the *Rhetoric.* So brilliant is Aristotle's treatise—it is certainly one of the great books of the Western world—that we can only regret the loss of the aforementioned *Theodectea* and of his history of rhetoric, *Gryllus,* named after Xenophon's son. For many years, the anonymous *Rhetorica ad Alexandrum* was thought to be another of Aristotle's rhetorical works. But scholars today are convinced that Aristotle is not the author of this sprawling work, and they are inclined to attribute it to Anaximenes of Lampsacus, an older contemporary of Aristotle. It was never an influential work in the history of rhetoric.

Another Greek rhetorical treatise that deserves mention here is a text that has come to bear the English title *On Style*. The date and authorship of this work are uncertain. For a long time it was attributed to Demetrius Phalereus, who governed Athens from 317 to 307 B.C. and who was invited by Ptolemy Soter to help collect books for the great library at Alexandria. On the basis of internal and external evidence, however, W. Rhys Roberts, who has made an English translation of *On Style* for the Cambridge University Press, concludes that Demetrius Phalereus did not write this text, that it was written sometime in the first century B.C. or the first century A.D. This text, which deals exclusively with the *elocutio* (style) division of rhetoric, is notable for being one of the first to analyze the "kinds" of style. Whereas most later rhetorics discussed only three styles (the elevated or high style; the elegant or middle style; and the plain or low style), the author of this text discusses a fourth type, the forcible style. Throughout his discussion of style, the author is interested particularly in the choice and arrangement of words.

Until the end of the fifteenth century, the *Rhetorica Ad Herennium* was thought to have been written by Cicero. Whether Cornificius is the author of this text, as some modern scholars maintain, is still being debated, but the *Ad Herennium*, written probably between 86 and 82 B.C., has the distinction of being the earliest extant Latin work on rhetoric and the earliest treatment of prose style in Latin. Futhermore, as Harry Caplan, who translated the treatise for the Loeb Classical Library, points out, the *Ad Herennium* offers "the oldest extant division of the kinds of style into three and the oldest extant formal study of figures." It should also be pointed out that the treatise presents the most complete treatment of *delivery* and *memory* that we have in any of the surviving classical rhetorics. Although virtually unknown in the ancient world, the *Ad Herennium* enjoyed wide currency in the Middle Ages and the Renaissance. Professor T. W. Baldwin reveals that it was the basic elementary text in the English grammar-school curriculum when rhetoric had its great revival during the Tudor Age.

Although Cicero was not the author of the *Ad Herennium*, he has enough titles under his name to assure his place in the history of rhetoric. Among his minor rhetorical works, written between 84 and 45 B.C., are *De Inventione, De Optimo Genere Oratorum, Topica,* and *De Partitione Oratoria*. His major rhetorical works are the *De Oratore*, the *Brutus*, and the *Orator*.

There is no room here for an exposition of any of these works, but some general word can be said about Cicero's contribution to rhetoric. Cicero was a skillful orator as well as an esteemed teacher of rhetoric; some literary historians hold that he gave more effective instruction by the example of his orations and epistles (*rhetorica utens*) than he did by his theoretical treatises (*rhetorica docens*). His works played a great part in mediating the controversy between the "Asiatics" (the exponents of the florid, highly mannered style) and the "Atticists" (the exponents of the plain, neat, severe style). Cicero's chief contribution, however, is probably his extension of the scope of rhetoric. Unlike Aristotle, who held that rhetoric had no proper subject matter, Cicero felt that the perfect orator had to be conversant with many subjects. In order to invent arguments, the perfect orator must have a command of a wide range of knowledge. Accordingly, under the Ciceronian system the study of rhetoric really became a liberal-arts course. This broadening of the scope of rhetoric helps to explain Cicero's appeal for the English and Continental Humanists when the study of rhetoric was revived during the Renaissance.

A later rhetorician whose name is invariably coupled with Cicero's is M. Fabius Quintilianus. Born in Spain about A.D. 35, Quintilian eventually went to Rome, where after completing his education he became a successful pleader in the law courts. In time he acquired such a great reputation that Vespasian established a chair of rhetoric for him at Rome. The prestige of this imperial endowment made him the supreme authority on rhetoric even after his death, about A.D. 96. About the year 88, he retired from his teaching post to write his great work on the training of the orator, the *Institutio Oratoria*. Fragments of this work seem to have been available throughout the Middle Ages, but after a complete text was discovered in the monastery of St. Gall in 1416, the *Institutes of Oratory* steadily gained popularity and firmly established itself in the European educational network. Between about 1475 and 1600, more than one hundred editions of the *Institutes* were published.

The twelve books of the *Institutio Oratoria* are divided as follows: Book I deals with the preliminary education necessary for a study of rhetoric. Book II defines the nature, aims, and scope of rhetoric. Books III–VII treat of oratory itself, with emphasis on the finding (*inventio*) and arranging (*dispositio*) of material. Books VIII-X treat of style (*elocutio*). Book XI deals with memory (*memoria*) and delivery (*pronuntiatio*). Book XII deals with the requirements for a perfect orator.

As the subject matter of Book I might suggest, Quintilian, like Cicero, regarded the broadly educated man as the fittest candidate for a course in rhetoric. Quintilian, moreover, emphasized a qualification that earlier rhetoricians had hinted at but did not belabor. Having accepted Marcus Cato's definition of the perfect orator as "a good man skilled in speaking" (*vir bonus dicendi peritus*), Quintilian insisted that in addition to being intellectually fortified for his office the orator must be trained to be a man of strong moral character. It was this insistence on the intellectual and moral training of the aspiring orator that made Cicero and Quintilian the two most potent classical influences on rhetorical education in England and America. The moral bias was especially important, because from the seventeenth through most of the nineteenth century the English and American school systems were dominated largely by clergymen.

Although the influence of the Roman rhetoricians had become dominant by the first century B.C., a few Greek works exercised a significant influence on the development of rhetoric. Dionysius of Halicarnassus, a Greek contemporary of Horace, taught rhetoric at Rome from 30 to 8 B.C. He wrote a monumental history and criticism of the great Attic orators and some minor rhetorical works which deal for the most part with a study of the style of such Greek luminaries as Plato, Thucydides, Herodotus, and Xenophon. But the work of his that influenced—or plagued—schoolboys was a work which bears the English title *On the Arrangement of Words*. Dionysius treated only one aspect of rhetorical style, the order of words. Although he realized that eloquent expression involves a due regard for *arrangement* and *choice* of words, he decided to confine himself to a study of arrangement because he felt that other rhetoricians had adequately dealt with the choice of words. Dionysius' particular contribution is that he made schoolboys aware of the inherent beauty of words and of the possibility of producing pleasing effects even with ordinary words if they were skillfully arranged.

Hermogenes and Aphthonius did not exercise as much influence on their contemporaries as they did on European schoolboys of the fifteenth and sixteenth centuries. Both of them published rhetorical texts entitled *Progymnasmata*. The *progymnasmata* were the first writing exercises, the "themes," that schoolboys attempted after they had learned their elementary rhetorical precepts. In addition to supplying technical rules for the construction of these minor forms of composition, the texts provided illustrations of the dozen or so common forms. These texts were clearly in the tradition of "formulary rhetoric"—the kind of rhetoric that taught by models. The *Progymnasmata* by Hermogenes and Aphthonius went through an astounding number of editions, in both Greek and Latin versions.

The mention of one more Greek text will end this survey of the more important classical rhetorics. This text is the famous *On the Sublime* by Longinus. Today, *On the Sublime* is for most students one of the cardinal documents of literary criticism. But one must not forget that this work was written by a rhetorician (earlier, about A.D. 260, he had written a now lost *Art of Rhetoric*) and that it has made a contribution to rhetoric as well as to literary criticism. "The object of the author," says W. Rhys Roberts, who has made one of the modern English translations of this treatise, "rather is to indicate broadly the essentials of a noble and impressive style." Three of the five sources of the sublime that Longinus discusses concern style: the appropriate use of figures of speech (chs. 16–29); nobility of diction (chs. 30–38); and dignity and elevation of word order (chs. 39–40). By making *enthusiasm* a respectable resource, Longinus encouraged the exploitation of emotional appeal in the suasive process, and by insisting that sublimity was "the echo of a great soul," he abetted the moralistic trend in later rhetorical education.

Rhetoric During the Middle Ages

Under the aegis of Hadrian and the Antonines (A.D. 117–80), the teachers of rhetoric attained a prestige and an immunity that they were never to enjoy again. These second-century Sophists acquired their unsavory reputation because they eventually abused their privileged office and adulterated their discipline. The object of the Sophists was to amaze an audience rather than persuade it. To effect this end, they encouraged all the flashy tricks of style and delivery. The schools of rhetoric during this period had two curricula: the "sophistic," which designated the academic study of rhetoric as an art; and the "political," which was concerned with the practical applications of the art. But because the "sophistic" school enjoyed greater prestige and higher emoluments, rhetoric took a turn that debased it.

Under the influence of the second-century Sophistic, rhetoric in the Middle Ages ceased to be pursued primarily as a practical art and became rather a scholastic exercise guided by the *compendia* of such medieval rhetoricians at Cassiodorus, Capella, and Isidore. Grammar, logic, and rhetoric constituted the *trivium,* the four-year undergraduate course of studies leading to the degree of bachelor of arts. Music, arithmetic, geometry, and astronomy made up the *quadrivium,* the three-year graduate course that led to the degree of master of arts. Scholastic logic held a decidedly superior position in the *trivium.* The province of rhetoric became principally a study of the art of letter writing (*ars dictaminis*) and of preparing and delivering sermons (*artes praedicandi*). True, the students were exercised in two forms of scholastic declamation—*suasoriae,* discourses on some historical or legendary subject, and *controversiae,* discourses on some classic legal question—but these declamations were conducted so much in the spirit of epideictic or ceremonial display that the product of such training was usually a glib, clever "entertainer" rather than a resourceful orator in command of all the available means of persuasion. Accordingly, the art of rhetoric stood still, if it actually did not retrogress, despite the prominent position that rhetoric held in the curriculum. As Richard McKeon has said in his essay "Rhetoric in the Middle Ages" (*Speculum,* 1942): "Yes, if rhetoric is defined in terms of a single subject matter—such as style, or literature, or discourse—it has no history during the Middle Ages."

Although St. Augustine (A.D. 353–430) is not chronologically of the Middle Ages, we might look at him as a representative figure in the development of rhetoric during the medieval period. Anyone who has read *The Confessions* knows that during the period of his "flaming youth" Augustine was a student of, and later a teacher of, the "pagan" rhetoric that derived largely from the second Sophistic of Rome. After his conversion, Augustine made a significant contribution to rhetoric in the Fourth Book of his *De Doctrina Christiana* (A.D. 426–27). Augustine was interested in rhetoric as a means of persuading Christians to lead a holy life. With that exclusive interest he can be said to have narrowed the province of rhetoric. But by rejecting the sophists' preoccupation with style and the other elements of display and by returning to the more comprehensive rhetoric of Cicero he can be said to have extended the province of rhetoric once again. He concentrated on Biblical texts and especially on the Epistles of that masterful rhetorical artist, St. Paul. Augustine's analyses of these texts, however, were concerned not so much with the "message" as with the rhetorical craftsmanship. Somewhat surprisingly, Augustine rejected Quintilian's notion that the rhetor must be a morally good man. He did not deny that a preacher's reputation for a virtuous life would have a persuasive effect on an audience, but he recognized that even a vicious preacher could induce his audience to follow Christ if he were skillful enough in the manipulation of his suasive resources.

Augustine's rhetoric laid the groundwork for the rhetoric of the sermon, the branch of study known today as homiletics—a science that was to command a great deal of attention during, and for many years after, the Renaissance and the Reformation. None of the classical rhetoricians, of course, had discussed the art of preaching, but the foundations for such an art lay in the epideictic variety of rhetoric.

Kenneth Burke, in his discussion of Augustine in *The Rhetoric of Motives,* pointed out that Augustine had noted the instructional function of rhetoric. Burke says that "once you treat instruction as an aim of rhetoric you introduce a principle that can widen the scope of rhetoric beyond persuasion. It is on the way to include also works on the theory and practice of exposition, description, *communication* in general." Following this lead, some modern students of rhetoric, like Donald C. Bryant, have seen the possibility of adapting classical rhetoric to cover at least two of the four forms of discourse— argumentation and exposition. As a matter of fact, there seems to be no reason why we could not develop a rhetoric of description and a rhetoric of narration too. As a case in point, Wayne C. Booth in his book *The Rhetoric of Fiction* (University of Chicago Press, 1961, 1983), has provided us with an excellent study of the rhetorical technique of non-didactic fiction.

Some Continental Rhetoricians

For the history of rhetoric on the European continent after the Middle Ages, we shall mention only a few Continental rhetoricians, confining our attention to the four or five who had a marked influence on the development of rhetoric in England.

The most influential rhetorician was Erasmus. Although this illustrious scholar spent only five years in England (1509-14), he set the pattern for the English grammar-school curriculum and for rhetorical training in the schools. He happened to be in England just at the time Dean Colet was founding St. Paul's school, and at the request of Colet he prepared a number of textbooks. Among these were *De Ratione Studii* and *De Duplici Copia Verborum ac Rerum*. Originally published in 1512, both of these texts went into an astounding number of editions in subsequent years. (The *De Copia*, for instance, had at least 150 editions—only a few of those, it should be pointed out, issuing from presses in England.) The *De Ratione Studii* is more a treatise on pedagogy than a rhetoric, but it is of interest to students of rhetoric for its incidental remarks about the language arts. It was not by endless drilling in rules that students learned to write and speak well, Erasmus maintained, but by discriminating reading and much practice. Erasmus is one of the early enunciators of that sanest of all precepts about writing: "write, write, and again write." He also recommends the exercise of keeping a commonplace book; of paraphrasing poetry into prose, and vice versa; of rendering the same subject in two or more styles; of proving a proposition along several different lines of argument; and of construing from Latin into Greek.

The *De Copia,* which became a widely used textbook of rhetoric in the Tudor schools, was designed to assist grammar-school students in acquiring elegance and variety of expression in Latin composition. This text was based on the traditional *res-verba* distinction (literally, the *thing* and *words;* more broadly, *matter* and *form*). The first book of *De Copia* showed the student how to use the schemes and tropes (*elocutio*) for the purpose of variation; the second book instructed the student in the use of topics (*inventio*) for the same purpose.

The matter of *copia* became one of the major concerns of Tudor education. The Latin word *copia* meant literally "plenty, abundance"; in a more particular sense, the phrase *copia dicendi* or *copia orationis* meant "fullness of expression." One achieved this fullness of expression by accumulating a number of things to say on a subject and by being able to say the same thing in a variety of ways. So *copia* was partly a matter of fertile invention and partly a matter of stylistic resourcefulness. By way of illustrating *copia,* Erasmus in Chapter 33 of Book One presents 150 variations of the sentence "Tuae literae me magnopere delectarunt" and 200 variations of "Semper dum vivam tui meminero."

The only other rhetorical work by Erasmus that we shall mention is his text on letter writing, *Modus Conscribendi Epistolas,* published in 1522. As we have seen, letter writing had been one of the favorite rhetorical exercises during the Middle Ages. During the Renaissance, it dropped to an inferior, but not insignificant, position in the curriculum. For Erasmus, letters became the first extended form of composition that the student wrote after he had mastered the fundamental rules of rhetoric. In that age which lacked our means of rapid communication and transportation, diplomatic and business affairs were promoted principally through letters. Accordingly, the man skilled in letter writing was as much sought after as the man skilled in oratory. And the number of letter writing manuals, both in Latin and in the vernacular, attests to the demand for this training in the sixteenth and seventeenth centuries. Today we also cannot afford to neglect formal training in this form of written discourse. Letters—friendly letters, business letters, promotional letters, letters to the editor—are the major form of written discourse that many of us will be called upon to produce after we leave school. There is as much rhetoric involved in some kinds of letters (the "begging letter," for instance) as there is in the most elaborate campaign oratory.

Along with Erasmus, Juan Luis Vives (1492–1540) stands in the forefront of those Continental scholars who spent only a few years in England but exercised an influence on the English grammar school that endured for well over a century. Born in Spain (and, for that reason, sometimes called the "second Quintilian"), educated in Paris and Flanders, he was appointed by Cardinal Wolsey in 1523 to the Lectureship of Rhetoric at Oxford. King Henry VIII entrusted the education of his daughter Mary to the joint tutorship of Vives and Thomas Linacre. Vives became *persona non grata* when Henry VIII was seeking a divorce from his compatriot, Catherine of Aragon, and he left England, never to return, in 1528.

Vives exercised an influence on English rhetoric, not so much from his textbooks as from his treatise on education, by which he helped to set the pattern of the rhetorical curriculum. Unlike Erasmus, Vives did not publish any rhetorical works during his sojourn in England, and none of his rhetoric texts that he later produced were widely used in the schools. Vives published the *De Disciplinis,* his major work on education, at Antwerp in 1531, three years after he left England. Three works on rhetoric followed soon after: *Rhetoricae, sive De Ratione Dicendi, Libri Tres* (Louvain, 1533); *De Consultatione* (Louvain, 1533), a short treatise on rhetoric that he had composed while he was teaching at Oxford; and *De Conscribendis Epistolas* (Basel, 1536), his contribution to the rhetoric of letter writing.

The *De Ratione Dicendi* and the companion *De Consultatione* provided a rich mine of material for Ben Jonson when he composed his own rhetorical work *Timber or Discoveries,* and it is highly probable that Shakespeare too was exposed to these works in his grammar school. But an examination of the statutes of the various grammar schools of the period shows that where Erasmus's textbooks are frequently recommended for the curriculum, Vives's textbooks are seldom mentioned. In his monumental study of Tudor grammar schools, *William Shakespere's Small Latine & Lesse Greeke,* Professor T. W. Baldwin accounts for the pre-eminence of Erasmus on the ground that he was the true Renaissance champion, whereas men like Vives and Colet belonged to the Catholic Reformation rather than to the Renaissance. Vives and Colet, he maintained, were more interested in moral reform than in literary polish.

Three other Continental rhetoricians who had a noticeable influence on English rhetoric deserve brief mention here. The first of these is Petrus Mosellanus or, to use his family name, Pierre Schade (1493–1524), a German professor of Greek at Leipzig University. He published a rhetoric text entitled *Tabulae de Schematibus et Tropis Petri Mosellani.* As early as 1530 the boys at Eton were using Mosellanus's text in the sixth form, and during the first half of the sixteenth century Mosellanus became the standard author on *elocutio* in the English grammar schools.

Philippus Melanchthon or Philip Schwartzerd (1497–1560), a professor of classics at Wittenberg and a close associate of Martin Luther, published three rhetoric texts: *De Rhetorica Libri Tres* (Wittenberg, 1519); *Institutiones Rhetoricae* (Hagenow, 1521); and *Elementorum Rhetorices Libri Duo* (Wittenberg, 1531). Whereas Mosellanus had concentrated on style, Melanchthon gave only a minimum treatment of the schemes and tropes, referring his readers, for a fuller treatment, to such rhetoricians as Cicero, Quintilian, Erasmus, and Mosellanus; he devoted most of his attention to *inventio* and *dispositio.* Melanchthon tended to relegate *invention* and *arrangement* to the province of logic, and by doing so, he laid the groundwork for the revolution that Ramus and Talaeus were to effect in rhetoric later on in the sixteenth century.

Joannes Susenbrotus's *Epitome Troporum ac Schematum* (Zurich, 1540) was an amalgam of Mosellanus and Melanchthon. The *Epitome,* with its collection of 132 schemes and tropes, had a printing in England in 1562, and thereafter, for the remainder of the sixteenth century, it replaced Mosellanus as the standard grammar-school text for the figures and served as the model for the later vernacular treatments of these stylistic devices.

English Vernacular Rhetorics of the Sixteenth Century

All of the rhetorics mentioned so far in this survey were written in either Greek or Latin, and most of the compositions by English schoolboys up to the second decade of the sixteenth century were in Latin. With the Renaissance, which began in Italy, spread to France, and eventually made its influence felt in England through the apostleship of Humanists like Roger Asham, Sir John Cheke, and Sir Thomas Elyot, there came a revival of interest in the pagan literature produced by the classical authors. When Aldus, in 1503, published the works of the chief Greek rhetoricians, classical rhetoric was assured of its share of this renewed interest. The cause of rhetoric was further aided, as we have seen, by the direction that men like Erasmus and Vives gave to the curriculum of the English schools. It was not long before rhetoric became the dominant discipline in the Tudor grammar schools and universities.

Although the rhetoric taught in the schools was basically Aristotelian, Aristotle's *Rhetoric* was never a prominent textbook. It was the Latin rhetoricians, especially Cicero, Quintilian, and the anonymous author of the *Ad Herennium,* who dominated the early teaching of rhetoric in the English schools. As the pride of the English people in the status and achievements of the nation grew, pride in their native language grew correspondingly, and it was natural that schoolmasters should begin to think of composing textbooks, and of getting their students to orate and write, in the vernacular.

It is common to classify the vernacular rhetorics produced during the English Renaissance into three main groups: (1) the Traditionalists—those who taught a full-fledged rhetoric, with attention given to the five parts: invention, arrangement, style, memory, and delivery; (2) the Ramists—those who assigned invention and arrangement to the province of logic and allocated only style and delivery to rhetoric; (3) the Figurists—those whose primary, if not exclusive, interest centered on the study of the schemes and tropes. Actually, these three groups differ more in their pedagogical approaches than in their fundamental conception of the art of rhetoric. The Ramists, for instance, believed as strongly in the importance of invention and arrangement as the Traditionalists did, but they believed that these subjects were more properly studied under logic. The Ramists may not have considered as many schemes and tropes as the Figurists did, but many figures that the Figurists studied under the aspect of style, the Ramists studied in connection with the topics of invention. Even from the brief exposition of the vernacular text-books that follows, the reader should be able to determine into which of these three groups the books fall.

Leonard Cox, a schoolmaster at Reading, has the distinction of having written the first rhetoric textbook in English, *Arte or Crafte of Rhetoryke* (1530). It is perhaps appropriate that this first English rhetoric should be of the traditionalist school. F. I. Carpenter, in a modern edition of Cox's text, demonstrates quite convincingly that it was based upon, even partly trans-lated from, the first book of Melanchthon's *Institutiones Rhetoricae*. Like Melanchthon, Cox was interested primarily in *inventio*.

In 1550, Richard Sherry, a headmaster at Magdalen College School, pub-lished through J. Day's press *A Treatise of Schemes and Tropes,* which has sometimes been called "the second book on rhetoric in English." It can cer-tainly lay claim to being the first English textbook on the schemes and tropes. Five years later, Sherry printed a Latin-English revision of the earlier text, changing the title to *A Treatise of the Figures of Grammar and Rhetorike* and treating about 120 figures. Sherry produced his text in the hope of cap-turing the grammar-school trade. But his hopes proved futile, for Mosellanus and Susenbrotus were at the time too firmly entrenched in the curriculum to be dislodged. The *Treatise of Schemes and Tropes* had only one edition.

Although the compilers of vernacular rhetorics found the competition with Latin texts disheartening, they continued to produce them, and although their texts did not at first replace the classical texts in the schools, English rhetorics eventually superseded the older texts, in sales if not in prestige.

The first of the vernacular rhetorics to gain wide currency was Thomas Wilson's *The Arte of Rhetorique* (1553). G. H. Mair, who has published a handsome modern edition of this rhetoric, says of Wilson that he was one of the Cambridge men "who ... did much to mould the course of the Renais-sance in England on its pedagogic side and who had no inconsiderable in-fluence on the development of English prose." Wilson's text is a "Ciceronian" rhetoric, in that it treats of the five parts, but as Russell H. Wagner, perhaps the chief modern authority on the *Rhetorique,* has pointed out, Wilson ap-propriated some of his rhetorical doctrines from Erasmus, Cox, and Sherry.

The *Arte of Rhetorique* has the careful organization and schematic form that characterized the best of the classical and medieval texts. Book I con-siders such matters as the five elements of rhetoric ("Inuention, Disposition, Elocution, Memorie, Utteraunce"); the seven parts of an oration ("Enter-ance, Narration, Proposition, Division, Confirmation, Confutation, Conclu-sion"); the three kinds of oratory ("Demonstrative, Deliberative, Judiciall"); and, in connection with these three kinds of oratory, the matter of Invention. Book II treats of Disposition and the Figures of Amplification. Book III deals mainly with Elocution (style) but gives also a summary treatment of Memory and Delivery. The chief appeal of the *Rhetorique* stemmed from the fact that Wilson had collected a great mass of sound classical doctrine and stitched it all together with his own observations, expositions, and illustrations, in an appealing English prose style. For native Englishmen there was something appealing too in Wilson's strictures on what he called "strange inkhorn terms."

Many vernacular rhetorics appeared in England from this point on, but the most popular were not necessarily the soundest rhetorics or the most venturesome ones. We will mention some representative texts of several kinds to show the vigor and variety of the rhetorical tradition in English schools (and later in American schools) up to about the end of the eighteenth century.

The rhetoric of letter writing, originating in the Middle Ages and continuing with the popular treatises of Erasmus and Vives, received another impetus late in the sixteenth century with the publication of Angel Day's *The English Secretorie* (1586). Day discusses some thirty different kinds of letters under four main headings: demonstrative, deliberative, judicial, and familiar. In the second edition of 1592, Day added a section on the figures of speech and provided marginal glosses identifying the various tropes and figures in the illustrative letters.

George Puttenham's *The Arte of English Poesie* (1589) is remembered by students of English literature as one of a group of Elizabethan treatises that attempted a defense of, or an apology for, poetry; but it also made a contribution to rhetorical theory. The third book of the *Arte of English Poesie*, with its elaborate treatment of figures, is operating in the tradition of Susenbrotus, Mosellanus, Erasmus, and Sherry. Puttenham made two contributions to English rhetoric: he invented vernacular names for the Greek and Latin figures, and, seeking a more rational basis for the classification of the figures, he decided to classify them according to the nature of their appeal. So we have the *auricular*, those figures which depend for their effect on alterations of "sound, accent, time" and therefore appeal primarily to the ear; the *sensable*, those figures which depend upon alterations of sense and therefore appeal primarily to the mind; the *sententious*, those that appeal both to the mind and to the ear. All in all, Puttenham treats 107 figures. George Saintsbury is not entirely right when he said of the *Arte of English Poesie* that it contained "the most elaborate treatment of rhetorical figures to be found, up to its time, in English literature," for Henry Peacham in his *The Garden of Eloquence* of 1577 distinguished 184 figures.

Richard Rainolde's *Foundacion of Rhetorike* (1563) was an English adaptation of Hermogenes and Aphthonius's *progymnasmata* exercises that proved so popular in the early Tudor schools. Rainolde, in fact, considers the same fourteen types of elementary compositions that Aphthonius treated, with examples that Rainolde himself had supplied. Rainolde's hope of replacing Aphthonius was doomed to disappointment, since only one edition of his text was published, and that has approached so close to oblivion that only five copies of the original edition exist today.

About this time a revolution in rhetorical studies was effected by the French scholar, Peter Ramus. Dissatisfied with the repetitiveness and vagueness that prevailed in the teaching of the subjects of the *trivium,* Ramus distributed the traditional parts of rhetoric between logic and rhetoric. *Inventio* and *dispositio*—that is, the discovery and arrangement of matter—he assigned to the province of logic. Rhetoric had a franchise only on *elocutio* (style) and *pronuntiatio* (delivery). The fifth office of rhetoric, *memoria*—the memorization of the speech—Ramus simply ignored. Style would confine itself to a study of schemes and tropes, leaving to grammar the study of etymology and syntax. Ramus was working for a strict departmentalization of knowledge, for he felt that a great deal of the error and confusion that had sprung up in the arts was the result of scholars' mistaking the proper subject matter of the arts. Although the teaching of the two arts would be kept separate, logic and rhetoric in practice would combine and work together. As Karl Wallace has pointed out, the effect of this Ramistic dichotomy was that henceforth such processes as discovery, arrangement, and judgment tended to be assigned exclusively to the intellect, while the "dress" or "ornament" that style gave to matter fell to the lot of the imagination. We shall see later what Francis Bacon is to make of this division of labor between the reason and the imagination.

Although Ramus himself never published a rhetoric text, he did inspire a number of rhetorics based on his philosophy. His most fervent disciple and propagator was Audomarus Talaeus (Omer Talon). Talaeus published in Paris in 1544 his *Institutiones Oratoriae* (or, as it is more familiarly known, *Rhetorica*) as a companion to Ramus's logic text, *Dialecticae Libri Duo.* As John Brinsley tells us in his *Ludus literarius; or The Grammar Schoole* (1612)—one of the most valuable primary sources of information about English schools in the late sixteenth and early seventeenth centuries—Talaeus's *Rhetorica* soon became the rhetoric text "most used in the best Schooles." The main reason for the popularity of Talaeus's text with schoolmasters seems to have been its brevity and simplicity.

In his extensive treatment of the Ramistic revolution (see *Logic and Rhetoric in England, 1500–1700,* pp. 146–281), Wilbur Samuel Howell has pointed out that it was Gabriel Harvey who first introduced Ramistic rhetoric to his countrymen, when he became praelector in rhetoric at Christ's College, Cambridge, in the spring of 1574, just about the time that Roland MacIlmaine was publishing in London the Latin text of Ramus' *Dialecticae Libri Duo*. Thereafter Talaeus and Ramus served as the model for the rhetoric and logic texts of Dudley Fenner (*The Artes of Logike and Rethorike*, 1584), Abraham Fraunce (*The Lawiers Logike* and *The Arcadian Rhetorike*, both in 1588), Charles Butler (*Rameae Rhetoricae Libri Duo*, 1597), and Thomas Farnaby (*Index Rhetoricus*, 1625; the fifteenth edition of this appeared as late as 1767). The appearance and success of these texts lend support to Professor Baldwin's contention that by the end of the sixteenth century the French-Calvinistic school of Ramus and Talaeus had scored a complete triumph over the German-Lutheran school of Melanchthon and Sturm.

English Rhetorics of the Seventeenth Century

During the course of the seventeenth century, we find English criticism gradually making the passage from the broad Humanistic ideals of the Italian Renaissance to the more rationalistic, stringent attitudes of the French critics. Renaissance critics had drawn eclectically from classical, medieval, and contemporary theory. No one authority or system was accepted as final or all-inclusive. It was the French critics of the second half of the century who induced the English to write and judge by a single, settled canon of rules. Since most of the French criticism of the seventeenth century was concerned with the epic and drama (largely as a result of the importation of the neo-Aristotelianism of such sixteenth-century Italian critics as Scaliger, Castelvetro, and Robortello), poetics began to absorb more attention than rhetoric. Furthermore, the line of demarcation between poetics and rhetoric began to blur. Consequently, it is sometimes difficult to point to a seventeenth-century textbook and say with any finality, "This is a rhetoric book" or "This is a treatise on poetics." One is just as likely to find rhetorical theory in Spingarn's collection of seventeenth-century critical essays as in a textbook whose title explicitly designates it as a rhetoric book. Another result of the shift in emphasis is that fewer rhetoric books were produced in the seventeenth century than in the previous period, and none of those that were produced exercised the influence or enjoyed the popularity of some Renaissance texts.

Besides the growing preoccupation with the rules, the seventeenth century exhibits some concern for the development of a simple, utilitarian style. The incipient interest in science—an interest created largely by Francis Bacon and fostered, after the close of the anti-science regime of the Puritans, by members of the Royal Society—encouraged the development of a "scientific" style. Coupled with this growth of the scientific spirit was the reaction against

"Ciceronianism," the movement that fostered the development of an ornate, highly mannered style by proposing Cicero as the principal, if not the sole, model for imitation. Morris Croll and George Williamson (see Bibliography) have traced out for us the counter development of the so-called "Senecan style," characterized by the relative brevity of the sentences, looseness of structure, succinctness and pithiness of phrasing, and jerkiness of rhythm. It was this movement that prepared the way for the development of the easy, colloquial style that graced so many eighteenth-century compositions. As might be expected, the growing interest in the "plain style" resulted in a diminishing concern for the schemes and tropes. But as we shall see in the discussion of the Royal Society's proposal for the development of a suitable expository style, John Dryden's development of an impressive "middle style" prevented the development of a prose style that would be as severely barren and denotative as mathematical symbols.

Our discussion of seventeenth-century rhetoric might well begin with Francis Bacon (1561–1626). Although Bacon wrote no systematic work on rhetoric, there are scattered throughout his writings remarks and discourses that throw light not only on his own literary practice but on the direction that rhetorical theory was to take in the seventeenth century. The chief loci for Bacon's rhetorical theory are *The Advancement of Learning* and the expanded Latin translation of this work, *De Augmentis Scientiarum*. Complementary material can be found in his *Colours of Good and Evil* and *Apophthegms, New and Old*. The best guide to Bacon's rhetorical theory is Karl R. Wallace's *Francis Bacon on Communication and Rhetoric* (University of North Carolina Press, 1943). Our discussion must be limited to two or three points.

"The duty and office of Rhetoric," Bacon says in *The Advancement of Learning,* "is to apply Reason to Imagination for the better moving of the Will." In a later work, Bacon says, "Rhetoric is subservient to the imagination, as Logic is to the understanding; and the duty and office of Rhetoric, if it be deeply looked into, is no other than to apply and recommend the dictates of reason to imagination, in order to excite the appetite and will." By viewing the imagination and reason as definitely distinct faculties, Bacon lays the groundwork for the great amount of subsequent discussion about the separate provinces and the separate cultivation of these faculties; and of course he is thereby fostering the Ramistic dichotomy between logic and rhetoric.

The view that imagination and reason were distinct and yet had to work together constituted the basis for Bacon's observations on style. Because he considered imagination subservient to reason, he advocated the precedence of *res* over *verba*. He took issue with the Renaissance school of rhetoric—the

Ciceronians especially—that was more concerned with words than with matter. As a result of this preoccupation with style,

> men began to hunt more after words than matter; and more after the choiceness of the phrase, and the round clean composition of the sentence, and the sweet falling of the clauses, and the varying and illustration of their works with tropes and figures, than after the weight of matter, worth of subject, soundness of argument, life of invention, or depth of judgment. (From *The Advancement of Learning*.)

Though preferring *res* to *verba,* Bacon did not entirely neglect the matter of style. The three stylistic features that he concentrates on were the conformity of the style to the subject matter, the use of simple words, and the cultivation of "agreeableness." Bacon's insistence on the integral relationship between style and content is one expression of his revolt against the Ciceronians, who tended to employ the copious style for all forms of address. Closely connected with this idea of style suiting the matter is Bacon's admonition that the style should be so adapted to the audience that "if a man should speak of the same thing to several persons, he should nevertheless use different words to each of them."

One of the seventeenth-century rhetoricians obviously influenced by Baconian doctrines was the Roman Catholic lawyer Thomas Blount (1618–79). In 1654, Blount published *The Academie of Eloquence.* As Professor Hoyt Hudson has demonstrated, the first forty-eight pages of this 232-page book are copied, without acknowledgment, from *Directions for Speech and Style,* a little book produced earlier in the century by another lawyer, John Hoskins, but never published under his name until the 1930's. Blount was one of the first English rhetoricians to draw his illustrative material from contemporary English writers, such as Sir Philip Sidney, Ben Jonson, and Edmund Spenser.

For Blount, the four virtues of style are brevity, perspicuity, "life" or wit, and "respect" or propriety. Note the premium that Blount placed on *brevity* (what other rhetoricians called *conciseness*). This emphasis and Blount's discussion of *sententia* and other figures connected with the "curt style" indicate that the Senecan manner was beginning to gain some attention. Blount was undoubtedly referring to the "pointed style" when he says in the section of the book dealing with commonplaces: "Eloquence is a way of speech prevailing over those whom we design it to prevail; That is, if we will take it in the short or Laconick way, a distilling our notions into a quintessence, or forming all our thoughts in a Cone and smiting with the point." Blount treats of only twenty-five figures (for the most part, those treated by Talaeus in his *Rhetorica*) and devotes about thirty pages of his book to amplification.

Blount's text concentrates on style, but it was style held under the tight checkrein of the reason. In the thirty years after the original publication of his work, five editions appeared. George Williamson, who has given us one of the most valuable studies of seventeenth-century rhetoric in his book *The Senecan Amble,* attests that "no other rhetoric of that time seems to have been quite so popular."

A number of rhetorics made use of the Scriptures. The most popular of these was *The Mysteries of Rhetorique Unvail'd* (1657) by John Smith, which defined rhetorical figures with special reference to the Scriptures; by 1709 nine editions of the work had appeared. With the ascendancy of the Puritans in the seventeenth century, rhetoric came more and more to serve as the tool of the sermon-writer and the expositor of the Scriptures. The subtitle of *Centuria Sacra* (1654) by Thomas Hall, a Puritan clergyman and schoolmaster at King's Norton, reveals the use to which rhetoric was being put during the Commonwealth period:

> About one hundred Rules for the expounding and clearer understanding of the Holy Scriptures. To which are added a Synopsis or Compendium of all the most materiall Tropes and Figures contained in the Scriptures.

John Prideaux, who was, successively, Rector of Exeter College, Oxford University, Regius Professor of Divinity at Oxford, and Bishop of Rochester, published a rhetoric in 1659 entitled *Sacred Eloquence: or, The Art of Rhetoric as It Is Laid Down in the Scriptures.* The names of John Smith, John Prideaux, and Thomas Hall have all but passed into oblivion, and although John Smith's book alone of these three enjoyed a spurt of success, neither the popularity nor the influence of these Scriptural rhetorics was ever widespread or long-lived.

One section of Thomas Hobbes's *Answer to Davenant's Preface to Gondibert* (1650), the section dealing with the "natural" style, has some pertinence to rhetoric and to the easy, colloquial style that Dryden was to "father" later in the century. True and natural expression is based, according to Hobbes, on two things, *to know well* and *to know much.* Hobbes goes on to examine the psychological effects of these two qualities:

> A signe of the first is perspicuity, property, and decency, which delight all sorts of men, either by instructing the ignorant or soothing the learned in their knowledge. A signe of the latter is novelty of expression, and pleaseth by excitation of the minde; for novelty causeth admiration, and admiration curiosity, which is a delightful appetite of knowledge.

To know much was taken care of by *inventio,* that part of rhetoric concerned with finding things to say. The invention of matter, however, eventually had its effect on style when there developed a great interest in amplification. *Copia* resulted in that variety of expression which pleased because of its novelty and ingenuity. *To know well* was originally more the concern of logic than of rhetoric. But here too the quality of one's knowledge was seen to have some effect on style. Many rhetoricians, both before and after Hobbes, insisted that an idea could not be *expressed* clearly if it were not *apprehended* clearly.

The natural style must also avoid words that are high-sounding but hollow (those "windy blisters") and phrases that express either "more than is perfectly conceived, or perfect conception in fewer words than it requires." Since Hobbes's consistent aim is to chasten the exuberance of a kind of prose that had been fashionable, one is not surprised to find that he devotes little attention to the figures and tropes. In general, his feeling is that while figures of speech add a certain grace and charm to writing they should be used sparingly and discreetly.

Although Hobbes may seem bent on undermining the classical tradition, he was in fact thoroughly steeped in the classics. He wrote several of his works in Latin, translated Thucydides and Homer, and published a helpful digest of Aristotle's *Rhetoric*. In his efforts to bridle rampant fancy, he may be said to be operating under the great classical principle of moderation. With his rationalistic aesthetics he is laying the groundwork for the "temperate" prose of the neo-classical period and for the psychological approach that was to figure in eighteenth-century rhetoric and criticism.

Another spur to the development of restrained prose was given by the activities of the Royal Society. In December 1664, two years after its founding, the Royal Society named a committee for the improvement of the English language. Among those named to the committee were John Dryden, John Evelyn, Thomas Sprat, and Edmund Waller. Their hope was that the authority of the Royal Society would help to refine, augment, and fix the English language. Although this project never advanced much beyond the planning stage, the Royal Society was to have some influence on the kind of prose written in the neo-classical period. The encouragement that Bacon had given to the formation of a "scientific" prose was to be supported by the Royal Society and given a new impetus. One section of Thomas Sprat's *History of the Royal Society* (1667) contains the manifesto of this reform.

The "superfluity of talking," Sprat said, had had such a devastating effect on the arts and professions that he could not help concluding that *"eloquence ought to be banish'd out of all civil Societies,* as a thing fatal to Peace and good Manners." The only remedy for this disease of "fine speaking" is "to reject all amplifications, digressions, and swellings of style; to return back to the primitive purity and shortness, when men deliver'd so many things almost in an equal number of words." In "An Account of the Life and Writings of Mr. Abraham Cowley" (1668), Sprat proposed Cowley aɔ an exemplar of this "proper style." In his choice of words, Cowley "neither went before nor came after the use of the Age," and he "forsook the Conversation, but never the Language, of the City and Court." Cowley, Sprat goes on to say, had mastered "the hardest secret of good Writing, to know when he has done enough." Despite the "new comliness" that Cowley achieved in his expression, he did not lose sight of *decorum*: "But it seems all to arise out of the Nature of the subject, and to be justly fitted for the thing of which he speaks."

It is regrettable that Cowley did not live long enough to write his projected "Discourse Concerning Style." Undoubtedly he would have said many sensible things about the plain style, for he was himself an admirable prose-stylist, one whom John Dryden himself took as a model. This "metaphysical" poet distrusted metaphysics, because he felt that the schoolmasters had reduced philosophy to a matter of mere words. Scattered throughout his poems are several instances of the sort of comment that might have figured in his proposed treatise on style.

Many of the same ideas about the plain style as those advanced by Sprat were presented by John Wilkins (1614–72), one of the pillars of the Royal Society and later Bishop of Chester, in his *Ecclesiastes* (1646) and *An Essay Towards a Real Character and a Philosophical Language* (1668). In the former essay he maintains that style should be "plain and natural, not being darkened with the affectation of *Scholastical* harshness, or *Rhetorical* flourishes." Obviously influenced by the doctrines of style in Seneca's *Epistles,* Wilkins recommends a style that follows a happy medium. Style, he says, "must be *full* without empty and needless Tautologies"; our expressions "should be so close, that they may not be obscure; and so plain, that they may not seem vain and tedious."

The extreme to which the Royal Society's advocacy of a plain, utilitarian style could be pushed is discovered in Wilkins's *Essay* where he proposes "a Real universal Character, that should not signify words, but things and notions." In other words, a series of symbols would be established, each symbol having a univocal, universal, and constant meaning. Literary symbols would thus approach the precision and stability of mathematical symbols. Fortunately for literature, this project never crystallized. Instead of words with rich associations and many-leveled meanings, our literary vocabulary might have been made up of "useful," universal ideographs.

Perhaps it was John Dryden, as much as anyone, who prevented the English language from taking that turn. Dryden preserved our language from taking on this mathematical character as much by his practice as by the rhetorical pronouncements scattered throughout his writings. He made *propriety* the central doctrine of his views on style. The propriety that Dryden called for is threefold: the language and style must fit "the occasion, the subject, and the persons." Closely allied to this concern for propriety is his discouragement of a "foreign" bias in our language. Dryden condemned Ben Jonson because "he did a little too much to Romanize our tongue." It is Dryden's move "to English" contemporary prose that has been largely responsible for his reputation as the father of modern English prose style. His advocacy of native words and his encouragement of the use of vernacular, rather than Latinate, syntax are part of his program to refine the language and to attain more naturalness, more ease, more spontaneity in writing. And in his recognition of the "beauties" and the "spirits" of writing he is preparing the way for the triumphant re-entry of the Longinian "transport" into the rhetorical criticism of the eighteenth century.

The documents we have been considering over the last few pages have not been, strictly speaking, rhetoric texts at all. They reflect rather the intellectual currents that contributed to the development and to the eventual decay of the rhetorical tradition in the eighteenth century. In their preoccupation with style, these texts indicate how much the Ramistic program had caught on: the province of rhetoric seemed more and more to be restricted to style alone. But these documents also indicate how the groundwork was laid for the development of the kind of easy, natural, colloquial prose style that prevails today. The kind of prose style that is most admired today is not the Euphuistic prose of the Renaissance nor the Ciceronian prose of the nineteenth century but rather the plain but elegant prose found in such magazines as *The New Yorker* and *Harper's* and exemplified in such writers as E. B. White, James Thurber, and George Orwell. And this kind of writing had its origin during the Restoration period with writers like Dryden, Bunyan, and Temple and its development during the Queen Anne period through writers like Defoe, Swift, and Addison.

English Rhetorics of the Eighteenth Century

As we pass to the eighteenth century, we confront the last full century in which rhetoric, in all its classical complexion, occupied a prominent position in the academic programs of the schools. During at least the first half of the eighteenth century, the influence of French critics, especially of Boileau, Rapin, and Le Bossu, was even more dominant than it had been in the last half of the previous century. The lamentable feature of this adulation for classical precepts was the uncritical manner in which they were accepted as absolute, inviolable law.

The questioning of Aristotelian and Horatian canons came with the appearance of editions and translations of Longinus. With the gradual emergence during this century of Longinus's *On the Sublime*, judgment came to be more a thing of taste and less a thing of rule. The new temper was displayed in such works as Leonard Welsted's *Dissertation Concerning the Perfection of the English Tongue and the State of Poetry* (1724), Robert Lowth's *De Sacra Poesi Hebraeorum* (1753), and Edward Young's *Conjectures on Original Composition* (1759). With the freer, more subjective type of criticism gradually claiming more and more adherents, the stage was being set for the appearance of the "romantic" writers.

These shifts in the perspective of criticism were reflected in the rhetoric books of the period. The eighteenth-century rhetoricians still paid allegiance to the classical precepts, but at the same time they urged their pupils to strike out on their own, to discover a style that was natural to themselves, to submit to the dynamic force of *enthusiasm*. They no longer felt it necessary to classify, define, and illustrate multitudes of figures and tropes. Delivery, that aspect of rhetoric which had been so long neglected in the schools, began to receive attention again, largely as a result of the elocutionary programs of such mentors as Sheridan and Walker. Pulpit oratory continued to be assiduously cultivated, inspired by the elegant practice of such famous English preachers as Tillotson, Barrow, Atterbury, and of the even more famous French preachers, Bossuet, Bourdaloue, and Massillon. By the end of the century, collections of sermons sold on the scale of popular novels today.

It can be said to the credit of eighteenth-century teachers that for the most part they regarded rhetoric as a practical art, much as Aristotle had conceived of it, rather than as a more speculative art. As in the seventeenth century, the line between poetics and rhetoric was hard to ascertain. Critics and rhetoricians drew on native belles-lettres for their illustrations. "In fact," George Saintsbury says, "Rhetoric, new dubbed as Eloquence, becomes the Art of Literature, or in other words Criticism." This merger of poetics and rhetoric helps to explain why the eighteenth century was the last great age of a serious academic interest in rhetoric.

At least fifty rhetoric texts produced during the eighteenth century are important enough to deserve being mentioned, but we will have to content ourselves with a look at only six or seven. Although a number of informative books have been published in recent years about English rhetoric in the sixteenth and seventeenth centuries (see the Bibliography), only a few surveys have been published about English rhetoric in the eighteenth century. A fairly exhaustive survey, but that only of the latter half of the century, is the unpublished doctoral dissertation that Harold F. Harding wrote at Cornell University in 1937, *English Rhetorical Theory, 1750–1800*. But in 1971, Wilbur Samuel Howell published his *Eighteenth-Century British Logic and Rhetoric*, a definitive treatment of at least the rhetoric of Great Britain.

John Stirling's very popular rhetoric, *A System of Rhetoric* (1733), only thirty pages long, contains in the first part a listing of ninety-seven figures and tropes. The Greek or Latin terms for the figures and tropes are translated into their English equivalents, and all are simply defined and briefly illustrated. The second part, entitled *Ars Rhetorica,* is nothing more than a Latin translation of the first part (apparently a concession to those schoolmasters who refused to use vernacular rhetorics in the classroom).

With its list of ninety-seven figures and tropes, *A System of Rhetoric* has the distinction of providing a catalogue of more figures than was given by any other rhetoric book in the eighteenth century—a century in which rhetoricians generally were defining and illustrating fewer and fewer figures. Among eighteenth-century rhetorics, only John Holme's *The Art of Rhetoric* (1739), with eighty-three figures and tropes, approaches this abundance.

Lectures Concerning Oratory was published in 1758 by John Lawson (1712–59), a Master of Arts from Trinity College, Dublin, and the first librarian of the University library. Lawson's book is firmly based on Aristotle's *Rhetoric* and is pieced out by examples, mainly from Cicero and Quintilian. The first six lectures give a short history of classical and modern rhetoric. Lecture 7 presents "some thoughts concerning Imitation." The remaining lectures treat of eloquence in relation to reason (chs. 8–9), to passion (chs. 10–11), and to the senses (chs. 12–18). It is in the seven lectures devoted to eloquence and the senses that Lawson treats of style "as it comprehendeth Ornament, Composition, Figures."

Lawson is a sensible, sometimes original, scholar, one who had absorbed a good deal of the learning of the past without closing his mind to the excellences of the present and the promises of the future. Following Aristotle as he did, he was deviating from the Longinian direction that criticism and rhetoric were taking in the eighteenth century. The encouragement Lawson gave to the cultivation of a simple, jargonless prose is remarkably akin to Jonathan Swift's pronouncements on style in *A Letter to a Young Clergyman* (1720).

John Ward served as professor of rhetoric at Gresham College in London from 1720 until his death in 1758. In the year after his death there appeared a two-volume collection of lectures on rhetoric, *A System of Oratory,* that Harold Harding in his survey of eighteenth-century rhetoric has called "the most elaborate and detailed synthesis of Greek and Roman rhetorical theory published in English." Although his greatest debt is to Quintilian, Ward acknowledges early in the first volume that he has borrowed "the finest precepts of Aristotle, Cicero, Quintilian, Longinus, and other celebrated authors, with proper examples taken from the choicest parts of purest antiquity." The fifty-four lectures cover 863 pages—a bulk that indicates the thoroughness of the work but which helps to explain why it never became a widely used school text. Ward's text is, however, the only English rhetoric published in the eighteenth century which came anywhere near matching the comprehensiveness of Hugh Blair's *Lectures on Rhetoric,* a text that we will discuss presently.

Ward's chief preoccupation is with style. Exactly one half of the lectures are devoted to *elocutio.* The other parts of rhetoric receive adequate, but less thorough, treatment. Disposition rates eight lectures; six lectures treat invention; four lectures are spent on delivery; memory is the subject of only one lecture. The last eight lectures deal with imitation, the nature of the passions, the character of the orator, and a brief history of oratory. This collection of lectures shows how seriously and exhaustively rhetoric was still being taught as late as the mid-eighteenth century.

We will turn now to a consideration of two men who were most responsible in the eighteenth century for quickening an interest in *pronuntiatio* or the delivery aspect of rhetoric. The most successful of these speech teachers (he might be called the Dale Carnegie of the eighteenth century) was Thomas Sheridan, the father of the dramatist Richard Brinsley Sheridan. Sheridan's works fall into three categories: those dealing with (1) reading and speaking; (2) pronunciation; and (3) education.

The most popular and probably the most representative of his printed works was *Lectures on Elocution* (1762). This book, which is a compilation of seven of his public lectures, deals exclusively with the problems of delivery —articulation, pronunciation, accent, emphasis, tone, pause, pitch, voice control, and gesture. His *Lectures on Reading* (1775) gives directions for reading prose and for reading verse. Archbishop Whately, in his rhetoric text published in the nineteenth century, lauded and recommended Sheridan's system of marking passages to be read aloud. Sheridan's success as an actor lent great weight to his pronouncements on matters of delivery. He is the chief figure in the late-eighteenth century elocutionary movement which resulted in the shift of meaning of *elocution* from *style* to *delivery* and in the later vogue of the "elocution contest" in the schools.

John Walker (1732–1807), the other eighteenth-century promoter of the art of delivery, was, like Sheridan, an Irish actor. In 1769, he gave up the dramatic stage, and after teaching for a time at Kensington Gravel-Pits School, he began a career of lecturing, at which he continued, with signal success, for the next thirty-five years.

Walker's first appearance in print came in 1777 when he published *The Exercises for Improvement in Elocution,* which was nothing more than a collection of readings from select authors for those seeking to acquire the art of reading or speaking in public. Perhaps the best and most popular of Walker's works was *Elements of Elocution* (1781). This two-volume work covered such matters as rhetorical punctuation, voice inflections, gesture, accent, emphasis, and pronunciation. The similarity of this work with Sheridan's *Lectures on Elocution* is apparent.

It should not be surprising that it was professional actors who gave a special impetus to a study of delivery, for all the spell-binding orators in history (men like Demosthenes, Churchill, William Jennings Bryan, Bishop Sheen, Billy Graham) have been, in a sense, great actors. Walker had the acting skill to qualify him as a teacher of delivery, but he lacked the grounding in the classics that Sheridan had and accordingly did not have the reserves to draw upon when it came to citing collaborative or illustrative material.

The history of British rhetoric in the second half of the eighteenth century is dominated by three Scottish rhetoricians. With the great cultural renascence that took place in Scotland after its union with England, Edinburgh soon came to be known as "the Athens of the North." During this period, in such fields as philosophy, aesthetics, psychology, history, economics, there are more eminent Scottish names than English names. And in rhetoric during this period, men like Kames, Campbell, and Blair had no serious rivals.

Henry Home, Lord Kames (1696–1782), a Scottish jurist and psychologist, published in 1762 the three-volume *Elements of Criticism,* a work that was frequently reprinted and that exercised a marked influence on subsequent poetical and rhetorical theory. The scope of *The Elements of Criticism* is much broader than that of most texts considered in this survey. Kames's book, as a matter of fact, makes its major contribution to aesthetics. In that regard, it is of a piece with three other Scottish works—Francis Hutcheson's *Original of Our Ideas of Beauty and Virtue* (1725), David Hume's *Of the Standard of Taste* (1757), and Alexander Gerard's *Essay on Taste* (1758). Only a small part of Kames's book deals with rhetoric in the traditional sense of that word. His purpose, he tells us, is "to examine the sensitive branch of human nature, to trace the objects that are naturally agreeable, as well as those that are naturally disagreeable; and by these means to discover, if we can, what are the genuine principles of the fine arts." Kames hoped that by probing human psychology he could find an immutable standard of taste by which to assess all works of art.

Despite its undeniable influence on literature, Kames's *Elements* was never widely used in the schools. His book was bulky, involved, and written in a rather ponderous style. Kames's influence was exercised indirectly, through the medium of those more popular Scottish rhetoricians whom he helped to form. As Helen Randall, who wrote a full-length study of Kames's critical theory, says: "If one may consider the direct influence of Blair as a secondary influence of Kames, one may almost say that the textbooks on this subject for about a hundred years owed their main outline and many of their rules to the *Elements of Criticism.*"

The second of the noted Scottish rhetoricians whom we are considering was George Campbell (1709–96). No less a critic than George Saintsbury has called Campbell's *The Philosophy of Rhetoric* (1776) "the most important treatise on the New Rhetoric that the eighteenth century produced." Campbell was at once more readable than Lord Kames and more profound than the other member of this Scottish triumvirate, Dr. Hugh Blair.

What was Campbell's peculiar contribution to the art of rhetoric? For one thing, he ventured the notion that rhetoric could have an end other than to persuade. In the first two paragraphs of his treatise, he defines *eloquence* (the term he prefers to *rhetoric*) as the "art or talent by which the discourse is adapted to its end," and he says that a speech may have any one of four ends: "to enlighten the understanding, to please the imagination, to move the passions, or to influence the will." This is reminiscent of Cicero's notion of the tripartite function of rhetoric: to teach (*docere*), to persuade (*movere*), to delight (*delectare*). Reversing the notion advanced by Aristotle and his followers that rhetoric was a mere offshoot of dialectic, Campbell proposed that logic be regarded merely as the tool of rhetoric. Campbell is perhaps best known to students of the English language as the one who proposed as the criterion of good usage the norm that locutions be *reputable, national, and present.*

Campbell's probing of the "philosophy" of rhetoric was so adventurous and original that his book exerted a fascination for students of rhetoric for many years after its original publication. More than twenty editions of *The Philosophy of Rhetoric* were demanded during the eighteenth and nineteenth centuries, and it was regularly used in American colleges until about 1870. His book might have proved even more popular if it had not been for the formidable competition it received from one of the most widely reprinted rhetorics ever written, Hugh Blair's *Lectures on Rhetoric and Belles-Lettres.*

By 1783, when Blair published his book, he had been delivering lectures to the students at the University of Edinburgh for twenty-four years. It was in 1759, at the urging of Lord Kames, that he agreed to deliver, without salary, a series of lectures on rhetoric. This series was so enthusiastically received that a group of his friends proposed to George III that he establish an endowed Chair of Rhetoric at the University and that Blair be installed as the first holder of the post. The reputation of the celebrated preacher of St. Giles in Edinburgh was already so high that the English monarch had no hesitation about commissioning Blair in 1762 as the first Regius Professor of Rhetoric. Blair was finally prompted to publish his lectures because for years handwritten copies of them had circulated freely among enthusiastic students and had been boldly offered for sale in the bookshops.

We will probably never get an accurate count of the number of editions and reprints of Blair's *Lectures,* but by 1835 there were at least fifty editions.

Later this text was translated into such languages as French, Italian, and Russian. It continued to be used in English and American schools until almost the end of the nineteenth century. William Charvat, a historian of American critical thought, has said that at one time Blair's *Lectures* was a text "which half the educated English-speaking world studied."

Why was Blair's text such a popular rhetoric? One reason was the amazing comprehensiveness of the forty-seven lectures in this two-volume text. In addition to the thirteen lectures devoted to belles lettres, there were discussions of taste, beauty, and sublimity (three of the key terms in eighteenth-century criticism); a survey of philology and a review of classical and English grammar; a detailed exposition of the principles of style, with special attention to the major figures of speech, and a detailed analysis of several pieces of prose composition; a history of oratory; and instructions for the composition of various kinds of speeches; discourses on poetry; and a compilation of the best classical and contemporary rhetorical doctrines. The marked religious tone of the *Lectures* also played a part in recommending Blair's text to schoolmasters. Blair's insistence that a man of eloquence must be a man of virtue became the warp upon which his lectures were woven. The mode and style of presentation also contributed to the popularity of the *Lectures*. Besides being clearly and systematically organized, the lectures were presented on an elementary level. Presuming in his students no previous training in rhetoric, Blair took great pains to define his terms, to elaborate on what might strike us as commonplaces, and to supply whatever background he deemed necessary for an understanding of the topic under discussion. As a result, Blair's *Lectures* could be used on several levels of the school curriculum.

The history of English rhetoric might well terminate with the end of the eighteenth century, but it is customary to carry the history one step further to include Richard Whately's *Elements of Rhetoric* (1828). Whately was one of that brilliant group of Oxford reformers that gravitated to Oriel College in the 1820's. Eventually he was made Archbishop of Dublin. In 1826, with some help from John Henry Newman, he published his *Elements of Logic,* which had grown out of an article he wrote earlier for the *Encyclopaedia Metropolitana.*

Whately's rhetoric has a strong Aristotelian flavor. Agreeing with Aristotle that rhetoric was "an offshoot of logic," Whately treated rhetoric as the art of "argumentative composition." His book is organized under four heads: (1) the appeal to the reason or understanding (this was the equivalent of Aristotle's logical proofs); (2) the appeal to the will (Aristotle's ethical and pathetic appeals); (3) style; (4) delivery. Among the notable features of Whately's *Rhetoric* were his elaboration of such Aristotelian concepts as sign, example, and probability, his brilliant analyses of argumentative fallacies, and his development of the function of presumption and burden of proof in the conduct of an argument.

Throughout the first three-quarters of the nineteenth century, Campbell, Blair, and Whately were the three modern rhetoricians most often used in the English and American schools wherever rhetoric continued to be taught. Although Blair proved to be the most popular of this trio, modern teachers of rhetoric speak with most respect of Campbell and Whately. Neither of them was a particularly original thinker, but both of them based their rhetorics on sound principles of logic and psychology. If their texts had come somewhat earlier, the tenure of rhetoric in the schools might have been extended for several more years.

Rhetoric in the Nineteenth and Twentieth Centuries

A review of the first hundred years of the Boylston Professorship of Rhetoric at Harvard University reveals what happened to rhetorical training during the nineteenth century and the early years of the twentieth century.* The Boylston Professorship, the most famous and influential chair of rhetoric in America, was made possible by a grant from Nicholas Boylston, a wealthy Boston merchant, in 1771 and was formally activated in 1806. The first two holders of the chair, John Quincy Adams (1806–09) and Joseph Mc-Kean (1809–18), adhered closely to the prescriptions of the original statutes, which charged that the training offered be solidly rooted in the classical tradition and that it be primarily concerned with eloquence in persuasive oratory. Edward T. Channing during his thirty-two-year tenure (1819–51) broadened the purview of his office to include lectures on literary criticism and abandoned the exclusively classical orientation of his lectures on rhetoric. The influence of Blair, Whately, and Campbell is especially evident in his exploration of psychological processes, in his concern with terms like *genius* and *taste,* and in his alliance of rhetoric with belles lettres. Having little interest in students' declamations, he gradually shifted the emphasis from speaking to writing.

The changes in scope and emphasis introduced by Channing were confirmed and extended by Francis James Child, who occupied the Boylston chair for twenty-five years, from 1851 to 1876. While doing graduate work at

* This account of nineteenth-century rhetoric is adapted from my article "What Is Being Revived?" *College Composition and Communication,* 18 (October 1967): 166–72. For the account of the Boylston Professorship, I am heavily indebted to Ronald F. Reid, "The Boylston Professorship of Rhetoric and Oratory, 1806–1904: A Case Study of Changing Concepts of Rhetoric and Pedagogy," *Quarterly Journal of Speech,* 45 (October 1959): 239–57.

the University of Göttingen, Child became enamored of German research in early English linguistics, literature, and folklore, and this philological interest profoundly affected the cast of his lectures and led eventually to the production of his great work, *The English and Scottish Popular Ballads* (1882–98). He used his podium to expound on Chaucer and to introduce his students to Anglo-Saxon, delegating instruction in oratory, for which he had no relish, to his assistants. When Charles William Eliot introduced the elective system at Harvard about 1875, Child found further encouragement for his slighting of composition, written and spoken, and for his concentration on philology and literary criticism. When Johns Hopkins, the first American university to be founded on the German model, tried to woo Child, the only way Harvard could keep him was to create for him the new office of Professor of English and to assign John Richard Dennett as his assistant to take over the rhetoric lectures. It was in the school-term of 1874–75 that Harvard established its first course in Freshman English, a course dealing with matters that previously had been taught only to sophomores, juniors, and seniors.

Adams Sherman Hill's twenty-eight-year tenure, from 1876 to 1904, rounds out the first century of the Boylston Professorship. During Hill's term, the Boylston Professorship was incorporated into the English department and the term *rhetoric* fell out of fashion, being replaced by the term *composition;* rhetoric's association with oratory was once and for all severed, and composition now dealt exclusively with written discourse; and the abandonment of textbooks in the rhetoric course reflected the shift from the theoretical approach to writing to the methods of imitation and practice. It was Hill too who introduced the use of literature to teach freshman composition and who resorted to the four forms of discourse—exposition, argumentation, description, and narration—as his way of approaching the process of composition. He paid a great deal of attention to style, but he made such a fetish of grammatical correctness that he soon reduced rhetoric to a set of "do and don't" prescriptions.

Part of the nineteenth-century development in the teaching of rhetoric, though not associated primarily with the Boylston Professorship, was the doctrine of the paragraph, stemming from Alexander Bain's *English Composition and Rhetoric* (1866) and fostered by such teachers as Fred Scott, Joseph Denney, John Genung, George Carpenter, Charles Sears Baldwin, and Barrett Wendell. Barrett Wendell's successful rhetoric texts helped to establish the pattern of instruction that moved from the word to the sentence to the paragraph to the whole composition. Henry Seidel Canby reversed that sequence, moving from the paragraph to the sentence to the word. It is to these men that we owe the system of rhetoric that most students were exposed to in the first half of the twentieth century—the topic sentence, the various methods of developing the paragraph (which were really adaptations of the classical "topics"), and the holy trinity of unity, coherence, and emphasis.

But even this kind of rhetorical approach to writing disappeared from our classrooms and our textbooks sometime in the 1930s. With the clamor from parents, businessmen, journalists, and administrators for correct grammar, correct usage, and correct spelling, rhetoric books began to be replaced with handbooks. By 1936 the study of rhetoric had sunk to such an estate in our schools that I. A. Richards, in his *The Philosophy of Rhetoric*, could say of it that it was "the dreariest and least profitable part of the waste that the unfortunate travel through in Freshman English," and W. M. Parrish, reviewing the situation in 1947, could say, in an article addressed to teachers of speech, "English teachers . . . have almost abandoned the very name of rhetoric, and the classical tradition is now completely in our hands."

It was the Speech Department at Cornell University that fostered the resuscitation of classical rhetoric in our time. In the fall semester of 1920–21, Alexander Drummond and Everett Hunt established a seminar at Cornell in which the students read and discussed Aristotle's *Rhetoric*, Cicero's *De Oratore*, and Quintilian's *Institutio Oratoria*. The effects of this classically oriented program began to be felt when graduates of Cornell's Speech Department took posts at universities in various parts of the country. The place to find articles on classical rhetoric during the 1930s and 1940s was not the journals directed to teachers of English but the *Quarterly Journal of Speech* and *Speech Monographs*. English teachers began to take notice when studies appeared of the rhetorical training of some of the great English writers—studies like T. W. Baldwin's *William Shakespere's Small Latine and Lesse Greeke*, Donald L. Clark's *John Milton at St. Paul's School*, and Karl Wallace's *Francis Bacon on Communication and Rhetoric*. The renewed interest in classical rhetoric was given another boost by the vogue of Mortimer Adler's *How to Read a Book* and by the post-war popularity of the New Criticism, for both Adler and the New Critics were applying rhetorical techniques to the reading process. In recent years, a number of books and articles have appeared that subject some of the literary masterpieces to a rhetorical analysis.

There has been sporadic talk during the last thirty years or so of a "new rhetoric." This "new rhetoric" is said to have profited by what it appropriated from the modern refinements in psychology, semantics, motivational research, and other behavioral sciences. Two of the names commonly mentioned in connection with the "new rhetoric" are I. A. Richards and Kenneth Burke. The roots of Richards's interest in rhetoric can be found in the book on semantics that he wrote with C. K. Ogden in 1923, *The Meaning of Meaning*. In 1936 he published *The Philosophy of Rhetoric*. One of his purposes in this work was to point up the limitations of the rhetoric of persuasion as it was taught by the ancients. To confine oneself to the persuasive aspect of language, he maintained, was to cut oneself off from some of the other uses of language. It was just because Bishop Whately had announced in his *Elements of Criticism* in 1828 that he was going to confine his study to "argumentative composition, generally and exclusively" that Richards chose him as the chief target of his strictures on the old rhetoric. George Campbell's *The Philosophy of Rhetoric,* with its concern for the psychology of the audience and its broadening of the function of rhetoric to include enlightening the understanding, pleasing the imagination, moving the passions, and influencing the will, represented for Richards a more desirable model for a twentieth-century rhetoric. We can epitomize Richards's approach to rhetoric by saying that he is interested mainly in how language *in any kind of discourse* works to produce understanding (or misunderstanding) in an audience. Something of this concern can be seen in the four terms he uses in his study of human utterances—sense, feeling, tone, and intention.

Kenneth Burke has more reverence for the classical rhetoricians than I. A. Richards does, but like Richards, he sees the possibility of extending the scope of rhetoric. In an article in the *Journal of General Education* in 1951, a year after the publication of his *A Rhetoric of Motives,* Burke said: "If I had to sum up in one word the difference between the 'old' rhetoric and a 'new' (a rhetoric re-invigorated by fresh insights which the 'new Science' contributed to the subject), I would reduce it to this: The key term for the old rhetoric was 'persuasion' and its stress was upon deliberate design. The key term for the new rhetoric would be *'identification,'* which can include a partially 'unconscious' factor in appeal." "Appeal" is the essence of communication for Burke. When people use symbols to induce co-operation in other human beings, they must *identify* themselves with the audience, must, in Burke's term, become *consubstantial* with them. Rhetoric becomes for Burke a study of the various modes of achieving identification. *Structure* of any kind is a mode of identification. The way we structure or arrange our discourse, for instance, could be one of the ways in which we adjust our discourse to fit the needs of our audience. Style, too, can be a mode of identification, since it can be a conscious or an unconscious attempt on our part to suit our language to the level of the audience. Burke's "dramatistic pentad"—act, agent, agency (means), scene (background), purpose—constitutes his critical apparatus for analyzing the motivation of human acts.

Another significant contributor to the "new rhetoric" is the Belgian philosopher Chaim Perelman.* Although Perelman had published books and articles in continental Europe for over thirty years, he only lately came to

---

* For a convenient summary of Perelman's "new rhetoric," see Ray D. Dearin, "The Philosophical Basis of Chaim Perelman's Theory of Rhetoric," *Quarterly Journal of Speech,* LV (October 1969), 213–24.

wide attention in America, mainly through the pages of the journal *Philosophy and Rhetoric,* founded at Pennsylvania State University in 1968 under the editorship of Henry W. Johnstone, Jr., and Carroll C. Arnold. Now English-speaking students of rhetoric can get a firsthand acquaintance with Perelman's major rhetorical work, *The New Rhetoric: A Treatise on Argument,* a translation of *La Nouvelle Rhétorique: Traité de l'Argumentation,* which Perelman and his colleague Madame L. Olbrechts-Tyteca published in France in 1958.

Like the English philosopher Stephen Toulmin, Perelman has been dissatisfied with the applicability of formal logic to the problems of decision-making in human affairs. Perelman contends that the development of a theory of argumentation suitable to the practical deliberations and decisions of public life has been hampered by the rigid allegiance in the Western world to Descartes's concept of reason and reasoning. "It was this philosopher," says Perelman in his Introduction, "who made the self-evident the mark of reason, and considered rational only those demonstrations which, starting from clear and distinct ideas, extended, by means of apodictic proofs, the self-evidence of the axioms to the derived theorems." But most things about which people argue exist in the realm of the contingent, the probable, the plausible, and in this realm, absolute, "scientific" demonstration based on self-evident premises is not always possible or effective. Perelman saw that the kind of "dialectical" proofs that Aristotle dealt with in the *Topics* and utilized in the *Rhetoric* provided the mode of nonformal logic that could "induce or increase the mind's adherence to theses presented for its assent."

Perelman, who also holds an advanced degree in law, found an effective model for this non-formal mode of reasoning in jurisprudence. In his book *The Idea of Justice and the Problem of Argument* (1963), Perelman says, "A thorough investigation of proof in law, of its variations and evolution, can, more than any other study, acquaint us with the relations existing between thought and action." He points, for example, to the use in courtroom trials of precedents, "the rationality of which is linked with the observance of the *rule of justice,* which demands equal treatment for similar situations." He goes on to say, "Now, the application of the rule of justice assumes the existence of precedents to teach us how situations similar to the one confronting us now have been dealt with in the past." Precedents, in other words, produce something less than conclusive proof, but they do constitute a *reasonable* basis for making crucial decisions. So do a host of other psychological, social, and cultural conditions, and it is with those operative conditions that the bulk of *The New Rhetoric* deals.

Chaim Perelman claims that "only the existence of an argumentation that is neither compelling nor arbitrary can give meaning to human freedom, a state in which a reasonable choice can be exercised. . . . The theory of argumentation will help to develop what a logic of value judgments has tried in vain to provide, namely the justification of the possibility of a human community in the sphere of action when this justification cannot be based on a reality of objective truth."

There are other developments in the "new rhetoric" that we might explore. We might look at the exciting work now being done in style and stylistics (the application of linguistics to literature), involving such men as Roger Fowler, Geoffrey Leech, and M. A. K. Halliday in England and Roman Jakobson, Seymour Chatman, Richard Ohmann, Louis Milic, and Francis Christensen in America. Noam Chomsky's transformational grammar and B. F. Skinner's psycholinguistics also have bearings on the "new rhetoric." The growing literature in communications theory has certainly put rhetorical behavior on a more scientific basis. Nor can we neglect the rhetorical dimensions of Marshall McLuhan's pronouncements about how the electronic media are altering the way in which we perceive, structure, and communicate our experiences. We must further explore all those manifestations of non-verbal rhetoric or "body rhetoric," as Franklyn Haiman terms it—marches, demonstrations, sit-ins in the political arena; music, the film, light-shows in the cultural sphere. We are even beginning to speak now of "the rhetoric of alienation" and "the rhetoric of black power" as new and distinctive styles of persuasive discourse. And not enough attention has been paid yet to the rhetoric of advertising, that pervasive influence on all our lives. But the mere mention of these "stirrings" should convince us that rhetoric —although perhaps of a different brand from what we have been studying in this book—is still very much alive.

Ever since the founding of the International Society for the History of Rhetoric in Zurich in 1977, students of rhetoric in North America have been discovering the work in rhetoric that is going on in Europe, where the kind of rhetoric discussed in this text began; and students of rhetoric in Europe have been discovering the work in rhetoric that has been going on in North America, where Western rhetoric emigrated sometime in the eighteenth century. Scholars on both sides of the Atlantic had supposed that the study of rhetoric was dormant, if not moribund, on the other side of the "pond." But just as there had been a vigorous revival of interest in rhetoric in the United States during the twentieth century, first in the Speech and Drama Department at Cornell University in the 1920s and then in English departments in the mid-1960s, scholars in various countries in Europe had been re-exploring rhetoric since about the 1950s.

At first, Europeans and North Americans interested in rhetoric began looking at scholars who were not rhetoricians primarily but who were philosophers, linguists, psychologists, anthologists, and literary critics, and they appropriated from these scholars insights about human communications that cast new light on rhetoric. And so in the literature about rhetoric published on both sides of the Atlantic, we encountered the names of people like Lev Vygotsky, A. R. Luria, Hans-Georg Gadamer, Paul Ricoeur, Roman Jakobson, Paul De Man, Jacques Derrida, Mikhail Bahktin. In the concluding chapter of his recent comprehensive history of rhetoric, *In Defence of Rhetoric* (1988), Brian Vickers discusses and assesses the ideas and influence on rhetoric of some of these authors and of other contemporary authors.

But thanks to some recent English translations, we on this side of the Atlantic have come to know the works of some continental authors who could really be considered rhetoricians. Three of these European rhetoricians who have figured prominently in discussions in our professional journals and scholarly books have been the Italian humanist Ernesto Grassi, the French philosopher Michel Foucault, and the German Marxist critic Jürgen Habermas. When the next chapter in the history of rhetoric is written, books like the following will have to be discussed: Michel Foucault's *The Archaeology of Knowledge,* trans. A. M. Sheridan Smith (New York: Pantheon, 1972); Ernesto Grassi's *Rhetoric as Philosophy: The Humanist Tradition,* trans. John Michael Krois and Azizeh Azodi (University Park: Pennsylvania State University Press, 1980); Jürgen Habermas's *Communication and the Evolution of Society,* trans. Thomas McCarthy (Boston: Beacon Press, 1979). Students can get a good overview of the work of these three continental rhetoricians, as well as of five other contemporary rhetoricians (I. A. Richards, Richard Weaver, Stephen Toulmin, Chaim Perelman, and Kenneth Burke) in Sonja K. Foss, Karen A. Foss, and Robert Trapp's *Contemporary Perspectives on Rhetoric* (Prospect Heights, IL: Waveland Press, 1985).

What has probably been very noticeable to many readers of this survey is the absence of the names of women. In fact, this absence has been a conspicuous feature of all histories of rhetoric. For instance, in both the French version (1958) and the English version (1969) of *The New Rhetoric: A Treatise on Argumentation,* L. Olbrechts-Tyteca is prominently listed as the co-author, along with Chaim Perelman, of this significant twentieth-century rhetoric text. If the first name of Olbrechts-Tyteca had been spelled out on the title page of this book, we might have learned that Luci Olbrechts-Tyteca was a woman. But whenever Perelman's rhetorical works are discussed in journals and books, there is no discussion—and hardly even a mention—of Madame Olbrechts-Tyteca. She was a colleague of Perelman's, and for ten years, she collaborated with Perelman in studying the ways in which writers in various disciplines used argument in their discourses. And yet, as far as the histories of rhetoric are concerned, she is just a name in a bibliographic entry.

One of the reasons for the absence of women's names in the histories of rhetoric is that for most of the 2500-year history of rhetoric in the Western world, there have been very few, if any, women who could be called rhetoricians, either as theorists or as practitioners. And the reason for the lack of women rhetoricians is that for most of that 2500-year span, women were denied access to formal education and to the public arena. Rhetoric is one of the most patriarchal of all the academic disciplines.

But because of the active feminist movement, we may be on the verge of recovering the names of women who could lay claim to being rhetors. Cheryl Glenn has written a dissertation at Ohio State University entitled "Muted Voices from Antiquity to the Renaissance: Locating Women in the Rhetorical Tradition" (1989). In the periods and the cultures that she investigated—from the time of the Athenian Greeks through the European Renaissance—she too did not discover many women who distinguished themselves as either practitioners of rhetoric or theorists of rhetoric. She turned up many bright, literate, forceful women, like Margaret More Roper (Thomas More's daughter) and Héloïse (the French abbess whose name is always linked with the medieval logician Abelard), women who managed to educate themselves despite being denied access to formal schooling, but she had a difficult time of it justifying a claim to their being regarded as rhetoricians in the traditional sense of that term. The closest she comes to finding a woman who could be regarded as a theorist and pedagogue of rhetoric is Aspasia of Miletus, who was reputed to be a teacher of, among others, Socrates. The closest Glenn comes to discovering a woman who could be regarded as an orator in the public arena is Hortensia. Hortensia was a patrician woman who about 42 B.C. protested vehemently but futilely in the Forum against an extraordinary tax that the Roman senate had levied against some 1400 widows of wealthy Roman citizens.

But when Cheryl Glenn investigates women in the nineteenth and twentieth centuries, as she intends to do, she will discover many women who can legitimately be classified as significant and effective rhetoricians. In the May 1989 issue of *The Quarterly Journal of Speech*, Karlyn Kohrs Campbell published "The Sound of Woman's Voices," an omnibus review of eleven books on women in rhetoric during the nineteenth and twentieth centuries. Some of these books present primary texts of speeches and written discourses by women of the nineteenth and twentieth centuries, and others of these books present historical or critical studies of women operating as rhetoricians. When it comes to the second half of the twentieth century, future scholars will find a plethora of women rhetoricians. Anyone who has been a regular reader of articles, scholarly books, and textbooks on rhetoric in the last twenty-five years would have an easier time ticking off a list of two dozen women, in

Speech or in English, who have made a significant contribution to rhetoric in our time than a list of two dozen men.

This survey of rhetoric, abbreviated as it is, has probably left readers' heads swirling with names and titles and dates. It is not so important that readers be able to recall and place all these details as it is that they be aware, in a general way, of the long and honorable tradition that classical rhetoric has enjoyed. Throughout that long history, rhetoric has risen and fallen periodically in public prominence, both in the political realm and in the academic arena. But even when it has been singularly inactive for a long period of time, it always stages a comeback. What once was so vital cannot be, even with the passage of time and the creation of a new world, entirely irrelevant and ineffectual. As long as human beings are permitted to utter or to write words, they will continue to act rhetorically.

BIBLIOGRAPHY

This selective bibliography will serve as a guide for those who may want to pursue further the study of rhetoric. The primary texts are listed chronologically; the secondary texts are listed alphabetically. The listing of primary texts has been limited to modern editions.

Bibliographies

James W. Cleary and Frederick W. Haberman, eds., *Rhetoric and Public Address: A Bibliography, 1947–1961*. Madison: University of Wisconsin Press, 1964.

Richard Enos et al., eds. *Heuristic Procedures and the Composing Process: A Selected Bibliography. Rhetoric Society Quarterly*. Special Issue.

Keith Erickson, ed. *Aristotle's Rhetoric: Five Centuries of Philological Research*. Metuchen, NJ: Scarecow Press, 1975.

Winifred Bryan Horner, ed. *Historical Rhetoric: An Annotated Bibliography of Selected Sources in English*. Boston: G. K. Hall, 1980.

———, ed. *The Present State of Scholarship in Historical and Contemporary Rhetoric*. Columbia: University of Missouri Press, 1983.

Albert R. Kitzhaber, ed. *A Bibliography on Rhetoric in American Colleges, 1850–1900*. Denver: Bibliographical Center for Research, Denver Public Library, 1954.

Erika Lindemann, ed. *Longman Bibliography of Composition and Rhetoric, 1984–1985*. White Plains, NY: Longman, 1987.

James J. Murphy, ed. *Renaissance Rhetoric: A Short-Title Catalogue of Works on Rhetorical Theory from the Beginning of Printing to A.D. 1700*. New York: Garland, 1981.

Primary Texts

Thomas W. Benson and Michael H. Prosser, eds. *Readings in Classical Rhetoric.* Davis, CA: Hermogoras Press, 1988.

D. A. Russell and Michael Winterbottom, eds. *Ancient Literary Criticism: The Principal Texts in New Translations.* Oxford: Clarendon Press, 1972.

Isocrates. Vols. I and II trans. George Norlin, Vol. III trans. Larue Van Hook. Loeb Classical Library. Cambridge, MA: Harvard University Press, 1928–29, 1945. All the Loeb Classical Library editions have the Greek (or the Latin) text on the left-hand page and the English translation on the facing page.

Plato. *Phaedrus.* Trans. W. C. Helmbold and W. G. Rabinowitz. Library of the Liberal Arts. Indianapolis, IN: Bobbs-Merrill, 1956.

———. *Gorgias.* Trans. W. C. Helmbold. Library of Liberal Arts. Indianapolis, IN: Bobbs-Merrill, 1952.

Demosthenes. *On the Crown.* Ed. James J. Murphy, with a new translation by John J. Keaney. Davis, CA: Hermagoras Press, 1983.

Aristotle. *Art of Rhetoric.* Trans. J. H. Freese. Loeb Classical Library. Cambridge, MA: Harvard University Press, 1959.

———. *The Rhetoric and the Poetics of Aristotle. Rhetoric* trans. W. Rhys Roberts, *Poetics* trans. Ingram Bywater. Introduction by Edward P. J. Corbett. Modern Library College Editions. New York: Random House, 1984.

———. *The Rhetoric of Aristotle.* Trans. Lane Cooper. Englewood Cliffs, NJ: Prentice-Hall, 1960.

———. *The Rhetoric of Aristotle.* Trans. E. M. Cope, revised and edited by John E. Sandys. 3 vols. Cambridge: Cambridge University Press, 1877.

Hermogenes. *On Types of Style.* Trans. C. W. Wooten. Durham, NC: Duke University Press, 1987.

Dionysius. *On Literary Composition.* Trans. W. Rhys Roberts. London: Cambridge University Press, 1910.

Ad Herennium. Trans. Harry Caplan. Loeb Classical Library. Cambridge, MA: Harvard University Press, 1954.

Cicero. *De Inventione: De Optime Genere Oratorum; Topica.* All three texts trans. H. M. Hubbell. Loeb Classical Library. Cambridge, MA: Harvard University Press, 1949.

———. *De Oratore.* Books I and II trans. E. W. Sutton and H. Rackham, Book III trans. H. Rackham. 2 vols. Loeb Classical Library. Cambridge, MA: Harvard University Press, 1942.

———. *Brutus: Orator.* Both texts trans. G. L. Hendrickson. Loeb Classical Library. Cambridge, MA: Harvard University Press, 1939.

Demetrius. *On Style.* Trans. W. Rhys Roberts. Cambridge: Cambridge University Press, 1902.

Longinus. *On the Sublime.* The Greek text edited and translated by W. Rhys Roberts. 2nd ed. Cambridge: Cambridge University Press, 1907.

————. *On the Sublime*. Trans. G. M. A. Grube. Library of Liberal Arts. Indianapolis, IN: Bobbs-Merrill, 1957.

————. *Longinus on Sublimity*. Trans. D. A. Russell. Oxford: Clarendon Press, 1964.

Quintilian. *Institutio Oratoria*. Trans. H. E. Butler. 4 vols. Loeb Classical Library. Cambridge, MA: Harvard University Press, 1920–22.

————. *Quintilian on the Teaching of Speaking and Writing: Translations from Books One, Two, and Ten of the Institutio Oratoria*. Landmarks in Rhetoric and Public Address. Carbondale: Southern Illinois University Press, 1988.

J. M. Miller, M. H. Prosser, and T. W. Benson, eds. *Readings in Medieval Rhetoric*. Bloomington: University of Indiana Press, 1973.

St. Augustine. *On Christian Doctrine (De Doctrina Christiana)*. Trans. D. W. Robertson, Jr. Library of Liberal Arts. Indianapolis, IN: Bobbs-Merrill, 1958.

Desiderius Erasmus. *On Copia of Words and Ideas (De duplici copia verborum ac rerum)*. Ed. and trans. Donald B. King and H. David Rix. Milwaukee, WI: Marquette University Press, 1963.

Leonard Cox. *The Arte or Crafte of Rhetoryke* (1530). Ed. F. I. Carpenter. Chicago Press, 1899.

Richard Sherry. *A Treeatise of Schemes and Tropes* (1550). With his translation of *The Education of Children* by Desiderius Erasmus, a facsimile reproduction with an Introduction and Index by Herbert W. Hildebrant. Gainesville: University of Florida Press, 1961.

Thomas Wilson. *Arte of Rhetorique* (1553). Ed. George H. Mair. Oxford: Oxford University Press, 1909.

Richard Rainolde. *The Foundacion of Rhetorike* (1563). Facsimile reproduction with an Introduction by Francis R. Johnson. New York: Scholar's Facsimiles and Reprints, 1945.

Henry Peacham. *The Garden of Eloquence* (1577, 1593). Facsimile reproduction with an Introduction by William G. Crane. Gainesville: University of Florida Press, 1954.

Abraham Fraunce. *The Arcadian Rhetorike* (1588). Ed. Ethel Seaton. Oxford: Oxford University Press, 1950.

George Puttenham. *The Arte of English Poesie* (1589). Ed. Gladys Dodge Willock and Alice Walker. Cambridge: Cambridge University Press, 1938.

John Hoskins. *Directions for Speech and Style* (1600). Ed. Hoyt H. Hudson. Princeton, NJ: Princeton University Press, 1935.

John T. Harwood, ed. *The Rhetorics of Thomas Hobbes and Bernard Lamy*. Landmarks in Rhetoric and Public Address. Carbondale: Southern Illinois University Press, 1986.

Francois de la Mothe Fénelon. *Fénelon's Dialogues on Eloquence*. Trans. Wilbur Samuel Howell. Princeton, NJ: Princeton University Press, 1951.

Giambattista Vico. *The New Science of Giambattista Vico*. Revised translation of 3rd ed. (1744) by T. G. Bergin and M. H. Fisch. Ithaca, NY: Cornell University Press, 1968.

John Lawson. *Lectures Concerning Oratory Delivered in Trinity College. Dublin*

(1758). Ed. E. Neal Claussen and Karl R. Wallace. Landmarks in Rhetoric and Public Address. Carbondale: Southern Illinois University Press, 1972.

George Campbell. *The Philosophy of Rhetoric* (1776). Ed. with a revised and expanded Introduction by Lloyd F. Bitzer. Landmarks in Rhetoric and Public Address. Carbondale: Southern Illinois University Press, 1988.

Joseph Priestley. *A Course of Lectures on Oratory and Criticism* (1777). Ed. Vincent M. Bevilacqua and Richard Murphy. Landmarks in Rhetoric and Public Address. Carbondale: Southern Illinois University Press, 1965.

Hugh Blair. *Lectures on Rhetoric and Belles-Lettres* (1783). Ed. Harold Harding. 2 vols. Landmarks in Rhetoric and Public Address. Carbondale: Southern Illinois University Press, 1966.

Adam Smith. *Lectures on Rhetoric and Belles-Lettres Delivered in the University of Glasgow by Adam Smith, Reported by a Student in 1762–63.* Ed. John M. Lothian. Landmarks in Rhetoric and Public Address. Carbondale: Southern Illinois University Press, 1971.

Richard Whately. *Elements of Rhetoric* (1828). Ed. Douglas Ehninger. Landmarks in Rhetoric and Public Address. Carbondale: Southern Illinois University Press, 1963.

James L. Golden and Edward P. J. Corbett, ed. *The Rhetoric of Blair, Campbell, and Whately.* Carbondale: Southern Illinois University Press, 1990.

I. A. Richards. *The Philosophy of Rhetoric.* New York: Oxford University Press, 1936.

Kenneth Burke. *A Rhetoric of Motives.* Berkeley: University of California Press, 1962.

Chaim Perelman and L. Olbrechts-Tyteca. *The New Rhetoric: A Treatise on Argumentation.* Trans. John Wilkinson and Purcell Weaver. Notre Dame, IN: University of Notre Dame Press, 1969.

Chaim Perelman. *The Realm of Rhetoric.* Trans. William Kluback. Notre Dame, IN: University of Notre Dame Press, 1982.

Richard E. Young, Alton Becker, and Kenneth L. Pike. *Rhetoric: Discovery and Change.* New York: Harcourt, Brace, and World, 1970.

History of Rhetoric

T. W. Baldwin. *William Shakespeare's Small Latine & Lesse Greeke.* 2 vols. Urbana: University of Illinois Press, 1944.

Charles Allen Beaumont. *Swift's Classical Rhetoric.* Athens: University of Georgia Press, 1961.

James A. Berlin. *Writing Instruction in Nineteenth-Century American Colleges.* Carbondale: Southern Illinois University Press, 1984.

———. *Rhetoric and Reality: Writing Instruction in American Colleges 1900–1985.* Carbondale: Southern Illinois University Press, 1987.

Stanley F. Bonner. *Education in Ancient Rome: From the Elder Cato to the Younger Pliny.* Berkeley: University of California Press, 1977.

John Brinsley. *Ludus Literarius: Or, The Grammar Schoole (1612).* Ed. E. T. Campagnac. Liverpool: Liverpool University Press, 1917.

Donald C. Bryant. *Ancient Greek and Roman Rhetoricians: A Biographical Dictionary.* Columbia: University of Missouri Press, 1968.

Donald L. Clark. *Rhetoric and Poetic in the Renaissance: A Study of Rhetorical Terms in English Renaissance Literary Criticism.* New York: Columbia University Press, 1922.

———. *John Milton at St. Paul's School: A Study of Ancient Rhetoric in English Renaissance Education.* New York: Columbia University Press, 1948.

———. *Rhetoric in Greco-Roman Education.* New York: Columbia University Press, 1957.

M. L. Clark. *Rhetoric at Rome: A Historical Survey.* London: Cohen and West, 1953.

William G. Crane. *Wit and Rhetoric in the Renaissance: The Formal Basis of Elizabethan Prose Style.* New York: Columbia University Press, 1937.

E. R. Curtius. *European Literature and the Latin Middle Ages.* Trans. W. R. Trask. Princeton, NJ: Princeton University Press, 1953.

Hugh M. Davidson. *Audience, Words, and Art: Studies in Seventeenth-Century French Rhetoric.* Columbus: Ohio State University Press, 1965.

Richard Leo Enos. *The Literate Mode of Cicero's Legal Rhetoric.* Carbondale: Southern Illinois University Press, 1987.

Ann Gunion, ed. *A Biographical Dictionary of Greek and Roman Rhetoricians: A Preliminary Survey.* Project Rhetor. Davis: University of California Press, 1985.

O. B. Hardison, Jr. *The Enduring Monument: A Study of Praise in Reniassance Literary Theory and Practice.* Chapel Hill: University of North Carolina Press, 1962.

Marvin T. Herrick. *The Poetics of Aristotle in England.* New Haven, CT: Yale University Press, 1930.

Charles Hoole. *A New Discovery of the Old Art of Teaching School (1660).* Ed. E. T. Campagnac. Liverpool: Liverpool University Press, 1913.

Wilbur Samuel Howell. *The Rhetoric of Alcuin and Charlemagne.* Princeton, NJ: Princeton University Press, 1941.

———. *Logic and Rhetoric in England, 1500–1700.* Princeton, NJ: Princeton University Press, 1956.

———. *Eighteenth Century British Logic and Rhetoric.* Princeton, NJ: Princeton University Press, 1971.

Lee S. Hultzen. "Aristotle's Rhetoric in England to 1600." Unpublished Dissertation. Cornell University, 1932.

Werner Jaeger. *Paideia: The Ideals of Greek Culture.* 3 vols. New York: Oxford University Press, 1943.

George Kennedy. *The Art of Persuasion in Greece.* Princeton, NJ: Princeton University Press, 1963.

———. *Quintilian.* Twayne World Authors Series. New York: Twayne Publishers, 1969.

————. *The Art of Persuasion in the Roman World, 300 B.C.–300 A.D.* Princeton, NJ: Princeton University Press, 1972.

————. *Classical Rhetoric and Its Christian and Secular Tradition From Ancient to Modern Times.* Chapel Hill: University of North Carolina Press, 1980.

————. *Greek Rhetoric Under Christian Emperors.* Princeton, NJ: Princeton University Press, 1983.

————. *New Testament Interpretation Through Rhetorical Criticism.* Chapel Hill: University of North Carolina Press, 1984.

Paul Oskar Kristeller. *Renaissance Thought: The Classical Scholastic and Humanist Strains.* New York: Harper Torchbooks, 1961.

Sister Joan Marie Lechner. *Renaissance Concepts of the Commonplaces.* New York: Pageant Press, 1962.

John H. Mackin. *Classical Rhetoric for Modern Discourse.* New York: Free Press, 1969.

H. I. Marrou. *A History of Education in Antiquity.* Trans. George Lamb. New York: Sheed and Ward, 1956.

W. F. Mitchell. *English Pulpit Oratory.* London: Society for the Promotion of Christian Knowledge, 1932.

M. Mooney. *Vico in the Tradition of Rhetoric.* Princeton, NJ: Princeton University Press, 1985.

James J. Murphy. *Rhetoric in the Middle Ages: A History of Rhetorical Theory From St. Augustine to the Renaissance.* Berkeley: University of California Press, 1974.

————, ed. *A Synoptic History of Classical Rhetoric.* Davis, CA: Hermagoras Press, 1983.

J. W. O'Malley. *Praise and Blame in Renaissance Rome: Rhetoric, Doctrine, and Reform in the Sacred Orators of the Papal Court, C. 1450–1521.* Chapel Hill: University of North Carolina Press, 1979.

Walter J. Ong. *Ramus, Method, and the Decay of Dialogue.* Cambridge, MA: Harvard University Press, 1958.

————. *The Ramus and Talon Inventory.* Cambridge, MA: Harvard University Press, 1958.

Herbert David Rix. *Rhetoric in Spenser's Poetry.* State College: Penn State University Press, 1940.

W. Rhys Roberts. *Greek Rhetoric and Literary Criticism.* New York: Longmans, Green, and Company, 1928.

Alexander Sackton. *Rhetoric as Dramatic Language in Ben Jonson.* New York: Columbia University Press, 1948.

William P. Sandford. *English Theories of Public Address, 1530–1828.* Columbus: Ohio State University Press, 1931.

Izora Scott. *Controversies Over the Imitation of Cicero as a Model for Style.* New York: Columbia University Press, 1910.

Jerrold E. Seigel. *Rhetoric and Philosophy in Renaissance Humanism: The Union of Eloquence and Wisdom, Petrarch to Valla.* Princeton, NJ: Princeton University Press, 1968.

David Shaw. *The Dialectical Temper: The Rhetorical Art of Robert Browning.* Ithaca, NY: Cornell University Press, 1968.

Robert W. Smith. *Art of Rhetoric in Alexandria: Its Theory and Practice in the Ancient World.* The Hague: Martinus N. J. Hoff, 1974.

Nancy S. Streuver. *The Language of History in the Renaissance. Rhetoric and Historical Consciousness in Florentine Humanism.* Princeton, NJ: Princeton University Press, 1970.

Lester Thonssen and A. Craig Baird. *Speech Criticism: The Development of Standards of Rhetorical Appraisal.* New York: Ronald Press Co., 1948.

Wesley Trimpi. *Ben Jonson's Poems: A Study of Plain Style.* Palo Alto, CA: Stanford University Press, 1962.

Rosemond Tuve. *Elizabethan and Metaphysical Imagery: Renaissance Poetic and Twentieth-Century Critics.* Chicago: University of Chicago Press, 1947.

Brian Vickers. *In Defence of Rhetoric.* Oxford: Clarendon Press, 1988.

———. *Classical Rhetoric in English Poetry.* Davis, CA: Hermagoras Press, 1988.

Karl R. Wallace. *Francis Bacon on Communication and Rhetoric.* Chapel Hill: University of North Carolina Press, 1943.

———. *History of Speech Education in America.* New York: Appleton, Century, Crofts, 1954.

Bernard Weinberg. *A History of Literary Criticism in the Italian Renaissance.* Chicago: University of Chicago Press, 1961.

W. H. Woodward. *Studies in Education During the Age of the Renaissance, 1400–1600.* Cambridge: Cambridge University Press, 1987.

Theories of Rhetoric

Charles M. Anderson. *Richard Seltzer and the Rhetoric of Surgery.* Carbondale: Southern Illinois University Press, 1989.

Walter H. Beale. *A Pragmatic Theory of Rhetoric.* Carbondale: Southern Illinois University Press, 1989.

Edwin Black. *Rhetorical Criticism: A Study in Method.* New York: Macmillan, 1965.

Wayne C. Booth. *The Rhetoric of Fiction.* Supplementary Bibliography, 1961–1982 by James Phelan. 2nd ed. Chicago: University of Chicago Press, 1983.

———. Wayne C. Booth. *Modern Dogma and the Rhetoric of Assent.* Notre Dame, IN: University of Notre Dame Press, 1974.

———. *A Rhetoric of Irony.* Chicago: University of Chicago Press, 1974.

E. M. Cope. *An Introduction to Aristotle's Rhetoric.* London: Macmillan and Company, 1867; rpt. Dubuque, IA: William C. Brown, 1965.

Frank D'Angelo. *A Conceptual Theory of Rhetoric.* Englewood Cliffs, NJ: Winthrop, 1975.

George Dillon. *Rhetoric as Social Imagination: Explorations in the Interpersonal Function of Language.* Bloomington: Indiana University Press, 1986.

Jacques Ellul. *Propaganda: The Formation of Men's Attitudes.* Trans. Konrad Kellen and Jean Lemer. New York: Knopf, 1966.

Daniel J. Fogarty. *Roots for a New Rhetoric.* New York: Columbia University Press, 1959.

Mary Amelia Grant. *The Ancient Rhetorical Theories of the Laughable: The Greek Rhetoricians and Cicero.* Madison: University of Wisconsin Press, 1924.

Ernesto Grassi. *Rhetoric as Philosophy: The Humanist Tradition.* University Park: Pennsylvania State University Press, 1980.

William M. A. Grimaldi, S.J. *Aristotle, Rhetoric I: A Commentary.* New York: Fordam University Press, 1980.

―――. *Studies in the Philosophy of Aristotle's Rhetoric.* Wiesbaden, Germany: Franz Steiner Verlag, 1972.

Elbert W. Harrington. *Rhetoric and the Scientific Method of Inquiry: A Study of Invention.* Boulder: University of Colorado Press, 1948.

Laura Virginia Holland. *Counterpoint: Kenneth Burke and Aristotle's Theories of Rhetoric.* New York: Philosophical Library, 1959.

Winifred Bryan Horner. *Rhetoric in the Classical Tradition.* New York: St. Martin's Press, 1988.

Sister Miriam Joseph. *The Trivium.* 3rd ed. South Bend, IN: McClave Printing, 1948.

James L. Kinneavy. *A Theory of Discourse.* New York: W. W. Norton, 1980. (Hardcover Edition: Englewood Cliffs, NJ: Prentice-Hall, 1971).

―――. *Greek Rhetorical Origins of Christian Faith: An Inquiry.* New York: Oxford University Press, 1987.

C. H. Knoblauch and L. I. Brannon. *Rhetorical Traditions and the Teaching of Writing.* Upper Montclair, NJ: Boynton/Cook, 1984.

A. D. Leeman. *Orationis Ratio: The Stylistic Theories and Practices of the Roman Orators, Historians, and Philosophers.* 2 vols. Amsterdam: Adolf M. Hakkert, 1985.

Karen Burke LeFevre. *Invention as a Social Act.* Carbondale: Southern Illinois University Press, 1987.

Erika Lindemann. *A Rhetoric for Writing Teachers.* 2nd ed. New York: Oxford University Press, 1987.

Marshall McLuhan. *The Gutenberg Galaxy: The Making of Typographic Man.* Toronto: New American Library, 1962.

―――. *Understanding Media: The Extensions of Man.* New York: McGraw-Hill, 1964.

Maurice Natanson and Henry Johnstone. *Philosophy, Rhetoric, and Argumentation.* University Park: Penn State University Press, 1965.

Jasper Neel. *Plato, Derrida, and Writing.* Carbondale: Southern Illinois University Press, 1988.

Marie Hochmuth Nichols. *Rhetoric and Criticism.* Baton Rouge: Louisiana State University Press, 1963.

Walter J. Ong, S.J. *Rhetoric, Romance, and Technology: Studies in the Interaction of Expression and Culture.* Ithaca, NY: Cornell University Press, 1971.

———. *Interfaces of the Word.* Ithaca, NY: Cornell University Press, 1977.

———. *The Presence of the Word: Some Prolegomena for Cultural and Religious History.* Minneapolis: University of Minnesota Press, 1981.

———. *Orality and Literacy: The Technologizing of the Word.* London and New York: Methuen, 1982.

Vance Packard. *The Hidden Persuaders.* New York: McKay Co., 1957.

D. Gordon Rohman and Albert O. Wlecke. *Prewriting: The Construction and Application of Models for Concept Formation in Writing.* Cooperative Research Project #2174, Cooperative Research Project of the Office of Education, U.S. Department of Health, Education, and Welfare, 1964.

Lev S. Vygotsky. *Thought and Language.* Trans. Eugenia Haufmann and Gertrude Vakor. Cambridge, MA: MIT Press, 1962.

Karl R. Wallace. *Understanding Discourse: The Speech Act and Rhetorical Action.* Baton Rouge: Louisiana State University Press, 1970.

Richard M. Weaver. *The Ethics of Rhetoric.* Davis, CA: Hermagoras Press, 1985.

Linda Woodson. *A Handbook of Modern Rhetorical Terms.* Urbana, IL: NCTE, 1979.

Richard E. Young and R. H. Koen. *The Tagmemic Discovery Procedure: An Evaluation of Its Uses in the Teaching of Rhetoric.* ERIC ED 024 951.

Collections of Articles on Rhetoric

Dudley Bailey, ed. *Essays in Rhetoric.* New York: Oxford University Press, 1965.

A. Baird, ed. *Essays from Selected British Eloquence by Chauncey Allen Goodrich.* Carbondale: Southern Illinois University Press, 1963.

J. Dean Bishop, Turner S. Kobler, and William E. Tanner, eds. *A Symposium on Rhetoric.* Denton: Texas Woman's University Press, 1975.

Lloyd F. Bitzer and Edwin Black, eds. *The Prospect of Rhetoric.* New York: Prentice, 1971.

Haig A. Bosmajian and Haminda Bosmajian, eds. *The Rhetoric of the Civil Rights Movement.* New York: Random House, 1969.

Robert L. Brown and Martin Steinmann, Jr., eds. *Rhetoric 78.* Minneapolis: University of Minnesota Center, 1979.

Donald C. Bryant, ed. *The Rhetorical Idiom: Essays in Rhetoric, Oratory, Language, and Drama Presented to Herbert August Wichelns.* Ithaca, NY: Cornell University Press, 1958.

———, ed. *Papers in Rhetoric and Poetic.* Iowa City: University of Iowa Press, 1965.

Don M. Burks, ed. *Rhetoric, Philosophy, and Literature: An Exploration in Honor of Frederick W. Haberman.* West LaFayette, IN: Purdue University Press, 1978.

Francis Christensen. *Notes Toward a New Rhetoric: Six Essays for Teachers.* New York: Harper, 1967.

Robert J. Connors, Lisa Ede, and Andrea Lunsford. *Essays on Classical Rhetoric and Modern Discourse*. Carbondale: Southern Illinois University Press, 1984.

Robert J. Connors, ed. *The Selected Essays of Edward P. J. Corbett*. Dallas, TX: Southern Methodist University Press, 1989.

Edward P. J. Corbett, ed. *Rhetorical Analyses of Literary Works*. New York: Oxford University Press, 1969.

Edward P. J. Corbett, James L. Golden, and Goodwin F. Berquist, eds. *Essays on the Rhetoric of the Western World*. Dubuque, IA: Kendall/Hunt, 1990.

Lionel G. Crocker and Paul A. Carmack, eds. *Readings in Rhetoric*. Springfield, IL: Charles C. Thomas, 1965.

Keith V. Erickson, ed. *The Classical Heritage of Rhetoric*. Metuchen, NJ: Scarecrow Press, 1974.

Aviva Freedman and Ian Pringle. *Reinventing the Rhetorical Tradition*. Urbana, IL: NCTE, 1982.

James A. Golden and Joseph J. Pilotta. *Practical Reasoning in Human Affairs: Studies in Honor of Chaim Perelman*. Dordrecht, Holland: D. Reidel Publishing Co., 1986.

Robert M. Gorrell, ed. *Rhetoric: Theories for Application*. Urbana, IL: NCTE, 1967.

Richard Graves, ed. *Rhetoric and Composition: A Sourcebook for Teachers and Writers*. Upper Montclair, NJ: Boynton/Cook, 1983.

A History and Criticism of American Public Address. Vols. I and II. Ed. William Norwood Brigance. New York: Russell and Russell, 1943; Vol. III. Ed. Marie K. Hochmuth. New York: McGraw-Hill, 1955.

Raymond F. Howes, ed. *Historical Studies of Rhetoric and Rhetoricians*. Ithaca, NY: Cornell University Press, 1961.

Lawrence W. Hugenberg, ed. *Rhetorical Studies Honoring James L. Golden*. Dubuque, IA: Kendall/Hunt, 1986.

Richard L. Johannesen, Rennard Strickland, and Ralph T. Eubank, eds. *Language is Sermonic: Richard M. Weaver on the Nature of Rhetoric*. Baton Rouge: Louisiana State University Press, 1970.

Richard L. Johannesen, ed. *Contemporary Theories of Rhetoric: Selected Readings*. New York: Harper, 1971.

George Levine and William Madden, eds. *The Art of Victorian Prose*. New York: Oxford University Press, 1968.

Ray E. McKerrow, ed. *Explorations in Rhetoric: Studies in Honor of Douglas Ehninger*. Glenview, IL: Scott Foresman, 1982.

Jean Dietz Moss, ed. *Rhetoric and Praxis: The Contribution of Classical Rhetoric to Practical Reasoning*. Washington, DC: The Catholic University of America Press, 1986.

James L. Murphy, ed. *The Rhetorical Tradition and Modern Writing*. New York: Modern Language Association, 1982.

Halford Ross Ryan. *American Rhetoric from Roosevelt to Reagan*. Prospect Heights, IL: Waveland Press, 1983.

Joseph Schwartz and John Rycenga, eds. *The Province of Rhetoric*. New York: The Ronald Press, 1965.

Martin Steinmann, Jr., ed. *New Rhetorics*. New York: Scribner's, 1967.

Studies in Speech and Drama in Honor of Alexander M. Drummond. Ithaca, NY: Cornell University Press, 1944.

Studies in Rhetoric and Public Speaking in Honor of James Albert Winans. New York: The Century Co., 1925.

William E. Tanner and J. Dean Bishop, eds. *Rhetoric and Change*. Mesquite, TX: Ide House, 1982.

Lester Thonssen, ed. *Selected Readings in Rhetoric and Public Speaking*. New York: H. W. Wilson, 1942.

Richard Weaver. *The Ethics of Rhetoric*. Davis, CA: Hermagoras Press, 1985.

Eugene E. White, ed. *Rhetoric in Transition: Studies in the Nature and Uses of Rhetoric*. University Park: Pennsylvania State University Press, 1980.

Theodore Windt and Beth Ingold, eds. *Essays in Presidential Rhetoric*. Dubuque, IA: Kendall/Hunt, 1983.

W. Ross Winterowd, ed. *Contemporary Rhetoric: A Conceptual Background with Readings*. New York: Harcourt Brace Jovanovich, 1975.

———. *Composition/Rhetoric: A Synthesis*. Carbondale: Southern Illinois University Press, 1986.

Style

Robert Adolph. *The Rise of Modern Prose Style*. Cambridge, MA: MIT Press, 1968.

Chris Anderson. *Style as Argument: Contemporary American Nonfiction*. Carbondale: Southern Illinois University Press, 1987.

J. L. Austin. *How to Do Things with Words*. Cambridge, MA: Harvard University Press, 1962.

Howard Babb, ed. *Essays in Stylistic Analysis*. New York: Harcourt Brace Jovanovich, 1972.

Richard W. Bailey and Dolores M. Burton. *English Stylistics: A Bibliography*. Cambridge, MA: MIT Press, 1968.

James R. Bennett. *Prose Style: A Historical Approach Through Studies*. San Francisco: Chandler, 1971.

———. *Bibliography of Stylistics and Related Criticism, 1967–1983*. New York: Modern Language Association, 1986.

Richard Bridgman. *The Colloquial Style in America*. New York: Oxford, 1966.

Huntington Brown. *Prose Styles: Five Primary Types*. Minneapolis: University of Minnesota Press, 1966.

Rollo Brown. *How the French Boy Learns to Write*. Urbana, IL: NCTE, 1963.

Frederick Candelaria, ed. *Perspectives on Style*. Boston: Allyn and Bacon, 1968.

Seymour Chatman, ed. *Literary Style: A Symposium*. New York: Oxford University Press, 1971.

David Crystal and Derek Davey, eds. *Investigating English Style*. Bloomington: Indiana University Press, 1969.

J. V. Cunningham, ed. *The Problem of Style*. New York: Fawcett, 1966.

Bonamy Dobrée. *Modern Prose Style.* 2nd ed. Oxford University Press, 1964.

Donald C. Freeman, ed. *Linguistics and Literary Style.* New York: Holt, Rinehart, and Winston, 1970.

Walker Gibson. *Tough, Sweet, and Stuffy: An Essay on Modern American Prose.* Bloomington: Indiana University Press, 1966.

Robert Graves and Alan Hodges. *The Reader Over Your Shoulder: A Handbook for Writers.* Macmillan Paperbacks. New York: Macmillan, 1961.

Donald Hall, ed. *The Modern Stylistics: Writers on the Art of Writing.* New York: Free Press, 1968.

Helen Heightsman Gordon. *From Copying to Creating.* 2nd ed. New York: Holt, Rinehart, and Winston, 1985.

Sister Miriam Joseph. *Shakespeare's Use of the Arts of Language.* New York: Columbia University Press, 1947.

Carl H. Klaus, ed. *Style in English Prose.* New York: Macmillan, 1968.

Richard A. Lanham. *Style: An Anti-Textbook.* New Haven, CT: Yale University Press, 1968.

———. *A Handlist of Rhetorical Terms.* Berkeley: University of California Press, 1968.

———. *Analyzing Prose.* New York: Charles Scribner's, 1983.

Edwin H. Lewis. *The History of the English Paragraph.* Chicago: University of Chicago Press, 1894.

Glen A. Love and Michael Payne. *Contemporary Essays on Style: Rhetoric, Linguistics, and Criticism.* Glenview, IL: Scott, Foresman, 1968.

Donald McQuade, ed. *The Territory of Language: Linguistics, Stylistics, and the Teaching of Composition.* Carbondale: Southern Illinois University Press, 1985.

Josephine Miles. *Style and Proportion: The Language of Prose and Poetry.* Boston: Little, Brown, 1967.

Louis Milic. *A Quantitative Approach to the Style of Jonathan Swift.* The Hague: Houton, 1967.

———. *Style and Stylistics: An Analytical Bibliography.* New York: The Free Press, 1967.

J. Middleton Murry. *The Problems of Style.* Oxford Paperbacks. London: Oxford University Press, 1960.

Frank O'Hare. *Sentence Combining: Improving Student Writing Without Formal Grammar Instruction.* Urbana, IL: NCTE, 1963.

Arthur Quinn. *Figures of Speech.* Salt Lake City, UT: Gibbs M. Smith, 1982.

Jacob Reed, ed. *The Computer and Literary Style.* Kent, OH: Kent State University Press, 1967.

R. A. Sayce. *Style in French Prose: A Method of Analysis.* Oxford: Oxford University Press, 1958.

Thomas A. Sebeok, ed. *Style in Language.* Cambridge, MA: MIT Press, 1960.

L. A. Sonnino. *A Handbook to Sixteenth-Century Rhetoric.* London: Routledge, 1968.

John Spencer, Nils Erik Enkvist, and Michael J. Gregory, eds. *Linguistics and Style.* London: Oxford University Press, 1964.

Style, Rhetoric, and Rhythm: Essays by Morris Croll. Ed. J. Max Patrick and Robert O. Evans with John Wallace and R. J. Schoeck. Princeton, NJ: Princeton University Press, 1966.

Warren Taylor. *Tudor Figures of Rhetoric.* Whitewater, WI: The Language Press, 1972.

Winston Weathers and Otis Winchester. *Copy and Compose: A Guide to Prose Style.* Englewood Cliffs, NJ: Prentice-Hall, 1969.

Joan Webber. *Contrary Music: The Prose Style of John Donne.* Madison: University of Wisconsin Press, 1963.

———. *The Eloquent "I": Style and Self in Seventeenth-Century Prose.* Madison: University of Wisconsin Press, 1967.

Paul C. Wermuth, ed. *Modern Essays on Writing and Style.* 2nd ed. New York: Holt, Rinehart, and Winston, 1969.

Thomas Whissen. *A Way with Words: A Guide for Writers.* New York: Oxford University Press, 1982.

Joseph Williams. *Style: Ten Lessons in Clarity and Grace.* Glenview, IL: Scott, Foresman, 1988.

George Williamson. *The Senecan Amble: A Story in Prose from Bacon to Collier.* Chicago: University of Chicago Press, 1951.

W. K. Wimsatt, Jr. *The Prose Style of Samuel Johnson.* Yale Paperbound. New Haven, CT: Yale University Press, 1963.

INDEX

DISCOVERY OF ARGUMENTS